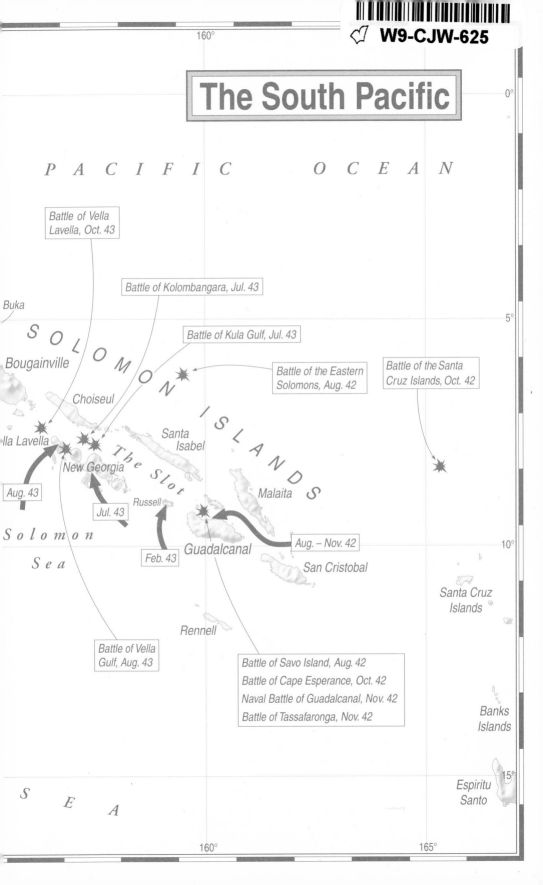

The South Pacific

160°

0°

P A C I F I C   O C E A N

Battle of Vella
Lavella, Oct. 43

Battle of Kolombangara, Jul. 43

Buka

5°

Battle of Kula Gulf, Jul. 43

S O L O M O N

Battle of the Eastern
Solomons, Aug. 42

Battle of the Santa
Cruz Islands, Oct. 42

Bougainville

Choiseul

I S L A N D S

Santa
Isabel

lla Lavella

The Slot

New Georgia

Malaita

Aug. 43

Russell

Jul. 43

Solomon

Sea

Feb. 43

Guadalcanal

Aug. – Nov. 42

10°

San Cristobal

Santa Cruz
Islands

Rennell

Battle of Vella
Gulf, Aug. 43

Battle of Savo Island, Aug. 42

Battle of Cape Esperance, Oct. 42

Naval Battle of Guadalcanal, Nov. 42

Battle of Tassafaronga, Nov. 42

Banks
Islands

15°

Espiritu
Santo

S   E   A

160°

165°

ADMIRAL BILL HALSEY

ADMIRAL BILL HALSEY

A NAVAL LIFE

Thomas Alexander Hughes

Harvard University Press

Cambridge, Massachusetts, and London, England

2016

First printing

Design by Dean Bornstein

Library of Congress Cataloging-in-Publication Data

Names: Hughes, Thomas Alexander, 1963– author.
Title: Admiral Bill Halsey : a naval life / Thomas Alexander Hughes.
Description: Cambridge, Massachusetts : Harvard University Press, 2016. |
Includes bibliographical references and index.
Identifiers: LCCN 2015040172 | ISBN 9780674049635 (alk. paper)
Subjects: LCSH: Halsey, William F. (William Frederick), 1882–1959. | United
States. Navy—Biography. | Admirals—United States—Biography. | World War,
1939–1945—Pacific Area—Naval operations, American.
Classification: LCC E746.H3 H84 2016 | DDC 359.0092—dc23
LC record available at http://lccn.loc.gov/2015040172

For Alicia, Elizabeth, and Katherine

CONTENTS

MAPS

ADMIRAL BILL HALSEY

Introduction

A Naval Death

THE WORLD WAR II naval hero Admiral Bill Halsey arrived at Fishers Island Country Club for his summer vacation on July 30, 1959. For years he had come to this sleepy islet three miles off the Connecticut coast near New London. The place soothed the old man, surrounded as it was by the seas he had plied his entire life. Swimming and reading filled days of relaxation, though he swam less vigorously than in summers past and cataracts complicated the reading. He took his suppers early, and he liked the fare simple. He was usually in his small but comfortable room by eight, asleep by nine. August 15 was like that, except, it being Saturday, he retired late from the parlor, where he enjoyed chatting with other guests. When he missed breakfast the next morning, the club manager went to his room. Halsey was unconscious. Shortly before noon, the sole physician on tiny Fishers Island pronounced him dead from an apparent heart attack. He was seventy-six years old.

Biography begins at the end, when judgments of a finished life are first possible. Within hours of Halsey's death, President Dwight Eisenhower mourned the loss of a "great natural leader." The next day the *New York Times* wrote of a man "born to a naval career" and of an "inspiring leader" of bold action. The *Baltimore Sun* called Halsey "a sailor's sailor" whose "formula for winning was simple—Kill Japs, kill Japs, and kill more Japs." The *Washington Post* proclaimed Halsey "a seadog of the old school. Known since his football days at Annapolis as 'Bull,' he was square of jaw, pungent of speech, audacious in combat, and original in his approach to naval tactics." In each account, only Halsey's intemperance at the Battle of Leyte Gulf, where he had abandoned an American invasion force to chase impotent Japanese aircraft carriers, had marred an otherwise brilliant career.

In the following days over 2,000 obituaries aped these characterizations. One columnist recounted Halsey's "monumental hatred of Japan," another called him "swashbuckling," a third said he was the "saltiest old salt of World War II." According to one widely circulated death notice, Halsey "was the Nathan Bedford Forrest of the seas— getting there fastest with the mostest." A West Coast writer said Halsey seemed to "violate all the traditional rules of naval warfare," and another championed the admiral's "daring, persistent, sometimes unorthodox" way of thrashing "the Japanese fleet clean out of the Pacific." These accounts repeated the same adjectives enough to constitute cliché: sea dog, salty, aggressive, audacious. In them, Halsey was a fighting man from a Navy family, simple in outlook, fierce in temperament, and colorful in expression. He was a wartime symbol for American enmity toward Japan, a favorite among the rank and file, and his moniker, Bull, had aptly captured a brusque sailor with plenty of fight. He had descended from a long line of mariners, and his wartime service had concentrated—on the positive side of life's ledger— on carrier attacks at the war's outset and the struggle for Guadalcanal in 1942, and—in the debit column—on fleet action at Leyte Gulf in 1944.[1]

History followed obituary. Samuel Eliot Morison's multivolume account of the naval war framed Halsey as a hard-hitting sea commander, sometimes brilliant, sometimes intemperate. *Sea Power,* the basic text read by midshipmen at Annapolis for years, described Halsey's "ready courage" in early carrier attacks and both praised and admonished his "aggressive" fleet command later in the war. In other leading books, Halsey was an "admiral inclined toward boldness to the point of recklessness," the Navy's "fire eating answer to George Patton," a "pugnacious" and "grizzled fighting admiral." Books prominently profiled the fighting admiral and clung stubbornly to, in the words of one, a "garrulous, boozing Halsey." Clark Reynolds, in his seminal *The Fast Carriers,* presents as good an example as any of this common view: Halsey was a gifted leader, a bull whose limited intellect prompted careless charges around the ocean. Reynolds wrote that Halsey "had at least as much salt water in his veins as any American naval officer of his generation" and, by World War II, had "personified the layman's vision of swashbuckling sea fighters."[2]

Biography followed history. In 1946, Ralph Jordan's *Born to Fight* repeated wartime accounts of seagoing exploits. In 1968, Chandler Whipple structured *William F. Halsey: Fighting Admiral* around what he claimed was Halsey's motto: "Attack, Repeat Attack." In 1974, Benis Frank's *Halsey* promised more, but in most respects delivered less. Two years later, James Merrill published *A Sailor's Admiral,* writing, "Bill Halsey was not one of the Navy's intellectuals," but he was a "fighting admiral without peer." In 1985, E. B. Potter's *Bull Halsey,* the best of the admiral's biographies, nonetheless sprang from an "image of witless bellicosity." The most recent biography, John Wukovits's *Admiral "Bull" Halsey,* published in 2010, never strays far from its first sentence: "William F. Halsey came by his combativeness honestly, for belligerence had nourished a family tree spotted with sea dogs and sinners."[3]

Popular culture followed history. In fiction, James Michener wrote of "old Bull Halsey who had guts" in *Tales of the South Pacific,* James Jones of the admiral who called the Japanese "yellow-bellied monkey meat" in *The Thin Red Line,* and Tom Clancy of "fighting Bull Halsey" in *The Hunt for Red October.* Hollywood mimicked this image in films such as *From Here to Eternity, Midway, Pearl Harbor,* and the one biopic devoted to Halsey, *The Gallant Hours,* whose 1960 poster slogan shouted, "They called him the Bull of the Pacific." Paul and Linda McCartney even made Halsey a musical namesake with their enigmatic song "Uncle Albert / Admiral Halsey."[4]

Almost seventy-five years of memory, then, have not advanced Halsey's portraiture beyond the depth reflected in newspaper obituaries at the time of his death. Halsey's service has reduced and solidified to one of bellicose sea command, the Patton of the Pacific. He is a stick figure and a marble man, his visage fixed and immovable, even as the wider war and many of its prominent actors have changed markedly from early retellings in the 1940s. This view of Halsey is a caricature, where truth is evident enough, but where distortion reigns everywhere. In growing larger than life Halsey became less than a man.

. . . .

There was so much more to him. Halsey never spent a day outside the cocoon of the American military, a trait he shared only with General Douglas MacArthur out of all the officers in the nation's history, and one that bequeathed to him a certain conservatism. Born to a naval officer in 1882, Halsey became a five-star fleet admiral following World War II, the highest rank given American military officers at midcentury. He spent his boyhood as a Navy junior and in 1900 he followed his father—hardly an audacious choice—into the Navy. After graduating from the Naval Academy, he commenced a life with destroyers and hunted submarines in World War I. In 1934, he became for a time the oldest man to earn Navy wings as an aviator. By World War II, he had more command time at sea than any other officer then serving and perhaps more than any officer in the nation's history.

He was there, at sea, leading an aircraft carrier task force, on the morning the Japanese attacked Pearl Harbor, and he vowed to fight until the "Japanese language is spoken only in hell." In the first months of 1942, as Japan raced across the equatorial Pacific and as America strained toward a war footing, Halsey directed the sole offensive actions the United States could then muster in that or any theater of operations. Before a single American formation saw action in Europe, Halsey joined MacArthur as the war's first heroes. Later, in April, he squired Jimmy Doolittle's airplanes toward Japan when no other admiral would risk his ships, making possible Doolittle's famous raid on Tokyo. In all of this, Halsey bestowed badly needed cheer on a home front reeling from the Pearl Harbor attack.[5]

From October 1942 to June 1944 he served as area commander of the South Pacific Forces, overseeing the epic struggle for Guadalcanal and the Solomon Islands. In its rush to treat Halsey as a seagoing fleet commander late in the war, history has left untilled this crucial period of Halsey's service, which was a time well before the massive weight of American military output bore down on Japan and well before the war's outcome was clear. There, he served ashore, leading Army, Navy, Marine, and associated air force troops in one of the war's most consequential campaigns. He mediated the disputes of policy and personality between the Army and the Navy and between MacArthur and Admiral Chester Nimitz that bedeviled the American war effort. In the South Pacific, Halsey exists in three dimensions, aggressive, yes, but also tentative and sometimes cautious. There, in the South Pacific, he was moderate in his judgments, circumspect in his command, human in his behavior. The Halsey of history is a cartoon, but there, in the South Pacific, he was a man.

Halsey's South Pacific service also illuminates broader contours of the war. Excepting the epic slugfest for Guadalcanal, the region has been a neglected corner of the war, without a champion then or a well-developed history now. No service but the Marines had much interest in recording its events: of the more than one hundred official Army histories, only one, *Cartwheel: The Reduction of Rabaul,* covered the region; the Army Air Forces concentrated on the bombardment of enemy homelands, devoting just portions of three chapters across seven volumes to the South Pacific struggle; and Morison's fifteen tomes on the Navy assign whole volumes to battles of a few days, but only a single book, *Breaking the Bismarcks Barrier,* to the region after Guadalcanal had been secured.[6]

A thousand or more secondary books on World War II mimic this topography. Eric Bergerud's tandem treatment of ground and air warfare, *Touched by Fire* and *Fire in the Sky,* and Bruce Gamble's trilogy treating the air war over Rabaul represent the outstanding examples among those few that treat the wider South Pacific, but even those shortchange high-level joint command as well as the fight for New Georgia, the battle for Bougainville, and the reduction of the Japanese position in the upper Solomons and New Britain. Collectively, these contests helped draw the United States and Japan into an attritional war that neither nation preferred but that only the Americans could possibly win. There, in the South Pacific, months of unrelenting

Imperial triumph finally met the red line of Allied resistance. There, Allied victory and Japanese defeat became all but foreordained, even as great questions of strategy and operations remained.

Halsey took to sea again in the last year of the war, as a fleet commander ordering the full weight of American naval might against a dwindling enemy. His strikes against Philippine, Formosan, and Japanese islands revealed his struggle to keep apace of the vast changes in sea warfare from the time of his raids in early 1942. At the Battle of Leyte Gulf he left an American landing force to chase Japanese aircraft carriers, and his miscues during two damaging typhoons were late stains upon his service that have been much explored but little understood, then or now, especially regarding the tension between loyalty to purpose and to person with which all military leaders must reckon.

. . . .

Halsey's was indeed a large life, capable of accommodating both Bull and Bill, the former a product of a wartime celebrity that the latter at first courted and then spurned. Halsey could be aggressive. He was a fighter, sometimes too much for his own good. On rare occasions, he was reckless. He was a masterful leader. But he was also more than a seagoing fleet commander at war, a task that occupied two of his seventy-six years and less than half of his World War II service. In nearly any environment beyond command at sea, he was hesitant in his judgments and uncertain in his relationships. Halsey's audacity was a professional skill honed over decades at sea, not a personal trait. After the war and in the quiet of his life, he tried the truth: for his autobiography, it was "Bill Halsey whom I want to get on paper, not the fake, flamboyant 'Bull.' "[7] But by then it was too late and few listened. He remains Bull to those who do not know him, a group that until now has included nearly everyone who has ever heard of him.

Chapter One

An American Aristocracy

BILL HALSEY, after he became famous, wanted to see in his ancestors what others saw in him. Sifting through the family tree for his autobiography, he found most Halseys had been "seafarers and adventurers, big, violent men, impatient of the law, and prone to strong drink and strong language." He liked to tell of a Massachusetts privateer named Captain John Halsey, prominent in the eighteenth-century book *A History of the Robberies and Murders of the Most Notorious Pirates,* who apparently met a swashbuckler's end: "He was brave in his own person, courteous to all his prisoners, lived beloved and died regretted by his own people." He told of Captain Eliphalet Halsey, who in 1815, sailing out of Sag Harbor, "took the first Long Island whaler around the Horn." And he told of the generations of merchant mariners on his mother's side, at least one of whom "died at the hands of outlaw pirates." Mostly, Bill Halsey liked the meaning these sailors bequeathed to his lineage. In the half century after Eliphalet, he liked to say, "a dozen other Halsey whaling masters sailed in his course. Following them, my father went into the Navy; I followed him, and my son followed me."[1]

Halsey's ancestors did include mariners, but among them were also men of prominence, wealth, and politics, with feet firmly rooted in the black dirt of the New World. He was, in fact, more closely related to founding fathers, American presidents, famous poets, wealthy merchants, college presidents, and leading preachers than to any pirate or whaler. Not until his father, William, entered the Naval Academy at Annapolis in 1869 did a current of sea salt truly run through Halsey's bloodline. This he knew, but Bill Halsey usually picked the

7

embellished script over the bare truth when it came to his sea-dog reputation.

. . . .

The Halseys had come early to the New World. Thomas Halsey and his wife Elizabeth left England for the Massachusetts Bay Colony in 1638, a scant eighteen years after the Pilgrims first crossed the Atlantic Ocean in the *Mayflower*. Two years later, Thomas helped found and later became a leading member of Southampton, Long Island. He died in 1679 as Southampton's largest land owner, with an estate of two homesteads, seven surveyed lots, over 350 acres of land, and a household inventory worth 672 pounds, considerably more than the 500 pounds then considered necessary for a good, substantial merchant in New York City. In life, he was rich enough to forgo the common practice of whaling to supplement farming income, and many descendants maintained a similar distance from the ocean for centuries.[2]

From Thomas, the family branch to the admiral reflects the prerogatives of primogeniture and the fancy of fortune, each generation adding to or subtracting from the family line in proportion to their industry and luck. Thomas's second son, Isaac, lived a comfortable life in Southampton, collecting farm rents. Isaac's second son, Joseph, moved to New York City, married his first cousin, Elizabeth, and tilled a modest acreage in northern New Jersey. Joseph's third son, also named Joseph, worked a small plot near his father and sired eleven children.

Subsequent generations lifted the admiral's bloodline from this mounting obscurity. Joseph's third son, Isaac, became a wealthy merchant, landowner, and prominent member of the Church of Christ in central New Jersey. During the American Revolution, he joined the local Council of Safety, became paymaster and quartermaster of the Essex Militia, and was among the few merchants to extend credit to George Washington's beleaguered troops during their sentinel winter at Valley Forge. When Isaac died in 1788, the *New Jersey Journal* opined that the public had "lost a respectful citizen and the church a liberal benefactor."[3]

Isaac's last son and ninth child, Jacob, devoted his life to the young republic. He published the *Newark Gazette,* championed the Federalist Party cause of a strong central government, and attracted a wide readership—President John Adams once praised the *Gazette*'s "intelligence, information, accuracy, and elegance." At home, Jacob wed Mary Wheeler, the daughter of an infamous revolutionary, Captain Caleb Wheeler, and broke from a generations-old pattern of New Jersey living, settling in the heart of Lower Manhattan in a house on Broad Street at the southwest corner of Washington Square. He joined the New Jersey militia during the War of 1812 and died while bivouacked at Camptown, near Newark. At the time, his three children were fifteen, twelve, and five years old. For a moment, the admiral's lineage teetered on the brink of destitution, at a time when few social structures protected the innocents left behind after death stole the family provider.[4]

Then it soared to new heights. Jacob's five-year-old son, Charles, was raised by his uncle William Halsey, a lawyer, judge, and longtime mayor of Newark. Emulating him, Charles first practiced law, but later turned to God and the New York Theological Seminary. Ordained a deacon, his uncle's good name gained a sinecure at one of America's most prestigious pulpits, New York's Trinity Church. In 1838, Charles married a beautiful young congregate, Eliza Gracie King, who was the daughter of Charles King, which made her the granddaughter of Rufus King.

Rufus King had been among the early republic's great servants. His signature adorns the Constitution, he served as one of New York's original senators, was the first U.S. ambassador to England, was the Federalist candidate for president in 1816, and, as either senator or diplomat, served through the administrations of the first six chief executives, a record equaled only by the sixth president himself, John Quincy Adams. When he died in 1827, King's substantial estate of $140,000 owed much to both his own capacities and his happy marriage to Mary Alsop, who was the daughter of the wealthy New York merchant John Alsop. If Rufus King did not occupy quite the same plateau as George Washington or Thomas Jefferson or James

Madison, he was nonetheless "foremost in the second rank of political figures in the early days of the republic."[5]

His son Charles was no slouch, either. He married Eliza Gracie, bringing yet more distinction to the family line because her father was the rich entrepreneur Archibald Gracie, whose home in later years became the New York mayor's official residence. From there, Charles earned his own prominence as a hero in the Great Fire of 1835, when he organized a makeshift fire brigade to save a large residential district, undoubtedly saving scores of lives and businesses. He published and edited the *New York American,* developing a reputation as "a scholarly editor and a finished writer" before merging the paper with the *Courier and Enquirer* in 1845. King then became the president of Columbia College, serving from 1849 to 1864 and overseeing the establishment of schools for law and medicine and the university's move from Park Place to Madison Avenue. He wrote two books, and was a director of the Bank of New York and a frequent speaker at civic events. Widely known around town as Charles the Pink due to his flamboyant dress, he retired in 1864 and moved to Italy, where a son served as U.S. ambassador in Rome. He died in 1867, two years before his grandson William Halsey, the admiral's father, entered the Naval Academy at Annapolis.[6]

It was Charles King's daughter Eliza Gracie (named after her mother) who married Charles Halsey. After honing his pastoral skills as deacon at Trinity Church, Charles Halsey became the rector of Christ Church and, with Eliza, raised a family. They had four daughters and two sons, in that order: Eliza Gracie (again!), Mary, Emily, Esther, Charles Henry, and William Francis. Mary died as a young child, but the five other siblings lived with their parents in the very heart of Manhattan at 9 East Eighteenth Street. On May 2, 1855, while inspecting a Christ Church construction project overlooking Union Square, Charles fell through a fourth-floor window. A half hour later he was dead at the age of forty-six. The *New York Herald* lamented "this disastrous event" that had "deprived the community of one of its most faithful, laborious, and consistent ministers of the gospel."[7]

At the dawn of his life nearly four decades earlier, Charles had been a boy of five when his own father had died. A happy association with his uncle helped save him from obscurity and propelled him in life to Eliza, the King family, six children, and the pulpit at Christ Church. Now, in 1855, his two-year-old son, William, faced much the same circumstance. As the youngest of Charles and Eliza's children, William would have to find his way without a father's guidance and support. Nine generations removed from Southampton's wealthiest citizen on his father's side, and three removed from Rufus King on his mother's side, William's chosen path into the Navy would be far different from the path of his ancestors, who as a group had never strayed far from New York City and had, as farmers, merchants, politicians, and preachers, lived lives sometimes of gentility and occasionally of wealth. There had been nary a strutting pirate or ship captain among them.

....

Bill Halsey's maternal lineage had scarcely more seafarer flair. When his father, William, married Anne Brewster in 1881, two of the oldest European families in America merged. Anne was a direct lineal descendant of William Brewster, *Mayflower* passenger and elder of the Pilgrim Church in New England. William Brewster was the primary author of the *Mayflower Compact,* the first written form of participatory government in British North America, and his signature appears fourth of forty-one names affixed to that famous agreement. He was for a decade the senior church official in the colony, and God's grace translated into tangible assets: at his death he held fine tracts of land totaling 212 acres, claimed other assets worth 150 pounds, and his library of 265 books was easily among the two or three largest private collections then in New England. William Bradford, the colony's celebrated governor, called him "my dear and loving friend," and the great Pilgrim chronicler Thomas Hutchinson believed Brewster "was, next to Bradford, the most significant figure in the Plymouth Colony." One hagiographic account called Brewster "the first Apostle of both civil and religious liberty on this continent." This was perhaps hyperbole, but maybe not, for William Brewster was quite the man.[8]

The line from him to Bill Halsey began with William's second son, Love, a leading member of Plymouth's upcountry settlement of Duxbury before he helped found the town of Bridgewater with his wife, Sarah Collier, daughter of one of Plymouth Colony's original London financiers. Then there was Love's youngest son, Wrestling, the last son of the second son of a family patriarch, who eked out a modest livelihood as a Duxbury carpenter. Wrestling's seventh child and second son, also named Wrestling, married Hannah Thomas and moved inland, first to the newer town and fresher promise of Pembroke and then to nearby Kingston, where he was active in local affairs and the church. When he died in 1767 at eighty-six years old, he had been the Kingston deacon for so long that many townspeople could recall no other. By then, if his station was not equal to that enjoyed by his great-grandfather William Brewster in the previous century, Wrestling had nonetheless stabilized the family line and saved it from a slide into hardscrabble subsistence.

Wrestling and Hannah's eldest child was the third consecutive Wrestling in Bill Halsey's Brewster lineage. This Wrestling married Deborah Seabury and settled on family acreage in Kingston in a sizable home that local historians later offered as an example of the region's substantial residences during the colonial era. Although he lived within the periphery of Boston's influence, Wrestling remained largely indifferent to the increasing tension between the mother country and the colonies prior to the American Revolution, living instead a quiet, idyllic, long life stretching into the early 1800s.

Martin, Wrestling and Deborah's fourth child and third son, was of prime age for military service during the Revolutionary Era. Though his name appears on none of the regional army service musters during the war, he may have served afloat because he emerged after the war as a sailor and became a merchant captain, skippering ships passing out of Boston and New York, bound mostly for other East Coast ports, sometimes for Europe and, on two occasions, for the Pacific Ocean. Martin married Sarah Drew, herself a descendant of William Brewster and Martin's fourth cousin, fathered eight children, and created a stable life in Kingston, by then the family home for generations.

For the first time, a member of Bill Halsey's family line had taken to the sea. In all the preceding generations, no one in either his paternal or his maternal line had sailed the oceans or been associated with the sea beyond the symbiotic relationship between landlubbers and maritime trade shared by all New Englanders.

Martin and Sarah's fourth child and third son, also named Martin, followed his dad down to the sea. Born in 1794, he was an apprentice merchant mariner by the War of 1812. He married Betsy Russell in 1823 and established a small apartment in the port town of Elizabeth, New Jersey, where he fathered two children before dying at sea in 1828. Over a century later, Bill Halsey ascribed his great-grandfather's demise to the hands of some ruthless degenerate, a pirate perhaps, but disease or accident was a far more likely cause of death than a gun barrel or knife blade. Widowed, Betsy took in wash and let a room to boarders to support four-year-old James and one-year-old Elizabeth until 1832, when she returned with them to Kingston, where she could lean on familial support.

Young James took to the road when he was able. In 1850 he was living in a boarding house in the New York borough of Queens, working intermittent jobs as a dockhand upon the quays or a day laborer along burgeoning New York avenues. Two years later he moved to Philadelphia, so recently the nation's premier city, before New York had rushed past it in the first decades of the Industrial Revolution. In 1853 he married Deborah Grant Smith, the daughter of a reputable farmer and prominent Congregationalist from Philadelphia County. With a small stake from his father-in-law, James established himself in a clerking house and clawed his family back into the respectable classes of society. He and his wife moved north, first to New York City, then Orange County, New Jersey, and ultimately coming full circle to the town of his birth, Elizabeth, where he settled into a large Victorian house at 134 West Jersey Street. From there, each day James traveled by streetcar to the Elizabeth Ferry pier, steamed across the water to Battery Park, and walked briskly to offices in Lower Manhattan, where he worked as a ship and freight broker.[9]

The couple had fourteen children. Their fourth, Anne, was born in 1859. She married William Halsey in 1881, and one year later gave birth to Bill Halsey, the future admiral. By that time, and dating to the *Mayflower,* the Brewster lineage had grown to well over 4,100 families. The extended family had produced exceptional persons, including Henry Wadsworth Longfellow and President Zachary Taylor. One family branch produced the town founder of Brewster, New York. Another branch begot James D. Brewster, who grew fabulously rich as his Brewster Carriage Company came to dominate the New England buggy market until the combustion engine and Henry Ford changed everything. Elsewhere, Benjamin Brewster, Anne's first cousin, became the attorney general of the United States during the administration of President Chester Arthur.

Anne's particular lineage after William the Pilgrim could not claim that sort of prominence. Still, her ancestors were never of the underclass and were only occasionally displaced from the middle class. For a time, her grandfather Martin's death had threatened to consign her father, James, to a life of hardship. But through his fortuitous marriage to Deborah Smith and his own diligence, James reached the respectable middle class during the Industrial Revolution, an era of momentous economic change in America. With the exception of two generations that had gone to sea, the Brewsters of Anne's bloodline had been preachers, farmers, carpenters, merchants, and money men. Like the Halseys, they had not built much of a reputation as military men or fighting sailors. Instead, their lives followed the classic pattern of industrious New Englanders as settlements became villages, villages became towns, and towns became cities. Along the way, Pilgrims became Yankees, and the Brewsters were distinguished in the pattern partly by their standing and mostly by their long association with the process.

. . . .

Two of the nation's leading Anglo-Saxon families mingled when William Halsey and Anne Brewster exchanged vows. To the 4,100 Brewster families the Halseys added 4,600 households, making William and Anne's family tree among the largest European lineages in North

America. Together, they could claim a New World heritage as deep as any and more prominent than nearly all save those with names such as Madison and Monroe or, in their own lifetimes, Edison and Rockefeller.

Yet their son Bill Halsey never exulted in this past, partly because he knew it imperfectly. "I know little or nothing about the Halsey family," he once explained to a genealogist. "My father went to sea as a young man and passed little to me in this regard." Throughout his life, the admiral referred to even first cousins as "distant relatives" and, astonishingly and somewhat incongruously, believed he had "only three immediate relatives" among the nation's many Halseys. Still, Bill Halsey had the essentials correct, especially as they related to well-known ancestors. On his father's side he knew he descended from a founder of Southampton, and on his mother's side he knew he came from *Mayflower* stock, which was always a matter of pride within the family. He knew Archibald Gracie was his great-great-grandfather, knew he carried the genes of Rufus King, and knew his great-grandfather Charles King was once president of Columbia University.[10]

When he became a famous admiral, however, Bill Halsey ditched what little he knew of his impressive pedigree and instead courted distant, imagined, or manufactured ties to shiftless mariners. He said he sprang from a "hard drinking, hard living set from around New York" so often that it became a cliché. To make his connection to the pirate John Halsey, he backtracked nine generations, all the way to Thomas Halsey, and then forward through another family line for six generations. Any relation, if it even existed, to the whaler Eliphalet Halsey predated Thomas's immigration to Massachusetts in 1638. As for the other dozen Halseys on the high seas for which he claimed kinship, Bill Halsey was as closely related to American presidents and famous poets as he was to any of them, and far closer in blood or marriage to Rufus King, John Alsop, and Archibald Gracie, to university presidents, prominent ministers, and successful newspapermen.[11]

As his celebrity grew in World War II, Halsey championed the legend of his seafaring bloodline to sustain his reputation for derring-do. Historians have adopted this patina, using it to frame Halsey's audacious temperament. Yet the truth was plain for anyone caring to look. Before he became famous, no disinterested observer would have characterized Bill Halsey's ancestry as swashbuckling. Four score before his birth, two successive Brewster generations had sailed the sea as merchantmen. But in New England family lines as deep as his, those were weak ties indeed to the sea. The truth of his family tree, and of his life itself, is at once more complicated and more compelling than the deception of his seafaring roots.

Chapter Two

The Admiral's Captain

BILL HALSEY'S father went down to the sea not to preserve a maritime tradition but to maintain a sense of place in American society. William Halsey was born in 1853 at his parents' home in Manhattan, a half a block west of busy Broadway Avenue. He came into the world a descendant of the great Alsop and Gracie fortunes, an heir to the political heritage of Rufus King, and with a virtual birthright into the respectable classes. Life was bright until his father, Charles, fell from that fourth-floor window, leaving two-year-old William to navigate life without a father's guidance. His family was never poor, and his grandfather Charles King, then president of Columbia University, provided a social footing in New York. But neither was the family rich. Widowed Eliza was never able, for instance, to move her family from their Lower Manhattan neighborhood, which during William's youth had steadily decayed as tens of thousands of destitute immigrants flooded New York, breaking across the city's social fabric. The circumstances of young William's life were not ruinous, but his father's death made him prone to take emotional and mental cues not from the stable, private world of hearth and home but from the broader, public world of city and society.

. . . .

At midcentury New York was a bewildering metropolis. It was a chaotic place, forever in some economic boom or bust. In 1857, amid a financial panic and in the wake of riots pitting immigrants against the city's native-born, the *New York Times* proclaimed the place the "worst governed city in the world." Then the Civil War sparked the New York draft riots of 1863, a multiday conflagration that was the "largest single incident of civil disorder" in the nation's history. Targeting the city's established interests, one rowdy mob stormed the grounds of Columbia College, intent on flaming President Charles King's house. Farther to the south, his daughter Eliza and her children, living a block from Union Square and sitting astride a fault line of native-born and immigrant neighborhoods, witnessed a major brawl less than 150 yards from their doorstep in which at least three people died. By the time he was ten, William was a veteran observer of mayhem, riots, and unrest.[1]

New York soared to new heights in the years after the Civil War. Central Park changed the city's footprint and skyscrapers transformed its profile. Industrialization offered treasure to an increasingly varied populace, many of whom, such as Cornelius Vanderbilt, Andrew Carnegie, and John Rockefeller, did not come from the blue blood that had for generations bestowed advantage on young men like William Halsey. For every fortune it fostered, however, the city battered hundreds of lives against capitalism's sharp shoals, and young William's experiences had taught him to fear more than to embrace the changing metropolis. Its episodic violence had threatened his physical security, its shifting economy his financial toehold, and its morphing demographics his birthright as a well-born native. As he approached adolescence, he looked elsewhere for a beginning.

For any boy interested in escaping the island of Manhattan, there was always and for a long time only the sea. During Halsey's childhood, over a hundred piers collared New York's southern tip below Fourteenth Street, making the waterfront a "restless wooden exoskeleton of ships, their long bowsprits nuzzling over the busy streets." The sea was the city's frontier, and it was there, on the periphery, "where a boy might turn his back on all that he had once known and step into an exotic dream of adventure, freedom, opportunity, and risk."[2]

An old family association gave William a chance to make the leap. Decades earlier, before his father, Charles, had left lawyering for preaching, he practiced law with George Robeson, who maintained an association with the Halsey family. When, in the spring of 1869, Robeson became President Ulysses Grant's secretary of the Navy, Wil-

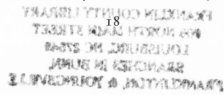

liam asked Robeson for an appointment to the Naval Academy in Annapolis, Maryland. The request might have amazed his mother, Eliza; family members had not strayed far from the confines of New York City for over a century, and years later his own son, the admiral, could only point to his dad's boyhood fascination with George Henty's adventure books to explain William's desire for the Navy. Lacking foreknowledge of the man he would become and the son he would have, in 1869 the Naval Academy probably held two great attractions for the youngster: it was not New York, and it was free—a crucial consideration given Eliza's financial circumstances. Robeson, who had already committed his allotted appointments that year, assigned William an Annapolis appointment from a congressional district representing southern Louisiana, a sleight of hand that benefited Yankee applicants in the decade following the Civil War, when Southern candidates were scarce. After he passed the admission examination, William Halsey, whose lineage was bereft of seafaring men, who had never ventured far beyond Manhattan Island, and who had surely never set foot in Louisiana, entered Annapolis in June of 1869, in his sixteenth year, representing the fair city of New Orleans.[3]

He and Annapolis were well suited to each other: each offered what the other needed, and took only what the other was willing to give. There, Halsey found a haven populated with familiar archetypes and a refuge from Manhattan's riptides. Most of Halsey's fellow students were, in the words of a Navy doctor, "blond-haired," "blue-eyed," and "Anglo-Saxon," eager to enter what one keen historian labeled a "naval aristocracy" of "proper characters" with the "right habits, principles, and feelings." Their careers, Robeson told Halsey's class in an opening address, rested on a Gilded Age social compact in which no one would grow rich in uniform, but in exchange for devoted service the Navy would provide "an adequate provision, in a most honorable calling, for your future support, of which, while you live, nothing but incapacity or misconduct can deprive you." Such a bargain sat in sharp contrast to the whims of New York City, where well-bred genes seemed to count for less and less and fortune appeared to fall randomly across an ever-wider swath of citizenry. In the many years that lay before him, William Halsey never once exhibited interest in the commercial world when the occasional opportunity passed his way.[4]

Halsey was at best a middling student. He earned grades below the median in both academic performance and military conduct. In the classroom, he had trouble with the hard sciences, did better in military studies, and achieved his best marks in humanities. His demerit record placed him near the bottom of his class in each of his four years as a student. He collected these admonishments earnestly, through an assortment of small offenses and instances of rowdy behavior. His dorm room rarely if ever made the grade, and he was routinely dinged for irregular behavior in ranks, visiting during study hours, and breaking curfew. On graduation day, Halsey's overall standing placed him nineteenth out of twenty-nine graduating midshipmen. In the end, his classroom work was unremarkable, and his conduct grade reflected a youngster fitting imperfectly into military life. There was no disgrace in any of this. Many a decent student did not endure the Annapolis grind at all—Halsey's classmate Albert Michelson finished ninth and later became the first American to win the Nobel Prize in Physics—and Halsey's demerit record, devoid of any serious shame, was one that many boys could be proud of, even as they grew into manhood.[5]

Halsey graduated to a moribund Navy, its fifty or so commissioned vessels barely one-tenth its Civil War size. His first meaningful cruise, begun in the summer of 1876 with twelve officers and 125 sailors aboard the *Alert,* took him to Shanghai and the Asiatic Station. Service in Asia could challenge a young man fresh from Annapolis. Officers of the era liked "smoking opium Chinese fashion" while ashore, and bluejackets pursued their own interests; one newspaper identified 688 houses of ill repute in Shanghai alone. With such prospects, sexually transmitted diseases ran rampant through ships, and less exciting scourges such as dysentery and malaria levied an almost constant tax on visiting crews. Quite aside from the degeneracy and filth, there were also chances everywhere for a bit of lawlessness as rambunctious and randy sailors clashed with local authorities.[6]

This smorgasbord of contagious disease and baneful opportunity placed a premium on officers with a hand firm enough to sustain discipline and a touch supple enough to compensate for the many small indignities of shipboard life. Halsey exhibited this balance from an early point in the cruise. As a watch officer, he was responsible for discipline and was free to report any seaman to the skipper for punishment at periodic hearings known as captain's masts. He exercised this power judiciously, reporting sailors less often than four of the other six watch officers, and almost always for fairly serious infractions such as insubordination or failure to fulfill essential duties. While with the *Alert,* Halsey never reported a sailor for spending extra time above deck at night, smoking at unauthorized times, or participating in the occasional shoving match, preferring to deal with these infractions without the formality of the mast. Although he risked ignoring serious problems, in the following years Halsey developed a reputation as a humane, perhaps even lenient, officer in his dealings with sailors in an era renowned for the martinet and macabre attitudes held by many officers toward enlisted men.[7]

Other opportunities for distinction emerged when in June 1877 the *Alert* chased the false rumor of a marooned crew in Dampier Strait, a channel between the small island of Waigeo and the northwest coast of Papua New Guinea. Although the ship's incomplete charts of the remote area dated to 1804, the *Alert* conducted an exhaustive two-week search of the strait, discovering many unmarked shoals but no shipwrecked souls, traveling 6,500 miles from Shanghai to Dampier Strait to Hong Kong. The cruise brought renown to the *Alert*'s skipper, Lieutenant Commander Albert Barker, and paid fewer public dividends for young Halsey. Leading up to and during the search, Halsey referred no sailor for a captain's mast, letting the mission itself focus the crew, but on the return leg to Hong Kong he reported a man for insubordination, a reminder to the crew to heed the requirements of a Navy ship afloat.

Once in Hong Kong's harbor, Halsey saved a man who had fallen overboard on the night of July 29. In Barker's words, "the night was dark and a strong current was running, but Halsey did not hesitate.

He sprang at once upon the hammock sail and from thence jumped overboard, at the risk of his own life, and grabbed the drowning man." Years later and by then a rear admiral, Barker believed it one of the greatest selfless acts he had ever witnessed. Others agreed. The Asiatic Squadron commander, Rear Admiral William Reynolds, thanked Halsey for his "prompt and heroic action," and the secretary of the Navy told young Halsey that he had "exhibited courage which is of the noblest character."[8]

William Halsey was an excellent junior officer. Upon his return from Asia in 1880 he was promoted to lieutenant, junior grade, and performed well on another cruise, this one with the *Iroquois* and the Pacific Squadron. He again saved the life of a bluejacket by jumping into the open sea, and he earned praise from both his skipper and local authorities for calming a near-riot between *Iroquois* sailors and townsmen in Auckland, New Zealand, a fight no doubt about the affections of local girls and fueled by liquor. Promoted to lieutenant in 1886, he turned in a third successful cruise, this one with the *Ranger* while she surveyed the Lower (Baja) California coast. Along the way, he garnered top marks in every category from every commander in officer efficiency reports, and collected an unbroken string of approbation. One skipper praised Halsey's "ability, zeal, and exceptional character"; another wrote of Halsey's considered judgment and calm temperament. One skipper's assessment was typical: Halsey had earned his "entire respect. He is a painstaking, conscientious and capable officer, strict, impartial and considerate in his management of men, and unhesitatingly and cheerfully obedient to orders. As a man, he is temperate in all his habits, and is a Christian gentleman."[9]

When in 1891 the Navy sent Halsey to Annapolis for a tour teaching, he could look back upon fifteen years of productive service and forward to a bright horizon. The future by then included a family. William had married Anne Brewster in 1881, during one of the few times he had traveled back to New York City as a young officer. How the two met is unknown, but the Halsey and Brewster families shared deep ties to Elizabeth, New Jersey, and they perhaps knew each other all along. Anne was an attractive, petite brunette. Bill, their son, recalled his mother "had the Spartan spirit" of the "tough gang of Puritans" from which she came. "She always held herself very straight and to people that did not know her she appeared very austere." His college friends at the Naval Academy remembered Bill's mom a bit differently, as a quiet if somewhat busy presence, and came to appreciate greatly her fondness for finding dates for the many students who were casting about for midshipman dances.[10]

. . . .

The elder Halsey entered midcareer in precipitous times. Industrialization changed the nation and its Navy as the nineteenth century drew to a close. New technologies, in the shape of steel and steam, altered the Navy's form while new ideas, from the pen of Alfred T. Mahan, remade the Navy's function. These changes shook the Navy, waking it from a long slumber following the Civil War, and confronted men of Halsey's generation like a squall line, presenting challenge and opportunity. Some would weather, even beckon, the storm. Others would endure it as best they could. Still others would find themselves cast ashore, pushed there by the wide wake of change that buffeted the Navy from every quarter in those years.

Following his teaching tour, Halsey met the new Navy in 1896 when he reported to Hampton Roads for duty with the *New York,* the Navy's newest cruiser, which boasted heavy guns, powerful steam engines, and an enlisted crew complement not of captains of the forecastle, tops, or afterguard but of machinists, oilers, and boilermakers. The *New York* was Halsey's introduction to responsibilities that extended at long last beyond those of a watch officer. As a division officer, his duties included the management of the bridge and the supervision of all watch officers, tasks that offered close contact with the *New York* skipper, Captain Winfield Schley. For the first time in his career, Halsey garnered something other than top marks in his fitness reports, earning only middling scores in "health" and "judgment in the handling of men." Time would tell if Schley's assessment was a passing blip or a harbinger of things to come, but one thing was certain: Halsey left little impression on his skipper. In his memoirs, Schley failed to include Halsey in his list of officers assigned to the *New York,* even though both men shared the bulk of their respective time aboard the ship.[11]

If the *New York* suggested something of the Navy's emerging shape, Halsey's next assignment, as a student at the Naval War College in Newport, offered a look at the Navy's changing purpose. Founded in 1885, the school and its faculty extolled the development of a U.S. fleet capable of decisive battle against the world's strongest navies, a concept at odds with the ideas that had for decades shaped the operations of a Navy of modest squadrons dispersed around the globe. Mahan had given voice to this new notion, and married it to the developing battleship, in *The Influence of Sea Power upon History,* published in 1890. Theodore Roosevelt, who as assistant secretary of the Navy delivered the opening address to Halsey's War College class, echoed Mahan. Dismissing the "schemes for defending the country by gun boats instead of by a fleet of sea going battle-ships," Roosevelt championed "a great navy, not primarily to fight, but to avert fighting, and maintain right by the show of ready might without the use of violence. Peace, like freedom, is not a gift that tarries long in the hands of cowards, or those too feeble or too short-sighted to deserve it."[12]

Roosevelt's premier biographer called it "the first great speech" of the future president's career. It was printed in every major newspaper and caused a nationwide sensation. "From Boston to San Francisco, from Chicago to New Orleans, expansionist editors and correspondents praised it, and agreed that a new, defiantly original spirit had entered into the conduct of American affairs." For the handful of War College students who had heard the speech firsthand, the wide reception of Roosevelt's words was confirmation that they stood on the precipice of a new era, a time marked by new steel warships and an emerging sense of national purpose. For them, Roosevelt's speech had placed into relief a wider constellation of forces calling the Navy to the horizon, to the new, and to the unknown.[13]

Halsey left no clear indication of his attitude toward the college and its desire to jettison old ways, though he confronted soon enough the consequences of a more aggressive American foreign policy and strengthening Navy. After Halsey left Newport and was teaching again at Annapolis in 1898, the battleship *Maine* blew up in Havana's harbor, sparking war between the United States and Cuba's colonial master, Spain. The conflict quickly escalated beyond the narrow matter of Cuba, and presented a chance to win Spanish possessions elsewhere, especially in the Philippine Islands. After Commodore George Dewey smashed a Spanish squadron in Manila Bay and Rear Admiral William Sampson helped rout Old World forces on Cuba, Spain consented to Cuban independence and agreed to sell Puerto Rico, the Philippines, and Guam to the United States for a paltry $20 million. At about the same time, America annexed Hawaii, parts of Samoa, and Wake Island. The Spanish-American War had birthed the American empire. Over the next five decades, the acquisition of new territory in the Caribbean and the Pacific brought in its train far-reaching consequences for the nation and its Navy. For William Halsey, the implications hit closer to home, and sooner.

The growing Navy needed more officers in every grade. In 1899 Halsey at last placed on his coat sleeves the braids, two broad and one narrow, of a lieutenant commander. He was forty-six years old, had served in the lieutenant grades for nineteen years, and had yet to skipper as much as a rowboat. The following year Halsey left Annapolis for San Diego to serve as executive officer aboard the *Adams,* a training ship for enlisted sailors. This should have been a familiar tour for him, given his long experience afloat and teaching tours at Annapolis. Yet, within weeks of becoming the *Adams* executive officer, he was in a hospital suffering insomnia, indicating something more than the occasional restless night and perhaps some serious emotional distress, physical pain, or drug or alcohol abuse.[14]

His duties as executive officer may have unnerved him. Bradley Fiske, one of the great officers of the era, found executive officer responsibilities "quite different" from lesser tasks, which were circumscribed either by time or task. The duties of an executive officer, by contrast, extended across the entire workings of a ship and would last "from midnight of one night to midnight of the next night, and then start in again." Looking back on it, Fiske felt fortunate to complete his own tour as executive officer "without loss of sleep or appetite and without having quarrels." For whatever reason, Halsey's own stint as an executive officer was more troublesome.[15]

In the summer of 1900 Halsey went to the Philippines and, at long last, took command of a naval vessel. It was not much. The *General Alvara,* a harbor hulk captured after Dewey's conquest some fifteen months earlier, was in every respect a mediocre war prize. She was 212 feet long, was capable of a modest ten knots, and embarked five officers—none save Halsey above the rank of ensign—and about forty sailors. The Spanish had used her in the Philippines as a lighthouse tender and utility transport, the same duties she now performed for the Americans. Essentially without protective armor, her modest battery consisted of three small smoothbore cannon. Any fighting the *General Alvara* would see during Halsey's tour would be pure providence, for no commander would deliberately place such an auxiliary in harm's way.[16]

The ship nevertheless plied dangerous waters, because Dewey's annihilation of the Spanish fleet had led to an unrelenting guerilla war between U.S. forces and Filipino insurgents. In early September, shortly after assuming his diminutive command, Halsey undertook a dozen mail, provision, and transport runs before returning to Cavite in October for dry dock maintenance. He took the *General Alvara* to sea again in November, commencing a monotonous series of mail and supply calls to lighthouses and garrisons scattered throughout the Philippines, usually spending two weeks running about the archipelago and then a few days at Cavite, replenishing and preparing for yet another run to garrisons, outposts, and lighthouses. By July the ship was back up on ways at Cavite. Since its maintenance the previous fall, the ship had steamed 17,180 miles, most of them in short passages. The *General Alvara* had visited seventy-four separate ports or lighthouses since its last dry docking, some of them more than once, and in only two instances did she spend more than ten days at anchor.[17]

Halsey's duties were routine, but over time their nature and regularity wore heavily. In and out of ports, around lighthouses, and nearly always in constrained water, the *General Alvara* contended with treacherous reefs, swirling shoals, heavy monsoons, and the occasional typhoon common to the region. Halsey was the only officer of any experience on board, so it fell upon him to navigate the uncertain seas, often with inaccurate charts. That the *General Alvara* never scraped bottom or had serious trouble moving through the Philippine littorals, even near lighthouses that by design sat near dangerous shoreline, was testimony to Halsey's considerable skill as a sailor.

In the climate and circumstance of the Philippines, the schedule was a constant grind. Tropical and maritime, the archipelago sported mean temperatures near one hundred degrees Fahrenheit and heavy humidity. Only the open sea offered relief. One officer lucky enough to escape the coastal war and join a "real ship" rejoiced as he "met the pleasant southern breeze." The *General Alvara,* however, rarely if ever enjoyed wide water, where the running was safer and the weather better. Officers with more varied duties could describe Manila as a "very gay place," comment on "bright and cheerful" Moro villages, or recognize "very attractive" landscapes where the bays and towns and mountains "were beautiful." No member of the *General Alvara* crew left similar descriptions. The ship's cruising schedule deprived them of the charms of Filipinas and sucked from them their enthusiasm. As for steaming the islands' beautiful byways, Halsey and his small band were more likely to be watching for dangers lurking below the waterline than for the beauty above the horizon.[18]

The *General Alvara* resumed her tedious rounds after slipping back into the water in late July. In September the Asiatic Squadron commander, Rear Admiral George Remey, joined the ship for a two-week inspection of the war zone. By that point guerilla tactics had transformed the fight into a vicious struggle, each side committing unspeakable atrocities. In some places, Americans captured by Philippine insurgents could expect to be buried alive, or have their eyes cut out or their feet amputated, or be cooked over a slow fire before being butchered and sometimes eaten. For their part, U.S. troops engaged in vigilante assassination, water torture, widespread burning, and sexual rampages. For Halsey, who sometimes witnessed these atrocities firsthand, not only while cruising with Remey but also in the course of his constant rounds throughout the Philippines, it may have been a searing experience. Combined with the slog of his own duties, the cruel spectacle of guerilla war would have assaulted many a man's sensibilities.

Halsey's humane attitudes toward sailors eroded in this hellhole. In December 1900, during his second captain's mast as a Navy skipper, Halsey sentenced a man to three days' solitary confinement, restricted his diet to bread and water, and demoted him in rank for being absent without leave—a lenient punishment given the conventions of the day. Soon, however, Halsey took to favoring a ten-day stint in double irons for the lesser offense of foul language. By early 1901 sailors inattentive to duty earned the same ten-day penance in shackles. Later that spring, merely reporting late to a formation on Halsey's ship meant three days in solitary confinement, bread and water, and a reduction in rank. By his last captain's mast aboard the *General Alvara,* Halsey was busting men two grades in rank for drinking from the officers' water cooler. In the end, solitary confinement, restricted rations, and shackles had become Halsey's favored means of punishment.[19]

Duties of command explained part of this pattern. Now a ship captain, Halsey's responsibility for discipline was surely greater than it had been while a watch or division officer. But as his time aboard the *General Alvara* lengthened, Halsey lost the balance between justice and punishment that had marked his earlier career. In this he was certainly no different from many other Navy skippers, but as he adopted the mores of his broader community he lost some of his distinguishing character.

He may simply have come too late to independent command. At the time, many observers and more than a few officers believed the slow approach to responsibility during the Gilded Age had robbed the Navy of commanders at appropriate, younger ages. "Long service in the lower ranks," opined one respected official in the Navy Department, "worked an injustice to the officers, and was detrimental to the navy since it unfitted the officers for command ranks. Men who had spent the best years of their lives in subordinate stations, occupied often with trifling and routine tasks, were not likely to have the executive habit, initiative, decision and resourcefulness, when having passed the meridian of life they became captains, commodores, and rear admirals." Yates Stirling, then a lieutenant skippering a small gunboat in the Philippines, recalled one lieutenant commander, perhaps Halsey because the two often crossed paths, as "none too sure of himself, having reached a position of responsibility at too old an age." Stirling believed this lieutenant commander had been "a capable man" and "excellent officer, but slow promotion had sapped his initiative as it had many others of his time." While Halsey was serving in the Philippines, his fitness reports became average: he was no longer judged "excellent" in every category, and Remey, who had ample chance to observe Halsey while aboard the *General Alvara,* marked Halsey's ability to command and his health both "very good" in December 1900 but downgraded these marks to "good" six months later.[20]

Halsey was probably happy for orders to return home to the comfortable environs of Annapolis in March of 1902. His ticket was the *Manila,* like the *General Alvara* a small, unarmored ship captured from Spain in 1898. For most of the war she had been confined to Cavite as a receiving hulk, and by early 1902 had not left her mooring for well over a year. Nevertheless, the Navy determined to use the *Manila* to run about 200 souls home. Halsey took command on April 1 and with seventeen officers, a crew of sixty-seven, and an additional 117 Army soldiers, left for Bremerton, Washington, on April 15.[21]

The trip was a test of seamanship from the start. "None of its officers had any experience with the vessel," Halsey remembered. "The records were incomplete, and as to what would be the performance of the ship and engines in a seaway no man could say." Within days of leaving the Philippines, horrendous weather assaulted the ship, tossing waves across the *Manila,* first cresting the bow and then sweeping the stern, over and over again. It seemed to Halsey the "vessel was never quiet for an instant, and combined more movements, at the same time, than had ever been observed on any occasion during a service of many years at sea." Compounding difficulties, the ship's steering gear worked miserably, her compass broke, and many of Halsey's passengers, who were unaccustomed to rolling seas, became violently ill.[22]

Then the real trouble began. On the afternoon of June 2 the *Manila*'s engines seized. Examining them, Halsey saw that all but one of the high-pressure steam pistons had simply worn away at the same time, breaking into fragments and destroying their cylinders. In one spot, the final stroke had bent the tail rod twice, cracked the inner lining of the high-pressure cylinder, and carried away the go-ahead shoe. "The wreck," Halsey marveled, "was complete in detail."[23]

The crew hoisted small auxiliary sails, which might have sufficed had the weather cooperated. It did not. From the afternoon of June 1 the barometer had fallen steadily. By 6:00 AM on June 4 the ship was tossing in a moderate gale, squall lines periodically passing over the hapless hull. Three hours later the small main trysail gave way, and with it went Halsey's ability to turn the *Manila* into the seas. The storm worsened, rolling the ship as much as forty degrees. By 11:00 AM the *Manila* was mired in a trough, "absolutely without control." Halsey feared that the wooden afterdeck house, badly rotten, would break away, flood the ship, and doom the crew. Soon sections belowdecks filled with water, giving the ship a starboard list of thirty-seven degrees. Halsey dropped the port anchor to compensate for that problem, but his ability to manage the crisis was fast slipping from his grasp. In the understated words of the official log, the *Manila* "was lying to with sea anchor over port bow, in trough of sea and unable to get out."[24]

The ship was helpless; her crew nearly so. The *Manila* was 1,200 miles past Honolulu, and midway between Bremerton and San Francisco, each about 1,100 miles distant, well outside normal shipping lanes. Although the ship possessed seven small lifeboats, only two could plausibly be of use for a relief expedition. That option "was carefully considered," Halsey recalled, "and there were many volunteers" for a dash in the small boats. But he sensed a better option lay with the stricken vessel. In the nearly three full days since losing power, the *Manila* had drifted in three directions, averaging fifty to sixty miles a day. Even if a relief expedition could find assistance, a rescue party could have a monumental task finding the *Manila*. Besides, despite all the ship's deficiencies, the storm had revealed one good quality: marked stability. At the height of the storm, Halsey bet the crew's fate on the *Manila*.[25]

The storm abated in the early afternoon. By some miracle of coincidence, engineers succeeded in turning the one remaining good cylinder, which was enough to coax the *Manila* slowly forward. Now the weather did cooperate. Altering course for San Francisco and more populated sea-lanes, the *Manila* encountered other vessels on June 8, sighted the Golden Gate on June 10, and reached the safety of Mare Island and land the following day.

Getting the *Manila* home was a singular achievement. Halsey may have missed the call to glory in the Philippines, but commanding the *Manila* set in relief his virtues: the seasoned sailor, the composed officer, the compassionate man. Whatever had turned him into a martinet in the Philippines faded: of the thirty-four sailors he disciplined on the *Manila*, only one received a penalty as harsh as solitary confinement, almost as if Halsey preferred to let the trial of the voyage impose its own regulation. Looking back on it, it is no exaggeration to say William Halsey saved hundreds of lives on the *Manila*. The Naval Institute found the voyage sufficiently noteworthy to publish Halsey's account in *Proceedings*. For Halsey, conning the *Manila* through her distress, on the open seas, alone and autonomous, was perhaps the last time he sailed as he imagined he would as a boy. It was his finest moment in uniform.[26]

. . . .

In the fall of 1905, by then a commander and following yet another teaching tour at the academy, the elder Halsey became the skipper of the cruiser *Des Moines*. Launched in 1902, the ship was one of the most thoroughly modern vessels on which he served. She measured over 300 feet, boasted ten five-inch cannon, was capable of a respectable sixteen knots, and her crew of 339, including twenty-seven officers, was at least five times larger than either of his previous two commands. To Halsey, the ship represented the new Navy that President Roosevelt was now hastily building.[27]

Much else had also changed since he last served afloat in American waters, before the war with Spain. Since 1902 the Navy had concentrated the North Atlantic, South Atlantic, and European Squadrons into a U.S. Fleet—the first time that moniker had been used—for annual maneuvers that exposed deficiencies in large-scale, combined ship tactics. Handling fleets of steam and steel required different competencies from those that had reigned in the days of sail and wood. Perhaps more important than the new technical requirements, however, was the fact that the formation of a fleet heralded a new mission for the Navy. With each passing year, the protection of American interests on far-flung stations became increasingly incidental to the task of meeting and defeating an enemy armada on the high seas. Mahan had come to the Navy.

The *Des Moines,* with the cruisers *Minneapolis, Denver,* and *Cleveland,* was part of the Third Squadron of the newly named North Atlantic Fleet. Halsey's commanding officer on the *Alert* in the 1870s, now Rear Admiral Albert Barker, commanded the fleet, while another former skipper, Rear Admiral Royal Bird Bradford, commanded the Third Squadron from the deck of the *Minneapolis.* Bradford was an exceptional naval administrator and reformer, having authored the most recent edition of the Navy Department's *Regulations,* established the Navy's Electrical Department, and written numerous professional papers extolling the challenges of a new Navy. His *Minneapolis* skipper, the remarkable Bradley Fiske, represented the prototype of the modern officer: technologically savvy, professionally adaptive, temperamentally decisive. With men such as these, the Third Squadron promised to lead the fleet as it developed the tactics for a dawning century.

The Third Squadron spent the spring of 1906 in ship drill off the Eastern Seaboard and in group exercises in the Caribbean. That summer, the squadron hosted 461 midshipmen, about two-thirds of the student brigade, for their summer practice cruise to the Azores in the central Atlantic. Halsey and the *Des Moines* dispatched their group of students at Annapolis on August 25 and headed to the Brooklyn Naval Yard for a period of refit, arriving on August 30.[28]

Within hours of the ship's arrival in New York, Halsey left the *Des Moines* and checked into the Brooklyn Naval Hospital, prodded there by the strong advice if not outright request of the ship's doctor, J. A. Murphy. According to the hospital admission report, Halsey was suffering from insomnia and gastritis, though there was surely something more to his condition. "For the past two weeks," Murphy reported, Halsey "has had great difficulty obtaining natural rest and is depressed and nervous." His appetite had been poor, the doctor recorded, and his bowel movements irregular. His prostration was marked and his pulse was weak.[29]

These were textbook symptoms of addiction withdrawal, something the medics soon faced forthrightly. Halsey's condition, a medical corpsman wrote in the early evening, had been "aggravated by excessive indulgence in alcoholic stimulants" a practice Halsey had evidently stopped cold turkey days earlier, right after the *Des Moines* had discharged its midshipmen at Annapolis. Halsey had self-medicated with sedatives to help him through the storm, and now the hospital staff gave him the much stronger chloral hydrate to calm his condition. Halsey surely had insomnia. His gastritis was real. But alcohol was his problem.[30]

The Navy tried to salvage something of Halsey's record. As Murphy explained in the medical report, Halsey "had been under a severe mental strain due to the demands of the practice cruise for midshipmen." A "great part of this cruise was spent at sea, and underway in inland waters, in bad weather and fog, throwing more than the usual amount of responsibility on the Commanding Officer." This was sympathetic. Halsey had long experience under more trying circumstances. Certainly no sea challenge aboard the *Des Moines,* for instance, matched his predicament with the *Manila* in the desolate Pacific. As for the unique responsibilities attendant on a midshipman cruise, mischievous students could hardly present an insoluble task to Halsey after all his years on the sea and at the academy. He handled men well, and this had been his ninth midshipman cruise, the first two as a student and three as a skipper of the academy's own practice sloop while serving on its faculty.[31]

The primary source of Halsey's crack-up coursed deeper through his veins than a summer cruise with boys. A Gilded Age naval career rested upon a social compact. As one of Halsey's peers described it, for a life of dedicated service, much of it spent in a "tiresome alternation of monotonous cruises at sea and profitless tours ashore," a naval man "might nevertheless live the kind of life that every man wants to live": a life of tenured service, financial security, honor, and perhaps glory; a "life in which he feels that he is doing the best he can with the one or five or ten talents committed to his keeping."[32]

This had been Halsey's agreement with the Navy. It had held fast through decades of broader social, economic, and political change in the late nineteenth century. His service had reflected a typical sequence of sea and shore duty; by 1906 he had spent nearly twenty years at sea, just over fourteen ashore, and two at home awaiting orders. His place on the Navy Register had been virtually constant his entire career. Since 1885 he had held the same spot within his year group, between Edmund Underwood and Frank Wilner. At once a testament to dismal promotion prospects and to sturdy employment, Halsey's name stayed on the same page of the register for nineteen years, a condition that surprised him not at all as he slowly accumulated the service that would at last yield senior rank.

Yet since the late 1880s momentous advances in technology and emerging ideas of naval strategy had worked to erode this steady life of a naval officer, creating a "crisis of career anxiety" among officers of Halsey's generation. The new Navy had sprung from the Spanish-American War with confidence, energy, and a hankering for change. Counting ships built, building, and authorized, the Navy grew nearly threefold in the last decade of Halsey's career. Almost overnight, the Navy went from a chronic surplus of officers to an acute shortage, a situation that persisted well into the twentieth century before the Naval Academy, which grew from 280 midshipmen in 1899 to 879 in 1906, could right the balance. With such growth, naval promotions quickened, stealing from many officers an orderly progression into the middle ranks and greater responsibility, which in turn exposed some officers' inability to adapt. As a result, the Navy's promotion system, based solely on seniority, came under assault as the insatiable reformer Theodore Roosevelt crusaded to base promotions on merit. For many men of William Halsey's vintage, who were at last nearing the high rank promised to them by longevity, Roosevelt's muckraking hit like a surprise squall line. For them, the new Navy promised better ships, greater prestige, and more chance for glory. But with change came reform, rendering the sea around these officers full of swift and uncertain currents.[33]

As Halsey aged through these reformist years, drinking may have provided an illusory reprieve. It did for others. Throughout the nation, alcohol consumption spiked around the turn of the century, as people from all walks of life struggled for footing in a churning, industrializing world. Urbanization and immigration placed drunkenness against a new backdrop, and temperance movements gained traction, eventually winning a ban on liquor consumption in the guise of the Eighteenth Amendment to the Constitution.

Now lying in a hospital ward, Halsey was a bit player on this national stage. The Navy had made drinking habits a formal inquiry in its officer efficiency reports in 1898, and since 1901 officials had worked with doctors to create what was for its time a progressive treatment for alcoholism. On the second day of his hospital stay, Halsey received a warm soda bath, began a light diet, and commenced a regimen of potassium bromide as a sedative and anticonvulsant. He was calmer by the third day, when he sat up in bed and later took a short outdoor stroll. He slept well that night and was discharged the following afternoon, September 3.[34]

Halsey never again served afloat. His alcoholism had probably bedeviled him for years. His hospital stay for insomnia in 1900, and another more recent admittance for an indeterminate respiratory problem, may have masked the problem. Eroding marks for health on his officer efficiency reports probably reflected his intemperance. Alcoholics can function well for decades, of course, but they cannot forever hide, especially in the close confines of a warship. Halsey fell completely apart during his command of the *Des Moines*. Maybe the ship's size and modernity unnerved him. Possibly service with Third

Squadron cruisers intent on developing the tactics for a new century, or comparisons with other ship captains better suited to the new Navy, proved too much to handle. His fellow cruiser skipper Bradley Fiske "had always heard that if a man arrived at a command position after the age of forty, he was too old to discharge his duties well." Recalling his time skippering the *Minneapolis,* and in remarks undoubtedly about Halsey, Fiske believed that "it was absolutely necessary for a man to become accustomed to independent responsibility early in life, and that if a man had those responsibilities fall on him when he had passed his prime, he was apt to break down under the load."[35]

After he left the hospital, Halsey was ordered to the Navy Department in Washington, DC, for less arduous duty. A medical board retired him a year later, just as his academy classmates who were still serving began making captain. He was fifty-three years old and had not known or cared about anything but the sea since he had first arrived at Annapolis some thirty-eight years earlier. Advanced on the retired list one grade to captain, as a civilian he continued to work for the Navy, responsible for supplying the Navy's ships with flags and pennants. He remained a thorough professional, contributing two more articles to *Proceedings* that revealed his essential conservatism: at a time when the magazine served as a sounding board for new ideas and experimental tactics, Halsey penned a sentimental history of the national flag and a romantic ode to a pennant stolen by the British Navy during the War of 1812.[36]

The Navy was Halsey's life. When asked in 1912 whether he had any special knowledge or experience outside of naval work, Halsey responded, "none worth considering." Even at that late date, he thought that the ability to "handl[e] men and ships tactically" was his greatest strength, though the time for that was long past. He continued to work at the Navy Department through the Great War and his son Bill's first two decades in uniform. He and his wife lived at the Marlborough in northwest Washington, an apartment complex popular with naval officers, even after his health began to deteriorate rapidly in 1918. That September, at the age of sixty-four, he left his Navy Department office and never returned. For another five years he and

Anne lived quietly in Washington, near other aging Navy friends. In October 1923 Halsey suffered a stroke and heart attack. Just shy of seventy, at the Marlborough, surrounded by old Navy friends, he died.[37]

William Halsey was a Navy man. The sea had always demanded physical courage from those who hoped to make from her a life, a requirement Halsey embraced. Annapolis had also impressed upon his young mind the compact between the nation and her naval servants. Yet his career had spanned the monumental shift from ships of wood and sail to fleets of steel and steam, upending the traditional calculus of a naval career. As the Navy modernized and expanded along with the boisterous nation it served, he failed to keep apace.

His son, the future fleet admiral, embarked on his own career as his dad's miscarried. The father's vocational choice anticipated the son's, and William's experiences framed Bill's outlook, attitude, and aspirations. As he took from his father sound traits in human relations, autonomous command at sea, and fidelity to nation and loyalty to the Navy, he also never forgot his dad's failure to navigate new waters surging around developing technologies. He inherited his dad's essential caution, and developed an audacious inclination only within the boundaries of command at sea. As the twentieth century proceeded, as William's death passed into memory, and as Bill's star ascended to fame, the family as well as the Navy were conscious always of William's service in uniform, and painstakingly, unfailingly, and forever referred to the elder man as Captain Halsey, a reminder of all that the father had attained, and all that he had not.

Chapter Three

A Carefree and Careful Boy

THE U.S. NAVY raised Bill Halsey. From his first breath, it determined his surroundings, decided his schools, and dominated his horizons. Because of the Navy, he moved seven times before his fifteenth birthday, living with relatives or camping from coast to coast in a succession of boarding rooms, hotels, and government-issued houses. Because of the Navy, his education came in fits, and almost always beside itinerant Navy boys like him, learning early the art of easy association but robbed of the richness of intimate friendship. And because of the Navy, his aspirations, which surely became grand enough as he grew to manhood, always encompassed only the sea.

. . . .

Bill Halsey was still in the womb when his father left for the *Iroquois* and a Pacific cruise from California to Peru and New Zealand. Anne, pregnant, went to live with her parents in the large Victorian house at 134 West Jersey Street in Elizabeth, New Jersey. There, in October 1882, Bill was born. He did not see his father until he was nearly three, when William Halsey began a shore tour at the Navy Yard in Brooklyn, moving his wife and son to a small house a short walk from the Brewster home. Shortly thereafter, in 1886, Bill's only sibling, Deborah, arrived. Despite his father's roots in Manhattan, the family spent little time in the city and continued a daily association with the many Brewsters in Elizabeth; already Anne's eleven siblings had produced for Bill twenty-three cousins in the immediate area. Until he was six he lived within a stone's throw of these relatives, and later, as a teen, he lived twice more with his grandparents while his father was at sea. As a man, some of Bill Halsey's cherished childhood memories were of his grandfather James Brewster, in a patriarch's chair near the fireplace, reading to whichever of his many grandchildren happened to be near.

This maternal link offered young Bill his only real glimpse of life outside the Navy. As a ship and commodity broker in Manhattan, his grandfather rode the riptides of industrialization. As it always had been, New York was a tornado of economic activity in the last decades of the nineteenth century, embodying what many observers called the destructive force of capitalism. Although New York's economic turmoil had pushed Bill Halsey's father to the Naval Academy and a life in uniform, it galvanized James Brewster. Brokers like Brewster sat in the eye of a commercial storm, sensitive to shifts stemming from Midwest wheat supplies, London commodity markets, or war near and far from home. The profession was not for the weak of heart, and New York City directories from the period reflect a wild array of brokers in and out of business. Men with cautious minds and careful constitutions failed while those with appetites for the exciting and unknown plied the trade with more lasting effect.

Brewster was of the latter sort. He had an office at 111 Broad Street as early as 1865, had moved to a bigger office at 118 Wall Street five years later, and jumped to even more trendy environs at 70 Beaver Street in 1880, about the same time he became president of the Cotton Exchange, the first futures exchange in the United States. He was established enough to underwrite his eldest son's appearance among New York's brokers, and was prominent enough that, when his daughter Anne married William Halsey in 1881, a Newark newspaper prominently reported the union. James Brewster never became fabulously rich, but he confronted the uncertainty of a changing world and survived well enough to provide for his outsized family and substantial household. It was an example his grandson Bill could have taken as a model, but the youngster never did, being always more Halsey than Brewster.[1]

When in 1888 the Navy posted his father to the *Ranger,* then in San Francisco Bay and slated to make a comprehensive survey of Lower California, the Halseys strode aboard a commercial steamer for the long trek to California, crossing the Panamanian Isthmus by railroad. During the passage to Panama, Anne doted on two-year-old Deborah, who had recently broken her back, and worried incessantly about the yellow fever and malaria that befell many travelers crossing Panama in those days. During their last sea leg on the way to San Francisco, six-year-old Bill vexed his parents by sneaking off to watch the slaughter of livestock for food; on one occasion his father found him standing in a pool of cattle blood wearing nothing but his skivvies. Eventually, the family arrived in San Diego without yellow fever, malaria, or hepatitis. William Halsey settled his family in the Hotel del Coronado, which had opened earlier that year and had swiftly become the swank place to board in Southern California, before himself proceeding to San Francisco and the Mare Island Naval Yard.[2]

The elder Halsey and the *Ranger* fell into a routine lasting two years: a week in San Diego to provision, followed by a month surveying the coast, followed each summer by a refitting at San Francisco. Young Bill, too, fell into patterns. There was kindergarten in Coronado, public school in Oakland, and a pleasant boarding establishment known the Navy over as the Bernard House near Mare Island. There were also playground mishaps, stitches, a scare or two with scarlet fever, and a concussion that required a weeklong hospital stay. Many years later a hotel steward in Coronado remembered a young Bill constantly racing through the hallways, and a Navy mother recalled the time the youngster upended a skiff in San Diego Bay, requiring rescue by a passing trawler.[3]

The Halseys trundled off to the Naval Academy in the summer of 1891, where William took up duties teaching. Young Bill became a man at the academy, spending more time there than any other place during the decade of his adolescence. During this first Annapolis tour, the family lived in a fine faculty apartment along Goldsborough Row, where Bill enjoyed the typical life of a junior on a naval base. He attended an Annapolis school designed to tutor Navy children, found trouble by breaking streetlights with slingshots, and helped form a neighborhood football squad called the Little Potatoes—so named because he and his friends thought themselves "hard to peel." His father had played baseball for Annapolis, and Bill avidly followed the academy's sports teams, beginning in his youth a sixty-year relationship with Academy athletics.[4]

At the academy, Bill formed lasting judgments about his dad. He recalled his father as "tremendously tactful" and "very thoughtful of others." The elder Halsey was a "good disciplinarian" who leavened firmness with kindness enough that the son never quite thought of his dad as stern. The old man was "very religious, being himself the son of a clergyman and raised by a very religious mother," yet also capable of "a good old sailorman's oath." More than anything else, Bill thought his father was a "very good wind-jamming sailing man" with a "tremendous amount of experience on sailing ships."[5]

This was common enough language by a child recalling a parent, though it was also heartfelt sentiment that the son carried throughout his life. His father's pocket watch was a treasured keepsake until it was stolen in 1941, and he hauled his dad's Annapolis yearbook with him during his own many decades in uniform, rebinding it thrice—the last time in 1948, just ten years before his own death. "I was proud of him always," Bill flatly declared, and it showed. When he became a full admiral in the midst of World War II, old friends wrote notes of congratulations, often adding phrases such as "wouldn't your dad be proud of you now!" For Bill Halsey, memory of his dad's tact helped guide and shape his own relationships with Navy men when his time came, and his ode to his father's sailing capacity reflected his own sense of a Navy man's most important skills, even as airplanes and submarines later changed so much of the sea service.[6]

As a twelve-year-old, in the summer of 1894, Bill moved with his mother and sister back to Elizabeth while William served aboard the *New York*. That fall, Bright's disease, a kidney dysfunction that can cause debilitating pain and death, aborted Bill's short career at Pingry Elementary School, the only school he ever attended that did not cater to Navy families. The following spring he was on the mend and into his first of three years boarding at Swarthmore Grammar School outside of Philadelphia. He remembered this period as the only extended ordinary time in his young life.[7]

Normal was relative, as few in turn-of-the-century America would have considered attendance at a distant boarding school full of naval officers' sons to be typical. But Halsey's was an unusual childhood. Swarthmore was the sixth of eight schools he attended, and as he approached his teenage years he had behind him a life passed in a series of Southern California hotels and Northern California boarding houses, on naval bases, and in his maternal grandparents' parlor in Elizabeth. He was in many respects a common kid: carefree, spirited, and sometimes stupid—in the summer of 1897 he was saved a second time from drowning by a fisherman. The few pictures dating to this period depict a playful, tousle-haired youngster, almost always in some baseball or football uniform, and already short in stature, thick of chest, and square of face. But even at this early age, the Navy's pace and patterns had etched deeply into his outlook and orientation.

In the fall of 1897 the boy moved back to Annapolis, where his father was once again teaching. The Halseys were by then thoroughly familiar with the academy and its rhythms. It was, increasingly, the place they called home. Father and son crewed sailboats together during regattas on Chesapeake Bay, and the entire family liked to spend Sunday afternoons in casual conversations with the sailors and midshipmen passing by their porch. As an adult, Bill could not recall a time when he did not know bluejackets, and all of his boyhood friendships sprang from Navy associations, many of them from faculty houses at the academy. There was Roy Ingersoll and Alex Sharp, teenage football buddies who later became admirals; Ned Newman, killed as a young officer in a turret accident on the old battleship *Missouri;* and Charlie Belknap, scion of a naval family and later president of the Monsanto Chemical Company.[8]

. . . .

Inevitably the Navy loomed as vocation for Bill. He never harbored any "thought except going into the Navy," once expressing surprise late in life that the ministry, a far stronger family tradition than the sea, never held for him much interest. As he approached fifteen, then the youngest age to enter the academy, he and his parents "began looking about for an appointment." They wrote to every politician they knew, some they didn't, and young Bill made a direct plea to President William McKinley in January 1898.[9]

"Dear Sir," the lad began. "I want to ask you, if you have not already promised all your appointments to the Naval Academy, that you will give me one." Arguing his merit by way of his father and as a kind of birthright, he added,

> I know people do not like to give important positions such as this away without knowing the person they are giving them to. But then you know that a naval officer would not keep his position long if he were not the right kind of man. I know plenty of respectable people that would testify to my good character. My father was appointed by Secretary Robinson [Robeson] of the Navy, who had been law partner of my grandfather. I have been with my father on shore and on ship board a great deal, and have always wanted to enter the Navy. My parents encouraged me in this desire and gave me their consent to enter if I could get the appointment. My father is now a senior lieutenant about 95 on the list for promotion.[10]

At first the Halseys received no answer from McKinley. In the summer of 1898 Anne arranged for supporting letters from the mayor of Elizabeth and the governor and attorney general of New Jersey. The next spring, Myron Herrick, a prominent Cleveland banker and later governor of Ohio and ambassador to France, wrote his fellow Ohioan McKinley on Halsey's behalf, invoking the concurrence of Mark Hanna, a political kingmaker and McKinley's political mentor. This prompted the president to write his Navy secretary, urging that every possible consideration be given young Halsey, which resulted in an alternate appointment for 1899 that came to naught when the lad with the primary appointment matriculated. During all this time, Bill was enrolled in an Annapolis school designed to prepare naval boys for the academy. There, while he waited, Halsey reviewed math equations, memorized geography facts, worked physics problems, and played pranks, one of which blew up the chemistry lab and garnered for Halsey a week's suspension.[11]

Bill grew desperate as time passed. Abruptly, he "decided that if I couldn't get into the Navy as a cadet, I could as a doctor." Though he had never expressed a medical interest, had displayed no aptitude for the field, and had no preparatory schooling, Bill's father approved this astonishing scheme, apparently as eager as the boy to have him in uniform. For a school he chose the University of Virginia for no other reason than that his good friend Karl Osterhaus, son of lieutenant and later admiral Hugo Osterhaus, was also slated to enter its medical program. Unsurprisingly, once at Virginia his makeshift motivation for medicine translated to poor grades and little real learning. Instead, he plunged into social activities. He played football well enough to join the practice squad, at left defensive end, and broke the varsity quarterback's leg during scrimmage, making Halsey a campus pariah for a time. He joined the Greek house Delta Psi, wearing its emblem on his watch chain for decades thereafter, and fraternity brothers Wiley Grandy, Lee Taylor, Billy White, and Pat Bryan became lifelong acquaintances.[12]

Meanwhile, in the Navy he longed to join, the aftermath of the Spanish War quickened changes already in motion. The naval expansion that had bestowed promotion, command, and challenge on the father now conferred opportunity on the son. In the spring of 1900, at about the time the elder Halsey went to the Philippines, Congress authorized a larger academy class, giving the president five additional appointments to Annapolis. This renewed hopes in the Halsey home. As Bill remembered it, his mother, Anne, hurried to Washington to "camp in McKinley's office" until she saw the president. Anne's cousin Benjamin Brewster, who had been Chester Arthur's attorney general, manufactured a meeting, and McKinley agreed to offer young Bill an appointment.[13]

Abandoning his medical studies, Bill made haste to Annapolis, joining again a school designed to prep boys for the admission test. He had but seven weeks before the July 2 test date to master the basics of a rigorous secondary curriculum in turn-of-the-century America.

He passed, and was sworn into the Navy on July 7, entering the Annapolis rolls two days later.[14]

Bill entered the Navy for the same reasons his father had stayed in
uniform: its familiarity, comfort, and security. For many youngsters,
Annapolis was designed to tear from them their sectionalisms and re-
cast them for service to the nation, often in traumatic fashion. This
had certainly been true for the elder Halsey, and it was surely the case
among many of young Bill's school contemporaries who would, like
him, gain fame in World War II: Ernest King, the son of a railroad
foreman, came from rural Ohio; Chester Nimitz, the son of hotel pro-
prietors of modest means, from the Texas hill country; Raymond
Spruance from his aunt's fading parlor near Baltimore; and Marc
Mitscher, the son of a widower, from Oklahoma. For them, and many
others, an unknown horizon beckoned at Annapolis, its gates symbol-
izing, in the words of one future admiral, "the beginning of a bewildering young life." For boys such as these, the decision to attend the
academy was a daring choice. But for Bill Halsey, Annapolis was home,
the Severn River his backyard, the Chesapeake his neighborhood. It
had always been so. Where the others had picked boldly, Halsey had
decided cautiously. At the dawn of adulthood, and forever thereafter,
Bill Halsey's personal inclination tended toward the careful. In the first
major choice of his life, Halsey followed the familiar path, drawn like
his father to the "twin shibboleths of every naval officer, reputation
and honor."[15]

....

In 1900 the academy was straining to keep pace with the transformations in the wider Navy. In the first decade of the new century, the
Navy added to the academy thirteen major buildings and laid plans
for many more. The great edifices of Dahlgren Hall, Macdonough
Hall, Bancroft Hall, and Mahan Hall all emerged, as did the school's
magnificent chapel, a new superintendent's residence, an administration building, and numerous smaller structures. The last remnants of
Fort Severn, the original occupant of academy land, were demolished
in 1909. With its disappearance, the only vestiges of the original institution were two small guardhouses at gate three. In each of Bill Halsey's

45

four student years at the academy, the clamor of construction projects was everywhere.

These were exciting times. The size of the student body grew, expanding from four companies to eight and becoming a brigade in 1903. Bill's class, entering in the summer of 1900, was the last to number under one hundred. By the time he graduated in 1904, there were nearly 700 officers-in-waiting at Annapolis. Even at that, the burgeoning fleet's need for junior officers was so great that from 1903 to 1907 the academy graduated its senior class at midyear to speed men to sea berths.[16]

The curriculum, too, lurched into the twentieth century. The midshipman confronted a dizzying array of classroom subjects. Halsey's freshman instruction included mechanical drawing, algebra, geometry, physiology, English, French, and Spanish. In his sophomore year the faculty added to this list chemistry, trigonometry, calculus, naval history, and maritime law. As juniors, Halsey and his classmates confronted the new Navy and its increasing technical demands, taking instruction in mechanical processes, theoretical mechanics, marine engines and boilers, and electricity and magnetism—all in addition to the regular college courses. In his senior year, reading, writing, and arithmetic faded as courses in naval tactics, gunnery drill, navigation, and naval construction came to dominate his days. In each of his four years, there was a conduct grade, which reflected as always a student's demerit tallies, and a newer mark labeled "efficiency," which aimed to judge a youngster's overall aptitude for Navy life.

All this left little freedom. The Navy regulated a midshipman's entire day. In Halsey's freshman year every moment from 6:30 AM until 9:55 PM was allocated. There was time scheduled for morning hygiene and breakfast. Class instruction commenced at 8:00 AM and continued until 3:20 PM, broken only by a short lunch. From 3:20 PM until 5:00 PM the midshipmen drilled, followed by dinner and formal study hall from 7:30 PM to 9:30 PM. Only the last twenty-five minutes of each day did the students have for themselves, before lights went out at 9:55 PM. So structured were their days, in fact, that even mild cases of diarrhea confined students to the infirmary, for there

46

was no time for irregular bowels in the course of a normal day at the U.S. Naval Academy. None of this surprised Halsey. Having grown up in the school's shadows and at his father's dinner table, he batted nary an eye as the academy ordered his life and told him where to purchase and how much to pay for the personal items in his locker, as well as dictating the brands of his underwear, soap, toothbrush, and comb.[17]

Like his father before him, Bill struggled in the hard sciences, did better with math, and appeared to enjoy English and history. He stood forty-second of seventy-five students after his first year, sixty-first of seventy following his sophomore year, forty-sixth of sixty-five as a junior, and settled at forty-third of sixty-two at graduation, ending his student days in the thirty-first percentile of his class, a pebble's throw from his father's spot at the thirty-fourth percentile in the class of 1873. In every year, vocational courses served as his ace, pulling him up into the wide middle of his class. His efficiency grades placed him thirteenth as a freshman, nineteenth as a sophomore, tenth as a junior, and eleventh as a senior. In seamanship, he stood ninth as a junior and fourth as a senior. Without such stellar marks, his overall class rank would have surely been in the bottom tenth of his class.[18]

Halsey's demerit tallies were a near perfect image of his father's record, placing him toward the bottom of his class. In Bill's freshman year, only ten of his seventy-five classmates garnered more than his 97 demerits. A mere three of seventy did worse than his 208 black marks during his sophomore year, when an incident of insubordination and unauthorized absence from the academy earned him a two-week stay on the *Santee,* the Annapolis receiving ship that doubled as a prison hulk for wayward students. As a junior, his 74 demerits placed him twenty-eighth of sixty-five, but he gave back some of this ground in his last year, when his 41 demerits placed him fifty-first out of sixty-two graduates. Like his father, an assortment of dorm-room offenses and a pattern of tomfoolery accounted for most of these black marks: he routinely ran a minute or two late, his room was usually on the messy side, his dress was often just a bit off, and he was notoriously ill disciplined at drill. None of these habits worked real harm. In time, all of them became hallmarks of his service.[19]

Neither his school standing nor his demerit record bothered him much. He recalled having "the usual struggles with the academic work" at Annapolis, but nothing many boys, including his father before him, had not overcome. Halsey took in stride the academic regimen, his attitude calibrated by moderate aspirations. Years later, he copped a posture of bravado common among mediocre students, telling a latter-day midshipman that he "remembered vaguely the English Department, where we studied various things. One was a course in Naval history. The text books were extremely poor. Another was a course in Logic, which was so elemental, that it was almost laughable." When he graduated, his class standing "didn't matter; what mattered was that I was now passed midshipman Halsey."[20]

He was never in serious jeopardy because of his demerits, either. Familiar with the Annapolis way, he knew a man's standing as an officer bore little relation to his demerit record as a student. His dad's career, after all, had thus far progressed unhindered by his conduct grades, and when it did crash it had little to do with sneaking cigarettes as a teenager. There was a difference between father and son, though. Whereas his father's demerits reflected an earnest boy's learning of the naval way, Bill's represented that of a youth already on intimate terms with sea service, confident such violations mattered little and, when necessary to attend a dance or obtain some leave, able to avoid demerits for weeks on end.

Athletics had always mitigated Annapolis strictures, and from the outset Halsey was an active sportsman, especially in football. In his freshman and sophomore years he played on the junior varsity and practice squad, activity that offered an occasional break from hazing, which in those years included such trifles as double-timing down the corridors as well as more serious episodes of fisticuffs and physical abuse. He made the varsity team his junior year. Just before the opening game, the starting fullback was injured and Bill took his place, a job he held all that year and the next, his last. Those teams were some of the poorest in Annapolis history. The Army beat them 22–8 in 1902 and 40–5 in 1903, the worst drubbing the Navy had received from the cadets at West Point to that time, although the game gave Halsey his one moment of glory on the gridiron. "Early in the second half," noted the *Philadelphia Public Ledger,* "little Halsey electrified the Navy contingent by making the longest run of the game. Catching the ball at his 4 yard mark he sprinted straight up the field, dodging and eluding half a dozen West Point tackles until he reached the 43 yard line, where he was brought to earth."[21]

Halsey's comfort at Annapolis was most evident during the academy's practice cruises, then taken in the middle three summers of a student's career. Reflecting both the transforming Navy and the burgeoning size of the student body, midshipmen spent one half of each cruise on a modern ship, usually a cruiser or battleship, and the other half on an old-style windjammer, which was almost always the *Chesapeake,* a three-masted bark serving as a station and practice vessel at Annapolis. In the summers of 1901 and 1902 Halsey embarked on the *Indiana* and the *Chesapeake,* spending six weeks during each year ranging the Eastern Seaboard. During the first cruise, he enjoyed ship liberty in the traditional manner, later spending eleven days in the academy infirmary recovering from gonorrhea. On the second, he and a few others managed to persuade a drunken coal passer on the *Indiana* to tattoo them with an image of an anchor and "USNA 04" in exchange for a fifth of whiskey.[22]

For many boys, these cruises were their first exposure to the sea, the trips looming large in their orientation to Navy life and their memory of the academy. For Halsey they were but familiar jaunts. He had already crossed the Americas via ship, had coursed along the beautiful California coast several times, and had sailed the Chesapeake Bay with his father on innumerable weekend afternoons. For him, "hardly a moment" of his practice cruises "was less than a delight," an opinion not shared by those prone to seasickness, a sensation Halsey, in all his life, never experienced.[23]

In Halsey's junior year his father returned for a third tour of duty on the faculty. Soon a commander and outranked at the school by only the superintendent, the elder Halsey and Anne opened their kitchen and parlor to their son and his friends on many a weekend. Few classmates could actually walk to their parents' homes from their sparse dorm rooms, and Bill enjoyed this unusual license. For most midshipmen, home leave was, in the words of the 1904 yearbook editors, "alloyed bliss" and "heaven." For Bill Halsey, it was about 200 yards to the west.[24]

The elder Halsey skippered the *Chesapeake* during the summer of 1903, Bill's last as a student. For perhaps the only time in academy history, father commanded son during a practice cruise. Bill acted as port captain of the maintop, the second ranking student position, and he was keen to show his dad that he "might become the fine all-around sailorman" that the elder Halsey was. He got his chance one stormy night off the Newfoundland coast, when he was among the first to climb into the ship's rigging and upon its cross spars, where the wind blew so hard that he could stand upright on the bell of the sail while he helped stabilize the vessel. The elder Halsey described the wild night as "excellent training," and three decades later the younger Halsey recalled the storm as "excellent experience," though other students were not sure as they tended nauseous stomachs and unsteady legs. For the entire month of July they sailed together, father and son, ship skipper and Navy wannabe. From Newport to Gardiners Bay, and from New London to Bar Harbor, the two served together afloat, in the U.S. Navy, for the first and last time.[25]

As they had for decades, the cruise welded generations of Navy men together, creating a kinship of naval officers often as strong as that of natural families. On the *Chesapeake* deck that summer, under the command of Commander William Halsey, toiled a veritable who's who of men who would be Admiral Halsey's World War II contemporaries: Dave Bagley, Roy Ingersoll, Bill Calhoun, Aubrey Fitch, Frank Jack Fletcher, Husband Kimmel, John McCain, Rollo Wilson, Robert Ghormley, Savvy Cooke, and Chester Nimitz. Alone among them, Bill Halsey had the advantage and burden of his father's being skipper.[26]

These were not the only academy contemporaries destined to play roles in Halsey's career. There was Ernest King, a senior and the cadet commander during Halsey's freshman year, and James Richardson, Kenneth Whiting, John Towers, Harold Stark, Charlie Belknap, William Pye, and Rufus Zogbaum—all fated for their own brand of latter-day prominence. Among the junior faculty were Lieutenant William Pratt, serving as professor of mathematics; Commander Charles Badger, the incumbent commandant of midshipmen; and Lieutenant Joel Pringle, who worked for Halsey's father in the Seamanship Department during Bill's senior year.

Halsey shone at the academy in his senior year. He exuded confidence and goodwill. He was fond of most of his classmates, and they of him. In addition to his play on the football field, he held more offices than any classmate except one, including positions on the Class Supper Committee, the Class Crest Committee, the Graduation Ball Committee, the German Class Committee, and the staff of the *Lucky Bag,* the class yearbook. As a battalion adjutant, he held respectable rank and a place in the class military order fairly near the top. He was elected president of the student athletic association, and was awarded the Thompson Trophy, which went annually to the senior who had done most to promote athletics at the academy. In common with all midshipmen, he had nicknames, among them Pudge, Willie, and Stud, the last of which was recognition for some vague talent with young ladies. "Started out in life to become a doctor," the *Lucky Bag* intoned, "and gained in the process several useful hints." And although at least twenty classmates shared paternal ties to the Navy, Bill Halsey had so adopted its mores that he alone earned from his peers the approbation of a Navy man. "A real old salt," his classmates proclaimed of him in the *Lucky Bag.* "Looks like a figurehead of Neptune." He was, it seemed, from his very birth a sailor.[27]

The essential Halsey emerged through these early years. Life on a series of naval reservations had fostered familiarity with distant places while it consigned much of America to the shadows. At home he lived within the Navy, inside its fences and behind its walls, where his father, between his many tours afloat, brought home the whiff of faraway lands, of China and Peru and Tahiti and New Zealand, and where American society, just beyond the gatehouse, existed only in vague outline. First as a boy and later as man, Halsey knew more about life in Shanghai than in Cincinnati, more about the sextant than the plough, and more about the workings of naval ships than about life on the

Great Plains, in the Deep South, or across the Mountain West. From birth to death, he never left the Navy's embrace, and seemed always to exhibit more comfort in the wardroom than the family room, more confidence afloat than on land, and more competence on the command bridge than in nearly any other circumstance in life.

The yearbook called him "everyone's friend," which was true enough. Camaraderie came easily to Halsey, and he was throughout life a great acquaintance. But as everyone's friend he was no one's intimate. His single sustained friendship through college was with his roommate, Bradford Barnette. Like Halsey, Barnette was a Navy junior familiar with the Annapolis way, a below-average student in the classroom, and one who "found the yoke of discipline a heavy one." Halsey and Barnette roomed together for each of their four years, an arrangement unusual enough to earn mention in the *Lucky Bag,* and a decade later Halsey named his daughter Margaret Bradford in silent tribute to the roommate that had lent familiarity and comfort to his academy dorm room.[28]

Halsey and his classmates were full of nostalgia as they prepared to leave Annapolis. "A few short days more and we will be scattered to the four corners of the earth, many of us never to meet again," the yearbook editors waxed. "Our period of probation is over and we must go. Good bye to our enemies, if we have them; au revoir to our sweethearts—God bless them. Others will soon fill our places and the old scenes know us no longer; but remember, remember, the Class of 1904."[29]

History has remembered, in large part because of Halsey, the class's most famous graduate. On graduation day, which had been moved forward to February 1 to meet the Navy's demand for officers, Bill Halsey was elated, ready to take on any task the service might ask. "I wish you all the luck in the world, Mr. Halsey," the academy's chief master-at-arms told him that afternoon. "But you'll never be as good a naval officer as your father."[30]

Chapter Four

New Officer, New Navy, New Century

PASSED MIDSHIPMAN HALSEY—as new Annapolis graduates were known—had less than a week to pack out his academy quarters, reach Hampton Roads, and report to Captain William Cowles and the battleship *Missouri,* a vessel that had left her Norfolk birthplace just weeks earlier. He and four other fresh Annapolis men reached the ship on February 7, 1904, as a windy sea began to swirl through the roadstead. Halsey and Barnette reprised their academy roles as roommates, stowing their gear before Halsey stood his very first watch as a regular Navy man late that evening, smack in the middle of a sleet storm. It was a harried start.[1]

The next morning the *Missouri* left for waters off Guantánamo Bay. There, Cowles, a family friend who two years later as the chief of the Bureau of Equipment would shelter the elder Halsey after his breakdown, paced the newest American battleship through sea trials before turning the ship toward Pensacola, where the Atlantic Fleet assembled for live target practice. On April 13, as the *Missouri* fired her twelve-inch main battery, a massive explosion rocked the hull as a main turret exploded, literally blasting one bluejacket skyward before he fell upon the quarterdeck, charred an outline upon the teak, and tumbled overboard. Cowles leapt toward the smoking gun casement, grabbing Halsey and another man as he went. Stench, fear, and bodies met them as they descended into the massive turret. It was, Halsey recalled, a "God-awful sight." He helped retrieve the dead while the ship made haste for Pensacola. Once there, Cowles tapped Halsey to supervise the death detail, composed of a handful of doleful sailors and six local undertakers. The catastrophe claimed thirty-four lives, including that of one of Halsey's boyhood chums and football buddies, Ned Newman, whose remains he escorted to Jacksonville and Newman's family. It was among the worst maritime disasters of the early twentieth century and was forever the greatest tragedy aboard any vessel Halsey served. It left an indelible imprint. In 1938 he recalled it as an "unimaginable grief," and ten years later, hardened by untold World War II catastrophes, the calamity still loomed "monstrous" in his memory.[2]

The disaster fueled a growing brouhaha in the press over a modernizing Navy. The blast figured prominently in two successive editions of the *New York Times* and in over 1,400 dailies across the nation. Like so many aspects of naval life, gunnery was then hastily evolving from the routine days of smoothbore cannon to the sophisticated science of big-gun rifles, a process not free from trial and, sometimes, costly error. This led to heated debate between reformers eager for change and traditionalists who believed the fleet's newest ships were "madhouses" run by gun fanatics, most of whom were quite junior and ought "to be put in straight jackets" before more ships blew up.[3]

Yet, as surely as the tide arrives, change came to the Navy, in ever-increasing waves. Throughout their careers, Halsey and his contemporaries would grapple with nearly continuous transformations. The *Missouri* reflected this dynamic, as her cavernous coal bunkers made her revolutionary for only a brief moment before the larger guns of the *Dreadnought* age made her obsolete. Indeed, the twentieth century's technological swagger spawned successive generations of battleships, destroyers, cruisers, submarines, and aircraft carriers, challenging officers and bluejackets alike. These changes swept across every deck afloat in the early twentieth century, and, by World War II, they had created a Navy accustomed to, but never quite comfortable with, a ceaseless cycle of innovation, ossification, and change. Still, despite this hubbub, from beginning to end naval officers of Halsey's generation remained committed to tradition and never broke faith with the timeless touchstones of patriotic duty and independent command. Successful officers of the era were bound to be those who kept pace with the Navy's morphing form while maintaining a fidelity to the enduring ethic of Navy life—for there could be no other way in a society as conservative as the Navy as it coursed through a great age of transition.

. . . .

Bill Halsey served aboard the *Missouri* for another eighteen months following the turret explosion, but nothing, not a cruise to the azure Mediterranean, not an audience with the king of Portugal, and not temporary detachments to help coach his beloved academy football team, compared to the drama of that sad moment. In December 1905 he left the battleship for the gunboat *Don Juan de Austria,* a Spanish relic sunk by the American Navy during the Battle of Manila Bay in 1898 and raised in 1900. The fleet had no great use for her, and the *Don Juan,* with her eight officers and nearly one hundred sailors, passed most of 1906 on detached duty in Dominican Republic waters, safeguarding American interests amid the baffling array of domestic intrigue then gripping that brittle Latin American polity. The vessel's chief yeoman recalled Halsey as an "earnest and sincere young officer who had his mind on his work," though Halsey himself remembered the tour as "stupefying in its monotony," marked mostly by his promotion to ensign, long stretches of repair in Norfolk, and a turn as the ship's wireless telegraphy operator, for in one of the discordant mysteries of naval administration, the decrepit *Don Juan* had one of the Navy's very first telegraphic sets. In the spring of 1907 the Navy ordered the ship into mothballs, righting in Halsey's mind an earlier error. "God knows what has become of her now," he recalled years later. "The greatest mistake the Navy ever made was raising the *Don* from Manila Bay."[4]

While serving aboard the *Don Juan,* Halsey began courting Frances Cooke Grandy, a Virginia belle and the niece of the chief engineer of the famous Civil War Confederate ironclad *Virginia.* With an image of his girl in his billfold, Halsey reported, for the second time in his infant career, to the Navy's newest ship, this time the *Kansas,* and to a skipper, Charles Vreeland, who knew Halsey's father well, having been a messmate of the elder Halsey on the *Alert* during the daring 1873 search of Dampier Strait.[5]

Vreeland rushed the *Kansas* through her shakedown cruise in the fall of 1907 and brought the vessel to Hampton Roads in early December. There, the crew made ready for the greatest peacetime pageant in American naval history. In an era of tension with an emergent Japan, President Roosevelt had decided to test the endurance of the nation's fresh battleship fleet and ordered as many as possible on a world cruise. Part preventative strategy and part technical training, in every respect the voyage of this Great White Fleet was a parade of power that rallied the nation. Thousands of people crowded into Norfolk and Hampton Roads as sixteen battlewagons gathered through the first weeks of December, a scene one correspondent believed would "be worth ten years" of life to see. To conjure a picture for readers, some newspaper reporters became mathematicians, counting the 691 large-bore barrels and the 14,762 men of the ships; others became electricians, equating the fleet's engine strength to the power needs of the entire Eastern Seaboard; still others became grocers, itemizing the 1.5 million pounds of flour, 1 million pounds of beef, 0.5 million eggs, and 40,000 pounds of English plum pudding taken aboard the vessels.[6]

Yet no poet emerged to capture the essence of the spectacle, for the world had rarely seen such an assemblage of iron, engine, and gun. Rear Admiral Robley Evans, an aged veteran of the Civil War, commanded the entire fleet, dividing his battleships into four divisions of four hulls apiece, each also commanded by a rear admiral. Evans took the first-division battleships *Connecticut*, *Kansas*, *Vermont*, and *Louisiana* for himself, and three other rear admirals divided the remaining dozen. Only once before, when the Union collected an armada for the assault on the Confederate Fort Fisher in 1865, and only once later, when the Navy embarked General George Patton's troops on their way to North Africa in 1942, did Hampton Roads witness a flotilla remotely as arresting. The panorama drove many observers to ill-disciplined drool. Franklin Mathews of the *New York Sun* compared the fleet to Lower Manhattan, the Dartmouth backfield, William

Howard Taft, and the Chicago Cubs in a single sentence. Amazingly, the entire scene had existed only in imagination a short generation earlier, and young Bill Halsey had been in the Navy longer than any of the sixteen battlewagons except one, the *Kearsarge*.

He probably cared more for the girl he was leaving than the sea change he was riding as a new officer in a new century. When, in the last days before the fleet sailed, Halsey was not busy aboard the *Kansas*, he was ashore, grabbing what time he could with Frances, whom he had taken to calling Fan. Local businessmen sponsored three lavish days of celebration to mark the fleet's departure, making use of many of the elaborate buildings left behind by the previous spring's Jamestown Exposition. As bands played and naval families promenaded and bluejackets frolicked, Halsey danced with Fan. Like many officers, he may have arranged to position her atop the Hotel Chamberlain roof so that, on the appointed day, he could see her among the thousands who crowded the windows and wharfs and ramparts for miles to wave the ships to sea.[7]

On December 16 the *Kansas* took her place, second in line behind the flagship *Connecticut*, braving a brisk north wind. Turning toward open water, each of the battleship prows bobbed in a swell of white water, nodding their own farewells to the crowded shore. On the *Kansas* the band played "Home, Sweet Home," "The Girl I Left behind Me," and "Auld Lang Syne." Belching black smoke into the crisp blue sky, the ships formed two lines of two divisions of four hulls apiece, and thundered cannon salutes to Roosevelt, who had arrived aboard the presidential yacht *Mayflower* to bid the juggernauts farewell. The scene brought the president to tears. "Did you ever see such a fleet?" he gushed. "Isn't it magnificent? Oughtn't we all feel proud?"[8]

Then the ships were gone, out of sight, heading south. The fleet's itinerary was the product first of coaling requirements and then of diplomacy, to solidify friendships and influence enemies. From the Virginia cape, the ships headed to Trinidad in the Caribbean, then on to Rio de Janeiro, followed by a stop at Punta Arenas, then through the Strait of Magellan and on to the Pacific Ocean. There, the ships planned to pass close by Valparaiso for a fleet review, pay a port call at Lima, and visit numerous California cities before coming to temporary rest in San Francisco in the summer of 1908, some eight months after they had left the East Coast. In July the vessels planned to head west, first to Hawaii and thence to Auckland, New Zealand, and on to Sydney, Melbourne, and Albany in Australia. Turning north, the ships intended to visit Manila before port calls in Japan and China. From there, the fleet planned to turn toward the Indian Ocean and Ceylon and the Suez Canal, followed by a series of visits to Mediterranean ports before it at last would slip past the rocks of Gibraltar, cross the Atlantic, and make for Hampton Roads and home, scheduled to come to rest some fourteen months after leaving Virginia. What a voyage!

Throughout the cruise Halsey found that his primary duty at sea was upon the bridge, where, as a watch officer, he was responsible for maintaining the *Kansas*'s course and speed relative to the other battlewagons of the First Division. At the time, keeping station in precise formation and prancing to the dictates of pennant flags was an obsession within the fleet. Maneuvers occupied much time at sea, and on any given day the ships might steam in a line of divisions, open order; then in a line of squadrons, natural order; then in a column formation, open order again. By the fleet's parade off Valparaiso, one admiral believed the ships had performed a "perfect exhibition of Marine Efficiency, power, and drill" of the like that had "never been witnessed on this Earth at any time in the World's history." As a junior officer, Halsey took his cue from older men and revered the station book and all the formulas, calculus, and signals that guided fleet maneuvers. Forty years later, he kept as his most vivid memory of the Great White Fleet a night off the Australian coast, when "a cherished wish of mine was fulfilled. From the time I relieved the watch one morning to the time I was relieved, four hours later, I kept the *Kansas* in perfect station without once speeding up or slowing down—the only time in my naval career I have been able to do so."[9]

Fleet precision had purpose beyond pride and pomp, however. Officers believed such discipline was necessary for victory in the battleship clashes Mahan had prophesied, and many an Annapolis man would have agreed with the British admiral Sir John Fisher, who believed fleet orchestration was a "plant of slow growth. Long and constant association of ships of a fleet is essential to success." Still, most officers had yet to recognize station discipline as merely a predicate to twentieth-century naval victory. In the future, triumph at sea would be the child of many factors, and if attention to fleet movement heralded how far the Navy had come in the few short years since distant, autonomous patrols had dominated its operations, mania about it also bore testament to how far the Navy was from a fighting unit worthy of modern maritime combat.[10]

The battleships possessed no better symbol of that modernity than their guns. Twice during their global trek, the vessels conducted large-scale gunnery drills, once in the spring of 1908 off Mexico's Pacific coast, and once that fall outside Manila Bay. During both these exercises Halsey was turret officer in charge of a casement of eight-inch guns, supervising one passed midshipman and perhaps a couple dozen sailors in the close confines of the turret. These were still dangerous drills; the *Missouri* turret explosion in 1904 had been followed by one aboard the *Massachusetts* in 1905, another on the *Kearsarge* in 1906, and yet one more on the *Georgia* in 1907, each of which killed ten men. Inside the turret, Halsey stood between two gun breeches, supervising the turret captain, a senior enlisted man; hoistmen, who carried the ordnance from the bowels of the ship up to the turret; loaders, who placed ammunition upon the breeches; plug men, who loaded the barrels; and rammer men, responsible for closing the barrel. Then, from the bridge, the gunnery officer, the irrepressible reformer and later pioneer aviator Lieutenant Henry Mustin, directed Halsey via telephone to set and fire the gun. In its brute labor, the whole process had roots in the past, but the math and physics that underpinned its ballistics, and the telephone that was then available in only the most sophisticated city homes, harkened the future.[11]

Wherever it went the Great White Fleet represented America's debut as a world power on the heels of the Spanish-American War, and it quickly became a phenomenon. Huge crowds greeted the ships. Perhaps 175,000 people covered Rio de Janeiro's cone-shaped hills to see the white battlewagons, and a quarter of a million souls gathered atop the slopes of Valparaiso to see them strut. Nearly two million people poured into numerous California ports, a collective throng about equal to the state's entire population. In San Francisco alone, officials estimated one million people congregated into the Bay Area as the behemoths approached, greatly straining the city's capacity as a host so shortly after the Great Earthquake of 1906. Later, in New Zealand, 10 percent of the nation's populace lined the shores of Auckland's harbor to see the ships emerge from an early morning mist, and in Sydney a multitude exceeding its 500,000 residents crowded the shoreline. In terms of sustained spectacle the world had never seen anything like it. At the dawn of the twentieth century most people still lived in rural areas, strewn and scattered around the globe. There existed few megacities, and gatherings of even a few thousand were unusual. The million people who had gathered in San Francisco perhaps matched anything humankind had mustered for a single event, ever.[12]

For the 14,000 men of the cruise, the crowds portended a torrid social schedule. Observing protocol had long been a part of Navy life, but the fanfare of the Great White Fleet supercharged these duties. At one port an admiral counted obligations to attend seventeen dinners, dances, and parties in a single day. In time, many officers grumped of "boredom" and "unintelligible speeches"; of parties that were "nightmares" and balls that were "dreadful." Aboard the *Kansas,* Lieutenant Commander Philip Andrews reported that the social whirlwind raised "serious questions as to how far our physical endurance can stand the wear and tear of such lavish entertainment." Once while in Rio, within the span of twelve hours, Halsey attended a luncheon atop Mount Corcovado, later the base of Brazil's famous Christ the Redeemer statue; a reception in Petrópolis, some thirty miles from the harbor quays; and a banquet at the American Embassy in the heart of Rio. The fleet's social demands wore heavily on bluejackets, too: one dinner in Australia planned for 3,000 drew exactly seven sailors, and by the time the fleet reached Manila in the fall of 1908, commanding officers had resorted to bribes of extra liberty to those willing to shoulder social responsibilities ashore. It was a Navy turned upside down.[13]

The human concentrate that enveloped the fleet at each port heightened chances for shore-liberty shenanigans. Navies had well earned their reputations centered on rum and riot, and there remained among the ships' crews enough of the perpetual dregs, outlaws, and misfits of the old Navy to raise the specter of wrecked cities in the fleet's wake. As a result, cruise officials relied to an unprecedented degree on shore patrols, which were squads of select enlisted men led by junior officers acting as police to corral disorderly sailors and whisk them back to their ships.[14]

Much of what Halsey took from the cruise came from his experience supervising shore patrols. As the first major port call, Rio de Janeiro's network of bright boulevards and dark alleys presented a Hobson's choice to thousands of bluejackets. At one point, two sailors in a cabaret sparked a brawl that spread first to dozens and ultimately to hundreds of participants and ignited a minor diplomatic rift. Punta Arenas, the small, desolate gateway to the Strait of Magellan, promised little better, made up as it was, in the words of one cruise participant, of the "backwash of humanity who had drifted there from shipwrecks: deserters, cutthroats, confidence men, beachcombers, and the like." Unsurprisingly, sailors soon found the town's small red-light district, on the top of a rise some two miles from the main wharf, where Halsey made his first arrests as a patrol officer, caging back to the ships a handful of randy bluejackets.[15]

By the time the ships reached California the fleet and Halsey had fallen into a shore routine. There were the huge crowds, the loud cheers, and the extravagant celebrations. A banquet held for junior officers at the Hotel del Coronado reminded Halsey of his time there as a youngster, when the Navy went largely unnoticed among the citizenry it served; and a large parade in Northern California evoked kindergarten memories. In Los Angeles, Halsey's shore patrol beat was the central police house, where he saw "drunk rollers," "dope fiends," and "hop heads," one of whom was a sailor whose rough treatment by the local police Halsey protested until he read what the man had done to earn arrest. In San Francisco, Halsey patrolled the city's embarcadero, then a line of whorehouses, drinking pits, and drug dens known as the Barbary Coast, regularly enough to earn the sobriquet "Big Bill." There, he detained a man thrice in a single day, the offender being a "little bit dirtier" and a "little bit drunker" each time, and later confronted one out-of-control sailor wielding a two-by-four like a switchblade. His few steps toward that man were "the longest miles I ever walked in my life." In such circumstances, Halsey learned swiftly to distinguish between those prone to persuasion and those "beyond the power of reason." Sailors in the latter category he confined promptly, but Halsey soon concluded that a bluejacket, "if handled properly and with decision, will rarely if ever get out of hand." Like his father, in time he developed a reputation as a sailor's officer, nearly always respectful of enlisted ranks and occasionally too tolerant of some of their shortcomings.[16]

Halsey's inclination to lead with reason fit well the emerging class of bluejackets then entering the ranks. By the world cruise, one *Kansas* officer believed sailors had become as different from the human flotsam of an earlier age "as the eagle is from the dodo." They were better educated and more even tempered, and in turn enjoyed a higher standard of living at sea and ashore. Despite ugly instances like the Rio riot, a street brawl in Santa Barbara, and another one in Auckland, desertion, the ultimate rejection of naval life, never shackled the world cruise. The fleet's desertion rate for the voyage represented less than 2 percent of its personnel, well below the clip of nearly 10 percent from earlier eras, and much lower than Army tallies during the same period, which, the *New York Times* reported, were "numerous enough to cripple whole companies and regiments." Halsey himself believed sailors ashore during the cruise behaved "far better than the conduct of the same number of college boys turned loose without supervision would have been."[17]

Halsey settled into a naval life of his own while cruising with the Great White Fleet. As a Navy junior he had known this life from the exterior, through his father's eyes. Now it was his as well, earned through watch duties, gunnery drills, and shore patrols. Life aboard a warship was a distant society, mysterious to outsiders and baffling to observers. An American battleship in 1908, for instance, used ninety-eight different bugle and whistle calls for internal communication, making it "one of the most discordant places in the world" to casual witnesses. Yet, from its 3:00 AM call for cooks to its 8:00 PM call to hammocks, a concealed regularity ran a man-of-war, making it a comforting cocoon to those who made a life at sea. Each day the same men gathered at the same place "under the eyes of the same officers with the same little notebooks, all at the same task." At appointed times each day men and officers collected together to eat and recreate at their respective messes, which served as guilds of the ship's larger citizenry, rendering small and comprehensible the ship's wide array of task and rank. Messmates lived together for months on end, placing a premium on men practiced in the art of close association, able to ignore the small peculiarities that grow conspicuous with time and capable instead of seeing the good points in every personality. In such circumstances, humor, card playing, board games, and music all acted as elixirs when, in the words of one officer on the cruise, "we have talked about all the people we know at home, and we have discussed every conceivable topic."[18]

Halsey came easily into this society, mentored in these first years by his father's friends. Three of the four ship captains in the *Kansas*'s division were close Halsey associates. Hugo Osterhaus of the *Connecticut* was the father of Bill's best friend and University of Virginia classmate, and he gave Halsey his start with the shore patrol. Richard Wainwright of the *Louisiana* had twice served with William Halsey, and he maneuvered during the cruise to keep Bill afloat when others thought he ought to return to America to help coach the Annapolis football team, something he had done in 1906 and 1907. And Vreeland, aboard the *Kansas,* guided the young officer from duty on the fifth watch to daytime watch officer, to turret officer, and eventually to division officer in the ship's engineering department, in the process making Halsey the sole ensign on the *Kansas* with division duties. Vreeland gave Halsey the highest possible marks in six formal evaluations, and once took the extraordinary step of publicly defending the young officer to the ship's second-in-command, who had berated Halsey for a badly organized mail call in Auckland.[19]

Long after newspaper accounts of the Great White Fleet had yellowed with age, Halsey recalled the routine of the cruise with the clarity of yesterday. There were the two Christmases at sea, where 14,000 souls had gathered, some of whom were rough, some refined, some educated, some illiterate, some Christian, and some with no religion at all. There were two New Years and a single July Fourth celebration, with fireworks, searchlight shows, and lighthearted shenanigans. There were five equator crossings, each marked, as had been tradition in the Navy from time immemorial, with adolescent tomfoolery. There were fantastic port calls at exotic locales, the sights, tastes, and sounds of each place leaving an imprint. There were souvenirs from various places, including tea from Ceylon that later served as reception trinkets at Halsey's wedding, and rugs from Punta Arenas and Auckland that warmed the family floor for years. Along the way were brilliant sunsets, snowcapped mountains, and glistening seas, sometimes placid, sometimes violent. Late in life Halsey remembered all this and more—the noise and thrill of gunnery drill, the challenges and triumphs of shore patrol, the pattern and pace of wardroom chatter—not in spite of their distance in time but rather because of their proximity to naval life. Across forty years in uniform, all of it had become common. As the Navy ran toward change in the twentieth century, it clung ever more to what it could from earlier times. In the future Halsey, too, would adopt where he must but stood unchanged where he could.

Eventually the cruise of the Great White Fleet neared its end. The ships passed through the Suez Canal in early January 1909, and spent a month at various Mediterranean ports. While the *Kansas* moored along the French Riviera, Halsey took leave and crashed his sister's honeymoon in Paris, and then, like the rest of the fleet, prepared for home. In early February the ships slid by Gibraltar, entered the Atlantic Ocean, and pointed toward Hampton Roads. At 11:00 AM on February 22 fleet lookouts spied the same American coast that had greeted the Jamestown pioneers, its vague outline growing darker as the morning fog cleared. Closer ashore, President Roosevelt, again aboard the *Mayflower*, now for the last time as president, strained his one good eye through a pair of binoculars. "Here they are!" he shouted, "feeling as much as seeing" the battle masts emerge from the seaward mist. The sound of the fleet's bands made him sanguine, and with each ship's salute he grew melancholic for the office he would soon relinquish to William Howard Taft. "Another chapter is complete," the president proclaimed, "and I could not ask a finer concluding scene for my administrations."[20]

Like the president, the crews were proud of their voyage. They had participated in the largest fleet circumnavigation of the globe in history. Across 434 days the Great White Fleet had traveled farther and had visited more continents and more countries than had any other navy on a single cruise. It had carried more men, consumed more coal, and expended more than thirty times the powder in salutes that the Navy had spent during the recent war with Spain. Halsey believed the cruise was a "success by every standard. Navally, it brought the fleet to the peak of perfection. Nationally, it increased the prestige of the United States in every country where we showed our flag. And diplomatically, it was not inconceivable that our appearance in Japanese waters at this time prevented war, or at least postponed it."[21]

That was claiming too much. The voyage had surely been a navigational and logistical triumph, yet it had at best a transitory effect on international affairs. The ships themselves, which had left Hampton Roads young in age, returned as near antiques. While the fleet had been away, navies around the world constructed the first of the *Dreadnought*-era behemoths. America had started its first such ship, the *Michigan*, while Halsey and the others had crossed the globe. The performance of the fleet's senior officers placed in relief this admixture of the old and new at the dawn of Halsey's career. Of the four admirals who began the voyage, only one finished it, and fully half of the sixteen ship captains failed to see the trip through to completion. Some left as a matter of normal rotation, but age, illness, and stress claimed many of the others, including Rear Admiral Robley Evans, whose decrepit body kept him cabin bound for weeks on end; Rear

Admiral Charles Thomas, who died of a heart attack; Captain E. F. Qualtrough, whose alcoholism earned him a court-martial; and Captain Hamilton Hutchins, who suffered a nervous breakdown.[22]

In many an age, a triumph such as the Great White Fleet would stand prominently for years. In the early twentieth century its accomplishments faded even as the ships still steamed. For the American public the spectacle of the white hulls had a short life. Covered extensively and excessively until it reached San Francisco, press reports of the cruise into the Pacific and beyond faded to mere pictures and extended captions in the country's newspapers and magazines. As the ships neared Hampton Roads in the early spring of 1909, accounts of the fleet's approach told not of the many thousands who had waved them good-bye but of the few hundred welcoming them home, a crowd woefully insufficient to represent even one person per every ten returning sailors. One short month after the vessels came to rest, *Harper's Weekly* published a ballad feting the cruise, so quickly had the voyage passed into folklore.[23]

Bill Halsey could not have asked for a better beginning. His father had donned the uniform as the Navy entered a long period of decline and routine, barely noticed by larger society, rarely challenged from within, and unaccustomed to wartime defense of the national interest. In contrast, the younger Halsey came to naval service as emergent ideas and developing technology gripped the nation and its Navy. In their respective times, both men had tackled well the challenges of junior officers. Both had passed from Annapolis, both had proved temperamentally suited to sea service, and both had met the early tests of watch and division duties. At the start, then, only their times distinguished them from each other, and only time would distinguish them again, in midcareer and at the end.

Chapter Five

A Naval Band of Brothers

HALSEY CARED LITTLE ABOUT the world cruise as he left the *Kansas* in the spring of 1909. His mind was on Fan. "There were many functions in Hampton Roads, and some in Norfolk," he recalled of the activity surrounding the fleet's return. "I dodged them as much as possible and spent all the time that I had free in Norfolk with Miss Grandy." He had bombarded Fan with ardent letters and souvenirs from every port on the world cruise, and now pressed hard for her hand in marriage. When in March the expanding Navy promoted him two ranks, to lieutenant, Halsey leveraged the double jump in pay to persuade Fan of a future. They agreed to marry later that fall.[1]

The horizon was bright. From the *Kansas* Halsey went to Charleston to take command of the *Du Pont,* one of the Navy's first torpedo boats. Commissioned in 1897, she was some 175 feet long and embarked a tiny complement of Halsey, Passed Midshipman Archie Allen, and twenty-two bluejackets. His father, William, had languished for a quarter century for a first chance at command, finally taking the reins of the *Manila* when he was forty-six years old, with graying hair, growing stomach, and the frayed, dull double stripes of an aging lieutenant. Bill reached command five times faster and twenty years earlier, his two lieutenant braids shimmering gold against the sea sun.

In June, with four other boats of the Reserve Torpedo Flotilla, the ship traveled north to Massachusetts for fleet maneuvers, where the *Du Pont* tended the gunnery range for the fleet's big guns. This modest task left ample free time, which Halsey and Allen filled with small parties aboard their floating empire with Allen's wife, who had followed the ship north for the summer; Halsey's sister, who was then married to a naval officer with the fleet; and, for a few weeks, Fan, who had escaped the Norfolk heat. In September the *Du Pont* and two other boats, led by Lieutenant Harold "Betty" Stark, plied the Hudson River from New York to Troy as part of the Hudson-Fulton Exposition, a festival of concerts and carnivals celebrating the river's history. By the fall the *Du Pont* was back at Jacksonville, Florida, preparing for winter. On December 1, Halsey married Fan at Norfolk's Christ Church. His best man was an Annapolis classmate, Lieutenant David Bagley, and his ushers were Lieutenant Commander Thomas Hart and Lieutenant Husband Kimmel, the latter an academy friend destined to play a central role in Halsey's life at the start of World War II.[2]

With command and a wife came a new chapter. Marriage brought fleeting thoughts of civilian life, and Halsey fished vaguely for something in the "engineering or business line of things." He wrote to a former officer then working in New York City, who told Halsey he would have great difficulty finding a salary to match his naval pay of about $3,000 per annum, even in good economic times. So Halsey stuck with the Navy, setting up a small home in Norfolk. There, he and Fan welcomed their first child in October 1910, Margaret Bradford.[3]

The Navy cooperated through these early years of domesticity. Halsey passed the first eighteen months of married life assigned to the Norfolk station ship *Franklin,* supervising successive classes of new enlisted recruits, where his superiors noted his "exceptional tact" and "executive ability" as well as his "painstakingly fair" attitude toward recruits. The job fit the Halsey liberal impulse with bluejackets, and the duty allowed Bill to live at home with Fan and Margaret.[4]

In the summer of 1912 he became the first member of his academy class to command a destroyer, initiating two decades of service in a type of vessel that had not existed when he had entered Annapolis. Destroyers, a byproduct and in many respects an afterthought of the battleship era, were about twice the size of torpedo boats but still flimsy, fast, and austere relative to larger ships. Quickly dubbed "tin cans," their precise role on the high seas would evolve along with the rest of the Navy in the twentieth century, but from the start their great agility attracted daring behavior among those who served upon their decks. Halsey had first boarded one as an Annapolis senior, when five prototypes steamed down Chesapeake Bay so close together that one sailor walked from the far starboard to the far port ship with nothing but a leap between hulls. From that moment, Halsey became "bitten with the desire to join the destroyers." In the following decades, he came to epitomize the tin-can Navy as much as any man.[5]

Halsey's ship was the *Flusser*. Launched in 1909, she was the twentieth destroyer and the sixth model since the first destroyers had appeared eight years earlier. The expanding Navy struggled to man these hulls, and nearly as soon as Halsey took command the *Flusser* went into reserve with four others, making Halsey the Navy's youngest division commander, with authority for five ships, at least on paper. Yet just twenty men and a single officer manned each vessel through the winter of 1913, an austerity that forced Halsey to gather a rotating work gang merely to fire the ships' engines.[6]

In the summer of 1913 he finagled two spots for his boats in fleet maneuvers off the New England coast. While there, the *Flusser* hosted Assistant Secretary of the Navy Franklin Roosevelt, then a vigorous man with much experience in small boats. When Roosevelt asked to take the helm of the ship, Halsey reluctantly complied. "The fact that a white-flannelled yachtsman can sail a catboat out to a buoy and back," Halsey thought, "was no guarantee he can handle a high speed destroyer." Yet Roosevelt proved a nearly "professional sailorman," handling the ship with skill and sparking an acquaintance between the Navy man and the patrician politician. Halsey hosted Roosevelt at sea twice more, once in 1918 when he escorted him across the English Channel, and once in 1920 near San Francisco during the Democratic Party's national convention, which nominated Roosevelt for vice president. Their cordial relations endured through the years until Roosevelt's death in 1945.[7]

By late summer Halsey had done well enough with the *Flusser* to win command of the *Jarvis,* a nearly new destroyer with the Atlantic Fleet's torpedo flotilla. This move ensured regular contact with the remarkable Captain William Sims, who had taken command of the flotilla that same summer. Sims had graduated from Annapolis in 1880 and had quickly grown restless in the moribund Navy. While still a lieutenant, he wrote directly to President Theodore Roosevelt to deplore the Navy's ritualized gunnery exercises, an impertinence that won him oversight of the Navy's target practice in 1902. Many of the Navy's old guard blamed Sims's radical gunnery methods for the turret explosions that had rocked the *Missouri* and other ships, but his techniques also led to dramatic improvements in gun accuracy. An insurgent in attitude and a muckraker in method, Sims next took aim at the Navy's decrepit promotion system, its inadequate administrative structures, and its draconian mores of discipline. Sims was intense and impatient and charismatic and clever, a volatile combination that sometimes made for stiff relations with senior officers but nearly always fostered enthusiasm among younger men. To Bill Halsey, Sims was a rebel proud of his periodic run-ins with authority and a man "loved by all his juniors."[8]

By the time the two men came to the torpedo flotilla, Sims was among the most influential of the Navy's reformers. He had just left the presidency of the War College, and he brought from that institution definite ideas of tactics and strategy as well as a crack staff, including Commander William Pratt, a future chief of naval operations, and Lieutenant Commander Dudley Knox, a man of atypical intellect who, even as a junior officer, was the Navy's leading authority on organization and administration. Sims and his staff had ambitious goals for the flotilla, hoping "to do for tactics" with the destroyers what Sims had earlier "done for gunnery" with the battleships. In the summer of 1913 there existed no American destroyer policy for division or squadron attacks against an enemy battle line, and most naval men loosely envisioned the small ships acting as scouts seeking out enemy dispositions, defensive screens for battlewagons, or suicidal attack boats in dire situations. Sims aimed to change all that and transform destroyers into deliberative, offensive weapons in their own right. To do so, he made the flotilla a seaborne laboratory for the study of command, leadership, and doctrine.[9]

By intellect and outlook, Sims was the antithesis of Halsey's father, who had been well suited to the Navy Sims had lambasted, and scant evidence beyond shared attitudes toward juniors suggested that Halsey's kid would have a fine turn working for Sims. The younger Halsey had first met Sims during a raucous wardroom party aboard the *Missouri* in 1904, and now, in the summer of 1913, Halsey found himself, with other flotilla skippers, aboard Sims's flagship for the first of innumerable discussions about the role of destroyers. This was in itself novel. Most senior officers of the day preferred solitude, at sea anyway, to the point that they often dined alone and, in Sims's words, "lived practically isolated lives in so far as organized and systematic discussion of military matters was concerned." Sims believed such seclusion was poorly suited to the complexities of modern war. From his very first days in command of the flotilla, he aimed to harness the collective competence of the twenty or so destroyer captains in his charge, not only to make the flotilla all it could be, but also to develop those within the group who, to paraphrase Napoleon Bonaparte and to quote Sims's premier biographer, perchance "carried an admiral's flag in his sea chest."[10]

At that first meeting Halsey and his peers heard not commands for ship movements or edicts about discipline but instead questions about the flotilla's purpose. This plea at first prompted such milk-toast replies as to "do all destroyer work," or to "make successful torpedo attacks," or, Halsey's meager contribution, to "help in the maintenance" of individual vessels. Over the course of many conferences in the ensuing months, and through frank talk, gentle persuasion, and sea drills, Sims massaged these ideas into a mission centered not inward on lesser chores but outward upon larger tasks, on the business and objectives of the fleet as a whole. In the age of Mahan, this could only mean, of course, the destruction of enemy battleships.[11]

So it was that in the 1914 winter fleet maneuvers off the Cuban coast, Sims's destroyers aggressively sought out the bigger ships. In earlier exercises destroyer attacks had been marred by errors, some of which the flotilla initially repeated that winter: detailed instructions proved unworkable in the swift pace of simulated war, tactical signals designed for peacetime parades worked poorly under more tense conditions, and attacks by multiple destroyers tended to dissolve once local situations became acute, usually because the boats lacked a common discipline to press strikes home. In the Caribbean warmth, Sims, his staff, and his destroyer skippers toiled toward solutions to these problems during intense exercises, long conferences, and occasional tennis matches or long walks along the shore, two of Sims's favorite pastimes.

To address the problem of overly detailed instructions they turned for inspiration to the British admiral Horatio Nelson, long a hero to naval men for his dramatic victories at the Nile, Copenhagen, and Trafalgar in the last century. As Knox explained it on behalf of the flotilla in the 1914 prizewinning essay for *Proceedings,* Nelson's most conspicuous characteristic during each of these victories had been self-restraint in communication, despite the temptation to issue voluminous instructions. Knox argued that Nelson was able to dispense with clumsy communiqués because, well before each of his signature victories, the British admiral had thoroughly socialized his skippers in tactics and strategy during visits aboard his flagship, where he much "preferred a turn on the quarterdeck with his captains, whom he led by his own frankness to express themselves freely, to the stiffness and formality of a council of war."[12]

To address the difficulty of coordinated movement among multiple ships, flotilla officers assaulted the Navy's signals book. Sims believed that a passion for prancing of the kind seen during the world cruise had created tactics deaf to the likely clamor of combat. For him, a battleship or destroyer division in exact column, with perfect interval and bearing, was no better than one slightly out of line from a military point of view, as long as ships maintained a capacity to shoot in every direction envisioned by the nature of a formation. Such a fleet might be less appealing from the vantage of adoring crowds ashore or high officials afloat, Sims acknowledged, but it would be "equally unsatisfactory from the point of view of an enemy on the beam."[13]

And to address the problem of ill-disciplined attacks, Sims and his flotilla officers courted doctrine, long an idea with little appeal among

Navy men because they feared it would erode a commander's traditional autonomy at sea. Yet, as Knox argued in the 1915 prize essay in *Proceedings*—the second year running that he and the work of the flotilla were so honored—the complexity, pace, and scope of modern war required some standard approach to combat. Knox and his destroyer cohorts believed doctrine could "harmonize methods, rules, and actions" and make possible "concerted action by a large force" amid the swirling circumstance of naval engagement. At first, and in deference to tradition, Sims and his skippers pushed doctrine gently, calling it a "general guide" rather than a set of "rigid and invariable rules." Anything beyond that they left to the practicum of the winter sea maneuvers to settle.[14]

For weeks in early 1914 the flotilla toiled, oftentimes alone on matters internal to its workings, sometimes at target ranges firing torpedoes, and occasionally with the battleships, either as a defensive screen or as an attacking force. The destroyer men lived for the latter challenge, when they fired dummy torpedoes at the battlewagons, a contest that Sims wrote his wife was "great fun." The first full weekend in March typified their activity. Halsey and the *Jarvis,* along with other destroyers, spent that Friday afternoon in division drills. At 7:00 PM, the overall fleet commander ordered destroyers to attack a battleship line with nothing more than a single position report to guide them, and required the strike before 2:00 AM Saturday. By 7:45 PM Sims had radioed a concise plan to the destroyers, ten of which quickly worked up to thirty knots. Finding their target, they breached the battleships' defensive screen at about 11:30 and broke off their mock attack two hours later, by which time Sims judged that each destroyer had had a turn firing torpedoes. Halsey's *Jarvis* simulated two direct hits, more than any tin can that evening. Then, at dawn, the destroyers split into two groups to join opposing battleship divisions, passing the morning attacking with torpedoes, defending with smoke screens, and jousting with one another. By midafternoon Halsey and other boat skippers were in conference aboard Sims's flagship, poring over the weekend's operations, tweaking, pruning, and shaping their operations for the next time.[15]

Six times that spring Sims aimed his boats at the battleships, each time improving, until finally the destroyers routinely pierced the battle line's defensive screen, which caused consternation among big-ship officers, who, as the destroyer men liked to say, had difficulty adjusting eight-knot minds to thirty-knot ships. While battleship officers toiled to digest tactical directives of over 500 words, destroyer skippers grew adept with Sims's increasingly brief missives, which eventually averaged about 60 words. When battleship radiomen flooded airwaves to interrupt destroyer signals, flotilla skippers reduced further the few messages passed among them. When the big ships moved evasively to disrupt the charging destroyers, the attackers adjusted adroitly, caring less for precise form and more for the purpose of maneuver, which for Sims was always to maximize the number of torpedo tubes that could train upon a battlewagon at any given moment. And when, at last, the big guns of the big ships turned their way, the destroyer men ran, closed ranks, and belched black smoke as a cloak, a nerve-racking stunt that reduced visibility to less than the length of a single ship. Nothing but simplified signals and "nothing but young men," Sims marveled, "could do such work with vessels going 30 miles an hour in close formation."[16]

Through the summer and winter of 1914 and beyond, Sims's ships made great strides. Before then, the Navy had not fully investigated the possibilities for destroyers, a ship type whose emergence had not followed upon the heels of extended imagination and formal thought of the kind Mahan had provided for battleships. Under Sims, destroyer men adopted an aggressive ethic based upon speed, agility, and daring. Destroyer doctrine, which continued to evolve, became formal in its structure and casual in its execution. It required strict adherence to scouting patterns, search plans, radio signals, and reporting procedures—and Sims always demanded a uniform acceptance of a general scheme to the point that he once relieved a skipper for infidelity to it. Yet Sims also championed individual initiative and delegated decision making, the two impulses that underlay his passion for officer conferences and that were, to one observer, a personal "fetish." To Sims and, eventually, most small-ship skippers, including

Halsey, adherence to a common doctrine was not inconsistent with individual enterprise. To the contrary, as the indefatigable Knox put it, "absolute loyalty to a general plan transformed intuition from a grave danger to a great asset," making doctrine "an indispensable element of command and an essential prelude to great success in war."[17]

Along the way Sims's skippers again found an appetite for the controlled melee, a concept long associated with scout forces in the Army but one that had atrophied in the Navy with the rise of formalist tactics in the battleship era. Sims believed the "object of all strategy and tactics is to strike the enemy in detail before he can concentrate," a common enough view to which he then applied doctrine to cohere the actions of many to that common purpose. To outsiders, including many battleship officers, the flotilla's strikes during exercises appeared chaotic. To the initiated, however, the cacophony was music; Halsey once called the attacks "orchestrated." As Sims explained it, "The Flotilla is the cavalry of the fleet and must act quickly and upon brief orders, and individual units must do the same. Consequently we must work as a team with a large measure of initiative. Some of the big ship people think these methods rather casual, and do not believe much in the doctrine, but perhaps in the course of time they will change their ideas." In this Sims foretold the early operations of the Pacific War, when aircraft carrier task forces commanded by Halsey hit at and then ran from Japanese forces in what appeared audacious and wild strikes, but which were also carefully calibrated wallops.[18]

In the torpedo flotilla Sims prepared Halsey and so many others for a war decades away, a contribution amplified by the quality of the destroyer men. In addition to staff officers such as Pratt and Knox, there was Lieutenant Commander Frank Evans, son of Admiral Robley Evans and one of the best boat handlers in the Navy, and Lieutenants Ernest King, Harold Stark, Rufus Zogbaum, Aubrey Fitch, George Cook, and John Newton, each one a future luminary and even then the cadre of the Navy's youngest skippers. Many of these men responded to the Sims touch, which was "not specifically naval or even professional, but instead applied more broadly to the leadership of men." Sims believed service aboard the small destroyers promoted esprit in ways not possible on larger ships. He was a master of the "little things by which human hearts are won," and he sought familiarity with bluejackets and courted camaraderie with junior officers without losing his dignity.[19]

In time, Sims and his destroyer men constituted what his biographer in 1941 called a "band of brothers," an idea Sims exemplified in a poem he wrote and hung in his wardroom. In part, it read:

> Destroyermen
> They're a lusty crowd that is vastly proud
>   Of the slim black craft they drive
> Of the roaring flues and the humming screws
>   Which make her a thing alive
> There's a roll and a pitch and a heave and a hitch
>   To the nautical gait they take
> For they're used to the cant of the decks aslant
>   As the white toothed combers break
> Oh, their scorn is quick for the crews who stick
>   To a battleship's steady floor
> For they love the lurch of their own frail perch
>   At thirty five knots or more.[20]

Halsey belonged in this world. He disliked formality, hated paperwork, and, even much later in life, preferred "conferences, which have the added advantage of encouraging free discussion." Halsey was not a Sims intimate—that status was reserved for the flotilla staff and senior skippers, and until the spring of 1914 Halsey was the junior ship captain in the flotilla. But Halsey shared Sims's intuition for command. In November 1913, at the same time that Sims complained that some of his skippers remained too immersed in administrative detail and too concerned with the polish of brass hardware, he described Halsey as a "calm, even-tempered, forceful" officer, "particularly well fitted for command and for handling men." In May 1914 Sims rated Halsey an "excellent" destroyer man, a judgment confirmed later that summer when no boat in the flotilla bested the *Jarvis*'s score in torpedo drills, a test that was a signature mark of a destroyer's efficiency. Above and beyond any of that, Sims believed Halsey was "specifically qualified for torpedo work," by which he meant that he believed Halsey had the gumption and guile to press home daring destroyer attacks.[21]

....

Halsey's fine start did not last. As with his father, Bill's health now conspired to abort his career, just as it was gaining steam. Except for common childhood diseases and his hospital stay for gonorrhea while a midshipman, Bill Halsey had enjoyed good health as a young man. He was not a fitness freak: when given the option during his annual physicals, he had always preferred a lenient bicycle test to a more strenuous run, and he had steadily gained weight through his twenties until, by his thirtieth birthday, he spread a meaty 195 pounds across his 5'9" frame. Still, from his graduation in 1904 to the summer of 1914, he had spent just two days on the sick list, in 1911, for laryngitis. Yet now, in late June 1914, in his thirty-second year, he contracted mumps, a condition that led to orchitis, a scrotal inflammation accompanied by painful testicular swelling. These maladies forced him off the *Jarvis* for three weeks, confined to his home in Norfolk and, for some strange reason, under the care of a private physician, Dr. C. R. Grandy, who occupied a distant branch on Fan's large Virginia family tree.[22]

That was the beginning. The mumps faded but Halsey could not shake a feeling of malaise. By autumn the same bugaboos that had bedeviled his father seemed poised to strike. By his own account, Halsey passed the month of August with a "marked loss of ambition and energy." On September 4 a Navy doctor expressed concern about Halsey's pulse, which at rest hovered near 120, and noted Halsey was "extremely nervous, easily excited and filled by vague fears. He is afraid of being in crowds and is totally different than former self." This was sufficient to hospitalize Halsey for a month with a diagnosis of neurasthenia, a popular turn-of-the-century verdict associated with anxiety, headache, impotence, and depression. Doctors of the day believed neurasthenia was caused by an exhaustion of the central nervous system, which they attributed to modernization and the pressures put on the genteel class by an increasingly competitive business environment. The condition was well known enough to earn its own moniker, Americanitis, and its own snake-oil cure, Americanitis Elixir, marketed by the Rexall drug company.[23]

The affliction threatened Halsey's command of the *Jarvis*. "I hope the trouble is not serious," Sims wrote upon learning of Halsey's illness, "for I would regret very much you leaving the Flotilla." Yet Halsey's condition deteriorated. In September his flotilla division commander complained that Halsey's "poor health had interfered seriously" with his duties. In January 1915 doctors noted Halsey suffered from insomnia, an "aloofness from his fellows," and a "general irritability." He was "depressed, emotional, and worries over trifles. He tires easily and is able to concentrate his mind on any particular subject only with some difficulty. Depression is so marked at times that he is unable to restrain himself and will weep." To earlier assessments of neurasthenia doctors now added a diagnosis of agoraphobia, an anxiety disorder characterized by extreme fear of panic attacks in public spaces. Halsey was now, quite literally, afraid of being afraid, and that scotched it. He was relieved of command of the *Jarvis* on January 15.[24]

He may have wondered if he shared his father's inability to cope with the modern world. From mid-January through March he lay in a Norfolk hospital bed, piddling about with small cares and large worries, his days broken by Fan's visits, sometimes with Margaret in tow. On March 23 a medical board concluded that Halsey was battling depression and suffered severe episodes of agitation, leading them to prescribe an additional three months of sick leave, completely "free from the cares and worries of active duty," after which another medical board would decide his ultimate fate. At that point, Halsey was in grave danger of forced retirement. He dismissed this period of time in his unpublished memoirs with a single sentence, and mentioned it not at all in *Admiral Halsey's Story*. But the spring of 1915 was surely a tumultuous period.[25]

He recovered enough. In early July Navy doctors cleared him for duty, and the Navy nursed him back to service. Captain Victor Blue, a long-standing friend of Halsey's dad and responsible for officer assignments in the Navy at the time, offered Halsey his choice of recruitment commands in Maine, Massachusetts, or New York City, adding that Halsey could "always go to the Naval Academy" if he desired. Halsey chose Annapolis, a duty that appealed to his familial roots but raised anew the specter of career derailment. By the early twentieth century many officers had come to regard a tour teaching midshipmen as "their personal contribution to the education of future officers," although most also recognized among their brethren a certain type, known as Naval Academy cruisers, who spent most of their shore duty teaching, finding it more pleasant and less taxing than the challenges of other tasks. Halsey's father was certainly one such officer, and Halsey's own path in the Navy was not yet sufficiently etched along any particular route to point reliably in another direction.[26]

Halsey loved the academy, as had his father. He had maintained close ties to the school's athletic department in the years since his graduation, having twice coached the football backfield, in 1904 and 1905, while on detached duty, and he had often spent leave in the Annapolis area. Academy duty allowed family time with Fan and Margaret and, after September 1915, a son, William Halsey III. They lived at 39 Upsher Road, the duplex adjoining the unit Halsey had lived in as a teenager during one of his dad's innumerable postings to Annapolis.

He was assigned as the officer in charge of midshipmen, responsible for the daily discipline of students. In this duty as policeman, Halsey did what he must and tolerated what he could, tempering "disciplinary severity with humor and tolerance," as one student recalled. But he soon tired of nursing young men, finding his second year at the academy a "stale repetition of the one before," especially as World War I, then raging in Europe, steered ever closer to American shores.[27]

When in April 1917 the United States allied with Britain and declared war on Germany, Halsey and other Annapolis officers jockeyed for sea duty. Instead, the war came to them, sort of. The Navy exploded from fewer than 70,000 men in 1916 to nearly 500,000 by the end of 1918, quickening promotions and making Halsey a lieutenant commander in January 1917, some fifteen years faster than his father's climb to the same rank. The war also shortened the academy school year in both 1917 and 1918 and brought a massive influx of reserve officer candidates, graduates from civilian colleges, to the academy for abbreviated summer instruction leading to commissions. Although Navy traditionalists disliked the reserve program, Halsey, who spent the summer of 1917 drilling a 400-man class of newbies, believed the college graduates were "the highest type of young Americans" and "a privilege" to train.[28]

Still, it was not the war, and Halsey hankered for action. The character of the conflict in Europe gave him some hope. On land, a contest envisioned as swift and decisive was in its third year of mud and blood. At sea, the battleship era drifted, stillborn. The Battle of Jutland in May 1916 was the war's sole major blow between dreadnoughts, and it left a wake of strategic indecision. Into the wash spilled a mixture of defensive sweeps, mine laying, and small fights, all swirling around the timeless stratagems of blockade and commerce raiding. The British Isles nearly starved due to sea blockade in the spring of 1917, making the destroyers that hunted submarines the sine qua non of Allied naval power. In the United States, all work on battleships stopped and plans for 273 destroyers sped their way toward shipyards. As perhaps only two dozen men in the U.S. Navy exceeded Halsey's command experience with destroyers, back in Annapolis, "every time the phone rang," he recalled, "I expected to be told to pack my gear."[29]

William Sims, by then a rear admiral, was running the American naval effort in London and begging for destroyers and experienced men. The first six tin cans had come promptly, arriving at Queenstown, Ireland, in early May 1917, followed by more, until in August there were thirty-five American destroyers and two tenders at the small Irish seaport. Halsey was not aboard any of them. On May 16 Sims had requested as many of his former skippers as possible, a plea he repeated on May 30, June 1, and June 19, along with a roster of a dozen names. Finally, in August, Sims asked by name for Halsey and a few others, which proved enough. He was off to war.[30]

Halsey reached Queenstown on January 18, 1918. Dangled from the southeast shore of Ireland, Queenstown was a small settlement of a few thousand people that was prominent as a debarkation for immigrants to the United States; it had been the *Titanic*'s last port call before she set off on her fateful journey in 1912. During the war, the region was a hotbed of Catholic separatism and free Irish sentiment, making the town a ripe target for German espionage and intrigue. Two para-political parties, Sinn Féin and the Irish Republican Brotherhood, had hatched from nearby hills the 1916 Easter Rebellion that left 450 people dead. By the time Halsey arrived there nearly two years later, relations between Allied naval forces and locals were strained; one British officer described the surrounding coast as nothing more than "rocks, sea, and Sinn Feiners." Technically friendly territory throughout the Great War, the political topography of Queenstown complicated operations emanating from an otherwise picturesque place, especially for American ship commanders with crewmen of Irish Catholic descent.[31]

The Queenstown command itself sprang from the unanticipated character of the war at sea. The local British commander, Admiral Sir Lewis Bayly, regarded his posting there in 1915 as purgatory, which was true enough before the submarine war dominated the ocean struggle and Queenstown became a hub for destroyers. Bayly was perfect for the fight. Before the war he had held a command analogous to that of Sims's torpedo flotilla, and, like Sims, he had nurtured a camaraderie among juniors and a cavalry mentality among his skippers. Sims commanded the U.S. forces in Ireland, but because he was in London, Bayly oversaw American operations in Queenstown, exercising his authority through Sims's local representative, Captain Joel Pringle, who had earlier worked for Halsey's father at the Naval Academy. In later wars and after longer experience in coalition warfare, these kinds of command irregularities attracted less attention, but at the time it was novel enough for Bayly to enter Pringle on the British Admiralty's Naval List, making him a de facto British naval officer—a happenstance with no corollary before or since. To navigate an odd blend of prerogative and obligation, Pringle himself relied upon a polished disposition. He was, as Sims's biographer put it, "a balanced, finished, sophisticated personality, well equipped to handle the difficulties of his peculiar position."[32]

It was to these men, in turn Sims, Bayly, and Pringle, that Halsey reported in January 1918. The submarine crisis that had brought America into the war the previous spring had abated somewhat, but had not dissipated. To better protect their precious supply convoys, the Allies had begun to convoy merchant shipping and escort them with destroyers. German U-boats, finding it increasingly difficult to sink Allied vessels on the open ocean, had then headed for coastal waters, where they were more likely to spy single ships either heading to or having just left ocean convoys. These littorals represented the convoy system's weak link—the danger zone, in Allied parlance—and were the areas to which Queenstown destroyers were increasingly devoted as Halsey piped aboard the *Melville,* a destroyer tender and Pringle's flagship, in the small but very busy Queenstown harbor.

Pringle assigned Halsey a familiarization cruise before giving him his own boat, the *Benham.* The *Benham* was the Navy's forty-ninth destroyer hull, and, as part of the eleventh class of tin cans, reflected the Navy's continuing experiment with the type. Like all destroyers, she was Spartan and provided little shelter from the wicked Irish Sea, which had over the centuries earned well its treacherous reputation. The U-boats added further danger. In words calculated to inspire diligence but that likely provoked fear, Bayly told his arriving destroyer skippers, "When you pass beyond the defenses of the harbor, you face death, and live in danger of death until you return behind such defenses. You must presume from the moment you pass out that you are seen by a submarine." If a skipper "relaxed for a moment," Bayly stressed, he would find his "vessel sunk" and his "men drowned." Unsurprisingly, this admonition translated into a laundry list of official warnings and proscriptions: periscopes could be floating lures attached to mines, distressed vessels might be disguised U-boats, destroyer skippers should eschew shipwrecked souls and disabled vessels, and skippers should not use searchlights nor expect nor rely upon lengthy radio transmissions or electronic navigation aids, a restriction that had the effect of denying the boats some of the best tools required for effective submarine hunting.[33]

Halsey's first patrols in the *Benham* were tentative. He refused to ram a periscope on March 22, depth charged empty waters on April 9, 11, and 14, and twice nearly fired upon American submarines. He backed the *Benham* from a Queenstown pier with a line still secure on April 26, throwing the ship first to starboard, bumping the sloop *Colleen,* then to port, brushing the destroyer *Shaw.* And as late as July, Halsey was still occasionally chasing phantoms, this time mistaking a sunken American merchantman for a U-boat, prompting his fellow skippers to dub him the "Duke of Aberdeen," composing for him his own ditty:[34]

> Last night Over by Aberdeen
> I saw a German submarine
> The funniest sight I ever seen
> Was old Bill Halsey's submarine.[35]

Like all skippers, Halsey struggled to meet inbound convoys. Typically, eight to ten destroyers escorted an outbound convoy to open sea for two or three days, then herded inbound merchantmen to some port in Ireland, England, or France. To locate arriving ships, a picket line of destroyers twenty or thirty miles long sometimes had nothing more than a position report within a degree of longitude and latitude, an area of some 3,600 square miles. Under those conditions, making a successful contact was, according to Halsey, "almost a matter of by guess and by God." He spent one March patrol searching for a convoy through weather as "thick as pea soup," risking high-speed collision with any of about thirty merchant ships before a barely perceptible shift in the wind alerted him to an immense object. Ordering the *Benham*'s engines to full reverse, he barely missed the huge troopship *Leviathan* as it emerged from the mist.[36]

Once matched with a convoy, the tension eased on the bridge but broadened through the ship. "The strain upon all grew greater," wrote one reporter who rode with Halsey's *Benham,* and the crew became "nervous, morose, and irritable. The eyes of the lookouts were red-lidded with constant and anxious watches," while "gunners, torpedo men, and depth charge hands crabbed at one another." High-speed chases and slow-moving convoys required exhausting attention, and in each of Halsey's first five patrols with the *Benham* he passed at least one thirty-six-hour period continuously upon the bridge deck, a tempo that often left him a "dead dog" and, on one occasion, sound asleep on the quarterdeck in the middle of an afternoon. Queenstown patrols, though they averaged but a week, were intense.[37]

The trial at sea made the time in port important. From the outset, little Queenstown was unable to accommodate the 6,000 or so U.S. Navy men under Bayly's charge. Most of these men lived aboard their vessels, but the influx nonetheless more than trebled the population of the town and required the construction of dozens of buildings, including barracks, torpedo repair shops, supply depots, and hospitals. Even an expanded Queenstown was too small to provide much in the way of recuperative charms, so bluejackets sometimes traveled to nearby Cork, spent freely, chased women, and, in Bayly's words, partook in "fair-sized brawls in the streets." Officers engaged in some of the same, except at better places such as the Royal Cork Yacht Club. Halsey and his peers "dubbed it the 'Royal Uncork Yacht Club,' and devised a special decoration, the F.I.R., for officers who had difficulty returning to their ships after an evening there. F.I.R. stood for Fell in River."[38]

This monkey business glossed over, or perhaps precipitated, problems. As early as September 1917 Pringle warned his skippers about the behavior of young officers ashore, believing "there was too much hanging around the Yacht Club." By the following May, and after many troubling reports, Sims agreed and extended his concern to a certain number of more senior officers, one of whom may have been Halsey. Sims's worries stretched beyond drinking, however, and extended to "very regrettable instances of immorality in connection with women" among his officers. Sims hoped a "word to the wise" would be sufficient, but he stood ready to act more decisively, and, in at least once instance, did.[39]

Local influences threatened more than American virtues, whatever they may have been. A newsman portrayed Queenstown as a village amok with petty espionage, where pretty girls with cheeks "red as apples," eyes "blue as the Irish Sea," and skirts "playing in the wind" preyed upon many a lad's loyalty. Bayly believed that "nine Irishmen out of ten cannot be trusted," committed as they were to Ireland's emancipation from Britain. Sims thought local Catholic clerics were "to all intents and purposes the enemies of the Allied cause," worried that American Catholics in Navy uniforms harbored confused loyalties, and agonized over the assignment of chaplains to the Queenstown command. When in the spring of 1918 a British Parliament plan to draft Irishmen for the European war threatened an open revolt, Bayly developed elaborate plans to protect Allied military interests at naval bases, airfields, and signal stations. When tensions peaked in March, Bayly noted an uptick in security breaches, and as Saint Patrick's Day loomed, the Queenstown command readied for some form of open hostility. Upon the *Benham*, Halsey ventured that the "Sinn Feiners might start something" and braced for what may come.[40]

Parliament eased its conscription plans and the crisis faded, replaced, in the fullness of time, by nostalgia. After the war one destroyer skipper recalled "the charming people" of Ireland, who were "always more than cordial" to the Americans. The truth was considerably muddier. Although the American component to the Queenstown command was puny compared to the astonishing overseas commands in World War II, these World War I footprints were among the Navy's first of any size upon foreign lands in a time of war. The experience of it stayed with Halsey and helped form his own command attitudes when fate once more placed him at a distant and troubled American station in a time of war.[41]

Back at sea, Halsey's summertime patrols washed away his combat inexperience. In mid-May he relinquished command of the *Benham* to Frank Jack Fletcher, himself destined for World War II prominence, and took charge of the *Shaw*. The *Shaw* had been commissioned just a year earlier, the Navy's sixty-eighth destroyer and part of the fourteenth model in the Navy's continuous tinkering with tin cans.

Halsey first conned her out of Queenstown in late May, and partici-pated in a three-destroyer attack on a U-boat on May 27. On June 7 he coolly checked his fire on a submarine, even after it refused a friend-or-foe challenge, until American markings emerged on its hull to confirm his reservations. Later in June he aggressively attacked a suspected German submarine, and, by virtue of seniority, found himself "king of the Irish Sea," with the destroyer *Beale* and two British sloops, the *Kestrel* and the *Zephyr,* under his control. By early July, Halsey was sure-footed enough to report directly to Sims a mer-chant ship captain who had conned his vessel erratically, telling his old boss that the civilian mariner should "be properly disciplined." Through all this Halsey kept a clean ship: the *Shaw* spent just five days in normal repairs during his command, a time considerably less than that of other ships and, in the case of some vessels, less than a tenth of the time. In one assessment, Sims specifically noted Halsey's knack for keeping the *Shaw* in service.[42]

Subordinates praised Halsey. When Halsey left the *Benham,* the ship's executive officer remembered how Halsey's "tremendous sense of confidence," ready smile, and "wonderful character" had infected the entire crew. By the summer, Halsey was regarded as "the best ship handler" in the command, capable of mooring a destroyer in a manner that an "egg between the ship and the dock wouldn't have broken."[43]

Peter Macfarlane, a *Saturday Evening Post* writer armed with a glowing endorsement from Franklin Roosevelt, spent two patrols with the *Shaw,* in part because his son Fred served aboard as a chief machinist's mate. In a series of fictionalized accounts, he used Halsey, who for operational security he called Captain Bradshaw, as his model destroyer skipper, an archetype representing a new Navy. Bradshaw was "a boyish-spirited, insuppressible hellion of the sea," Macfar-lane wrote, "who handle[d] his ship with a dash and reckless daring that would get him courts-martial in any other branch of the ser-vice." He was "no conservative battleship-bred captain, but a typical cowboy of the sea, all but worshipped by his men." As a result, the *Shaw* "was a happy ship—and an efficient one. She never lost a con-tact, never lost a convoy; month after month had fought the combing seas, performing her assignments with a skill and sureness that made her conspicuous as one of the most reliable of the destroyers." If some of that was hyperbole, some was real. In a report to London, Pringle told Sims that Macfarlane had "spent most of his time on Old Bill's ship. If he can not absorb the spirit of the sea from Bill, he can not be expected to get it from anybody else."[44]

Halsey's formative experiences in wartime command were nearly devoid of direct combat. He dropped depth charges just four times, never once fired his deck guns in anger, and, through ten patrols on the *Benham* and eleven on the *Shaw,* was not sure he ever came into contact with a U-boat. None of this was unusual. Submarine hunting was a lean business in World War I, the function of patience and stamina. Destroyers operating out of Queenstown sank less than a handful of them during the entire war, despite techniques that relied upon sophisticated hydrophone technology, advanced radio intelligence, and joint operations with the world's first air forces, which often flew maritime patrol with the tin cans. Fighting is but one aspect of military operations, and the ultimate lesson Halsey took from Queenstown concerned the administration of American forces there and the cordial, effective relations forged between American and British personnel, who not only became "comrades in arms, but close friends." After the war, the destroyer men of each nation formed the Queenstown Association and held yearly galas. In 1921 the American Queenstowners hosted Bayly in both San Francisco and New York, and Halsey's sentiment for his British boss prompted the only professional writing Halsey ever accomplished, a book review of Bayly's memoir for *Proceedings.* The Queenstown Association held reunions in occasional years until 1957, when sixty members, including Halsey, met in New York at the Harvard Club for one last gathering of ancient World War I tin can sailors.[45]

. . . .

In August the Navy ordered Halsey to Philadelphia to commission the *Yarnall,* one of the nearly three hundred wartime destroyers nearing completion. A member of the 110-strong *Wickes* class of tin cans, the *Yarnall* and her sisters marked the end of adolescence for

Navy tin cans, her 314-foot length, thirty-five-knot speed, four-inch battery, twelve torpedo tubes, and 125-man crew a fair approximation of the destroyers that performed a wide variety of missions for the Navy across the next two decades. Halsey commissioned the ship on November 29, two weeks after the war ended. He and the *Yarnall* sailed for Europe anyway and stayed for six months, ferrying dignitaries and patrolling the English Channel. Promoted to commander, Halsey once again hosted Franklin Roosevelt, twice took leave in Paris, and, in rough seas one black night, lost two men overboard, one a reservist whom Halsey had helped train in the previous year.[46]

In June 1919 the *Yarnall* sailed for Hampton Roads, where Halsey became a division commander, responsible for six ships, and joined an armada setting course for San Diego. With a bevy of other destroyers, the *Yarnall* passed through the newly completed Panama Canal, which made the journey across the isthmus and to California quicker and safer than it had been in Halsey's youth. In San Diego, the *Yarnall* joined a growing aggregation of vessels dubbed, for the first time, the Pacific Fleet, which represented a momentous operational shift for a Navy that had for decades focused its attention east, toward Europe, and south, toward the Caribbean and South America. A collision of American and Japanese objectives in China and along the far Pacific Rim had precipitated this reorientation, and for Halsey it meant a new strategic horizon.

Once on the West Coast, Halsey faced the brunt of a demobilizing Navy. On the *Yarnall,* he lost his executive officer, a fourth of his officer complement, and nearly a third of his crew to discharges. It was the same throughout the fleet. Rear Admiral Henry Wiley and Captain William Pratt, outstanding officers who held successive command of the Pacific Fleet destroyers during Halsey's California tenure, had about half the men required to crew their 170 boats, so they mothballed over one hundred vessels and organized the rest into three squadrons of eighteen hulls, each squadron further separated into three divisions of six vessels, and instituted among these ships a rotating reserve system, whereby full crews moved often among ships to keep them in working order.

Halsey moved swiftly among four ships—the *Yarnall, Chauncey, John Francis Burns,* and *Wickes.* That December, he took command of the *Chauncey,* a quirky vessel hastily built during the war. On a squadron cruise to Honolulu the following spring, *Chauncey*'s boilers seized without warning, causing the *Aaron Ward,* commanded by Raymond Spruance, to slice a gash into the *Chauncey*'s fantail. A court inquiry absolved both men of any responsibility in the collision, allowing an infant friendship to prosper between Halsey and Spruance, the two men who most influenced the Navy's tactical operations in World War II. While the two men bonded at sea, their wives established a friendship over picnics and dinners. Margaret Spruance was fond of "Billy" and, especially, Fan, who had not always found ready friends within the close confines of Navy life. The two men were different, Halsey assertive and outgoing, Spruance quiet and thoughtful. But they appreciated each other. Halsey believed Spruance was "one of the best all around officers" in the Pacific Fleet destroyers, "quiet, efficient, always on the job, and with a clear thinking brain always working." For his part, Spruance admired Halsey's "aggressive, exhilarating, skillful leadership."[47]

In September 1920 Halsey assumed command of the *Wickes* and another six-ship division. With them, he managed some semblance of habit and its corollary, accomplishment, in the postwar Navy. The division passed January and February 1921 cruising off the Latin American coast, and spent March in drills near Southern California, typically leaving San Diego at midmorning and returning by nightfall. Years of destroyer duty had given Halsey advanced ideas about their employment, and with his squadron commander and old flotilla mate, Captain Frank Evans, Halsey devised a daring high-speed anchor technique to stop a destroyer in less distance than the length of its hull, as well as a series of innovative formations that could be accomplished by ship whistle alone. "When a squadron of nineteen destroyers maneuvers by whistle, at night, blacked out, at 25 knots," Halsey wrote, "it's no place for ribbon clerks," a judgment underscored two years later when seven other destroyers crashed upon the California coast near Santa Barbara, wrecking ships, ruining careers, and killing twenty-three sailors in the Navy's worst navigational mishap of the interwar years.[48]

In April, the Pacific Fleet held live fire exercises that pitted destroyers against battleships in maneuvers reminiscent of the torpedo flotilla drills off the Cuban coast before the war. In one attack, Halsey, in temporary command of Evans's eighteen-ship squadron, split his force to each side of an oncoming division of four battleships. With instructions to close within 3,000 yards, Halsey crept to 700 yards behind a deep black smokescreen before firing thirty-six dummy torpedoes, scoring twenty-two hits, and causing over $1 million of very real damage to the big ships after a few torpedo air flasks accidentally exploded on contact. The following day, as the fleet's battleship skippers complained of the damage, a California newspaper screamed "Destroyers Decisively Defeat Battleships" in a headline.[49]

Halsey's career suffered no perceptible ill effects. Instead, assessments of his performance with Pacific Fleet destroyers constituted a valedictory of his time with the tin cans. Rear Admiral Wiley believed Halsey "was a splendid destroyer captain." Pratt thought him an "excellent officer" and a "fine ship handler" who always had "his division closed-up, in hand, and smart." Frank Evans wrote that Halsey was "preeminently a seaman and ship-handler of high order" who "was always courteous" and "a true seaman of the old school." Those with only a passing chance to evaluate Halsey came to similar judgments: Captain L. R. Sargent, who observed Halsey during fleet exercises in the fall of 1920, thought he "displayed, in full measure and rare combination, the essential qualities of initiative, decision, judgment, leadership, loyalty, and technical skill." Six months later, Sargent went out of his way to add that Halsey was "a leader of men of the first rank, an exceptional destroyer and division commander with the necessary qualifications for big ship command."[50]

If Halsey could have commented on this last assessment, he would have eschewed the path toward big ships. He had found his professional home, and it was a destroyer. Robert Carney, then an executive officer with the Pacific Fleet destroyers and later Halsey's wartime chief of staff, believed Halsey had "found an outlet for his command talent, his inherent boldness, and his gift for dealing with people" on the smaller ships. Halsey himself believed the Pacific destroyers were the "proudest ships in the fleet." Among them, the *Wickes* was the best. In the summer of 1921 the ship placed first in battle efficiency and in general excellence among all fleet destroyers, a performance that helped propel Halsey's division to first place, which in turn helped his squadron to the top of the fleet, a singular honor. "I can not too highly praise," President Warren Harding wrote Halsey, "the earnest and efficient manner in which you, your officers, and your men, performed their assigned duties." The note was perfunctory for Harding, but Halsey was the only destroyer skipper who got it that summer. With him in the Pacific destroyer force was Spruance, and over the months there had also been Joseph Taussig, Charles Blakely, David Bagley, Rufus Zogbaum, Arthur Carpender, Frank Jack Fletcher, and John Shafroth, all future admirals. Halsey had served alongside some of the Navy's best young officers, and had come out on top.[51]

Destroyers fit him. The close interaction among a destroyer crew suited his personality and fostered a tactile, almost intuitive practice of shipboard discipline. Halsey typically wielded a lenient orb as a ship captain, often after some initial show of sternness. As early as his first mast as a skipper with the *Du Pont,* for instance, he hammered one sailor for overstaying shore liberty, sentencing him to six weeks' confinement and a reduction in pay; later during the same tour it took the far more serious transgression of drunkenness at sea to earn the same penalty. When he commanded the *Flusser,* Halsey chose to describe as "misplaced" a sailor who could have reasonably been labeled absent without leave, and he later cut short a rear admiral's suspension of a junior officer in the name of ship exigency. Throughout his career, Halsey disciplined lightly for transgressions indirectly related to ship efficiency, such as shabby uniforms or low-stakes gambling, but he could come down hard on sailors whose offenses assaulted naval mores. Those caught lying or stealing consistently won stiffer penalties than those who drank too much, he was generally tougher than other skippers on scandalous behavior of an illicit character, and he once went to extraordinary lengths to ensure one bluejacket's dishonorable discharge for urinating in a messmate's bowl of break-fast oatmeal. Like all skippers, he developed idiosyncrasies; he was far less tolerant of salty language than other captains and, within a few years of his first command, he had adopted an inclination for proba-tionary sentences a full two decades before the practice became com-monplace throughout the Navy.[52]

Halsey's supple hand sometimes risked a lax ship. Frank Jack Fletcher awarded a general court-martial, a bad-conduct discharge, and seven summary courts-martial the day after he took command of the *Benham* from Halsey. More often than not, however, Halsey's way led to happy and efficient ships. His mast and muster calls meted fewer disciplinary sentences than had been registered on the same ves-sels with skippers preceding or succeeding Halsey—a happenstance especially true with Fletcher and the *Benham* and, later, when Halsey and Spruance swapped commands not once but twice. Halsey never quite flouted the guidelines or the customs of naval discipline, but for him an increasing comfort with command translated into a restrained, sparse, and elastic use of a skipper's hard hand.[53]

By 1921 the truth was this: in something under a decade Halsey had gone from a psychiatric ward to command of the proudest de-stroyer in the Pacific. William Sims had been as responsible as any doctor for this transformation. Sims surely knew Halsey's dad had broken under the strain of command, but he had also seen enough of young Bill Halsey while with the torpedo flotilla to recognize promise. When he commanded American naval forces in Europe during World War I, Sims did not ask for Halsey first or second or even third, but ask for him he did, which garnered for Halsey orders for Queenstown and another chance. In that encore, Sims rated Halsey "excellent" and described him as an officer possessed of "good judgment, tact, and ability."[54]

In the fall of 1921 Halsey left California for a desk job in Wash-ington, but in all the years that followed, his view of sea life and naval combat changed little from that which he developed while with the destroyers. Of all the old shipmates who wrote to him in World War II, a disproportionate number stemmed from the destroyer force and from his acquaintances made during the years 1912–1920. There was a steward from the *Benham,* a yeoman from the *Shaw,* a petty officer from the *Chauncey,* a lieutenant from the *Yarnall,* and a gunner from the *Wickes* who recalled how Halsey "gave the battleships hell" in the live fire exercise off the California coast. In 1942, in the midst of the campaign for Guadalcanal, a harried Halsey took time to write a dying Admiral Henry Wiley to say his tour with the Pacific Fleet destroyers was "the happiest and most profitable I have had." The horizon held new experiences, new ships, new challenges, and even an airplane or two, but through all the years that followed, destroyers remained Halsey's favorites, and, right to the very end, in temperament and outlook, he never really left the tin cans.[55]

Chapter Six

Becoming Bill Halsey

THE PUNCTUATION OF WAR distorts military biography. Combat is an inferno, drawing the biographer's pen ever forward, ever nearer, and tempting a rush past golden embers that better illuminate human dimension. This is surely true with accounts of Bill Halsey, which race by the first six decades of his life to concentrate on the four years of World War II. But Halsey was thirty-nine years old when he left the Pacific Fleet destroyers in 1921, his personality and temperament fully formed. They had existed in seed before he was born, and grew with him to maturity athwart the first decades of the twentieth century. By the end of his fourth decade, he was far enough along life's path for personal traits to endure whatever the future might hold, yet unknown enough for others to see him clearly, without the distortions that would come with celebrity in World War II.

Halsey was flamboyant, superstitious, and sentimental. He liked trinkets and accoutrements. He used a gaudy fraternity keychain throughout his life; was partial to jewelry, especially gold bracelets and silver necklaces; and was drawn to loud neckties when choosing civilian clothes. For many years he sported a New Zealand tiki bracelet of greenstone, bought while a youngster with the Great White Fleet, until a friend suggested he looked like Carmen Miranda, a flashy stage and film actress. In his wallet he carried a four-leaf clover mounted in isinglass long before the press was interested in such trivialities. The *Missouri* turret explosion had occurred on Friday, April 13, 1904, and he ever after dreaded Friday the Thirteenth. By World War II his favorite keepsake was a delicate Hawaiian good-luck symbol, a tiny strip of white linen on a thin straw staff. As an admiral, he refused to fly with Chester Nimitz for no other reason than that he believed Nimitz was bad luck in the air. Unusual for a Navy man, he was a pack rat and lugged around immense stores of junk. Halsey's household moves routinely exceeded the weight allowances for officers, and no sofa was too busted, no table too worn, "no lamp shade too wrecked, no souvenir too cheap, and no cap, pin, or button from old cruises too inconsequential to haul from place to place." He grew teary-eyed easily and freely, often confessing to "being a wretch" or "crying like a baby" when relinquishing command of a favored ship. His face flushed easily, often with little emotional cue. A fellow officer declared him "the finest example of an extravert I've ever known," and in temperament and psychology his personality was an exoskeleton, exposed to the world.[1]

He was physically awkward. A tolerable athlete as a boy, as a man Halsey's large head, thick chest, and slender legs invited exaggeration well before the caricaturists took up his portrait, after which an association of illustrators proclaimed Halsey's bust "one of the six most startling in the world," the others being those of Ernest Hemingway, Ernest Bevin, Walter Reuther, Tyrone Power, and J. Edgar Hoover. His seven-and-seven-eighths cap size required special orders, and only the hefty 200 pounds he carried on his 5'9" frame through the fleshy middle of his life brought his body into some semblance of proportion. His exercised modestly, favoring walks, an occasional round of golf, and swimming—usually in loud red trunks that became something of a joke among his peers. He had a habit of spilling drinks and dropping plates, and, if a lifetime of military service had produced by midcareer a dignified bearing when he stepped onto a ship bridge, he nevertheless lacked the physical grace and height required for a truly imposing presence.[2]

He was tight with a dollar, and a bit of a square. In 1913 financial fears kept him in uniform the single time he considered leaving the Navy, which turned out to be a good bet when the Great Depression later settled across the land. In numerous instances, he was not above trading on friendships to secure inexpensive ship passage for his family as they traveled here and there during his many career moves.

In 1924 he penned seven letters in a failed bid for reimbursement of a $23 dental bill, in 1935 he disputed a Navy commissary bill for $1.68, and in 1938, as a rear admiral, he battled the Navy Mutual Aid Association for a $5.36 premium overpayment on a $9,000 life insurance policy. Despite such care, he failed to file his 1938 tax return, an oversight never resolved after the rush of war overtook him and, apparently, the Internal Revenue Service. His automobile purchases were conventional, spaced nearly uniformly four years apart. At first he owned Fords, then later Oldsmobiles, and at last Buicks, following the path marked for American families by Detroit automobile marketers. He cared meticulously for each, and drove them carefully. He was involved in just two minor fender benders, each of which prompted letters with insurance companies and repair shops over amounts as little as five dollars.[3]

Halsey was correct but not passionate in his family relationships. Despite his sincere sentiment toward his father, the elder Halsey's death in October 1923 merited not a mention in his memoirs and, as if an afterthought by his ghostwriter, a single, transitory paragraph in *Admiral Halsey's Story*. His relationship with his mother was warmer, especially as she aged, to the point that in 1947, just months before Anne Masters died, Halsey warmly ascribed to her his traits of empathy and loyalty, as well as the tendency to see "problems only in black and white, without intermediate tones." Halsey remained on good terms with his sister Deborah, though his contact with her grew less immediate as the years passed, a common enough pattern among siblings, exacerbated in their case by Deborah's two divorces and three marriages, each one taking her a bit further from naval life. As for him and Fan, by the time Halsey was forty he had lived with his wife and their children for less than half the lifetime of his eleven-year-old daughter, and about a third the lifetime of his six-year-old son. He had provided for them honorably, but from an emotional distance. All of this was usual for men of his time, and his absence from home was typical in the Navy.[4]

Despite the strong current of clergyman in his lineage, Halsey was not religious. When duty or custom compelled attendance at church, he preferred an upper-class Episcopalian ethos, as did the preachers in his bloodline. He believed in God, but as He was not in the Navy, Halsey had little time for Him. Halsey was never anything other than a Navy man. By midlife, naval mores had become part of his fiber. He had no abiding friendships beyond naval circles, no outside interests, no hobbies. To him, the second story of a home was the upper deck, the rear seat of a car the stern sheets, his baggage his gear. He read, but haphazardly, and nearly always for professional purposes.

He knew little of civil society, and as his competence and confidence in things naval grew, his unease in unfamiliar circumstances became more apparent. The occasional request to speak to civic groups usually prompted a disproportionate amount of preparation. For a twenty-minute overview of the Navy presented to a group of Knoxville hardware store owners in 1935, for instance, Halsey, by then a senior captain, tapped the expertise of the Navy's public affairs office, employed two Navy yeomen as writers, privately engaged the services of a journalist, and dress-rehearsed his performance four times. He would have delivered the same chat to a group of officers with nary a blink. Like other military men deeply embedded in uniformed service, he understood well the ethic of service, but occasionally copped a sanctimonious attitude toward those he served. In the 1920s, when domestic politics and various international treaties constrained the size and composition of the Navy, he complained often and sometimes bitterly of a meddling Congress and of weak presidential leadership. When an elite boarding school solicited an opinion about a fellow captain's financial responsibility attendant to an application for admissions, Halsey brusquely replied that the man "was a high ranking officer in the United States Navy" and "such a statement" was "entirely unnecessary."[5]

Halsey was a quintessential company man. He was largely apolitical, voting irregularly and in accordance with service interest, not political philosophy; he voted for Franklin Roosevelt for president in 1936 and for Dwight Eisenhower in 1952 because he thought they would do more for the Navy than their opponents. He perfected early the duality of service ashore and afloat, favoring crisp khaki in the office, crummy Annapolis letter sweaters on the bridge, and certain Navy standards in any circumstance. He was never late with a haircut, tended to excessive personal pruning, and, when uniform regulations became passé among ranking officers in World War II, reserved just one personal privilege: the miniature naval aviator wings he pinned on his garrison cap.

His relationships with officers senior to him were marked by appropriate regard but unencumbered by false or undue deference; with juniors, he, like his model Sims, courted camaraderie without sacrificing dignity. He could be blunt and was often plainspoken, sometimes to a fault, but peers rarely heard him criticize seniors even as they witnessed tolerance toward juniors. Halsey once dismissed a fellow officer as "a nut on the subject of leadership, about which he knows nothing," and derided the so-called experts then beginning to pollute the academy classroom and the ship wardroom. He felt leadership could be learned through example but not taught in any formal sense, and by his fortieth year his style sat firmly upon a foundation begun by his father and finished by his own experience. In his view, leadership and command were not brothers but cousins, linked by loyalty to the Navy. He grasped intuitively that the writ of command arrived by fiat and from above, and the warrant of leadership came slowly and was bestowed only from below. When push came to shove, he, again like Sims, valued the latter more than the former, there being, he wrote a friend, "not much choice" between the two: leaders more effectively established morale and esprit, the essential ingredients "to make each ship and unit of the fleet better, day by day, and finally to make the Navy more efficient by every possible means." Unsurprisingly, juniors responded to such an outlook: from his own perch as chief of naval operations some thirty years later, Admiral Thomas Moorer remembered "everyone" in those days "was crazy" about Halsey, who shunned the "separation" between junior and senior officers that was otherwise common.[6]

In the clubby interwar Navy, he and Fan entertained infrequently, though the wives of other officers remembered him as an ideal guest: prompt, pleasant, and appreciative. The Navy was Halsey's life, he being an extension of it. He refused to join a lawsuit against the Navy over flight pay reductions during the Great Depression, even as other officers did so, including the vast majority of Army Air Corps fliers, and, on his annual officer appraisals, he always listed his current duty as his preferred job until, given his knowledge of naval custom, he knew it was time to move on, whereupon he listed whatever duty he thought the Navy next had in mind.[7]

. . . .

This is how he came to Washington in 1921. By then, just two of his academy classmates had more time at sea than he, and many had served in substantial staff positions ashore. Although he loved ship life, Halsey intuited that the Navy wanted him ashore for beach duty somewhere besides Annapolis and he listed a desire for staff work on the East Coast in his fall 1920 appraisal. He landed in the Office of Naval Intelligence, one of the Navy's newer agencies, perhaps because his old destroyer flotilla mate, Dudley Knox, then a retired captain, worked there and had told Captain Luke McNamee, who ran the office, of Halsey. Settling his family into the same Marlborough apartment building where his parents lived, Halsey reported to McNamee in October and began commanding, as he recalled years later, a "large steel desk."[8]

He did not like pushing paper. In March 1922, less than six months after reporting, he applied for and received orders to become the naval attaché in Berlin, reaching the German capital in the fall of 1922 with his wife, twelve-year-old daughter, and seven-year-old son. In many respects he was an odd fit for attaché duty, most of which was tedious. Spying on Germans was verboten, and Halsey only once sleuthed, on Grover Bergdoll, a notorious American draft dodger living in Germany who Halsey suggested should be assassinated. Rather, the vast majority of information an attaché gathered was the product of an explicit quid pro quo with host nation officials or it came from newspapers, journals, and professional proceedings. Teasing out truly valuable information in such a circumstance typically required an unusual mix of talents centered upon excellent language skills, a working knowledge of local norms, a solid grounding in diplomacy, and a strong sense of international law, none of which Halsey possessed. For his tour, then, he would have to rely upon social skills, personal industry, and good luck.[9]

In mid-October the Halseys settled into a Berlin brownstone and confronted a desolate Germany. Five years after World War I, the nation remained a mess. The war had confined one in ten Germans to a grave or hospital ward, and the Treaty of Versailles had committed the nation to debilitating reparation payments, stripped it of substantial military force and industrial capacity, and eviscerated its monarchical form of government. Into the hollow had risen the Weimar Republic, a regime utterly unable to salve the many wounds of war. Hyperinflation transformed a single German mark in 1918 into a trillion by 1923, creating one financial calamity after another. Horrendous spikes in infant mortality and chronic malnutrition conspired with the collapse of social and educational services to produce widespread cultural despair. Within a few short years, a rising class of malcontents, radicals, and revolutionaries emerged to prey upon a weary and broken populace. Through it all, geography alone endured. In a paradox worthy of Voltaire, busted and beaten Germany retained her place at the heart of European affairs. "No where else in Europe," wrote Robert Murphy, the astute American consul in Munich at the time, "was the past, present, and future of that continent more dramatically revealed." For any attaché up to the challenge, Germany constituted a rich and important landscape.[10]

Halsey was busy soon enough. He reported to the American ambassador, Alanson Houghton, a scion of the Corning Glass Company fortune, on October 27, and he sent his first report, an assessment of a delayed-action fuse developed by the Krupp Munitions Works, to Washington on November 28. A deluge followed. From that first report to his last as an attaché, 559 days later, he authored 770 communiqués. Although a few dozen were the product of specific requests from the Navy Department, most stemmed from Halsey's sense of the kind and scope of information Washington might find helpful.[11]

In this way his reports constitute a collage of his worldview, which was then, as it was always, primarily naval. He dutifully forwarded German naval histories of the Great War, assessed the capabilities of the once great German Navy, opined on submarine development, and authored reports on oil gauges, pneumatic tubes, hull coating, naval binoculars, and stereoscopic range finders. He was a frequent visitor to the Zeiss and Goerz optical works in Jena and Munich and toured the Krupp munitions plant in Essen and the Draeger naval works in Lübeck.[12]

His interest in naval technology ranged beyond the vocational and extended to the scientific. He penned half a dozen reports on wireless telegraphy, which was rapidly maturing, and voice radio, an advancement then being pioneered by the Dutch and the Germans. In February 1923 he reported the success of two Dutch scientists who had discovered the electrical attractions between metal and semiconductors; this Johnsen-Rahbek effect later enabled revolutionary advancements in telephone technology. In January 1924 he alerted the Navy Department to German experiments with bituminous compounds that, in his opinion, could render coal useful again, even for a Navy swiftly converting to oil. In February 1925 he informed Washington of developments in aluminum alloys and authored an assessment of radioactive materials that displayed an intuitive sense of a technology destined to remake war two decades later. He grasped the German acumen for scientific inquiry and engineering, and he regularly compiled extensive lists of German patents whose use no one could reliably foretell but knowledge of which his instinct told him may someday be valuable.[13]

In all this Halsey lacked the educational and intellectual discipline for discriminating judgments about which advances were consequential and which were not, but he embraced the technical progress of the twentieth century and displayed an appreciation of the lengthening line of modern marvels that had so bedeviled his father. As early as his time aboard the *Don Juan de Austria* as an ensign, he had dabbled in telegraphy. Later, in 1926, he adopted electrical razors nearly as soon as they hit the market, and in his life's twilight he owned one of New York City's first color televisions shortly after CBS broadcast its first color images in 1950. Halsey was a technophile, a man well suited to his century.[14]

Halsey penned 147 letters and reports on developments in aviation. His earliest musings on naval aviation had dated to 1910, during wide-ranging dinner conversations with Spuds Ellyson, who in December of that year had become the first naval aviator, and Ken Whiting, who became the Navy's sixteenth flyer in 1914. Halsey had first flown as a passenger in 1913, at the Naval Academy with Pat Bellinger, who later commanded the first transatlantic air crossing. The following year at Pensacola he flew again, with the future admiral John Towers, the Navy's third aviator.[15]

He could not have been oriented to aviation by a stronger group of pioneers, and now, in Germany, he put this introduction to good use. He told the Navy Department of German achievements in rotary engines and airfoils, and wrote with confidence of variable-pitch, counter, and soft-iron propellers. Across nearly two years as an attaché, Halsey reported on seaplanes, balloons, and dirigibles; fuels, alloys, and instruments; and training, doctrine, and theory. At regular intervals he sent, without comment and often without translation, German aeronautical publications by the box load, a practice that prompted the State Department to ask the Navy to bear some costs for its courier service in Berlin.[16]

Halsey's appetite for aviation information encouraged more bartering with German officers than did his interest in any other matter. In early 1923 he sought specifications of an engine made by the Wright Aeronautical Corporation and collected information about the *Langley,* then the only American aircraft carrier, for the German Admiralty; and in September he helped a German officer secure a visa to tour the Martin aviation works in Cleveland, Ohio. In return, Halsey cultivated a robust sense of German aviation. He made a thorough assessment of the nation's airline industry, creating a comprehensive map of German routes, pricing, and passenger loads, delving so deeply into the matter that he could, for example, ascribe the success of a new

Berlin–Danzig flight to the fact that Polish visas were not necessary for air passengers but were for rail travelers. He attended university lectures on aerodynamics and emergent theories of flight stabilization, gleaning what he could with his shaky German. He authored reports on aviation practices in other European countries, including Britain, France, and the Netherlands. On three occasions in the spring of 1923, he related German and Russian aviation activities, reports that became the backdrop to a communiqué he sent that August in which he presciently suggested that Germany was flouting World War I treaty restrictions pertaining to aviation, particularly as they related to building small, single-engine planes "of dangerous speed and power." He authored reports on the role of aviation in naval warfare, forwarded a set of rules for air combat, and, from start to end as an attaché, reported on aviation matters more thoroughly than he did for any subject.[17]

In all this, some of America's foremost aviation experts continued to tutor Halsey. For a time, his assistant attaché in Berlin was Lieutenant Commander Zachary Lansdowne, who had earned an excellent reputation flying with the Royal Air Force in World War I and who would perish in 1925 in the infamous crash of the Navy airship *Shenandoah*. Towers, by then like Halsey a commander, occasionally left his perch as attaché in London to pass through Germany to inspect a dirigible being built for America, a project that also brought to Germany Lieutenant Commander Jerome Hunsaker, who had developed the first American university course in aerodynamics at the Massachusetts Institute of Technology and had already served as the Navy's chief aircraft designer. From Lansdowne, Halsey got something of the infectious enthusiasm of young aviators; from Towers, an increasingly senior perspective on the possibilities of naval aviation; and from Hunsaker, a preamble into the complexities of aeronautics when the science stood at the edge of human understanding. All helped inform his attaché reports from Berlin, and the ideas they imparted to Halsey would serve him well in the coming years.[18]

If his attaché accounts of naval and air matters were thorough and detailed, Halsey's analysis of political issues was perfunctory and pedestrian. He managed fewer than a dozen reports on the combustible mix of economic calamity and political intrigue that gave rise to National Socialism and Adolf Hitler. He wrote only once of the Nazi Party, and then conflated it with Communism, political ideologies at profound odds. Only two nations beyond Germany really sparked his interest: Soviet Russia, mostly after a brief trip he took in 1923, and Japan, a nation that even then appeared to grab his gaze. He reported Japanese nationals living in Germany, especially those who held American visas, and forwarded hard-to-find topographical data on the Mariana, Caroline, and Marshall Islands, South Pacific atolls Germany had ceded to Japan following World War I. In February 1924 he ferreted out a clandestine German program to produce diesel engines for Japanese submarines, but failed to relate this to any broader Japanese-German cooperation that may have existed. Like most officers of his generation, Halsey's focus circumscribed a strictly maritime arc, and his occasional assessments of wider issues were heavily influenced by their effect on naval policy and procurement. He was uninterested in the larger world and, despite—or perhaps because of—increasing rank, his horizons never extended far from the Navy's boundaries.[19]

In Washington, Halsey's superiors judged him as they always had. Despite his paltry knowledge of German and of Germany, officials in Naval Intelligence thought Halsey's reports reflected "care and thoroughness in preparation," and McNamee believed Halsey "made an excellent attaché. He is a good mixer and has the personality and initiative to accomplish anything he starts out to do." Halsey himself did not stress his time as an attaché in later years, devoting a meager three paragraphs in *Admiral Halsey's Story* to his nearly three years working for the Office of Naval Intelligence. Still, in a career spanning four decades, it was his sole substantial tour ashore outside Annapolis, and the only time he would serve, and learn something of, the burgeoning Navy staff that grew apace with his own career in the early twentieth century.[20]

When he was not writing reports, life for Halsey and his family in Berlin was pleasant, at least at first. Germany's economic collapse was for him a windfall, and he escaped the financial straits often experienced by attachés elsewhere—the pecuniary strain on John Towers in London helped ruin his marriage. Halsey's salary and $300 monthly allowance for expenses purchased about two million marks when he took up his duties. By the summer of 1923 he could exchange a single dollar for first millions and then billions of marks. The Halseys lived in a fashionable walk-up in one of Berlin's best neighborhoods, Fan sprinkled cooking and equestrian lessons through her days, and they employed private tutors for Margaret and young Bill. By the end of 1923, the occasional game of poker Halsey played with other embassy staff reached farce; one of them recalled years later that it was "quite a thrill to raise a trillion" holding nothing more than an ace-high hand.[21]

In early 1924 Halsey's daughter contracted acute tuberculosis. In March Fan hurried to Switzerland and admitted Margaret to a renowned hospital in Davos. In Berlin, Halsey was granted an extended leave, making his anticipated summertime return to West Coast destroyers improbable. Rear Admiral Philip Andrews, an old shipmate from the *Kansas* and the Great White Fleet who was now leading what remained of American warships in European waters, offered Halsey the command of the *Dale*, a destroyer arriving from Philadelphia and scheduled to ply Mediterranean waters on diplomatic duty. Halsey grabbed the offer, and Andrews named Ray Spruance, the *Dale*'s current skipper, Andrews's chief of staff. It was an elegant solution that kept Halsey in Europe, near Margaret, and did no real harm to Spruance, offering him valuable staff experience.[22]

Halsey assumed command of the *Dale* on July 6 at the German port of Swinemünde, about the same time that Margaret began a long, slow improvement. He spent the next year and a half pacing first the *Dale* and then the destroyer *Osborne* through battle practice drills and goodwill calls, mostly in the Mediterranean Sea, and trekking to Davos when time in port allowed. During one visit to Malta, he saw an aircraft carrier for the first time, the British flattop *Hermes,* which struck him as an "off-center, ungainly bucket, something a child had started to build and had left unfinished." Commanding a destroyer on routine sea duty and in sundry diplomatic chores presented few challenges for Halsey, who was able to rely upon seasoned executive officers of long acquaintance aboard both ships. Andrews, a famously crusty critic throughout the fleet, gave Halsey glowing marks during this stopgap service, crediting Halsey with "great improvement in the appearance and condition of the *Dale*," and telling others Halsey had "marked executive ability and force." When, in late 1926, doctors pronounced Margaret well enough for transatlantic passage, Halsey relinquished command of the *Osborne*, this time to Spruance, and gathered his family on a steamer bound for New York. From there, he settled his family in Asheville, North Carolina, and placed his daughter under the care of Dr. Charles Minor, a national authority on tuberculosis, before returning to the Brooklyn Naval Yard to assume duties as the executive officer of the battleship *Wyoming*, under the command of Captain Austin Kautz.[23]

This posting kept Halsey close to family. The *Wyoming* never ranged far from the East Coast and spent a long period refitting at the Philadelphia Naval Yard, giving Halsey opportunity to reach Asheville on holidays, leave, and many a weekend. Kautz believed Halsey was an "exceptionally gifted" officer of "high moral and mental attainment," a man of "unfailing firmness, courtesy, and tact." Kautz routinely described his executive officer as "brilliant" and gushed that Halsey's most admirable trait was "the ability to command a cheerful compliance with his orders and instructions." This ovation continued a long string of praise for Halsey as a seagoing naval man, only this time as an executive officer. The same duty that had exposed his father's weaknesses decades earlier now highlighted the son's strengths. On the heels of a year as an executive officer, Halsey was promoted to captain, a rank his dad never achieved on active duty. Whatever challenges lay ahead, Bill Halsey had surely grown confident and comfortable with responsibility at sea.[24]

Instead, other trials marked Halsey's *Wyoming* tour. There was, of course, Margaret, recovering but still quite frail. The ordeal had taken its toll on both parents. Fan's largely lonely vigil had intensified a fragility that had until then only sporadically surfaced. By the time she was in Asheville, Fan was tired, irritable, and restless. She suffered extended periods of insomnia and became prone to erratic behavior. The symptoms were pronounced enough for formal evaluation, and doctors mused about Graves disease before ascribing her difficulties to stress.[25]

Halsey's health had also flagged. While in Europe, ad hoc travel between his ship and Switzerland had worked against a decent diet and regular exercise, which translated into chronic gout and hospitalized him twice. Then, with the *Wyoming*, he developed a rash on his legs, groin, and scrotum. Reminiscent of numerous milder outbreaks in previous years, the inflammation was now bothersome enough to require medical care. Doctors suspected acute lymphangitis, a painful, itchy infection, and sent him to a naval hospital for ten days. Three months later, he was hospitalized for what the doctors guessed was erysipelas, another bacterial skin contagion. The medics never settled upon a firm diagnosis, however, and considered elephantiasis when a moderate enlargement of his left testicle developed. Whatever the cause, Halsey's troubles were almost certainly aggravated by the same stress that was buffeting Fan as a result of their daughter's illness. Fan's irritability hinted at what became in later years a debilitating mental illness. Bill's skin inflammations would bedevil him for years.[26]

....

The four gold braids of a captain necessitated a job beyond that of executive officer. In January 1927 Halsey took command of the *Reina Mercedes,* which was, like his father's *Manila* and his own *Don Juan de Austria,* a relic prize from the Spanish-American War. Since 1912, she had served as the Naval Academy's receiving ship, its skipper charged with berthing the school's enlisted force, confining students on detention, and overseeing the academy's marina. It was an odd quasi-command, but skippering a permanently moored hulk compensated Halsey in other ways: alone among Navy vessels, receiving ships housed captains' families, and the Halseys enjoyed spacious quarters, a cook, a steward, and an attendant. Academy life offered ample diversion for Halsey, who had always followed its athletic teams and now became the faculty representative for the boxing squad, then in the midst of an eleven-year undefeated run under the auspices of the incomparable Hamilton "Spike" Webb, a dynamo of a man who also coached Baltimore kids, including, at one point, Walker Smith, better known as Sugar Ray Robinson. Overall, Halsey's duties were hardly onerous, with the exception of a few salacious episodes between *Reina* sailors and, in the secretary of the Navy's words, "a number of civilian perverts," a problem that involved Halsey in the "disagreeable but very important duty to protect the men under your command from the degenerative practices of older men." In this instance, Halsey's investigations produced indictments and convictions in both state and federal courts.[27]

Working a regular day, Halsey's health improved. He got eight hours of steady rest, ate and drank moderately, fell ill to nothing more than a head cold, and took regular exercise in the form of golf, swimming, tennis, or walks. He dropped fifteen pounds. He limited his coffee to four cups daily and cut his cigarette smoking from thirty sticks a day to a pack of twenty, which was moderate enough for the time. His duties allowed more time with his family than any other posting in his career. Both Margaret and young Bill, moving through their early teenage years, attended schools in adjacent Annapolis, his son taking a prep course for academy admission just as his father had decades before. From a personal perspective, duty aboard the ship was "the most delightful tour" of Halsey's long service in uniform.[28]

The school also acted as bellwether for professional things to come. In 1926 the Navy instituted a summer orientation course in aviation for each graduating class. The following year, the academy's aviation detachment, headed by Lieutenants Dewitt Ramsey and Clifton Sprague, moved to the *Reina Mercedes,* which placed Halsey in command of airplanes for the first time. The two young pilots sometimes took Halsey aloft, and, like so many others of the era, he was hooked. "The arrival of the aviation detachment changed my whole career," he later remembered. "Soon I was eating, drinking and breathing aviation."[29]

By the time Halsey left the *Reina* in 1930, some 60 percent of each class hoped to become aviators, making it by far the most desirable posting among the midshipmen and, as it happened, some captains, too. Since 1926, the Navy had required aircraft carrier commanders to have aviation training, a rule that had sent some senior officers to Pensacola to take a half-baked course leading to an air observer certificate until men who had grown up as aviators reached the required rank for such commands. In the summer of 1929, the Navy's chief personnel officer asked Halsey if he'd like to take the observer's course. With the prospect of a carrier command, Halsey "jumped at the chance," but for the first time in his career he failed a physical, on account of his eyes.[30]

. . . .

So the Navy sent him to destroyers again, this time as a commander of an eighteen-ship squadron of the Atlantic Fleet, working for Rear Admiral William Leahy, an old family acquaintance who had once, while a captain in the Bureau of Navigation, shielded Halsey from fallout stemming from problems with the *Wyoming*'s electrical machinery while Halsey was the ship's executive officer. Now, Leahy found nothing wanting in Halsey as a commander of a destroyer squadron. He was a "resourceful, daring, and energetic" officer, one "particularly well qualified by experience and temperament to command a Destroyer Squadron or flotilla in war." Without a doubt, Halsey's abundant time with destroyers would pay dividends in a time of crisis, although service aboard them had long since ceased to be a catalyst for his professional growth.[31]

In the summer of 1932 Halsey received orders to attend the Naval War College in Newport, which did mark a new turn in his career. After a brief stop in Annapolis for their daughter's marriage to Preston Spruance, the son of well-heeled parents and at the time a senior at Princeton University, Bill and Fan moved into a small cottage in Jamestown, Rhode Island. From there Halsey took the brief ferry ride to the War College each day, crossing the narrows of Narragansett Bay, the same waters that had nearly claimed his life as a boy while his dad attended the course in 1897. In the intervening years, the course at the War College had become an important component to a naval career, growing in class size to nearly one hundred students, in length to a year, and importance, as every admiral qualified to command at sea but one was a graduate by the time World War II arrived.

On the first day of class, the college president, Rear Admiral Harris Laning, told Halsey and his eighty-seven classmates that the War College offered the sole "broad basic preparation for high command" they would likely get. The school's primary aim was to develop "sound and able thinking," and Laning warned the students not to expect all matters pertaining to war to be presented to them "on a platter." Instead, the curriculum nurtured a deliberate decision-making process to sharpen command judgments and codify action throughout the fleet. As one astute historian wrote, the methodology was a "tool by which a commander and his subordinates could order data, relate them to ultimate purpose, and ascertain the best or most likely means of producing the desired effect." In such a situation, "juniors would still exhibit proper subordination," but, armed with a commander's intent, "they would be able to adapt to the fluid and ever-changing conditions of war while still pursuing the objective their seniors sought." William Sims, then living in retirement near the War College, could not have said it better, and Halsey was surely at home with such a philosophy.[32]

War games dominated the curriculum. The major game that year postulated a Japanese seizure of the Philippines and assigned the American fleet to recapture the islands. For the game, the American fleet commander was played by the senior student in the class, Captain Ernest King, recently selected for promotion to rear admiral. King favored a swift strike through the central Pacific to reach Manila before the Japanese could consolidate their gains. Laning disapproved, and students debated, as they had for years, the wisdom of a bold, swift counterstrike across the Pacific, which would expose salient flanks to Japanese attacks, or a more deliberate approach, a prudence that would offer the enemy more time to fortify their Philippine defenses.[33]

Halsey judged the problem to be a classic case of positional warfare. America needed a stronger and more mobile fleet to dislodge the Japanese, who, fighting defensively, were tactically stronger and held interior lines. Japan, he argued, would use aerial reconnaissance by day and destroyer and submarine attacks by night to harry any American naval advance before attacking on a large scale just outside Philippine waters when American forces would be tired. Halsey believed the Navy should sleuth its way across the Pacific along as direct a route as possible, avoiding enemy contact until near Manila, before unleashing a powerful blow. In this way, he believed Japan's strategy would be "evasive and protective," America's "secretive and offensive." Once America "took to sea," he wrote, the "fleet must keep to the sea until it reached the Philippines." He wanted no part in a deliberative approach to the Philippines that courted a quagmire of attritional battles near and around distant islands of which, at the time, only geographers, dreamers, and whalers knew anything.[34]

For Halsey that year, and for naval planners throughout the interwar period, the problem was this: the Navy could strike quickly or strongly on the far side of the Pacific Ocean, but not both. This was the conundrum of War Plan Orange, the Navy's operational scheme for a Pacific war. Much of what the Navy thought or bought in the interwar years was a function of this puzzle: the characteristics of submarines, destroyers, cruisers, and battleships—along with the operating doctrine that would guide their commanders—all sat against the canvas of an imagined war with Japan. The rise of the aircraft carrier, perhaps more directly than any other interwar development, was the product of efforts to project power across the wide Pacific. For officers such as Halsey who had not served on planning staffs, their War College year was their introduction to this paramount issue. Years later, Raymond Spruance declared that his two tours teaching at Newport were the pillars upon which he relied as a wartime fleet commander, and many ranking officers would have agreed with Chester Nimitz, who claimed that his student year at Newport made nothing of World War II, except the campaign in the South Pacific and Japanese kamikaze attacks, "strange or unexpected."[35]

Halsey never went that far, in part because in World War II it would fall to him to work out a rare blind spot in War Plan Orange—the Solomon Islands campaign—and in part because he did not take to scholastics. War College hours were modest, stretching from 9:00 AM to 3:30 PM, six days a week, with afternoons free on Wednesdays and Saturdays. This left time for students to make what they might of the school year. Halsey relaxed. "Few years in a naval officer's life are more pleasant than this one," he recalled of his Newport tour. "It is restful because you have no official responsibilities, and it is stimulating because of the instruction, the exchange of ideas, the chance to test your pet theories on the game board." Halsey never took from the library a book on the school's supplementary reading list. His eleven-page thesis, "The Relationship in War of Naval Strategy, Tactics, and Command," began with a two-page quote and relied upon trivialities to define strategy ("that which precedes contact"), tactics ("that which follows"), and objective ("get there the firstest with the mostest") before moving on to an extended discussion on command, surely his comfort zone after so many years at sea.[36]

Unusual among officers of his rank, he'd get another year in school. He was considered for a second year of Naval War College instruction, but when the longer course did not materialize the Navy proposed first to make him the station commander at Guantánamo Bay, then to let him stay at Newport to teach, and finally to assign him command of the recruiting station in New York City. Halsey served in this shore billet for nineteen days in July before orders sent him to the Army War College in Washington for another year as a student, making him one of a handful of senior World War II officers to attend both the Army and Navy schools in the interwar years.[37]

A second year of academics likewise left little impression. He participated in numerous staff studies relating to war preparation, wrote a couple of mediocre historical analyses dealing with past campaigns, contributed to a hypothetical national war plan, and participated in map maneuvers and a command post exercise. He dispatched all of it in a short paragraph in his memoirs, but grasped well enough the essential difference between the Navy and Army schools, recalling, "At Newport we had studied the strategy and tactics of naval campaigns," while "at Washington we studied on a larger scale—wars, not campaigns—and from the viewpoint of the top echelon." He remembered his classmates Omar Bradley and Jonathan Wainwright, later Army commanders in World War II, though he neglected to mention Courtney Hodges, another future Army commander, and the incomparable Lewis Hershey, who directed the nation's selective service system through three wars, serving thirty-three years as a general officer without ever seeing combat but surely intimately involved in war "from the viewpoint of the top echelon."[38]

Halsey busied himself with other endeavors while in Washington. Reflecting the hurried state in which he had arrived in Washington, he and Fan stayed briefly first with his mother at the Marlborough, and then for a few weeks at the Brighton Hotel before settling into a home at 1516 29th Street NW, between Georgetown and Rock Creek Park. Toward the end of his school year he bought a stately Victorian at 312 Queen Street across the Potomac River in Alexandria, Virginia, the only house he ever owned. It is not clear why he bought the place. He perhaps craved roots after an itinerant life of half a century, though Annapolis would seem a more logical home; maybe he hoped to settle his wife as he continued to serve here, there, and everywhere, but surely there were more years behind him in uniform than in front of him; possibly he saw a chance to buy at a market bottom, in the depths of the Great Depression—already the average home price in the nation had dropped from $7,100 in 1930 to $4,400. But Halsey was not a speculator by nature. Otherwise careful with a dollar, he stretched mightily, and awkwardly, to meet the $15,000 purchase price, using savings, two small loans against life insurance policies, a third loan from his new son-in-law, and a three-year balloon mortgage of $7,500.

Whatever his motive, home ownership was a bust. Halsey leased the place to a succession of businessmen and government officials, including Edwin Smith, an inaugural member of the National Labor Relations Board, and George Kennan of the State Department, later famous as a Cold War diplomat. Halsey rarely got his asking price, which hovered around $125 a month, failed to hold a single tenant beyond a year, and two renters broke their lease early. As for the house itself, it seemed continually in need of repairs. In 1938, during Kennan's year in the home, an army of rats infested the place, collapsed the sidewalk and front steps and created a crater four feet deep, a condition that led to terse letters between Halsey and Kennan over the pace and cost of repairs. The house often appeared "very shabby," according to one realtor, a condition Halsey blamed first on tenants, especially the Smiths, with whom he bickered constantly, and then on a succession of rental agents. He renewed his balloon mortgage twice, in 1937 and in 1940, without paying a penny in principle. By the latter year, living in Honolulu and busy with fleet exercises, Halsey had grown tired of the house, in which he had spent few nights, and listed it for $20,000, an absurd price given that housing values had continued to decline in the half decade he had owned the place.[39]

From the start, the house was probably part of a retirement scheme Halsey hatched as he contemplated his seventh year as a Navy captain in 1934. Always a careful reader of the Navy Register, during his War College years Halsey could see as plainly as others his chance for admiral rank. For all the changes since his father's time, seniority still dominated the Navy's promotion system. Halsey had entered the Navy List in 1904 at number forty-two of his sixty-one classmates. He and fifty-seven classmates had become ensigns two years later, he and fifty classmates reached lieutenant in 1910, and he and the remaining thirty-seven of his classmates still serving placed the stripes of lieutenant commander on their sleeves in January 1917. Lockstep advances loosened slightly in World War I, with its opportunities for heroics and temporary advancements, and Halsey lost a few steps. Nine members of the class of 1904 reached the permanent rank of commander in January 1921, though Halsey did not garner his third broad braid stripe until that June, among the last cohort of his twenty-nine classmates. In the summer of 1926 the first of his classmates made captain, and seventeen of them wore four stripes before Halsey did so in February 1927, placing him well below the middle of his classmates still serving. Absent extraordinary service as a captain, this made the rank of admiral a long shot at a time when any given academy class produced perhaps half a dozen flag officers.[40]

By 1934 little of his time as a captain promised a late sprint past those ahead of him. With the exception of eighteen months at sea leading a destroyer squadron—something he had done regularly on a temporary basis as early as 1920—he had spent the past seven years as the skipper of an Annapolis hulk and in school. He did not have big-ship command or any substantial staff or shore duty, something most other senior World War II admirals had by similar points in their careers. Ernest King, for example, had helped establish the Naval Postgraduate School and authored a groundbreaking study on the education of naval officers, and Chester Nimitz had served on the staff of the chief of naval operations, established the nation's first naval reserve officers training course, and served in the Navy's all-important personnel bureau.

Halsey had more time at sea than any of these others, but even this had begun to work as a detriment. His Naval War College thesis had opined at great length that a senior officer's primary responsibility, at sea or ashore, was to acculturate juniors to basic ideas and specific plans through the conference method, which was "the most important part of an officer's training," so that they could operate freely without "complicated instructions" or "irksome signals," both of which tended "to interfere with a subordinate acting independently." This was vintage Sims from the old destroyer flotilla years, and in some places Halsey copped the exact language of Dudley Knox's essays written some two decades earlier for *Proceedings*. As a senior captain, then, Halsey had not significantly altered his view of command at sea or service ashore from that which he had possessed as a lieutenant. He could have written his Newport essay in 1915. In 1936, when the Navy would first consider members of the class of 1904 for admiral, and look for those few who had continued to grow through the middle ranks, Halsey's name would probably escape the list. In all likelihood, he could look forward to some long-delayed duty ashore and then retirement and twilight, apparently at 312 Queen Street. Unless, of course, something broke in his favor.[41]

Chapter Seven

The Oldest Aviator

A MONTH AFTER Halsey purchased the Alexandria house, Rear Admiral Ernest King proposed Halsey take the naval observer course at Pensacola and assume command of the aircraft carrier *Saratoga,* among the world's largest combat ships. The chance to enter aviation had passed Halsey by in 1929 when he failed his eyesight test, but friends now gave him a second chance. Rear Admiral William Leahy ran the Bureau of Navigation and controlled the Navy's personnel. King, Halsey's Naval War College classmate, had become head of the Bureau of Aeronautics. Both knew of Halsey's interest, and the Navy would remain short of senior men to skipper aircraft carriers for another few years, when at last a sufficient cadre of early aviators would reach ranks commensurate with the commands. Leahy had hinted at flight training in Halsey's officer efficiency report in 1932, and was probably responsible for the unsettled series of orders Halsey received in 1933 following his Naval War College tour. For Leahy and King, Halsey's year at the Army War College perhaps constituted a holding pattern while they maneuvered him to aviation.

Fan was skeptical. Halsey would turn fifty-two that autumn. In the years since the passage of laws requiring aeronautic training for aviation command, maybe two dozen senior men had trekked to Pensacola for the observer course. Most had been lieutenant commanders or commanders, ten to fifteen years younger than Halsey. A few, including King himself, had been captains, and only two of those had been older than Halsey. To assuage Fan's concerns, Halsey agreed to seek Leahy's informal advice, an officer "for whose judgment we had enormous respect." Unsurprisingly, given his hand in the whole affair, "Bill Leahy not only agreed, he was enthusiastic."[1]

After his War College graduation, Halsey settled Fan into a summer rental in Rhode Island and began the long drive south. He knew as well as she did that there would be challenges aplenty in coming so late to an adventure so new. Orville Wright had first flown at Kitty Hawk just thirty years earlier, in Halsey's junior year at Annapolis. World War I then grew American naval aviation from next to nothing to some 7,000 officers, 30,000 enlisted ranks, and 2,000 planes, some of them operating out of European bases in the same antisubmarine duties that had occupied Halsey in the Great War. Demobilization in the 1920s had sapped these tallies, but the birth of the Bureau of Aeronautics in 1921 and the Naval Aviation Expansion Act of 1926 brought to naval aviation enough stability and money to flourish. Throughout the nation, both within and beyond military circles, a golden age of air power in the late 1920s bequeathed generations of quicker, bigger, and more powerful aircraft, a development that made Charles Lindbergh an international icon, helped make aviation the most requested duty among graduating midshipmen, and begot for airplanes a central place in the Navy's planning for war in the Pacific, where the new technology promised novel ways to project power across the vast ocean.

For all its growth, however, aviation remained a wild child as Halsey motored through the South toward Florida. About one American in 140,000 was a pilot, and perhaps one in 1,000 had ever been a passenger. A Travelers Life Insurance study in 1931 guessed the annual death rate of pilots at nearly 15 per 1,000 fliers, with a higher incidence among military men, making flight one of the nation's most dangerous activities. In the 1930s, Navy experts assumed one in thirty pilots would experience a catastrophic accident at some point. Halsey probably balanced these risks against the rewards he knew awaited him if he met Pensacola's challenge: already, all four captains who had taken the first observer course in 1925 had become admirals. Yet the uncertainty of the air sobered him. Settling into a Tallahassee hotel on his last night on the road, he reflected, "Bill, you're fifty-one years old and a grandfather, and tomorrow morning you'll begin competing with youngsters less than half your age." At dinner that evening he enjoyed a favorite libation, a whiskey and water. He did not drink again for a year.[2]

On July 1, 1934, Halsey reported to the Pensacola commandant, Captain Rufus Zogbaum, an old friend from the destroyer flotilla and himself a latecomer to aviation. Established as a Navy yard in 1826, Pensacola was the place to which Halsey's father had first reported following his academy graduation in 1873, and was the shore to which young Bill Halsey had raced with the *Missouri* following the horrific turret explosion in 1904. Now it represented yet another beginning. Zogbaum assigned an affable lieutenant named Bromfield Nichol as Halsey's instructor for a makeshift observer course, essentially a gentlemen's audit of the first three months of the yearlong aviator's course. Pioneer aviators, men who had grown up in aviation, often resented older students such as Halsey, viewing their presence in Pensacola as legerdemain allowing others to garner the fruits of aviation's growth in the interwar years. By the time Halsey arrived in Pensacola, those tardy to aviation like him had been tagged by longer-serving pilots as either Kiwis, for a New Zealand bird that did not fly, or Johnny-come-latelies, an appellation that needed no translation, then or now.

After a few weeks as Nichol's passenger, Halsey itched for the full course in aviation leading to pilot wings. That, he believed, would offer a better "understanding of a pilot's problems and mental processes" than a mere observer's badge. This proved delicate. Leahy and King had managed to slide him into an observer's billet without a full flight physical, something more difficult to accomplish with bona fide pilot hopefuls. When a Pensacola physician conducting what the doctor himself called a "superficial" exam found Halsey fit for flight training on July 20, Halsey squeezed both ends of bureaucracy, carefully cutting out the aeronautics office in Washington. On July 24, he asked Zogbaum to propose to Leahy that Halsey enter the aviator's course, and petitioned Leahy to tell Zogbaum the same thing. Leahy and Zogbaum both tentatively complied pending the other's concurrence, their respective correspondence crossing in the mail in early August. Wanting Halsey to "obtain the maximum varied experience in aviation" possible, Leahy suggested that Zogbaum allow Halsey to partake in as much pilot training as could be "accomplished without undue hazard." Zogbaum acquiesced on August 20, something Leahy knew immediately but did not formally recognize until months had passed, in late November. Halsey later professed ignorance of all this handiwork. "My eyes still could not pass the tests for a pilot," he wrote in his autobiography, "and how I managed to become classified as one, I honestly don't know yet, and I'm not going to ask."[3]

But he was surely in on the swindle from the start, the murkiness and timing of which had been calibrated to bypass the clerks in the Bureau of Aeronautics and allow Halsey to claim observer status if physicians later raised holy hell about the fait accompli. This they did, first within months, and then for years thereafter when physicals consistently found Halsey unfit for pilot duty. Halsey kept his wings, although doctors made stick their insistence that he always fly with a copilot. By the end of the decade the whole matter had become infamous throughout the Bureau of Aeronautics as "a long and complicated story." Even some doctors came to admire the skulduggery of it all.[4]

So it was that Halsey took his place among the fifty-seven student naval aviators of the class of 34-3, virtually all either ensigns or junior lieutenants and only one, besides Halsey, over the age of thirty. He managed the course, barely. He was the last student in his class to solo, twice overturned taxiing aircraft, and once led astray a three-plane formation to the point that naval authorities alerted crash crews at nearby civilian airfields. In the words of one instructor, during landings Halsey made too many "violent maneuvers too close to the ground." In the opinion of another, he failed to reach "the standard in all phases of primary land plane flying." A fellow student recalled Halsey was "awfully difficult" to accompany in formation, and seemed not to "know how fast he was going, nor where he was going, nor his altitude." By his own admission, Halsey never "mastered any stunt that required delicacy." Before long, he developed the "impression that whenever I got in the air, my base was always anxious until I returned."[5]

His instructors recognized his rudimentary skills but consistently recorded his deficiencies in performing the full range of tasks required of rookie naval aviators. He won the Flying Jackass award, a rotating trophy of an aluminum breastplate in the likeness of a rabbit, when in the spring of 1935 he jumped a plane across a taxiway and onto an active runway, destroying runway lights and wreaking havoc. Presented "with the greatest feeling of felicitation and humbuggery," Halsey was exhorted by Lieutenant Commander Matthias Gardner of the instructor staff to wear the award until another jackass came along, and to thereafter let its memory become "an ever constant guide for you in your future actions and relations."[6]

Humor acted as a salve for Halsey, but the truth was the training taxed him. As he had with the official Navy, Halsey did not tell Fan of his switch to the aviation course until he had to, in October 1934, when instead of arriving back in Rhode Island he sent for her to come to Florida. She headed south in December, where Halsey's appearance prompted concern. He had lost nearly fifty of his 200 pounds, leaving him looking like a "sick turkey buzzard." Half of the weight returned, but the course never became easy. He woke every morning at 6:00 AM. "With flying and ground school," he wrote his son, then an eleventh grader at the Lawrenceville School in New Jersey, "I am plenty tired by the time evening rolls around." This pace frustrated Fan as she found her husband had little free time. Even those precious moments often evaporated: Halsey was the only captain at Pensacola besides Zogbaum, and he was sometimes pressed into social obligations and official duties, twice serving as the president or presiding officer of a court-martial or board of inquiry. Years later, another World War II admiral, Joseph "Jocko" Clark, recalled Halsey had more trouble getting through the course than any other Johnny-come-lately, which was probably true enough.[7]

He did so with grit, charity, and grace. He worked hard, and did well, where he could. He finished thirteenth in the ground school portion of training. He courted ribbing from his juniors, submitted to their antics, and declined the small privileges of rank. He took his place among them during Saturday morning inspections. Fellow students tossed him into the drink when he soloed last in the class, a time-honored tradition. He refused the prerogative of early morning flight slots, coveted because of generally better weather. He kept the Flying Jackass trophy long after another had earned it, replacing it with a replica, and later hung the original on the bulkhead of his *Saratoga* sea cabin as a mark of humility. In these and other ways, one student remembered, Halsey "endeared himself to everyone by being one of the boys."[8]

In the end, seven of his fifty-seven classmates failed the course outright, and another four were sent back a class. It is hard to imagine each of these laggards being poorer pilots than Halsey. But the old captain had a knack for marshaling personal goodwill, a trait he leveraged every time he took to the skies. On May 28 Zogbaum designated Halsey a naval aviator. At fifty-two years, six months, and twenty-nine days old, he became at the time the oldest newly minted Navy pilot.

If it was a stretch to say he was of a similar ilk to that of the ensigns and lieutenants wearing the same shiny gold wings, it was also a distortion to call his training a farce. He knew he was not one of the young pilots. He never thought of himself as a flier after his Pensacola year, being too thoroughly acculturated to the Navy officership to parse his service in such a way. He never qualified for carrier flight operations, and in later years he piloted only as much as was necessary to maintain flight status and its accompanying pay, usually a small handful of short hops each month for a total of something under ten hours of flight. By World War II he rarely if ever handled the controls, and some who served with him during the war believed Halsey was a naval observer and not an aviator.[9]

For him, flying was a way to understand the men he would command. His leadership was always more tactile than cerebral, and he exercised it best through direct interaction and close association. This was easy in the destroyer Navy, for it had been a small fraternity, and he was of them then. But now, as the Navy grew and changed around him, so too did he, as much as he could, anyway. His father had failed in an analogous test of adjustment, and Halsey was determined to hurdle the obstacles that had bedeviled his Dad.

In June Halsey and Fan scurried from Florida to California. On a sunny July 6 he reported to Vice Admiral Henry Butler, one of the first four naval air observers from 1925 and now the fleet's senior carrier commander. The next day Halsey took command of the *Saratoga* from his old friend Ken Whiting, with whom he had had his earliest conversations about aviation in 1910. The *Sara* was massive. Twelve feet short of three football fields, the ship carried a complement of nearly 3,400 men and displaced 33,000 tons, making her three times longer, ten times more populous, and eleven times heavier than a destroyer.

Where he could, Halsey fell back upon familiar habits. He ship-handled as he always had, comfortably and aggressively, even perfecting a flying anchorage, an audacious trick with destroyers and one unknown in vessels the size of the *Saratoga*. He governed as he had grown accustomed, strictly at first, loosely thereafter. He delegated as of old, leaving, in the words of the ship's navigator, "a great many things to his staff." Most of these practices were in sharp contrast to those of both his predecessor and his successor on the *Saratoga*—John Towers followed Halsey as the *Sara*'s skipper and arrived inclined to tighten up "the more lax routine of the Halsey regime." Although they risked permissive behavior, Halsey's command habits begot a happy ship and the coveted E for standing number one in engineering in the entire fleet in 1936. In time, Halsey came to view the *Sara* "as simply an overgrown destroyer." He told Zogbaum, who had earlier skippered the ship, that he "was enjoying this fine command in every way and can appreciate how you loved it." As an officer, Halsey was still of the Navy, and as a ship, the *Sara* was still of the sea.[10]

Yet the flattop surely marked a new horizon. In 1908, four years after Halsey had graduated from Annapolis, aircraft carriers had escaped even the fertile imagination of H. G. Wells, whose classic *The*

War in the Air dreamt of air dirigibles, not sea ships, as plane carriers. Things had then moved quickly. The Royal Navy invented the aircraft carrier in the midst of the Great War, and in the early 1920s others followed, notably Japan and the United States. In 1922 the American Navy converted a collier into the experimental carrier *Langley,* and began work transforming two partially built battle cruisers into the powerful *Lexington* and *Saratoga,* which first sailed later that decade. The *Ranger,* the first American ship designed from the keel up as a carrier, followed in 1934 and two more, the *Yorktown* and the *Enterprise,* began building as Halsey was learning to fly.

Together with their officers, pilots, and crews, these ships undertook the complex task of first inventing and then developing naval air power. Yet, by the time Halsey piped aboard the *Saratoga* in 1935—a short seven years before Japanese carrier planes devastated the American fleet at Pearl Harbor—aviation had promised much but had accomplished very little. Five days after he took command, Halsey traveled to San Diego, where the *Saratoga*'s four flight squadrons homeported. There, his education in fleet aviation began in earnest, tutored by the ship's executive officer, Forrest Sherman; its navigator, Donald Duncan; its air operations officer, Thomas Sprague; its squadron commanders, which included Felix Stump; and Matthias Gardner, who had followed Halsey from Pensacola to serve as liaison officer between the *Saratoga* and the San Diego Naval Air Station. Among the early aviators, Sherman was known as "brilliant," "quiet," and "well-read"; Duncan had a "keen administrative sense" and was already "much sought after for his mind"; Sprague wore well a reputation as an "aviator's aviator"; Stump had behind him a graduate education in aeronautical engineering from the Massachusetts Institute of Technology; and Gardner provided for Halsey a ledge of familiar footing in an otherwise new world. To a man, all later earned stellar war reputations and flag rank: Sherman became Chester Nimitz's deputy chief of staff and helped outline the triumphal march across the Pacific Ocean, Duncan helped hatch the famous Doolittle Raid on Tokyo, Sprague turned in a hero's performance in the Battle of Leyte Gulf, Stump eventually commanded the entire Pacific Fleet, and Gardner became the model for Matt Garth, the beau ideal naval aviator played by Charlton Heston in the Hollywood blockbuster *Midway*. Collectively, it was an outstanding group of fliers, balanced in experience and temperament, well versed and unified in their enthusiasm for naval aviation.[11]

Halsey's comfort with delegated authority helped him settle into the carrier Navy and learn, as he put it, "from others, while bearing responsibility for their actions." Some lessons he immediately grasped. He quickly developed awe at the demands placed upon fleet aviators, who operated from mobile airfields a fraction the size of Pensacola's airstrips, over large expanses of water devoid of landmarks, and performed daily a task even now considered among the most challenging in all of flight: landing planes upon the unsteady surface of a moving deck. Other lessons required more tutoring. Within months of taking command, he wrote of "a close analogy" between carriers and destroyers and proposed combining the *Saratoga*'s gunnery, air, and air operations departments into one large deck compartment, as existed on smaller ships, to ensure speedier accomplishment of shipboard tasks. In a series of conferences, Sherman, Duncan, and Gardner managed to abort this scheme, agreeing it would pay dividends in internal efficiency but undercut aviation's wider versatility, which extended far beyond the wake of a single hull.[12]

Halsey's primary classroom for carrier operations became the Navy's annual maneuvers. Fleet Problem XVII, held in the spring of 1936, was for the flattops a conservative affair off the California coast. Fleet Problem XVIII, held the following spring, brought the fleet out beyond Pearl Harbor. Halsey and the *Saratoga* left Long Beach on April 16, reached Hawaii on April 23, and made for a point northwest of Wake Island on April 30. There, with the *Lexington* and *Langley*, they joined the Black force, a notional American enemy assigned to attack the French Frigate Shoals, Midway, and Hawaii, which were defended by the *Ranger* and the rest of the White force. The game across the first week of May relied heavily on aviation, with 412 planes assigned a variety of roles, including patrol and search missions, attacks on shore defenses and enemy ships, and close support of amphibious landings. No exercise to that point had aggregated anything like that number of aircraft or their assigned tasks, and few had contemplated as a general scheme not a battle in confined waters but rather a coordinated campaign across a vast expanse of ocean.[13]

In after-action conferences, the maneuvers invigorated debate about carrier action separate from the battle line. Admiral Arthur Hepburn, commanding the entire U.S. Fleet, had kept the Sara and Lex tethered to battleships and criticized aviators' preferences for "independent operations" and "a private war between the opposing air forces, often with complete disregard of contribution to the success of the entire operation." For their part, carrier men, led by Vice Admiral Frederick Horne, thought tying thin-skinned carriers to other combatants left them vulnerable and constrained their true value to the fleet, which they believed was "to obtain and maintain control of the air" for offensive operations. For airmen, this much was becoming plain: "Once an enemy carrier is within striking distance of our fleet no security remains until it—its squadron—or both, are destroyed."[14]

The debate introduced Halsey to the signature issue of carrier doctrine in the interwar period: the relationship of aircraft carriers to the traditional battle line. It also marked the relative positions of battleship officers and naval aviators, one a group he had never joined, the other but a new acquaintance. To make sense of it he fell back on his service in Sims's destroyer flotilla, where suspicion of traditional tactics was strong and confidence in the new reigned. He viewed intrepid naval aviators as the 1930s analogue to earlier destroyer men, and as he voiced that opinion with increasing confidence while commanding the Sara, others took note. Within his first year with flattops, Halsey had, in Vice Admiral Henry Butler's words, "grasped the intricate duties" of aviation well.[15]

His inaugural years in aviation paid other dividends as well. In 1934, the year he entered flight training, Halsey had stood fourteenth among the twenty-one members of his academy class still serving and, among those of the line, had the least time at sea as a captain, a function of his long tour aboard the hulk Reina Mercedes. The top man in the class was selected for flag rank in 1935, signaling to other 1904 graduates they had one more year to make rank before the Navy moved on to the class of 1905. Halsey did not stand a chance, except that by the mid-1930s most of the old-time naval observers had passed from the scene, leaving King the sole qualified aviator wearing flag rank, at a time when the *Yorktown* and *Enterprise* were nearing completion, the *Wasp* keel had been laid, and plans for another, the *Hornet,* were well along. In December 1936 the Navy tapped the remaining 1904 winners: David LeBreton; Husband Kimmel; Forde Todd; David Bagley, who had been Halsey's best man a quarter century earlier; and Halsey himself, who leapfrogged ten of his classmates, easily one of the largest jumps to admiral in the interwar Navy. Not every latecomer to aviation made flag rank, of course, but it is hard to conjure an Admiral Halsey absent Captain Halsey's move to carriers. He would not put on the broad gold stripe of a rear admiral until March 1938, but as 1937 dawned, Halsey knew he had reached an exalted plateau, one of which his father could have only dreamt, and one that promised an entirely new lease on his naval career. Two decades earlier, Sims had salvaged Halsey from a hospital ward. Now, Leahy and King had saved him from obscurity. The house in Alexandria would have to wait.[16]

. . . .

Following his first lessons in fleet aviation, Halsey left the *Saratoga* and took command of the Pensacola Naval Air Station in the summer of 1937. He had not paid much attention to its inner workings during his student year, but now it became his job to know the place, which was in the midst of rapid expansion. From 1933 to 1938, the station's annual budget grew sixfold, from about $1 million to nearly $6 million; its flight hours per annum had quadrupled, from 54,000 hours to 194,000 hours; its aircraft and squadron complement had nearly doubled, from five squadrons aggregating 260 planes to eight of 405 aircraft; and its annual production of pilots had exploded five times over, from 137 to 720. As he and Fan settled into Quarters A, the station comprised 407 buildings and permanent structures; counted one primary, one auxiliary, and two planned secondary airfields; employed nearly 4,000 people; and was firmly established in the hearts and minds of naval aviators everywhere as the Annapolis of the Air.[17]

The place initiated Halsey to the issues facing major shore installations. For the first and only time, he oversaw a large number of civilians, some 1,500, whose lives did not orbit ship and sea, and whose supervision could not be the function of the mast (for years after his Pensacola time he was bemused about the civil servant whose punishment for trying to blow up the naval hospital was a three-month work suspension). For the second and last time, he stood for the Navy in a federal district court, this time over a lease dispute regarding an airfield easement. And on three separate occasions, he wrestled with the Bureau of Aeronautics over aviation training, where he represented the more specific concerns of a station commander against the more general aspects of policy emanating from Washington. He did most, but not all, of this well. On the one hand, the veteran head of a Washington inspection team declared the air station in "better condition than I have ever seen it." On the other hand, Halsey was more aggressive than wise when, against the advice of Florida senior U.S. senator Park Trammell, he undercut labor union efforts to organize Pensacola's civilian employees.[18]

As commandant, Halsey rated an aide. He chose Lieutenant Bill Ashford, whom he had first met as Ashford passed through aviation orientation as a midshipman in the summer of 1927. A small-town North Carolinian, Ashford had attended the University of Georgia, where he played quarterback and joined the Kappa Alpha fraternity, before entering the Naval Academy. There, he excelled as a wrestler—his brother represented the United States in the 1932 Olympics in the same sport—and finished in the exact middle of his Annapolis class. He became an aviator in 1929 and, since then, had served as the aviation officer aboard the *Texas,* earned a coveted life-saving medal for rescuing a drowning chaplain, passed a pleasant tour with a patrol squadron in Panama, was a dive-bomber pilot with the *Ranger* and *Lexington,* and, right before reporting to Halsey, was a scout pilot flying long search missions out of Pearl Harbor. Ashford stayed with Halsey for six years as aide, flag lieutenant, tactical officer, and operations officer, accompanying Halsey as the latter went from the four stripes of a captain to the four stars of an admiral. A superb athlete and middling student, Ashford was a good social mixer and had a well-balanced aviation résumé as a young officer. He would become the archetype of the junior subordinates Halsey gathered around him as his own increasing seniority granted him an ever-greater license to do so.[19]

At Pensacola Halsey was the Navy's senior aviation trainer. In this capacity he relied upon the counsel of his deputy, Gerald Bogan, a pugnacious officer already well on his way to becoming "a thorough teacher in the ways of carrier combat," and the expertise of seasoned squadron commanders, including Thomas Sprague, who had served Halsey as the *Saratoga*'s air operations officer. Halsey nearly always hewed to the recommendations of these experienced subordinates, and together the Pensacola team minted 714 pilots and failed 98 during Halsey's tenure. Only once did Halsey ignore their counsel on training matters, in a case where Sprague's desire to dismiss an enlisted student related more to personal misconduct than to flying acumen. Then as later, Halsey usually listened to others when his judgment was not rooted in long experience, but without exception he moved with assurance when he found himself on familiar ground, traits that endeared him to Bogan, who found Halsey "a good commandant" and a "very sound, fine person."[20]

Pensacola afforded regular family life, the first since Halsey's school tours at Newport and in Washington some five years earlier. Margaret, married and now with two children, was living in Wilmington, Delaware, where her husband, Preston Spruance, had become a boy wonder executive at the DuPont chemical company. Young Bill was in his junior year at Princeton, where he had alighted after poor eyesight precluded his attendance at Annapolis. Both of Halsey's children spent extended breaks in Florida, where their parents enjoyed a grand home of five bedrooms, three living areas, two kitchens, and separate servant quarters. The place came with a couple of maids, a Navy cook, two cars, a chauffeur, and its own plane.[21]

Despite these comfortable surroundings, Fan sank into an abyss at Pensacola. Her temperament had grown uneven since the first vague hints of mental illness surfaced in 1926, as her daughter battled tuberculosis. During Bill's tour aboard the *Saratoga,* she had established house in a small Long Beach apartment, but increasingly erratic behavior had made her presence a growing problem at West Coast public functions. In Pensacola, Halsey began shielding her from a great many events, including the February 1938 Mardi Gras celebrations in New Orleans, long a staple of the commandant's calendar. In April, she fell apart, suffering what Halsey forthrightly told a select few was a "nervous breakdown." Taking emergency leave, Halsey placed Fan in a Philadelphia mental ward associated with the renowned Pennsylvania Hospital, in part because of its location near their daughter Margaret's home, and in part because of its humane treatment of mental maladies. There, she came under the care of Dr. Edward Strecker, who had earlier been among the nation's first psychiatrists to treat alcoholism not as a moral failing but as a disease, a progressive stance Halsey valued by way of his father's experience. By the 1930s, Strecker was pioneering the treatment of psychoneuroses to lighten the everyday strain of modern life. Fan spent the summer in his care, and following her discharge in early October, Halsey reported to friends she was "in excellent shape," adding his "intention to be overcautious in being quiet for some time to come. We are both hoping the cure will be complete." It was not, and the summer of 1938 marked the start of a long, painful, and sad decline.[22]

Fan's illness harried Halsey's move back to sea command that summer. He had assumed the rank of rear admiral in March, and was in line to stand up Carrier Division Two, composed of the *Yorktown,* which had just completed her shakedown cruise, and the *Enterprise,* scheduled for her own inaugural voyage later that year. Distracted with Fan's breakdown, Halsey devoted little preparatory time to his impending duties and knew little about the carriers themselves, whose size and design were different from those of the *Saratoga* and *Lexington.* He managed to bring Ashford with him to his new command, but, as he admitted in May to Ernest King, by then a vice admiral and Halsey's prospective boss, he had "little first-hand knowledge of the *Yorktown* and *Enterprise* at the moment. However, during my leave I shall try to get in touch with affairs in Norfolk and in Washington to learn what I can."[23]

He took command of the two ships in late June, flying his flag from the *Yorktown*. By the end of World War II the Navy had over a hundred flattops, but in 1939 it owned five commissioned carriers: the *Saratoga* in the Pacific, the *Lexington* and *Ranger* of Carrier Division One in the Atlantic, and now the two ships of Halsey's Carrier Division Two, the *Yorktown*, led by Captain Ernest McWhorter, and the *Enterprise*, skippered by Captain Charles Pownall. Making these last two ready for fleet service occupied Halsey over the next months. Sea trials, tactical data tests, and technical assessments filled many days at sea while the air squadrons assigned to each flattop gathered near Norfolk. The pilots trained with the ships when they could, but mostly they operated from nearby airfields. Sometimes, Halsey gathered them in a hangar, where Lieutenant Commander Miles Browning, a brilliant, prickly pilot with an outstanding grasp of naval aviation, moderated discussions of various tactical problems upon a large, makeshift game board of the kind used at the Naval War College. In November Halsey told King the Norfolk Yard would not finish fitting out both flattops until December 30, making their planned January rendezvous with the fleet near Panama problematic. "As you can imagine, it is going to be a scrap right up to the last minute to get these ships clear from the material bureaus and the Navy Yard," he explained to King. "However, every time an objection is raised, we listen and say, 'Fine, the ships will leave on 3 January.' I hope it works."[24]

The strategy performed well enough. The ships, with four destroyers, left Norfolk on January 4 with paint crews still aboard. Near Saint Thomas four days later, Halsey began drilling the green ships and their air groups. Although no lives were lost, those days saw, on the *Yorktown* alone, one pilot catapult his plane across the deck, two others ram the crash barrier, a fourth ditch into the water, and two more scrape the deck when their landing gear collapsed. "I'm sorry we smacked up so many planes, but it was almost inevitable under the circumstances," Halsey wrote Rear Admiral Arthur Cook, chief of the Bureau of Aeronautics. The carriers themselves were "grand," he added, and his only complaint regarded the flag bridge, which afforded no view of the flight deck and was, in his view, "the worst abortion that the Bureau of Construction and Repair has ever brought forth." On January 22 the ships reached Guantánamo Bay, where Halsey reported to King aboard the *Lexington* that the cruise "had been strenuous work for all hands but excellent practice." For the next month, King drove his collective command hard, exercising for the first time four American carriers in unison: the *Ranger, Lexington, Saratoga,* and *Yorktown.*[25]

February 20 brought the annual maneuvers. Fleet Problem XX was designed to test the Navy's control of the Caribbean, pitting a defending Black force of some fifty surface ships, the *Ranger,* and nearly one hundred shore-based planes against a similarly sized attacking White force and the carriers *Lexington, Enterprise,* and *Yorktown.* The exercise revealed the carriers' uneven but generally increasing steam in the last years of peace. Aviation accounted for the bulk of damage inflicted by the White fleet, a fact that led one observer to claim multiple carrier operations had "reached a new peak in efficiency" and caused the usually reticent Ernest King to applaud, especially considering, in his words, the "relative inexperience" of Halsey's ships.[26]

Still, the flattops had mostly operated squarely within the fleet and between battleship columns. Moreover, indiscriminate expectations for aviation among surface officers continued to manifest a limited sense of carrier operations. One operational order for Halsey's ships, for instance, had the *Yorktown* and *Enterprise* simultaneously scouting a 180-degree sector, maintaining air patrols and pickets, destroying enemy ships, and providing air support for troop transports, a smorgasbord that constituted nearly every possible use of aircraft. To airmen, it seemed, surface officers had a knack for asking too much of carriers in the way of routine operations and too little in the way of offensive punch. This proclivity prompted Halsey to comment that "any full understanding of carrier operations requires an informed sense of what they can and, importantly, what they can't do," a refrain that become one of his favored aphorisms.[27]

Thus began Halsey's command of multiple carriers. Occupying a seam between King, who held operational command of White's three flattops, and the skippers of the *Enterprise* and the *Yorktown,* Halsey exercised deft control of Carrier Division Two. Twice he redirected aircraft from defensive cover above the flattops to offensive strikes, not only provoking one battleship skipper to complain Halsey was cheating but also revealing Halsey's growing skepticism that land-based patrol planes posed mortal danger to carriers. Throughout the exercise Halsey hewed to a long pattern of delegated authority, leaving great initiative to his subordinates. On its last day, for instance, Halsey's tactical signals averaged 17 words while King's messages averaged 144. One *Yorktown* officer felt sorry for Halsey, who "seemed to be along for the ride" as King micromanaged the war game. But the invisible hand of leadership often masquerades as the laconic exercise of command, and the old destroyer man William Sims, who died in 1936, would have been proud of what Halsey had retained through the years.[28]

This was also Halsey's inauguration working for King. They had known each other for decades: King had been the senior ranking midshipman during Halsey's freshman year, the two had overlapped for some months as destroyer skippers in Sims's flotilla, and they had spent a year together as students at the Naval War College. The two were different, Halsey being casual and lenient, and King more formal and firm—King once explaining that even excellent subordinates required "a good kick in the ass every six weeks." At sea, according to one who served with both, Halsey's mess was "lively and stimulating" and King's was tight-lipped, dominated by King's towering intellect. During the fleet exercise, King had composed "every word of the instructions he intended to use," according to his biographer. "He did not want advice or suggestions from anybody, not his staff, not even Halsey," who he believed was a "competent naval officer but inexperienced in carrier tactics." At the time, Halsey agreed, thanking King upon the latter's departure from sea command the following year "for your patience of me personally and for the professional lessons you have given me. I should be proud to serve under you anytime, anywhere, and under any conditions."[29]

In the spring of 1938 Halsey settled into flag command upon long-established pillars of his sea service: a comfort with independent responsibility, an expectation of the same among subordinate officers, and a liberal impulse toward enlisted sailors. When a mistake on the *Yorktown* hangar deck delayed a strike launch during the fleet exercise, an angry King demanded the offending officer's name. Me, Halsey replied by radio, a signal that elicited admiration throughout the ship. "He's got broad shoulders," recalled one sailor. "He takes it without passing it on." When McWhorter once worried an approaching squall could upend air operations, Halsey at first responded, "Well, Mac, I don't care. If you're not in a hurry, why don't you go around?" but he later vowed to scuttle the captain's career when McWhorter then timidly asked, "Admiral, shall I use right or left rudder?" And when Halsey himself insisted not once but twice on an incorrect protocol for a visit by a Marine officer, he publicly apologized to the junior officer of the deck. "Andy," he rasped, "I'm sorry. I'm sorry as hell. I really fucked up your honors. I'll never do that again." Then, as before and later, most officers serving with Halsey would have agreed with John Hoover, for a time Halsey's chief of staff in 1940, who recalled that "Admiral Halsey was very pleasant. He was a man who was very easy to get along with."[30]

. . . .

A war scare with Japan and sabotage threats against the Panama Canal rushed Halsey's carriers and other vessels to the Pacific later that spring. There, on the last day in May, Halsey took command of Carrier Division One, taking the place of Charles Blakely, who in turn replaced King as the Navy's senior air officer afloat. In this new role, Halsey commanded the *Lexington* and *Saratoga*, flying his flag from the latter, whose familiar confines served as a metaphor for his growing awareness of carrier aviation. He had served as the *Saratoga*'s skipper for two years, and now he commenced another two years as an embarked admiral. "The *Saratoga* was my first love in the carrier Navy," he recalled later. In the end he lived aboard her longer than he lived in any other place his entire life, either afloat or ashore. "She is," he declared, "a Queen to me."[31]

The *Sara* and *Lex* passed the remainder of 1939 in ship drills, aviation training, and overhaul, all with an eye on the next major maneuvers. Fleet Problem XXI, in the spring of 1940, was easily the most ambitious and complex of the interwar exercises. Encompassing six weeks, the maneuvers comprised eight distinct scenarios sprawled over a vast expanse of the eastern Pacific, from close offshore California to the international date line. The exercise entailed substantial aerial operations, including a mock fleet raid on Hawaii to test carrier vulnerability to shore-based air defenses, and a contest for the central Pacific between the United States, thinly veiled as Purple, and Japan, designated Maroon.[32]

Throughout the maneuvers' six weeks Halsey led his flattops imperfectly but confidently. In the exercise's first phase he launched planes too early to maximize a strike on an opposing battle line, and later he held planes on carrier decks too long to inflict much damage on Hawaii airfields. In an increasingly prominent pattern, he used few words: his operational dispatches during the problem averaged nineteen words, less than half the average of his immediate superior, whether Vice Admiral William Pye or Admiral Charles Snyder, who collectively averaged forty-five words. In one instance, Halsey reduced from ninety-six to thirty-six words a communiqué from Pye, and established in the process a full day of operations for two carriers. He championed radios and common frequencies for ship-to-plane communications instead of Morse code, a change that eliminated intermediaries and risked mayhem but also promised swift strikes in fast-paced battles. In echoes of Dudley Knox's exhortations for doctrine, Halsey believed getting information of enemy movements to "every air and surface unit of the force instantly" would not court ill-disciplined attacks as long as subordinate commanders hewed to a collective scheme of action.[33]

In conferences following the exercise, aviators worked again to free the carriers from the battle line. They had made some inroads. The *Yorktown* had operated as far as seventy-five miles from the battleships early in the exercise, and the *Lexington* served as a detached carrier toward the end of the maneuvers. Mostly, however, the flattops continued to cruise in tandem with the battlewagons, tied to the behemoths' slower speed and poorer agility. For fliers at that late interwar date, independent operations had become the sine qua non of effective carrier employment. Halsey argued that flattops needed to approach their targets "at maximum speed," then "expedite" their attacks and "retire from danger" with great dispatch. In this belief he was no different from most airmen, but other issues were more his own and demonstrated a growing comfort with the parameters of naval aviation. Across four fleet problems, two as the *Saratoga* commander and two as a carrier division commander, Halsey concluded that land-based scout bombers were rarely able, on their own, to inflict significant damage to carriers, a judgment at odds with prevailing opinion that later freed him to strike aggressively in the early carrier raids of World War II.[34]

In a break from established patterns, following Fleet Problem XXI in May 1940, the fleet remained in Hawaiian waters as a deterrent against Japan, whose war with China now threatened American interests in the Philippines. Europe had descended into general war the previous autumn, and as the possibility of global conflagration with enemies on two continents developed, Congress conceived a true two-ocean Navy, allocating money for nearly 300 ships, including several fast battlewagons and a dozen carriers designed to spearhead a drive across the Pacific. Substantial as it was, this growth merely represented the bow wave of massive wartime expansion. By August 1945, the Navy was twenty times larger in personnel, twenty-four times larger in naval aircraft, and sixty times larger in ships compared to its prewar footprint. Only vigorous minds could hope to stay apace with such growth, and only the most intellectually agile of men would master the attendant change that expansion brought in its wake.[35]

Halsey, who replaced Charles Blakely on the *Yorktown* as the commander of all carriers and their air groups in June, rode the wave as best he could. With this new job came a promotion to vice admiral, making Halsey one of the seven most senior officers afloat and, in his words, a "naval Pooh-Bah" responsible for virtually all carrier operations of the Navy. Across the next few months, the European war drew the *Ranger, Yorktown,* and *Wasp,* the Navy's newest carrier, to the Atlantic, leaving Halsey with the *Enterprise, Lexington,* and *Saratoga* to prepare for what might come in the Pacific. Amid the turmoil, Halsey wrote Rear Admiral Arthur Bristol, the commander of the Pacific Fleet Air Detachment in San Diego, "that the present world situation does not admit any delay whatsoever in adequately outfitting the Carrier Force," a sentiment he reiterated in an exhortation to Rear Admiral Aubrey Fitch, then in command of Halsey's old Carrier Division One, to rush the *Enterprise* through a short refit in San Diego, embark whatever air squadrons Fitch could lay his hands on, and return the flattop to Hawaii "as quickly as God will let her and just a little bit quicker."[36]

In the spring of 1941 Halsey's Annapolis classmate Admiral Husband Kimmel became the Pacific Fleet commander. Shortly after assuming the post, Kimmel canceled Problem XXII, allowing his force to concentrate on assimilating the legions of recruits pouring toward the sea to crew new vessels. He ordered the fleet to strip ships, removing all gear not needed for fighting, and to step up war training exercises of all types. He also reshaped the Pacific Fleet, for years organized into type commands with battleships, cruisers, destroyers, and carriers operationally separate from one another, into composite task forces centered upon the *Saratoga, Lexington,* and *Enterprise,* naming three vice admirals, William Pye, Wilson Brown, and Halsey as their respective commanders.

In the process, Kimmel created the lineup of senior sea commanders that first met the Japanese at war. Pye, a 1901 academy graduate and former director of the Navy's War Plans Division, was an intellectual and a master tactician, though his classmate King always thought he "operated in something of an ivory tower," unable "to condense his ideas to reasonable dimensions." Brown, Annapolis class of 1902, was discreet, judicious, and a paragon of old-school manners. He had been a serial naval aide to presidents, including Calvin Coolidge, Herbert Hoover, and Franklin Roosevelt, and had served as the superintendent at Annapolis for three years before reporting to the Pacific Fleet in February 1941. Of the three, Halsey could claim by far the longest contiguous sea service, and was the only one with carrier service afloat. Although he retained his administrative responsibility for all fleet carriers and their air groups, for Halsey, these changes meant a heightened focus on the operational readiness of the *Enterprise* task force, now composed of the carrier, three battleships, five cruisers, and eighteen destroyers.[37]

The sense of urgency that year saved Halsey from an inglorious end. In "the ordinary course of events," Bureau of Navigation chief Rear Admiral Chester Nimitz had informed Kimmel in the spring, the coming summer's rotation should see Arthur Cook replace Halsey as the senior carrier commander afloat, and Halsey's assignment to the Norfolk Navy Yard as commandant. Kimmel, who had been an usher at Halsey's wedding some three decades earlier, demurred, not wanting to switch a key subordinate at a delicate time. This decision disappointed others who coveted Halsey's sea slot, including Cook, who thereafter spent the war anonymously as the Tenth Naval District commandant, and Halsey's old friend John Towers, who from his perch as the chief of the Bureau of Aeronautics in Washington took to telling friends Halsey "ought to retire."[38]

Instead, Halsey hurried to the future. Kimmel typically kept two task forces at sea at any given time. This meant Halsey and his *Enterprise* were at sea about two-thirds of the time in the months before war. On most of these training jaunts, the *Enterprise* and her escorts headed southwest, in the direction of the Marshall Islands, the nearest Japanese possessions and the location from which she would presumably sortie in case of actual war. Unaware of greater strains that lay ahead, these last prewar cruises were grueling for Halsey and others as they peeled away the long habit of peace. He dropped eighteen pounds in the summer and fall of 1941. The continuous need for training and an increasing imperative to fight took most of the energy he could muster, a task eased somewhat by the arrival of his friend Rear Admiral Ray Spruance, who that fall took command of Halsey's cruiser division, flying his flag atop the *Northampton*. Since last serving with Halsey in the mid-1920s, Spruance had had two tours teaching at the Naval War College; had made admiral rank the traditional way, as a battleship skipper; and had commanded the yard at San Juan, Puerto Rico. For Halsey, Spruance would be a source of calm and confidence in the months ahead.

So too would *Enterprise* officers. Her skipper, Captain George Murray, was a terrific Navy man. He represented the first generation of true aviators to command the big flattops, having earned his wings in 1915 as just the fifteenth Navy pilot. Halsey's flag staff, which numbered twenty-one officers and sailors, included many destined for distinguished service with the admiral. In addition to Ashford, there was Lieutenant Bromfield Nichol, Halsey's sociable flight instructor at Pensacola, who had served as Halsey's tactics officer since 1939. Lieutenant Commander Leonard Dow, a standout offensive guard on the 1925 and 1926 academy football teams and widely regarded as the best communications officer afloat in the Pacific Fleet, served as Halsey's signals officer. Lieutenant Horace "Doug" Moulton, a Kansan from the Annapolis class of 1931 who had traded the Navy for a junior executive position with the U.S. Steel Corporation and later returned as a reserve officer, was Halsey's flag lieutenant. His intelligence officers included a Marine lieutenant colonel, Julian Brown, whose charm hid an inclination toward self-promotion, and Lieutenant Gilven Slonim, a remarkable Japanese linguist whose training in Japan had concluded in June, making him among the last of the American officers to serve in prewar Japan. Slonim brought to the *Enterprise* four veteran radio operators, giving the flattop the most robust and able mobile communications unit then afloat. Yeoman Herbert Carroll, prized among top Navy officials for his efficiency, decorum, and discretion, kept the staff files. With the exception of

Slonim, Halsey knew each personally, well before they had joined his flag allowance, and he had exhibited considerable care in placing them together.

Commander Miles Browning presided over this group as Halsey's chief of staff. Browning had graduated from Annapolis in 1918, saw early service in destroyers, went into aviation in 1924, skippered both a scouting and a fighter squadron, attended the Naval War College, taught naval aviation at the Air Corps Tactical School, and had taken up duties as the commander of the *Yorktown* carrier air group at the same time that Halsey first flew an admiral's flag from its bridge in the summer of 1938. From that point forward, the two had formed an unusual bond, Halsey the aviation neophyte, Browning one of the most gifted and natural air tacticians in the interwar Navy. Unquestionably brilliant, Browning was also "one of the most irascible and unstable officers" in the Navy, a disagreeable drunk prone to irrational and sometimes immoral behavior. Although Browning "drank too much, too often, and had a capacity for insulting" behavior, Halsey valued his expertise and trusted his own ability to channel Browning's abilities in productive ways.[39]

After large-scale carrier operations in 1944 and 1945 called into question Halsey's grasp of modern war, it became common to find fault in his prewar service, his late instruction in carriers, and even his leadership style. Halsey's career had left blind spots: he never did much more than salt his sea service with significant shore duty, did not have the administrative experience of King or Nimitz, had never served in the Navy's War Plans Division, and did not share Spruance's accomplishment of conducting long tours teaching at Newport, postings that gave Halsey's longtime friend an unmatched cerebral anticipation of the war to come. He was ignorant of some aspects of aviation: in the months prior to war Halsey discounted severe deficiencies with the fleet's aerial torpedoes, seemed agnostic about the possibilities of dive-bombers before they transformed air combat at Coral Sea and Midway, and urged the accelerated production of the Brewster Buffalo, the Navy's "best airplane," apparently ignorant of the far better Grumman Wildcat, then merely months from its operational debut.[40]

After he became famous for his pugnacious character, many attributed his early war success to a style particularly suited to the crisis and called him a late bloomer. "What would have happened to him," went one typical refrain from a contemporary, "in peacetime?" Yet, across nearly four decades he had accumulated more command time at sea than anyone of comparable rank, was a natural leader nearly without peer, and, without the war, he would still have had a record second only to those few who commanded the entire U.S. Fleet—even if far less fame would have attached to his name. By the fall of 1941 Halsey had acclimated to naval aviation more than any other latecomer. His time in carriers had coincided with crucial periods of aviation advances, including the first systemic experiments with multiple-carrier tactics and their independent use in exercises around Wake, Midway, and the near edges of other faraway places that would soon enough become known to so many others. On the eve of war, he knew the 350 or so carrier pilots in the Pacific Fleet better than any other senior officer: ten of twelve squadron commanders and nine of twelve executive officers had first oriented to flight as midshipmen in the academy program Halsey had supervised in the late 1920s, some 70 percent of the Navy's senior line pilots had passed through Pensacola proximate to Halsey's time as either a student or commandant, and virtually every junior pilot in the fleet had arrived during Halsey's continuous service afloat since 1938, keeping him abreast of their initiation on the flattops.[41]

This personal knowledge offered Halsey a tactile sense of who his fliers were, what they could accomplish, and what was beyond their grasp. When in 1939 *Popular Aviation* aired aviator complaints of "the desk pilot who got into aviation by the grace of politics and a lenient instructor," Halsey eschewed a defensive crouch and commended the article to the senior officer afloat as well as the chief of naval operations. In December 1940 Halsey pushed John Thach, destined to become one of the war's outstanding aviators, into squadron command well before his time, telling others Thach was "a man of particular ability and it might be well at this time to initiate the practice of employing younger men in the top positions." Six months later, and based upon little more than Thach's impassioned plea, Halsey supported a fundamental change in fighter tactics to incorporate a two- instead of a three-plane formation, a profound doctrinal adjustment that later accommodated the Thach Weave, a famous tactical maneuver that mitigated the Japanese Zero's dogfighting advantages early in the war.[42]

From Halsey's arrival at Pensacola in the summer of 1934 to the fall of 1941, he had been continuously in aviation. For more than half that time, he had served at sea in command, a record unsurpassed among the senior officers that went to war and of immense importance after the Japanese laid waste to the Pacific Fleet's battleships. His late arrival to aviation had produced a man profoundly of and from the Navy who was nonetheless alive to the possibilities and capabilities of naval air. This had been the essential purpose of those who had decades earlier insisted on bringing midcareer officers into the new arm. Halsey admired aviators, learned their craft as best he could, and championed their just cause without aping the more fantastic claims sometimes made for pilots and their planes. In 1941 he wrote that those who clamored for independent air power were either "theorists, no doubt honest, who have been blinded to reality" or "pseudo-experts who serve some narrow interest at the expense of national welfare." The development of naval aviation had seen remarkable progress in the short decades since its birth, Halsey proclaimed, but the elemental truth of aviation "could be summarized in a few words: *Airplanes are not a fighting team by themselves.*"[43]

In reality, by World War II the old destroyer man had conformed his long-standing ideas of naval command to the particulars of carrier aviation. "Carriers realize their maximum potential when employed to deliver swift blows in unexpected quarters and at unexpected times," he told fellow admirals assembled at the conclusion of Fleet Problem XXI. "In adverse circumstances it might well be that a major force, compelled in all other respects to accept the tactical defensive, could, by the energetic exploitation of the carriers' mobility and range, restore a favorable balance." A year later, and just months before Japan's pilots laid low battleship row, he told a gathering of Southern

California aircraft manufacturers that "the first blow is half the battle" in carrier warfare. "The most sluggish imagination must stir to the picture of these splendid ships steaming silently and completely darkened at express train speed throughout the night, to rain trip-hammer blows again and again on enemy ships or coasts a half-thousand miles or more from their starting point of the night before. This is the destiny of our carriers." In the days before Pearl Harbor, that was about the fairest anticipation of the early Pacific War one was likely to hear from American quarters.[44]

William Halsey Sr. as a midshipman, Annapolis, circa 1871.
Courtesy of the Library of Congress.

Assistant Secretary of the Navy Theodore Roosevelt at the Naval War
College, 1897. *Front center:* Roosevelt; *rear, five from right:*
William Halsey Sr. United States Naval Institute.

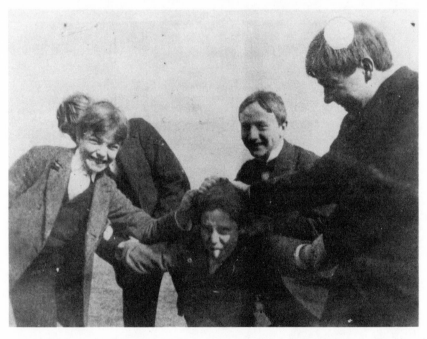

Bill Halsey *(far left)* at fourteen years old at Swarthmore Preparatory
School, 1896. Courtesy of the Library of Congress.

Halsey as Annapolis plebe, 1900.
United States Naval Institute.

The Great White Fleet at Hampton Roads, 1907.
Department of the Navy. Courtesy of the U.S. National Archives.
Photo 19-N-12897.

William Sims, circa 1918.
United States Naval Institute.

Halsey as skipper of USS *Shaw,* 1918. Courtesy of the
Library of Congress. Photo: F. E. Sellman.

Task Force Eight/Sixteen Staff, early 1942. *From left:* Julian Brown, Doug
Moulton, S. E. Burroughs, Miles Browning, R. Gardner, G. E. Griggs,
William Halsey, B. T. Holcomb, Leonard Dow, B. Groesbeck, H. G. Gibson,
Bill Ashford, Bromfield Nichol, William Buracker, P. T. Hunt,
Herb Carroll, and I. N. Bowman. Department of the Navy.
Courtesy of the U.S. National Archives. Photo 80-G-464485.

Lt. Colonel James Doolittle's plane leaves the USS *Hornet*, April 18, 1942.
Department of the Navy. Courtesy of the U.S. National Archives.
Photo 80-G-41197.

Halsey at sea.
Department of the Navy. Courtesy of the
U.S. National Archives. Photo 80-G-47116.

USS *Hornet* under attack, Battle of the Santa Cruz Islands, October 26, 1942.
Department of the Navy. Courtesy of the U.S. National Archives.
Photo 80-G-33947.

Aerial view of Nouméa, New Caledonia, January 1943.
Courtesy of the U.S. National Archives.

Halsey's quarters and former Japanese consul home, Nouméa, circa 1943.
Courtesy of the U.S. National Archives.

Chapter Eight

The First Fighter

BILL HALSEY'S OBLIGATIONS at home remained deaf to his expanding naval responsibilities. His children were grown and gone, young Bill having graduated from Princeton University in 1938. But Fan's instability had grown worse since her nervous breakdown in 1938. She broke a leg stepping off a California curb in 1940, prompting Halsey to set up quarters in a two-room suite at the Halekulani Hotel. Thereafter, routine family affairs fell on his shoulders. He went to some length to clear up many small obligations Fan had incurred but not paid, and he asked a brother-in-law to oversee the rental of the Alexandria house. He made arrangements to collect his household goods, scattered across four storage facilities in Virginia and Florida. Although he had made no will, and would not until after the war, he believed the time was ripe "to get affairs in shape, just in case." He simplified his finances, which then included only his naval pay of $10,647 per annum; four life insurance policies aggregating $30,000, each of which was pledged against debt totaling $14,000; a personal loan from his son-in-law for $2,500; and his home in Alexandria, for which he had not yet paid a penny toward the principal. According to Halsey's flag lieutenant, Fan's illness intensified in the months before the war, perhaps as a result of the growing responsibilities laid upon her husband's shoulders and the consequent diminishment of the time they could spend together. In November, a setback returned Fan to inpatient care, this time at Queen's Hospital in Honolulu, from which she was not discharged until December 19, twelve days after the Pearl Harbor attack.[1]

Thus, it was with one eye toward Fan's hospital suite and another toward the sea that Halsey reported to Kimmel's headquarters in the early morning of November 27, prior to yet another sortie with his task force, the sixth since the first of September. This trip was not a training jaunt. Kimmel intended to reinforce the outpost garrisons on Wake and Midway islands, planning to send the *Enterprise* to Wake early the next day to deliver Marine fighter pilots and planes, and using the *Lexington* for a similar mission to Midway some days later. By then, the Japanese had made their fateful choice for war, and before Halsey left Kimmel that evening a "war warning" message from Washington had reached Pacific Fleet headquarters, proclaiming, "An aggressive move by Japan is expected within the next few days." Recent sightings in the Far East had placed Japanese forces in the South China Sea, and American officials in Washington and Hawaii agreed that Japan's long-anticipated assault into oil-rich British Malaya and the Dutch East Indies was probably imminent. As evening fell on November 27, Kimmel and Halsey discussed the possibility of encountering Japanese warships between Hawaii and Wake. In such an eventuality, "how far do you want me to go?" Halsey asked. "Use your common sense," Kimmel replied. Halsey considered that the finest order he ever received.[2]

The *Enterprise* left her berth in the darkness before dawn on November 28, 1941, taking cruisers and destroyers but leaving slower battleships behind. As soon as they reached open sea, Halsey placed his force on a war footing, astonishing many, including members of his staff, who remained unaware of recent intelligence. Their trip westward was uneventful. On December 4, some 200 miles from their objective, the Marine fighters flew off the carrier to meet their fate on Wake. Halsey's ships then turned to dash back to Hawaii. They had planned to arrive at 7:30 AM on Sunday, December 7, but poor weather put them on a trajectory to reach Pearl Harbor some six hours later, in the early afternoon. The predawn stillness of December 7 found the *Enterprise* 200 miles due west of Oahu. Shortly after 6:00 AM Commander Howard Young, the air group commander, with Bromfield Nichol in the backseat carrying Halsey's report on the Wake mission, led fourteen dive-bombers off the flattop and headed to Pearl Harbor. After watching them into the air, Halsey retired from the flag bridge and, for the first time since leaving Hawaii on November 28, went below decks for a proper shower and shave before having breakfast with Moulton.[3]

Shortly after 8:00 AM the *Enterprise* watch officer informed them of an air raid on Pearl Harbor. Halsey at first thought anxious Pearl Harbor gunners had fired upon the *Enterprise* dive-bombers, due to reach Hawaii at that time. He held this suspicion even after Dow handed him the actual dispatch from Kimmel's headquarters, stamped at 8:12: "Air Raid Pearl Harbor. This is no drill," as well as another, stamped at 8:23: "Alert. Japanese planes attacking Pearl and airfields on Oahu." Halsey recalled in his autobiography that he called the ship to general quarters almost immediately, but in truth he and so many others stirred to hostilities somewhat slower. "It took me an appreciable interval of time," he acknowledged in his unpublished memoir, "before I became convinced that this was war." Throughout the task force it was the same. Ashford thought it took "three times longer to send and receive signals" that first day of war. "There seemed to be a mild daze that pervaded the entire force. People did not seem to be quite able to comprehend just what was happening, and their minds were functioning very slowly."[4]

Three additional messages from Kimmel left no doubt the fight had come, one at 9:03 AM repeating news of the air raid, one at 9:21 placing all ships then at sea anywhere near Hawaii under Halsey's operational control, and one at 9:42 reporting "some indication" of a Japanese fleet northwest of Hawaii. At 11:05, two additional national ensigns, one of which was the largest American flag most *Enterprise* sailors had ever seen, ran up the foremast and main mast of the carrier, helping form, for the first time in the Pacific Fleet's history, the battle flags of an American man-of-war on the open sea.[5]

The situation was confused. In addition to the *Enterprise* and her three cruisers and nine destroyers, Halsey now had Wilson Brown's Task Force Three, then split in two groups: the *Lexington* and her escorts under the command of Rear Admiral John Newton, approaching

Midway to deliver Marine fighters; and Brown's smaller collection of surface ships conducting training near Johnston Atoll. With the Japanese strike, both groups raced back toward Hawaii, the *Lexington* abandoning its task to deliver the Marines to Midway. By the early afternoon, Halsey also had another cruiser-destroyer force, under the command of Rear Admiral Frank Jack Fletcher, maneuvering south of Oahu; the rump of his own task force, which was left behind when he had sortied for Wake; and a handful of ships that had managed to escape the carnage of Pearl Harbor, under the command of Rear Admiral Milo Draemel. Together, Halsey had two carriers, eleven cruisers, and twenty-four destroyers, in four disparate groups flying the flags of six admirals, with little to no practice operating together, spread across an ocean stretching from 600 miles to the northwest to 500 miles to the south of his position, which remained 200 miles due west of Oahu. The Americans began the war with nothing more than a scattered pickup team at sea.[6]

They had no idea where the Japanese were, nor any good way to find out. The *Lexington* was too distant to act in concert with the *Enterprise*. Halsey, who had dispatched that morning half his dive-bombers, reserved his remaining planes for an offensive strike if the Japanese were found. This left land-based planes for scouting, but aircraft and airfields on Oahu had suffered staggering damage in the morning air raid. The search reports that did reach Halsey were inconsistent, incomplete, and incorrect. Although an initial guess placed the enemy to the north of Hawaii, by midmorning a panicked report put two Japanese carriers near Barbers Point, a mere twenty miles west of Honolulu, and multiple indications throughout the day placed an enemy force south of Pearl Harbor. Halsey flung strike aircraft in every direction, but focused on supposed enemy ships to the south, which to him "looked like the real thing," consistent as their location was with prewar concern about the Japanese presence in the Marshall Islands. At 4:00 PM he launched all his remaining aircraft in that direction, leaving the *Enterprise* without planes, a suicidal circumstance if a melee should erupt anywhere near the flattop.[7]

The American searches never came close to the Japanese, who had arrived early that morning from the north with six carriers. As Halsey had watched the *Enterprise*'s last peacetime launch at 6:00 AM, the Japanese were over 200 miles due north of his position and about 240 miles to the northwest of Oahu. From there they had launched and recovered 350 planes before promptly turning back whence they had come and to the northwest, where the North Pacific's gray winter promised a safe retreat. By dusk, the darkened silhouettes of carriers *Akagi, Kaga, Soryu, Hiryu, Shokaku,* and *Zuikaku* steamed silently, their battleships and cruisers and destroyers beside them, carrying home the world's best carrier air groups, diminished yet intact after their lightning strike at the heart of the Pacific Fleet. Also at dusk, the last of Halsey's planes still in the air landed, some upon the *Enterprise* deck and some making for Pearl Harbor, where one six-plane formation of fighters suffered four aircraft destroyed and three pilots killed at the hands of jittery American antiaircraft gunners. This final ignominy of December 7 made it the costliest day for the *Enterprise*'s fighter squadron across their entire first war tour, which extended through the Battle of Midway in June 1942.[8]

It was a bitter end. The day's "confusing and conflicting reports" had succeeded "only in enraging" Halsey. That night, he waited for "the straight word" and reviewed his situation. Of his air group, he had slightly less than half aboard, intact. The rest were scattered across three Oahu airfields or shot down—he did not exactly know. Of the ships in his immediate force, the *Enterprise* had less than half her fuel stores remaining, the cruisers less than a third, the destroyers only a fifth. The *Lexington* and her air group were still too far off to provide mutual support. Although Halsey later liked to say, "On the opening day of war, I did everything in my power to find a fight," it was fortunate he never encountered the far more powerful Japanese fleet. By sunrise on December 8, as knowledge dawned that the Japanese had escaped, Kimmel ordered the *Enterprise* group to Pearl for quick replenishment, leaving only the *Lexington* and her escorts at sea should another foe approach.[9]

Halsey's officers and men were unprepared for the scene awaiting them. Just before darkness on December 8, the *Enterprise* entered the long outer channel into Pearl Harbor. The ship slid past the crippled *Nevada,* the sole battleship to get under way the previous day only to beach along the channel's western edge. On the eastern shore rested the remnants of one of the *Enterprise*'s own planes, shot down the day before. Coming around Ford Island, the carrier inched past the remains of the *Utah,* lying in mud. Now near the harbor center, the carrier crew could see in the fading light the charred skeletons of airplanes and hangars ashore. Off to starboard sat the carnage of battleship row, fire and smoke still spewing from the half-drowned battlewagons. The air was foul with roasted paint and burnt flesh; the water sullied with bloated bodies and dark oil, so thick that motorboat wakes resembled, in the words of one sailor, "sullen little folds that fell back at once into the overall black melancholy." An eerie quiet enveloped the whole scene, punctuated only by an occasional shout from the shore: "Where the hell were you?" and "You better get out of here or the Japs will get you too." High above the nightmare, on the *Enterprise* flag bridge, stood Halsey, silent as well, except for this, to no one in particular: "Before we're through with them, the Japanese language will be spoken only in hell."[10]

In the months, years, and decades that followed, commissions, scholars, and conspiracists passed judgment on the day. Most found varying degrees of fault with senior military officers in Hawaii for America's stinging defeat, but the best among them attributed the disaster to a calamitous constellation of a daring enemy in Japan, complex command relationships in Hawaii, and poor communications emanating from Washington. Halsey never dwelt much on the matter, though he vigorously defended Kimmel after Roosevelt relieved Kimmel of command on December 13, vouching for him first to the Roberts Commission, a formal congressional inquiry, then to the Hart Inquiry, the Navy's investigation into the debacle, and then to anybody who would listen, writing in his autobiography that no one could have "worked harder, and under more adverse circumstances" to prepare the Pacific Fleet than his old friend Husband Kimmel.[11]

All that lay in the future on the night of December 8 as Halsey reached Kimmel's headquarters, where officers still wore uniforms from the day before, their faces haggard and unshaven. In those first days of war, American jitters were such that senior men believed carriers were safer on the open sea, chasing submarines, than at Pearl Harbor, behind torpedo nets. As a result, on December 9 Halsey and the *Enterprise* force hurriedly returned to sea, where it was not difficult for U.S. flattops and Japanese submarines to find each other because in the first fortnight of war as many as twenty-five Japanese subs plied nearby waters. On December 10 an enemy submarine spied the *Enterprise* off the eastern shore of Kauai, initiating a two-day skirmish between the carrier and at least two and perhaps three enemy submarines. The *Enterprise* dodged two separate torpedo tracks, destroyers delivered several depth charge attacks, the cruiser *Salt Lake City* engaged a submarine with gunfire, and scout bombers attacked the *I-70*, sending her to the bottom. Japanese submarines managed to sink five American merchantmen in the first weeks of war, but they missed the *Enterprise*. The flattop returned to Pearl Harbor on December 15, credited with the first enemy warship sunk in the conflict.[12]

The following day Halsey visited Fan at Queen's Hospital to arrange for her return to the mainland. Three days later she was discharged to the care of civilian friends in Honolulu, with whom she then awaited passage to California. At about the same time, Halsey gave his daughter, Margaret, all legal authority over his affairs. In early January, he thanked Rear Admiral William Calhoun, who had helped oversee Fan's travel to San Francisco, for his close attention to the delicate matter. "Mrs. Halsey arrived safely and is now being looked out for by my daughter—thank God." This, Halsey added in his first contemporaneous reference to the Japanese as subhuman, left him "free for one job and one job only—to get these yellow bastards."[13]

. . . .

It would be a long slog, commencing as it did with the catastrophe at Pearl Harbor and an unrelenting string of Japanese conquests elsewhere. On the opening day of war, Japanese aircraft had bombed the Philippine Islands and invaded Malaya and Thailand. On December 9,

Japan occupied Makin and the Gilbert Islands, outcroppings south-east of the Marshall Islands and athwart a line stretching between Hawaii and Australia. By December 10 Thailand had surrendered, Japanese forces had captured Guam, and the Imperial Army was on Philippine soil. That morning off Malaya, the Japanese Navy sank two principal British ships, the *Prince of Wales* and the *Repulse,* effectively ending British naval obstacles to Japanese designs. That evening, Germany and Italy declared war on the United States, ensuring for America the conundrum of a global, multifront war. On December 15, Japan invaded British Borneo, reaching, in a little more than a week of staggering success, the distant, oil-rich shore upon which its whole motive for the Pacific War rested.

The swift advance rocked the American spirit and engendered open talk from senior American officials of a retreat from Pearl Harbor and even worse. Chief of Naval Operations Admiral Harold "Betty" Stark told Washington officials the Japanese could blockade Oahu at will and attack the West Coast, Alaska, or Panama, a picture, he declared, that "was not overdrawn." The Army general in charge of West Coast defenses went so far as to warn San Franciscans that Japanese carriers lurked beyond the horizon and "death and destruction are likely to come to this city at any moment."[14]

At this dark juncture the Navy shirked the relief of the besieged garrison at Wake. Pye, in temporary charge of the Pacific Fleet after Kimmel's ouster, had sent Rear Admiral Frank Jack Fletcher and the *Saratoga* force toward Wake with reinforcements, using Brown's *Lexington* group for a diversionary raid in the Marshalls. But Fletcher, worried about his fuel supply, made a tentative approach to Wake, and Brown's resolve to strike the Marshalls eroded at the first signs of Japanese defenders in that vicinity. When the Navy Department in Washington radioed doubts about the plan's feasibility, Pye recalled the two carriers to Pearl Harbor, leaving Wake, which had become something of a modern-day Alamo to America in the first days of war, to the Japanese, who occupied the small atoll and captured its gallant garrison on December 23. It was a debacle with blame aplenty: at sea, Fletcher and Brown had proved wanting in seamanship and aggression. At Pearl Harbor, Pye had oscillated. And in Washington, the Navy Department had intruded from afar.

Roosevelt rebuked the entire Navy, his reaction tempered only by the words of a visiting Winston Churchill. "It is dangerous," the prime minister told the president, "to meddle with admirals when they say they can't do things. They have always got the weather or fuel or something to argue about." From friendly sidelines came the harshest words: retired admiral Joseph Reeves, father of American carrier aviation, thought the Wake fiasco a disgrace worse than Pearl Harbor. "By gad," he exclaimed, "I used to say a man had to be both a fighter and know how to fight. Now all I want is a man who fights." Halsey, watching from the perch of his second wartime patrol chasing submarines northwest of Hawaii, likely agreed. The aborted Wake relief "caused bitter disappointment to all hands in the fleet," he recalled later. "Why it was cancelled, I still do not know." The war was a mere fifteen days old, "and already we had lost Guam and Wake."[15]

The stench of the war's early weeks lingered. At Pearl Harbor the senior intelligence officer wrote, "Despair filled Pacific Fleet headquarters." Elsewhere, more than a few would have agreed with the fleet's chief planner, who declared the Navy "was in great need of a victory." Observers, both in and out of uniform, worried that two decades of peace had left the Navy "over-organized, over-theorized, over-administered, and over-complicated." *Time* magazine piled on, taunting, "Where Is the Navy?" in one early war headline. By February, Roosevelt openly wondered "about the failure of top naval leaders to deliver some kind of triumph in the ten weeks since Pearl Harbor." About the same time, the president's closest adviser, Harry Hopkins, confided in his diary that Roosevelt "was going to have many of the same problems that Lincoln had with generals and admirals whose records look awfully good but who well may turn out to be the McClellans of this war," referring to the cautious Civil War general.[16]

The Navy haltingly found its footing, aided greatly by two officers. In Washington, Ernest King became the commander of the U.S. Fleet and the chief of naval operations, making him the most powerful officer since George Dewey, who had won glory destroying the Spanish Fleet in Manila Bay in 1898. In Hawaii, Chester Nimitz arrived on Christmas Day and took command of the fleet on New Year's Eve, the same day Halsey returned with the *Enterprise* from his second war cruise. One year behind Halsey at Annapolis, Nimitz had been a submariner, specializing in diesel engines, before passing through cruiser and battleship billets in the 1920s. He had made his mark across two tours in the Bureau of Navigation in the 1930s, the last as its chief. Although he had never exercised senior command at sea, he had exquisite administrative and interpersonal skills. His Annapolis yearbook had dubbed him a man of "cheerful yesterdays and confident tomorrows" and, thirty-five years on, Nimitz arrived in Hawaii with a pleasant demeanor and steady temperament. He had, the dean of American naval historians Samuel Eliot Morison wrote, "the patience to wait through the lean period of the war, the capacity to organize both a fleet and a vast theater, the tact to deal with sister services and Allied commands, the leadership to weld his own subordinates into a great fighting team, the courage to take necessary risks, and the wisdom to select, from a welter of intelligence and opinion, the strategy that defeated Japan."[17]

For King, the Allied cause in the Pacific centered on two vital tasks: first, to secure Hawaii, and second, to preserve Australia and New Zealand as springboards for a later offensive. The former mission implied some sort of continuing fleet action in the central Pacific; the latter required protecting a lifeline that ran south from Hawaii through Samoa, Fiji, the New Hebrides, New Caledonia, and on to Sydney and Auckland. Translating these strategic aspirations into operational missions required careful balance, however, because in the early months of 1942 Nimitz had but two resources: the fleet submarine flotilla, sent deep into Empire waters, and the carrier task forces, soon without the *Saratoga,* lost for many months to a torpedo attack, but including the *Yorktown,* recently rushed from the Atlantic and given to Frank Jack Fletcher. To these tasks King subordinated all others, persistently encouraging action even as battleships continued to settle in the Pearl Harbor mud. In January he exhorted Nimitz "to undertake some aggressive action for effect on general morale," in February he badgered him to make "every effort" to damage Japanese ships and bases, and in March he demanded that Nimitz distribute to his senior officers a *Saturday Evening Post* article titled "There Is Only One Mistake: To Do Nothing." As late as April, King continued his quest to rid "Pearl Harbor of pessimists and defeatists," and had undertaken to find Roosevelt a fighter, much as Lincoln had eventually found Ulysses S. Grant, the sledgehammer that was needed to bring the Confederacy to its knees in the Civil War.[18]

. . . .

Nimitz had his first extended meetings with Halsey on January 9 and 10. The two were as different as men who had attended the same college, chosen the same career, and thrived in the same closed society could be: Nimitz thoughtful, reserved, incisive; Halsey outgoing, sentimental, decisive. They knew each other, but not well. Like nearly every Halsey contemporary, Nimitz knew Halsey's dad had failed aboard the *Des Moines,* and, due to his tenure as the Navy's senior personnel officer, was probably aware of Halsey's own brush with mental strain as a young man. For his part, Halsey understood Nimitz to be technically proficient and an outstanding manager, skills he surely did not possess to the same degree, and ones he did not particularly value. At the outset of their wartime association, nothing indicated Nimitz and Halsey would have anything other than a professional and correct relationship. In fact, if anything, the trials of war suggested that a strained interaction between them was as likely an outcome as any other.

Nimitz ordered Halsey's *Enterprise* force and Fletcher's *Yorktown* group to strike Japanese positions in the Marshalls, with Halsey in overall command. Early on January 11 the *Enterprise* slipped down the channel to open sea for her third war cruise, making a course southward to rendezvous with the *Yorktown,* at the moment steaming toward Samoa with Marine reinforcements. Off the *Enterprise* bow steamed the destroyers *Dunlap, Balch, Maury, Ralph, Talbot, Blue,* and *McCall;* bestride and behind the carrier were the fleet tanker *Platte* and the cruisers *Chester, Salt Lake City,* and *Northampton,* the last flying Spruance's flag. Their luck was lousy from the start. On January 13 an ill-advised radio transmission by a pilot revealed their position. On January 14 the *Blue* lost a man overboard. January 16 brought a trifecta: a sailor on the *Salt Lake City* died in a turret accident, a machinist perished aboard the *Enterprise* in an airplane crash, and a torpedo plane failed to return from patrol, its three-man crew presumed lost until thirty-four days later when they washed ashore a tiny island alive. On January 17 a scout plane ditched in the water, killing the radioman. On January 20, as the *Enterprise* group reached a position one hundred miles northwest of Samoa to link up with the *Yorktown* force, a *Salt Lake City* patrol pilot broke radio silence again, updating the force's position to anyone caring to listen.

All the while, the Japanese had continued their onslaught. The same day Halsey had left Hawaii for Samoan waters, Japan pushed down toward Singapore and into Borneo. On January 23 Imperial forces moved into the Bismarck Archipelago just east of New Guinea, occupying Rabaul on New Britain and Kavieng on New Ireland and becoming a dagger directly north and immediately athwart the center of an Allied supply line between North America and Australia. Eight weeks into the war, the Japanese had nearly completed a massive defense perimeter across the central and southern Pacific, guarding from the Americans their onslaught deep into the Far East. By the time Halsey had met Fletcher near Samoa and pointed the two carriers toward the Marshall Islands, he "had never been on an operation cursed with worse luck." It was an inauspicious way to commence the Navy's first strike of the war.[19]

The Marshalls beckoned. Some 2,500 miles southwest of Hawaii and the nearest Japanese possession, war games before the war had suggested that American carriers might be mauled in a raid there, and that possible outcome had dissuaded Brown from pressing an attack with the *Lexington* as part of the Wake relief fiasco. Probably for that reason, Nimitz had given Halsey wide latitude to make his attack and Miles Browning first proposed a probing strike in the Gilberts, 600 miles southeast of the Marshalls and only recently occupied by the enemy, before plunging deep within the Marshalls chain. When a submarine reconnaissance suggested meager Japanese defenses in the area, however, Halsey doubled down, splitting his carriers, making each more vulnerable, but promising strikes against a wider array of targets. To Fletcher and the *Yorktown* he left the original objectives in the Gilberts and assigned himself and the *Enterprise* three targets in the Marshalls: Wotje, Maloelap, and the large anchorage and suspected airfield at Kwajalein, which became the prime objective of the mission. Aboard the flattop, Browning, calculating American and Japanese aircraft ranges and using maps dating to the antebellum Wilkes Expedition, "put a pencil on the chart and indicated the ideal spot" where the *Enterprise* could best strike targets strewn across the three scattered atolls: smack dab in the midst of the islands, 150 miles east of Kwajalein, 100 miles northwest of Maloelap, and a mere 25 miles due north of Wotje.[20]

Developed, modified, and promulgated within a span of days aboard the *Enterprise,* it was an aggressive plan eschewing strikes on outlying atolls and aiming instead at the heart of Japan's easternmost Pacific toehold. Aboard the *Yorktown,* Fletcher "likely gave a shake of his head in amazement when he discovered how Halsey intended to rampage the northern Marshalls." On the *Enterprise,* one pilot thought the plan "half-cocked," a second proclaimed he knew "not a damn thing" about his targets, and a third declared the entire scheme "ominous." Yet they all desired the fight, and one *Enterprise* diarist wrote, "We'll be heroes or bums by this time next week." Prominent historians believed the planned strike "was by all odds the most hazardous operation yet undertaken by the Pacific Fleet," and called Halsey's intentions "the first true demonstration" of the admiral's "boldness as a war leader." In 1947, Halsey recorded in his autobiography that the scheme "was one of those plans called 'brilliant' if they succeed and 'foolhardy' if they fail."[21]

The scheme was bold, but it was not reckless. Halsey had long since concluded that dispersed shore-based enemy planes of the type probably stationed in the Marshalls did not pose inordinate risk to raiding carriers, provided surprise could be achieved and the flattops retreated before defenders massed for a counterstrike. Although

Halsey did not know the precise composition of other Japanese forces in the area, the region was a vast tract of ocean and sand-spit isles unlikely to harbor concentrated defenses, and even less likely to host Halsey's only real concern, opposing carriers. In fact, the Japanese had only a small surface flotilla, a moderate submarine force, and just fifty-one assorted planes in the area. American timidity since Pearl Harbor had accentuated the scheme's claim to audacity, but in his unpublished memoirs Halsey was less dramatic than he and others were in their public pronouncements. Of the plan to strike the first American blow of the war, Halsey said simply, "We weighed the advantages and disadvantages, then took a chance."[22]

On January 31 the Yorktown and Enterprise groups began their sprints, Fletcher heading to a point equidistant between Mili and Makin, Halsey to Browning's pinprick on the map directly atop Wotje. The Enterprise crew was tense. Halsey was anxious, bouncing about in his emergency cabin just behind the flag bridge, drinking coffee, reading cheap mystery novels, and smoking cigarettes. Two decks below, the ship's executive officer composed a ditty to headline the following morning's plan of the day: "An eye for an eye, a tooth for a tooth / This Sunday it's our turn to shoot / Remember Pearl Harbor."[23]

At 5:00 AM the first aircraft took off, led by the carrier's air group commander, Howard Young. By 7:00 the carrier had but a small reserve of fighter planes still on deck, and for short periods in mid-morning the ship had every plane aloft, indicating Halsey's fervent desire to hit the Japanese. The attacks on Kwajalein were timed for the moment of half light just before dawn, late enough for pilots to see targets, early enough to find the enemy asleep; and the air strikes on Maloelap and Wotje were to coincide with a bombardment by Spruance's cruisers.[24]

The subsequent action resembled a melee as Enterprise aircraft hit four targets across an area of some 15,000 square miles while Spruance's cruisers and destroyers bombarded shore fortifications on five islands. Across seven hours the Enterprise launched and recovered fourteen distinct strikes aggregating 133 sorties. "These young pilots acted as if they were playing football," Halsey marveled later. "They'd fight like the devil, take a short time out, and get back into the fight again." From sunup to high noon, the ship maneuvered inside a five-by-twenty-mile rectangle, sometimes within sight of land, often within range of enemy shore guns, and always vulnerable to enemy planes aloft.[25]

Japanese defenders struggled all morning to marshal assets against a carrier they had not yet found by midday. They sortied two carriers and ten bombers from faraway Truk, and seven submarines from Kwajalein scurried to sea, but the enemy misreported American positions and misread coded messages in the morning's excited tension. "Surely," Morison mused, "some kind of angel was guarding" the *Enterprise* force. Still, at about 1:00 PM, after the *Enterprise* bombing squadron skipper made his third report to Halsey upon the completion of his third mission of the day, Halsey gathered his force and shaped a course northward, racing against the moment the Japanese would finally overcome their shock and organize a focused defense.[26]

One *Enterprise* wag dubbed the retreat "hauling ass with Halsey," which became something of a rally cry in subsequent raids. Near 2:00 PM five Japanese planes found the flattop, and a couple of hours later two more appeared overhead. Murray's deft handling of the ship's rudder foiled the first attack, however, and fighter patrol planes intercepted the latter threat. As dusk approached, Halsey's task force slipped behind a squall front, the haze and coming darkness giving succor to the withdrawing Americans.[27]

Halsey later told Nimitz the Japanese planes had attacked his force with "ferocity and accuracy," and Murray believed the carrier's escape could "only be described as miraculous." This was first-time giddiness that faded with longer time at war. The truth was this: except for two brief moments, the Japanese had failed to challenge Halsey, and by evening the American task force was making nearly thirty knots and had slipped into the murk of a storm. Indeed, before either side had worked out the intricacies of fighter direction, it was very difficult to gather sufficient air forces amid fluid combat without deliberate and prolonged planning, something an aggressive, high-speed

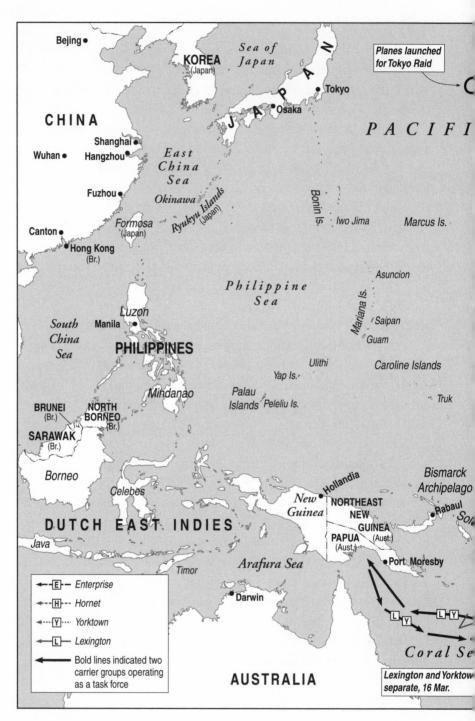

U.S. carrier raids, January to May 1942.

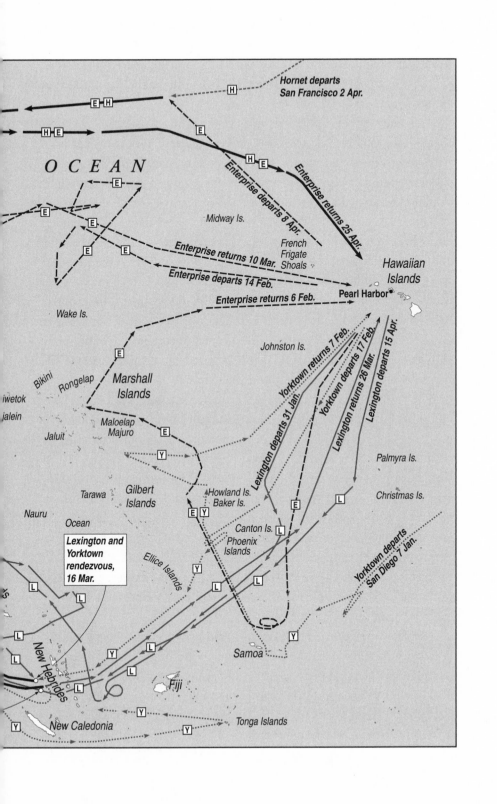

Hornet departs
San Francisco 2 Apr.

E H

H E

O C E A N

E

E

E

E

E

Midway Is.

French
Frigate
Shoals

Enterprise departs 8 Apr.

Enterprise returns 25 Apr.

Hawaiian
Islands

Enterprise returns 10 Mar.

Enterprise departs 14 Feb.

Enterprise returns 6 Feb.

Pearl Harbor

Wake Is.

Johnston Is.

Yorktown returns 7 Feb.

Yorktown departs 17 Feb.

Yorktown departs 26 Mar.

Lexington returns 26 Mar.

Lexington departs 15 Apr.

E

Bikini   Rongelap

iwetok
jalein

Jaluit

Marshall
Islands

Maloelap
Majuro

E

Lexington departs 31 Jan.

Palmyra Is.

Y

Christmas Is.

Tarawa

Gilbert
Islands

Howland Is.
Baker Is.

E

L

Nauru

Ocean

E   Y

Canton Is.   L

Phoenix
Islands

L

Yorktown departs
San Diego 7 Jan.

**Lexington and
Yorktown
rendezvous,
16 Mar.**

Ellice Islands

Y

L

L

L

L

L

L

New Hebrides

Y

L

L

L

Y

Samoa

Fiji

Y

Y

New Caledonia

Y

Tonga Islands

carrier strike followed by a quick withdrawal made nearly impossible, as Halsey had prophesied before the war and as the Japanese had demonstrated at Pearl Harbor.[28]

The material effect of the raid was slight. Halsey believed the enemy had been "struck an extremely heavy blow," reporting a cruiser, two submarines, and fifteen auxiliaries sunk; another cruiser, two submarines, and three transports severely damaged; and twenty-eight airplanes destroyed. Fleet intelligence officers reduced this to one transport and a small subchaser sunk, eight ships damaged, eighteen aircraft destroyed, and about ninety men killed, including the rear admiral in charge of the area. Postwar analysis adjusted the physical score lower still: three small auxiliaries sunk, six additional vessels damaged, and fifteen planes shot down or blown up on the ground. Against this total, the Americans counted four two-man scout bomber crews lost, including a squadron skipper, Lieutenant Commander Halstead Hopping, and eight deaths aboard the cruiser *Chester*, incurred when enemy aircraft found the ship with a single bomb.[29]

The raid had an outsized effect on defenders and attackers alike, however. For the Japanese, the raid suggested the vulnerabilities of outlying Japanese possessions. Admiral Isoroku Yamamoto's chief of staff, Admiral Matome Ugaki, and his chief of operations, Admiral Yoshitake Miwa, believed the raid constituted a reproach of the samurai code and agreed that the Americans would "probably continue such attacks in the future." More unsettling still, for both men the raid raised the ugly specter of a strike on Tokyo, which could cost the Imperial Navy the emperor's confidence, a thought that made Ugaki "shudder." Across the next weeks, an American strike against the Japanese capital became an increasing and nearly obsessive concern for the Japanese.[30]

For the Americans, the Marshalls raid bolstered the Navy's badly bruised morale and became a bright light for a home front in need of confidence. Although poor weather and what some observers felt was Fletcher's "excessive caution" undermined the *Yorktown* raid, Nimitz publicized Halsey's strike and the *Enterprise* met a hero's welcome as it traversed Pearl Harbor's channel on February 5. Salvage men in dungarees crowded the rails of half-submerged battlewagons, troops at Hickam Field and patients at Hospital Point cheered, and everywhere ship whistles filled the air. The display overwhelmed Halsey, who from his perch on the carrier bridge "cried and was not ashamed." In accounts widely replicated elsewhere, the *New York Times* devoted no fewer than ten prominent articles across three days to the raids, telling readers the Navy's "devastating striking power" had struck at the heart of Japanese naval strength, bagging thirty-eight warplanes and sixteen ships, including an aircraft carrier, a cruiser, a destroyer, three large tankers, two submarines, and five cargo vessels. The raid, Miles Browning boasted to one reporter, had "fairly well repaid" Pearl Harbor. Unbridled exaggeration is an occupational hazard of war, and in time Halsey himself realized the Marshalls strike amounted to "at best a nuisance raid" essentially barren of physical spoils. But he then and forever understood the raid's morale value: "When our task forces sortied for the Marshalls raid, you could almost smell the defeatism around Pearl. Now, the offensive spirit was re-established; officers and men were bushy-tailed again."³¹

Within a week Nimitz returned Halsey's *Enterprise* group to sea to strike Wake to avenge the December debacle, although the superstitious Halsey recoiled at orders renaming his ships Task Force Thirteen and sending them to sea on Friday the Thirteenth. So the *Enterprise* steamed from Pearl Harbor on Valentine's Day as Task Force Eight, with almost the same escorts she had had for the Marshalls strike, Spruance again in the *Northampton*. At sea, Browning produced a plan using the Marshalls' raid as a template, sending cruisers and destroyers forward to bombard Wake and assigning the *Enterprise* a quick hit-and-run role. On February 23, Spruance peeled off with two cruisers and a pair of destroyers to make a roundabout approach to Wake from the west, the darkest portion of the horizon at dawn, while the *Enterprise* commenced a thirty-knot run to a spot 175 miles north of the island. Early the next morning the strike went off with few adjustments, Spruance lobbing nearly 2,500 shells and Halsey flinging thirty-six planes at Wake with but modest reaction from Japanese defenders. By afternoon, and again reminiscent of the Marshalls strike, Spruance and Halsey were beating a retreat to a rendezvous point behind a storm front.[32]

The following day Nimitz suggested by radio that Halsey strike Marcus Island "if practical" before returning to Hawaii. As one *Enterprise* bluejacket recalled, "anything was practical to Halsey," so the *Enterprise* force pointed northwestward toward tiny Marcus, a Japanese possession less than a thousand miles from Tokyo. Browning and Halsey planned another swift strike, this time from a point 125 miles north of the target, but without an accompanying shore bombardment. Horrendous weather threatened a necessary refueling on February 28, but then offered concealment as the *Enterprise* began a high-speed run toward Marcus on March 2 with two cruisers, leaving the destroyers behind with an oiler. On March 4, another predawn launch of aircraft, another midmorning recovery, and another hasty retreat marked Halsey's third wartime raid.[33]

As military operations, the Wake and Marcus strikes were uneventful and yielded little fruit. At Wake, Halsey claimed three airplanes destroyed, a handful of airfield buildings damaged, and two vessels, each no larger than personal pleasure yachts and about as important, sunk—a measly tally shrunk by postwar analysis to two paltry planes and a boat. Marcus was sparser still, reducing Halsey to calling a couple of outbuildings and a radio shack the "jack pot" and leaving his force to cling to the emotional consolation that the strike had triggered air raid warnings across portions of southern Japan. The strikes were hardly worth the four planes and three airmen lost, but Nimitz had ordered the missions in part to placate King's desires for offensive action. Across the ocean, Yamamoto and his staff dismissed the raids over dinnertime chitchat. "Only their bold practice of bombing at close range," Ugaki recorded in his diary, "should be called quite daring." As public relations, however, the raids were again ballyhooed at home. At least 700 newspapers reported the strikes, proclaiming that the Navy had "smashed the daylights out of two Jap bases" and left survivors to stew "among the smoking shambles."[34]

The *Enterprise*'s next sortie promised more. After returning to Hawaii on March 11, Halsey learned of an audacious scheme to bomb

Tokyo. Avenging Pearl Harbor had been a singular American ambition since about 8:00 AM on December 7, and in January a small
handful of officers had outlined a plan to launch long-range Army
medium bombers from a carrier, strike Japan's capital city, and land at
airfields along the Chinese coast. Through February, the Navy prepped
the carrier *Hornet,* undergoing sea trials under the command of Captain Marc Mitscher, while Army Lieutenant Colonel James Doolittle,
a famous interwar air racer, readied a group of Army B-25 pilots. By
mid-March the *Hornet* and Doolittle's fliers were ready.

King then sent Captain Donald Duncan, who had served under
Halsey aboard the *Saratoga* in 1937, to disclose the scheme to Pacific
Fleet commanders. On March 20, Nimitz and Duncan discussed the
plan with Halsey and Browning. By then, despite nearly ten weeks
of preparation, the plan remained an aspiration: the B-25, chosen
because of a combination of range, payload, and wingspan, remained
utterly untested in combat; none of Doolittle's Army pilots had made
an actual carrier takeoff; no steaming approaches to Japan had been
identified; no broader task force had been assigned; no targets in
Japan had been earmarked; and, owing to security concerns about
Chinese discretion, no international coordination could ever exist beyond cryptic messages about American planes landing at a half-built
airdrome near Zhuzhou, 1,100 miles beyond Tokyo. "Do you believe
it will work, Bill?" Nimitz asked. "They'll need a lot of luck," Halsey
replied. "Are you willing to take them out there?" Nimitz quizzed.
"Yes," Halsey said. "Good," Nimitz replied. "It's all yours."[35]

Halsey and Browning then traveled to San Francisco to settle details with Doolittle. On March 31 they met in Halsey's suite at the
Fairmont Hotel for three hours to, as Doolittle put it, "think of every
contingency that might arise and have an answer for it." They established steaming schedules for the *Hornet* out of San Francisco and the
Enterprise out of Pearl Harbor, a rendezvous point in the empty North
Pacific, a protection plan using *Enterprise* aircraft for both flattops,
and a spot about 400 miles from Tokyo to launch the Army bombers.
If the Japanese spied the force before then, Doolittle's planes would
lift off toward Tokyo, Hawaii, or Midway, or be pushed fruitlessly

into the sea to free the *Hornet* deck for her air group. Although Doo-little's aviators had staked the project with their lives, the Navy's material risk was far the greater with two carriers so close to Japan. If it came to a fight, Halsey's force would need the full capabilities of both flattops, meaning a sacrifice of the Army planes and perhaps their crews to the gods of war.[36]

On April Fools' Day *Hornet* crewmen gingerly lifted the Army bombers from a Mare Island quay and onto the carrier deck. The following morning the carrier, two cruisers, four destroyers, and a tanker made way for the Golden Gate and open sea, bound, as the story went, for Hawaii. Once clear of land, Mitscher told the force their mission, eliciting cheers. "Heigh-ho, heigh-ho, we're off to Tokyo!" went one instantly contagious ditty. "We'll bomb and blast and come back fast, heigh-ho, heigh-ho." As they steamed silently through the dreary North Pacific, the Army fliers pored over the few suggestions for targets they had received from Washington, picking for themselves industrial or military targets in the built-up sprawl between Tokyo and Yokohama in a manner befitting the mission's hopscotch character.[37]

Back at the Fairmont Hotel, Halsey languished in bed, grounded by bad weather and the flu. He and Browning finally got away on April 5, reached Pearl Harbor on April 6, garnered Nimitz's approval of their operational plan on April 7, took the *Enterprise* force to sea on April 8 as Task Force Sixteen, and revealed their part in the mission to ship crews on April 9. When on April 13, at a spot nearer Siberia than Hawaii, the *Hornet* emerged from the dawn mist to join the *Enterprise,* the task force made one formation of two carriers, four cruisers, eight destroyers, and two tankers, bound for Japan, 2,500 miles distant, along a route not wholly different from the one Imperial forces had traced in the days immediately before and after their Pearl Harbor attack.

The Japanese knew the Americans were there. Halsey's tardy departure from San Francisco had required adjustment to the *Enterprise*'s rendezvous with the *Hornet,* necessitating increased radio traffic. On April 10 the enemy tracked some of these transmissions to American carriers in the North Pacific, stoking anxiety of a strike on their homeland. Since Halsey's Marshalls raid, Japan had bolstered a picket line of converted fishing trawlers arrayed along a line 600 miles from its shores, a fact unknown to the Americans, and had established a powerful home guard force with a nominal strength of four battleships, a cruiser, two carriers, and five destroyers. Elements of this guard force had sortied three times in response to potential American raids on Japan's main islands, including in the immediate aftermath of Halsey's Marcus strike in early March, and now, in the second week of April, news of American carriers in the North Pacific stirred them into action again. Knowing nothing of Doolittle's longer-range bombers, they calculated that American carriers would launch a strike about 300 miles off Japan's coast. Well before that, they surmised, their picket boats would find the raiders, offering a window for Japanese shore-based aircraft to obliterate the Americans before Halsey could do a thing.[38]

Battling deteriorating seas, the American ships sliced west at sixteen knots. To Robert Casey, a newspaper correspondent embarked on the *Salt Lake City*, they looked like "a procession of Gothic cathedrals" in the murky light. On April 16 the Army bombers were made ready for takeoff. On April 17 an intensifying storm rolled the carrier decks sixty feet from sea top to trough, halting all *Enterprise* flight operations and denying Halsey eyes beyond the range of his radar. That same day, Halsey fueled the two carriers and four cruisers, left his destroyers and tankers behind, and began a bruising twenty-five-knot sprint in the rough swell, planning to reach his launch point in the late afternoon of April 18. Up to that moment, Doolittle recalled, time had "hung heavily" in the air, but now the pace quickened. "Jim, we're in the enemy's back yard now," Mitscher told him. "Anything can happen from here on in."[39]

At 3:10 AM on April 18 it did. *Enterprise* radar picked up two small vessels about twelve miles to the southwest. Frenzy followed. Near 7:45 *Enterprise* lookouts spied the Japanese trawler *Nitta Maru* bobbing in the billowing water, part of Japan's picket line. The *Hornet* was then 670 miles from Tokyo, at the extreme outer limits of a feasible strike, and in a near gale. But Halsey's force had surely been spotted. At 8:23 he adhered to a decision made weeks earlier in a San Francisco hotel suite, signaling the *Hornet*: "Launch planes. To Colonel Doolittle and gallant command good luck and God bless you."[40]

As the Army fliers sped down the flight deck, Halsey remembered, there was not a "man topside in the task force who didn't help sweat" them into the air. Hours later, the raiders appeared over Tokyo, Nagoya, Kobe, and Osaka, their bombs damaging a warship in dry dock, lighting fire to about ninety buildings, killing perhaps fifty people, and wounding another 250. Winging toward China, Doolittle's fliers either ditched into the sea or crash-landed in China. Eight crewmen fell into Japanese hands. Three were executed. Every Doolittle raider passed the threshold of glory. Doolittle earned an immediate double promotion to brigadier general. "The hats of Task Force SIXTEEN are on high for you," an exultant Halsey wrote the Army flier on April 24. "I do not know of any more gallant deed in history than that performed by your squadron." In the second contemporaneous example of his foul descriptions of the Japanese, Halsey concluded by telling Doolittle to "keep on knocking over those yellow bastards."[41]

Three minutes after he saw the last of Doolittle's raiders off the *Hornet*, Halsey turned his ships about, racing for safety at twenty-five knots. The *Nashville* had spent 924 six-inch shells and needed the help of *Enterprise* planes to sink the *Nitta Maru*, an extravagance the Americans could not afford to duplicate often during their escape. For the next three hours, they attacked sixteen additional small vessels in the area, sinking three, while Japan rushed five carriers, six cruisers, nine submarines, ten destroyers, and 208 shore-based attack planes to pursue the retreating Americans. Few of these had any real chance to catch Halsey. In an autobiographical exaggeration, he remembered Japanese planes "chased us all the way home." For a day there was surely danger enough, but thereafter the vast ocean and poor weather provided ample cover. Weeks later, a Pacific Fleet analysis calculated that just one enemy submarine, fourteen patrol craft, and three attack bombers had even entered a defensive screen of 130 miles surrounding Halsey's force. On April 20, admitting defeat, the Japanese abandoned what had become a wild goose chase.[42]

On that same day, Halsey's strike force of two carriers and four cruisers met its destroyer escort and tankers. Together, they made a course for Hawaii, entering Pearl Harbor on April 25 to very little fanfare. The raid had ranked among the most guarded secrets of the entire war. Only a handful knew of its particulars beforehand, and even President Roosevelt was ignorant of its details until Doolittle's fliers had left the *Hornet* deck. Yet the strike itself had little meaning without publicity. Later, newsreel footage of the bombers taking off, taken by the film director John Ford from the *Hornet,* provided the succor for the American people that Roosevelt had intended from such a mission. Doolittle became a national hero, Roosevelt placing a Medal of Honor upon his breast on May 18. Within a year, one Doolittle raider, Ted Lawson, penned the bestselling book *Thirty Seconds over Tokyo,* and inside another year an Oscar-winning film by the same title championed the feat. Initially, however, the Navy's role in the raid was secret. When asked how the planes reached Tokyo, Roosevelt replied they had come from a covert base at Shangri-la, a mythical place prominent in James Hilton's 1933 novel *Lost Horizon.* The part played by Halsey's carriers in the mission was not revealed for a year, by which time the attack had passed into history as the Doolittle Raid.

As had sometimes been the case with other early carrier strikes, American military reviews of the raid were at odds with the Japanese reaction. Nimitz was lukewarm about its success. His intelligence officer believed the "effects of the raid were not momentous, nor commensurate with the American risk of two of our four precious aircraft carriers in the Pacific." Spruance recalled the "Doolittle raid was a spectacular operation, good for American morale," but did not impress him "as particularly valuable from a military point of view."[43]

But the raid shook Japanese confidence and had far-reaching consequences. After disbelief, "pandemonium ruled" in downtown Tokyo among a populace repeatedly assured of the impunity of the capital. The effect on military men was great. Yamamoto's personal mess attendant never saw the admiral as downhearted as he was in the raid's aftermath. "Even though there was not much damage," Yamamoto lamented, "it's a disgrace that the skies over the imperial palace should have been defiled without a single enemy plane shot down." Fallout from the air strike sparked a devastating Imperial Army rampage across that portion of China whose population had aided Doolittle's fliers, killing nearly 250,000 civilians as retribution. At sea, Doolittle's bombs drew the Japanese Navy closer to home to guard against further attacks, and never again did Japan venture far into the Indian Ocean, denying the Axis powers their only real possibility for a coordinated global strategy. The "emotional shock of the Doolittle Air Attack on the Government and the people of Japan was extremely large," according to one official Japanese account, and it added impetus to existing plans to extend Japan's defensive perimeter farther across the North Pacific to the Aleutian Islands and Midway, which in turn promised the Americans a chance to truly avenge Pearl Harbor.[44]

. . . .

The Doolittle Raid's major levy upon the American Navy was opportunity cost. The mission had left but two carriers under the command of Frank Jack Fletcher, the *Yorktown* and the *Lexington,* for important duty in the South Pacific, where intelligence officers had correctly guessed Japanese intentions to further menace American supply lines to Australia by occupying Port Moresby in New Guinea and Tulagi in the Solomon Islands. On April 30, five days after returning from the Tokyo raid, Halsey's *Enterprise* group raced from Pearl Harbor to augment Fletcher's two flattops.

By then, Halsey and his task force had become old hands together. He and the ship's skipper, Captain George Murray, had forged an effective partnership aboard the *Enterprise,* Halsey pleased with Murray's ship keeping, and Murray's self-assurance rendering Halsey's habit to roam the vessel beyond flag country in mild violation of custom nothing more than a benign habit. At sea and upon the flag bridge, Halsey wore a simple khaki uniform, sometimes without rank insignia. On bright days, he took to a white sun helmet; on crisp evenings, he favored an aviation windbreaker with a leather breast patch stenciled simply with "Bill Halsey." The admiral was too senior and his command too large for him to retain a personal touch with every sailor, but he maintained an image as a sailor's admiral through those first months of war, especially among the *Enterprise* crew. Shortly after the Marshalls raid, the entire carrier crew gave him a standing ovation prior to the screening of a movie upon the flight deck, bringing him to tears. Weeks later, the ship's newsletter recounted a vignette where one sailor had remarked to another that he'd follow "the old son-of-a-bitch" to hell and back, which prompted Halsey, nearby and unseen, to protest that he was not that old. Beyond the carrier, aboard the *Northampton,* Spruance probably spoke for many in the task force when he told his wife, "Bill Halsey is a grand man to be with. He is a splendid seaman and will smack them hard every time he gets a chance."[45]

Indeed, Halsey emerged in those months after Pearl Harbor as the senior sea admiral most willing to fight, his derring-do a stark contrast to that of his task force contemporaries. William Pye, for instance, had lasted a single war patrol before the Wake relief fiasco consigned him to the presidency of the Naval War College, where he could better apply his considerable cerebral gifts. Wilson Brown had followed his failure to strike the Marshalls in December with a hesitation to raid Rabaul in February so pronounced that an Australian admiral wondered if the war had "shook Brown's nerve." Although he redeemed himself by a successful strike against a Japanese force in New Guinea, his persistent gripes about provisions so thoroughly eroded his standing that at one point King scolded, "Carry on as long as you have hardtack, beans, and corn willy," before he relieved Brown outright in March, sending him to the White House, where Brown's manners could better serve the war effort as the president's naval aide. This left Frank Jack Fletcher as Halsey's most competent task force peer, but his tentative approach to Wake in December and an obsessive worry over fuel supplies in subsequent months made it clear to most observers that he lacked the flair that had become Halsey's hallmark.[46]

Of the eight carrier raids the Americans attempted in the war's early months, Halsey had led four and had abandoned none. Across those months, his *Enterprise* group had used nearly three times the ordnance used by Brown's *Lexington* force and about two-thirds more than Fletcher's ships—sometimes to the chagrin of friendly ships, because *Enterprise* pilots attacked the submarine *Pompano* in December and the submarine *Gudgeon* in March. Among superiors, King believed Halsey was easily the most aggressive of the Navy's task force commanders. Among peers, a secret committee impaneled by the secretary of the Navy in the spring of 1942 to identify the best flag officers placed Halsey fifth; no other officer of comparable rank in the Pacific Fleet sat higher, and Nimitz did not break into the top forty. Among subordinates, "Wild Bill will try anything once" had become a typical boast among bluejackets, with *Enterprise* pilots bragging that danger "didn't mean anything to Admiral Halsey." And among the enemy, the lead pilot of the Pearl Harbor raid, Mitsuo Fuchida, later testified that if "the Japanese Navy had had a half dozen Halseys throughout the war and just one at Pearl Harbor, the story of the war in the Pacific would have been entirely different. Defeat is not only a matter of economics and material; it is a question of aggressive leadership. This would have saved the situation for us many times during the war. What we needed was a Halsey."[47]

Now racing south to join Fletcher's carriers, Halsey had a quickly emerging reputation as a brawler for a nation starved for good news. Following the Marshalls raid, the *New York Times* wrote he had the "fighting blood of the Navy" in his veins. In the prop wash of the Wake and Marcus strikes, news reports had citizens everywhere waiting "hopefully for the next time Bill Halsey's task force turned up." In early April, *Time* magazine opined that the weary men defending Bataan in the Philippines "should look not south, to Australia and General Douglas MacArthur, for relief but east, to the central Pacific, where Halsey's potent force lurked." In its wide-ranging appraisal of the first six sorry months of the war, *Time* ascribed to Doolittle and Halsey America's only significant battle victories and praised Halsey for his "brilliant raids." By then, press accounts had taken to cliché: Halsey was a "sea dog," a "salt-water warrior," and a "bulldog." Such bluster sometimes bred blushes among Halsey's peers, but the media attention served to make meaningful for a democratic citizenry the sacrifices borne upon the factory floor and in home-front living rooms.

Spruance, as sober an officer as existed in the Navy, encouraged his wife to read *Life* magazine's account of Halsey's Wake and Marcus strikes. He knew the article was a vast exaggeration, but understood also the purpose it would serve.[48]

Drawing upon long service aboard destroyers and his time with carriers, Halsey had managed, to an extent unmatched by his peers, to place tactical calculation before strategic caution. Over the course of a few months, he and the *Enterprise* had perfected the hit-and-run carrier raid, descended from the darting tactics of Sims's destroyer flotilla and foreshadowed by interwar fleet exercises. Bold as they were, however, these raids were not foolish, their risks underwritten by a sound belief that the Japanese could not collect sufficient force to counterpunch surprise raids, a calculation appreciated by Halsey's pilots: one wrote that Halsey was "a daring man but he uses his head," and another reported that "the attitude of the admiral, a pilot himself, was nicely understood aboard his carrier flagship, above the flight deck and below."[49]

Halsey's confidence in carrier aviation survived even in the darkest early moments of the war. At a time when the American spirit waned and naval confidence slipped to the point that one carrier skipper described the war as "defeat, retreat, and frustration," Halsey stood steady, telling one old Navy friend his force did "not suffer from ennui" and relating to another that at times of tragedy and disaster it was "necessary to keep your chin up and tell the other fellow to go to hell." As he raced through the equatorial doldrums in the first week of May to join Fletcher's *Lexington* and *Yorktown*, America had found its fighting admiral, at the moment it most needed him. As Nimitz's chief intelligence officer wrote, the "American public needed a hero" in those gloomy days, and Halsey "was it." Roosevelt, it seemed, had found a fighter. Over the course of innumerable weeks, many months, and a handful of years to come, this first impression held fast among the American people, for good reasons and bad, with positive and negative consequences for Halsey, his peers, and the nation.[50]

Chapter Nine

The Right Man

MAKING SPEED TO THE SOUTH in early May, 1942, Halsey's task force entered for the third time in as many months the equatorial doldrums, where the hot sun, still air, and warm sea conspired to pulse heat through the gray steel of ships. In the midday boil, the *Enterprise* deck melted rubber soles and fried exposed flesh. Belowdecks it was hotter. The ship sweat with condensation as if alive. People wilted. Across the first six days of May the *Enterprise* sick bay filled with no fewer than one hundred heatstroke victims. Halsey escaped the worst of this environment, but the heat and high humidity recognized no naval rank and assaulted his body as it did those of sailors forty years his junior.[1]

The *Enterprise* was late coming south to partake in the Battle of the Coral Sea. On May 7 and 8 Fletcher's forces battled a large Japanese fleet in the war's first major carrier air engagement. In a confused and muddled clash, both sides suffered significant losses, including the carriers *Lexington* and *Shoho*. The Japanese claimed a tactical victory with a greater material score, but the Americans parried Japan's drive southward, which had been Fletcher's strategic objective. Halsey, hundreds of miles from the action when it occurred, milled about for a week to augment Fletcher's depleted force should the Japanese reappear. They did not. In mid-May, Nimitz recalled Halsey and Fletcher to Pearl Harbor for impending action elsewhere. Halsey was surely disappointed to miss the Coral Sea action, where his *Enterprise* might have proved decisive in the evenly matched contest. The war was young, however, and other chances would come his way.

Halsey was sick by the time the *Enterprise* returned to Pearl Harbor on May 26. For two decades, skin maladies, exacerbated by heat and humidity and usually in the form of dermatitis on his palms, feet, and scrotum, had bedeviled him. Now, in the spring of 1942, weeks at sea prompted a general eruption. Since early March a Honolulu dermatologist had treated him with modest success, but in the tropical Coral Sea Halsey's condition worsened to the point that he could sleep only in short fits, naked and without cover sheets, upon a bed covered with talcum powder. By his own reckoning, he had lost twenty pounds since the first of the year, was lucky to get two hours of sleep in twenty-four, and had tried every "remedy in the pharmacopoeia" until he "nearly went out of my mind." When he reported to Nimitz at midday on May 26, Halsey could hardly bend his arms and legs at the elbow and knee, and crossing his fingers or toes was impossible. Only his face and two round contiguous spots on his chest and belly were spared, transforming his torso into a canvas depicting, one nurse later remarked, a white snowman against a bright red background. He was gaunt, exhausted, and irritable.[2]

He could not continue in task force command. This presented a quandary to Nimitz. The Pacific Fleet commander was reasonably sure the Japanese meant to attack Midway in early June, and he wanted Halsey, his most successful carrier commander, to help bait a trap. Instead, Nimitz placed Fletcher in overall command and gave the *Enterprise* task force to Spruance, a bold choice not based upon seniority or aviation experience, for Spruance had not enough of the former and none of the latter. Days earlier, however, Halsey reported that Spruance had "displayed outstanding ability" across the war's first months and was "fully and superbly qualified to take command of a force comprising mixed types and to conduct protracted independent operations." It was in effect a letter of recommendation for his old friend Spruance, and in its writing Halsey helped set the trajectory of one of the great World War II admirals. On June 4 Spruance, with Halsey's *Enterprise* staff and his own considerable talents, helped win the crucial carrier battle of the war at Midway, where American forces sank four Japanese carriers against the loss of the *Yorktown*.[3]

Halsey was on a slow boat home when the battle occurred, heading toward Dr. Warren Vaughan of Richmond, Virginia, one of the nation's foremost dermatological allergists. Nimitz, loath to risk losing Halsey permanently to a stateside sick leave, had sent him there with artifice, telling King by dispatch that Halsey had been "temporarily incapacitated" by some "obscure allergy" and adding in a subsequent letter that he expected "Halsey to be somewhat rested and relieved of the worst part of his itching in a few days, at which time I will give him orders to proceed, via air, to Washington" to report "for temporary duty—upon completion of which he is to return to Pearl. This will be my way of giving him a complete change of scenery and the relaxation he needs. He is now in the best of spirits, full of vim and vigor, and anxious to get going again, but he does need a short period of rest. He is neither ill nor on the sick list."[4]

Halsey, with Ashford in tow, reached Richmond on June 14. Nearly a month of tests followed, finally revealing streptococcus and staphylococcus in five teeth. Halsey's underlying dermatitis stemmed from any number of issues and was probably fungal in origin, but his recent inflammation had most likely been sparked by this infection. After dentists removed the infected teeth, antibiotics improved Halsey's condition. Discharged from the hospital on July 21, he stayed in Richmond another month for observation, during which time Vaughan prepared injections of strep and staph bacteria as prophylaxis and perfected topical solutions of menthol and benzocaine, a rub of calomel, a special soap, and an ointment of coal tar to treat Halsey's skin on an ongoing basis. A brief inflammation in January 1943 led to a hurried use of Vaughan's injections and a more liberal application of the special lotions to Halsey's scrotum, a regimen that elicited ribbing from those members of Halsey's staff close enough to the admiral to tease him of such things, but his dermatitis never again assaulted his skin as it had in the spring of 1942.[5]

Throughout this period King had acquiesced in Nimitz's subterfuge. Halsey was never, as an official matter, sick during this Richmond interlude. He retained his administrative post as commander of the Pacific carriers, even in the face of Bureau of Personnel efforts to replace him in July. Ashford, shuttling between Washington and Richmond, kept Halsey tethered, barely, to his official duties. For a time, Halsey's presence in Richmond was secret, and not even Fan, in Wilmington with Margaret and her family, knew his whereabouts. As he improved, however, he emerged. In late July he partook in a charity fundraiser, visited schoolchildren, and attended a high-society dinner given in his honor. In early August he saw his wife and daughter in Delaware, where he was reminded of his growing renown when a young grandson, upon seeing a newspaper cartoon of Halsey, exclaimed, "Grand daddy, you're famous!" At a garden party on August 10, Halsey met a number of Margaret's friends, one of whom, a Navy Reserve lieutenant named William Kitchell, soon joined his staff. Later that month, Halsey addressed the midshipmen at Annapolis, his first public duty with the Navy since leaving Hawaii in early June.[6]

As Halsey's health improved, others confronted the question of what to do with him. He remained the Navy's most successful fighting admiral, even after sitting out the Battle of Midway and the entire summer of 1942. Both King and Nimitz desired him at sea again, and in early September he attended one of their periodic San Francisco conferences to reorient him to the war. On September 11 he flew from San Diego to Pearl Harbor with Ashford and Kitchell. By then, Miles Browning and Julian Brown had also joined the small group, their beloved Enterprise in Pearl Harbor undergoing repairs to damage suffered in the Battle of the Eastern Solomons in late August. On September 12, during an awards ceremony on the Enterprise, Nimitz announced Halsey's return to spontaneous cheers. Later that day, Nimitz delighted Halsey by producing young Bill Halsey, now an ensign in the Supply Corps reserve and, like his dad, a recent arrival from the West Coast. On September 15, when Ashford rejoined the Enterprise flag allowance as assistant air operations officer, Kitchell became Halsey's aide. That same day, Halsey renewed his administrative duties with an eye toward reclaiming his old task force when the Enterprise returned to the fight.[7]

The carrier was ready a month later. On October 13, the day before the Enterprise left for the South Pacific, Nimitz sent Halsey,

Browning, Brown, and Kitchell ahead on an aerial inspection through the South Pacific to familiarize them with the area they would presumably soon prowl. On October 18 Halsey arrived at Nouméa, New Caledonia, the headquarters of the South Pacific Command of Vice Admiral Robert Ghormley, who at that moment was immersed in directing the epic battle for Guadalcanal, then in its tenth week. Upon landing, Halsey was handed an eyes-only dispatch from Nimitz directing him to relieve Ghormley and assume at once the responsibility for the tenuous American toehold on Guadalcanal. "Jesus Christ and General Jackson," he exclaimed to no one in particular as his party made their way to Ghormley's command ship, the *Argonne*, bobbing in Nouméa's picturesque harbor. "This is the hottest potato they've ever handed me." Taking command from Ghormley, an Annapolis football teammate and friend of forty years, was bittersweet. Afterward, he immediately ordered trusted members of his *Enterprise* staff, including Ashford, Nichol, Dow, and Moulton, to join Browning, Brown, and Kitchell aboard the cramped *Argonne*. Upon arriving late on October 25, these *Enterprise* men went to Halsey's small shipboard office, where the admiral sat alone reading dispatches, a half-eaten ham sandwich and a full ashtray competing for space atop his little desk. Drawing his glasses down the bridge of his nose, Halsey remained seated and did not as much as pause for handshakes. "Look around and see what is to be done," he said. "It's a goddamn mess."[8]

That it was. Before the war, neither Japan nor the United States anticipated the scope of the fighting south of the equator. Japan's wild success in the war's first months, however, had pushed Imperial forces southward, to Rabaul and its commodious harbor at the northwest end of New Britain in January and to the northern coast of New Guinea and into the Solomon Islands in March, with momentum sufficient to birth embryonic ambitions for Australia and New Zealand, too. This astonishing march threatened Allied supply lines linking the United States and Australia, by then sacrosanct as a feeding tube because the war in North Africa had cut Britain's Mediterranean routes to her Oceanic commonwealths. Suddenly, sleepy South Pacific isles, heretofore known only to natives, whalers, and coconut planters, became important. While the Japanese Navy probed farther south, Americans moved to guard tenuous sinews to Australia. As many as 80,000 U.S. troops sailed for the southwest Pacific between January and March, four times as many as had left for Europe during the same period, and another 200,000 arrived by the end of 1942, with their planes, tanks, and guns in train, a development that would have astounded any respectable prewar strategist in either Washington or Tokyo.[9]

Jurisdiction for this surprising corner of the war bedeviled both combatants. Geographically a maritime theater dominated by ocean, the area contained enough land to make any fight thoroughly joint in character, presenting both Tokyo and Washington with the thorny problem of interservice command. From the start the Japanese failed to fully integrate their Army and Navy in the region, and settled instead upon separate areas of responsibility, with the Army generally controlling New Guinea operations and the Navy running affairs in the Solomons, a bifurcation that worked against a smooth and coordinated offensive.

The Allies did little better. As early as 1924 planners in Washington had concluded that a Pacific war would require a single authority, and divided Army/Navy command in Honolulu was widely seen as one culprit in the catastrophic attack on Pearl Harbor. As 1942 dawned, Washington officials established joint commands in the Panama Canal Zone, then of signal concern to strategists, and overcame not only interservice but also intra-Allied anxieties to create an integrated American, British, Dutch, and Australian command in the far Pacific— an achievement they later duplicated with Allied commands in the Mediterranean and European theaters. But in the South Pacific, this comity "foundered on the sharp crags of service jealousies and rivalries," as an official Army history put it. The Navy steadfastly guarded prerogative in the ocean area, long considered its special domain, while the Army rejected any command that subordinated General Douglas MacArthur, then the most celebrated and senior American combat leader, to an admiral, even Nimitz, whose stature was not

177

then what it would later be. Through the early months of 1942, even Roosevelt failed to break this impasse, which produced some of the most intense interservice sniping of the entire war, straining the good-will of King, the Army chief of staff, General George Marshall, and their subordinates to the breaking point.[10]

Weariness overcame reason in March, when Roosevelt and the Joint Chiefs agreed to two sovereign organizations, the Southwest and Central Pacific theaters, led respectively by MacArthur and Nimitz. They further divided Nimitz's command into the North, Central, and South Pacific commands, the last promising both the most urgent action, because it encompassed much of the supply route to Australia, and the most delicate coordination, because it abutted MacArthur's zone of authority along the 160th meridian below the equator. To command the South Pacific sub-theater, King and Nimitz chose Ghormley, a 1906 Annapolis graduate with long service in battleships who, most recently, was the Navy's top representative in London, a position analogous to William Sims's in the days before American entry into World War I. Ghormley was well respected, contemplative, and genial. He was also something of a natural diplomat, a skill he deployed with great success in London, and a bit of a worrier, a trait not well suited to the tasks that now rose from the horizon in the South Pacific.

In early May, as Halsey had raced south in his futile dash to join Fletcher for the Battle of the Coral Sea, Japan occupied Tulagi in the lower Solomons and soon thereafter began building an airfield on nearby Guadalcanal, from where its planes could threaten Allied supply lines to Australia. This quickened the American impulse to drive back Japanese forces and regain Rabaul, whose fine natural harbor, growing airfield complex, and location at the apex of the northern Solomons and western New Britain made it the linchpin of Japan's entire southern thrust. Guadalcanal, however, sat exactly athwart the 160th meridian, so recently identified as the boundary between MacArthur and Nimitz, rendering local plans the function of Washington debate.

In early July, the Joint Chiefs divided the task to regain Rabaul into three sequential phases, to begin in early August: Phase One, an attack on Tulagi and Guadalcanal, under Nimitz's command; Phase Two, a double-pronged strike up the Solomons chain and through New Guinea under MacArthur's direction; and Phase Three, a final assault on Rabaul, presumably but not explicitly under MacArthur's command. In each phase, Ghormley would control South Pacific forces in the Solomons, but his relation to higher authority was variable and ambiguous. In Phase One, Nimitz was to be his administrative and operational superior, MacArthur a coordinating authority. In Phase Two and, implicitly, in Phase Three, Ghormley would report to MacArthur operationally and to Nimitz administratively. In every instance, Ghormley's naval forces would come from Pacific Fleet allotments, giving Nimitz an outsized privilege even in later stages when MacArthur's command prerogatives were the greater.

The arrangement saddled the South Pacific commander with two bosses wearing different uniforms. It was hazy enough to prompt continuous problems in the coordination of combat operations. Only months of fruitless negotiations made this organizational smorgasbord palatable. Although control over the entire area was vested collectively in the Joint Chiefs of Staff, unified command of the theater existed only in the Oval Office, for no single authority short of the presidency could arbitrate the many questions of strategy throughout the Pacific, and no single person except the president could command the movement of men and material throughout a theater destined, by its sheer size and basic medium, to require great fluidity in the prosecution of war. Unity of command had long been holy writ among military men, but in the South Pacific of World War II it proved elusive.

Through July, as Halsey emerged into Richmond society, forces in the South Pacific collected for a counterstrike at Guadalcanal. At sea, Frank Jack Fletcher assumed duties as the task force commander. Rear Admiral Richmond Kelly Turner, recently of King's war plans staff in Washington, became the amphibious force commander, responsible for first bringing and then sustaining Major General Alexander "Archie" Vandegrift's First Marine Division on Guadalcanal. Their collective preparations were hurried: Fletcher had mere weeks to shape some eighty ships spread across the Pacific into a single force; Turner had to effectuate from scratch the first major seaborne landings of the war; and Vandegrift, promised when his division left its East Coast home weeks earlier that no combat operations loomed until 1943, had to make do without his most experienced regiment—a full third of his force—and grope toward a plan with no knowledge of Guadalcanal beyond a few plantation managers' scattered reports, a makeshift map derived from reconnaissance photos, and an old *National Geographic* article. A brief dress rehearsal in late July was in Vandegrift's view "a complete bust," and to anyone acquainted with the facts it was no surprise when those responsible for America's first major counteroffensive of the war had in colloquial conversation replaced the operation's formal code name, Watchtower, with one better suited to their circumstances, Shoestring. Still, the imperative for action increased as the Japanese edged ever nearer to a complete airfield on Guadalcanal and a firm grasp on the Solomons. So, as the most careful historian of the looming battle put it, in early August Watchtower commenced "at a velocity that mocked all conventions and under conditions that affronted a fair portion of the principles of war."[11]

On August 7, as Halsey visited Fan and his daughter Margaret's family in Wilmington, Turner delivered Vandegrift's Marines to Guadalcanal. Surprising the few Japanese in the area, the Marines quickly occupied the budding Japanese airstrip and christened it Henderson Field in memory of an aviator killed at Midway. Fletcher, skittish at keeping the bulk of the Navy's carrier force in a confined area, left for open sea the following evening, leaving behind a greatly diminished force to protect Turner's supply ships and the Marines on the beach. Later that same night, Japanese warships stole into the narrow strait between Guadalcanal and Savo Island to inflict, in the Battle of Savo Island, the American Navy's worst defeat since 1812, leaving four Allied cruisers sunk and three other hulls ablaze. The calamity forced Turner's supply ships, now exposed along Guadalcanal's littorals, to evacuate with much of Vandegrift's provisions still aboard, consigning the Marines to many weeks of hardscrabble survival. Americans evened the naval score somewhat on August 24 in the Battle of the Eastern Solomons where, at the cost of extensive damage to the *Enterprise*, they deflected major Japanese reinforcements meant to recapture Henderson Field and sank a carrier, a destroyer, and an auxiliary. Still, at month's end, Fletcher's reputation lay in tatters, never to recover, and the defenders of Henderson Field clung, barely, to a tiny coastal plain surrounding the airstrip, the sea to their back and surrounded on three sides by an increasing number of Japanese.

By early September, as Halsey rejoined the Navy in Pearl Harbor, the fight for Guadalcanal had etched a pattern across the Solomons' sky, sea, and jungle that stretched well into November. A few dozen pilots based at Henderson Field gave the Americans control of the air and the tactical advantage during daylight hours; after dusk, Japanese talent at night operations gave to them the initiative. In twelve-hour increments the tide of war changed hands, creating an oscillating siege marked by unremitting jungle clashes, desperate daytime dogfights, terrifying night banzai charges, unbearable naval bombardments, and, mercifully, moments, usually in the breaking of dawn or the coming of dusk, to collect the wounded, bury the dead, snatch some rest, and fortify for what would surely and relentlessly come next. In mid-September a fierce fight for a ridge bordering Henderson Field killed thousands of Japanese and hundreds of Americans, and throughout the month a series of bloody battles along a flanking beach rendered untold more dead, many half-buried in the surf, unwitting stars in some of the war's most haunting photographs. Amid the fighting, both sides managed to supplement their forces: the Americans sporadically and in larger increments—the Seventh Marine Regiment in September and the Army's 164th Regiment in October; the Japanese routinely and in smaller additions—arriving at night in dribs and drabs by destroyer or barge in operations quickly dubbed the Tokyo Express by some American wit.

By early October, as Halsey waited on *Enterprise* repairs in Honolulu, the fight had become a debilitating stalemate. On the battlefield and along both sides of the line, malaria, mud, and misery connived with vicious combat to sap morale. In the air, the October sky witnessed ferocious combat, costing 321 Japanese and 234 American planes at a time when every airframe counted. At sea, major clashes with decisive tactical results, such as the Battle of Cape Esperance in early October, which sent four Japanese warships to the bottom at the cost of a single American hull, constituted nothing more than an interruption to the gridlock ashore. By then, the ground fight had become what strategists call a meeting engagement, the point at which two forces collide, at a place neither wanted for its intrinsic value, much like the Battle of Gettysburg in the Civil War. In the process, Guadalcanal had become the site of a death struggle with no clear or present resolution, rendering commonplace a sentiment carved upon the cross of a simple Marine grave: "And when he goes to heaven / To Saint Peter he will tell / Another Marine reporting, Sir / I've served my time in hell!"[12]

As Halsey prepared for his South Pacific orientation tour, both sides reconciled themselves to the unenviable requirement to take the fetid island. In Tokyo and at Rabaul, the Japanese prioritized the Guadalcanal fight over their preferred thrust into New Guinea. Over the first fortnight of October, they undertook Herculean preparations for a decisive assault on the beleaguered American airstrip: over a hundred trips by destroyers and cruisers working the Tokyo Express delivered 160 tons of provisions and something over 10,000 men to the island, bringing the Japanese total to 15,000 effectives against 22,000 Americans, less than half of whom were fit to fight on the heels of nine weeks of torment. In probably the most concentrated bombardment of the entire war, in any theater, at any time, two Japanese battleships punctuated this effort with a point-blank shelling of small Henderson Field on the night of October 13–14, rendering prostrate even the indefatigable Vandegrift, who recalled, "A man gets close to himself at such times."[13]

Intelligence reports of even more Japanese racing down from Rabaul heightened American anxiety. In Pearl Harbor, Nimitz acknowledged on October 15 that his forces no longer controlled the sea near

Guadalcanal, making the American position untenable. From Brisbane MacArthur wired Marshall, "It is now necessary to prepare for possible disaster in the Solomons," an outcome he believed likely "unless the Navy accepts successfully the challenge of the enemy surface fleet." Throughout Washington and at the White House, the fight was quickly becoming the most pressing military concern, even as the Allied invasion of North Africa, slated for early November, drew near. From mid-October to mid-November, Roosevelt, whose son James served as a Marine officer on Guadalcanal, paid more attention to the Solomons fight than he would any other operation except for the Normandy invasion later in the war. On October 16, the *New York Times* published what amounted to a eulogy to the struggle for Guadalcanal, a name, the editors wrote, that "will not die out of the memories of this generation. It will endure in honor."[14]

Forceful leadership may have stayed such gloom. Since the summer, however, Ghormley had seen problems rather than solutions to his many difficulties. He had called the directive to take Guadalcanal "disconcerting news." He had told Nimitz the stalemate was due to forces beyond his control, including a strong Japanese naval presence making it "too dangerous" to supply the Marines; Washington officials who "did not understand" the campaign; an American Army that had not "backed up" the fight; New Zealand leaders who were "afraid" of lending aid to the operation; and a British government that had all but jettisoned its sovereign responsibility to its Solomon Islands protectorate. He was always acutely aware of deficiencies in carriers, cruisers, destroyers, and transports—and at one point he laid upon Vandegrift's shoulders the choice to surrender the island if the Marine position on Guadalcanal became untenable, a remarkable abdication of moral responsibility.[15]

Ghormley had not grasped his mission. From the start he had split his resources between the fight for Guadalcanal and the wider objective to secure supply lines between America and Australia, failing to see the defense of Henderson Field as the sine qua non of both missions. This diffusion kept three carrier groups, centered on the *Saratoga,* the *Wasp,* and the *Hornet,* in dispersed ambivalence, steaming south of the Solomons and north of New Hebrides, where they were ill positioned to either harass Japanese on Guadalcanal or cover trans-pacific supply lines, but where they were increasingly vulnerable to a growing concentration of Japanese submarines in an area soon dubbed Torpedo Junction. On the last day of August, a Japanese submarine found the *Saratoga,* knocking her out of the war for three months, and two weeks later another sank the *Wasp,* leaving the Pacific Fleet with only the *Hornet* to supplement the Guadalcanal fight before the *Enterprise* could re-enter the fray in late October. Across his entire time as South Pacific commander, Ghormley never found time to leave the *Argonne* for even a brief sojourn to Guadalcanal, despite visits to the region by officials as far away as Pearl Harbor and Washington, including tours by Chester Nimitz and General Hap Arnold, America's senior airman and a member of the Joint Chiefs. And through it all, Ghormley penned long letters to his wife, twice and sometimes thrice weekly, wherein he commiserated with her daily home-front grind, recorded his growing frustration with his mission, wrote of his increasing exhaustion, and, improbably and in great detail, described the emergence of a toothache.

Nimitz's trip to the South Pacific, from September 24 to October 5, was meant to bolster sagging morale and evaluate Ghormley. In a single ceremony he awarded twenty-three Navy Crosses, fourteen Distinguished Flying Crosses, and eleven Silver Stars. In meetings with the South Pacific commander and his staff aboard the *Argonne,* Nimitz posed pointed questions: Why were idle Army troops on New Caledonia not rushing to Henderson Field? Why had warships not more forcefully challenged nighttime Tokyo Express runs? How could a growing bottleneck of supply ships, destined for Guadalcanal but languishing in Nouméa's harbor, be alleviated? Hearing no satisfactory answers, Nimitz's confidence in Ghormley eroded further when, during his quick sojourn to Guadalcanal, Vandegrift told the Pacific Fleet commander, "Out here too many commanders have been far too leery about risking their ships." On October 15, back in Pearl Harbor, Nimitz received yet another glum dispatch from Nouméa, where,

Ghormley reported, Allied forces were "totally inadequate to meet" the impending Japanese assault on Henderson Field.[16]

At long last, that evening Nimitz concluded that Ghormley lacked the personality to rouse subordinates to the heroic measures now required. He asked King for permission to replace the South Pacific commander with Halsey, who was then at the front end of his South Pacific aerial orientation tour. It was a momentous proposition. In only one other instance during World War II was an American of equivalent rank relieved of combat command for cause, and Ghormley was a personal favorite of the president. But concerns about Ghormley had already extended beyond Nimitz. Hanson Baldwin of the *New York Times* had recently told Nimitz that the poor results in the Solomons stemmed from "overcaution" and identified Ghormley as "completely defeatist." Arnold had returned to Washington from his own trip to the South Pacific believing Ghormley had a "bad case of the jitters," the only solution being "new leaders who know and understand modern warfare; men who are aggressive and not afraid to fight their ships." Moreover, King and Nimitz had discussed Ghormley during their September San Francisco conference, and Nimitz had just days earlier sent King thirty-four verbatim transcript pages of the disquieting *Argonne* conferences. To Nimitz's request to trade Ghormley for Halsey, King replied promptly and simply: "Approved."[17]

While at Pearl Harbor, Halsey had gleaned hints of Nimitz's unease with Ghormley but he had no inkling of his impending task before reading Nimitz's dispatch upon landing in Nouméa on October 18. Nimitz had made a bold and not wholly logical choice. Halsey's known talents as a seagoing carrier commander were at a high premium, his skill for desk work was weak, and his aptitude for area command, serving ashore, was a complete mystery. By his own admission, the job put Halsey "back on my heels." He "knew nothing about campaigning with the Army, and much less with New Zealand and Australian" forces. Like most officers, he had little experience with combined or joint operations and, by virtue of a prewar career devoid of significant staff experience anywhere near Washington, had

less familiarity with Army officers than nearly every naval contemporary. Just days shy of his sixtieth birthday, Halsey had long
since established a command style predicated upon knowledge of the
tasks before him, and had perfected a brand of leadership resting
upon personal familiarity with those in his orbit. Neither circumstance would pertain in the vast South Pacific. At the time of his appointment, and over the many years that followed, Nimitz never told
Halsey why he had chosen him for the difficult task. Nimitz did, however, confide to his wife that Ghormley had been "too immersed in
detail and not sufficiently bold and aggressive at the right times," and
once told Ghormley's son that his father's "panicky and desperate"
dispatches had raised the ugly specter of a mental collapse. By impli-
cation, then, Nimitz perhaps believed Halsey would steer clear of
minutiae, his command would remain daring, and his leadership steady,
all reasonable bets. Only time could tell, however, whether Halsey
would also focus upon those few particulars of great consequence,
choose wisely moments of restraint amid aggressive action, and worry
when worry was right.[18]

. . . .

When he assumed command on October 18, Halsey confronted not
only the impending Japanese assault on Henderson Field that had so
unnerved Ghormley but also two simmering South Pacific issues demanding immediate focus: a long-planned occupation of Ndeni, an
island in the Santa Cruz group some 330 miles east of Guadalcanal,
where an airstrip could offer important cover for ongoing naval engagements; and a scheme to land Marine forces near Aola Bay, on the
Guadalcanal coast, behind enemy positions in an audacious attempt
to turn the Japanese lines. Turner and Vandegrift had sparred over the
plans for weeks, Turner advocating for each, Vandegrift pleading for
a single-minded focus on the defense of Henderson Field. Within days
of taking command, Halsey had canceled the Ndeni operation, freeing
the crack Eighth Marine Regiment for duty with Vandegrift, and had
placed in motion the Aola Bay landings, committing a scarce Marine
battalion, precious Army troops, and prized Navy construction engineers to the task. Canceling Ndeni was a brilliant stroke: the Eighth

Marines later proved crucial to the defense of Henderson Field. The Aola Bay operation was a disaster: the swampland there was utterly unsuited to airfield construction, making meaningless the efforts of so many Americans. Within days of his arrival in the South Pacific, then, Halsey had made one prescient and one pitiful command decision, a record suggesting something of the learning curve he now faced.

On October 23 Halsey summoned staff officers and commanders to the *Argonne*. The small assemblage included the two main American protagonists in the Guadalcanal fight, Turner and Vandegrift; Army Major Generals Millard Harmon and Alexander Patch, who were, respectively, the area's senior ground representative and the commander of the Americal Division, then performing garrison duty in New Caledonia; and Marine Brigadier General DeWitt Peck, the South Pacific war plans officer. It was Halsey's first collective look at the few senior subordinates with whom he would now toil.

He had known Kelly Turner tangentially and by reputation for years. Four years behind Halsey at Annapolis, Turner entered aviation in 1927 as a Johnny-come-lately but had left the air arm a decade later for service in battleships. Early in the war he was King's chief plans officer, and then in the South Pacific he essentially made up the Navy's first ship-to-shore doctrine on the fly. Like King, Turner had a razor-sharp mind, likened by many to a computer before that analogy was common, that made little allowance for lesser brains. He was parsimonious in praise, deficient in generosity, and devoid of magnetism. Already he had clashed repeatedly with Vandegrift, his nominal subordinate, over Guadalcanal operations. A binge drinker and probable alcoholic, he had by the fall of 1942 well earned his moniker, Terrible Turner. His biographer wrote that he was "greatly loved by some and greatly hated by others," but that was sympathetic. Most thought Kelly Turner was a brilliant son of a bitch.[19]

Halsey had met Vandegrift in the small prewar Navy Department, but did not know him well. A native Virginian, Vandegrift attended the University of Virginia for three years before earning a Marine commission in 1909 through a competitive examination. Nearly dismissed from the corps for disciplinary infractions as a young officer, he matured through assignments in Latin America and China and staff duty in Washington. Southern refinement and an understated sense of humor masked a ferocious determination. He resented Turner's meddling in ground operations on Guadalcanal, and encouraged more gripes among Marine grunts aimed at Turner than was perhaps wise. His Virginia roots, alma mater, and grasp of aviation made him a quick Halsey favorite, and ten weeks into the epic brawl for Guadalcanal, his steady leadership had already preordained the Medal of Honor he later received for the defense of Henderson Field.

Halsey knew neither Harmon nor Patch before the war. Harmon was an anomaly. An Army Air Forces pilot, he was a flier through and through and had before the war supported the Air Corps' independence from the ground Army. As Arnold's chief of staff in the war's first months, he impressed both Arnold and Marshall with a considered judgment and moderate personality. He was easily their consensus choice for the senior administrative Army post in the South Pacific, where Marshall needed the soldier to protect Army equities in the overwhelmingly naval theater and Arnold needed the airman to guard Air Forces interests. This made Harmon the Army Air Forces' senior officer serving overseas in a ground billet anywhere on the globe, and he deployed both tact and energy to infuse naval plans with a wider aperture. In contrast, Patch was more typically an Army general, but like so many of the new division commanders that filled a growing roster of slots, he was almost a complete unknown, even to many Army officers in the region.

Halsey's plans and operations officer, Marine Brigadier General DeWitt Peck, was a holdover from Ghormley's command. He had served in Shanghai before the war, where he established knowledge of and friendships with many Japanese officers, and, in the months following the Pearl Harbor attack, he had served in the Navy War Plans Division under Turner, his duties tending to add insight to Halsey's strategic calculations about the enemy in the South Pacific. All these men had toiled together over Guadalcanal for months before meeting Halsey as a group on October 23, when they craved the energy and feared the ignorance that sometimes accompany new commanders.

During the conference with Halsey, Vandegrift and Turner jostled over recent operations. The Marine relayed the challenges attendant on ten weeks of restricted diet, sleepless nights, incessant enemy attack, and the assault of nature: in the past seven days alone, 678 new cases of malaria had been diagnosed, and across October his Marines suffered a staggering illness rate of 2,500 per 1,000 per annum—meaning each man would average 2.5 attacks of debilitating illness per year. To compete for the island, he told Halsey, his depleted force required the bulk of the American Division then guarding New Caledonia, at least another regiment from the soon-to-arrive Second Marine Division, and more fighter and bomber support for Henderson Field. Vandegrift's litany was a direct critique of Turner, who protested that the Navy had done all it could to feed the troops ashore with a tight supply of transport and supply vessels, still fewer combat ships to protect them, no open water for evasive tactics, and an enemy presence that had transformed even modest supply runs to Guadalcanal into treacherous missions.[20]

Halsey believed that "what Kelly had said was of course true." It was, however, "also true that Guadalcanal *had* to be held." To him, the whole conversation "began to echo the question the public had asked in the panicked weeks following Pearl Harbor, 'Where is the Navy?'" After two hours of talk, Halsey, gray eyebrows bristling, abruptly asked Vandegrift, "Are we going to evacuate or hold?" The blunt query startled Vandegrift. "I can hold," he replied, "but I've got to have more active support than I have been getting." Halsey drummed the table with his fingers for a moment. "You go back there, Vandegrift. I promise you everything I have."[21]

The Marine returned to Guadalcanal as the enemy's feared October offensive commenced. After sunset on October 24 and amid a merciless rain, the Japanese launched a triphibious assault on Henderson Field. The worst of the ground attack crashed down upon the battalion of Lieutenant Colonel Chesty Puller, whose immortal reputation stemmed from these Guadalcanal nights. For hours, powder flashes alternated with jungle darkness in a mad menagerie, the Americans defending resolutely, the Japanese coming relentlessly, some breaching the Henderson defense perimeter. By dawn of October 25, Admiral Isoroku Yamamoto, who had planned the Pearl Harbor attack and whose position as the commander of the Combined Fleet made him a Japanese amalgam of King and Nimitz, believed that from his Combined Fleet anchorage at Truk a further push from the sea and a pull from the air would at last propel the Japanese across the runway. Carrier planes and a nine-ship bombardment force then raced to the scene, only to be stymied by a small band of Henderson pilots who sank one and wounded four of the marauding ships, leaving, as night came again, ground forces to reprise their night battle. In darkness the Japanese stormed the airfield in some of the most brutal and dense combat of the campaign. As morning broke on October 26, American deaths approached 100 but aggregate Japanese losses exceeded 3,000, comparable to the Allied tally for D-Day at Normandy later in the war. The effort produced easily the nearest thing to a breach of American defenses the Japanese had yet mustered, but at prohibitive cost, and all for a ramshackle airfield that would have been, even in good repair, the shame of even a small American city in 1942 had it been on its corporate outskirts.[22]

The fight then turned to the sea. Days earlier, Yamamoto had turned out Vice Admiral Nobutake Kondo and no fewer than nine embarked admirals, spread among three task forces totaling four carriers, four battleships, ten cruisers, twenty-five destroyers, and nearly 200 land-based airplanes, to annihilate any American ships approaching Guadalcanal. To parry this massive force, the largest yet arrayed in southern waters, Halsey, at the tail end of his inaugural week in command, first had the small collection of planes at Henderson, at the moment exhausted, eighty-five land-based warbirds at distant Espiritu Santo, the carrier *Hornet,* the battleship *Washington,* seven cruisers, and twelve destroyers organized into two task forces: Task Force Seventeen, the carrier group under the command of the *Enterprise*'s old skipper, now Rear Admiral George Murray, and Task Force Sixty-Four, a battleship group led by Rear Admiral Willis

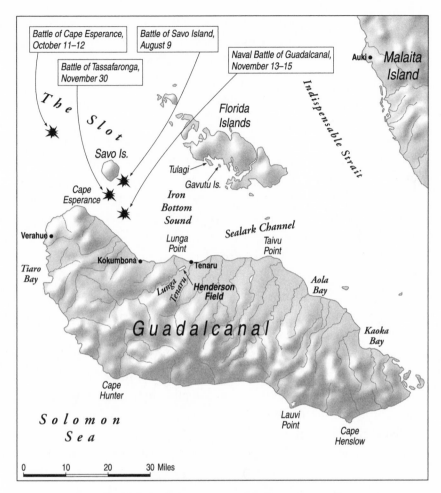

Battle of Cape Esperance,
October 11–12

Battle of Savo Island,
August 9

Battle of Tassafaronga,
November 30

Naval Battle of Guadalcanal,
November 13–15

Auki • *Malaita Island*

The Slot

Savo Is.

Florida Islands

Tulagi

Gavutu Is.

Cape Esperance

Iron Bottom Sound

Indispensable Strait

Verahue •

Sealark Channel

Lunga Point

Taivu Point

Kokumbona •

Tiaro Bay

• Tenaru

Lunga

Tenaru

Henderson Field

Aola Bay

Guadalcanal

Kaoka Bay

Cape Hunter

Solomon Sea

Lauvi Point

Cape Henslow

0   10   20   30 Miles

Guadalcanal, August 1942 to January 1943.

"Ching" Lee, one of the era's great battleship officers. As the battle drew near, Task Force Sixteen, under the command of Thomas Kinkaid and with the *Enterprise*, arrived following the *Enterprise*'s long convalescence at Pearl Harbor, augmenting Halsey's force by another carrier, a battleship, two cruisers, and seven destroyers. Though still outnumbered in every ship category, Halsey now warmed to his chances. From his considerable time in aviation since 1934, he had come to think that carrier strength "varies as the square—two carriers

are four times as powerful as one," because each flattop could concentrate in turn on strike, search, or defense in a manner difficult for
one carrier to accomplish simultaneously. "Until the *Enterprise* arrived," he remembered of these October preliminaries to what became
the Battle of the Santa Cruz Islands, "our plight had been nearly hopeless. Now we had a fighting chance."[23]

Leaving Lee's battleship group to the south to await opportunity,
on October 24, in a taut twenty-eight-word directive, Halsey ordered
Kinkaid's *Enterprise* and Murray's *Hornet* to make a daring sweep
north of the Santa Cruz Islands and east of the Solomons, the farthest
north that American carriers had ventured since August and within
range of land-based Japanese aircraft, before meandering to the southwest, where they would slip beyond the range of enemy pilots but
could still hit the flanks of any Imperial Navy strike at Guadalcanal.
This bold thrust and dilatory withdrawal struck one latter-day observer
as a "dangerous, foolhardy gesture," but it suggested to Yamamoto
a potential trap, and the Japanese temporized for a moment. Both
sides embraced the fight soon enough, however. Near midnight, after
surveying intelligence reports, Halsey concluded that action was now
"obviously a matter of hours." He radioed a dispatch to Kinkaid and
Murray that directed, simply, "Attack, Repeat, Attack," leaving, as he
recalled, "the rest in their hands."[24]

Perhaps not even William Sims would have been as succinct. Halsey's
inclination toward sparse instruction had reached an apogee. After
weeks of hesitancy under Ghormley, Halsey's assurance reverberated
through the South Pacific Force. Vandegrift believed the message "inspired us all by its aggressive brevity," and a historian wrote that the
order, "bereft of any operational specificity or doctrinal nuance and
apropos of no particular target," nonetheless placed a "clean vector
through everyone's mind that ordered their next moves." Aboard the
Argonne, having placed his ships upon the sea as best he could, Halsey
retreated into his cabin, paged through a dime-store detective novel,
and tried, without success, to sleep.[25]

Eight hundred miles to the north, Kinkaid and Murray sprang to
action. Kinkaid, the tactical officer in charge, represented a study in

contrasts when compared to Halsey. After graduating from Annapolis in 1908, an emotionally rich marriage and a genuine enjoyment of staff work kept Kinkaid ashore in the prewar decades. When he reached flag rank in the summer of 1941, he had fewer years at sea than any line officer from his class and had served a paltry two years in command. Admiral Husband Kimmel's brother-in-law, Kinkaid was a cruiser division skipper in the war's early months, escorting carrier task forces under Wilson Brown, and he believed the Navy's retreat from Wake in the war's first weeks and Brown's hesitation at Rabaul in February had been sound, given the circumstances at the time. He became the *Enterprise* task force commander after the Battle of Midway, when Spruance left to become Nimitz's chief of staff, and would have returned the carrier to Halsey had Nimitz not sacked Ghormley. That he, and not a naval aviator such as Murray, now had charge of two flattops revealed the Navy's devotion to seniority and bespoke the unfinished efforts to promote aviators to flag rank and give them command of carrier operations.

Kinkaid and Murray would need the initiative to overcome a 136 to 199 deficiency in aircraft. The Americans and the Japanese did not spot each other on October 25, but the following morning each found their prey. A daring American scout hit the *Zuiho* at 7:40 AM, destroying the carrier's arresting gear, rendering her useless, and forcing her retreat from the battle before it had begun. Within the hour, 75 U.S. and 110 Imperial planes were flying reciprocal courses, sometimes within visual distance of each other. Japanese pilots found the *Hornet* at 8:55, the crowded sky masking their approach from American radar. Slashing their way through an unsuspecting combat air patrol, in a span of twenty minutes they ruined the carrier's flight deck, gashed her hull, and smashed her superstructure, leaving the flattop that had delivered Doolittle's raiders to Tokyo earlier that spring aflame, flooded, without power or propulsion, and soon to be abandoned. A mere ten miles distant, only a passing rain squall saved the *Enterprise* from a similar fate.

At 9:15 AM American fliers reached the *Shokaku* and *Zuikaku*. A group of *Hornet* fliers hit the *Shokaku*, veteran of the Pearl Harbor attack. By 9:30, her flight deck was ruptured, her hangar deck was aflame, and, like the *Zuiho* before her, she lay utterly incapable of further combat operations. Although the *Zuikaku* escaped significant damage, pilots found the cruiser *Chikuma*, inflicted severe damage, and sent her, too, into full retreat.

Back in the American sector, rain had abandoned the *Enterprise*. Shortly after 10:00 AM, another Japanese strike plunked bombs through her flight deck, damaged her superstructure, and immobilized her forward elevator, greatly reducing the ship's effectiveness. They also damaged the destroyer *Smith* and the cruiser *San Juan* and ruined the forward sixteen-inch gun turret on the battleship *South Dakota*. Through it all, the *Enterprise* fighter direction control had been awful, relaying to defending American pilots incorrect velocities, vectors, and altitudes of Japanese planes. Days earlier, Halsey's request for members of his former staff had culled from the carrier a cadre of experienced communications experts, most especially Leonard Dow. Given the swarm of enemy planes striking the *Enterprise* that morning, some damage to the flattop was likely, but Halsey's drain of experienced men had surely increased the vulnerability of his favorite fighting ship. "The fighter direction during the battle," a defensive Halsey later wrote Nimitz, "was apparently not all that could be desired." Halsey had "debated a long time" before ordering Dow from the *Enterprise,* and he did so in part because the former head of the Navy's communication school was by happenstance on the carrier and able to take Dow's place. "This is not an alibi," Halsey meekly concluded, but "merely to give you my reason in the matter."[26]

The violent morning then gave way to a stalking Japanese hunt to finish the crippled *Hornet*. The damaged *Enterprise* took aboard what planes she could, and near 1:30 PM Kinkaid, as the senior officer afloat, turned his carrier and her consorts to the southeast, putting water between them and the Japanese, leaving the *Hornet* to her fate, which she met, almost mercilessly, shortly after midnight, when the last of her slipped beneath the waves. Kinkaid was later criticized for this retreat, but at the time he knew the *Hornet* was unable to fight, he did not yet know the extent of damage to his *Enterprise*—the only

American carrier now moving under her own power in the entire Pacific—and he believed, correctly, that the Japanese retained a superior force, including undamaged carriers.

The harried morning had found Halsey pacing the *Argonne,* disquieted in his inaugural role as bystander. Snippets of information dribbled his way. At midmorning, and already through his first pack of cigarettes, a dispatch informed him, "*Hornet* hurt." In the early afternoon, well into his second pack of smokes, Halsey learned Kinkaid had retired, his *Enterprise* "unable to give *Hornet* fighter coverage." A little later this unsettling news arrived: "*Hornet* in tow. No aircraft." Along the way, vague reports suggested something of the American air attacks on the Japanese carriers, but definitive news on that score was at least twenty-four hours away.[27]

Throughout the day, habit and training overcame the desire to seek the comfort of participation. Halsey remained mute in the face of most dispatches, even as Nimitz chimed in from Pearl Harbor with suggestions, and only sometimes did Halsey send simple radio acknowledgments. The battle was properly in Kinkaid's hands. Eventually Halsey learned more of the drama and sorrow of the morning, including the loss of his son's best friend aboard the *Smith,* a Navy junior who as a child had many times taken dinner at Halsey's table. But only at 3:00 PM did Halsey issue an action directive, authorizing a general withdrawal from the battle, a dispatch that did little but confirm what Kinkaid had ninety minutes earlier put into effect. Later, he told Nimitz that Kinkaid had been too cautious launching search patrols and had kept his speed and heading too long in a misguided effort to help returning *Enterprise* pilots at unnecessary risk to the ship, and concluded that Kinkaid needed a rest. But Kinkaid, in his debut as tactical officer in charge during a battle, had plunged headlong into a hornet's nest and had retired only after he was left with the sole remaining American carrier in the Pacific Fleet.[28]

Had he known it then, Halsey would have warmed to Japan's air losses. Against an American tally of eighty-one planes and twenty-six aircrew lost, the ferocious Japanese strikes had cost the Imperial Navy ninety-nine aircraft and a whopping 148 aircrew, including two dive-bomber group leaders, three torpedo squadron leaders, and eighteen other section or flight leaders. Forty-nine percent of the Japanese dive-bomber crew members were killed, along with 39 percent of the torpedo bomber crews and 20 percent of the fighter pilots. In fact, the Japanese lost more aircrew at the Battle of the Santa Cruz Islands than they had in the war's three previous carrier battles—Coral Sea, where they lost 90; Midway, which cost them 110; or the Eastern Solomons, where the tax was 61. By the end of the battle, at least 409 of the 765 elite carrier aviators who had attacked Pearl Harbor less than a year earlier were dead. Worse, Japan had no sustained way to make up the loss. Although no ships flying the Rising Sun had sunk in the battle, the *Zuiho* would not return to action until late January, the *Shokaku* would not return until the following summer, and aircrew loss caused the two undamaged flattops to retreat to Japan, idled for months. Certainly, American losses were also severe: a precious carrier and a destroyer sank, with heavy damage to another carrier and two additional destroyers, meaning that for weeks thereafter Halsey would have only the wounded *Enterprise* as a flattop if the Japanese pressed another attack. But when the Battle of the Santa Cruz Islands ended, it was not Halsey who found himself relieved of command but Chuichi Nagumo, who had led the Japanese carriers. Later, Nagumo acknowledged that the battle had been "a tactical win, but a shattering strategic loss for Japan. Considering the great superiority of our enemy's industrial capacity, we must win every battle overwhelmingly."[29]

Halsey deduced Japanese losses soon enough. In an extended letter to Nimitz on October 31, the first of dozens he penned across the next eighteen months, Halsey suggested something of the battle's favorable exchange of aircraft and pilots, surmised the de facto loss of Japanese carriers for some considerable time, and vowed to return his ships, including his sentimental favorite, the *Enterprise,* promptly to the fight. He would "patch up what we have and go with them," he told Nimitz. "I will not send any ship back to Pearl Harbor unless it is absolutely necessary. This may mean operating the *Enterprise* with a slightly reduced complement of planes and under difficulties, but under the present circumstances, a half a ship is better than none."[30]

Two weeks into his new job, Halsey had spied a design in enemy operations. "I have about reached the conclusion that the yellow bastards have been playing us for suckers," he told Nimitz. The Japanese "pattern of attack has been practically the same" during each of the four major naval engagements in Solomon waters since early August. A scouting force of cruisers and sometimes battleships, generally approaching Guadalcanal from the northeast, would clear a path for a main force of cruisers, destroyers, transports, and supply vessels, approaching from the northwest, while a strike force of carriers and their consorts would lurk farther to the east, north of the Santa Cruz Islands, eager to pounce on any American ships arriving to block the main force. In this manner, Halsey believed, the Japanese "have sucked us out beyond the easy reach of our shore based aircraft and are willing to play attrition tactics with us."[31]

This assessment guessed incorrectly about enemy intentions, which centered consistently on seeking decisive battle, but it got their particulars right. The Japanese tended toward dispersed, multipronged thrusts to land supplies on Guadalcanal, and they often aimed to lure American ships beyond the range of aircraft flying from either Guadalcanal or Espiritu Santo, whose airfields constituted the one indisputable American advantage in the lower Solomons, and into the orbit of waiting Japanese carriers, of which Japan still had more. In the future, aided by an intelligence advantage derived from long-range search planes, coast watchers on surrounding islands, and signal intercepts that usually gave the Americans two to three days' notice of an approaching Japanese force, Halsey told Nimitz he intended "to keep my forces, particularly carriers" farther from Guadalcanal and closer to Espiritu Santo, to make the Japanese "come to us." When that certain eventuality next arrived, Halsey would close quickly on Guadalcanal and "begin counter punching" much like a boxer in a close brawl, with a powerful combination of shore- and carrier-based aircraft, destroyers, and cruisers.[32]

This approach heralded a renewed emphasis on surface fighting. Thus far in the war, carrier operations had dominated the contest and had relegated cruisers and destroyers and what few battleships there were to roles as mere adjuncts, as Ray Spruance's experiences with the *Northampton* alongside Halsey's *Enterprise* in the war's first months had made manifest. As a result, American surface ships had lost their independent fighting edge. Through September, six of the seven Allied cruisers that had fought Japanese ships muzzle to muzzle had sunk, and destroyers had become more adept at submarine hunting than high-speed torpedo runs. In the South Pacific, Halsey had already surmised among destroyers a general "reluctance to illuminate and engage" the enemy, and his chosen strategy would require something more. As a good disciple of Sims, he meant to get it.[33]

Promising an informal letter at least once a week, Halsey concluded this first note to Nimitz: "I was completely taken aback when I received your orders on my arrival here. I took over a strange job with a strange staff and I had to begin throwing punches almost immediately." Still, Halsey and his officers were "not the least downhearted or upset by our difficulties, but obsessed with one idea only, to kill the yellow bastards." Six days later, he reiterated this sentiment, telling Nimitz his occasional "growls and grouches" that had already appeared in message traffic were merely "the privileges of an old sailorman. We are not in the least downhearted and are going to continue to knock hell out of the yellow bastards."[34]

These letters heartened Nimitz. He recited parts of the first to his staff and remarked in its margins, "This is the spirit desired." He sent the second on to King in Washington: "I am sending to you, for your personal use, Halsey's personal letter of November 6th to me, which I think you will enjoy reading." To Nimitz and King, Halsey's nerve and headlong thrust at Santa Cruz, as costly as it had been, had "more than justified" the decision to switch South Pacific commanders. There was, of course, much more to accomplish in the South Pacific. The end was neither foreordained nor, for that matter, anywhere in sight. But there was now belief that the Americans had placed the right man, at the right time, in the right place.[35]

Chapter Ten

The Thin Red Line

THE EXHAUSTING OCTOBER battles forced an interlude. Japan relented, briefly, and the Allies replenished. Concurrent with Ghormley's relief at midmonth, Nimitz had urged Washington officials to rush men and materials "not now in sight" to the Solomons as a "matter of national security." On October 24, 1942, the president chimed in, expressing "anxiety" over Guadalcanal's plight and directing the diversion of all possible resources to the region, especially air power, even at the expense of prior commitments to England if necessary. The Navy and Army then pushed over 400 planes toward the region; Ernest King ordered a battleship, six cruisers, a pair of destroyers, some two dozen submarines, and nearly fifty cargo and transport hulls to follow; and Marshall identified the Twenty-Fifth Division, then in Hawaii and slated for MacArthur's zone, for potential diversion. It would take time for these forces to reach station, but they were now in sight. When Nimitz asked Halsey what more he could do, Halsey simply thanked him for "sending everything," a sentiment surely never shared by Ghormley during his time in Nouméa.[1]

This flood tide exacerbated a burgeoning logistics mess in the South Pacific. The nearest major harbor, at Auckland, was distant enough to render it "as much use as last year's bird nest," Halsey told Nimitz, and the remote destinations, austere ports, and voracious appetite of battle created a bottleneck nearer the fight. At one point that fall in Nouméa's small port, where before the war perhaps a handful of medium-sized vessels came and went each week, ninety-one ships lay waiting for transshipment, eighty-three of them holding needed provisions for Guadalcanal. At times, Halsey had as few as four cargo vessels free of logjams. Up the line, serious materiel shortages were ubiquitous, and there were days when lack of fuel all but halted air operations from Henderson Field. This shipping crisis had global ramifications at a time when a huge armada was also committed to the invasion of North Africa, and as the situation festered the president and the Joint Chiefs expressed dismay that a fair portion of the nation's merchant marine bobbed in a watery queue at a tiny French port in the middle of nowhere.

This prompted Nimitz to lend to Halsey Rear Admiral William Calhoun, the Pacific Fleet's senior logistician. A great-grandson of Vice President John C. Calhoun, Admiral Calhoun arrived in Nouméa to find supply methods "as primitive as Robinson Crusoe" had used. Forsaking Auckland as a major supply port and developing the facilities at Nouméa paid swift dividends. The monthly discharge of cargo at Nouméa jumped nearly fourfold from November to December, from 34,327 tons to 126,216 tons, a miracle prompting Halsey to declare that logistics in Nouméa had been accomplished "by guess and by God" before Calhoun appeared, but had now become a "smooth running organization." It was not that quite yet, and it would take time to unravel the massive logistics knot, build port facilities, and untangle very different Army, Navy, and Marine supply organizations. But Calhoun had made a very good start.[2]

The lack of an imminent Japanese assault on Henderson Field also laid bare the fault lines between the South and Southwest Pacific areas. These were the consequence of a divided Pacific command structure as well as nearly inbred differences between Army officers, accustomed to ground campaigns upon continents, and Navy men, inclined to view warfare across vast oceans. Yet, fighting in the Solomon Islands was neither continental in scale nor oceanic in scope. The men charged with operations there confronted instead a war in the littorals, upon a canvas equal parts land, sea, and air, and focused, while the Guadalcanal campaign raged, on an airfield a bit larger than New York City's Central Park. Groping for a kind of war few anticipated, sailors often felt it was "very difficult to interest the Army in the war in the Pacific," as Nimitz's command diarist put it, while soldiers believed, to paraphrase MacArthur, that their brethren on the quarterdeck could see nothing beyond the fabled broadsides of a Mahanian clash. These worldviews collided in the South Pacific, becoming manifest in the types of warfare that most often crossed command seams: submarine and air operations.[3]

By the fall of 1942 the American submarine war emanated from three unequal commands: one at Pearl Harbor, controlled by Nimitz, and two in Australia, at Freemantle on the far side of the continent, controlled by MacArthur, and at Brisbane along the near coast, whose boats were often but not always controlled by Halsey even though they homeported in MacArthur's zone. Over time, the Pearl Harbor and Freemantle commands became proxies through which Nimitz and MacArthur sparred, becoming "independent rival organizations, competing for Japanese shipping rather than cooperating," and in the middle, the Brisbane command became nearly a "unique" task force subject to Halsey's and MacArthur's sometimes competing directives. As a result, submarine leaders in Honolulu, Freemantle, and Brisbane sometimes spent more energy "bellyaching" and trading "petulant letters" between themselves than they did concentrating on the enemy, a level of infighting that contributed to ineffectual South Pacific submarine patrols across the entire campaign. Of Brisbane's twenty-four patrols in the last months of 1942, eighteen went through Solomon waters, where they hunted with little success the many Japanese ships then engaged in the Guadalcanal fight, in stark contrast to the stunning success Japanese submariners had had in nearby locales such as Torpedo Junction.[4]

Similar organizational muddles marred the air war. In the summer of 1942 there were nearly 3,000 Allied aircraft of all kinds in the Pacific, twice the roughly 1,500 Japanese warbirds throughout the same region. But service jealousies conspired with other factors to constrain these planes deep within either Nimitz's Central Pacific or MacArthur's Southwest Pacific boundaries. At one point, over 2,100 of 2,400 land-based fighters and bombers were based either in Hawaii or in Australia—many, particularly those in Hawaii, far from the front lines. Fewer than 200 were on New Caledonia or South Pacific airfields closer to Guadalcanal, where they could do more immediate good but where the exigencies of battle might siphon them between theaters, in one direction or the other, into the orbit of Nimitz or MacArthur.[5]

This paucity made Halsey a chronic supplicant for air support. Until more planes arrived in larger numbers, he and Harmon repeatedly implored Washington officials for additional aircraft, especially in the form of B-17 heavy bombers and P-38 fighters. Although most of these requests "foundered on the hard rock of prior commitments," South Pacific commanders won two concessions: permission to divert a handful of heavy bombers destined for MacArthur, a license airmen in Australia resented, and a small allotment of P-38s from Washington coffers, an allowance that earned for Harmon the ire of Arnold, who did not wish to send the planes to the South Pacific but was forced to after Harmon had "shouted to high heaven until every brass hat in Washington heard the echo."[6]

These modest adjustments still left Halsey short of operational requirements for some time. From MacArthur he routinely solicited aid from the Southwest Pacific's Fifth Air Force, for many months the best-resourced air unit within range of Rabaul. Across four days in late October and two days in mid-November, for instance, Halsey made six separate requests for bombing strikes against Rabaul, its Simpson Harbor, and enemy vessels at sea. The Fifth Air Force commander, Major General George Kenney, met these requests when he could but viewed MacArthur's own ground campaign in New Guinea as his first obligation. "There was," he believed, "no use talking about playing across the street until we got the Nips off our front lawn." When he did support South Pacific operations, Kenney tended to exaggerate results, crediting one late October and another early December raid with sinking four ships and leaving another dozen ablaze, results improbable to the point of impossible with the paltry twelve bombers devoted to each mission but impressive enough to help Kenney earn his turn on the cover of *Time* in January 1943. Across the span of some months, South Pacific officers came to believe Kenney "was a cocky guy," and Halsey took to collecting the airman's operational claims in a special leather dossier, sending copies to Navy Department officials in Washington without comment but with clear meaning.[7]

For his part, Halsey could be parsimonious in his own support for MacArthur's fighting, especially when it involved warships, which the admiral had in greater supply than the general, whose Seventh Fleet that fall consisted of as few as four cruisers, eight destroyers, seven shallow draft patrol boats, and twenty submarines, some shared with Halsey. MacArthur had gamely defended Port Moresby, the linchpin to Allied presence in Papua New Guinea, from sustained Japanese attacks since late summer, and in November he attacked the Japanese rearguard at Buna and Gona in a daring scheme to envelop the enemy. But when that battle devolved into a stalemate every bit the match of Guadalcanal in death, disease, and despair, MacArthur asked Halsey for ships necessary to aid his flailing offensive. Yet Halsey proffered only a handful of patrol boats, suggesting instead that MacArthur mount a defense while the Allies concentrated in Halsey's sector. "My greater contribution to our common effort," he told the general, "would be to strengthen my position and resume our advance up the Solomons as soon as possible."[8]

MacArthur coldly thanked Halsey for his opinion and bitterly told Marshall the bifurcated command arrangement in the region mocked "the basic and fundamental principles of the art of war." Gona fell to Allied forces in December and Buna followed in January, but at horrible cost: the Allied casualty rate exceeded that at Guadalcanal, and the American Thirty-Second Division required a full year's recuperation. Buna and Gona are widely seen as MacArthur's low ebb during the war, his command there "reminiscent of the worst generalship of the First World War." But Morison, not often sympathetic to the Army general, wrote that the battle had been fought "within sight and smell of the sea," and that "the main reason for this heavy price in life and suffering was the want of Allied sea power." For that, King and Nimitz, who had limited Seventh Fleet assets in the first instance, and Halsey, who had tendered but tightfisted aid in the second instance, must together shoulder some burden.[9]

. . . .

Fortunately for the Allies, the Japanese command structure in the South Pacific exceeded American defects. Their division of the area between Papua New Guinea and the Solomons, with the Army responsible for the former and the Navy in charge of the latter—though each not exclusively so—was worse than the American split. At Rabaul, debate between Japanese Army and Navy officials routinely hampered the smooth execution of operations, and Yamamoto's decision to retain the bulk of the Combined Fleet some distance away at Truk further complicated the flow of orders and directives. In the lower Solomons, this meant Japanese commanders were often responsible to multiple superiors; Rear Admiral Raizo Tanaka, the primary force behind the intrepid Tokyo Express, was at times subject to orders from the Combined Fleet, the Eleventh Air Fleet, and the Eighth Fleet, a circumstance he found "confusing at best" and, when directives were incompatible, "confounding at worst."[10]

Still, the imperative to fight was as strong among the Japanese as it was among the Americans, and even the emperor pined for the recapture of Guadalcanal. So by the end of October Japan laid plans for yet another midmonth onslaught in November. Across the first fortnight in November, it brought a steady stream of supplies and men to the island, harnessed 220 land-based aircraft for the effort, and quickened development of an airfield at Munda Point on New Georgia Island to mitigate the advantage of proximity American pilots enjoyed in the skies above Guadalcanal, all of which propelled, in the undulating pattern of the campaign, Japanese strength in the region to yet another peak.

On November 8 and 9 Halsey set foot on Guadalcanal for the first time. With Vandegrift, he surveyed the Marines' tiny domain, an area yet to reach beyond the immediate confines of the Henderson complex and still, in its entirety, within range of Japanese field guns. His appointment as South Pacific commander three weeks earlier had been met by whoops, hollers, and, quite literally, somersaults among the Guadalcanal rank and file, and now his "personal magnetism brightened the scene wherever he went, which was about everywhere," recalled Colonel Merrill Twining, Vandegrift's operations officer. Vandegrift added that the visit was a "wonderful breath of fresh air" for his troops and an eye-opener for Halsey, who "talked to a large number of Marines, saw their gaunt, malaria-ridden bodies, their faces lined from what seemed a nightmare of years." Halsey listened carefully to Twining's explanation of operations, and asked "very sensible questions as to why we were doing what we were doing." The visit marked the first time Halsey came under enemy attack on land, in the form of a midnight destroyer salvo, and was the first time he saw dead Japanese, which, he was soon fond of saying, were the only "really good Japs, a spectacle equaled only by the Bay of Naples or the Grand Canyon." The short trip beyond the cramped *Argonne* had provided the kind of tactical, visceral experience Halsey had always valued over cerebral assessments, and he returned to New Caledonia resolved to press the fight and, as soon as possible, find relief for Vandegrift's weary First Marines.[11]

At midmonth the next major Japanese assault arrived. At that moment, each antagonist mustered about 30,000 soldiers on Guadalcanal, although the Americans were healthier. To swing the advantage to the Japanese, Yamamoto had gathered eleven transports to carry 7,000 men of the veteran Thirty-Eighth Infantry Division to the island, spearheading the convoy with the most Japanese power the South Pacific would ever see: Vice Admiral Hiroaki Abe's battleships *Hiei* and *Kirishima,* a cruiser, and fourteen destroyers as close escort; the carrier *Junyo,* three escort flattops, four battleships, twelve cruisers, and fifty-four destroyers steaming in reserve; and over one hundred planes of the Eleventh Air Fleet on hair-trigger alert on Bougainville airfields. Abe's force planned to reach Guadalcanal near midnight on November 12, bombard Henderson Field into ruin, and pave a path for the transports the following day. Only a large fleet carrier force, made impossible by their Santa Cruz losses, was missing in the gathering Japanese constellation.[12]

For nearly a week Halsey had been aware of these preparations through an astonishing ability to decode enemy radio traffic. In addition to Vandegrift's defenders, he had about sixty planes at Henderson Field, a complex that by then included the original runway and two nearby auxiliary airstrips, and could count on perhaps thirty-five Army bombers from Espiritu Santo to pitch in and, possibly for short bursts in an emergency, carrier planes from the *Enterprise,* then in Nouméa undergoing repairs to damage suffered at Santa Cruz. On November 4, elements of the Eighth Marine Regiment, previously slated for the Ndeni operation, had also reached the island, providing desperately needed fresh men. But at sea Halsey was still seriously outgunned, especially after the Battle of the Santa Cruz Islands had cost him the *Hornet* and before the first wave of reinforcements from outside the region arrived. In deference to the *Enterprise*'s wounds, he held in reserve his old Task Force Sixteen, consisting of the battered flattop; the battleships *South Dakota* and *Washington;* the cruisers *Pensacola, Northampton,* and *San Diego;* and six destroyers. He gave nearly everything else he had to Kelly Turner, with orders to rush perhaps another 5,500 reinforcements, scraped together from other locales, to Guadalcanal to counter Yamamoto's additions.

In contrast to Halsey's sparse missives, Turner issued an eleven-part order, augmented by a five-part addendum, stretching across five typescript pages. He divided the bulk of his forces into two unequal groups to escort the troop convoy of half a dozen ships. One was composed of the cruiser *Atlanta* and three destroyers under the command of Rear Admiral Norman Scott, and the other of the cruisers *San Francisco, Portland, Helena,* and *Juneau* as well as ten destroyers under Turner's own command and that of Rear Admiral Dan Callaghan. These task forces traced different routes to Guadalcanal, were harried along the way by air attack, and had by the morning of November 12 delivered their human cargo to Henderson Field amid a ferocious air battle above, beating the planned arrival of Japanese reinforcements by twenty-four hours. Combined Fleet officers surmised that Turner's ships would "stick around" for the day but "go away as usual" at dusk, leaving darkness to the ships of the Rising Sun in a pattern consistent with the three-month campaign. But the Americans now chose a bolder course. Turner retreated with most of his supply ships to Espiritu Santo and directed a pickup force to block Abe's approaching ships: five cruisers and eight destroyers, embarking both Scott in the *Atlanta* and Callaghan in the *San Francisco*.[13]

It was not much in the face of the enemy. Abe's task force had operated together on numerous occasions, enjoyed a considerable night-fighting advantage, entered the fray arrayed in two fluid columns, and could fire a broadside five times more potent than that of the American line. In contrast, the American vessels had neither trained as a group nor sortied together to the fight. Moreover, custom had placed the senior but inexperienced Callaghan, among the best-liked admirals in the Navy, in command in lieu of Scott, who another remembered was "kind of like a junior Halsey." He "had balls. He was smart. And he was shrewd." Callaghan had recently registered a lackluster few months as Ghormley's chief of staff, while Scott had drilled his *Atlanta* force mercilessly in night operations and had laid claim in the October Battle of Cape Esperance as the Navy's only successful surface force commander against Japan. For the coming fight, the inexperienced Callaghan then deployed his vessels in a rigid column reminiscent of an eighteenth-century set-piece clash, rendering Scott and his *Atlanta* mere supernumeraries of the line. When the Americans entered the early darkness of August 12, a *San Francisco* deck officer remarked that the mission against such a superior force was tantamount to suicide. "Yes, I know," Callaghan replied. "But we have to do it."[14]

The battle was brutal. Shortly after midnight the two antagonists steamed into the confined waters between Guadalcanal and Savo from opposite directions. Callaghan's initial directives confused subordinates, giving the Japanese the jump and transforming the contest, in the words of one American skipper, into "a barroom brawl after the lights had been shot out," precisely the sort of scrap favoring the more agile fleet. In the chaos, the *San Francisco* shelled the *Atlanta*, before itself coming under ferocious attack by a swarm of Japanese destroyers, so close abeam that the American cruiser could not depress her guns enough to strike back. Within forty minutes, two American destroyers lay on the bottom while three more destroyers and two powerful cruisers limped from the scene, nearly incapacitated. The Americans had managed to damage the *Hiei* and sink one destroyer and injure another, but U.S. material losses were the greater and the human ledger favored the Japanese as well, partly because both Callaghan and Scott had perished, the only time in the war two American flag officers died at sea in the same action, in this case just minutes apart, and Scott in all probability by friendly fire.[15]

Incredibly, the victors then undermined their tactical advantage. At about 2:30 AM Abe, unnerved by the ferocious battle, fled, forsaking his primary objective, the bombardment of Henderson Field. This forced Yamamoto to delay the transports steaming toward the island and some days later to relieve Abe, a humiliation from which Abe never recovered and a recompense, in part, for the lives of two U.S. admirals and so many others.

Through most of it Halsey had paced the *Argonne*. "We had little to no sleep that night," he remembered. Bits of information indicated a ferocious battle had taken place, but nothing else. "The waiting was hard, as usual. I walked the decks, re-examined reports and charts, and conferred with my staff. I must have drunk a gallon of coffee and smoked two packs of cigarettes. When the tension became unbearable, I skimmed through the trashiest magazine I could find." It was midmorning before dispatches told of grievous American losses and suggested the deaths of Callaghan and Scott, the latter, in Halsey's view, "the fightingest flag officer" in the South Pacific. When it was confirmed later that day, Scott's death hit hard. "I had known and loved Norm Scott for years," Halsey later wrote. "His death was the greatest personal sorrow that beset me in the whole war."[16]

By the evening, Halsey knew as well the battle's broader aftermath. Henderson pilots had found and sunk the injured *Hiei*, *Atlanta* had succumbed to her wounds, and an enemy submarine had literally blasted the cruiser *Juneau* from the water, taking the great bulk of her crew, including five brothers from the same Sullivan family, to their watery graves. To a fellow World War I destroyer skipper, Halsey reported that the battle's intensity had been "almost unbelievable." As he wondered if such a mortal investment could pay sufficient dividends, he learned that Captain Gilbert Hoover of the *Helena* had cut short a search for *Juneau* survivors. Incensed, he summarily relieved Hoover of command, although he later found reason in Hoover's action and concluded, after the war, that he had made a "grievous mistake." Hoover, holder of three Navy Crosses, never overcame the stigma of the wartime dismissal, however, and the episode revealed that Halsey had not yet become accustomed to the more deliberative knack sometimes required for command far from the heat of battle.[17]

The day's seesaw had been, in Samuel Morison's words, "the wildest, most desperate sea fight since Jutland." It was a battle, Richard Frank added, that stood "without peer for furious, close-range, and confused fighting during the war." Yet it had purchased exactly one day's reprieve for Henderson Field. Yamamoto retained his massive reserves, including most of the Combined Fleet at Truk, and remained committed to landing major Japanese reinforcements. On the forenoon of Friday, November 13, he reset plans for the following day, sending Vice Admiral Gunichi Mikawa with six cruisers and six destroyers to accomplish the nighttime bombardment Abe had abandoned; directing Vice Admiral Nobutake Kondo to use the battleship *Kirishima,* four cruisers, and nine destroyers to sweep Iron Bottom Sound and confront the remnants of the battered American fleet; and readying again Tanaka's eleven packed transports for a sprint toward Guadalcanal.[18]

To dissuade Yamamoto, Halsey primarily had the *Enterprise* task force now at sea in reserve near Nouméa, clear of the lurking dangers within Torpedo Junction. Well over a hundred repairmen still clambered on these ships. The *South Dakota*'s number one turret remained useless from damage suffered at Santa Cruz, and the carrier's continuing maladies included an inoperable deck elevator and a hull that leaked oil like a sieve. On November 14, Halsey ordered the flattop to close within range of Guadalcanal and dispatched Rear Admiral Willis Lee, with the *South Dakota, Washington,* and four destroyers, into the narrow waters near Savo to confront Kondo.

This decision flouted orthodoxy by committing capital ships to constricted waters, negating the powerful reach of their big guns and rendering them vulnerable to the torpedoes of an enemy skilled in night fighting. Halsey knew this, but made his decision instinctively. He held no dictum of warfare more firmly than Lord Horatio Nelson's exhortation before the Battle of Trafalgar, learned so long ago as part of Sims's destroyer flotilla: "No Captain can do very wrong if he places his Ship alongside that of an Enemy." To now do anything less, Halsey believed, would riddle the morale of his whole command, especially the tenacious and exhausted Marines of Guadalcanal. Besides, he had been sent to the South Pacific to fight, and there was at the moment no reasonable alternative.[19]

Halsey's scheme to transit Torpedo Junction only when necessary now worked against him. Neither Kinkaid nor Lee reached Savo Sound before Mikawa's cruiser bombardment shortly after midnight on November 14, when nearly 1,000 eight-inch shells slammed into the Marine encampment, wreaking havoc but, in a seeming miracle, mostly missing Henderson's runways. Believing the raid had destroyed the airstrip, Tanaka's transports then began the day's dash south to Guadalcanal. They learned differently shortly after noon, when the first of seven separate Henderson and *Enterprise* air attacks appeared overhead. In one of the Pacific War's most spectacular aerial strikes, the U.S. fliers sank one cruiser and six transports, damaged others, and forced nearly 5,000 Japanese soldiers onto destroyers. Of the twenty-three vessels that had formed a tight formation that morning, by early evening Tanaka had nine. Halsey described the day to Nimitz as "a dive and torpedo bomber paradise," and the strikes underscored the importance of local air superiority and the abiding advantage Henderson Field, a de facto unsinkable carrier, had given the Americans over many weeks of fighting. Tanaka's dogged direction of the Tokyo Express had kept the Japanese on Guadalcanal tethered to their supply lines, but days such as November 14 were enough to sap resolution from even the stoutest Imperial determination.[20]

For Yamamoto, the arrival of Lee's battleships offered a chance to retrieve something from this emerging catastrophe. He ordered Kondo's warships south into the breach, along with the four undamaged transports from Tanaka's convoy. Between Guadalcanal and Savo Island, Lee waited with his improvised force. The damaged *South Dakota* and the *Washington* had never before maneuvered together, the four destroyers came from different divisions, and Lee operated without prepared plans. Yet he proved as adept as Halsey at sparse communications. For only the second time that fall, the Americans employed a loose formation that took maximum advantage of Allied superiority in radar and freed destroyers to act as an active screen beyond the range of larger ships. This deployment countered Kondo well, who had achieved the ultimate in Japanese dispersion tactics with fourteen ships divided four ways within a square barely a dozen miles on each side.

Shortly after 11:00 PM Kondo's ships wedged into the narrow confines between Guadalcanal and Savo to confront Lee. The opposing battlewagons fired the first shots before torpedo and gun sallies by Lee's four destroyers dominated the beat of the battle. The tin cans fared poorly. The *Walke* and *Preston* sank and the *Benham* limped, gravely damaged, from the scene before Lee ordered the *Gwin* to withdraw. But the tin cans had screened well their larger charges and, by illuminating the skirmish, had offered Lee in the *Washington* a portrait of Kondo's deployment, allowing him to mortally wound the battleship *Kirishima*. This forced Kondo's retreat and bedeviled again an increasingly desperate Japanese attempt to land reinforcements. Incredibly, Tanaka brought his remaining four transports to Guadalcanal at dawn anyway, sacrificing them upon a beach before scurrying away with his thin-skinned escorts—though a subsequent attack from Allied airmen meant most of the embarked troops never reached inland. The whole brawl had cost Japan a battlewagon, a destroyer, and her remaining supply ships against a tally of three American tin cans. The old destroyer man Halsey blanched at this loss, but, as he told Nimitz later, he would barter destroyers for battleships "any time the yellow bastards ask for it." For just the second time in the constrained waters of the Solomon Islands, the Americans had won a surface engagement. The first had been Scott's triumph at Cape Esperance. Now Lee had come out ahead.[21]

This Naval Battle of Guadalcanal, as history dubbed it, had been the war's wildest three-day stretch at sea. For Halsey, who had come to believe the "bad news always comes first," the early reports throughout November 13 and into the next day had indicated a clash slipping away: the mauling of Callaghan and Scott's force, Mikawa's uncontested shelling of Henderson, the news of the massive Japanese convoy making steam for Guadalcanal. Keeping a clear head in such circumstances was, Halsey recalled later, "the hardest thing for an area commander in the rear." It was also the most crucial requirement. In those moments, Halsey discovered that a lifetime's preparation to risk his own life had left him unready to sacrifice others. He had long ago subordinated his life to duty, but risking other Americans without himself facing some commensurate hazard was another matter. Aboard the *Enterprise* earlier in the war, he shared the dangers of the ship's company. Now insulated well behind the battle, he confronted the "great mental agony" of calculating acceptable American loss against the prospect of Japanese success. Yet, he concluded, that was "what a commander is for." Everything depended upon "his judgment at this moment."[22]

The *Hiei*'s demise was the first distinct good news that reached Nouméa sometime in the early afternoon of November 14. As further reports that day mitigated American losses and increased Japanese damage, Halsey's spirits brightened. By the time he ordered Lee into the narrow waters of Savo Sound against the advice of subordinates, he believed they "had the bastards licked." The whole affair had been "nip and tuck," he later wrote, but fortunately "tuck won."[23]

Tuck killed, actually. If the verdict of Santa Cruz was muddled, and if deciphering relative tallies in Guadalcanal's near-constant land combat was tedious, the slaughter of Tanaka's transports made manifest a resounding American victory. Both antagonists had intended to burnish their flagging troops on Guadalcanal. The Americans delivered nearly 6,000 men and many tons of provisions without losing a supply ship. The Japanese deposited maybe 2,000 troops, a four-day ration of rice, and a single day's supply of ammunition at the cost of most of the Japanese cargo vessels in the area. Personnel losses were even at about 1,800 seaborne deaths each, although Japanese materiel losses were the greater by far: against two American cruisers and seven destroyers sunk, the battle cost Japan two battleships, a heavy cruiser, three destroyers, and ten transports, a loss equating to a monthly cost of over a million tons of shipping, some sixteen times beyond what Tokyo officials had calculated as sustainable in the war with the Allies. Operationally, the victory belonged to the determination of Callaghan and Scott, the acumen of Lee, and the fliers of both Henderson Field and the *Enterprise,* whose planes, as they often did in the otherwise evenly pitched battles of the lower Solomons, arbitrated who had won and who had lost. Strategically, the Japanese failed to land anything like the force required to overrun Henderson Field, while the Americans strengthened their presence.[24]

Appraisals on each side of the line came swiftly. "It must be said," read a Japanese assessment written about this time, "that the success or failure in recapturing Guadalcanal Island, and the naval battle related to it, is the fork in the road which leads to victory for them or for us." Following the battle, the fork bent in the American direction. Ugaki recognized that the clash had been an utter defeat, Yamamoto never again contested control of the seas near Guadalcanal, and attempts at Japanese resupply grew more modest before they faded completely away.[25]

American sentiment was a mirror image of Japanese attitudes. On Guadalcanal, Vandegrift, who had criticized Navy leadership before Halsey's arrival, thanked Lee "for his sturdy effort," Kinkaid "for his intervention," and paid his "greatest homage" to Scott and Callaghan, "who with magnificent courage against seemingly hopeless odds drove back the first hostile stroke and made success possible." In Nouméa, Halsey was sure the battle would "go down as an epic in Naval warfare." At Pearl Harbor, where gloom had pervaded as late as November 12, elation loosened Nimitz's traditional reserve and prompted his command diarist to call the clash "*the* decisive battle of this campaign." In Washington, the battle deaths of two rear admirals at first created apprehension, matched, Assistant Secretary of the Navy James Forrestal remembered, "only by the tension that pervaded Washington the night before the landings in Normandy." This sense of doom faded fast. In a speech on November 17, Roosevelt found purpose in the death of his former aide Callaghan. Speaking of both Guadalcanal and the recent Allied invasion of North Africa, he reported to the nation "a great deal of good news," adding, "It would seem that the turning point in this war has at last been reached."[26]

Halsey basked in the battle's immediate wash. Nimitz expressed his "admiration beyond expression" for the "offensive spirit of your fighting forces." In an officer efficiency report soon thereafter, Nimitz wrote that Halsey had a "rare combination of intellectual capacity and military audacity" that could "calculate to a cat's whisker the risk involved" in military operations. In Washington, the president suggested Halsey's promotion to full admiral on November 18, despite a tradition of and, until just months earlier, the legal provision for only the four full admirals then on the active list: King; Nimitz; Harold Stark, at the time serving in London; and Royal Ingersoll, Nimitz's counterpart as the commander of the Atlantic Fleet. On November 26, after placing makeshift four-star insignia upon his collar, Halsey gave his three-star pins to Rear Admiral William Calhoun. "Send one of these to Mrs. Scott and the other to Mrs. Callaghan," Halsey directed. "Tell them it was their husband's bravery that got me my new ones." Halsey had reached the pinnacle of his profession, measured in rank anyway, and, calculated in responsibility and authority, a plateau so far beyond the plane once occupied by his father that it boggled his mind. To his South Pacific Forces he radioed, "Your names have been written in golden letters on the pages of history. No honor for you could be too great. My pride in you is beyond expression. Magnificently done. To the glorious dead: Hail heroes, rest with God."[27]

. . . .

Although the tide at Guadalcanal may have turned, waves still slapped hard upon American hulls for some time to come. Across the last fortnight of November, U.S. ground attempts to capitalize upon the mid-November triumphs faltered as now the Japanese, not the Americans, enjoyed the tactical advantage of defense. At sea, on November 30 the Japanese inflicted a sharp defeat at the Battle of Tassafaronga, where eight Japanese destroyers ferrying cargo bested a superior American force of five cruisers and six destroyers, sinking one cruiser and damaging three against the loss of a single destroyer. Long-standing defects in American torpedo design partly explained this lopsided result, but there were other factors: Nimitz had recently pulled Kinkaid from the South Pacific for duty in the Aleutians, and Halsey had placed newly arrived and untried Rear Admiral Carleton Wright in charge of the pertinent American group. Wright's battle plan kept destroyers tight by cruisers in a manner consistent with early war practice but deaf to the emerging patterns in the Solomons, and some destroyer skippers remained tentative. Commenting upon Wright's after-action report, Halsey deplored Wright's poor use of destroyers and told Nimitz the tin cans had fired torpedoes from too great a range and had not sprung into the battle independently. "As a destroyer sailor of long service," he wrote, "it has broken my heart" to see the offensive potential of those ships "abused"—a judgment shared, ironically, by Japanese officers, one of whom later opined that the Americans should have been more aggressive in Solomon surface battles. "Annihilation of our reinforcing units would not necessarily have been difficult even for a few destroyers," this officer believed, "if they had chosen to penetrate our lines and carry on a decisive battle." Remaking the pattern of American operations, however, would take, as Nimitz's own comments on Wright's report made clear, "training, training, and more training," and this sound remedy required time, a commodity Halsey had had precious little of since arriving in the South Pacific six weeks earlier.[28]

Halsey probably needed more resources as well, even with recent battlefield victories. In late November the reinforcements that had begun their journey to the region the previous month at last began reaching the South Pacific in significant numbers. In the air, the 29 operational planes at Guadalcanal in late October grew to 188 by the end of November, and as the New Year approached Halsey could call upon another 150 at nearby fields on Espiritu Santo and 330 seaborne aircraft as well. At sea, the *Saratoga,* two battleships, four cruisers, and a squadron of destroyers came, followed, by the end of December, by the bulk of the Pacific Fleet then afloat: two fleet carriers, six escort carriers, six battleships, thirteen cruisers, forty-five destroyers, and two dozen submarines, allowing Halsey to establish five task forces, two centered on the carriers, two organized around the battleships, and one a powerful cruiser-destroyer mix designed to continue the close fight in the Solomons. And on the ground, the remaining elements of the Americal Division from New Caledonia arrived on Guadalcanal, augmented later by the Twenty-Fifth Infantry Division, under the command of a dynamo major general named Joseph Collins, diverted from Australia with such dispatch that its soldiers were astonished and more than a little disappointed to greet Guadalcanal mud instead of Australian women as they disembarked.

These soldiers were sufficient to replace Vandegrift's Marines, who at last had lost their battle edge, becoming, in the words of one of their own, "short tempered and unable to coordinate" even rudimentary maneuver. They were very sick to boot: a medical survey revealed a 75 percent malarial rate and raised the specter of widespread battle fatigue bordering on neurosis. On December 9, Major General Alexander "Sandy" Patch and the Americal Division relieved Vandegrift, who then took his depleted Marine division to Australia for a period of well-deserved rest. On Guadalcanal, the influx of troops increased the Allied tally to nearly 50,000 by late December, a number large enough to bestow upon Patch the command of a new Army corps, the XIV. This development introduced an additional command layer between Halsey and the front line. From that point forward, the Army exercised greater prerogative over ground operations, a circumstance Halsey explicitly recognized when, at about the same time, he limited Turner's responsibilities to the support of the Guadalcanal garrison and conferred on Harmon, his senior Army representative in Nouméa, authority over tactical operations on the island, exercised largely through Patch's corps headquarters, making Harmon the only Army flier of the war with de facto control over an Army ground corps.[29]

As American power waxed, Japanese power waned. Japan could still call upon a powerful collection of Navy ships in the area, but its carrier strength had not recovered from the fall's expenditures of flight crews. Its South Pacific land-based air forces were likewise impressive on paper, totaling over 400, but many were devoted to tasks in New

Guinea, where they faced Douglas MacArthur's forces. The disparity between the two Guadalcanal combatants became greatest on the ground, where, from a peak of perhaps 30,000 men in mid-November, Japanese strength had rapidly dwindled by two-thirds. For those remaining, food rations shrank to one-sixth of normal levels for men on the front lines and to one-tenth for all others. A report to Tokyo on December 7, the first anniversary of the Pearl Harbor attack, indicated fifty men died each day from starvation or sickness. The survivors increasingly ate roots, grass, and, according to a few gruesome reports, each other. One staff officer wrote that the force had reached "the very bottom of the human condition," and another morbidly calculated the life expectancy of his compatriots in a scale that ranged from "those who can stand—30 days" to "those who can blink—tomorrow." By the New Year, among the Japanese there, Guadalcanal had earned in spades its morose moniker, Starvation Island.[30]

. . . .

With this emerging balance sheet of relative strength, the Army took its turn fighting the enemy. As it had been for the Marines, Guadalcanal proved a hard teacher. Harmon, new to ground operations; Patch, new to corps command; and Collins, eventually one of the United States' best leaders in Europe but now in his baptism of fire, first planned to clear a series of enemy positions on high ground to the south of Henderson Field whose guns had long harassed American positions. The task took five times the troops—five battalions—and twice as long—until late January—to accomplish, a job so sapping that at one point a regimental commander took the extraordinary step of recommending his own relief. In early January, Patch, then with the equivalent of three infantry divisions at his disposal, initiated a second drive to the west of Henderson Field, using Collins's Twenty-Fifth Division as a spearhead. The campaign's largest and most conventional offensive, this thrust managed in a week to claim nearly two miles and gain important high ground just inland of resolute enemy positions near Point Cruz, long an important Japanese defensive anchor on the coast. This paved the way for the Second Marine Division, recently created from elelments of other Marine regiments, to push the remaining Japanese back beyond Point Cruz, laying bare another stretch of coastal lowlands to the north and pressing the enemy toward an ever-shrinking patch of soil near the island's northern apex. For a time, the XIV Corps did not use a single tank, perhaps the only occasion in the war that an entire Army corps engaged in combat lacked that singular symbol of conventional strength. But by the last week of January, Patch's men had at long last cleared the entire coastal plain surrounding Henderson Field and had established a contiguous line sufficient for a general, coordinated offensive to chase the last Japanese from the island.[31]

Halsey had observed these operations with an unusual detachment. Although distance from the area's naval battles had vexed him, he more readily accepted a senior commander's remove from tactical matters when it came to the ground fight, especially as it grew beyond the grasp of a single Marine division and became more bureaucratized and regularized with the arrival of more Army troops. His operational dispatches and war diary through January indicated an abiding interest in naval matters, as did his letters to Nimitz, wherein he recorded Navy personnel assignments, seagoing organizational changes, and even individual ship training schedules but offered parsimonious assessments of the continuing fight on Guadalcanal. "The situation with the Nips" on the island, he told Nimitz on December 20 almost as an afterthought, "is as obscure to me as it probably is to you," adding, in mid-January—just as the Army began making real progress on the ground—"the situation in regard to the Japs is a bit baffling."[32]

Navy Secretary Frank Knox chose this propitious moment to visit. He and an aide, a young Adlai Stevenson, future two-time Democrat nominee for president, had arrived in Pearl Harbor on January 14, inspected Midway Island two days later, and reached Espiritu Santo on January 20, where Halsey and John McCain, now the chief of the Bureau of Aeronautics, met them aboard Rear Admiral Aubrey Fitch's flagship, *Curtiss*. That night, a few Japanese bombs, the first that had fallen on the area for weeks, harassed their sleep. The next morning, Knox, Nimitz, Halsey, and McCain left for Guadalcanal, where Nimitz was impressed by the signs of progress since his visit in October. Henderson Field was now an all-weather airstrip, living areas approximated civilization, and fighting men no longer resembled the walking dead. That evening, another Japanese air strike pestered the group, chasing Knox, Halsey, and McCain into slit trenches while Nimitz, denied sleep the evening before, clung stubbornly to his bed and mosquito lattice, a display of courage that improbably netted him, alone among the group, a bout of malaria. The successive air strikes at Espiritu Santo and Guadalcanal sparked suspicions, never confirmed, of Japanese intelligence on Knox's travels. When on the morning of January 23 the group left for Nouméa, some wit in the radio hut suggested sending the departure report in plain Japanese. "I want 'em to know for sure the high-priced hired help has left."[33]

In Nouméa, Halsey's operations officer, DeWitt Peck, and his Army commander, Miff Harmon, joined the group to review the situation in the South Pacific. Nimitz asked what everyone wanted to know: When will the Japanese abandon Guadalcanal? Peck estimated April 1. Halsey agreed. Others nodded. Nimitz thought that was a conservative timeline, until he was reminded of the dogged Japanese resistance along every sector of their lines to date. The meeting was serious business, but the proceedings were interspersed with friendly banter and outright laughter. It was a stark contrast to those who had also attended the downcast Nimitz-Ghormley conferences the previous fall, a difference attributed, according to Nimitz's biographer, to Halsey's infectious confidence. Unlike those earlier meetings aboard the *Argonne,* no one now seriously doubted the final outcome in the lower Solomons, though everyone present concurred that the remaining days on Guadalcanal were likely to be bloody.[34]

This last judgment was underscored by a spate of intelligence. January had seen a large increase in enemy forces in the region, including an uptick in aircraft on nearby fields and a threefold surge of ships at Rabaul, to about one hundred vessels. By midmonth, radio intercepts suggested a looming enemy carrier presence in Solomons waters as well, which would be their first foray into those seas since the bruising battles of October and November. By the time Knox and Nimitz left Nouméa on January 24, the Americans knew Truk harbored the headquarters of the Combined, Second, Third, and Fourth Fleets, a major Japanese submarine command, both her active carrier divisions, and no fewer than a score of flag officers. Beyond all that, the emperor's New Year's rescript had promised that "the finest of the Japanese Army, Navy, and Air units" were heading "toward the Solomon Islands where a decisive battle is being fought between Japan and America."[35]

The Americans took him at his word. Nimitz alerted Halsey to an impending "Jap push," and nearly everyone expected an imminent strike. From as far as Washington, King warned of a "Jap offensive operation now in full swing on a major scale primarily directed against Southern Solomons," and from as near as Nouméa, Halsey believed a "major attack" on Guadalcanal was "materializing" in the "same general pattern as mid-November," and he asked for emergency air support from the Southwest Pacific. Among those with access to intelligence, it seemed only MacArthur in Brisbane withheld judgment, believing the enemy was surely poised to strike but was as likely to hit within his sector as Halsey's zone. As a result, he refused Halsey's plea for aviation, noting that the admiral already controlled far more airplanes than MacArthur did if carrier decks were included in calculations.[36]

All this prompted Halsey in late January to protect to the gills four Guadalcanal-bound troopships carrying replacements for the last of the Marines on the island. In a testament to his swelling strength, five American task forces, aggregating two fleet carriers, two escort carriers, three new fast battleships, twelve cruisers, and twenty-five destroyers took to the sea with orders to flank the troopship quartet. It was the largest single fleet the U.S. Navy had yet put to sea, and one not likely to escape detection, spread as it was over thousands of square miles. On the afternoon of January 29, it did not. During the brief Battle of Rennell Island, Japanese pilots crippled the cruiser *Chicago,* which, following bumbled attempts to shepherd her home, succumbed to further attack the next day. Both Halsey and Nimitz decried the series of local errors that had contributed to this stunning loss, but each had played a role in the *Chicago*'s demise: both had endorsed estimates of a major Japanese offensive, and Halsey had put to sea a force widely disproportionate to the specific task of escorting four vessels to Guadalcanal.[37]

As it was, gathering Japanese forces at Rabaul and Truk were not a spearhead but a rearguard. The Naval Battle of Guadalcanal had crystalized two paths for Japan in the lower Solomons: launch yet another major offensive or accept defeat. When planners determined a large January attack would require shipping on a scale as to upset Japan's entire war economy, Japanese leaders agreed to quit Guadalcanal, establish a defensive line in the middle Solomons, and concentrate upon a renewed thrust into New Guinea. This represented a return to their original scheme, but was a reversal of recent emphasis so monumental that it required two meetings with the emperor to effectuate.

This plan was fraught with danger, as is any retreat in the face of an active opponent. If Halsey as much as sniffed Japanese backtracking, the retreat could easily become a catastrophe. Indeed, the uptick of Japanese force in January was, in fact, part ruse to cover the withdrawal, and Japanese leaders did not disclose their plans even to their troops on Guadalcanal until about mid-January, the same time they feigned offensive preparations from Rabaul. On February 1, with the bulk of the American Navy still in nearby waters, twenty Japanese destroyers formed the vanguard of three successive runs to Guadalcanal, where survivors had gathered near Cape Esperance on the island's north shore, protected by a few hundred of their strongest soldiers still fighting Patch's advances from Point Cruz. Three days later, and again on February 7, sets of twenty destroyers made the same intrepid run, whisking, in the end, about 10,000 soldiers from Starvation Island. In the judgment of a scholar of the Japanese Navy, it was an amazing feat, and one "almost impossible to explain."[38]

The clandestine operation was not without casualty. The Americans sank one of the destroyers and damaged three. Throughout the first week of February, however, Halsey and others stubbornly believed the Japanese were preparing an offensive, a judgment that tethered massive American sea forces farther south of Guadalcanal, perched for opportunity, while the Tokyo Express evacuated the island.

"Although we had a veteran group of cruisers and destroyers within range of the Express' track," Halsey later explained, "we considered it wiser to hold them against the major threat" of an offensive strike. For a week, then, the bulk of Halsey's fighting sea power cruised nearby, "awaiting developments," as Nimitz's command diarist put it, while the Japanese escaped. On February 9, when two of Patch's pincers met near the point of Japanese evacuation, the unthinkable and unbelievable firmly dawned on the Americans: the Japanese had left. That evening Patch sent a jubilant note to Halsey: "Total and complete defeat of Japanese forces on Guadalcanal effected 1625 today," he wrote. The "Tokyo Express no longer has terminus on Guadalcanal."[39]

American participants excused the failure to interdict the Japanese withdrawal, but there was responsibility aplenty. Radio intercepts had indicated the establishment of a Japanese encampment on Bougainville for "forces evacuated from Guadalcanal," and Patch's advance in late January had overrun abandoned enemy positions with radios, machine shops, and working artillery intact. Yet Halsey never considered a Japanese retreat because it was inconsistent with enemy behavior to date, in the Solomons or anywhere else. For him, the "enemy's obstinacy, the desperate plight of his troops on Guadalcanal, and the long lull since his last offensive" all led him to suspect attack, not retreat. King and Nimitz demonstrated no better foresight, the latter believing a Japanese carrier move into the Marshalls in early February was nothing more than a diversion for a push toward Guadalcanal, and they later excused Allied miscalculation by crediting the Japanese with "skill in keeping their plans disguised and bold celerity in carrying them out." Yet the episode represented, in the judgment of a prominent historian of American code-breaking efforts in the Pacific, "the most significant intelligence failure on the Allied side throughout the Guadalcanal campaign." In Nouméa, Honolulu, and Washington at the time, however, no one was able to point a finger anywhere without directing it everywhere, so the Americans contented themselves with congratulations.[40]

. . . .

The fight was finished. The tide had turned. Before Guadalcanal, the Japanese were on the march everywhere. Afterward, they took the offensive with growing irregularity, and rarely again enjoyed success in a general campaign anywhere on the globe. The battle's human cost was modest, though never inconsequential. Perhaps 29,500 Japanese and 6,000 Americans died on the island and in surrounding waters, a toll far smaller than the tallies of Eastern Front battles raging about the same time. The materiel score was more substantial. Each side lost twenty-four warships and about 650 aircraft, a symmetry suggesting the attritional nature of the Solomon Islands fight, a type of war that both sides eschewed, but that only the Americans could win.

It had been an epic struggle. Tallies of lives, ships, and planes could not fully convey its meaning. "Guadalcanal is not the name of an island," one Japanese general wrote, "it is the name of the graveyard of the Japanese army." Americans agreed. "Guadalcanal is not a name but an emotion," Morison declared, a sentiment amplified by James Michener in his singular *Tales of the South Pacific,* wherein he wrote that the memory of Guadalcanal would surely fade but would never disappear, becoming instead distant, rather "like Shiloh or Valley Forge" on the American ear.[41]

Halsey did not write with such flourish, but he was more succinct: "The grim, ugly, bloody, expansive campaign was finished." Although he had come late to the fight, he had been as responsible as anyone for the victory. He had arrived at a moment of crisis, and American defeat was strongly possible well into November. Of Guadalcanal's six major sea clashes, each more bloody than any American naval battle from 1814 to 1941, four occurred on his watch. Not until he succored the Marines did Vandegrift's men stem Japanese pressure on Henderson Field, and not until he provided Army replacements did the Japanese flee the island. Halsey had gone head to head with the famed Yamamoto, and he had won.[42]

His performance had been imperfect. He had settled uneasily into area command, far from the active front. His grasp of ground operations, especially as the Marines gave way to Army units, was tentative.

He had failed to harry a tenuous Japanese evacuation of the island. But Halsey's leadership had exercised a powerful tonic upon a beleaguered force at the crucial moment, leaving the Americans hungry for more of it. As the epic battle ebbed, one Marine general spoke for many when he wrote that there "was only one Halsey, and we need many victories." *Time,* in a review of the war's first full year, "found few opportunities for great achievement" among military men. "Outstanding among Americans for accomplishment in battle," however, "stood the name of Admiral William Halsey, who, not once but again and again & again, took his task force into swift encounters against the Japs." James Jones, of Company F, Twenty-Seventh Infantry, Twenty-Fifth Infantry Division, in the sequel to *From Here to Eternity,* wrote of Guadalcanal as "the thin red line" separating life from death, for people and for nations. Halsey did as much as anyone to keep America on the right side of that wire. In February 1943, the great glow of victory surely obscured struggles yet to come, but what a bright ember it was, while it lasted.[43]

P-38 fighter planes moving from harbor dock to airfield, Nouméa, New Caledonia, October 1942. Courtesy of the U.S. National Archives.

Auguste Montchamp *(left)*, Halsey *(center)*, and Millard Harmon *(right)*,
celebrating liberation of French North Africa, June 1943.
Courtesy of the U.S. National Archives.

South Pacific Staff, January 1943. *Front row, from left:* Julian Brown, DeWitt Peck, William Halsey, Miles Browning, and A. H. Dearing. *Back row, from left:* Bill Kitchell, Leonard Dow, Doug Moulton, G. E. Griggs, Bromfield Nichol, J. U. Lademan, J. W. Smith, Marion Cheek, Lem Bryan, Bill Ashford, and J. W. Roper. Courtesy of the U.S. National Archives.

Kelly Turner *(left)* and Archer Vandegrift at sea near Guadalcanal, August 1942. United States Naval Institute.

Japanese cargo vessel wreckage, Naval Battle of Guadalcanal,
November 1942. United States Marine Corps.
Courtesy of the U.S. National Archives.

Theodore Wilkinson *(left)* and Millard Harmon at sea near New Georgia, July 1943. Courtesy of the U.S. National Archives.

Lieutenant Robert Carney Jr. places rear admiral insignia upon
his father's uniform as Halsey looks on, July 1943.
Courtesy of the U.S. National Archives.

American landing on Rendova Island, June 30, 1943.
Department of the Navy. Courtesy of the U.S. National Archives.
Photo 80-G-52573.

Unloading supplies, Rendova Island, July 1943.
Courtesy of the U.S. National Archives.

Soldiers on New Georgia Island, July 1943.
Courtesy of the U.S. National Archives.

Rehabilitating the Munda airfield following American capture, New
Georgia Island, August 1943. Courtesy of the U.S. National Archives.

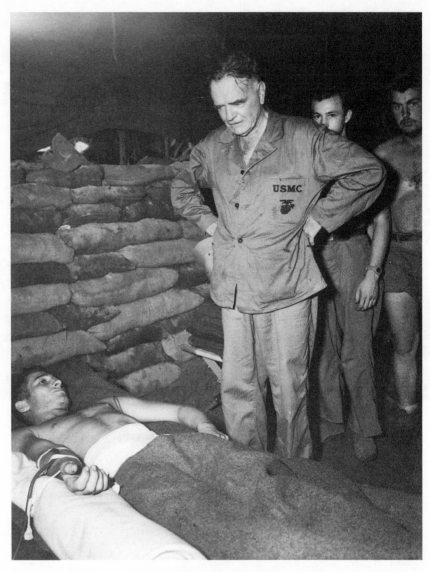

Halsey visiting wounded Marines, Bougainville Island,
November 10, 1943. Courtesy of the U.S. National Archives.

Halsey confers with ground commanders. *From left, seated:* Brigadier
General Allen Turnage, Halsey, and Major General Roy Geiger, Bougainville
Island, November 10, 1943. Department of the Navy.
Courtesy of the U.S. National Archives. Photo 80-G-161595.

Press interview. *From left:* Halsey; Marine Lieutenant Sanford Hunt; Frank Tremaine, United Press International; Fred Hampson, Associated Press; and Lieutenant Jonathan Rice, Bougainville Island, November 11, 1943. Courtesy of the U.S. National Archives.

From left: Chester Nimitz, Ernest King, and Halsey, Pearl Harbor, September 1943. Courtesy of the U.S. National Archives.

Halsey at sea, December 1944.
Admiral Carney Collection. Courtesy of the
U. S. National Archives. Photo 80-G-470894.

Chapter Eleven

Real Tales of the South Pacific

THE WAR'S FIRST YEAR made Halsey famous. Springtime carrier raids had splashed his name in American newspapers, and when
he assumed command in Nouméa the *New York Times* greeted the
announcement with an eight-column banner, a *Los Angeles Times*
headline lauded the choice of an "Aggressive Commander," and the
Washington Post proclaimed, "Admiral Halsey, Unorthodox Fighter,
Takes Over Navy's Toughest Command." Following the mid-November
Naval Battle for Guadalcanal, correspondents appeared at Halsey's
headquarters with growing regularity. A *Detroit Free Press* article
proclaimed Halsey "the country's new naval hero, whose name will
be remembered in naval annals along with those of John Paul Jones,
David Farragut, and George Dewey." In a two-week span, a political
cartoon depicting the ghosts of Jones, Farragut, and Dewey admiring
Halsey appeared in no fewer than one hundred newspapers and magazines. On November 20, 1942, Halsey made the first of two appear-
ances on the cover of *Time* for, the editors wrote, having "saved
Guadalcanal." Months before Dwight Eisenhower's name became
ubiquitous, nearly a year before George Patton earned universal renown, and well before publicity machines could parade a continuous
series of heroes before the home-front crowd, Halsey was eclipsed
only by Douglas MacArthur as *the* commander at the fighting front,
at sea or in the field. In time, this wartime polish enveloped Halsey's
service, and he adopted a kind of celebrity that distorted as much as it
clarified the myriad facets of his personality, his South Pacific command, and his environs—especially the tiny town of Nouméa, which
was the most peculiar host of any wartime Allied headquarters.[1]

Halsey at first embraced the adulation that came his way. In late November he explained to correspondents that he strived to do "the exact opposite" of what the Japanese expected, and to do it fast, a philosophy that one reporter wrote "will do nicely as a maxim of naval operations until a better one comes along." At a New Year's Eve press conference, Halsey predicted the war would end within a year, a bombast he repeated during an early January trip to Wellington, where the *New Zealand Herald* declared that Halsey had become a "legend for enterprise and hard hitting." Soon, Halsey's daily regimen, including ocean swims in loud red trunks and noisy evening meals, earned wide retelling. In the summer of 1943, Marshall Field and Company reproduced a favored necktie, long since out of style, and marketed it as the Halsey Tie through its department stores.[2]

Publicity netted Halsey fan letters, sometimes a hundred or more each week. Many arrived with presents: shoes, saddles, belts, boots, buckles, and, by the end of the war, at least five sweaters embroidered "Bull." The director of the Ralph Waldo Emerson Museum sent an ebony cribbage board once owned by the poet. Others offered crackpot ideas for weapons, tactics, and strategy. A few produced songs, some of which became popular radio ditties. Residents of Halsey's birthplace of Elizabeth tried to deed him a house, but when naval regulations intervened they proffered a parade instead, attended by Halsey during leave later in the war, moving an eleven-year-old girl to poetry:[3]

> Admiral Halsey had a parade
> The crowds were vast and gay
> To see the face of someone true
> On Admiral Halsey's Day
>
> Admiral Halsey had a parade
> The crowds all shouted and waved
> To see his beaming, shining face
> On Admiral Halsey's Day
>
> Admiral Halsey had a parade
> The mothers all cried and prayed

For the man who was so brave and true
On Admiral Halsey's Day

Admiral Halsey had a parade
His eyes were filled with tears
To see the ones that waved and prayed
On Admiral Halsey's Day[4]

By midwar Halsey's many fans assumed a kinship that belied their distance from the admiral. "Well Bull," began a letter from a Kansan who believed Halsey had all the attributes of a Western cowboy. A North Carolinian proclaimed Halsey akin to the farmer and the store clerk, to the coal digger and the laborer, and to "every walking decent American." Another declared him simply "so doggoned democratic, bold, and fearless." Women joined this love fest, one beginning her letter with "My dear sir, good friend, and great leader," another excusing her "presumption" in writing because "we Americans should have the fraternal feeling toward each other," and a third confessing she had hung a portrait of Halsey in her bedroom, an "indiscreet" act she meant to compound if someday she could meet Halsey and show him "what's in my heart."[5]

This was heady stuff. In the seventh decade of life, Halsey had deservedly become a hero and was certainly famous, phenomena that predated his birth by centuries and had long been touchstones of naval service. But he also became a celebrity, an invention of the age in which he lived, and one for which he had no good archetype. According to a leading social historian, by 1940 a plethora of new media—movies, radio, news magazines—had bred a kind of renown based not upon achievement but upon personality, creating a false familiarity between the public and the famous, and begetting, in the process, celebrities, who became stick figures reflecting "nothing but ourselves in a magnifying glass." *Time* was a prime mover of this trend. Founded in 1923 upon a "basic premise" that "people are interesting *per se,*" as one early advertisement put it, the magazine "prized the nuggets of information, the unexpected facet, that make newsmakers come alive on the page." Thus, in that first cover story on Halsey, *Time* reported that the admiral's face "was itself like a battlefield. Everything about it was big, broad, strong. The weather had been on it, and personal suffering behind it. The huge mouth looked like command, and above it, the nose was pugnacious. The eyes were aggressive. They and their screen of brow above and the weariness below were as impressive and busy looking as a couple of task forces."[6]

This renown came upon Halsey nearly without warning. His first war interviews, with Joseph Harsch of the *Christian Science Monitor* and H. R. Knickerbocker of the *Chicago Sun* in late January 1942, before the Marshall Islands raid, had produced insufficient color to see much news ink. As late as November 1942, just days after the Naval Battle of Guadalcanal, a North Carolina newspaper identified a photograph of Halsey as that of a Nazi spy wanted by the FBI. Weeks later, no news editor in America could possibly repeat the error. By then, Halsey was a reporter's dream, "a likable fellow who could be built up into a national hero," according to Nimitz's biographer. Thereafter, the "press lost no time enshrining him as the nemesis of the Japanese, a half-fictional character whom they named 'Bull,'" a moniker whose origins remain shrouded: some thought it dated from World War I, some claimed it was an adaptation from an interwar aviator admiral, and most, including Halsey himself, believed it a wartime invention of an adoring media, perhaps stemming from a typographical error of his first name. In time, Halsey's press conferences assumed "the atmosphere of a movie premiere," complete with hordes of correspondents, introductory music, and Navy Department pamphlets titled *Halsey the Man, Halsey the Fighter,* and *Halsey the Phrase Maker.* For Halsey, an extrovert prone to external cues who had nonetheless spent his life in the cloistered Navy, stardom brought the home front close, long after his temple hair had first gone gray. As distinction came to his doorstep, he proved a willing press partner, ready to confirm popular conceptions of sea command and salty leadership. And along the way, he became a caricature, some traits exaggerated, others ignored, a portrait true enough in broad outline and inaccurate in nearly every particular.[7]

. . . .

Halsey, as a plain-talking, hard-drinking rabble-rouser, helped sketch this cartoon. As the son of an alcoholic who had crashed within the same naval fraternity in which he now lived, Halsey had always been keen to demonstrate a capacity to roughhouse. While a young man, he took a beer or two or three on occasion, and he later graduated to liquor, even as Prohibition outlawed imbibing. In World War I, he was among those whose habits at the Royal Cork Yacht Club concerned William Sims, and in the early 1920s he partook in boisterous picnics while serving with the Pacific Fleet destroyers. When newsmen arrived in 1942, Halsey boasted of benders and hangovers. "There are exceptions of course," he liked to say, "but as a general rule I do not trust a fighting man who does not smoke or drink." His favorite toast, repeated enough to become cliché, was "I've drunk to your health in company / I've drunk to your health alone / I've drunk to your health so many times / I've damn near ruined my own." By war's end, Halsey's endorsement of drink was known enough to spark a backlash among temperance movements, prompting his only hate mail and at least one petition to President Harry Truman, from a Methodist association of some 700,000 members, for his relief from command and removal from public life. Since the war, historians have emphasized this aspect of Halsey, liking to repeat, for instance, the story of the time he excused a destroyer's booze run to Sydney but would have cashiered the skipper had the diversion been for repairs.[8]

Halsey was no teetotaler, but, excepting his early career, his rowdy reputation was overdrawn. A shipmate from his stint aboard the *Wyoming* in 1925 recalled him as a moderate drinker, and a decade later Halsey shunned alcohol without ill effect while in flight training. At midwar, the Army Force fleet surgeon in New Caledonia, Colonel Arthur King, never knew Halsey to overindulge and suspected the admiral was a bit of a faker with a drink in his hand, which he nursed with almost "professional skill." A staff officer remembered that the admiral "used alcohol as a social elixir to great effect, but hardly ever to a point that would have prevented him from safely driving a car."[9]

Halsey himself wrote movingly of the deplorable effects of alcoholism on family life, something he knew instinctively, and civic life, where he believed liquor contributed to such "grave national problems as delinquency, crime, and pauperism." From his first mast as a skipper with the *Du Pont* in 1909 to his last aboard the *Saratoga* in 1937, he had less patience for public intoxication than he had for many other common bluejacket infractions. He appreciated liquor's tonic benefit, and made certain it was available to front-line troops, but he also understood its side effects. In the early 1920s he often chided Ray Spruance, who was prone to bad hangovers, that he needed "to learn how to drink." As the South Pacific commander, Halsey encouraged courts-martial for any sailor drunk at sea, once upbraiding a cruiser skipper for failing to do so. Through most of his adult life, Halsey kept a diverse and well-stocked personal bar, but upon its shelves sat the inventory of a man who enjoyed social libation, not of one chugging relentlessly, habitually, and to excess.[10]

Halsey's informality and irreverence added other layers to his wartime veneer. His dislike of stuffy regulations was legendary, but he also was a stickler for military customs and courtesies. Failure to render a proper salute often earned rebuke, and with his shore patrol duty during the cruise of the Great White Fleet in mind, he prescribed strict rules for ships visiting Nouméa: liberty parties were limited to no more than 5 percent of a ship's company at a time, and bluejackets were to dress in regulation uniform, return to their vessels by 5:00 PM, and be chaperoned by a patrol with a petty or commissioned officer in charge.[11]

Never a regular churchman, Halsey poked fun at organized faith. He told others of the Irish Catholic priest who "cussed and drank us all to shame," of the "Jew tailor" who made his uniforms, and called Julian Brown, for a while his intelligence officer, a "Hebraic so-and-so." But he also revered the priest as a "fighting Irishman," assisted the tailor's son far more than duty required when the latter found a fair amount of trouble in wartime London, and praised Brown "as an outstanding example of what an American should be." As he once told an acquaintance, World War II "had been born of prejudice and hatred and brutal ambition," and he was proud of "the Stars of David scattered amongst crosses" in American war cemeteries, where "Christian and Jew slept peaceably side by side, brothers in arms and brothers in death."[12]

His contempt of the Japanese became the most prominent feature of Halsey's wartime veneer. Before the attack on Pearl Harbor no utterance matched his wartime diatribes, and even in the war's early months he limited colorful commentary to close friends. This changed with fame and the slugfest on Guadalcanal. After that, Halsey routinely described the Japanese as descendants of female apes and male criminals. His favored descriptions of Japanese became "yellow bastards," "yellow bellied sons of bitches," "Japtards," and whatever simian or rodent metaphor he could summon: "yellow-bellied monkey meat," "monkeymen," "yellow monkeys," "monkey bastards," "rat bastards," "slant-eyed gopher meat," and "mole dwelling rat bastards." One letter to an old friend was typical: "These yellow bastards are beasts all right," he proclaimed. "In order to save the world, I am going to advocate at the peace table for the few yellow bellies that are left—emasculation for the males and spaying for the females." According to the leading chronicler of race and the war, by the summer of 1943, "Halsey was the most notorious" among all Allied leaders "for making outrageous and virulently racist remarks about the Japanese."[13]

His repugnant sentiment did not make him an outlier, however. Some may have disliked his outspokenness; Spruance, for example, "did not think we should be calling our enemies a lot of names the way Bill does." But Halsey's intellect was not strong enough to conjure these attitudes on his own. Stereotypes of Japanese long preceded Pearl Harbor, something the indiscriminate internment of Japanese-Americans at the war's onset revealed, and even urbane commentary trafficked in racism well before Halsey did: in the first months of war the New Yorker depicted Japanese as yellow monkeys and the Nation likened Japanese fatalities to "a rat's death." Life magazine once published—and treated as a human-interest story—a full-page photograph of an attractive blonde posing with a Japanese skull that her fiancé had sent as a battlefield souvenir. Halsey's race baiting, then, merely reflected and amplified American attitudes, a fact made manifest by much of Halsey's fan mail, including one letter thanking the admiral for "giving the yellow rice-chewers a heck of a licking," a second for "killing all the mole animals of the monkey tribe," a third for "chasing the yellow mice" from their burrows, and a fourth that solicited from Halsey evidence that the Japanese descended from apes, so that the writer, a teacher, could incorporate such insight into his high school biology course.[14]

For combatants on each side, racial invective reflected that most important ingredient of war: enmity, so necessary when mass killing becomes state policy. Halsey's mantra to "kill Japs, kill Japs, and kill more Japs," first muttered in the depths of the Guadalcanal crisis and later placed on billboards greeting Allied soldiers to other islands in the Solomons, was consistent with widely held strategic calculation in the midst of a death match. By the time Halsey promoted such rage, most Americans believed, as one best-selling book put it in 1943, the Pacific War would end only with Japan annihilated, "its men dead and its women and children divided and lost among other people." So as the war moved from Guadalcanal to other Solomon Islands killing fields, and then on to Tarawa and Iwo Jima and Okinawa, Halsey took to saying, about the same time that America took to believing, "The only good Jap is a Jap who's been dead for six months."[15]

Halsey's vitriol was also a function of leadership. He had arrived in the South Pacific on the heels of unrelenting Japanese triumphs. The onslaught had shaken Allied confidence and created among everyday servicemen and high officials alike an image of the enemy, in the words of *Yank*, the U.S. Army weekly, as "a born jungle and night fighter," or, in the words of Joseph Grew, the prewar ambassador in Tokyo and America's preeminent Japan expert, as "sturdy," "Spartan," "clever and dangerous." They "will not crack," Grew informed his fellow Americans, and "only by utter physical destruction or utter exhaustion can they be defeated."[16]

Halsey's outrageous statements were designed to rally his troops from this nadir. In the first week of his South Pacific command, he told a ship's crew, "Don't do your bit in the future—do your best. There will be blood and sweat and tears—but we have proved we can take it—and that we come back fighting harder than ever. You are battle-tried veterans. Go forth and preach the faith of our objective. Be an inspiration to the new and untried men who are just joining us." His outlandish prediction in early 1943 that the war would end within the year was "proffered in the interests of good combat psychology," he told a congressman. "We can certainly not shorten this war if everyone concerned is prepared to advance and support the thesis that it is going to be a very long and drawn out one." To Nimitz he explained, "These yellow bastards are no 'super men,'" and the sooner Americans understood this, the better. At a time when American spirit was low, "Old Bull Halsey," Michener wrote in *Tales of the South Pacific*, had the "guts to grunt out, when we were taking a pasting, 'We'll be in Tokyo by Christmas.' None of us believed him, but we felt better that we were led by men like him."[17]

After peace returned and Halsey had no need for it, his bile ebbed. In 1947, to an officer he had once cheered "for the hill blasting, cave smashing extermination of 11,000 slant-eyed gophers" at Palau, he now expressed gratitude for "taking such an active part in the rehabilitation of Japan" as a part of Douglas MacArthur's occupation force. In the late 1940s, he struck up a respectful correspondence with Japanese officials. In 1949, at a time when he lent his name to very few endeavors, he raised funds for a consortium of Japanese universities. The next year, he hosted a visiting Japanese delegation in New York. In 1953, he backed out of two long-standing naval engagements—including the annual dinner of his beloved World War I Queenstown destroyer association—to attend a banquet in honor of Japan's crown prince. Two years later, he helped place a group of Japanese exchange students in American schools. By then, and "curiously enough," as he confessed to a friend, Halsey had "lost all hatred" of the Japanese. His wrath had been real, his personal animus toward Japanese was genuine, and his wartime outlook was racist. But the intensity of his bigotry was temporal. During the war he concluded, as had most Americans, that Japan would not surrender short of total destruction. He believed what he said about the Japanese, and thought his troops needed to hear it, loudly, often, and with intensity.[18]

. . . .

Careful observers recognized Halsey's Janus face. From afar, Ernest King thought Halsey a "bit of a show-off." One long-standing staff officer in Nouméa believed the "Old Man can put on a good show. He's a sea-going Hamlet." DeWitt Peck felt Halsey "had very unfortunate publicity. I understand the impression that people got from newspaper stories and so on that he was impulsive and a damn-the-torpedoes-full-speed-ahead type. He wasn't." Peck "never saw Halsey make any lightning damn-the-torpedoes decision at all. He was a thoughtful, intelligent, forceful leader. The impressions he gave were all wrong." Perceptive journalists grasped this. One noted that the admiral "obligingly" spewed "the appropriate curses" whenever reporters were hungry for good copy, and another, Joseph Bryan, who was the son of a Halsey fraternity brother at the University of Virginia, wrote of the dichotomy in "Four-Star Sea Dog," a two-part cover feature in the *Saturday Evening Post*. Bryan paid homage to all the Halsey stereotypes: the admiral was casual, audacious, to the point; he had "never been a spit and polish officer"; his hatred of the Japanese was "ancient and integral and cold." Yet, with fame Halsey had also become "a perfect embodiment of that wartime fiction: the gruff sea dog. He is a direct plagiarism from Robert Louis Stevenson and Howard Pyle, from his blue water oaths to the foul anchor tattooed on his left shoulder."[19]

Halsey was an ambivalent partner in this charade. His unpublished memoir, a typescript of an oral history given in 1946 for Bryan, who ghostwrote Halsey's 1947 autobiography, contains no worse slang for the Japanese than "Nips" and just two direct instances of foul language, and revealed personal aspirations to cook, play piano, and speak a foreign language. In contrast, in his published autobiography Halsey spoke more of drinkers, brawlers, and fighters. He bragged of requisitioning bourbon for carrier pilots, and bemoaned the prohibition of alcohol on ships. He called the Japanese "rat bastards" and "monkey men," mocked "Hirohito's protruding teeth," and described a mass drowning of Japanese sailors as a "rich, rewarding, beautiful slaughter."[20]

As the war neared its finish and yet another round of press requests for interviews arrived, Halsey told a public affairs officer that he had "made a monkey out of myself many times, and I will gracefully submit to other people making a monkey of me if it is necessary." But he did not like it. By war's end, he was thoroughly fed up with his renown. In 1952, he "tore to pieces" a sketch of his wartime service, bemoaning a public portrait that stressed, just "as the correspondents did during the war—a 'Roaring Bull.' I didn't then, nor do I now, like that picture." But from start to finish he was as responsible as any other for the image, and whenever he went looking to assign blame for the phenomenon he never needed to look beyond his wardroom mirror.[21]

. . . .

The legend of Bull Halsey obscured broader truths about the war. Contemporaries and historians claimed his "offensive spirit" and "transparent confidence" had invigorated the Allied fight on Guadalcanal, influenced his headlong commitment of carriers at Santa Cruz and his placement of battleships in confined Solomon waters at the Naval Battle of Guadalcanal, and fueled his devotion to Marines near Henderson Field. This picture is incomplete. American fortune on Guadalcanal did turn with Halsey's appearance in Nouméa, but it was also proximate to the arrival of massive reinforcements, some coming from locales as distant as the Mediterranean and much of them emerging only after Roosevelt himself so ordered. Halsey's decisions to court battle at Santa Cruz in late October, accept it off Guadalcanal in mid-November, and sustain it across many weeks near Henderson Field were the function of policy before they were the product of personality. After Ghormley had failed, Nimitz had sent Halsey to fight. Fight Halsey did. By October, given the strategic path set in both Washington and Tokyo, there was no reasonable alternative for a local commander, American or Japanese. As Halsey told the men of the *Boise* within the first week of his South Pacific command, their collective "course has been charted. We must avenge and avenge and avenge. The way to accomplish this is simple. We must hit and hit and hit and then hit again with everything we have and keep on hitting. The thought and the word defense must be abhorrent to us. Offense must be written on our brain in letters of fire. Steam ahead full speed in the face of every obstacle and do not stop till the foe's back is broken."[22]

Halsey's outsized personality also consigned to history's shadow the complex political and social landscape of his South Pacific headquarters in Nouméa. In 1946 James Michener, who as a wartime reserve lieutenant had been assigned to write the administrative history of Halsey's command, abandoned the task, almost as if he could not tell the truth about the place while adhering to the conventions of accuracy. Two years later, his fictional *Tales of the South Pacific*, describing a region full of intrigue, shenanigans, and farce, won a Pulitzer Prize. Halsey's South Pacific, centered on the small French colonial capital of Nouméa, New Caledonia, was every bit as strange as Michener's, and, for Bill Halsey, quite a bit more challenging in the months after the Guadalcanal fight ebbed and as the struggle to reach Rabaul gained new steam.

New Caledonia had always been different. The largest of all South Pacific islands, from the start its size and large deposits of nickel and chrome promised to European imperialists something more than standard aspirations of copra and coconut. France claimed it for Catholicism and a penal colony in 1853, and for the next seven decades Parisian officials dumped upon its shores some 15,000 common criminals and political exiles, including many from the ill-fated Paris Commune of 1871, as well as about 2,500 respectable settlers engaged in coffee growing and cattle ranching. After World War I, French, German, and Japanese mining companies arrived, accompanied by a growing French functionary class and imported Javanese and Tonkinese indentured laborers, necessary after native Kanaks proved uncooperative workhands. By World War II the island housed a rich concentrate of humanity, sheltering the descendants of hard-core criminals, political dissidents, settlers, industrialists, civil servants, native Kanaks, and displaced Asians among its population of

60,000, of which 10,000 called compact Nouméa home. Although it was, according to credible authority, acre for acre "probably the richest land in mineral resources in the world," metropolitan France had always treated New Caledonia rather like Tahiti's ugly sister, and, by the 1930s, a combination of geological accident and French design had made the island "like none other in the South Seas."[23]

Then World War II arrived. As in other locales where the tricolor flew, France's swift defeat in June 1940 precipitated a scramble for local control as Caledonians aligned with the Vichy regime, with the vanquished yet official government, or with an incipient Free French fighting movement operating from a London hotel suite and under the direction of a brash, unknown junior general named Charles de Gaulle. Ham-handed threats, two-bit conspiracies, and very real riots involving nearly half the Nouméan populace produced a shaky foundation for the Free French and de Gaulle but left the business community, the landed elite, and a Communist clique at loggerheads for local prestige. Wartime shortages and the territory's stubborn commitment to its increasingly worthless scrip then propelled a slide in New Caledonia's economic life. By early 1941 basic food staples were scarce, and even the island's mining interests had difficulty navigating the otherwise routine accounting of international credits and debits. According to Australian diplomats, New Caledonia was then a basket case, its internal political situation complex to the point of comedy, its economy isolated, its currency barter, its citizenry obsessed with hoarding when not consumed with trifling intrigue every bit the equal to—and a good bit more real than—that portrayed in the wartime blockbuster movie *Casablanca*.[24]

Into this cauldron of petty ambition and economic lethargy strode the Americans. In March 1942, 15,000 troops, the progenitors of Patch's American Division, disembarked from seven transports and spilled through Nouméa's narrow streets. This cascade upset fragile alliances among locals, some of whom cheered the newcomers and others who feared U.S. presence would overwhelm French sensibilities. In early May street riots again gripped the town, prompting Patch to seek martial law, a petition that rocketed through War Department channels, across to the secretary of state, on to Roosevelt, and thence to de Gaulle in London. Indignant and pragmatic, the Free French leader acquiesced to military rule in Nouméa if necessary, but forever after suspected American imperialism at play in New Caledonia.[25]

The crisis passed without martial law, but the episode foreshadowed much of the American experience in New Caledonia during the war. French colonial and American newcomer never became comfortable neighbors, and the Allied presence in Nouméa was never free from the larger, often confused, and always delicate relations between the United States, the Free French, and the Vichy regime. On a human scale, as many as 300,000 Americans reached New Caledonia in the following years, to live there as part of the South Pacific command apparatus or to pass through on the way to or from battle, creating a complex social tapestry. Men such as Halsey, military officers with scant experience in civil affairs and uneven talent for diplomacy, struggled to grasp Caledonian political intrigue and its relationship to wider coalition warfare while managing a lonely and sometimes randy American force so far from home.

Halsey's efforts to trade the dank *Argonne* for healthier billeting in Nouméa served as his introduction to nutty New Caledonia. In the fall of 1942 Auguste Montchamp, the colonial governor, deflected three requests to come ashore, citing concerns for Free French prerogative, a recalcitrant attitude probably fueled by U.S. accommodation of rival Vichy interests in North Africa following Allied landings there on November 8. In what Halsey told Nimitz was "more or less a jackass arrangement," the Americans eventually finagled the use of an elementary school, then between terms, as an expedient toehold in the town. Facing eviction by returning grade-schoolers as the new year approached, however, Halsey solicited Montchamp's help for a fourth time, suggesting (rather erroneously) that New Caledonia's small militia was a component of his command, arguing (somewhat dubiously) that he could merely requisition quarters if it came to that, and revealing (quite ominously) a heavy hand that did not sit well with the French, who came to believe Halsey "would throw out the Governor himself to occupy his residence." To Nimitz, Halsey explained that local officials feared a large American presence "would not uphold the dignity and sovereignty of the Fighting (not here) French," and to the secretary of the Navy Halsey declared that his "principal difficulty" in the South Pacific was not the killing Japanese on Guadalcanal but rather "the non-cooperative 'business as usual' attitude of the French."[26]

Halsey's squabble with Montchamp reached the White House in mid-January 1943. Roosevelt, who viewed de Gaulle as a difficult, pugnacious, and important ally, authorized an entreaty to the Free French leader to prod Montchamp into action and quietly indicated to the Navy Department that he would again support the imposition of martial law if necessary. Montchamp blinked. By early spring, Halsey had a parcel of land to build a structure adequate for 250 staff members. For senior officer quarters, he secured two Quonset huts and a ramshackle French house and, for himself, the former Japanese consulate, of all places. It "was one of the few brick houses in Noumea," Halsey explained, "and its cool, airy hilltop commanded one of the most superb views I have ever seen." The house contained the "usual watercolor of Fujiyama, the usual embroideries of goldfishes and geishas, and the usual dwarf pine in the corner," all of which Halsey quite improbably kept. For the next year and a half, he took great pleasure when, each morning, "the Marine guards raised the American flag over this bit of property which had once belonged to a representative of Japan."[27]

From this modest footprint the American military presence grew enormously. Eventually some 30,000 to 40,000 Americans occupied the immediate area, outnumbering Nouméan inhabitants by three or four to one. The imprint made a mockery of French rule. The visitors assumed many responsibilities of civil government, including the up-keep of harbor facilities, road maintenance, public health and hygiene, and the water and electrical supply. Soldiers, sailors, and Marines seeped into every corner of Nouméan life. They took over the town's three little hotels, boarded in every available private home, controlled all quay space in the harbor, and established twenty-six separate head-quarters, medical units, and administrative offices within the twenty square blocks of the town center. American officials censored information, restricted travel, controlled the lone radio station, and for a while made secret even the weather report, all in the name of a war that was all too real for Halsey and military men but had become an abstraction for the majority of Caledonians after the immediate threat to the colony passed in the spring of 1942. In May 1943, in response to a biting French claim that he had failed to build necessary facilities for his men, Halsey told the Navy Department that since he had arrived the previous fall his command had constructed 2,186 buildings, had under construction an additional 336, and had plans for untold more. For every 1,000 American troops on the island, he added, 905 lived in tents, 90 were housed in structures built by or for the Americans, and only 5 were billeted in French buildings, mostly high-ranking officers renting homes or hotel rooms or boarding with French families. All of this was true, but it also underscored to Caledonians what they already knew: American faces, influences, and effects had washed upon their insular shore like a tidal wave, and would not soon recede.[28]

Wartime surveillance further undercut relations between the two groups. Nouméa and its port promised valuable information to a skilled enemy agent, and by early 1943 there was enough known of Japanese espionage in Honolulu prior to the war to put Americans on high alert. Moreover, the complicated political topography of Nouméa reminded Halsey of the confused loyalties in Queenstown during World War I. So within weeks of moving ashore he expanded his command's counterintelligence force and requested weekly updates on their findings.[29]

These investigations uncovered spies real and imagined. There was the German settler who was found with a sketch pad inside a restricted boundary near an American encampment; the clerk for the French Bank of Indochina who had passed information on local Allied lend-lease transactions to the home office in Saigon, then under de facto Japanese control; and the woman who, through an affair with an American, had learned of and passed on details about U.S. ship movements to a Japanese mine laborer, himself an enemy agent. But there was also the firebrand publisher of a weekly newsletter accused of fascist loyalties who was guilty of nothing but local muck-raking; the promiscuous lemonade stand attendant, "the best looking native girl in town" in the eyes of one counterintelligence agent, whose affections extended without prejudice to locals and indentured laborers and both white and black American servicemen, no doubt offending certain sensibilities; and the local barber, whose Communist sympathies and penchant for braggadocio had fueled a four-month investigation only to find him to be a man of petty ambition and ambivalent sexuality. A surveillance report on a nearly professional troublemaker typified these misplaced security concerns: "Suspect man in late thirties with wooly hair. Typical malcontent and work shirker who goes in for political agitation. Caledonian born. Father a convict named Marcaeder, a bootmaker, and mother a Caledonian native. Before war went to France and spent 3 or 4 years in low quarters of Paris with leftist loafers."[30]

As his familiarity with New Caledonia grew, Halsey recognized the insidious influence of intramural Nouméan machinations, now fueled by legitimate wartime anxieties, as well as the makings of a runaway U.S. counterintelligence operation. The Americans conducted over 1,000 investigations on the island by early 1944, counted as informants nearly 500 Caledonians, and identified 294 suspicious persons, of which nearly 150 were suspected of being enemy agents. These tallies represented one in ten, one in twenty, one in thirty-five, and one in sixty-five Nouméans, respectively. Halsey concluded that they were a gross improbability and the function of overzealous "sleuth-hounds," an assessment he used to rebuff a personal emissary of Bill Donovan, head of the Office of Strategic Services—forerunner to the Central Intelligence Agency—and a judgment upon which he relied to reduce the counterintelligence investigations on the island in late 1943.[31]

While it lasted, however, widespread spying infused already turbulent relations between everyday Americans and Caledonians otherwise linked by commerce and sex. The war brought an economic boom to the island. Before hostilities, Nouméa had two laundries, three small movie houses, three undersized hotels, and six modest restaurants. After Pearl Harbor, a plethora of laundries, sandwich shops, soft drink stands, improvised bars, and makeshift cafés sprang up. In wartime Nouméa, a single establishment routinely sold 18,000 beers and 5,100 hamburgers each day. A thriving black market emerged, in everything from gasoline to milk to counterfeit currency, fueling a petty criminal element that in at least one instance drew American supply troops into a long-running scheme to pilfer official stocks. A vibrant trade in opium among the few Chinese on the island ensnared more than a few servicemen, and American influx disturbed local labor relations as indentured Javanese and Tonkinese fled their servitude at twenty times the prewar rate to sell souvenirs or clean GI clothes. According to the Australian consul in Nouméa, by the first anniversary of the Americans' arrival every aspect of Nouméan life had become "overshadowed by the prevailing occupation of making money out of the Americans. There must be few people, white or black, who are not benefiting from them directly or indirectly."[32]

Reciprocal benefits for Americans were often found in the bedroom, where enough activity was immoral or illegal to catch Halsey's eye. His command dishonorably discharged one sailor for menacing a thirteen-year-old girl, and courts-martialed three others for the sexual enslavement of two Javanese domestics. A farmer's allegation of sailors molesting and then killing sheep made its way from outrageous claim to an offer of nearly $4,000 to cover damages. In late 1943 a volatile accusation by the local governor that black American servicemen had become "the terror of the white women in New Caledonia" found voice in *Time* magazine and prompted Roosevelt's personal request for information. In an eight-page letter supported by fourteen enclosures, Halsey related that eight white and eighteen black servicemen had indeed been tried for sexual crimes in 1943, resulting in twice as many convictions as acquittals and relatively harsh penalties for the guilty, even when, Halsey rather ineptly added, "the plaintiffs were known prostitutes or 'easy' women."[33]

Halsey, who believed "fighting men are frolicking men," thought these numbers represented neither a large military force running wild nor a problem that a bit of sanctioned intercourse could not solve.

Prostitution, from time immemorial the handmaiden of military camps the world over, thrived in Nouméa. For the price of fare, taxi drivers brought servicemen to any number of underground bordellos, where Americans could expect to pay fifty cents for native companionship and three to four dollars for French women. For a while venereal disease was as common as the prostitutes and, across some months, as likely as dysentery among the American troops. To combat this malady, the U.S. Army established and Halsey condoned underground ties to the main French bordello, known locally and infamously as the Pink House, where military police kept order and Colonel Arthur King, the Army Force surgeon general, set up a prophylactic station. Through the spring of 1943 and beyond, about 6,000 visitors a month patronized its ten bedrooms. While it operated, the French maintained a pretense of ignorance for the sake of their wives and daughters, American authorities used the guise of French sovereignty as a veil, and the Pink House thrived in broad daylight with a queue of men sometimes a block long shuffling ever nearer to its Potemkin delights. Years later, Arthur King recalled that not a single case of venereal disease traced its origins to the place.[34]

The industry of working girls failed to satiate all sexual ambition. In the late summer of 1943 a court inquiry into the homosexuality of two naval officers grew into a veritable dragnet. Military police raided parties, picnics, and parks, especially one near the town center known colloquially as Triangle Gardens. The investigation enmeshed a wide assortment of suspects, from those of lowly enlisted ranks to a Marine colonel, from dispossessed Caledonians to local luminaries, and painted Nouméa as a sort of homosexual wonderland or, as one suspect put it while being interrogated, a place well known as "hot" for "us gay people." By October, many dozens of servicemen filled a makeshift brig known as the Queer Stockade, and the whole affair had become something of a witch hunt, memorialized in *Tales of the South Pacific,* where an accusatory whiff could cause panic: "From time to time, horrifying stories would creep around a unit: 'Two men down at Noumea. Officers, too. Dishonorable discharge! Couple years at Portsmouth!' And everyone would shudder . . . and wonder."[35]

The issue was no fiction to Halsey. Some accused were innocent, and all would be considered harassed in the light of latter-day sensibilities. In the milieu of 1943, however, many were also guilty. As these cases reached his office, Halsey exchanged at least twelve cables with Washington officials to gauge his command prerogative and obligation. In the end, he was as lenient as law and rule allowed. The probe had implicated thirty-nine Navy men, sixteen Marines, and forty-four soldiers, tallies Halsey reduced to seven sailors, two Marines, and five soldiers, largely by eliminating hearsay evidence and, in three instances, because the offender "was entirely passive" or "so drunk he didn't know what he was doing." Although some staff officers felt this tact established an insufficient deterrent, Halsey also recommended where he could the least severe discharge available to the offenders: dishonorable for sailors and Marines, undesirable for soldiers. As he always had, Halsey displayed a liberal impulse toward his charges, but judged harshly those who had broken faith with central tenets of military service. He toiled hard, for instance, to ensure a sentence including hard labor for one Marine lieutenant who had used his rank to coerce sexual relations with a subordinate. But mostly, he had a war to fight, and preferred to keep his gaze upon the Japanese to his front rather than the bathhouses and park benches to his rear.[36]

. . . .

This was the perspective he would have conveyed to staff officers unhappy with his adjudication of the salacious cases. By the summer of 1943, the twenty-five men Halsey had brought ashore the previous November had swelled to over 300, 95 percent of whom were naval officers, most of the rest Marines, and just two who wore Army khaki. In early 1943 came a deputy commander, Rear Admiral Theodore "Ping" Wilkinson, who had won the Medal of Honor for bravery off the coast of Veracruz in 1914 and had an excellent reputation within the Navy. Many others reaching Halsey's inner circle did so upon compatible personalities as much as vocational capacity. His prewar cohort of Browning, Ashford, Dow, and Moulton had already grown with the arrival of Herb Carroll, the admiral's yeoman, Benedicto Tulao, the admiral's mess attendant, and William Kitchell, by 1943 well established as Halsey's flag lieutenant. Others now followed. Lieutenant Commander Gene Markey, a screenwriter, movie producer, and husband to some of Hollywood's great beauties, including Joan Bennett, Hedy Lamarr, and Myrna Loy, was for a time Halsey's assistant intelligence officer, and Robert Montgomery, a prominent actor already nominated twice for Academy Awards, served on the South Pacific staff before transfer to the European theater. Halsey collected people, and he often held fast to those who fit his temperament: Dow and Moulton stayed with him to the end of the war, Tulao until Halsey retired, Kitchell and Carroll to Halsey's death, and Markey and Montgomery beyond even the grave—Markey, as a business partner with Halsey's son, and Montgomery, as the producer of *The Gallant Hours,* a 1960 film starring James Cagney that depicted Halsey's command of the Guadalcanal fight.[37]

As Halsey's command grew, his inner circle of associates shrank. This was the result of the rigors of wartime work and the intense personal loyalties Halsey elicited. As was his wont, he usually embraced a handful of valued men and then spoiled them. In fitness reports Halsey wrote that Ashford had "excellent military and personal character"; Kitchell had taken to naval life with "ability, adaptability, interest, and enthusiasm"; Moulton was "superior in every respect"; and Dow was "well balanced," had "a keen grasp and excellent military judgment," and, like Moulton, was "superior in every respect." Halsey's men returned his devotion, sometimes to the point of hero worship. By the middle of the war, Ashford believed Halsey was a "very good" pilot, a preposterous judgment, and by the end of the war another believed Halsey's "whole mob" was "so vigorously loyal" to the admiral "that nothing should be permitted to ever dim that feeling."[38]

Sometime in the spring of 1943 this admirable sentiment began to erode the free and frank exchange of ideas upon which Halsey's command and leadership had always relied. As early as December, Halsey battled the Navy to get Commander Oliver "Scrappy" Kessing, one of his "oldest and best friends" but a well-known drinker throughout the Navy, promoted to captain and transferred from sleepy duty as an ROTC instructor to take command of the burgeoning Guadalcanal naval base. Ernest King refused, believing Kessing's record barely merited his current post, let alone an important wartime job. This produced half a dozen heated exchanges between Halsey and Navy Department officials, after which Kessing finally arrived on Guadalcanal, but without the four stripes of a captain. "I do not know why he was passed over nor do I care," Halsey complained to Nimitz. "I know him well and personally. He is a fighting man. Peace time and war time standards have small relationship. He will make good in any man's war, and this is every man's war." Weeks later, when Halsey saw Frank Knox and Nimitz in late January, he declared that if Kessing's promotion had not occurred by the time Halsey returned to Nouméa he would merely order Kessing to "assume rank, uniform, and title, of Captain, U.S. Navy." Nimitz "had a fit," Halsey remembered. "For God's sakes," the Pacific Fleet commander implored, "don't do it. You'll foul up everything." Kessing's promotion came through normal channels soon thereafter, but the episode fostered an impression of a senior intensely loyal to his subordinates, sometimes to the point of ill-considered judgment.[39]

From his short time with Halsey during his January Pacific tour, Knox had warmed to the admiral as a fighter but had grown cold on his administrative abilities, an intuition reinforced not only by the Kessing fracas, but also by Halsey's feud with New Caledonian officials over housing, then reaching its zenith, and by the "saturnine character" of Miles Browning, who had, in the words of Nimitz's biographer, "succeeded in offending Knox as he had so many others." Concluding that Halsey's staff was, in the words of one distinguished postwar observer, "a casual, slipshod organization of brilliant individualists," Knox determined Halsey needed a new chief of staff, and he found willing conspirators in King, who had long believed Browning was "no damn good at all," and Nimitz, who had the previous month already suggested to Halsey a switch, especially since a recent affair Browning had had with a fellow officer's wife had wrecked Browning's already shaky reputation beyond the point of repair.[40]

Halsey acknowledged his chief of staff's shortcomings. He disliked Browning's hair-trigger temperament and would not have disagreed much with one description of Browning as a "lean, hawk-like man" who "drank too much, too often" and who "had a capacity for insulting behavior." Sometimes, Halsey told Nimitz, "I should like to wring his neck." But Halsey also appreciated Browning's operational acumen, especially as it related to aviation, and credited him with many of the Navy's meager successes in early 1942 during Halsey's carrier raids, which was a fair assessment. Following the Guadalcanal crisis, and confident in his ability to channel Browning's energies in positive directions, Halsey was "almost superstitious" about not replacing his chief of staff "now when things appear to be smoothing out." Such was Halsey's prestige in the springtime of 1943 that three successive levels of seniority—Nimitz, King, and Knox—accepted his rebuff, for the time being.[41]

. . . .

Devotion such as this made for a merry band of brothers in Nouméa. Although some observers judged Halsey lazy, the admiral believed in steady rather than frenetic work and grasped that the nation kept him in uniform not for what he did but for what he thought, a task he accomplished better while well rested. He usually woke near 6:30 AM and was at his desk by 8:30. Meetings with his chief of staff and close aides began the day, followed by reading dispatches, preparing or endorsing reports, and catching up on correspondence. After a light lunch, Halsey took an hour's walk before presiding at administrative or operational staff conferences. He tried to finish each day with visits to various military establishments around Nouméa, and at least three times a week he capped daylight with an ocean swim. Halsey dined at dusk with a handful of staff officers, subordinate commanders, and visitors, the food being good enough to expand his waistline to thirty-eight inches, requiring new trousers. He retired for the day shortly after dinner and almost never later than 10:00. Altogether, the New Caledonia routine harnessed his sixty-year-old energies for those explosive moments of combat that would surely come his way.[42]

For his younger subordinates Halsey valued tomfoolery as an outlet for wartime stress. Nearly as soon as he had moved ashore, he commissioned a foraging expedition to San Francisco's Fairmont Hotel, a mission netting a commercial kitchen, bar supplies, furniture, and a baby grand piano. He also established a secure alcohol supply, a delicate task at one point requiring the surreptitious labeling of a hundred cases of liquor as pineapple juice, and at another point demanding a near-conspiracy between Halsey and the executive director of the National Distillers Association to overcome tightening home-front stocks. Soon, the two Quonset huts and French home used by senior staff became known, respectively, as Wicky-Wacky Lodge and Havoc Hall, and together they became something of a war zone fraternity row.[43]

Parties were popular with visiting ship skippers, Red Cross volunteers, and military nurses. Some nights were worthy of fiction. Years after the war, Rear Admiral Arthur Ageton set his potboiler *The Jungle Seas* amid the "bistros and flesh-pots of Noumea," including Massacre Manor, which was a thinly disguised Havoc Hall, where raging benders were the norm. Reading the book in 1953, Halsey told Ageton he thought descriptions of Massacre Manor were "a bit lurid and sexy" and "might hurt some people, especially if they have a guilty conscience." This latter category perhaps included his friend and fellow admiral Bill Calhoun, whose marriage dissolved during the war, and probably a lower-ranking officer on his staff whose wife once implored Halsey to intervene to save her marriage.[44]

It may also have included Halsey himself. By that point in the war his marriage was barren of physical or emotional spoils. Kitchell had taken over the admiral's perfunctory correspondence with Fan, to the dismay of Halsey's two children. A natural flirt, Halsey enjoyed the company of Red Cross girls and Army nurses in Nouméa and kept a ready supply of nylon stockings as party favors, at one time hoarding thirteen pairs of various sizes. Halsey became particularly close to four women, arranging travel and billeting for them as the war progressed, and grew especially friendly with two: a New Zealander to whom he quietly returned "some personal clothing" near the end of the war, and an Army nurse, a little older than most, who was, in the judgment of Arthur King, a "most attractive and sophisticated" lady. As Halsey prepared to leave the South Pacific in the summer of 1944, his friendship with this nurse was worrisome enough to prompt an Army major general to direct King, as her senior medical commander, to either send her home or "take her out on the beach, shoot her, and bury her." After the nurse returned to the United States she wrote Halsey, "Many people have served you, on your staff and under your command in the South Pacific, but I doubt exceedingly if the duty performed by any of them has been more pleasurable than has mine. I feel deeply honored and shall be eternally grateful for the privilege of having served 'COMSOPAC,' " an abbreviation meaning Halsey in his role as commander of the South Pacific.[45]

Whatever distractions these friendships provided Halsey, they did not keep him wedded to Nouméa. In stark contrast to Ghormley, Halsey traveled regularly to the far reaches of his command, especially after the Guadalcanal crisis passed. His first trips to Guadalcanal, in early November and late January, and his orientation to New Zealand right after the New Year, commenced a pattern that held throughout his time in the South Pacific. In 1943 he traveled to Brisbane, Canberra, Sydney, and Melbourne in April; to Efate in May; to Espiritu Santo, Guadalcanal, the Russell Islands, and Efate in June; to Guadalcanal, New Georgia, Espiritu Santo, and Pearl Harbor in September; to Brisbane in October; and to Guadalcanal, Bougainville, and Brisbane again in November. New Year's Day 1944 found him at Pearl Harbor, from where he traveled on to the West Coast, Fort Worth, and Washington; he was at Guadalcanal, the Russell Islands, New Georgia, the Treasuries, and Green Islands in February; he went to Brisbane, Guadalcanal, and Bougainville again in March; to Brisbane one last time in early April; to Pearl Harbor and San Francisco in May; and, when he left the South Pacific for good, to Pearl Harbor in mid-June 1944. In what was in later decades called leadership by walking around, Halsey spent 159 of the 609 days he commanded in the South Pacific traveling, a practice that required two personal pilots and a stable of four planes and that accentuated his strengths as a visceral, hands-on leader.[46]

Visitors came to him, too. At first a trickle during the Guadalcanal crisis, in early 1943 they arrived with increasing regularity, to the point that, one local admiral remembered, Nouméa was "overrun with them." Across the first five months of the year, no fewer than eleven groups, varying in size from two to seventeen dignitaries representing the War, Navy, State, and Treasury Departments, traipsed through Nouméa. When Congress entered summer recess, the politicians came: separate groups of five and seven in June, four in July, and three in each of August and September. At one point Halsey asked Nimitz to limit these trips because they occupied valuable time, but the Pacific Fleet commander demurred, sardonically explaining there were "quite a few people in Washington and elsewhere who think that this is a people's war belonging to the United States and not just to you and me."[47]

One guest in late summer vexed Halsey. On August 25 Eleanor Roosevelt arrived in Nouméa, sent there by her husband, who, contrary to Halsey's belief, felt that that part of the world had been "rather neglected in the matter of visitors." Halsey admired the First Lady but dreaded her arrival, thinking the visit a political gesture. He warmed watching her. Across two days, she visited New Caledonian hospital wards, Red Cross facilities, and recreational centers. In one twelve-hour stretch, she toured three large infirmaries and an officers' rest home, reviewed a Marine raider battalion, twice spoke before thousands of enlisted troops, and was the guest of honor at a dinner with senior military officers. Following a three-week sojourn to New Zealand and Australia, where she kept up the same frenetic pace, she traveled to Guadalcanal, where Halsey had also alighted with Senators Henry Cabot Lodge Jr., James Mead, and Ralph Brewster, a distant maternal cousin. There, in a single day, the First Lady toured a hospital ward, paid respects at a makeshift cemetery, and conferred with commanders. She also managed to see, on three separate occasions— once near noon, a second in midafternoon, and a third late in the evening—a thirty-three-year-old enlisted Army weatherman, Joseph Lash, who had been a friend of the First Lady for years. Before the war, Lash had spent weeks with Eleanor at Hyde Park, the president's New York estate, passed weekend getaways alone with her in Chicago, and enjoyed a third-floor bedroom in the White House set aside for his exclusive use. Although Halsey believed her visit to his command paid important dividends with the rank and file, he blanched at her open affection for Lash. Publicly, Halsey marveled at her energy and her effect on the grievously wounded men she visited, "a sight," he later wrote, he "would never forget." Privately, he wished the First Lady had never visited Guadalcanal.[48]

....

There was not much Halsey could have done about the First Lady's visit, and many other aspects of his South Pacific tour fell beyond his grasp. Although he proved a willing partner with newsmen who conjured the legend of Bull Halsey, like many a celebrity he tired of the private intrusions that accompanied public adulation. As for New Caledonia, he could not dictate the circumstances of life in that distant French colony, a place as eccentric in real life as it was in Michener's imagination, and at least as peculiar as the town portrayed in the film *Casablanca,* beset by the same wartime pressures as Nouméa. De Gaulle himself came to believe that Nouméa was a "cesspool of intrigues," the resident American consul thought the place engulfed in "political pot-boiling," and to Patch the outpost resembled "an island full of Hatfields and McCoys." Halsey would have agreed with all of them, and his challenges with French officials did not fade. As late as December 1943 he found himself explaining away an official complaint filed by de Gaulle over whether Halsey or Montchamp should have occupied the left side of a rear seat in an automobile during a military parade—a farce repeated in May 1944 over the precedence of official cars in a procession to a memorial for American war dead.[49]

As a young destroyer skipper in Queenstown during World War I, Halsey had glimpsed more than appreciated the challenges of fighting from a small outpost far from American shores. The intervening years had bequeathed wisdom and patience in unequal dollops. In New Caledonia, these were sometimes enough, as his adjudication of South Pacific homosexual investigations demonstrated, and sometimes insufficient, as he never mastered relationships with his French hosts. Life in Nouméa made clear to Halsey that war was much more than combat, but the fighting was the feature he was best at. As the interlude following the epic contest for Guadalcanal lengthened, he almost longed for an active fight, where he could again confront the Japanese freely, aggressively, and boldly.

Chapter Twelve

The Crossroads of Command

SOUTH PACIFIC OPERATIONS built slowly after the exhaustion of Guadalcanal. Halsey's first step following the epic battle was a cakewalk. On February 7, 1943, he directed Turner to take the Russell Islands, two isles a mere thirty miles from the northwest tip of Guadalcanal. The Japanese had used them to stage forces heading south, and the Americans now wanted them for the same purpose going north. For the task, code-named Cleanslate, Halsey tapped some 9,000 men, mostly from the newly arrived Forty-Third Infantry Division, to confront a paltry 400 Japanese garrison troops. Arriving on Russell shores on February 21, the Americans discovered that even those few defenders had left. Although they met no resistance until March 6, when the first of five modest air raids materialized, the Americans took until April 17, poking cautiously over undefended ground, to proclaim the place pacified, ready to serve as a tiny stepping-stone.[1]

This two-month plod irked Ernest King. To "what ends are these operations a means?" he queried Nimitz on March 1. The campaign was indeed an "overstuffed affair," to use Morison's phrase, but it nevertheless revealed much and foreshadowed more. For the Japanese, defeat at Buna and Guadalcanal meant retreat farther up the northeast coast of New Guinea in MacArthur's zone and to the middle Solomons in Halsey's sector. Falling back upon interior and shorter defensive lines, however, they grew tactically stronger even as their strategic position weakened, promising any opponent a long grind toward the prize of Rabaul. For the Americans, the bloat of Cleanslate indicated neither a clear sense of nor a strong consensus on how best to leverage grueling triumphs in the lower Solomons and New Guinea. This confusion amplified interservice quarrels stretching from Washington to Brisbane, mostly about which admixture of Southwest and South Pacific operations could now best propel the Allied advance, and in early 1943 disputes over command and strategy in the Pacific came to dominate American discussion and undercut battlefield momentum. Halsey, removed two degrees from Washington officials and subordinate in one way or another to both MacArthur and Nimitz, was as much an observer to these debates as he was a participant. While he readied his own forces for whatever might come, however, he was never far from these high-level discussions. As they developed, he became an essential conduit between the general in Brisbane and the admiral in Honolulu, making effective a series of half-baked compromises stemming from crucial midwar deliberations.[2]

. . . .

Crises through the fall of 1942 had sublimated the Pacific's muddied command relationships. According to the Joint Chiefs' July 1942 directive, Nimitz and the Navy had directed, and MacArthur and the Army had supported, Phase One operations to capture Guadalcanal. This relationship was to flip for Phase Two, the advance up the New Guinea coast and through the remaining Solomon Islands, and Phase Three, the capture of Rabaul itself. But command interaction during Phase One had proved more opaque in practice than prospect, as deficiencies in air and naval support between MacArthur and Halsey indicated, and promised to remain so in subsequent operations, when MacArthur would have operational command but remain even more beholden to Nimitz for maritime support across a broader area. No one much liked this command sophistry, and as combat exigencies faded on Guadalcanal and at Buna, who commanded what, and where, became contentious once again. In December, Marshall bemoaned the "mutual support by lateral liaison" in the far Pacific and argued that MacArthur should control not only all operations but also a significant part of Nimitz's fleet, a position he believed consonant with the age-old dictum of unity of command. King agreed the Pacific command setup was "an unsound military structure," but he and every senior admiral then in uniform refused to broker the wholesale transfer of capital ships to MacArthur's control. His solution, to grant Nimitz command of the entire Pacific, place MacArthur in subordinate oversight of the far Pacific, and leave Halsey tactical control of operations in the Solomons, served only to widen the moat between Army and Navy officials as 1943 approached.[3]

All this left the South Pacific at loose ends. Halsey's planners needed clarity for operations, not only to know "if we are to operate under MacArthur's direction" or to "proceed on our own," but also to infuse future operations with a sound rationale. "Merely to be directed to push up the Solomons is not enough," Peck told Halsey. If the purpose was to capture Rabaul, "our plan might well be to assemble sufficient force and strike directly" at the Japanese stronghold. "If, on the other hand, the basic motive" was one of "containment and attrition" astride MacArthur's and Nimitz's flanks, "then our plan might well be based upon a step-by-step move up the Solomons, bringing steadily increasing pressure to bear on the Japanese, relying heavily on land based air support and conserving to the maximum our own seaborne forces." Halsey sympathized with Peck, though he also knew the Joint Chiefs were far from a consensus over higher command. For him, the occupation of the Russell Islands was an effort to do something—anything—while his seniors in Brisbane, Honolulu, and Washington bickered through their impasse. In the same vein, he also began planning an early April invasion of New Georgia farther up the Solomons, which at least provided his force a guiding star while strategic disputes raged elsewhere.[4]

Hoping a focus on strategy might ease debate over command, in January Washington officials asked MacArthur and Nimitz to update campaign plans. MacArthur held fast to the three-step scheme to capture Rabaul, but, given dogged Japanese resistance, now spread prospective operations over more months than originally conceived and contemplated more force, especially in air power, which had become an arbiter in the region's many battles. Absent "long preparation and great resources," he told the Joint Chiefs, any campaign in the far Pacific would "inevitably lead to disaster," a point of view from which he never wavered. This sensible position did nothing to resolve delicate matters of command or even plans, especially for King, who was anxious for a quick strike to compound the Guadalcanal victory. On the last day of January, the chief of naval operations complained to Nimitz and Halsey that the South Pacific campaign seemed locked in a "status of delay, linger, and wait," tying up the vast bulk of American naval assets in the entire Pacific.[5]

In February Halsey sent a representative to Brisbane to coordinate plans with MacArthur. These deliberations produced a more detailed outline to take Rabaul, code-named Elkton, after the Maryland town popular for Depression-era shotgun weddings. But the plan further delayed immediate operations, especially for New Georgia. This infuriated King, who worried that disheveled Japanese defenses were gaining precious time to rebuild. In early March, he banned Navy ships not already assigned to MacArthur's Seventh Fleet from Australian ports except in cases of grave battle damage, lest they fall into MacArthur's languid orbit, and openly flirted with a complete abandonment of the region in favor of what was then and always had been the Navy's preferred course: a thrust through Central Pacific atolls under Nimitz's direct command, starting with the Gilbert Islands. MacArthur blew up upon learning this, relating to Marshall a long-held figment of his imagination centered on a Navy conspiracy to eliminate the Army entirely—lock, stock, and barrel—and take over sole control of national defense. As spring loomed, then, months of wrangling over command had produced, in the senior American admiral, a willingness to undermine the design of the larger war, and had reignited, in the senior American general serving overseas, an outright delusion. And still the debate over command had yet to stake any middle ground, as indeed there was precious little of that real estate to be found.[6]

At loggerheads, Marshall and King called representatives of each command home for direct consultations. This Pacific Military Conference convened on March 12 in Washington and included Navy and War Department planners as well as representatives from each Pacific area: Major Generals Richard Sutherland—MacArthur's chief of staff—and Kenney came in MacArthur's stead; Harmon, Twining, and Browning for Halsey; and Spruance and Captain Forrest Sherman represented Nimitz. Washington officials were astonished to learn of Elkton's requirements to reach Rabaul—twenty-three divisions, forty-five air groups, and as many warships as the Navy could muster—a force beyond that then in Europe, despite the Allied policy to defeat Germany first, and tallies well above what was remotely possible for the Pacific anytime in 1943. However, in a rare display of intratheater solidarity, the Pacific representatives held firm to these requirements, forcing the Joint Chiefs to temporize. They limited far Pacific goals in 1943 to the approach but not the capture of Rabaul, and gave MacArthur and Halsey a total of seventeen troop divisions and twenty-four air groups, inclusive of Australian and New Zealand contributions. Of these, for his drive through the Solomons, Halsey could draw upon five Army, two Marine, and one Kiwi division as well as six American air groups and whatever small amount of air power New Zealand could supply, a proportion of force befitting his status as the junior partner in the far Pacific. The whole scheme firmly delayed Halsey's April invasion of New Georgia until MacArthur initiated major operations in New Guinea, a result a disappointed King agreed to only after Halsey promised to pounce on New Georgia sooner if any fleeting opportunity emerged.[7]

Amazingly, all this left untouched the basic question of Pacific command that had so vexed the debate. From the first weeks of war, Marshall, King, and their proxies had wrestled with the issue. Resolution had evaded them and compromise had proved temporary, even ephemeral. Now exhausted with the issue, the Joint Chiefs at last resigned themselves to what they had arranged the previous summer, vesting MacArthur with strategic command in the Southwest and South Pacific areas, giving Nimitz control of the vast bulk of Pacific warships, and leaving Halsey between the two and subordinate to both.

King thought this setup undermined smooth operations. Nimitz felt the arrangement obtuse. MacArthur claimed that of "all the faulty decisions of the war, the failure to unify the command in the Pacific" reigned supreme: it violated fundamental principles of doctrine and command, and could not "be defended in logic, in theory, or even in common sense." Others called the command arrangement a "monstrosity." In the war's first desperate weeks, Marshall had told his American and British peers "there must be one man in command" of each major theater because control through cooperation would surely founder upon the shoals of "human frailties"; and only unified command could "solve nine-tenths" of the myriad challenges global war would surely bring. The Allies achieved integrated command in every other corner of the globe, overcoming not only interservice but also intra-Allied prerogatives. In the end, however, neither Marshall, nor King, nor even Leahy or the president proved willing to force unity of command in the Pacific. They were simply unwilling to harm their relationships with each other over this one issue when they needed each other's goodwill on so many other matters of world war. Only time could tell if the dividends of such a trade would exceed its tax.[8]

. . . .

Amity in Washington burdened Pacific officers with this convoluted arrangement. MacArthur and Nimitz could not rely upon fealty to smooth the way. Neither knew the other well, and mutual distrust far outweighed shared devotion. As Army chief of staff in the early 1930s, MacArthur had battled Navy interests in Depression-era Washington, and a quarrelsome relationship with Admiral Thomas Hart, the ranking Navy officer in Manila at the war's outset, had encumbered him with a naval phobia to the point of hysteria. Nimitz's attitude toward MacArthur was less freighted with personal baggage, but bashing the Army general was accepted, encouraged, and rewarded among Nimitz intimates in Honolulu. Throughout the active fighting in the far Pacific, the two commanders exchanged few direct messages. Despite numerous entreaties from Washington officials, neither found opportunity to cross the Coral Sea to see the other during Nimitz's three trips to the South Pacific, in October 1942 and January and June of 1943. Astonishingly, their first wartime conference did not occur until the spring of 1944, well after the major fighting in Halsey's area had concluded. By then, a "veritable wall" divided the theaters, a demarcation known as the "Pope's Line" among staff officers in both Brisbane and Honolulu.[9]

All this begged intermediaries. At first Nimitz used Vice Admiral Arthur Carpender, leading MacArthur's small Seventh Fleet, for influence in MacArthur's zone, lobbying for a naval sweep through the Torres Strait, an air strike on Palembang oil fields, and a blockade of Borneo oil supplies, all of which extended far beyond the horizon of MacArthur's existing plans. When the Army commander banned Carpender from direct communications with Honolulu, Nimitz turned to the occasional refugee from MacArthur's area. A Seventh Fleet cruiser division commander recalled that whenever he "passed through Pearl Harbor, Nimitz would question me very thoroughly about MacArthur," and even junior officers on the heels of short tours in Brisbane were "greeted like a Marco Polo" upon their return to Hawaii, "debriefed like a prisoner of war," and released only after "supplying twenty-five pages anatomizing MacArthur country." This modus operandi could hardly prove satisfying, however, and increasingly Nimitz turned to the one conduit he had all along: Bill Halsey. In the late spring of 1943, Nimitz took to describing Halsey as his "agent in all dealings with the Southwest Pacific Area," began including Halsey on his meager correspondence with anybody within MacArthur's orbit, and told all Pacific Fleet subordinates to do the same.[10]

Fitting easily between MacArthur and Nimitz would strain Halsey's considerable interpersonal skills. He too had never met MacArthur, and his early wartime impressions of the general reflected Navy animus as well as particular frustration with the meager air support from the Southwest Pacific during the Guadalcanal fight. In a February 1943 letter to Nimitz, Halsey called MacArthur "Little Doug" and a "self-advertising Son of a Bitch," a reference to recent Southwest Pacific press releases trumpeting MacArthur's victory at Buna but slighting success at Guadalcanal.[11]

As he laid plans for a mid-April conference in Brisbane with MacArthur to flesh out Elkton's operational details, Halsey knew not what to expect. MacArthur's seniority far outpaced the two years of age separating the men. In World War I, as Lieutenant Commander Halsey skippered a single destroyer off Ireland's coast, Brigadier General MacArthur commanded an infantry division at the fighting front. In the early 1920s, as Commander Halsey filed attaché reports from a Berlin desk, Major General MacArthur revolutionized education at West Point as its superintendent. In the early 1930s, as Captain Halsey traded the floating hulk *Reina Mercedes* for yet more routine destroyer command at sea, General MacArthur became the Army's chief of staff, the four stars upon his collar outranking every soldier in the nation. In the later 1930s, as Halsey cut his teeth in naval aviation alongside lieutenants, MacArthur became a de facto Philippine field marshal in Manila, where he helped reverse long-established American plans to retreat from the archipelago should war come. After Pearl Harbor and before America's military altar became cluttered with icons, MacArthur was the only senior officer whose visage eclipsed Halsey's bust. MacArthur's defense of Bataan and Corregidor begot a thriving industry in buttons, pendants, photographs, and film. Within weeks of the Pearl Harbor attack, MacArthur was the namesake of parks, streets, buildings, and babies from New York to Los Angeles. Within months, the first of many adoring wartime biographies became a best seller, and before they even met, MacArthur had made his third appearance on the cover of *Time*, a full half year before Halsey made his debut.[12]

They were dissimilar men. MacArthur outclassed Halsey in brainpower. Indeed, few men in uniform could match the general's cerebral talent and none could boast of anything close to his personal library of 6,000 books. A lifetime of thought and decades of senior staff and command experience had made MacArthur unique even among the handful of military geniuses who bestrode the global stage of World War II. But the Army general lacked Halsey's open, democratic approach and its corollary, personal rapport. According to one biographer, MacArthur was simply "too aloof and too correct in manner, speech, and dress" for that favored Halsey stratagem to work. Whereas enlisted men loved Halsey, even when he made mistakes, they occasionally respected MacArthur. Sometimes they called him Dugout

THE CROSSROADS OF COMMAND

Doug, recalling MacArthur's reluctance to leave Corregidor's tunnels for Bataan's mud, and they were known to heckle his image on movie newsreels, a reaction rare if not outright inconceivable among Halsey's charges at midwar.[13]

They used their staffs differently. The men closest to Halsey were his compatriots and comrades, sometimes to their collective detriment, and acted fundamentally as a sounding board. MacArthur, inclined to keep his own counsel, used his juniors as a shield from wider input. A Renaissance man from an earlier century sitting atop a modern military machine, MacArthur had not so much a staff as he did a court, led by Major General Sutherland, an efficient, egotistical Yale graduate; personified best by his intelligence officer, Brigadier General Charles Willoughby, a German immigrant with aristocratic airs and an uneven capacity for analysis; and dominated through and through by a small collection of fellow Philippine escapees, known, among themselves affectionately and by others derisively, as the Bataan Gang, a band of loyalists and sycophants. Many outsiders saw in Sutherland an insecure and ruthless gatekeeper, in Willoughby an example of loyalty trumping competence, and in most of the rest a mediocrity abetted by MacArthur's peccadilloes and redeemed only by his singular gifts as a commander and strategist. MacArthur's relations with subordinate commanders were more regular, but his nickname for them also signaled insularity: the Ku Klux Klan, reflecting the names of his ground forces commander, Walter Krueger; his Fifth Air Forces commander, George Kenney; and Thomas Kinkaid, who had left the South Pacific for Aleutian operations in late 1942 before replacing Carpender as the Seventh Fleet commander in the summer of 1943.

Beyond all that, the organizations in Brisbane and Nouméa were poorly suited for interaction. Halsey's staff of 300 was overwhelmingly naval in composition and outlook, and nine in ten of MacArthur's 400 wore an Army uniform. As a result, one senior South Pacific officer confided in his diary, in neither place did "the actual mechanics" of coordination exist, even in those instances where everyone was "willing and anxious for team work." In all the months of campaigning in the region, South Pacific and Southwest Pacific staff contingents met but twice to detail operational plans, and most in either locale would have agreed with an assistant gunnery officer in Nouméa, who recalled that there was little to no interaction on an ongoing basis. Those links, he maintained, occurred at "primarily a pretty high level."[14]

All this meant that Halsey and MacArthur relations would constitute diplomacy. As Halsey winged his way toward Brisbane on April 15 for their first meeting, yet another Army-Navy tempest played out. In early March, Fifth Air Force planes had obliterated a Japanese convoy of eight destroyers and eight transports ferrying 6,900 troops from Rabaul to Lae, sinking every troopship, half of the destroyers, and killing or turning back all but 1,200 of the Japanese badly needed in New Guinea. But MacArthur's thirst for publicity and Kenney's penchant for hyperbole marred this decisive victory with wild claims of the destruction of twelve transports, three cruisers, and seven destroyers and the deaths of over 12,000 Japanese, an exaggeration that even the Army Air Forces in Washington quickly recognized and that a subsequent investigation confirmed. At the time, however, MacArthur used the victory to needle the Navy, telling reporters on the eve of Halsey's arrival the "control of the sea no longer depends solely or even perhaps primarily upon naval power, but upon air power operating from land bases held by ground troops."[15]

When they first shook hands on the tarmac of a Brisbane airfield, MacArthur and Halsey shared only the ties of a life in uniform and a tenuous link dating to the Philippine-American War, where Halsey's father, skippering the *General Alvara,* had been an acquaintance of MacArthur's father, the general commanding American ground forces in Manila. Yet, alone among the eight Americans to earn five-star rank from the war—a group including George Marshall, Dwight Eisenhower, and Hap Arnold in the Army and William Leahy, Ernest King, and Chester Nimitz in the Navy—only they had been born into military households and would never spend a day outside the cocoon of military life. This would have to serve as an elixir if the two men were to mesh and not tangle across the meaty middle of World War II.

Their conference, held across three days, went well enough to produce a detailed plan to capture Rabaul. Code-named Elkton III to distinguish it from earlier iterations, the scheme called for three phases and thirteen distinct operations in a campaign to be called Cartwheel. Its major components would commence with MacArthur's early summer occupation of Woodlark Island and Kiriwina for airfields, followed by operations to take New Georgia in Halsey's zone and the New Guinea coastal towns of Lae, Salamaua, and Finschhafen in MacArthur's area. In the fall, Halsey's invasion of Bougainville and MacArthur's jump from New Guinea to Cape Gloucester on New Britain would follow in quick succession, and the capture of Kavieng and the isolation of Rabaul would mark the arrival of the New Year. Then, sometime in early 1944, the Southwest and South Pacific forces were to converge and seize the Japanese citadel itself.

The only real sticking point concerned New Georgia. MacArthur's designs had already delayed Halsey's plans for the island, and now the general described its prospective assault as a "non-convergent" operation. Instead, he wished Halsey's forces to pass it in favor of a larger jump to Bougainville. Halsey the sailorman would have jumped at the chance, but his initial growth as an area commander urged caution. He argued that Japanese positions in the Solomons still constituted mutually supporting strong points, and the Allies did not yet possess the preponderance of force necessary to justify such a move without an intermediate base within fighter-plane range of Bougainville. MacArthur relented, but only after securing from Halsey another delay of New Georgia operations, to King's ongoing dismay. Described by official Army historians as "complicated but flexible," the final Cartwheel plan envisioned a series of incremental and alternating steps between the South and Southwest Pacific to unsettle Japanese defenses, and would demand as close an integration of relatively independent commands as any campaign of the entire war.[16]

This interdependence would have puzzled those who had labored without success for a cleaner command arrangement in the region. MacArthur and Halsey, however, emerged from their first wartime meeting optimistic. MacArthur said he liked Halsey "from the moment we met." He perceived the admiral as "blunt" and "outspoken," and the fear of losing ships, which MacArthur judged "the bugaboo of many sailors," was "completely alien to his conception of sea action." Halsey was "a real fighting admiral. He has some faults, likes a head-line, thinks a lot of himself, but he's not dumb. Neither is he brilliant and sometimes he might be erratic. He has color and he's a showman. However, he is a fighter and as a general rule people like him. Lots of them will follow him blindly." For his part, Halsey felt as if the two "were lifelong friends." Seldom had a man made a "quicker, stronger, more favorable" impression on Halsey. MacArthur "was then sixty-three years old, but he could have passed for fifty"; his "hair was jet black; his eyes were clear; his carriage was erect"; and he spoke in "a diction I have never heard surpassed." Others noticed the mutual attraction, and press reports fawned over a budding friendship. "Halsey's visit was most welcome and did a world of good," Carpender re-ported to Nimitz, and the "good effect of his personality and sound common sense can hardly be overestimated." Having failed to estab-lish a strong entente with the general himself, an appreciative Nimitz teased Halsey with a *Honolulu Advertiser* clipping on the Brisbane conference, noting, as the article relayed, "General MacArthur and Admiral Halsey are kindred souls." Whether this comity, which al-most alone promised to redeem the disjointed command arrangements for the far Pacific, would prove enough was, in early 1943, anyone's guess.[17]

. . . .

In Washington, King would not then have placed much faith in the prospect. Elkton planning had now postponed Halsey's New Georgia invasion four separate times, moving it from April 1 to May 15, and in early May MacArthur would delay it further, first to June 4 and then to June 15 before finally setting the assault near the end of the month to align the operation with strikes in his own sector. Although Halsey diplomatically claimed this procrastination "made little differ-ence to him," it elicited heckles among South Pacific planners and sent King into near apoplexy. By the spring of 1943 the Navy had placed the lion's share of the American Navy in Halsey's hands, including, most of the time, five carriers, six battleships, thirteen cruisers, dozens of destroyers, and the bulk of the troops and supply ships then flying an American ensign, organized into seven task forces. Adding the nearly 287,000 airmen and soldiers ashore at various South Pacific bases, Halsey controlled over 600,000 men in uniform, effectively as large of an American command as any then deployed anywhere in the world. But this powerful punch sat distressingly idle across the spring of 1943. At sea, a few ships thrice lobbed shells at the Munda airfield on New Georgia, on four occasions a task force did the same to an airfield being constructed near Vila on Kolombangara, and once Rear Admiral Tip Merrill's cruisers and destroyers managed to sink a pair of Japanese destroyers. For King, this fell short of the hard hits that could win the war for the Allies anytime soon, a judgment Nimitz shared. They knew MacArthur had dictated most of the delays, but believed "their cause must be shared" by Halsey. In early April, these men earmarked three cruisers and four destroyers from the South Pacific for operations elsewhere, the first time since the previous summer that Navy strength in the region fell for reasons other than battle loss.[18]

Worse, the springtime lull allowed the reeling Japanese time to solidify their defensive positions, the very thing King most feared. In MacArthur's sector they built or substantially expanded airfields in New Guinea and New Ireland; in Halsey's zone they did the same on Buka Island, at Buin on Bougainville, and at Munda. At Rabaul, the Japanese stronghold had been bothered very little by Kenney's irregular air raids, and by the time MacArthur and Halsey had finalized Cartwheel plans, the Japanese had planted there a force of nearly 100,000 men, greatly improved the two existing airfields and added four more, and placed in the surrounding hills nearly 400 antiaircraft guns, dozens of automatic cannon, hundreds of fixed beach positions, and coastal defense batteries housing thirty-eight massive barrels.[19]

The reprieve bequeathed to Yamamoto the tactical initiative, an increasingly rare luxury for the Japanese. In late March he and his Third Fleet commander, Admiral Jisaburo Ozawa, committed nearly 350 aircraft to Operation I, a counterattack upon Allied positions on Guadalcanal and in New Guinea. On April 7 some 224 planes set off for Guadalcanal in the emperor's largest air strike since Pearl Harbor. On April 11, 12, and 14, Yamamoto aimed at New Guinea with 100-, 173-, and 186-plane raids, a shocking display of latent Japanese might in the region. These raids produced dogfights of the likes not seen since the previous fall but they yielded little. Against fifty-five airplane losses of their own, the Japanese sank a destroyer, a small corvette, a tanker, and two transports and destroyed perhaps thirty-five aircraft.

Japanese pilots, however, claimed a cruiser, two destroyers, twenty-five transports, and over a hundred planes. This score left Yamamoto with a short-lived glimpse of better things to come. To thank his fliers, he traveled to select airbases. On April 14 American cryptanalysts learned of Yamamoto's itinerary and his exact arrival time on tiny Ballale Island, just off the bottom end of Bougainville: 9:45 AM on April 18. This sparked a flurry of dispatches between Washington, Honolulu, and Nouméa. Could the Americans intercept the flight? Should they try to kill Yamamoto? Could the Japanese replace him with a better officer? Would the mission reveal the Allied ability to decode Japanese communications, a secret so valuable it was guarded well into the 1970s? The president's sense was to "get Yamamoto." King concurred, though not wholeheartedly. Nimitz believed Yamamoto could not be replaced with a better officer, adding that any attempt would be "down in Halsey's bailiwick. If there's a way, he'll find it." Halsey, who had with typical bombast earlier claimed Yamamoto as public enemy number three, behind only Hirohito and Hideki Tojo, urged swift action.[20]

This the Americans did, reflecting Halsey's temperament in the name given the plan: Operation Vengeance. Early on April 17 Halsey ordered Rear Admiral Marc Mitscher, the air commander at Guadalcanal, to assassinate the Japanese commander. By midmorning Mitscher's operations officer, Marine Major John Condon, determined that the Army's P-38 Lightning was the only plane with the range, even with drop tanks, to intersect Yamamoto's flight path, precluding use of the Navy and Marine Corsairs that had recently debuted to universal acclaim. By midafternoon, Mitscher had selected Army Major John Mitchell to lead the mission, Mitchell had identified the best pilots from multiple squadrons for the task, and Condon had prescribed a complex five-legged route of nearly 600 miles to, and then some 400 miles from, the Japanese flight, placing Mitchell's men at a right angle to Yamamoto's descent to land at precisely 9:35 AM. As dusk neared, ground crews hustled to retrofit eighteen Army fighters with Navy navigation aids and Marine drop tanks, some rushed from rear areas with but moments to spare. In the darkness, Mitscher, Condon, and Mitchell relayed the scheme to the chosen fliers. Although the mission had been explained to others as the byproduct of coast watcher reports on the movements of unnamed senior Japanese officers, to "provide additional incentive" Mitscher now secretly told the assigned pilots that Yamamoto was the target.[21]

Mitchell's Lightnings rose from Guadalcanal at 7:25 AM on April 18, the first anniversary of the Doolittle Raid and less than twenty-four hours after Halsey had helped place in motion the longest fighter intercept of the war. Shortly thereafter, Yamamoto began his journey from Rabaul, his chief of staff Ugaki in a trailing aircraft, and another six fighter planes flying high escort. Mitchell's reckoning brought the Americans to the intercept point a minute early, at 9:34, where they found two planes descending from 6,500 feet, "almost as if," according to one account, "the affair had been pre-arranged with the mutual consent of friend and foe." Ugaki survived a sea crash, but an American bullet pierced Yamamoto's skull well before his plane smashed into the Bougainville jungle. Japanese officials, fearing Yamamoto's death might spark infectious panic, did not acknowledge the tragedy until May 21, and a four-day Shinto funeral in early June had the feel of a royal interment, complete with a rare Imperial address. Throughout Japan, Yamamoto's loss, according to one Japanese admiral, "dealt an almost unbearable blow to the morale of all military forces."[22]

The American pilots returning to Guadalcanal were more upbeat. Upon landing, one of them exclaimed he had killed Yamamoto, fueling gossip already extant at Henderson and sending it reverberating throughout the South Pacific. News of the strike appeared in correspondents' accounts submitted for press censor review before Tokyo announced Yamamoto's death, placing in jeopardy the entire Allied code-breaking effort. This incensed higher commanders. Interservice finger pointing reached as far as King and Marshall, and ensnared a rear admiral and a corps commander. Halsey began a security investigation even before dispatches from Knox, King, and Nimitz directed him to do so, but he was not interested in a witch hunt. The inquiry, he told Nimitz, would likely finger as culprits "the men who did the splendid job," leaving senior officials with "a bear by the tail." In the weeks that followed, Halsey, as the responsible local commander, was able to modulate more senior and more irate opinion, and when news of the mission finally leaked later that summer, he was able to parley Mitchell's award of a Navy Cross instead of a Medal of Honor, as had been initially suggested, as retribution enough. A full year after the shoot-down, King and Marshall remained concerned about possible leaks compromising Allied code-breaking efforts, but Ugaki, and presumably other ranking Japanese, never had an inkling the American attack had been based upon such intelligence.[23]

Back in August of 1942 Yamamoto had moved his flagship, the super battleship *Yamato*, from home waters to Truk lagoon in response to the American landings at Guadalcanal. Since then, he had been a near constant presence as Halsey's adversary. At Guadalcanal, the American admiral bested the Japanese icon, and now Halsey had killed Yamamoto with one of the most audacious missions of the war. Made possible through code breaking, it had been contemplated in the Oval Office, debated at the Navy Department, passed on from Pearl Harbor, and ordered from Nouméa inside of three days. On Guadalcanal, within twenty-four hours, a Navy rear admiral oversaw it, a Marine major planned it, and an Army squadron commander led eighteen fliers, many barely beyond high school curfews, along a flight route as precise as, and hundreds of miles longer than, anything demanded of better-prepared pilots over the Normandy beaches the following year, to ambush the war's most important Japanese admiral. The brouhaha over security concerns helped obscure from plain view the astonishingly versatile command structure that had enabled this feat that hurled American planes toward Yamamoto on the second most consequential Sunday of the entire Pacific War.

....

Indeed, despite the long spring of discontent expressed in some corners over operational delays in the far Pacific, Halsey had used the time to provision and codify his forces. In February, he launched Operation Drygoods to transform rear echelons into massive storehouses. In May, he established a South Pacific Joint Logistics Board composed of senior logisticians from every service to coordinate the interchange of resources and manage the many supply vessels plying South Pacific waters. Between those months, 50,000 tons of provisions, 80,000 barrels of gasoline, and over 100,000 tons of equipment reached camps across the region, enough of it at Guadalcanal that the place changed its code name from Cactus to Mainyard. These large stockpiles earned derision from some quarters as overpreparation amid belated operations. "This criticism is thoroughly justified," Halsey told Nimitz, though he made no excuse for the prodigious accumulation of supplies. "This may worry the boys back in Washington, but it does not worry me in the slightest." When he next struck the Japanese, Halsey wanted every possible advantage.[24]

He also restructured his command, which had grown, he recalled after the war, "like Topsy." When Halsey had first arrived in Nouméa, his ground forces were irregularly organized. Major General Millard "Miff" Harmon was the South Pacific's senior Army officer, though Harmon's portfolio included only administrative authority with no firm voice in the operations of either Vandegrift's Marines, who reported directly to Halsey, or Patch's Americal Division, which for a time reported directly to Marshall in Washington, the only deployed division to do so in the war. It was no more conventional in the air, where three sovereign commands flew: Rear Admiral Aubrey Fitch directed the area's ground-based aircraft; seagoing task force commanders controlled carrier planes; and Brigadier General Roy Geiger, through Vandegrift's authority, commanded the aircraft taking off from Henderson, regardless of what service markings happened to adorn their aluminum skins. Only at sea was Halsey's authority clean and direct, as he grabbed for himself de facto tactical command of all ships Nimitz sent his way.

Over a number of months Halsey moved to regularize this polyglot. He gave to Harmon more authority over Army operations, and welcomed the arrival of the XIV Corps in December. He championed the establishment of the I Marine Amphibious Corps in early 1943, and he supported the birth of the Thirteenth Air Force about the same time. Together, these changes created analogous organizations within the Army, Army Air Forces, and Marines, promising a more standard administration of South Pacific units.

Operationally, Halsey grew his amphibious force and remade his air force. Although War Plan Orange had for decades implied a march across Pacific islands, the Navy had done little to prepare for littoral combat and entered the war deficient in the special assault craft, tactical technique, and doctrinal underpinnings such combat required. All this was slowly rectified in the spring as Turner's amphibious force grew to eighteen large troop transports, a dozen escorting destroyers, and well over a hundred landing vessels for tanks and infantry, types of ships unknown to the prewar Navy.[25]

In the air, the prewar years had placed a premium on strategic bombing in the Army Air Forces, close air support of ground troops among Marines, and fleet defense and shore strike in the Navy, leaving Halsey with contesting views about how, where, and with what equipment to fight the Japanese in the South Pacific. Harmon, one of the war's most broad-minded generals, believed the Solomon Islands' geography and austerity had obliterated standard ways of thinking about air power, organizationally and doctrinally. Whereas wings, groups, and squadrons devoted to particular missions codified operations elsewhere, in the distant jungles of the South Pacific that approach was "impossible" and "one must still think in terms of the individual airplane." The frenzied fight for Guadalcanal, for instance, had thrown the region's three separate air commands toward Henderson Field at such velocity that pilots often had no idea what outfit his wingman called home: on one typical October 1942 day, the morning saw five dive-bombers from four different organizations rumble into the air to attack a retreating Tokyo Express, while the afternoon witnessed the scramble of nearly three dozen fighters from five squadrons representing Army, Navy, and Marines. And beyond all that complexity there were New Zealand squadrons, first a couple, then six, and ultimately nine in the front lines, bringing to the South Pacific air war the challenges of not only joint but also combined operations.[26]

Such circumstances demanded integrated command. Halsey's commander of land-based aircraft, Aubrey Fitch, was the only prewar Johnny-come-lately with deeper service in aviation than Halsey, having before the war commanded the tender ship *Wright;* the Navy's first aircraft carrier, *Langley;* the large flattop *Lexington;* two naval air stations; an air patrol wing; and a carrier division. Through the spring of 1943, he molded the compact Marine air organization at Henderson Field, known colloquially as the Cactus Air Force, into the Air Solomons Command. Staffed by Marine, Army, Navy, and New Zealand officers, its command rotated in two- to five-month increments among some of the best American airmen of every service, including hard-charging Marine Major General Geiger, who later commanded a field army on Okinawa and finished the war with a combat record equal to any senior Marine in history; Rear Admiral Mitscher, who became the war's best fast carrier task force commander; and Major General Nathan Twining, later an Air Force chief of staff and chairman of the Joint Chiefs of Staff. Down ranks, Air Solomons comprised fighter, strike, bomber, and reconnaissance components, each equipped with aircraft and personnel without regard to service affiliation or national origin, and aggregating, at its height, over 700 land-based airplanes stretched across fifty airfields.[27]

In other locales, the Air Solomons' unusual amalgam might have been a recipe for the ambiguous employment of air power, especially from separate service perspectives. Although it was inconsistent with prewar doctrine, the command was nonetheless well fitted to the air tasks at hand in the South Pacific: maritime search and interdiction, suppression of enemy forces, close air support, and the nullification of Japanese strongholds. Its hallmarks, according to one modern assessment, were "a willingness to improvise, a subordination of service doctrine and mission biases to urgent operational demands, and the emergence of a truly joint operations organization" that, in most respects, the Americans did not attain again until the Persian Gulf War of 1991.[28]

To Halsey, its hodgepodge made manifest the fruits of integrated command. "We are the South Pacific Fighting Force," he often lectured subordinates, adding, "I don't want anybody even to be thinking in terms of Army, Navy, or Marines." To underscore the point, he directed Navy and Marine officers to discard neckties because the Army already had, in the hopes that "uniformity of appearance would encourage uniformity of action." If that failed, he threatened to "issue coveralls with 'South Pacific Fighting Force' printed on the seat." He forbade tallies of enemy aircraft shot down by service, both because he was "opposed to the publication of any box score that would divide credit between the Army, Navy, and Marine flyers," and because, as a practical matter, South Pacific air forces were "so thoroughly integrated" that it was very difficult to maintain distinguishing records. Later, whenever he heard blather about interservice difficulties, he liked to tell of his air forces during the height of operations, where Army, Navy, Marine, and New Zealand airmen "fought with equal enthusiasm and excellence under rear admirals, then under a major general of the Army, and finally under a major general of the Marines." Official Army Air Forces historians agreed. Air Solomons operations, they wrote, were marked by a "healthy spirit of cooperation," a happy circumstance for which "a large share of the credit must go to Adm William F. Halsey."[29]

. . . .

Whether such sentiment could overcome the nearly universal deficiency in joint backgrounds among American officers in World War II remained a question as the summer of 1943 approached. High officials in Washington had failed to unify control in the Pacific, though there, amid the vast ocean, MacArthur and Nimitz had found Halsey. A career of shared experiences with Nimitz and an immediate chemistry with MacArthur suggested he might be able to lubricate personal and operational fault lines between Brisbane and Honolulu. As for his own command, Halsey had readied his force as best he could that spring, a fact appreciated by Nimitz during a mid-June tour of the South Pacific. "The outstanding impression of my visit," he reported to King, was of "great improvement in all matters of organizational and material development." There now existed a "discernible workable organization of the complex elements" constituting Halsey's forces, especially within air and ground units, and, logistically, gone were "the days of congestion" at ports that had undermined earlier operations.[30]

None of this carried much consequence until major combat operations resumed, of course. Although the early months of 1943 constituted the foundation for subsequent Solomon Islands operations, by May Halsey found he had little to do but bluster and pine for the next "chance to kill YELLOW BASTARDS," as he put it in a note to Nimitz. It was an uncomfortable stance for a fighter such as Halsey, who continued to stew through June or, as he commiserated with Calhoun on June 29, "sit here and squeeze the left one."[31]

Chapter Thirteen

Low Tide

NEW GEORGIA BECKONED, at last. The next major island along the interior line of the Solomons chain, it sat directly between Guadalcanal and Rabaul. The conventions of twentieth-century combat had obviated much of warfare from bygone times, but no invention had yet supplanted geography's prerogative, especially at the far edges of the globe. In the Solomons, each antagonist knew strategy sprang from the map, and both had long recognized New Georgia as a potential flash point. The Japanese had first reconnoitered the island in October 1942, as Halsey arrived in Nouméa, and had commenced construction of the Munda airfield the next month under a veil lifted only by Donald Kennedy, maybe the greatest of the Solomon Island coast-watchers. A trio of B-17 bombers struck the airstrip on December 9, marking the first of some 120 raids by South Pacific planes through the spring months, some of them also aimed at a strip on nearby Kolombangara at Vila after Japan had begun construction there. Along with naval bombardments by cruisers on January 23, March 5, and March 15, 1943, these raids rendered the two airstrips suitable only as shuttle points for Japanese planes, even as they continued to be siren songs for Americans looking to spring toward Rabaul. Halsey sent the first of numerous reconnaissance teams to New Georgia in late February, and passed the following months waiting only for MacArthur's approval for an invasion.[1]

American intentions surprised no one. By late spring there were over 10,000 Japanese defenders on New Georgia and Kolombangara, more than at any other place in the Solomon Islands. Evenly divided between the two islands, most of them were clustered near the Munda or Vila airfields, making those the most guarded Japanese parcels in the South Pacific outside of Rabaul. With reinforcements, Japan had more than 300 aircraft in the region, and could quickly put to sea a potent task force of cruisers, destroyers, and submarines to play havoc with American invasion convoys. Moreover, in testimony to New Georgia's import, the Japanese had broken practice and unified the island's Navy and Army units under a single command, held by General Noboru Sasaki, whom scholars have described as one of "the most wily and resolute Japanese generals of the Pacific war" as well as "the finest field commander faced by the Americans in the South Pacific." He and his force would be prepared when the Allies arrived.[2]

Halsey readied the invasion under the code name Toenails. His resources dwarfed Japanese coffers. At sea, he had five carriers, three battleships, nine cruisers, twenty-nine destroyers, eleven submarines, fifty-two motor torpedo boats, forty-one supply and troop ships, and sixty-nine landing craft. On the ground, the venerable First Marine Division was gone but in its stead stood elements of the Second and Third Marine Divisions; the Twenty-Fifth, Thirty-Seventh, and Forty-Third Army Divisions; the Americal Division; a detached Marine Raider regiment; and four naval construction battalions, whose exploits building airfields had already transformed the acronym CB into the famous "Seabee." In the air, and without counting carrier aircraft in the region, Halsey controlled over 600 planes, most assigned to the Air Solomons command then under Mitscher and most operating from Guadalcanal and Russells airstrips. In aggregate and at the time, Halsey's command was the largest and most balanced Allied command in the Pacific.[3]

Planning, ongoing for months, fell principally to Turner and Marine Major General Barney Vogel, commander of the I Marine Amphibious Corps, which had been established in Nouméa the previous fall to oversee the growing number of Marines in the area. New Georgia was an ill-shaped blob some forty-five miles long and twenty-five miles wide, with rugged coast, dense jungle, and jagged mountain spines. Natives had forever avoided the deep interior, living near the coast and traveling along the shore in skiffs. Even along the waterline the island was forbidding, ringed as it was to an atypical degree by small islets, sharp coral, and shallow lagoons. The plain at Munda made a defensive ally of the entire area, nestled between impregnable jungle to the north and east and, to the south and from the west, rugged coast barring watercraft much larger than patrol boats. Turner thought the Munda airfield was the "most magnificent defensive area" in the entire Solomons. The plan Vogel eventually championed entailed both Marine divisions, elements of an Army division, seven detached battalions, and 14,000 support personnel, escorted by the great bulk of Halsey's extant fleet, all aiming to land near Segi Point before commencing a thirty-mile sweep through the jungle to Munda.[4]

Halsey blanched at the prospect of an extended jungle march with more than half his total ground force. King and Nimitz already suspected Halsey's strength had undermined sound South Pacific planning, and Halsey believed Cartwheel's intricate sequence of assaults in the Solomons and New Guinea made a large ground force at New Georgia a bad bet, lest resources be unavailable for his subsequent invasion of Bougainville—a potential deficiency he knew MacArthur would not make good. For Halsey, prudent allowance for operational reserves limited the New Georgia assault to a single division and maybe a few additional detached forces. As he explained it to Nimitz, Vogel's plan was "wholly unacceptable, primarily because it was unrealistic and ignored the forces available and called for means considerably in excess of those available in the South Pacific." Vogel's planners, however, felt that any smaller force flirted with failure. They described Halsey's position as "obdurate" and, as the weeks passed, some of them wondered aloud at what point the fighting admiral had traded the tactical demands of local circumstance for the strategic druthers of higher commanders.[5]

New Georgia planning crystalized misgivings that Halsey harbored about Vogel. The Marine's bluff personality had made the two fast friends, but as early as April the admiral had asked Peck, while on temporary duty in Washington, to relay concerns to the Marine Corps commandant, Lieutenant General Thomas Holcomb. Vogel lacked "initiative and punch," Peck explained to Holcomb, and Halsey pined for the return of Vandegrift, who was then slated to replace Holcomb as Marine Corps commandant upon the latter's retirement that coming fall. Halsey wanted the Marine commandant to recall Vogel rather than initiate Vogel's relief from Nouméa, a subterfuge that struck Holcomb as "so unlike Halsey," who he knew "as a courageous frank type" surely possessed of the rectitude to fire Vogel himself. Following Peck's return to Nouméa, Holcomb sought Nimitz's advice. Fresh from his brief visit to Nouméa, Nimitz reiterated Halsey's "definite lack of confidence" in "Vogel's military and professional competence." These were strong words, and with them Holcomb recalled Vogel to Washington and placed Vandegrift in temporary command of the I Amphibious Corps while he searched for a more permanent replacement.[6]

Halsey's dissatisfaction with Vogel was just—when Vandegrift arrived in Nouméa he confronted problems in the I Amphibious Corps so widespread as to require the replacement of its chief of staff, the relief of a division commander, and a wholesale reorganization of the command's logistics operations. But Halsey's ham-handed dismissal of Vogel sat at odds with his forthright ways, and as Vogel left the theater Halsey told him that dissatisfaction in Washington, not Nouméa, had led to his relief, hiding his hand in the whole affair. Halsey's dodge disappointed Vandegrift, and Holcomb found the episode "most disturbing and confusing." The incident left Nimitz cold too, though, as he reported to King, "as long as we trust Halsey to do the big job" in the South Pacific, "we must also trust his judgment in a matter like this." Unsurprisingly, Halsey devoted only an oblique half sentence to the regrettable incident in his autobiography. The episode, however, reverberated through the entire New Georgia campaign.[7]

Just weeks before a late June assault, Vogel's relief placed primary Toenails planning in Turner's lap and thrust the Army's Forty-Third Division, an untried National Guard division, into the heart of the operation. Compounding matters, Turner was not well, and was in any event slated to leave the South Pacific for duty in Honolulu in mid-July, just two weeks into the prospective operation. He spent nearly two weeks in June confined to the hospital ship *Solace* with either malaria or dengue fever, and his binge drinking had reached a periodic peak. His new plan was a complex scheme to envelop Munda using the Forty-Third Division, a detached Marine regiment, and a few scattered battalions. Turner envisioned a quartet of small landings slated for June 30: one far to the south, on the island of Vangunu to secure Wickham Anchorage for small ships; another at Segi Point to establish a fighter strip; a third at Viru, a small harbor about five miles from Segi, to serve as a motor torpedo base; and a fourth on small Rendova Island, just seven miles south of Munda, to range the Japanese airfield with artillery and posit Major General John Hester's Forty-Third Division. Days later, Hester's men would then traverse the small lagoon to a point east of the Munda plain while yet another landing at Rice Anchorage on the island's north shore by Colonel Harry Liversedge's Marine regiment would interdict Japanese reinforcements from Kolombangara, sealing the fate of Munda field.[8]

This mouthful of a plan atomized Halsey's forces. He divided his large warships and submarines into six task groups as covering forces, leaving half his destroyers and the troop, cargo, and landing ships to Turner's designs. Turner then split these amphibious forces into two sections and five subgroups to accommodate the myriad landings before they would converge to lift forces to Rice Anchorage and Munda. The hurried plan maintained Halsey's direct control of covering forces, and in turn failed to vest Turner with command of all South Pacific vessels operating in the immediate area. Moreover, the scheme did not identify the conditions required for the essential shift of command from Turner to Hester once troops were ashore, the very circumstance that had undercut Turner's relationship with Vandegrift at Guadalcanal. Beyond all that, Harmon, Halsey's senior Army officer, worried that Hester's inexperienced division staff could not oversee Toenails's far-flung operations. He alerted the XIV Corps commander, Major General Oscar Griswold on Guadalcanal, to stand ready should the National Guard division falter. In its complexity and nuance, the entire scheme was uncharacteristic of Halsey, who acknowledged to Nimitz the plan's "lack of homogeneity" but insisted that "necessity, not desire," had made it so. In its optimism, however, Toenails was pure Halsey. Planners anticipated few difficulties getting ashore at any point, and estimated that Munda would fall quickly and certainly by July 10.[9]

The preliminary landings on Vangunu, on Segi Point, and near Wickham Anchorage went well. So too on Rendova, where nearly 6,000 Americans made landfall in what Harmon called a "splendidly executed" operation, astonishing the 120 Japanese defenders and Sasaki, who, surveying the scene through binoculars from Munda, had not expected the Americans to trifle with outlying locales. On July 2 Turner then catapulted some 5,000 of Hester's men across the sound between Rendova and New Georgia, landing them at Zanana, a small village six miles east of Munda. Three days hence, in the final Toenails landing, a task force of ten cruisers and destroyers under the command of Rear Admiral Walden "Pug" Ainsworth brought Liversedge's 2,600 Marines to Rice Anchorage, losing the destroyer *Strong* to an impromptu clash with patrolling Japanese tin cans. At both Zanana and Rice Anchorage, as with all the other landing points, planners had eschewed stronger Japanese coast defenses for more desolate areas, trading a fight getting ashore for jungle slogs to their objectives, an exchange consistent with thinking then current in amphibious doctrine.[10]

The advantages of defense then conspired with Japanese resolve to extract a toll. At sea, in the narrowing waters between Rice Anchorage and Vila, Ainsworth tangled with ten Japanese destroyers rushing reinforcements to New Georgia in the early hours of July 6. In the darkness, American cruiser guns confronted Japanese destroyer torpedoes, as they had done many times. In weight, the American broadside of nearly 2,500 six-inch rounds dwarfed Japanese fire, and Ainsworth believed he had swiftly dispatched an entire group of enemy warships. Then the first Japanese torpedoes arrived, fired before the American guns had come alive, and blew up the cruiser *Helena*. Despite this loss, Halsey reported that the scuffle had intercepted supplies and "virtually annihilated" the Japanese force, sinking a "minimum of eight enemy ships."[11]

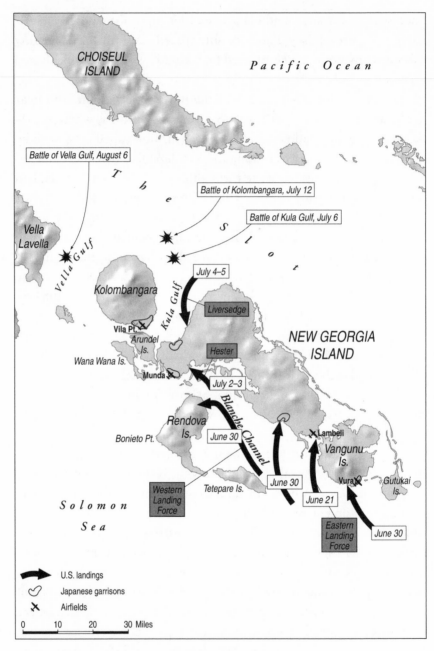

New Georgia, June to August 1943.

He was spectacularly wrong. Nearly all 1,600 Japanese reinforcements reached land at a cost of just two Japanese destroyers. Ainsworth had hesitated to press his attack at the crucial moment and, rather incredibly at this late date, had tethered his destroyers to his cruisers, diminishing their ability to swarm with their own torpedoes. "By the standards of 1942," one historian put it, "Ainsworth had fought a decent battle." But it was mid-1943, and in this Battle of Kula Gulf, as the contest became known, he had "lost more tonnage than the enemy and failed to accomplish his mission."[12]

A week later he got a second chance to intercept a Tokyo Express in the Battle of Kolombangara. He had better odds this time, counting three cruisers and ten destroyers in his fold against a Japanese cruiser, five destroyers, and an assortment of small transports carrying 1,200 soldiers. Yet, meeting in the same waters as before, Ainsworth did no better by any measure, and much worse by some, than he had in the first engagement. He struck hard in the early hours of July 13, sinking the cruiser *Jintsu* before torpedo wakes once again appeared. For the loss of *Jintsu*, the Japanese delivered their human cargo, sank the destroyer *Gwin,* and knocked out all three Allied cruisers, two for months and the third for the remainder of the war.

Halsey believed the two naval battles had "been costly to our forces" but, even well after the war, argued they had been "well worth the price." Nimitz disagreed. "Night encounters in those narrow waters," he wrote Halsey, were justified only if they interdicted Japanese supplies, escorted American ground forces, or inflicted greater relative damage on the enemy. None pertained in either action. Ainsworth hewed to Nimitz's views. "Looking back over one's shoulder," he confessed to Nimitz, "one can always see how we should have done things differently." But no two sea clashes of the war were more alike than the Battle of Kula Gulf and the Battle of Kolombangara, and Ainsworth had no reasonable claim to hindsight's shield in the second engagement, foreshadowed as it was by the first. There were many factors for the failure in the waters between New Georgia and Kolombangara, but mostly the Americans were learning that the isolation of a determined adversary holding a defensive position ashore was simply a very tall task—a hard truth that had aided them on Guadalcanal but now redounded to Japan's favor on New Georgia.[13]

Across the first two weeks of July the Japanese had managed to grow Sasaki's garrison by 5,700 men. Exploiting their nighttime dominance in the sound between New Georgia and Kolombangara, they then ferried smaller numbers of additional troops on July 19, July 22, and August 1. In the second half of July, Halsey resorted to torpedo boats to hunt this traffic, a method that interrupted few Japanese supplies but did, on the night of August 2, produce a hero when PT-109 sank, consigning its skipper, Lieutenant John F. Kennedy, and its small crew to a week's hardship before rescue. Afterward, Kennedy's father, Joseph, Roosevelt's prewar ambassador to Great Britain, lobbied the Navy Department for a Navy Cross for his son, creating a mild quandary and a special inquiry. Halsey believed young Kennedy had displayed courage and resourcefulness, "but such conduct is general in both large and small ships operating in enemy waters and does not appear to have been of such character as to warrant special awards." His dad's doggedness, however, netted for Kennedy the Navy and Marine Corps Medal, a noncombat decoration for heroism, though a far cry from the Navy Cross.[14]

On land the Japanese reinforcements added to already stout defenses. To the north, Liversedge's valiant efforts to stop the stream of Japanese migrating toward Munda failed, foiled by too much mud, not enough food, too little intelligence, and not enough manpower. In the south, Hester's main body of Forty-Third Division troops fared worse. Tangled terrain and shrewd defenses befuddled the National Guardsmen, who had arrived on New Georgia's shores hardened only by the unopposed landings in the Russells. By day, the Americans mistook cockatoo calls for Japanese. At night, large land crabs became enemy infiltrators. On three successive evenings, bivouacked units battled supposed Japanese in blind melees only to find, when light arrived, dead Americans, bayonetted by U.S. steel or shredded by American shrapnel. When the Forty-Third did advance, the jungle's understory made soldiers more lumberjacks than warriors. Within a week, every man was disheveled, most were dispirited, and some were outright spooked. On July 9 some sixty Allied aircraft roared overhead and an entire destroyer division pumped five-inch shells toward Japanese positions, but not even the support of combined arms could punch the division through enemy defenses and onto Munda's plain, just four miles away.[15]

Rumblings of trouble reached Halsey in Nouméa almost as soon as problems wafted from the mildew of New Georgia. From Harmon he learned the Forty-Third was cracking. Troops were leaving the line suffering exhaustion, many crying, some hallucinating, and a few showing, according to the XIV Corps surgeon, symptoms of "true psychoneurotic complexes." By late July these numbers reached perhaps a hundred a day, and throughout the month another 1,000 soldiers fell to dysentery or malaria. The division became a mental basket case, prominent in the annals of the Army's medical histories. Psychiatrists attributed the calamity to poor leadership, discipline, and fitness.[16]

But blame could not be laid solely upon the Connecticut citizenry whence the division hailed. In the Southwest Pacific, MacArthur had had similar problems with the National Guard's Thirty-Second Division, whose introduction to combat at Buna was marked by a series of blunders, calamities, and tragedies. Halsey now confronted the same issues. He had been largely uninterested in his ground forces since the fight for Guadalcanal had broadened to a corps-sized operation the previous December. In the months before Toenails, he proved too ready to accept optimistic assessments of the Forty-Third Division's readiness, and his relief of Vogel had thrust the unit into the viper pit of New Georgia without adequate preparation. The result was a large-scale unit breakdown nearly unique in the American World War II experience. Through most of July, as New Georgia operations languished, only Allied aviation kept a steady drumbeat of progress. Some 200 planes struck Bougainville on July 17 and again on July 18, Kahili was bombed on July 20, 26, and 27, and Vila was victimized on July 26 and July 31.[17]

The crisis worsened as Halsey turned his full attention to its solution. His first inclination was to view the troubles on New Georgia as "no serious menace." Soon, however, his letters and dispatches suggested otherwise. He requested that Nimitz postpone Turner's long-planned July 15 transfer to the Central Pacific. He asked the Pacific Fleet commander to delay the return of escort carriers to Hawaii. He requested cruisers to replace those lost or damaged at Kolombangara and Kula Gulf. He implored MacArthur for the early return of a few South Pacific destroyers on loan. He beseeched both Nimitz and MacArthur for six submarines to augment his existing six. And he asked Nimitz for a new fast battleship.[18]

Requesting the kitchen sink got Halsey nothing except skepticism and rebuke. Nimitz and MacArthur rejected his entreaties. King told Halsey he was "appalled at the slowness of progress in the area where you are now working," and advised more "will to do the best you can with what you've got." Between Southwest Pacific operations and emergent Central Pacific plans, Halsey in fact lost resources in the midst of the New Georgia mess, including four submarines to MacArthur and much-needed amphibious tractors to Nimitz. Eyeing his own drive through the Gilbert and Marshall Islands, slated to start that fall, Nimitz took Turner right on schedule, forcing Halsey to substitute the South Pacific deputy commander, Rear Admiral "Ping" Wilkinson, who, in his own words, was "ill-fitted by experience and knowledge" for the job.[19]

Nimitz told Halsey his task was to conduct operations congruent with his allotted forces and to economize wherever and whenever possible. The Pacific Fleet commander suggested that the Japanese were on the "strategic defensive" in the South Pacific, that they were unlikely to engage large or heavy forces for Munda's survival, and that neither American battleships nor carriers could now be "profitably employed" in the Solomons. Nimitz told Halsey that as "the responsible Commander on the spot," Halsey was of course free to employ his force as he deemed best, but he should neither request nor expect more resources. Such a rebuke from the senior admiral in the Pacific represented a far distance from the previous fall, when material riches flowed toward Halsey at the height of the Guadalcanal fight.[20]

So Halsey did what he could with what he had. He started with commanders. Realizing the Forty-Third Division was "feebly led," he authorized Harmon to clean house. Two battalion commanders and an entire regimental command section were sacked, and veterans from Griswold's XIV Corps began to augment Hester's beleaguered staff. Still, the division continued its mental collapse, and Halsey directed Harmon "to assume full charge of and responsibility for ground operations in New Georgia." Harmon placed Griswold in direct command of New Georgia forces but, for the time being, retained Hester as Forty-Third commander as a sop to whatever was left of divisional morale. These changes were a start. Griswold transferred a 250-bed hospital from Guadalcanal to address a backlog of psychiatric cases, and after he surmised that four hardened battalions of entrenched "Munda moles" blocked his path, he worked to codify his front, improve his logistics, and keep pressure on the "slant eye" enemy while awaiting reinforcements.[21]

Heretofore loath to commit additional force, into New Georgia Halsey now sent most of the Thirty-Seventh Division, like the Forty-Third a National Guard unit, but better led by Major General Robert Beightler, and elements of the crack Twenty-Fifth Division, led by the incomparable Joe Collins. By July 25 enough new troops had arrived for a multidivision lunge toward the Munda plain, still about two miles distant. They were aided by massive naval and air support, including 4,000 shells from offshore destroyers and 500,000 pounds of explosives from over 300 air sorties.[22]

Such combined arms made Japanese victory on New Georgia unlikely, though it did not translate into an easy ground advance against entrenched defenders. As a measure of intensity, all three American Medals of Honor for New Georgia stemmed from action in the last days of July. The Forty-Third Division continued to register meager results, exhausting Halsey's patience with Hester, whom he fired on July 29, replacing him with John Hodge, a star apprentice of Joe Collins. Afterward, when a mild rebuke from Nimitz raised the possibility that the removal of an Army division commander by an admiral could inflame interservice relations, Halsey attributed Hester's relief to stomach ulcers, though the truth of the matter was plain for all to see.[23]

Still defenders stood their ground, forcing Griswold to ask for yet more attackers. This put Halsey and Harmon in a bind. Their only substantial ground reserve until Vandegrift whipped the Marines into better shape was the rest of the Twenty-Fifth Division, the seed corn for the subsequent assault of Bougainville. Neither man had any real choice, however. Harmon acknowledged that New Georgia had become "much tougher" to subdue "than we had thought," and he understood the Americans had to prevail "as quickly as possible." So into New Georgia went most of the rest of Collins's division, with neither a guarantee that it would turn the tide nor a clear sense of how to replace it in subsequent campaigns.[24]

. . . .

American intelligence at New Georgia was as bad as its planning or execution. Unbeknown to Halsey, by August 1 Sasaki's dogged defenses had dwindled to perhaps 3,000 men near Munda and another 2,000 facing Liversedge in the north, most in a state of physical shambles after weeks of desperate fighting. They could not last forever against a burgeoning American force then 35,000 strong and hurtling toward 50,000. Across the first days of August, Griswold's men at last made progress. On August 5, the Thirty-Seventh Division cut Sasaki's supply lines north of the airfield and the Forty-Third Division washed at last across the western portions of the runway. That evening, three weeks later than first envisioned, Griswold radioed Halsey that the admiral was "the sole owner" of Munda field, a message Halsey acknowledged as a "custody receipt." For the rank and file, capture of the strip was more bitter than sweet. One grunt wrote it was a "shitty little airfield," littered with bomb craters and burned-out enemy planes. Another said it looked like a "slash of white coral in a Doré painting of hell," lying "like a dead thing" between the blue lagoon to the south and the green hills to the north and east, with red blood still running fresh through its soil.[25]

Men of the Twenty-Fifth Division passed the remainder of August chasing a fleeing enemy from New Georgia, a thankless task Collins described as the "worst physical ordeal" he endured in the war. They finished by August 24, when the last of nineteen enemy barges teeming with Japanese made off to Vila, leaving only the outlying island of Arundel in enemy hands. That sore required two battalions, an anti-tank company, Marine reinforcements, and an additional month to cauterize. At the finish, the New Georgia campaign took longer, devoured more supplies, and created more problems than anyone in the South Pacific had envisioned at the start.[26]

Hollow applause followed upon the hard victory. Harmon, who had first raised the alarm on Hester and his division, counted the Munda operation as a signal triumph in a report to Hap Arnold. Griswold, who had rushed in to redeem the emergent calamity, called the campaign "the finest example in all my experience of a united, all service, all-American team." Halsey, who had vainly begged for all manner of additional force in the midst of the mess, praised his charges for their "teamwork" and "unrelenting offensive spirit."[27]

In truth, the New Georgia campaign ranks among the worst-managed Allied affairs of the entire war. However just, Halsey's circuitous relief of Vogel thrust an ill Kelly Turner, a green John Hester, and the inexperienced Forty-Third Division deep into Toe-nails planning. Turner splintered his forces across small operations, forcing the piecemeal commitment of troops "in a manner," according to an official Army history, "no experienced Army commander would have tolerated." Of the initial landings, neither the roadstead at Wickham, nor a makeshift airfield at Segi Point, nor the harbor at Viru became of any real consequence. Liversedge's Marines at Rice Anchorage endured extreme hardship and displayed personal courage, but without more of them they never could have interdicted significant Japanese reinforcements. Once ashore, entire American units buckled under the mental strain of jungle war, forcing Halsey, who had planned to take Munda inside of two weeks and with fewer than 20,000 men, to devote five weeks and nearly 50,000 men to the task. The fight had cost the Allies the cruiser *Helena,* the destroyers *Strong* and *Gwin,* and nearly 2,000 men, with perhaps 4,000 more wounded, not counting the many lost to disease and mental calamity.

These tallies were probably—and most unusually for the Pacific War—close to par with enemy losses. Sasaki and many Japanese managed to slip across the narrow waters to Kolombangara to fight another day. The triumph had advanced the Americans another 50 or so miles to Tokyo, with only another 3,000 to go. It had exhausted the South Pacific Force, leaving it unable to springboard swiftly toward Bougainville, which in turn jeopardized Halsey's Cartwheel commitments to MacArthur. After the war, freer to speak the truth, Halsey acknowledged these problems and more. "Looking back" on the campaign, he wrote, "the smoke of charred reputations still makes me cough."[28]

. . . .

He could have added his own name to the pyre. Halsey's limited insight into the workings of other services and his near total inexperience with combined arms meant he confronted unfamiliar horizons in the South Pacific. All officers, if they become senior enough, oversee operations with which they are not expert. Halsey, unlike many, did so in the face of a determined enemy across the most contested period of the war. His command instincts had carried him through the war's early months, where his deep sense of Navy matters enriched judgment, calculated risk, and fostered bold, decisive action. But in the South Pacific, with its unanticipated political, strategic, and operational environment, he found he needed more.

Staff changes in the summer of 1943, some the product of routine rotation and others more directly remedial, promised help. Rear Admiral John Shafroth replaced Wilkinson as Halsey's deputy when the latter took up Turner's duties, and Shafroth was then replaced in the fall by Vice Admiral John Newton. DeWitt Peck, who had cast a long shadow as Halsey's planning and operations officer, left to become assistant commandant of the Marine Corps. Into the void came Captain Raymond Thurber, one of the few holdovers from Ghormley's staff, and new arrivals, including Marine Colonel William Riley and Navy Commander Ralph "Rollo" Wilson. This was an outstanding quartet. Newton, a brusque officer who had served a successful prewar tour as Halsey's chief of staff, increasingly shouldered the administra-

tive burdens of the South Pacific command, freeing Halsey for operations. Thurber was an original and imaginative thinker with wide
knowledge of cutting-edge weapon systems. Riley arrived with a reputation for brilliance and with Holcomb's personal approbation. And
Wilson had recently left the helm of the destroyer *Buchanan,* where
he had earned for himself a Navy Cross and for his ship a Presidential Unit Citation at the Battle of Cape Esperance.[29]

These men would toil under new staff leadership. After months
of trying, Navy officials at last forced Halsey to replace Miles Browning.
The issue had never been far from Nimitz's mind. In the spring, he
had exploded upon learning that Halsey had sent Browning home to
recover from malaria or dengue fever—the record is unclear—via the
same artifice Nimitz had employed with Halsey's illness the previous
summer, and for the same reason: to ensure Browning's return. "I have
used this method once and in your case only," Nimitz scolded, "and
that was from Oahu and not from the South Pacific." The prospect of
replacing Browning during his convalescence was a powerful consolation for Nimitz, however, and in June he again proposed relieving
Browning, whom he admitted was brilliant but an altogether toxic
agent. Halsey did "not fully accept the idea," Nimitz reported to King,
but "it is at least working on his mind, because he has tentatively
chosen Duke Ramsey if for any reason he cannot keep his present
chief of staff."[30]

In Washington, King was merely biding time when Browning's
illness combined with Halsey's New Georgia stumbles to provide an
opening. Bribing Halsey with a carrier command for Browning, a
plum that Halsey would never deny a valued subordinate, King
maneuvered into Browning's spot not Ramsey, who as a qualified
aviator was needed at sea, but Robert "Mick" Carney. A third-
generation naval officer and 1916 Annapolis graduate, Carney had
served aboard the *Fanning,* one of the few World War I Queenstown
destroyers to sink a German U-boat while most, including Halsey's
ships, had searched in vain. Between wars, he had commanded destroyers, served significant tours ashore, and had evidenced an abiding
interest in naval administration via no fewer than eleven articles in

Proceedings, including "Staff Organization Afloat" in 1930 and "Material Administration Aboard Ship" in 1938, in the process gaining King's attention, who had himself once won *Proceedings'* prize for best article with "Some Ideas for Organization Aboard Ship." Through the war's early months, as chief of staff to the admiral responsible for convoys in the Atlantic, Carney earned a Distinguished Service Medal—at the time just one of two awarded to officers below flag rank. Promoted to captain and command of the *Denver* in the fall of 1942, Carney was twice decorated for combat action in the South Pacific, once in March, earning a Legion of Merit for action near the Russell Islands, and again in June, winning the Bronze Star for combat near Bougainville. In July King ordered Carney to Nouméa, where on July 26 he was promoted to rear admiral and became chief of staff.[31]

Halsey and Carney appeared an odd pair. Carney was more cerebral and analytical, came more deliberately to judgments, and expressed himself far better, both orally and in writing, than did his new boss. In sharp contrast to Halsey's charismatic style, Carney believed knowledge was the sine qua non of leadership, insisting that a commander need not "be a Barrymore on the naval stage" if he lacked a "flamboyant or inspiring personality." In fact, even "the Hunchback of Notre Dame could do a hell of a job as a force commander if he knew enough." Carney had left the *Denver* with "great reluctance," and had never served closely with Halsey until he arrived in Nouméa. As he took up duties, he understood Halsey "was an inspirational character, and actually was becoming a legend in his own lifetime," but that was about it.[32]

Yet similarities between the two men fashioned their differences into complements. Both were sons of naval officers and were thoroughly acculturated to Navy norms. Both prized athletics as a laboratory for leadership. Both appreciated the distinction between salty language and vulgar expression. Both had matured in destroyers, where each had perfected the casual flair so prized among the interwar tin can crowd—Carney once told a lieutenant asking for his daughter's hand in marriage that "if my daughter's hand is all you are interested in perhaps we should review the entire courtship." Herman Wouk, in his wildly successful novels *Winds of War* and *War and Remembrance*, modeled his naval hero Pug Henry after Carney, who represented to Wouk "not a great leader destined for CNO, but a naval officer who would perform well wherever he was," becoming in the process the "backbone" to victory. It was King's great insight to see that Carney's strengths could backstop Halsey's weaknesses and promise no significant tension with Halsey's fighting ways. Carney quickly became Halsey's indispensable mainstay, and only "when Bill Halsey quits fighting," King told Carney later in the war, would the younger admiral ever get another job. Looking back upon it decades later, Halsey's son came to the same judgment. "Despite being quite different in temperament," he believed his father and Carney "worked very well together."[33]

Secretary of the Navy Frank Knox also contrived to send others toward Nouméa that summer. Harold Stassen had been elected governor of Minnesota in 1938 at the age of thirty-one. He earned distinction as a Republican ally of Roosevelt's prewar foreign policy, and hints of greatness as the keynote speaker at his party's 1940 convention. In early 1943, he resigned the governorship to report for duty as a lieutenant commander in the Navy Reserve. This unusual circumstance caught Roosevelt's eye and sparked Knox's imagination. With the president's blessing, Knox sent Stassen to Halsey without a specific portfolio but sure that the governor's managerial skills and political talents would find a place. Arriving in August, Stassen became the assistant chief of staff for administration and quickly won Halsey's praise as a "constructive, entirely frank, and loyal" officer endowed with "efficiency, dispatch, and rare tact." Nearly everyone agreed: Nimitz later solicited Stassen's expertise on civil affairs as more Pacific islands came under American control; James Forrestal, who replaced Frank Knox as secretary of the Navy in 1944, sought his insight on a whole host of issues; and Roosevelt, after flirting with the idea of Stassen instead of Forrestal as the secretary of the Navy, appointed the Minnesota boy wonder as one of eight American representatives to the San Francisco conference that produced the United Nations charter in the spring of 1945.[34]

Stassen exercised a rare degree of influence with Halsey, who grew fond of saying, "If they make better men than Harold Stassen, I've not yet met them." Following Roosevelt's victory over Thomas Dewey in the 1944 presidential election, Halsey recommended Stassen to Charles Belknap, a fellow World War I destroyer skipper, prominent Republican, and president of the Monsanto Chemical Company. Stassen was "a fast and solid thinker, and has a broad view of both national and international affairs," Halsey wrote. "He is gifted with a fine personality, he is an excellent mixer, has a keen sense of humor, and is an all-around he-man." With an eye toward 1948, Halsey told Belknap, "You cannot start too early to bring him forward," adding, "nothing must be done to embarrass him in any naval work. He is determined, and rightfully so, to be a naval officer until the war is finished." As was Halsey, who reminded Belknap that his name was "not to be connected with this in any way." The only explicit political note extant among Halsey's papers, the missive served to underscore the wartime bond between the old admiral and the young governor and, if its topic was unusual, reflected Halsey's characteristic affection for the men near him.[35]

With this cadre, Carney restructured Halsey's headquarters. He split Peck's duties, making Riley the plans officer, Thurber the operations officer, and Wilson the assistant operations officer. Carney moved Army and Air Forces officers into more prominent positions. He split the intelligence division into an analytic branch, led by an Army officer who was expert in ground combat, and an operational branch under joint Navy and Air Forces leadership because, in Carney's view, the airmen of each branch had the best grasp of the fluid nature of modern, combined arms operations. To Stassen, Carney assigned the informal role of Halsey's gatekeeper, a delicate task because, as Carney quickly surmised, the South Pacific commander "would see the janitor if he wanted to come in," a habit that provided Halsey the tactile contact he craved but sometimes distracted him from the essential task at hand. From the more than 300 officers on the South Pacific staff, Carney also established the skeleton of an advanced headquarters, with a nucleus of men ready to leave Nouméa within twenty-four hours and able to direct surface, air, and sea operations. These changes broadened the resident expertise and perspective within Halsey's inner circle and tended to make South Pacific headquarters more professional and less fraternal, although no group led by Halsey would ever trade ease for ceremony.[36]

Reorganization transformed Halsey's staff from one centered on operational and naval tasks to one alive to theater and joint responsibilities as well, an administrative archetype with no strong American antecedent and a makeover occurring, unevenly but everywhere, in high Allied echelons the world over. Some months earlier, a communiqué from the Joint Chiefs had championed the creation of integrated staffs and, to foster a disinterested perch to adjudicate interservice wrangles, implored joint commanders to divest direct control of their air, sea, and ground units to subordinate service commanders. Allied headquarters in Italy and England aped these instructions closely, but intramural tension between MacArthur and Nimitz made their wholesale adaptation difficult in Brisbane, Honolulu, and Nouméa. As Halsey explained it in 1947, his "sensitive position" relative to MacArthur and Nimitz had "complicated normal command" of air and sea forces, the most mobile and most likely units to cross command boundaries. To maintain comity with both men, he never combined into a single unit all his aviation, which in effect kept carrier-based aviation beyond MacArthur's orbit, and he never relinquished to a subordinate all South Pacific naval vessels, as the delicate "dance" between MacArthur and Nimitz regarding the allocation of warships was "hard enough to navigate with four stars" and would, he believed, have been impossible to manage with less standing.[37]

As a result, Halsey continued to exercise command through a fluid admixture of naval, amphibious, Marine, and air task forces even as his Army ground command became more regularized through Griswold's XIV Corps headquarters. Wilkinson, who controlled the amphibious forces directly involved in island assault but never had the many covering task forces within his portfolio, acknowledged that the setup was "strange-looking and strange seeming" but nonetheless "tailored to fit the situation." The arrangement "did not have the virtue of simplicity," Halsey acknowledged, but now with a strengthened staff he believed he had complied with "the spirit of the Joint Chiefs directive." The new setup also preserved a relaxed habit of command, by then a nearly intrinsic part of Halsey's personality. "I don't like a rigid organization for a flexible war," he once explained. "It is too easy to build a pyramid of command in which everything flows to the top through channels neatly bordered with red tape. That red tape is soon wrapped around the commander. I prefer a free interplay of ideas and exchange of information through all echelons. If you have the right kind of commanders, you don't have to kick them in the pants or pull them back by the belt."[38]

. . . .

With New Georgia behind them, Halsey and those around him doubled efforts to enliven a languid campaign. They received an immediate spark at sea. On August 5, the day Munda airfield fell, Commander Frederick Moosbrugger and six tin cans intercepted four destroyers bringing a rearguard of 900 Japanese to aid Sasaki's retreat from New Georgia. Completely free from duty as either carrier escorts or cruiser adjuncts for the first time since the Battle of Balikpapan in Philippine waters eighteen months earlier, American destroyers wrecked the Japanese column in a silent torpedo attack near midnight off Kolombangara, leaving, in the paraphrased memory of one Japanese skipper, a "tower of flame" on one ship, a "pillar of fire" on another, and a "giant conflagration" on a third. Three of the four Japanese destroyers were below water almost immediately, the fourth was fleeing, and not a ding had marred a U.S. ship. Over 1,200 enemies died, and just 310 survived. This Battle of Vella Gulf was as controlled a fisticuff as Sims had envisioned. The result was sweet vindication for American destroyer men and "catastrophic for the Japanese, both materially and psychologically." For the first time, American destroyers had independently engaged in surface night battle, and for the first time, the Imperial Navy had lost a torpedo action after sunset. The battle was evidence that destroyers sometimes worked best as offensive platforms unfettered by screening duties, and suggested that enough trial and sufficient error had accumulated on the American ledger of combat to weed out the poor ideas, bad practices, and ineffectual leaders of a peacetime force.[39]

For Halsey, the victory coincided with a moment of personal travail and triumph. On August 11 his son, serving as a supply officer aboard the *Saratoga*, disappeared when the plane he was aboard ditched in the South Pacific. Although Halsey remembered insisting on no special search for his son beyond the standard efforts, his staff directed an exhaustive hunt using the bulk of an entire scouting squadron flying out of Efate. For three days Halsey, who believed his son likely lost, quietly carried on; when told of the ordeal some weeks later, Nimitz doubted the report's veracity as he surely "would have heard" from Halsey had it been true. On the evening of August 14, a patrol plane spied four rafts and ten men upon the shore of tiny Eromanga Island, fifty miles from Efate. The next day, seaplanes rescued young Bill and his compatriots. In his autobiography, Halsey shifted these dates backward across the date line to accent the dramatic. Reporting his son saved on Friday the Thirteenth, Halsey, at least for a moment, "spit in the eye of the jinx that had haunted me on the thirteenth of every month since the *Missouri's* turret explosion thirty-nine years before."[40]

Good as they were, neither the Battle of Vella Gulf nor his son's rescue changed Halsey's immediate calculus in the South Pacific. New Georgia's crisis was past, but a long line of similar cesspits loomed, most immediately Kolombangara, now home to Sasaki's remaining Munda garrison and swelled with as many as 12,000 defenders centered, again, on an airstrip, this one near Vila. "The undue length of the Munda operation and our heavy casualties made me wary of another slugging match," Halsey recalled, "but I did not know how to avoid it." Reflecting on the Cartwheel plan, Halsey could see "no victory without Rabaul, and no Rabaul without Kolombangara."[41]

But his staff could. The New Georgia fiasco resurrected a springtime suggestion, first made by Thurber, to bypass Kolombangara for the island of Vella Lavella, thirty-five miles farther to the northeast. To the extent that Seabees had perfected airfield construction, Halsey's men saw no inherent value to Kolombangara if another island suitable for a landing strip existed. An irregular splotch of land like New Georgia, Vella Lavella was guarded by neither a formidable coral sheath nor the Japanese, who maintained a sparse garrison of maybe 200 soldiers. On July 28, with Munda still in Japanese hands, Halsey, with Carney, Thurber, and Riley, discussed the gambit to jump to Vella Lavella over Scotch whiskey and water following dinner. A few days later, a reconnaissance party led by an Anglican bishop and two natives identified a suitable airfield site. By August 11, Halsey had scratched Kolombangara and ordered Wilkinson to occupy Vella Lavella with a disproportionate force meant to redeem his sin of parsimony in New Georgia: most of Fitch's land-based aviation, nearly all of two carrier air groups, and task forces of cruisers and destroyers and submarines to screen 4,600 men under the command of the Twenty-Fifth Division assistant commander Brigadier General Robert McClure.[42]

This force came ashore on August 15, overwhelming the few dozen Japanese in the immediate vicinity and leaving a fleeting enemy air strike to register the day's few American casualties: twelve killed and forty wounded. Across the next six weeks the only real battle for Vella Lavella took place on the sea and in the air. On September 18, to rest American forces for the invasion of Bougainville and succor Allied harmony, Halsey assigned Major General H. E. Barrowclough and the New Zealand Fourteenth Brigade to the fight. The Kiwis, as a percent of manpower and treasure, had contributed more resources than did the United States to the South Pacific, and Halsey was keen to reward them with action. Once ashore at Vella Lavella, the New Zealanders harried the last 600 forlorn enemy soldiers, pinning them against a small strip of beach by early October. The entire campaign had cost fifty-eight American and New Zealand lives and one small landing craft.[43]

For that Halsey now had two airfield complexes in the central Solomons. At Munda, Seabees transformed the wrecked Japanese airstrip into a 6,200-foot coral runway suitable for the largest bombers in the region. The place quickly became home to a parade of rotating squadrons, an advanced Air Solomons headquarters, a large fuel tank farm, and storage for over 9,000 tons of bombs. That fall, it was the best and busiest airfield in the entire region, frequently hosting over 250 airplanes, its complexity and operational tempo greater than that of all but the largest commercial airports in the United States until the early 1960s. The field at Vella Lavella, hacked from scratch out of the dense foliage, could not boast all that, but by early October it too could accommodate over a hundred planes each day, just in time for the next jump up the Solomons chain.[44]

Vella Lavella redeemed Halsey from the wreck of New Georgia and in the process emancipated the bulk of his depleted force for operations farther up the Solomons chain. According to the Army's official history, it was "a major and completely successful departure from the original Toenails plan." Observers then and chroniclers since have viewed it as the first significant example of island hopping, a modus operandi soon commonplace in both the Southwest and Central Pacific, and often credited, along with submarine deprivations and fast carrier forces, as a principal factor in Allied victory. Although a cottage industry arose to identify the South Pacific officer most responsible for the idea, the general notion of island hopping was neither novel nor even especially American. The Japanese had bypassed Allied positions in the opening months of the war, and then had leapt over the upper and middle Solomons to alight at Guadalcanal. For the United States, bypassing some islands and fighting for others had for decades been a basic assumption of Plan Orange deliberations, Roosevelt himself mused about it early in the war, and MacArthur would champion the tactic, and in fact bypassed a Japanese strongpoint at his first opportunity, just weeks after Halsey's move into Vella Lavella, when in early September he landed forces at Lae instead of Salamaua.[45]

The real consequence of bypass was not in the circumvention but in the isolation of enemy strongholds, something Wilkinson, a geography buff, understood, as he had long been eager to "by-pass the strongest Japanese garrisons, seal them off by air and sea, and leave them to wither on the vine." Here Halsey and his force fell short. With New Georgia gone, the Japanese had abandoned the central Solomons and regarded the American invasion of Vella Lavella primarily as a threat to the evacuation of their 12,000 men on Kolombangara. During the dark moon commencing in late September, barge and destroyer traffic whisked these men north to Bougainville.[46]

Alive to this possibility, South Pacific planes attacked enemy airfields and ports by day, and at night motor torpedo boats and cruiser-destroyer task forces covered escape routes. Halsey believed those measures sank as many as ninety troop barges in late September and early October, sending Japanese by the fifties and hundreds to Neptune's grave. But he overcounted enemy barge losses by perhaps two times. Nearly 3,800 Japanese escaped on September 29, and similar numbers reached safety on October 2 and 3. By October 6, the 600 troops trapped by Barrowclough on Vella Lavella constituted the sole organized Japanese force in the area, and even a destroyer clash in the Battle of Vella Lavella failed to prevent these men from reaching refuge to fight another day. In the end, nearly 10,000 enemy troops, including the incomparable Sasaki, slipped the loose Allied noose. In late 1943, the Americans had achieved advantage enough to bypass Japanese strongholds, but had not yet the wherewithal to isolate those enemy troops and render them superfluous to future contests. As he had at the conclusion of the Guadalcanal campaign, Halsey failed to punctuate his victory by snaring a large contingent of enemy forces on the run.[47]

. . . .

For the Japanese, this tactical success capped a long, strategic retreat. With it, the emperor's only remaining representatives in the central Solomons were a small contingent operating a barge station on Choiseul. The central Solomon fight had cost Japan seventeen warships, innumerable sailors, something over 2,500 soldiers dead and countless more wounded, and important real estate. For the Americans, the campaign had taken from February to July to prepare and from July to October to execute. New Georgia, planned as a one-division undertaking, had required elements of four. At sea, America had lost six warships and, counting sailors, soldiers, and Marines, there were over 2,000 dead, 4,000 wounded, and nearly 3,500 lost to disease or war neurosis.

For both combatants, the greatest consequence of the slow central Solomon slog was in the air. Japan had lost a modest 110 planes across the spring, most in the air battles of early April. But June, July, and August alone had cost them 790, meaning 2,500 Japanese aircraft had been destroyed in the year since Guadalcanal was invaded. This emasculation, long in the making but peaking during the New Georgia campaign, marked the end of an effective air force along Japan's outer defense perimeter. As Navy Corsairs and Army P-38s, some from such celebrated squadrons as Major Gregory Boyington's Marine "Black Sheep" and the Navy's "Jolly Rogers," came to dominate the skies, the Allies claimed general air superiority in the region. Henceforth, as a rule, Halsey's forces knew they could count on pilots overhead being friendly or, if Japanese, compromised by fatigue and inexperience, so that any roar from the sky meant help or at worst a nuisance.[48]

No single battle or massive dogfight trumpeted this outcome. It emerged from the attritional muck that had characterized South Pacific battles. But it was real enough as both contestants looked to further combat. The emperor grasped this despite the heavy filter of information reaching him. The day Munda fell he proclaimed, "We can't continue being pushed back inch by inch." Three days later he asked, "What in the world is the Navy doing?" and throughout August he pleaded with whoever was within earshot, "When are you going to wage decisive battle?" To be sure, the Japanese Army and Imperial Fleet remained intact, but Japan's military machine and its outer defense perimeter had been punctured.[49]

For Halsey, New Georgia was the trough of a wartime learning curve. His keen eye had redeemed his inattention to detail in naval combat early in the war, but it failed him when it came to joint operations and ground war. A requirement to act as fulcrum between MacArthur and Nimitz not only placed strictures on his command prerogatives but also introduced unrealistic assumptions into his South Pacific plans. His bungled relief of Vogel put Marines, his only real experts at amphibious war, at the periphery of the New Georgia campaign and placed a green National Guard unit in the center of the inferno. Once the fight faltered, his calm deserted him and, in a near panic, he requested a glut of supplies and men from MacArthur and Nimitz that he knew neither man was willing or able to give. Stirred to action, Halsey then poured prodigious force onto the small island to wrest control of Munda field and sent excessive strength ashore at Vella Lavella. It is hard to imagine Halsey committing these errors of calculation at sea, but in combined arms and ground fighting, where neither long service nor intimate experience fostered confident assertion, Halsey's steps were first tentative, then frantic, and rarely certain. A resolute enemy had caused some of this trouble. Within his own orbit Halsey's inexperience and his murky position between Nimitz and MacArthur had greatly contributed to these difficulties. How well he next surmounted these issues would determine the trajectory not only of his contributions to the war but also of broader Allied success in the South Pacific.

Chapter Fourteen

High Tide

WAR COMPRESSES TIME as few endeavors do. It would cure Halsey of inexperience soon enough. But his rickety perch between MacArthur and Nimitz promised no similar solution. As Allied advances registered in late 1943 and early 1944, Halsey's South Pacific jurisdiction between Southwest and Central Pacific commands narrowed. The war would eventually pinch his command from the map, but until then Halsey would need better footing astride the two big Americans of the Pacific War. As MacArthur and Nimitz vied for control of the Pacific contest, Halsey worked to manage his friendly flanks as much as he endeavored to capture Bougainville in late 1943 and to isolate Rabaul in the spring of 1944.

. . . .

The interminable issue of command had festered through the hot summer months. King had used the slow slog through the middle Solomons as a bludgeon in high Washington councils to quicken planned assaults in the Central and North Pacific. The eight battleships, forty-five carriers, 400-plus cruisers and destroyers, and eighty-eight submarines that joined the American fleet in the two years following Pearl Harbor could not possibly be employed in the far Pacific alone, and King believed a broader tableau of operations from the Aleutians to New Guinea could whipsaw dwindling enemy resources along a 4,000-mile arc, confounding Japanese strategy to concentrate for decisive battle at a specific time and place. MacArthur and Halsey disagreed, but Nimitz warmed to the proposal as more ships, planes, and tanks reached him. By the summer of 1943, Washington officials had authorized a drive through the Central Pacific, and by the fall they had agreed to isolate and not capture Rabaul, purchasing MacArthur's acquiescence by approving the general's long-cherished desire to return to the Philippines via a drive northwest along the New Guinea coast.[1]

These shifts upended Cartwheel operations and obviated what had been Halsey's central objective. He had gleaned something of these plans when his pleas for reinforcements during the New Georgia crisis had fallen on deaf ears. In subsequent weeks he lost the Marine Second Division and an increasing number of ships to a new Fifth Fleet in the Central Pacific under Ray Spruance, who since the Battle of Midway had served as Nimitz's chief of staff. Halsey had long understood his role as the junior partner in the Pacific command triumvirate, but he now knew without a doubt his task lay not in strategic objectives, trophies reserved for MacArthur and Nimitz, but rather, as he put it, in the application of "the maximum pressure on the enemy with the minimum amount of troops, ships, and supplies." Among his South Pacific staff, a growing sense "of a great big Nimitz on our right and a great big MacArthur on our left" took root, "while we were squeezed in a little funnel, the Solomon Islands, working like hell and fighting every day."[2]

Granted separate axes of attack toward Japan, MacArthur and Nimitz had even less impetus to act in concert. MacArthur unleashed a new round of anti-Navy diatribes and roundhouse critiques of naval strategy, derisively pronouncing Nimitz "Nee-mitz" whenever animus reached a boiling point, which was often. Nimitz, who had long starved MacArthur's Seventh Fleet of capital ships, now outright forbade his staff from "gallivanting to Australia" when duty brought them as far as Nouméa. From Washington, King piled on, restricting the use of flattops in operations near Japanese land-based aviation, a stance the Navy would violate routinely in the Central Pacific but designed, as Nimitz's command diarist frankly acknowledged, "to prevent the use of our carriers" along the New Guinea coast as part of MacArthur's pending campaign toward the Philippines.[3]

In the midst of all this, MacArthur and Nimitz called upon diminishing South Pacific resources to serve their own designs. In September

Halsey conducted diversionary operations to support MacArthur's invasion of Salamaua, Lae, and the Huon Peninsula. In Ocotber he did the same for Nimitz's first salvos in the Central Pacific, Spruance's carrier strikes on Marcus, Tarawa, and Wake. Each complicated Halsey's march into the upper Solomons, still necessary for Rabaul's isolation if not outright capture. The original Cartwheel plan had contemplated using two divisions to capture well-defended Japanese airfields in southern Bougainville in operations commencing in mid-October, but now Halsey believed he lacked the force to attack at the appointed time and place. Instead, he suggested delaying the operation to mid-November or, more radical still, bypassing the island altogether and using air attacks to "contain and strangle" the enemy airfields.[4]

This plan ran afoul of intentions on his either side. From Brisbane, MacArthur complained that the scheme failed to place South Pacific ground-based fighter planes within range of either Rabaul, a prerequisite for neutralizing the Japanese citadel, or Cape Gloucester in his own sector, always a Cartwheel objective but now necessary to anchor MacArthur's right pivot as he turned left toward Manila. The Army general was willing to accept a delay in operations until November, but he insisted on a South Pacific assault somewhere along Bougainville's midriff to make South and Southwest Pacific positions mutually supporting. At the same time and from Honolulu, Nimitz maintained that Halsey should strike southern Bougainville in mid-October, in line with original plans, mostly to free Halsey's troop transports for use in the Central Pacific's invasion of the Gilbert Islands in November.[5]

This double squeeze irked Halsey. He had anticipated it in late August when, in an unusual cable direct to King and sent also to the White House, where his old friend Admiral William Leahy would read it as the president's chief of staff, he complained that Pacific command arrangements had long bedeviled the smooth orchestration of operations and now required "decision from outside" the region. In mid-September, he wired MacArthur that he was "in a most difficult position as to planning," admitting that strictures from Pearl Harbor had hobbled his desire for "the closest possible teamwork" with the general. To Nimitz, he professed abiding subordination but begged that his "command relations be clarified" so he "may know" whether to invade southern Bougainville in mid-October to satisfy Navy druthers or attack farther north on the island a bit later to meet MacArthur's desires. Believing the issue had reached a head, Halsey sent Harmon to Brisbane and planned to dispatch Carney to Honolulu to work through these entanglements.[6]

Harmon met little success. MacArthur rejected Halsey's notion to slip past Bougainville, believing the admiral had grown gun shy in view of the tough New Georgia fight. He thought the South Pacific retained force sufficient to assault the island, and he firmly held that only operations aimed at central Bougainville would comply with existing Joint Chiefs directives to both isolate Rabaul and aid his incipient steps toward the Philippines.[7]

Harmon's failure in Brisbane prompted Halsey to travel to Honolulu himself rather than send Carney. He arrived on September 23 and stayed for ten days, armed with a general defense of South Pacific operations. For a year, he had been closer to the fight than any naval officer of similar rank. His experiences had produced assessments at odds with Nimitz's judgment. In meetings with Nimitz, Spruance, and nearly everybody else of high rank, including King, who was coincidentally in Hawaii, Halsey was less sanguine about the Japanese defensive crouch in the South Pacific than was the Pearl Harbor commander. Bristling at recent criticism that he had been too profligate in his use of force, Halsey used a favored Nimitz phrase to explain he had been "continually governed by the balance of calculated risks," taking "every opportunity to inflict damage on the Jap" as long as "our losses can be replaced more quickly and in greater force." He thought the enemy had proved "fairly adaptable" and believed there remained plenty of productive fight left in his region. He denounced the "interception" of South Pacific resources by Central Pacific authorities, and decried the "hazy command lines" and the "uncertainties" regarding his obligations and responsibilities to Southwest and Central Pacific campaigns. "I serve three masters," he concluded, referring to the

Joint Chiefs, Nimitz, and MacArthur, and "am pulled sideways," a circumstance he believed courted calamity, sooner or later.[8]

History has marked poorly this tumult, caring more for Mac-Arthur's first steps back to Manila and Nimitz's initial thrust into the middle Pacific. But this was as close to a wailing complaint as Halsey came during the war. Carney remembered the fall of 1943 as a "difficult period." John Towers, who attended the Pearl Harbor conferences, confided that Halsey's protestations had produced "strong exception" among participants, particularly Halsey's old friend Spruance. Nimitz felt Halsey had overplayed his hand and succeeded mostly in unnecessarily riling MacArthur. Grievance is a risky stratagem among senior officers, who by inclination, acculturation, and duty solve problems without complaint. Halsey understood this, and neither expected nor received immediate relief to his conundrum. But he also meant to make manifest his frustrations, hoping to encourage reticence among those with the rank to pick and to poke at South Pacific operations. Probably, too, he believed his decades in uniform and time in the Solomons blaze had granted him an old sailorman's license to grumble and groan among friends without undue cost.[9]

Unsurprisingly, South Pacific operational planning for Bougainville proceeded in fits while these larger issues intruded. Bougainville was more regular in shape than New Georgia; a jagged mountain spine divided its 125-mile length and 30-mile girth, splitting the north, east, and south shores, where most of its few natives lived, from a forlorn west coast, where an alluvial plain sat miserably between jungle-clad foothills and gray-black beaches seldom more than fifteen yards wide. Five enemy airfields and a number of naval outposts dotted the island, augmented by additional airstrips in the Shortland Islands to the south and Buka to the north. The 40,000 Japanese defenders, concentrated along the southern seaboard, hailed from the Seventeenth Army, under the command of Lieutenant General Haruyoshi Hyakutake of Guadalcanal renown, and included the Sixth Division, the infamous brutes responsible for the rape of Nanjing in 1937. Had it been the first and not the last of the major South Pacific operations, its inhospitable topography and strong enemy presence might have confounded Allied troops every bit as much as had Guadalcanal. As it was, however, Bougainville loomed as just another pile of sludge in the long Solomons slog.[10]

Planners had first prepared to invade southern Bougainville in accordance with the Cartwheel outline. In August they abruptly focused upon Halsey's stillborn desire to bypass the island. By the middle of September they stood becalmed, "at a figurative crossroads" according the official Marine history, "uncertain about which road to take" while commanders in Brisbane, Honolulu, and Nouméa tussled. Merrill Twining, watching operational objectives flit about, believed strategic debate was "a ball and chain" to planning and rendered detailed operational preparations about as realistic "as a four year old's letter to Santa Claus."[11]

In late September Halsey told staff officers to focus on two paths. Both schemes required the Treasury Islands for an airfield and as a feint toward Bougainville's southern coast. One plan then called for invasion of the west coast near Empress Augusta Bay, the other for a strike on the east coast at Kieta. Both places were lightly defended, though they posed dissimilar challenges to an invading army: Kieta required a longer sea train and its soil was poor for airfield construction; Empress Augusta Bay was an open roadstead and sat within a thirty-minute flight of five Japanese airfields. As his staff weighed these relative disadvantages, Halsey grew weary of debate "day after day" and became frustrated as "talk took the place of action," a circumstance he never long countenanced. On October 1 he decided for Empress Augusta Bay and set a date, November 1, admitting that the area exposed his flanks at sea and in the air but knowing any subsequent battle would, in itself, "greatly further the overall Pacific Plan." In the end, his decision was the product of pressures emanating from Brisbane and Honolulu, and he chose a path more congruent with MacArthur's demands than with Nimitz's conceptions, for his operational responsibilities ran through the Army general and not the service of his birth. Years later, recalling the myriad influences bearing upon the South Pacific that fall, Halsey wrote that Bougainville plans "probably caused as much discussion as a convention of Philadelphia lawyers."[12]

For the task, he owned a fraction of his springtime riches. There was Fitch's land-based aircraft. Wilkinson's amphibious force counted twelve attack transports, ten of them aged veterans of the Guadalcanal landing, and a modest screen of eleven destroyers, a dozen minesweepers, and a couple of seagoing tugs. Halsey's covering forces included a single carrier group led by Rear Admiral Frederick Sherman and consisting of the venerable *Saratoga* and the new light flattop *Princeton*; Rear Admiral Tip Merrill's veteran but worn cruiser task force; a crack destroyer squadron under Captain Arleigh Burke; and a small handful of submarines. Days before the invasion, Nimitz agreed to augment this meager assortment with another carrier division and a new cruiser force, but these would not reach Halsey's area before the operation commenced. As the campaign approached, memory of Guadalcanal's first thin days prompted many veterans in Nouméa to dub the operation Shoestring II rather than employ its formal code name, Cherryblossom.

The Third Marine Division, elements of the Army's Thirty-Seventh Division, and a portion of Halsey's New Zealanders constituted Cherryblossom's ground force. Detailed planning for these units fell to Major General Charles Barrett, who had replaced Vandegrift as the I Marine Amphibious Corps commander two weeks earlier. Barrett, new to combat command, struggled with Cherryblossom's calculated risk. Well liked, soft spoken, and intellectual, he tended, as Vandegrift later noted, to conjure "all kinds of imponderables" to whatever task was at hand. It took him no time to conclude that the Bougainville plan was "too fraught with uncertainty." Three weeks into command and a week after Halsey had declared for Empress Augusta Bay, Barrett had yet to add any tactical detail to Halsey's general scheme, wasting time the South Pacific commander did not have. In frustration, Halsey relieved Barrett on October 7, asking yet again for Vandegrift, then touring Central Pacific Marine units before taking up duty as the commandant of the Marine Corps, to return for a second encore while Major General Roy Geiger, of Cactus Air Force renown and himself now in Washington, made his way to the region as a more permanent replacement.[13]

Barrett's relief led to tragedy. The day after he learned of his pending removal, but before it was widely known or effectuated, the Marine died in a fall from a second-story bedroom in Nouméa. An inquiry promptly proclaimed it an accident, a conclusion Halsey hastily accepted on October 19. But Barrett had, with trademark Marine discipline, plainly hurtled himself headlong toward a concrete slab some twenty-five feet below his windowsill. A close observer told Vandegrift that Barrett had been "worn and gray and haggard" and had simply "cracked." To Holcomb, Vandegrift asserted, "There by the grace of God goes any one of us," adding, "Halsey knows the straight story."[14]

For those few who knew, there were reasons aplenty for a charade. Honesty would have demoralized Marines, still smarting after missing much of New Georgia, at a time when Halsey needed their grit for Empress Augusta Bay. With echoes of Vogel's relief in his ear, Halsey did not want another bungled removal of a Marine general on his hands, especially a respected one, before a shot had been fired on Bougainville. Holcomb agreed and most Marines, he told Vandegrift, would have seen Barrett's relief as precipitous. The truth, these men reasoned, was simply too coarse for the moment, and even after the war Halsey and Vandegrift kept the pretense of Barrett's death in their respective memoirs, a story that held for sixty-five years.[15]

Whatever the merits of the deceit at the time, Halsey probably thought little of the dividends that unvarnished reality offered history's long arc. Confronted for the third time with the necessary relief of a general in the South Pacific, Halsey was, as with Vogel's removal in June, less forthright than his reputation might otherwise indicate, but he acted, in contrast to Hester's relief in August, swiftly, in a manner consistent with his renown for action. To the historian who uncovered the whole affair, Halsey had acted imperfectly in cover-up but correctly at core. To him, given the bad start at New Georgia and the lives now at stake on Bougainville, Halsey's removal of Barrett "must be counted among his most audacious—and correct."[16]

When Vandegrift returned to Nouméa he was surprised to find Bougainville plans had shifted to a penultimate assault in the Treasury Islands followed by a charge into Empress Augusta Bay in the middle of Bougainville, or, as Geiger later put it, a right jab followed by a roundhouse left hook. Vandegrift convinced Wilkinson to accelerate the deposit of all forces to the beachhead, and added a feint into Choiseul to further deflect defenders from Empress Augusta Bay, but otherwise mostly—and quickly—fleshed out details in accordance with Halsey's general directive.

The entire gambit depended heavily on aviation to suppress Japanese air power and repulse any counterattack, and Kenney's Fifth Air Force bombed Rabaul six times in October, claiming 275 planes destroyed and as many as fifty merchant and small warships sunk. On November 2 he claimed bombers ruined another eighty-five planes and scored direct hits on a heavy cruiser, a destroyer tender, three destroyers, three Navy auxiliaries, three minesweepers, sixteen merchant vessels, two tankers, and a tug, resulting in 114,000 tons of shipping sunk, all, Kenney wrote, within "the period of twelve minutes." Never in "the long history of warfare," he added, "had so much destruction been wrought upon the forces of a belligerent nation so swiftly at such little cost."[17]

These claims were wildly inflated, an occupational hazard of war that particularly afflicted Kenney. His raids had destroyed perhaps eighty planes and, on November 2, sunk 5,100 tons of shipping, less than a twentieth of Kenney's assertions. By this point in the campaign, South Pacific officers regarded Kenney as "a very loud and careless promisor of things." Publicly, Halsey muttered that the airman had launched "helpful attacks on Rabaul every now and then," which was true enough, but privately Halsey was far blunter, recording that Kenney's October claims were "another example of that lying son-of-a-bitch's braggadocio."[18]

South Pacific land-based air forces did better. By the fall, Fitch had nineteen Navy, fourteen Marine, ten Army, and three Kiwi squadrons spread across bases on Espiritu Santo, Guadalcanal, the Russell Islands, New Georgia, and Vella Lavella. From October 15 to 31, these units flew sixty-three missions and nearly 4,000 sorties against Japanese fields on and near Bougainville, principally at Kahili, Kieta, Buka, the Shortlands, and Ballale. By November 1, just thirty-one operational Japanese planes called these airstrips home, a number that dwindled to zero two weeks later. In this accomplishment, Halsey's forces were aided by an early dividend from King's strategy to whiplash Japanese defenses along a wide front: Admiral Mineichi Koga, who had replaced Yamamoto as commander in chief of the Combined Fleet, wanted to rush aircraft of the Third Fleet from Truk to Rabaul as Allied preparations for Bougainville became clear, but Spruance's carrier raid at Wake Island on October 6 held these planes in place until October 28, when 173 fighters, dive-bombers, and torpedo bombers raced to Rabaul, too late to interfere with Allied air preparations for Cherryblossom.[19]

As his air forces pounded Bougainville, Halsey moved closer to the front as well. On October 23 he arrived at Guadalcanal with the advanced headquarters echelon Carney had created in July, and established himself near Wilkinson and Vandegrift. It had never been Halsey's habit to supervise subordinates closely, but a growing comfort with joint operations and his experience during New Georgia operations, when his distance to the active front had dampened his tactile sense of command, underlay the trip, and Halsey intended to stay put until forces were securely ashore at Empress Augusta Bay.

. . . .

On October 27 the Navy brought the leading edge of 7,700 troops, many from New Zealand's Eighth Brigade, to the Treasury Islands and then placed on Choiseul's northeast coast some 700 Marines under the command of Lieutenant Colonel Victor "Brute" Krulak, a man of legendary intensity who in Halsey's words "had guts and muscle enough for six men." The large Treasury force quickly overwhelmed about 200 defenders. On Choiseul, the small Marine contingent wreaked havoc disproportionate to its size, at one point attacking a garrison of 1,000 evacuees from Kolombangara, and generally feigned a force far larger than Krulak possessed, which was its purpose.[20]

Meanwhile, Wilkinson's amphibious force of a dozen transports and their screen of destroyers whisked 14,000 Marines to Bougainville, reaching the waters off Empress Augusta on October 31. That evening, Tip Merrill's cruisers and Sherman's carriers bombed Bougainville airfields before, in the case of Merrill, retiring near Vella Lavella to rearm and, in the case of Sherman, heading to open sea to refuel and await developments. In the predawn darkness the following morning, Wilkinson's force reached Cape Torokina and turned inland, where the sea gave way, as it had at Guadalcanal, the Russells, New Georgia, and Vella Lavella, to the coarse sand, dense jungle, and forbidding mountains of yet another island of mildew and mud.

Halsey's plan had traded exposure to Japanese air and sea attack for a paucity of ground defenders, a gamble that required the swift discharge of Marines and then the quick retreat of thin-skinned transports. Nearly all 14,000 Marines and 6,200 tons of supplies reached shore by evening, aided by equipment and technique refined through a year of amphibious South Pacific assaults. Fewer than 300 defenders and a single large artillery piece offered momentary resistance in the immediate vicinity, leaving 2,000 Japanese a middling distance to the south as the sole serious ground threat to Vandegrift's men. Four waves of enemy planes, totaling 120 aircraft, posed an initial threat but were batted back by air combat patrols, and the only real obstacle to the landings came from the heavy surf that claimed over eighty small landing craft.[21]

The open water to the west posed the greatest threat to the lodgment. Aiming to reprise Japan's stunning Savo Island victory a year earlier, at Rabaul Koga ordered four cruisers under Vice Admiral Sentaro Omori and six destroyers led by Rear Admiral Matsuji Ijuin, victor of the Battle of Vella Lavella, to sortie with 1,000 reinforcements. Under weepy skies in the morning darkness of November 2 they met Merrill's four cruisers and two divisions of four destroyers under the command of Arleigh Burke, at a point some thirty miles from the Marines ashore.

The Battle of Empress Augusta Bay was a messy affair. Merrill smartly sent his destroyers ahead armed with torpedoes while his cruisers hovered nearly ten miles distant, waiting for opportunity with their larger guns. But his charges fought poorly. Within thirty minutes, neither destroyer division was under effective control, one suffering

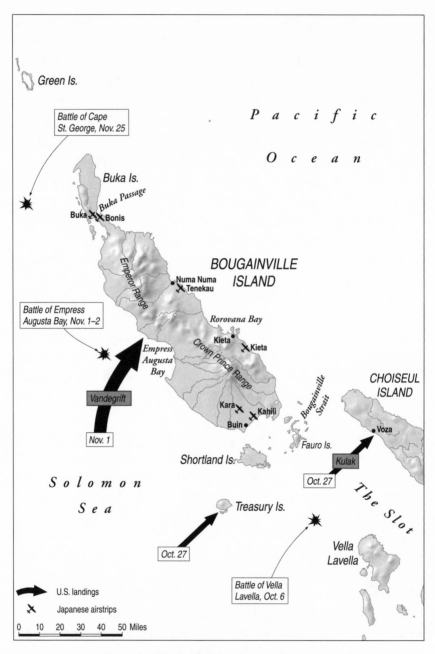

Green Is.

Battle of Cape
St. George, Nov. 25

Buka Is.

Buka Passage

Buka ✕✕ Bonis

P a c i f i c

O c e a n

Emperor Range

BOUGAINVILLE
ISLAND

Numa Numa
✕ Tenekau

Battle of Empress
Augusta Bay, Nov. 1–2

Rorovana Bay

Kieta ✕ Kieta

Crown Prince Range

*Empress
Augusta
Bay*

Vandegrift

Kara ✕ Kahili

Buin

*Bougainville
Strait*

CHOISEUL
ISLAND

• Voza

Nov. 1

Fauro Is.

Kulak

Shortland Is.

Oct. 27

S o l o m o n

S e a

T h e   S l o t

Treasury Is.

Vella
Lavella

Oct. 27

Battle of Vella
Lavella, Oct. 6

➤ U.S. landings

✕ Japanese airstrips

0   10   20   30   40   50 Miles

Bougainville, October to November 1943.

battle damage to three ships and the other disoriented in darkness, while the cruisers failed to do much but lob promiscuous amounts of ordnance in the general direction of Omori's force. The Japanese, however, fought worse. Following initial hits on American destroyers, Omori grew tentative, his indecision nurtured by the sheer weight of the American broadside, which had caused ship collisions in his line. Withdrawing from the battle, Omori had damaged two U.S. cruisers and three destroyers, but only one of them seriously, and had failed to get reinforcements to Cape Torokina, his central objective. He had, moreover, lost a cruiser and destroyer to the ocean depths and incurred damage to four additional vessels. Merrill retired to the south knowing victory was clearly his, though it had been ugly. The Americans scored with just two of fifty-two torpedoes and perhaps twenty of over 4,600 six-inch shells. At Rabaul, Omori's failure cost him his job, though the Japanese were not yet finished with the Marines now nestled along Bougainville's jungle edge.[22]

Koga next sent from Truk Vice Admiral Takeo Kurita with core elements of the Second Fleet: seven hardened heavy cruisers, a destroyer squadron, and a fleet train of supply, tanker, and transport hulls brimming with reinforcements. Halsey had little to oppose this dagger aimed at the exposed Marines. Far to the north, Spruance harnessed over 200 ships—including twelve battleships and eleven fast carriers—for pending operations in the Gilbert Islands, but Halsey had only Merrill's light cruisers and destroyers, at the moment totally spent, and Sherman's carrier group, consisting of the *Saratoga,* the light carrier *Princeton,* and a tiny band of smaller escorts. Kurita's force could plow past this brittle line and annihilate the Allied position on Bougainville. For Halsey, this was "the most desperate emergency that confronted me in my entire time" in the South Pacific.

Ray Thurber thought Sherman's carriers, with luck, weather, and the wind, might catch Kurita unawares while the Japanese were provisioning at Rabaul before plunging south. The prospect of carrier strikes against powerful shore defenses had sullied the reputation of more than one American admiral early in the war, and in the fall of 1943 Rabaul remained a citadel, its offensive punch diminished but its defenses in many respects stronger than in early 1942, when first Wilson Brown and then Fletcher had shied from its teeth. Yet, as at Santa Cruz and Guadalcanal and so many other places, Halsey saw but one choice: to fight. "We could not let the men at Torokina be wiped out while we stood by and wrung our hands," he recalled. Directing Sherman to strike Rabaul, Halsey fully expected the carriers and their air groups "to be cut to pieces" and probably "stricken, if not lost." He tried to forget that his son, Bill, so recently presumed lost, served aboard the *Saratoga,* but he failed. After issuing Sherman's orders, he slumped at the foot of his Guadalcanal cot, suddenly looking, Carney recalled, "150 years old" and very conscious of fatherhood.[23]

Sherman's flattops had just finished refueling far to the south, beyond Guadalcanal, when Halsey's directive arrived. The *Saratoga,* Halsey's queen, had become a hard-luck ship, twice torpedoed and with enough time in repair yards to earn derision with names like the Pond Lilly or the Sara Maru. Now she sped through the night, reaching a point 60 miles off Bougainville and 230 miles south of Rabaul by midmorning, November 5. She and the *Princeton* launched all ninety-seven airplanes they had, and relied upon Allied land-based aircraft from Munda for combat cover, marking the first time the Americans used such a defensive shuttle. Late that morning Sherman's fliers caught the Japanese ships at Rabaul flat footed, as Thurber had wagered, one cruiser still drinking fuel from a tanker. With rain enough to shroud their advance and clouds enough to hide their initial dive toward Simpson Harbor, they destroyed twenty-five aircraft and damaged six cruisers and two destroyers. The raid sullied Kurita's plans and "stunned" at least one Japanese skipper, who decried the "disgrace" the strike had brought to the Imperial Fleet.[24]

When Nimitz's carrier reinforcements reached Halsey in the following days, the South Pacific commander launched another mobile raid of 275 planes on November 11, the silver anniversary of World War I's armistice. That strike sank a destroyer, damaged a cruiser and three other tin cans, and left just fifty-two aircraft at Rabaul fit for further operations. Both raids revealed the changing calculus of carrier strikes on shore bastions, and underscored the possibilities additional flattops in the region promised, a point Halsey drove home, telling Nimitz afterward that he only wished "it might have been possible, while the Japs were hanging on the ropes, to have smashed their cripples" with more American carriers.[25]

A late-November sea battle highlighted the growing Japanese plight in the region, when five enemy destroyers brought nearly 1,000 ground troops to Buka and evacuated 700 aviation support personnel, useless since Allied air power had ruined the nearby airstrip. On November 24 Halsey radioed Burke to intercept them with five U.S. destroyers, penning in the process a classic dispatch: "Thirty-One Knot Burke, get this," he wired, using a moniker Burke had earned scurrying about the upper Solomons. "Put your squadron athwart the Buka-Rabaul evacuation line about 35 miles west of Buka. If no enemy contacts by early morning, come south to refuel at same place. If enemy contacted you know what to do. Halsey."[26]

Indeed Burke did, in the dark, rainy, early hours of November 25, Thanksgiving. With "true instinct for the chase," he pounced on the Japanese tin cans, sinking three before breaking off for want of fuel unless, as he cracked, he could gas up in Rabaul. This Battle of Cape St. George produced nary a dent on an American hull. It was accomplished without much preparation, with little tactical intelligence, and with ample intuition for and indoctrination to destroyer ways. It was an "almost perfect action," declared Admiral William Pye at the Naval War College, one "that can be considered a classic," an assessment almost no one then or since has challenged. It was also the last of the major surface actions in the middle Solomons. The first had occurred in March near Kula Gulf, and nine more concentrated in late summer and early fall. Together, they marked the passing of a powerful Japanese surface force.[27]

For the Japanese, Halsey's daring November carrier raids had been especially calamitous. The first forced most of Kurita's cruisers back to Truk or home waters; the second ruined Japanese air power in the region and left Koga worried about not having even a "skeleton force around which to rebuild" Japan's carrier air power. Never again would a Japanese warship larger than a destroyer grace Rabaul's

Simpson Harbor. No longer would aircraft from her airfields pose a significant threat to Allied operations. It would take more to render the fortress impotent, but the early November raids spelled the end of the garrison's ability to project power beyond its immediate environs. MacArthur radioed acclaim, King and Nimitz sent applause, and the Army Air Forces offered praise from faraway Washington, where Hap Arnold called Sherman's strikes "magnificent." Afterward, Halsey rushed to the *Saratoga* deck to backslap and enthuse, proclaiming that the raids had struck "a funeral dirge for Tojo's Rabaul."[28]

Lost in the din were the risks inherent in multiple Allied fighting fronts. Halsey's entire strategy at Bougainville was imperiled by seven enemy cruisers solely because he lacked sufficient capital ships, which were plentiful in Spruance's zone. With less luck, Sherman's two carriers and their planes could have been destroyed while attacking Rabaul, and the Marines on a thin, exposed Bougainville beachhead torn to pieces. If the American scheme to stretch Imperial forces across an oceanic front promised great recompense, it also offered the Japanese a chance to concentrate upon a weaker Allied element for decisive engagement, a gambit that increasingly became the emperor's best chance to salvage something from the war. In the months to come, the Americans would have to underwrite carefully their whipsaw strategy if the benefits of such an approach were to outweigh its costs.

. . . .

While South Pacific naval and air forces secured sea and aerial flanks, the small coastal plain edging Empress Augusta Bay quickly fell to Halsey's designs. Learning from the mistake of distance at New Georgia, he visited the beachhead on November 10, where he conferred with commanders, swam with troops, visited with newsmen, and tripped over a foot protruding from the muck, belonging, he wrote, to a dead "Private Watanabe or Corporal Yamatoya." By November 13, Halsey deemed the lodgment firm enough to shift command of the operation from Wilkinson to Geiger, who had arrived from Washington to relieve Vandegrift of ground command on November 9. Geiger commanded 44,000 men by mid-December, when he in turn relinquished control to the Army's XIV Corps, under Gris-

wold's direct leadership and Harmon's supervision. The first Bougainville airstrip was ready for operations on November 23, and within
weeks three Air Solomons squadrons called the island home, one more
knot in the noose around Rabaul. A furious battle the following
March briefly threatened the Allied position, but well before that no
contest on Bougainville could have affected the wider war.[29]

In his Christmas 1943 message to his command, Halsey struck a
satisfied tone, crediting his "jungle-smashing sea sweeping sky blazing
crew" for success at Empress Augusta Bay. He expanded this sentiment in a local Red Cross magazine article, praising the intrepid
"Army Liberator," the "fearless destroyer man," the selfless "Marine
corporal," and the "inspired Sea Bee," who together on Bougainville
had drawn the "dividing line between Yesterday and Tomorrow
in this bloody business of whipping the Jap." Cherryblossom was in
many respects the high tide of operations wholly within Halsey's
South Pacific. Vandegrift, three times a redeemer of South Pacific operations, believed the Bougainville campaign revealed "how much we
had progressed in both means and techniques since the Guadalcanal
landings." The assault, he wrote, "went off beautifully," supporting
air and sea operations had been "perfect," and subsequent operations
had never veered far from script.[30]

From start to finish on Bougainville Halsey benefited from strong
subordinates, themselves sifted by the grist of combat. As an amphibious force commander, Wilkinson had matured to the point that, in
Morison's phrase, he had gone "into Bougainville as if he had been
preparing for it all his life." Tip Merrill was a seasoned commander
of cruiser groups, having led them in Halsey's sector with increasing
agility since early 1943. Frederick Sherman was, like Halsey, a newcomer to aviation in 1936 at age forty-seven, a brilliant tactician and
a somewhat showy fighter. Arleigh Burke became one of the war's
great destroyer skippers in the South Pacific, a reputation that propelled him to chief of naval operations in the 1950s. Roy Geiger,
two-time winner of the Navy Cross, was, in the words of his best
biographer, "the most influential Marine aviator in the history of the
United States Marine Corps," with a war record the equal of "any

Marine in history." Griswold, a careful planner, was well suited to fortify the Empress Augusta Bay perimeter in December and then well able to repulse the Japanese counterattack when it came the following March.[31]

With this strong cast, Halsey's relaxed command habits, which had been a detriment at New Georgia, became strengths again. Once his forces reached Bougainville, he told one postwar audience, he "didn't meddle" in operational and tactical matters. "It was my job to define the objective and outline the mission. But I was never concerned for a minute with the administration of their forces or the modus operandi they employed to reach those objectives." This left Halsey free for the one remaining task in the Solomons left to him as 1943 faded and 1944 loomed: the isolation and reduction of Rabaul.[32]

. . . .

That became his focus. On November 17 he returned to Nouméa from his month-long sojourn at Guadalcanal. From November 23 to 25 he was in Brisbane to coordinate plans to neuter Rabaul. By then, tension with his left flank had reached ebb tide, enabled in part by a cordiality Halsey and MacArthur always maintained even when events mocked such sentiment. Happy circumstances also abetted intratheater relations. Carney's son, Robert Jr., a Marine lieutenant, had in midwar married Sutherland's daughter, Natalie, uniting the South and Southwest Pacific chiefs of staff in a way no official directive could. Thereafter, Sutherland's legendary animus was never aimed at Carney, and Carney recalled no difficulty dealing with Sutherland, a nearly unique memory among all the outsiders that brushed against the coterie of men who surrounded MacArthur in Brisbane. As insurance for good tidings, in early November Halsey appointed Captain Felix Johnson as his personal representative to MacArthur's staff, charged with maintaining an entente between the two commands. Johnson, whose "diplomatic qualifications" Carney believed were "perhaps outstanding in the entire Navy," won MacArthur's trust almost immediately, serving as the general's de facto naval aide and one of only four messmates in the spring of 1944 when MacArthur briefly took to sea. Mostly, however, relations between Brisbane and Nouméa sat at high tide in November 1943 because Halsey had done as Mac-Arthur wished at Bougainville, invading at a place, Empress Augusta Bay, and at a time, early November, to allow South Pacific support for MacArthur's pending December assault at Cape Gloucester.[33]

Busy with those pending operations, MacArthur offered little aid in the aerial reduction of Rabaul. Kenney launched no significant air strikes against the citadel after early November, leaving the garrison of perhaps 80,000 effective defenders and some 150 operational aircraft to South Pacific designs. The first American airfield on Bougainville brought Rabaul within range of ground-based fighters, and a December 17 sweep of seventy-six planes led by Marine Major Gregory Boyington's famed Black Sheep Squadron commenced Rabaul's death knell. Two days later, Thirteenth Air Force heavy bombers from Guadalcanal attacked. Air Solomons then managed three or four strikes per week, usually in groups of forty to fifty fighters or ten to forty bombers, in formations of mixed types and services in a pattern long familiar in the South Pacific, extending the war's celebrated ace contest between Boyington, Marine Captain Joe Foss, and Army Major Dick Bong, the troika representing the best American pilots in the region.

The pace quickened in early 1944. Heavy bombers moved north to Munda, and fighter planes began regular operations from not one but two Bougainville airstrips and yet another in the nearby Treasury Islands. Almost every day elements drawn from twenty-five squadrons converged on the once proud Japanese bastion. In January and February they aimed nearly 6,000 sorties against Rabaul, an onslaught that overwhelmed enemy strength, including 140 additional warbirds rushed to Rabaul as a stopgap. February 19 witnessed the last significant aerial battle above the Japanese citadel, leaving perhaps a dozen flyable enemy planes anywhere near Rabaul. By early March the outpost was a shambles, denuded of warships and planes, severed from Empire waters, cut off from even mail. Although a store of provisions guaranteed the garrison's survival to the end of the war, Rabaul soon became essentially the war's largest Japanese prisoner of war camp, its nearly 100,000 inhabitants locked in a cage sealed shut by Halsey's air and naval forces. At long last, the wake and wash of the Allied advance had rendered Rabaul a forlorn place.[34]

. . . .

Halsey had been away much of the time his air forces pummeled Rabaul. He had turned sixty-one in October, making him the oldest admiral serving in an active combat billet. Alone among all American officers, he had been continuously at sea or in a combat billet as a flag officer for six years, since the spring of 1938. Slated for a twilight tour commanding a sleepy naval district shortly before Pearl Harbor, only his forced convalescence in the summer of 1942 had provided rest. Although his stamina ranks among his greatest wartime traits, his staff recognized he needed a break. In December, Thurber floated the idea of leave for Halsey during a meeting with King in Washington, and Carney did the same with Nimitz during a conference in Honolulu. On December 26 Halsey flew to Pearl Harbor, where he passed four days discussing with Nimitz the South Pacific campaign and future operations. He reached the West Coast on New Year's Eve, where Fan had come from Margaret's home in Delaware to see her husband for the first time in sixteen months, and saw also his son, Bill, still with the *Saratoga,* then at the Mare Island Navy Yard. In California, Halsey attended one of King and Nimitz's periodic planning conferences, partook in war bond rallies, and made speeches. He spent two days in Washington, conferring again with King, and reached Delaware and his daughter's home on January 13 for two weeks' rest.[35]

The trip underscored his celebrity. On New Year's Day he was mobbed at the annual East-West collegiate football game. At the Fairmont, long his favorite hotel in San Francisco, he took to a kitchen entrance to avoid a throng of lobby well-wishers. In Los Angeles, he spoke before a large, influential group of West Coast industrialists. On January 7, he recorded triumphal remarks for the National Broadcasting Corporation, telling the country the South Pacific had been a "war laboratory" where the Americans first learned to "project a combined air-land-sea campaign" across "70,000 square miles of the Pacific Ocean." Along the way, he said, the hesitancy of Guadalcanal had been replaced by the confidence of Bougainville, and Allied forces now had the "tools and the know-how" to beat the Japanese. In Washington, he attended a Senate luncheon in his honor, held a Navy Department press conference replete with a Marine Corps band, and met with President Roosevelt, renewing an old acquaintance. At every stop, young children sought attention, old men wanted handshakes, and seasoned press correspondents solicited autographs.[36]

Fan struggled with this hubbub, her behavior toward Halsey swinging from fawning to ferocious, sometimes in front of other officers and, once, in the presence of young grandchildren. Shortly following Halsey's return to Nouméa on February 3, Margaret hospitalized her mother until Fan regained a modicum of mental footing. Returning to Nouméa, Halsey could only wonder what their future together held, when the war's battlefields would yield to peacetime kitchens, living rooms, and bedrooms.

. . . .

Back in Nouméa, the question of how best to cauterize Rabaul without derailing MacArthur's reorientation toward the Philippines or Nimitz's Central Pacific thrust sparked yet another tempest among senior officers. The Joint Chiefs had long intended South Pacific forces to capture Kavieng, on the northern tip of New Ireland, and Southwest Pacific troops to take Manus in the Admiralty Islands and drive farther into New Britain toward Rabaul. Neither Halsey nor Mac-Arthur supported these plans now that Rabaul was impotent, Halsey fearing an unnecessary slog to capture Kavieng, like Rabaul unable to project Japanese power but capable of a robust defense, and MacArthur viewing any further incursion from Cape Gloucester as a fruitless drain on resources—though he did covet Manus, but now only to anchor his right pivot toward the Philippines.

The Army general also raised, for good measure, the whole ugly matter of command. The "loose coordination" that had heretofore governed Southwest, South, and Central Pacific forces now risked catastrophe in his and Halsey's rapidly converging areas, where the "constant coordination of air and naval forces" required "immediate decisions" involving the "intermingling" of all Pacific forces in the shrinking region. In this, MacArthur believed Nimitz was completely unable to "exercise unbiased judgment" and suggested himself as savior, or at least overall commander. Having failed at every turn to create unified command in the Pacific, the Americans were in no danger of doing so now. In late January, the joint chiefs belayed MacArthur's march from Cape Gloucester but directed his capture of Manus, ordered Halsey's strike at Kavieng, required Nimitz to support MacArthur's operations, and all but washed their hands of further command intrigue in the area, telling both Nimitz and Mac-Arthur they should henceforth function by "mutual arrangements" rather than "operate by frequent directives" emanating from Washington. Nimitz then augmented Halsey's and MacArthur's navies to tallies not before seen in those waters—fourteen carriers, four battleships, ten cruisers, fifty-three destroyers, and nearly 200 supporting vessels—but only in March, after Spruance's force replenished from Central Pacific strikes at the Marshall Islands, and only under the proviso that Halsey retain direct control of the bulk of the capital ships, the necessary predicate that had long greased the fault line separating his and MacArthur's sectors.[37]

Halsey was in Delaware with his family during this imbroglio, but he could see it from 10,000 miles away. He had long suspected such issues would delay South Pacific operations in early 1944 just as they had a year earlier in the spring of 1943, a dalliance "repugnant to his temperament and at variance with his conception of Pacific strategy," to use Morison's phrase. The short hop from Guadalcanal to the Russell Islands had kept things moving then, and now Halsey looked for an analog at the other end of the Solomons chain. In late December he had told Wilkinson that any impending delay in Allied movement worked "more to the advantage of the Jap bastards than to us" and suggested that control of the lightly defended Green Islands, 115 miles due east of Rabaul, could keep a New Zealand brigade profitably employed and support yet another airfield.[38]

On February 5, two days after returning from the United States, Halsey committed Wilkinson to the task, telling him that the broader state of the war remained "very confused all the way up the line." Ten days later Wilkinson's amphibious force delivered nearly 6,000 Kiwis to the Green Island of Nissan, where they obliterated a paltry one hundred defenders. A month later nearly 17,000 men had reached the island, where already a fighter and a bomber airstrip were operational, essentially obviating the need for Kavieng. The South Pacific had been a hard laboratory for nearly two years, but this assault had been planned to the last detail and executed with precision within a matter of weeks. Such an operation could not have occurred in even the relative calm of an exercise just eighteen months earlier. To a group of staff officers two months later, Wilkinson called the affair "a very simple operation" that had demonstrated that the Japanese "were ready to quit" the area.[39]

MacArthur was reaching the same conclusion. His design for Manus envisioned a late-March attack with an entire division. On the heels of Halsey's Green Islands coup, however, he rushed a 1,000-man reconnaissance team to snatch the place on February 29. This windfall prompted the sharpest exchange between MacArthur and Halsey of the entire war. Because Halsey's staff had prepared the plans and would supply the manpower to transform Manus into a major fleet anchorage, Nimitz now suggested placing the island within Halsey's operational orbit. This blew MacArthur's top. Nimitz's proposal was an "artificiality" to "perpetuate the South Pacific Force" beyond its natural terminus at Rabaul, MacArthur bellowed in cables and letters to Washington officials. For two gut-wrenching years, MacArthur declared, he had toiled toward the fruit of far Pacific victory. Now, with "the moment of success in sight," Nimitz's proposal could not be other than "a serious reflection on my capacity to command." If it came to pass, MacArthur's "professional integrity" and "personal honor" demanded an audience with the president before "determining my own personal action in the matter." What leeway MacArthur, an active duty officer during wartime, had in the event was unclear, but already the thunder of a draft to make him the 1944 Republican presidential nominee could be heard in the distance.[40]

Awaiting Marshall's response, MacArthur summoned Halsey to Brisbane. On March 3 the admiral flew to Australia. In MacArthur's Spartan office the two had it out. MacArthur "was fighting to keep his temper," Halsey recalled. "He had lumped me, Nimitz, King, and the whole Navy in a vicious conspiracy to pare away his authority." In retaliation, MacArthur intended to restrict construction at Manus until jurisdictional matters were settled. Halsey replied that such a remedy "hampered the war effort" and believed a fit of pique had clouded MacArthur's judgment, a suggestion that drew audible gasps from those present, including Sutherland and Kenney. Command of Manus "did not mean a whit" to Halsey, and an "enlisted cavalry man could boss it" for all he cared—as long "as it was ready to handle the fleet" when the Allies pushed toward the Philippines.[41]

The following day the debate enjoyed two encores and threatened to erupt a fourth time before MacArthur agreed to proceed with large-scale construction. This entire tumult came to nothing when the Joint Chiefs ignored Nimitz's proposal, although Marshall chided the Southwest Pacific commander for his tantrum about "professional integrity and personal honor." These were "in no way questioned or, so far as I can see, involved," he told MacArthur, adding, coyly, that MacArthur was welcome to see "the President at any time on this or any other matter." So construction of the Admiralties' complex went forward, MacArthur never relinquished operational control, and the whole affair served mainly to remind anyone caring to notice of the nasty undercurrents that swirled still around the screwy command compromises attendant to far Pacific military operations, even in an hour of great triumph.[42]

. . . .

For those present across interminable months of sludge and trudge, the Japanese collapse in the Bismarck Archipelago came quickly. On the heels of swift success in the Green Islands and at Manus, the Joint Chiefs canceled Halsey's assault at Kavieng and substituted undefended Emirau as just as good a knot in Rabaul's noose. On March 20 Wilkinson deposited a Marine force on the island. Not an enemy plane, submarine, or ship appeared, and soon another Allied airfield sprang from a spit of land to become consequential for a moment. Although it was the final amphibious operation of the South Pacific campaign, Wilkinson saw Emirau forever not as culmination but as anticlimax, so easy had ship-to-shore movements against an extinct foe in the region become.[43]

Cartwheel operations, begun in the clamor of Guadalcanal and Buna, ended in the quiescence of the Green Islands, Manus, and Emirau. South Pacific battles were not the largest nor the longest nor the deadliest of the war, though they involved some of the most brutal fighting. For both combatants, they occurred at the far end of supply lines and among the most challenging of geographic conditions. The battles included the most compressed and hence the most complex triphibious operations of the war, relying as they did on the intimate interplay of ground, sea, and air operations in a manner nonexistent when the war began. The Pacific War was fought almost exclusively in this area for eighteen months after the Battle of Midway in June 1942. The campaign commenced at a time when opposing forces were evenly arrayed, and when the outcome of war hung in the balance. Although global war is too complex, its actors too numerous, and its events too interrelated for hoary maxims regarding turning points, the truth is this: at Cartwheel's completion, Allied victory in the Pacific War was virtually foreordained, even as great questions of strategy still sat beyond the horizon, where they awaited MacArthur's march to the Philippines, Nimitz's Central Pacific drive, the bombing and blockade of Japan proper, and a dozen other things.

Attritional combat, long derided as a dithering cousin to decisive engagement, bore this Allied triumph. No signal battle marked the changing tide. Instead, in the South and Southwest Pacific, the war turned inexorably against the Japanese, marked first by begrudging retreat in New Guinea and the lower Solomon Islands and last by the collapse of the Empire's outer defense perimeter. Neither the United States nor Japan desired a war of attrition. Its possibility would have provoked ridicule among prewar strategists in both nations. Once engaged, however, a long, slow slog greatly favored America, with its industrial capacity and manpower reserves. In 1943 alone, thirty-nine carriers of all types, two battleships, eleven cruisers, 363 destroyers and destroyer escorts, and fifty-six submarines had joined the fleet, their tonnage equal to the Japanese Navy at its wartime peak, in late

1941. By the spring of 1944, some 350,000 Japanese were trapped in MacArthur's and Halsey's sectors, a number in excess of those deployed in the entire Central Pacific. More defenders languished on Bougainville than defended Saipan and Iwo Jima combined, and more regular infantry were shipwrecked at Rabaul than later protected Okinawa. Given how bloody these contests were in 1944 and 1945, it is difficult to calculate Allied victory had Japan relocated even a portion of their trapped South Pacific troops.[44]

In Washington at the time, and in literature since, Cartwheel operations after Guadalcanal and Buna were often seen as a prelude to the main contest, whether that was, for the Army, the return to the Philippines or, for the Navy, island hopping across the Central Pacific. One eminent historian went so far as to describe much of the period from March to October 1943 as the war phase "when nothing happened." But operations in the far Pacific were more than that. There, the war became a total struggle not only in name but in deed, and there, more than in the immediate wash of Pearl Harbor or the dramatic victory at Midway, the Allies accepted the unlimited character of the fight, expended prodigious resources in blood and treasure, and met the Japanese, push for push and shove for shove. When that happened, Japan was doomed.[45]

In such an environment, Halsey's sea daring mattered less than other attributes. Although naval action was ubiquitous throughout his command of the South Pacific, his perch as an area commander meant other admirals honed American fighting skills on the grindstone of sea combat. Instead, it was in different corners that Halsey counted in the South Pacific. His late embrace of aviation at fifty-two had nudged his mind toward three dimensions and other domains, and his careful attention to the structure of South Pacific air commands paid enormous dividends in the march up the Solomons. His command of ground troops traced a more uneven learning curve, from a simple recognition of Vandegrift's talents at Guadalcanal, to a halting and nearly deceitful stewardship at New Georgia, to bold action at Vella Lavella, and finally to mature, reasoned judgment at Bougainville. Halsey had long known how to dare at sea. In the South

Pacific, in his seventh decade, he learned to calculate risk in amphibious and ground warfare as well.

Most fundamentally, in the South Pacific Halsey accepted unrelenting and brutal battle after Ghormley could not and before some others in high command could. It is hard to imagine many admirals exposing the nation's only operational carriers as bait in the Battle of the Santa Cruz Islands, or flinging precious ships into the confines of Iron Bottom Sound in the Naval Battle of Guadalcanal on three successive nights at a time when Japan ruled the nighttime sea. Yet those weeks sealed the fate of the Japanese on Guadalcanal and turned the trajectory of the South Pacific, and indeed the Pacific War, on its head. The war demanded that the Allies fight the Japanese forces at some point and at some time. In nearly every circumstance he confronted as the South Pacific commander, Halsey believed fighting them farther from Japan and as early as possible redounded to America's benefit.

Most importantly, in the South Pacific Halsey was the sinew connecting MacArthur and Nimitz. When Washington officials failed to unify command in the Pacific, someone had to navigate the boundary between the Southwest and Central Pacific sectors. MacArthur and Nimitz exchanged nary a letter or cable across the entire campaign. Their one meeting in April 1944 occurred well after any significant South Pacific operation and was marked by stiff pleasantries. Their respective staffs likewise interacted little and traveled between Brisbane and Honolulu even less. Halsey filled the gap. He met Nimitz six times during the South Pacific campaign, and their near-weekly correspondence was full of substance, nuance, and detail. He established an immediate rapport with MacArthur upon their first meeting in April 1943. Four additional conferences, in October and November 1943 and March and April 1944, helped maintain amity when difficult matters of strategy and operations intruded. More than any other person or command, Halsey and the South Pacific bridged the chasm of strategy and personality that divided the Pacific at the 159th meridian during the war's crucial middle years.

As 1944 stretched into late spring Halsey increasingly knew he had run out of war in the South Pacific. Nimitz and King both wanted him returned to sea command, but where or how remained unknown to the point that Halsey joked about next running an "old ladies home." In April, Nimitz indicated that Halsey and Spruance would alternate Pacific Fleet command, changing not the ships but their skippers, keeping the force as the Fifth Fleet under Spruance and as the Third Fleet under Halsey, an arrangement confirmed in early May when King, Nimitz, and Halsey met in San Francisco. It was a bit unorthodox and offered little prospect for rest among the rank and file, but the setup had the virtue of employment for the two best seagoing fleet commanders in the American Navy and represented, as Halsey later explained, a sort of pony express in reverse, where the riders and not the horses changed at predetermined moments.[46]

At midmonth Halsey undertook a farewell tour of the South Pacific, surveying many of the twenty-five major and a few of the eighty-two minor South Pacific installations via some of the region's fifty-five airfields. He visited Brisbane one last time to finalize the transfer of his Army divisions, the Thirteenth Air Force, and the remnants of the once mighty South Pacific naval force to the Southwest Pacific. He exchanged heartfelt sentiment with MacArthur and solicited an autographed photo, the sole time he engaged in this common wartime practice. "You and I have had tough sledding with the enemy," Halsey wrote the Army commander, "and we have had some other problems nearly as difficult," a reference to the many issues of divided command. Yet, Halsey felt that "in every instance" the two men had "licked" their "difficulties." MacArthur agreed, adding that Halsey left behind "the unforgettable memory of a great sailor, a determined commander, and a loyal comrade." Victory obscures all kinds of defects, of course, and in the afterglow of far Pacific success even Nimitz became blind to the ills of fractured command, writing in a widely circulated dispatch that "coordination between the various services and their component parts" had proven "united military effort can be obtained under a democratic government. To all concerned I say well done."[47]

That summer in Nouméa, the Pink House disappeared into lore. In time, the canteens would also empty, the laundries close, and the street-side cafés blow away. In his end-of-tour report, Halsey praised the "unified but decentralized" nature of South Pacific operations. The wide dispersion of forces, their dissimilar composition, and difficulties in communications required as much, and it was a happy circumstance that Halsey's inclination toward strong leadership and laconic command matched the region's peculiarities. He believed the "successes of the South Pacific Force were not the achievements of separate services or individuals but the result of whole-hearted subordination of self-interest by all, in order that one successful 'fighting team' could be created." Forwarding the report to King, Nimitz thought that last sentiment "might well be a guiding directive to all armed services of the United States, now and in the future." Halsey had arrived in Nouméa when the entire Allied position in the Pacific "hinged on our tenuous foothold" at Guadalcanal, Nimitz wrote, and Halsey's achievements there had been "impressive and complete," so much that the record, in his view, needed no further "embellishment or eulogy" from him.[48]

On June 14 Halsey gathered a small group of longtime staff officers. They toasted their success and knew more work lay ahead. Reminded of the tough early days, when morale had been low and material scarce, Halsey suggested that any future South Pacific shoulder patch "should have as a motif a rusty nail and a frayed shoestring." The next morning, American and New Zealand troops lined the roadway to the fleet anchorage as he bade farewell. "Their cheers and the bands and the flags stung my eyes," Halsey remembered. His part in the South Pacific was his finest hour, and in Nouméa, behind a desk far from the front and safe from the fight, Halsey joined, in the judgment of the South Pacific's most careful chronicler, "the great admirals of history." As his plane lifted from the harbor, however, and New Caledonia faded from view, Halsey's gaze was forward, to a new chapter of coveted fleet command upon the high seas. He never saw Nouméa again.[49]

Chapter Fifteen

At Sea at Last

HALSEY ARRIVED AT PEARL HARBOR on the forenoon of June 17, 1944. With him came a contingent of loyalists. Carney continued as chief of staff; Riley and Dow remained the duet responsible for plans and communications; Doug Moulton stayed as Halsey's air operations officer; Stassen, Kitchell, and Herb Carroll rounded out Halsey's flag secretariat; and a handful of bluejackets, led by Benedicto Tulao, constituted seed corn for a seagoing mess. Thurber left as the operations officer, but his longtime assistant Rollo Wilson fleeted up, maintaining continuity in that important position. Within two weeks, this Third Fleet nucleus grew to sixty officers, including Commander Marion "Mike" Cheek as Halsey's intelligence officer; Lieutenant Commander John Lawrence, Lieutenant John Marshall, and Ensign Carl Solberg in flag plot—the nerve center of a seagoing fleet—and Commander Carnes "Piggy" Weeks as medical officer.

Two-thirds of Third Fleet officers were reservists, reflective of the wartime Navy's citizenry. Cheek was an Annapolis graduate who had left the Navy for business in the Far East and returned to duty as war arrived; Lawrence, Marshall, and Solberg were New England Brahmins with Ivy League educations; and Weeks had been in private practice in New York City until a cocktail party introduction to Halsey landed him with the Third Fleet. They and the South Pacific holdovers knew little of large seagoing fleets. Many had not served afloat across the middle years of the war, when the American Navy reinvented itself, and Halsey's staff retained the whiff of area command: Riley, a Marine brigadier general, now planned fleet operations. As they settled into office space within Nimitz's headquarters atop Makalapa

Hill, with views of Pearl Harbor below and the colorful Koólau range above, how well Halsey's cohort adjusted to new challenges would to a large extent determine his success or failure.

The latest imbroglio over command in the South Pacific that spring had spawned the general plans from which they now worked. Ongoing debate between George Marshall and King in Washington and MacArthur and Nimitz in the Pacific had produced in March an outline for operations stretching to the New Year. MacArthur detailed his return to the Philippines via a hopscotch campaign northwestward along the New Guinea coast, while Nimitz was to both secure the general's seaward flank and continue his own drive through the Central Pacific. Spruance's springtime strikes at Truk and invasions in the Marshalls were an amalgam of this agreement, designed to cover MacArthur's mid-April invasion of Hollandia and springboard Nimitz's forces into the Marianas in mid-June. After the Marianas fell, Halsey would in early fall conquer the western Caroline Islands and the small Palau chain, from where he could cover MacArthur's approach to the Philippines via Morotai and on to Mindanao, the largest southern Philippine island. Whether the Allies would then invade other Philippine places or jump directly to Formosa was left to another day and another debate, but given the difficulty of joint planning for the Pacific, this March directive constituted as much coherence as was then likely. It was, as one distinguished historian called it, a delicate "reconciliation among conflicting strategic and tactical concepts" and one that required the ongoing interaction of Southwest and Central Pacific forces, now without the benefit of the South Pacific command as intermediary.[1]

In a series of brilliant amphibious jumps through the summer, MacArthur advanced a thousand miles up the New Guinea coast at a cost of about 2,000 battle deaths, only twice what tiny Tarawa had earlier extracted from Nimitz, leaving the Southwest Pacific forces just short of Morotai and the approach to Mindanao as September dawned. In Nimitz's sector, Ray Spruance spent the summer invading the Marianas' islands of Saipan, Guam, and Tinian with a Fifth Fleet swelled to fifteen carriers, seven battleships, nearly 600 additional vessels, and 127,000 assault troops. This vast armada prompted Vice Admiral Ozawa to sortie in June with the bulk of Japan's punching power—nine carriers, five battleships, and many cruisers and destroyers—eager for the decisive victory the Japanese had sought since Pearl Harbor. In the ensuing battle Spruance adopted the operational defense, holding Mitscher's flattops close to the American amphibians. Although Spruance won a lopsided victory, claiming three enemy carriers sunk and about 600 planes destroyed against negligible losses in a clash known formally as the Battle of the Philippine Sea but dubbed the Great Marianas Turkey Shoot, the contest vexed many Americans who were sure a freer pursuit of Ozawa could have wiped out the Japanese Navy. At sea, carrier officers seethed at Spruance's caution, and at Pearl Harbor regret pervaded Pacific Fleet headquarters, a sentiment amplified in Washington. Weeks later, Spruance discharged such critiques as "ancient history," though after the war he admitted that "instead of waiting in a covering position," he should have "steamed to the westward in search of the Japanese fleet." In the battle's wake, King and Nimitz vowed to never let a similar opportunity slip, an oath magnified as the capture of the Marianas took far longer, well into August, and cost far more, nearly 5,500 American and as many as 70,000 enemy lives, than anticipated.[2]

. . . .

While the Fifth Fleet covered the capture of the Marianas, Halsey and his Third Fleet staff prepared for sea duty. They knew they were rookies again. Central Pacific amphibious operations were so far beyond the scale of Solomons campaigns as to render them incomparable. The Navy had grown from 902 to 6,359 vessels since Pearl Harbor, and was six times greater in destroyers, ten times larger in carriers, and counted in the thousands whole classes of auxiliaries and landing ships unknown when Halsey was last at sea. Moreover, flattops no longer operated alone, as they had during Halsey's *Enterprise* tour early in 1942, and instead steamed in multiple groups of four and sometimes five, nearly a score operating in close unison, a change requiring new doctrine and battle managers bent over the pale light of radar scopes, looking more like scientists in laboratories than officers of old upon the quarterdeck. Immersed in area command in the South Pacific, Halsey and his staff had been but distant observers and only occasional participants in these developments, leaving them agnostic at best and ignorant at worst about the myriad changes industrial apogee had brought to sea combat.[3]

They learned what they could from Spruance, embarking four staff members aboard Fifth Fleet ships. Stassen had hitched a ride on the *South Dakota,* the one American battleship to sustain damage during the Turkey Shoot, and concluded that Fifth Fleet operations had been too stiff and fighter direction too disorganized. As a remedy, Stassen convinced his superiors that Halsey should retain the capacity to command directly the entire fleet if the need arose, a practice inconsistent with Spruance's habit aboard his flagship, the cruiser *Indianapolis,* and at odds with Halsey's own comfort with delegation. Because only a battleship had the space for the kind of flag plot, combat information center, and communications suite robust enough to micromanage the fleet, the *New Jersey,* the second of four *Iowa*-class battleships and among the finest fighting hulls the U.S. Navy ever commissioned, became Halsey's flagship. Into early August, Pearl Harbor workers cut through bulkheads and across decks to clear room for ten transmitters and forty-two radio receivers over the ship's normal machinery, as well as berthing for the forty-four staff officers and nearly 150 bluejackets Halsey took to sea, a third more than Spruance's coterie and a number requiring the loss of fifteen of the ship's regular officer complement and a proportional number of sailors. Since first arriving in the South Pacific ten months earlier, Stassen had proved a quick study and a nearly unique talent, but that this gifted amateur had attained such a trusted status by the summer of 1944 spoke volumes of the Third Fleet staff's idiosyncratic nature.[4]

Much of this occurred while Halsey was in Delaware on two weeks' emergency leave in the middle of July tending to Fan, who had suffered another mental collapse and, for the first time, memory loss, a worrisome development that prompted a physician to "marvel" at Halsey's "ability to stand up to worries at home" while serving as a wartime fleet commander. Back in Hawaii near month's end, Halsey added detail to Third Fleet designs for the Caroline and Palau Islands. This process proceeded in fits, partly because Halsey's habits from his South Pacific days, when his strategic prerogatives had been greater, died hard. He initiated planning with a warning order, for instance, a privilege reserved for area commanders, and then proposed bypassing Palau for a jump directly into the Philippines, a product of his confidence in carrier aviation but a suggestion at odds with the Joint Chiefs of Staff. As Halsey was no longer an area commander and would never be a member of the Joint Chiefs, Nimitz countermanded the warning order until he himself was ready to begin preparations and ignored the suggestion to bypass Palau.[5]

Continuing debate over long-range plans also hindered Halsey's preparations. The Joint Chief's March directive authorizing the Palau, Morotai, and Mindanao invasions left unsettled what would come next: either the capture of additional Philippine islands, MacArthur's preference, or a jump directly to Formosa, King's desire. When a flurry of memos and dispatches stretching from Washington to Australia failed to resolve this issue, Roosevelt traveled to Honolulu to discuss the matter with MacArthur and Nimitz, arriving on July 26, just days after the Democratic National Convention in Chicago had nominated him for an unprecedented fourth term. MacArthur and Nimitz regarded the meeting as a political campaign appearance, and MacArthur especially resented the summons to Pearl Harbor from his Brisbane headquarters.

But Roosevelt came to Honolulu not so much to grandstand as to settle difficult strategic issues. His trip was the natural, even necessary, result of a divided command in the Pacific that had provided MacArthur and Nimitz no single superior short of the presidency. In Honolulu, and with only himself; his chief of staff, Admiral William Leahy; and the two Pacific commanders present, the president clearly favored operations farther into the Philippines, pulled perhaps by MacArthur's powerful oratory to liberate the American commonwealth. Military planners, unaccustomed to such direct presidential intervention, continued to debate the issue for weeks as if the matter remained undecided, but as the days passed, a scheme calling for the invasion of Mindanao in October, Leyte in mid-December, and Luzon, the major island and home to Manila, in the spring of 1945 took hold, leaving the whole matter of Formosan operations bureaucratically in limbo but essentially dead.

This decision at last freed local commanders to design in detail more proximate operations. Halsey assigned two divisions to assault Palau and an Army corps to capture Yap and Ulithi, slating the first task for September 15 to coincide with MacArthur's attack at Morotai and the second for early October, allowing the bulk of Third Fleet combatant vessels to support each assault. Beginning in late August, Halsey intended to strike the Bonin and Volcano Islands between the Marianas and Japan as a diversion, and then focus upon Japanese airfields in the Philippines to suppress enemy planes capable of reaching Palau and Morotai. Meanwhile, MacArthur's Fifth and Thirteenth Air Forces under Kenney were to blanket Japanese airfields in the Carolines to cover Halsey's approach into the region. Together, these air plans constituted interwoven operations between Southwest and Central Pacific Forces, and, in the words of an official Army historian, constituted the Pacific War's "most widespread and thoroughly integrated series of strategic air support missions yet undertaken."[6]

. . . .

All this required Halsey to be at sea soon. On August 24 he and his staff boarded the *New Jersey,* under the command of Captain Carl Holden. Together with three destroyers, the battleship cleared the channel buoys and turned west. Two days later, Nimitz placed Halsey in command of the main portion of the Pacific Fleet, still in scattered formations near the Mariana Islands, and directed Spruance and his flagship *Indianapolis* to Pearl Harbor. With that, the ships and men of the Fifth Fleet became the Third. The very next day Halsey, who always suspected the Japanese of chicanery, directed a destroyer to board and to verify that an enemy hospital ship bound for Truk was indeed a mercy ward and not a de facto troop transport. This cheered others, including Mitscher, who wrote to "praise the lord" for Halsey's hardline, but it worried Nimitz, who feared the action would subject Allied mercy ships to the same treatment. He countermanded the order, making Halsey "mad as hell." It had taken exactly two days for Nimitz to feel the need to channel Halsey's aggressive instincts.[7]

Not since early May 1942, at the front end of his lost race to the Battle of the Coral Sea, had Halsey rode a proud flagship on the way to battle. His home as an embarked fleet commander was in the *New Jersey* superstructure, directly below the captain's perch, and comprised a flag bridge, flag plot, sleeping quarters, offices, and a large room for conferences and meals. Halsey usually woke early. He spent enough morning time in the washroom readying for the day that staff suspected he was a bathroom dawdler, clipping, shaving, bathing, and brushing twice and perhaps three times. When he emerged he was immaculate, his shoes polished and his heavily starched khaki uniform shorn of all trinkets but collar rank and small wings above the left breast pocket. A spectacle case hung from his belt, above the right pant pocket, and he often wore shorts to keep his sensitive skin cool and dry. A small army of attendants met his every whim, and white linen, silver flatware, and fourteen plates emblazoned with four blue stars dressed his mess three times a day. When not at battle station, he passed time in flag plot, where as many as twenty bluejackets kept track of the fleet's movements and the enemy's whereabouts, or on the flag bridge, where sailors in nearby ships delighted in his appearance. "Look," they would shout, "there's Bull Halsey." In contrast to Spruance's marched walks aboard the *Indianapolis,* he sometimes played deck tennis on nice days and read detective novels when weather was lousy. "Though not a large man," Solberg recalled, Halsey "had a head so big and shoulders so wide that he seemed almost to lurch as he walked," nearly "like a boxer, rising on the soles of his feet." Solberg suspected there had been times in the South Pacific when Halsey had stepped more heavily, but at sea again, "he strode with a spring. At 62, he was like a man going to a tryst." Indeed, as Halsey himself told Nimitz, it was "a grand and glorious feeling to be at sea again."[8]

As the *New Jersey* sliced westward, dozens upon dozens of steel silhouettes began to crest the horizon. Near Manus the Third Fleet surface combatants appeared: six battlewagons, nearly twenty cruisers, and dozens of destroyers under the command of Vice Admiral Willis

Lee. In the seas surrounding Eniwetok, Vice Admiral Marc Mitscher and his carriers came into view, divided into four groups of four or five flattops a piece. Nine fleet carriers, most of the powerful new *Essex* class, and eight light carriers, all from the wartime *Independence* class, had become the modern Navy's battle line, commanded, at long last, mostly by officers with long service in aviation. There was of course Mitscher, and the task groups were commanded by Rear Admirals Frederick Sherman, Gerald Bogan, Joseph "Jocko" Clark, and Ralph Davison. Halsey needed little reminder of Mitscher's vast talents, and had taken to calling the wizened aviator "a fighting fool"; Sherman remained Halsey's favorite carrier commander; Bogan, who had been one of Halsey's teachers in carrier ways at Pensacola and aboard the *Saratoga* before the war, had since blossomed into an outspoken, tenacious, capable combat leader; Jocko Clark, a full-blood Cherokee and the first Native American to graduate from Annapolis, may have been the best of them all; and Davison, like Bogan early to aviation at the age of twenty-four in 1920, was more deliberate and quiet—but that a man of his halcyon disposition had climbed high in carriers was itself a mark of the growing maturity of naval aviation. They were soon all joined by Vice Admiral John McCain, like Halsey a latecomer to aviation and a natural scrapper who had opened the South Pacific campaign as Ghormley's air commander. At some point to Halsey's liking, McCain was to relieve Mitscher of overall carrier command, a plan that soon prompted Halsey to relieve Clark to make room for McCain to learn the ropes.[9]

It was a magnificent fleet. When Halsey first laid eyes upon the flattops, he zoomed by zip line and hanging chair from the *New Jersey* to the new *Hornet*, perhaps the sole time in the war a four-star admiral went over the side at sea. "I hadn't been with the fleet for more than two years," he explained, and "I wanted to see what the new carriers and planes looked like." For all the innovation the flattops represented, however, the most revolutionary character of his armada related more to beans than bullets: a Sea Logistics Group of thirty-four fleet oilers, eleven escort carriers, forty-five destroyers and destroyer escorts, ten fleet tugs, twelve ammunition ships, fourteen dry and four fresh provision vessels, and six freshwater tankers rode shotgun for the Third Fleet, able to keep the combat ships at sea indefinitely, a capacity so far beyond the steaming radius of the Great White Fleet at the dawn of Halsey's career that it boggled the mind. Once all together, this Third Fleet constituted the preponderant striking power of the American Navy and counted about a hundred major combatants. In regular cruising formation, it extended some forty miles in length and nine miles flank to flank, literally stretching well beyond what Halsey's eye could spy from the *New Jersey* bridge.

The carriers commenced their work on the last day of August. Davison's force, consisting of four carriers, two cruisers, and eleven destroyers, peeled north toward Chichi Jima and Iwo Jima, where over three days 250 warbirds shot up some forty enemy planes and sank a dozen small auxiliaries before proceeding to strike Yap on September 8. At the same time, the three other carrier groups under McCain, Bogan, and Sherman aimed their thirteen flattops and 850 aircraft at Palau for three days beginning on September 6 before striking Mindanao airdromes on September 10 and 11. These collective strikes destroyed many ground installations and a few naval auxiliaries but few enemy planes. Looking for better remuneration, Halsey struck deeper into the Philippine archipelago, hitting Cebu, Leyte, and Samar with 2,400 sorties on September 13, 14, and 15, destroying some 200 planes, a few more small ships, and ground targets at a cost of just eight planes.[10]

This impunity astounded both Halsey and his carrier commanders. Allied intelligence suggested that as many as 650 Imperial aircraft waited in the southern Philippines, but Third Fleet pilots had not seen anything like that number. On September 13 a pilot from the *Hornet,* shot down over Leyte and returned to the fleet by friendly Filipinos, reinforced Halsey's suspicions of modest enemy defenses in the central Philippines. Halsey's experience in the South Pacific had sensitized him to "symptoms of Japanese weakness," and he now sensed an opportunity to pounce and punch hard "the vulnerable belly of the Imperial dragon." The air strikes had dealt a "crippling blow to the enemy," he wrote Nimitz, and revealed that the Japanese "were operating on a shoestring in these areas." By dispatch, he made a bold proposal: skip the assaults at Palau, Yap, Morotai, and Mindanao, and plunge headlong toward Leyte, months earlier than planned. This radical suggestion was wholly beyond his portfolio as a fleet commander; it essentially repeated the Carolines bypass he had earlier recommended and Nimitz had previously rejected; and any change now would upset the carefully laid plans of higher authorities, including the president. Halsey's proposition was bold to the point of crazy.[11]

Nimitz summarily rejected as impossible the abandonment of Palau operations, which were slated to commence within twenty-four hours. Halsey's invasion fleet was then approaching Palau's shores, and minesweepers and frogmen were already in waters near the target islands. But the Pacific Fleet commander was willing to nix the October invasion of Yap, and sent Halsey's missive to MacArthur and the Joint Chiefs for their consideration. MacArthur could not stop Morotai's invasion, also slated to commence within a day, though he jumped at the chance to trade Mindanao for an early invasion of Leyte. The Joint Chiefs, then with Roosevelt in Quebec for the Quadrant Conference with their British counterparts, huddled briefly and decided quickly to cancel the Yap and Mindanao invasions and advance the Leyte assault by a couple of months, to October 20. "Having the utmost confidence in General MacArthur, Admiral Nimitz, and Admiral Halsey," George Marshall recounted, "it was not a difficult decision to make." In his State of the Union address the following January, Roosevelt recognized Halsey for a "major change in plans" that "saved lives that would have been expended in the capture of islands which are now neutralized far behind our own lines." Morison, well after the war, credited Halsey with a "brilliant strategic suggestion."[12]

Many Americans would now have to make changed plans work, starting with those slated to take Morotai and Palau, operations deemed too imminent to forgo even as the rationale for their capture—to cover the invasion of Mindanao—had eroded with the leap to Leyte. At Morotai, MacArthur's forces faced little difficulty. In Halsey's sector, it was different on the Palau islands, especially Peleliu.

Recent Japanese reinforcements there had ballooned enemy ranks to some 10,500 men, many from elite Army units and some from Japan's finest infantry regiment, led by Colonel Kunio Nakagawa, whose eye for terrain and gift for close combat forebode ill for the Americans.

For the nearly 50,000 American soldiers and Marines embarked upon Third Fleet ships, only their first few steps ashore at Peleliu on September 15 were easy. Pushing inland, they met a cross section of mortar, artillery, and automatic fire. By September 18, the fight had become "savage and costly," according to the official Marine history. The Japanese fell back to Umurbrogol Ridge, a coral badlands where they had excavated some 500 caves impregnable to air or artillery attack. In that tortured terrain, the Marines slugged well into October. There, flamethrowers made their debut as ubiquitous weapons, and eight Medals of Honor were won, five posthumously. Each Japanese killed cost the Americans an astonishing 1,500 rounds of small-caliber ammunition, fifteen mortar shells, and twelve hand grenades. Nakagawa gave his life in defense, but so doggedly had he fought that the emperor granted him a graveyard promotion from colonel to lieutenant general. At one point, Halsey told Nimitz that poison gas might be needed to roust the enemy from their perch. It was a mess.[13]

Peleliu fell in early November, but at terrible cost. The Japanese lost 11,000 men; the Americans 2,000, with another 8,000 wounded. Bloody Peleliu, as history remembers it, lasted longer than the desperate Marine assault at Tarawa earlier in the war and at Iwo Jima later, but it produced fewer rewards. Its possession mattered little for subsequent operations, and only the occupation of Ulithi atoll, taken on September 23 almost as a byproduct of the fight, yielded significant advantage when its lagoon later served as a forward anchorage for as many as 600 ships. The great Marine memorialist Eugene B. Sledge spoke of deep anguish over Peleliu and the National Museum of the Marine Corps called it "the bitterest battle of the war." Most historians judge Peleliu among Nimitz's rare blunders. He never visited the island, the sole Central Pacific beachhead he skipped, and after the war he rarely spoke of the campaign. Halsey, who had twice suggested bypassing the place, feared "another Tarawa" as costs mounted, and, in a rare example of introspection, wondered aloud upon the *New Jersey* flag bridge if he should not have pressed Nimitz harder to skip the place. For those many observers who saw in Halsey mostly a ferocious fighter, the whole episode revealed that the old admiral could think, too, sometimes better than Nimitz.[14]

. . . .

While Peleliu burned, Leyte loomed, for defenders and attackers alike. Their June defeat in the Great Marianas Turkey Shoot had left Japanese officers dispirited. In midsummer, Ozawa limped back to home waters to repair his remaining carriers and to train replacement pilots. The battleships and cruisers, under Vice Admiral Takeo Kurita, retreated to Lingga Roads, near Singapore, where they could lie near the Empire's oil sources. For the fall, the Japanese redoubled efforts for a decisive battle. Four related contingencies, dubbed the Sho-Go plans, anticipated American strikes at the Philippines, which they guessed most likely, or, in descending probability, Formosa and the Ryukyus, the southern home islands, or the northern home islands. For Sho-Go 1, once the Americans committed to battle in the Philippines, four separate Japanese naval forces drawn from the surface combatants in Lingga Roads and the carrier fleet in Japan would converge as multiple pincers to crush the invaders and destroy whatever American fleet might appear. The scheme encompassed nearly the entire Japanese fleet then extant, including four of six carriers, nine of nine battleships, twenty-one of twenty-two cruisers, and thirty-one of thirty-five modern destroyers. Even then, air power was necessary to thwart American strength, and the whole plan hinged on a large reserve of aircraft, then collectively stationed in the northern Philippines, Formosa, and upon the flattops, to mass at the correct point and the precise moment of maximum impact. Very fine historians have described the Japanese plan as "realistic and feasible," but the truth was the entire gambit relied upon a complex and precise interplay of scattered forces, exquisite timing, and near-total surprise, conditions not usually proximate to one another amid the cacophony of combat. Sho-Go was a long shot from the get-go.[15]

For the Americans, the leapfrog into the middle Philippines hurried their own preparations. A mere five weeks separated the Joint Chiefs' decision to bypass Mindanao and assault Leyte from the invasion itself. It would take two weeks merely to distribute the plans to participating ships then scattered from West Coast ports to the Indian Ocean, leaving but three to work out an amphibious plan among Southwest and Central Pacific commands every bit the equal of the Normandy landings some months earlier for which Allied navies had had nearly a year in London to prepare. Complicating matters, Nimitz remained agnostic toward intertheater coordination, relying upon a yellowed 1935 regulation, "Joint Action of the Army and Navy," to guide his staff's interaction with MacArthur, and the Army general, busy with land preparations for Leyte proper, had little time to devote to intertheater naval interaction. All this meant that Halsey would reprise his South Pacific role as the de facto conduit through which MacArthur and Nimitz effected their respective plans.[16]

His partner would be Vice Admiral Thomas Kinkaid. Since leaving the South Pacific, Kinkaid had performed well in Aleutian waters and in November of 1943 had become MacArthur's Seventh Fleet commander, replacing Vice Admiral Arthur Carpender. Kinkaid had then won accolades for his deep devotion to and support of MacArthur's brilliant march along New Guinea's coastline through the summer of 1944, months that also saw the Seventh Fleet's long-delayed growth into a formidable organization of submarines, destroyers, cruisers, battleships, and, for short periods, allotments of Nimitz's fast fleet carriers. Though Halsey and Kinkaid were, as one distinguished historian put it, "antipodal" in temperament and disposition, they shared the objective to marshal the many assets of the Seventh and Third Fleets to propel MacArthur's ground forces toward Leyte.[17]

Because the massive invasion required the assault ships of both fleets, Kinkaid assumed temporary command of Wilkinson's Third Amphibious Force to augment his own Seventh Amphibious Force, under Rear Admiral Daniel Barbey. Meeting at Hollandia in late September, Kinkaid, Barbey, and Wilkinson hammered out a scheme by which 420 transport, supply, and landing ships would carry 203,000 men of the Sixth Army and three million tons of supplies to the Philippines. A Seventh Fleet bombardment group of six battleships, five cruisers, and fifteen destroyers under the command of Rear Admiral Jesse Oldendorf, and eighteen small escort carriers led by Rear Admiral Thomas Sprague, would escort them to their landing points.

Gathering these forces constituted a monumental challenge. They staged directly from no fewer than nine different places scattered across the Southwest and Central Pacific, including Pearl Harbor, 5,120 miles from Leyte; Finschhafen on New Guinea's southwest coast, 2,075 miles distant; Manus, 1,565 miles away; and Hollandia itself, 1,240 miles away. The overall plan was more than an inch thick. Its distribution list spanned four pages. It took six pages to list assigned ships and units, seven more to outline various tasks and missions, twenty-five to describe the movement schedule for all units, and another twenty-five merely to list assigned radio frequencies and call signs. "The staff work" involved, recounted one authority, "was almost unbelievable." Kinkaid recalled that he, Barbey, and Wilkinson had to "work fast," but, he remembered, "it was the only time" in the Pacific War "that I saw plans properly made. We had the ideal physical set-up. Everyone was [at Hollandia]. We were able to get together and work out an excellent plan while looking over each other's shoulder. Each man had his chance to get in his oar."[18]

Such was not the case with Halsey's combatant vessels. With Mitscher's carriers and Lee's battle line, he was to cover the operation, but neither Kinkaid nor Halsey worked for the other and their respective superiors, MacArthur and Nimitz, coordinated poorly. When Halsey assumed command of the Third Fleet, he had only a vague sense that his carriers were to backstop Kinkaid's mission at Leyte. He had met Kinkaid aboard the *New Jersey* nearly as soon as he arrived in the western Pacific, and on September 17 representatives for Nimitz, MacArthur, and Halsey met once at Hollandia. Ten days later, Halsey met Kinkaid and MacArthur in the same locale, and from these hurried deliberations emerged the basic contours of Halsey's mission.

Nimitz authorized Halsey to support the Leyte assault by "destroying enemy naval and air forces threatening the Philippines area," with one important caveat: if "major portions of the enemy fleet" emerged, their annihilation would become "the primary task," a clear indication of Nimitz's lingering disappointment over Spruance's caution in the Marianas. With Kinkaid's and MacArthur's concurrence, Halsey translated this directive into Third Fleet plans to strike as far north as Okinawa in the week before the invasion, then work southward to Formosa, where more lucrative targets existed, before finally taking station far off the Philippine coast to pounce should major Japanese naval units challenge Kinkaid's powerful force.[19]

The freedom to lie in wait was music to Halsey's ears. His staff had already outlined plans "to seek out the enemy and attempt to bring about a decisive engagement," regardless of budding responsibilities to MacArthur and Kinkaid. Now, "inasmuch as the destruction of the enemy fleet is the principal task," Halsey reported to Nimitz, "my goal is the same as yours—to completely annihilate the Jap fleet if the opportunity offers," writing that he meant to "move smartly" if required and "to deny the enemy a chance to outrange me in the air" or employ "an air shuttle" between their carriers and their many land bases in the region against the Third Fleet. To Kinkaid, Halsey expressed hope that the Seventh Fleet might early blow open a "back door" into the South China Sea via Surigao Strait, through which the Third Fleet could utterly wreck enemy supply lines between Southeast Asia and Japan. Nimitz, gaining a sense of that scheme, prohibited Halsey's transit of the strait without his express permission, but otherwise offered tacit support of Halsey's aggressive drive, telling the Third Fleet commander he was "always free to make local decisions in connection to the handling of forces placed under your command."[20]

As MacArthur, Kinkaid, and Halsey bid good-bye at Hollandia, Third Fleet designs to hit enemy airfields as far north as Okinawa were clear enough to withstand the exigencies of war. But intentions to then park Halsey's powerful flattops and battleships in the Philippine Sea to await developments were murky enough to court confusion and, in extremis, calamity should MacArthur, hell-bent on returning to the Philippines, Kinkaid, duty-bound to stay close aside, and Halsey, itching for a crack at the Japanese fleet, interpret the many cues of combat differently. Compounding matters, MacArthur had forbidden Kinkaid to communicate directly with Nimitz, which in effect officially denied Kinkaid and Halsey direct radio contacts. Nimitz, moreover, never gained a strong grasp of developments and plans from his faraway perch at Pearl Harbor, and, in the weeks before the invasion, he and Halsey would cross wires over Clark's relief to make room for McCain, misunderstand each other as to the control of submarines and land-based Navy planes in the region, and work at cross purposes toward a basing plan for the Third Fleet in the far Pacific. Halsey attributed these miscues to "freakish" radio reception in the area and a communications net overwhelmed by the sheer volume of messages, prompting him to complain that "these long range conversations" between Nimitz and himself were "pretty unsatisfactory." The upshot of all this, for Marc Mitscher and likely many others, was that right up until the invasion, each senior commander remained somewhat "in doubt as to what support he can ask for when he can ask for it and under what conditions it would be given" in the ensuing clash.[21]

. . . .

For the rank and file in Halsey's fleet, no sharp line divided Third Fleet operations supporting the Palau and Leyte invasions. Ebbing operations in the former locale and looming plans for the latter place both meant relentless air strikes along the far Pacific Rim from Okinawa to the Philippines. The Japanese had, on paper anyway, many planes throughout the region: some 1,425 aircraft operating from nineteen airfields on Luzon and twenty-six on Formosa, with as many as 400 planes scattered through the middle Philippines despite Halsey's recent plunder there. Halsey concentrated first on targets in the central and northern Philippines, placing his four carrier groups on a rotating replenishment schedule, provisioning and refueling one while three struck. On September 21 and 22 his fliers hit Clark and Nichols airfields near Manila, the first air raids on the Philippine capital since the war's early months, and on September 24 they attacked ships at Coron Bay, a popular enemy anchorage just north of Palawan thus far largely immune to American reprisals. Nimitz judged the strikes "brilliantly conceived and splendidly executed," and according to the best historian of the carrier war, the operations capped a month of "magnificent" pillage through the archipelago, costing the Japanese some 893 planes and sixty-seven ships totaling 224,000 tons. Halsey could "scarcely believe" such success, and on September 28 he directed with satisfaction the bulk of his carrier forces as well as Lee's battle line to well-deserved rest at Manus, Saipan, and Ulithi, their first collective relief since Halsey had assumed command of the operating fleet in August.[22]

He hoped to offer them a week's respite. A typhoon chased those at Ulithi to sea after a couple of days, however, prompting the rest to sortie as well and, all together, head north on October 6. For the first time since assuming command in August, Halsey's entire force now maneuvered together. There were the four carrier groups of seventeen flattops and over 1,000 planes. There were the six battleships, fifteen cruisers, and fifty-seven destroyers in Lee's battle line, and the massive fleet train along the periphery. In all, ninety-five major combatants and hundreds of auxiliaries marched to Halsey's beat, making it perhaps the greatest fighting fleet in history, and he the most powerful admiral the sea had ever seen.[23]

By then Halsey's Third Fleet staff had congealed into a group similar to his South Pacific cohort in function but quite different in their interaction. Having added another few months to their fellowship, and now living amid the confines of a ship's wardroom, pronounced cliques had developed. Among Halsey's old-timers, this process had seeds in Nouméa, where Thurber had drifted from the inner circle to the point that Carney, who had first judged Thurber "a chap with a great deal of imagination and of enormous brilliance," now "never quite understood either how he got into the picture or how he stayed in it," adding after the war that Thurber "was a sorry specimen" and "certainly a misfit among the two-fisted and can-do people that Admiral Bill had collected."[24]

Newcomers fitted unevenly into these morphing patterns. Weeks had joined the staff at Halsey's personal request, but others viewed

Weeks as an agreeable social climber prone to talk and sloth in equal measure. Cheek, who had won the Navy Cross for intelligence work in the Philippines before taking one of the last planes out of Manila in 1942, was shy and careful, hardly ingredients to mix easily with the jocular informality of Halsey's staff—One fellow officer viewed Cheek as among the "most phlegmatic men I have ever known," which was too harsh, but Cheek's gentle voice had fostered a habit as intelligence officer on the *New Jersey* "to submit little notes" to Carney during meetings, "who might or might not pass them to Halsey." In a group that relied upon informal interchange, these fault lines were dangerous. As his merry band grew old in amity, Halsey's skills as a commander remained clear and his brand of leadership strong, but a chink had emerged: Halsey was a poor manager of men. His comfort with camaraderie had, after years of war, made those around him a little less of a military staff and a little more of a fraternal club. Along the way, Halsey had paid too little attention to the proper ordering of the human capital closest to him and upon which he relied to transform his nearly unparalleled instincts into sound judgment and smart decision.[25]

Halsey's inner circle, principally but not solely Carney, Wilson, Dow, Moulton, and Stassen, fashioned themselves as the "dirty tricks department," and it was, Carney boasted, a "poor day when we could not think up something" to "bitch up the enemy's plans." A diversionary shore bombardment on Marcus Island on October 9 failed to mask Halsey's intention to hit Okinawa with carrier aircraft the next day, but did no real harm. From dawn to dusk on October 10, and from a position nearer Tokyo than the closest American base at Saipan, the Third Fleet launched 1,396 sorties against Okinawa, destroying four cargo ships, a couple dozen smaller vessels, and nearly one hundred aircraft at a cost of twenty-one planes and just three crewmen. With the exception of the Doolittle Raid, no American planes had yet ventured this near to Japan proper, and in Tokyo, the commander of the Combined Fleet, Admiral Soemu Toyoda, recognized "the start of something important." He placed Imperial naval forces on alert for Sho-Go 1 and Sho-Go 2—American invasions of either Leyte or Formosa—and ordered Admiral Shigeru Fukudome's 230 fighter planes on Formosa as well as scarce elite aviation units in the home islands to muster all-out counter attacks.[26]

The next day Halsey's dirty tricksters tried again to shield plans from this gathering challenge, mounting a raid over northern Luzon airfields to conceal their real objective, the many well-stocked Formosan airstrips reserved for multiday strikes commencing on October 12. Again the sham accomplished little except to offer the Japanese on Formosa a day's grace, something Halsey acknowledged after the war but of which he remained ignorant during the fight. Beginning before dawn on October 12, from point-blank positions one hundred miles east of Formosa, Third Fleet flattops launched the first of three strikes, totaling 1,378 sorties, at Japanese airfields and shipping. Although he knew they were coming, Fukudome was overwhelmed, his fighters "nothing but so many eggs thrown at the stone wall" of attacking planes. One-third of his pilots were consumed in the first American wave, only sixty rose to oppose the second wave, and none defended the Empire as the third wave arrived. It was more of the same the following day, when the Americans launched another 974 sorties against a paltry thirty-two defending planes, and so fantastical were the claims of American pilots that Halsey, aboard the *New Jersey,* nearly forgot it was Friday the Thirteenth.[27]

This aerial hurricane forced Japanese plans. Now knowing that the bulk of the American carrier fleet was parked within easy range of dozens of airfields, Toyoda redoubled defenses in the region, rushing to the area another 200 planes from other islands, 250 from northern Japan, and, in a directive with profound consequences, some 175 carrier planes from the mobile fleet. Japanese fliers damaged the cruiser *Canberra* late on October 13, leaving her dead in the water some 1,300 miles from the nearest Allied base and a mere 90 from Japanese arms. On the following day, Fukudome marshaled 400 more planes toward the juicy American armada, hitting the *Houston,* leaving not one but two cruisers stricken deep inside enemy waters. In Japan, this success sparked euphoria over what Radio Tokyo claimed was the destruction of eleven carriers, two battleships, three cruisers, and one destroyer, with at least another eight carriers, two battleships, four cruisers, and a destroyer aflame—altogether a tally worthy of the mythical divine wind said to have thrice saved Japan from ignominy in past centuries. The emperor celebrated with an Imperial rescript, and in later years Halsey even liked to tell of the Tokyo zookeeper who proclaimed that a special cage awaited the Third Fleet commander upon his imminent capture. The Japanese, Halsey concluded, "were peerless liars," and only abject desperation could have prompted such delusion.[28]

Still, Halsey was in a pickle. Two cruisers now sat "squarely in the Jap dragon's jaws," he recalled, "and the dragon knew it." Some wag on the *New Jersey* dubbed the damaged vessels and a handful of destroyers standing watch the CripDiv, naval shorthand for "crippled division." Halsey's first inclination was to cut his losses and scuttle the two cruisers, but his dirty tricks department convinced him to use the wounded ships as a trap for the Japanese fleet, transforming them into the BaitDiv with a screen of five cruisers, a dozen destroyers, and a pair of light carriers as additional inducements. He sent two powerful carrier groups seaward, ready to attack whatever enemy force appeared, and informed MacArthur he would temporarily suspend air operations supporting the coming Leyte assault, judging the chance to destroy an enemy fleet more important. Playing off Radio Tokyo, Halsey notified Nimitz that the Third Fleet's "sunken and damaged ships have been salvaged and are retiring at high speed toward the enemy."[29]

The scheme might have worked. On October 15 a powerful cruiser and destroyer group under Vice Admiral Kiyohide Shima sortied from the Inland Sea in accordance with Sho-Go 1, and now looked to pick off what the Japanese assumed were distressed flattops. Enemy patrol planes exposed the American ruse, however, and Shima wisely turned from what would surely have been his demise. The *Canberra* and *Houston* reached Ulithi and safety on October 27, their safe arrival marking, somewhat ironically, Third Fleet failure to manufacture a decisive clash in waters favoring the Americans.

Halsey's carriers returned to their supporting tasks. Commencing October 15, they pummeled Luzon airfields, gradually working southward toward Leyte in the ensuing days as the invasion neared on October 20. By then, and beginning with strikes at Okinawa on October 10, the Third Fleet had tallied an incredible score. The Japanese had committed some 1,400 aircraft against Halsey's ships, flying hundreds of sorties for days, an aerial force greater than any the American Navy had ever encountered, even in the dark weeks in the Solomons in 1942. They managed but a dent upon the Third Fleet at colossal cost: nearly 600 Imperial planes and as many pilots gone, about equal to their losses against Spruance in June. At the time enough of this was known that even Roosevelt sent personal congratulations, telling Halsey the nation had watched with "pride" his "fleet's magnificent sweep into enemy waters."[30]

Perhaps more importantly, Halsey's aggressive strikes had forced Toyoda to commit precious aircraft prematurely, creating "something closely akin to the destruction of the entire land-based air part" of Japanese plans and denuding Ozawa's flattops of all but 116 aircraft, far less than half their normal complement. Imperial plans to repulse the Leyte invasion and turn the tide of war required an immaculate interplay of air and naval formations, and now one arm of that plan was essentially gone. After the war, one Japanese carrier admiral remembered that the few days prior to the Battle of Leyte Gulf divided the naval air war into two, between a time when Japan could mount significant air opposition and a time when it could not, a judgment that echoes across the decades: the week and a half preceding the Leyte invasion had, in the words of one prominent historian, "brought the Americans success on a scale" unimaginable. Before MacArthur's force reached Leyte, Halsey's "knock-down, drag-out fight," as he put it in a report to Nimitz, had greatly and maybe fundamentally undermined Japanese schemes.[31]

Halsey had achieved a lopsided victory, but his costs were also considerable. The one hundred American planes lost in the fortnight before October 20 represented a tenth of his carrier strength. Daily sortie rates reflected this dissipation, as the nearly 1,500 flights on the first day over Formosa slackened to fewer than 500 by the fourth. This pace frayed more than a few nerves—one flattop skipper cracked under the pressure—and prompted three of four of Halsey's carrier group commanders to register alarm: Bogan reported that the fighter squadron aboard the *Bunker Hill* was "a sad picture" of "practically 100% combat fatigue," McCain relayed that the air group on the *Wasp* was in much the same shape, and Sherman added that *Lexington* pilots were near the end of their tethers. Collectively, the fast carriers were approaching nearly ten months at sea, even if Halsey's staff was new in the saddle. "Probably 10,000 men have never put a foot on shore" during those months, Mitscher reported, and "no other force in the world has been subjected to such a period of constant operation without rest or rehabilitation." This, in Mitscher's view, had left a force with sluggish reactions that was "not completely effective against attack."[32]

Six weeks of nearly continuous operations had worked on Halsey, too, spawning a case of the flu on October 18. On the heels of Bogan's report, Halsey sent the *Bunker Hill* to Ulithi for rest and permitted McCain's group to withdraw momentarily for refueling, but he refused relief for others, including himself, and reminded skippers of obligations to "instill and maintain a resolute spirit in overworked pilots when stakes are high," a sentiment that struck some ears as mere shibboleth. Pacing flag plot aboard the *New Jersey,* Halsey was not blind to the limits of pilot endurance. "Damn it," he muttered to no one in particular, "I know they're tired and need a rest." But there, in the sea east of Leyte Gulf, a lifetime of sensitivity to bluejacket welfare crashed upon the shoals of other commitments: "We would have liked to rest awhile," Halsey recalled years later, "but there was no time. There was a battle over the horizon, and we went to meet it."[33]

Chapter Sixteen

Bull's Run

FROM NEARLY A DOZEN different locales throughout the western Pacific, the 700 ships of the Leyte amphibious force marshaled. Commencing formation in early October 1944 and reaching full strength by midmonth, this armada steamed toward the Philippines under the careful gaze of Kinkaid's warships. Just after midnight on October 20 the invasion convoys slipped into Leyte Gulf and headed toward the assault beaches along the northeast coast of the island, Barbey's Northern Attack Force aiming at Tacloban, Wilkinson's Southern Attack Force heading some fifteen miles down the shore to the small town of Dulag. As the dawn sun rose behind heavy clouds to the east, MacArthur, from *Nashville*'s bridge, discerned Tacloban's squat outline to the west, where as a second lieutenant he had first alighted some four decades earlier, fresh from West Point. Shortly before 7:00 AM Kinkaid's battleships and cruisers opened fire, though Leyte's soft shore and absorbent jungle harbored nothing like the tough defensive crust of small coral islands. By midmorning elements of four divisions were well ashore. At 1:00 PM MacArthur, glorious in pressed khakis, trademark sunglasses, and with corncob pipe, waded ashore with Philippine president Sergio Osmeña, starring figures in one of the war's most famous photographs. More conscious of reporters than snipers, MacArthur strode to a radio transmitter and microphone. "People of the Philippines," he exclaimed, "I have returned. By the grace of God our forces have returned to stand again on Philippine soil."[1]

From there they would fight, kill, and die, on Leyte for the better part of two months and on other Philippine islands until the end of the war. But history's gaze did not tarry long upon them, focused almost from the beginning on the Japanese fleet, already slipping protective sheaths in ports, harbors, and anchorages in response to the invasion. Neither Halsey nor Kinkaid really expected a vigorous enemy response to the landings—with the exception of the Marianas in June, the Japanese Navy had not sortied in major strength since the crisis at Guadalcanal two years earlier; the Japanese could reach Leyte Gulf only through the narrow and treacherous Surigao and San Bernardino Straits; and Halsey's pilots had shattered local enemy air strength in recent weeks. Two days after the initial assault, Halsey told Nimitz that although the "prudent view" held that the Japanese carriers could still upend calculations, he was "now only waiting" for MacArthur to "achieve sufficient consolidation" ashore before withdrawing the Third Fleet "to rearm and get ready for future operations" aimed squarely at Japan proper. No American sensibility, however, could then fathom the despair of Japanese officials as they chased illusions of redemption or, in the words of one senior naval officer in Tokyo, at least "a fitting place to die" with "the chance to bloom as flowers."[2]

So the Japanese Navy came. Toyoda ordered four task forces to the fight. From the home islands came Vice Admiral Jisaburo Ozawa's group of six carriers, counting the two battleship hybrids *Hyuga* and *Ise,* and a dozen escorts. From Okinawa and Borneo came a potent collection of four cruisers and eleven destroyers in two groups under the commands of Rear Admiral Kiyohide Shima and Vice Admiral Shoji Nishimura. And from Lingga Roads, Vice Admiral Takeo Kurita sortied with a massive line of fifteen destroyers, a dozen cruisers, and seven battleships, including the monsters *Yamato* and *Musashi,* whose eighteen-inch guns, housed in turrets weighing more than an entire destroyer, made them the most powerful battlewagons ever produced. Nishimura and Shima were to force their way through the Mindanao Sea and Surigao Strait and then up the coast of Leyte, the southern half of a pincer aimed not at the American battle line but at the thin-skinned amphibians near shore, a new twist on the eternal Japanese quest for decisive engagement. Kurita's massive force constituted the other arm, pushing though the Sibuyan Sea and San

Bernardino Strait and down the east coast of Samar before crashing into Leyte Gulf from the north. Ozawa's carriers, meanwhile, had first meant to annihilate any covering American forces in the region, but their aircraft losses in recent weeks compelled them to accomplish their mission not by confrontation but through deception, acting as a lure to sweep supporting American forces from the area.

Thoughtful Japanese officers knew the plan was the province of desperation. The four Japanese fleets reported through different intermediate channels to Toyoda in Tokyo, courting confusion. There had been very little coordination with Japanese ground forces anywhere in the Philippine archipelago, inviting dispersion. The two offensive pincers would have to traverse the Surigao and San Bernardino narrows with little to no air cover, risking disaster. At Brunei on October 21, Kurita gathered his skeptical skippers. Few of them liked trading warships for transports as targets, and many believed the Sho-Go plan was too complex to work. From them Kurita could marshal little beyond resignation. "Would it not be shameful to have our fleet remain intact while our nation perishes?" he asked, pleading that the coming battle was a "glorious opportunity" to "remember there is such a thing as miracles."[3]

Divine favor did not long steam with the converging Japanese forces. In the predawn hours of October 23 two American submarines spied Kurita's force as it traversed the western coast of Palawan en route to the Sibuyan Sea. The *Darter* and *Dace* damaged one cruiser and sank two, including Kurita's flagship, plunging the Japanese admiral headlong into oil-slicked waters before rescue deposited him aboard the super battleship *Yamato,* where Ugaki was embarked. The *Darter* was lost in the clash, but it was one of the spectacular submarine attacks of the war, forcing Kurita to detach two tin cans to guard the damaged cruiser as he forged ahead with five battleships, nine cruisers, and thirteen destroyers, still more than enough to inflict serious damage should he reach Kinkaid's amphibians.

The most important result of this opening salvo in the Battle of Leyte Gulf was the information it provided Halsey and Kinkaid about Japanese dispositions. At about 2:00 AM the *Darter* had sent a flash message of Kurita's position and composition, a report reaching Kinkaid and Halsey near dawn, giving the two American commanders their first sense that the Japanese meant to counter the American landings with capital ships. Carney and the Third Fleet staff recalled the message as "one of the most significant contact reports of the Pacific war," its contents reinforcing vague indications of enemy ship movements from other sources, including a dispatch from Nimitz received the day before that suggested Japanese carriers had probably sortied from home waters.[4]

Halsey gathered his staff around his *New Jersey* wardroom table. He had previously believed that the Japanese were likely to reinforce their Tacloban forces with small Tokyo Express runs, but now wondered about a Japanese attack on Kinkaid's vulnerable amphibians, mimicking their great success at the Battle of Savo Island, or the likelihood of a general engagement with Third Fleet combatants on the high seas, much like Spruance's Fifth Fleet battle in the Marianas. Following a lively discussion, Halsey reoriented his four carrier task forces, keeping McCain's refueling appointment far to sea but drawing the remaining three groups closer to the Philippines to cover northern approaches to the archipelago and the two straits through which the Japanese could spring upon Leyte, placing Sherman's four flattops to the north, about a hundred miles from Luzon; Bogan's carriers, with the *New Jersey,* to an area east of San Bernardino Strait; and Davison's carriers, with the battleship *Washington* flying Lee's flag, due east of Leyte Gulf near the exit of Surigao Strait.

Early on October 24 Halsey's flattops launched an extensive hunt to lay bare Japanese plans. A vast search arc extending 300 miles to the west and covering all navigable channels in the region required so many planes that Sherman, near Luzon's many Japanese airfields, worried that too few aircraft remained in reserve to defend his flattops should the Japanese appear, a concern he shared with his own staff but not, at the time, with Halsey. Aboard the *New Jersey,* excitement mounted as the dawn sky brightened. At 8:10 AM came electrifying news: a search team from the *Intrepid* had spied Kurita's large force off the southern tip of Mindoro, bound inferentially for the

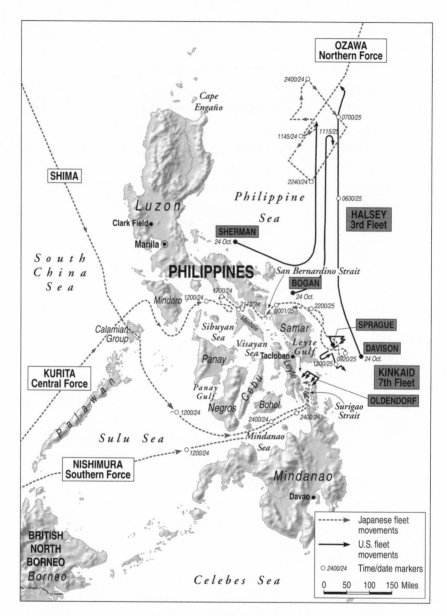

Battle of Leyte Gulf, October 1944.

Sibuyan Sea and San Bernardino Strait. Again benefiting from one of the war's best contact reports, Halsey sprung to action. At 8:22 he grabbed a radio headset and repeated the reconnaissance information to nearby ships. Five minutes later, and bypassing Mitscher as the intermediary commander, he ordered Sherman's flattops to the north and Davison's flattops to the south to tighten up on Bogan's flattops in the center. Five minutes after that, he took to the headset again. "With obvious excitement in his voice," one scholar imagined, Halsey ordered all three task groups to "strike, repeat, strike," words reminiscent of his "attack, repeat attack" formulation at the front end of the Battle of the Santa Cruz Islands. With them, the Battle of Leyte Gulf began in earnest.[5]

Halsey's aspirations were immediately complicated by other events. A dispatch from Nimitz indicated that the Japanese carriers were now likely nearing the region from the north, and a search plane from Davison's group to the south had located Nishimura's seven ships, including two battlewagons, steaming across the Sulu Sea in the direction of Surigao Strait. This information armed Halsey with a sense of three distinct and unequal Japanese groups converging on Leyte Gulf: Kurita's massive force, already in his crosshairs, and Nishimura's smaller fleet to the south of Kurita, the two evidently aiming to hit American landing forces from the north and the south in a coordinated pincer; and another force, as yet unseen but strongly surmised, of enemy flattops to the north, ready to pounce at any opportunity that a distracted Third Fleet might present. The Japanese had never attempted anything of similar scale and scope, anywhere, at any time. At midmorning Halsey reached three reasonable judgments, directing McCain's carriers to abort their refueling to rendezvous with Halsey the following morning, surmising that Kinkaid's combatants inside Leyte Gulf were sufficient to repulse Nishimura should the enemy force Surigao Strait, and maintaining like a laser beam his focus on Kurita's armada, unquestionably the most dangerous Japanese force then known to the Americans.[6]

If only events had cooperated. Instead of zooming off to strike Kurita, Sherman's remaining eighty or so aircraft became entangled with about 150 attacking Japanese warbirds from Luzon airfields and Ozawa's carriers, still not definitively detected by the Americans. Amid furious dogfights, some directed from the *Essex* by a young John Connally, later secretary of the Navy and governor of Texas, Commander David McCampbell shot down nine attackers and Ensign Roy Rushing added seven, earning both ace status and Mc-Campbell the Medal of Honor. Near 9:30 AM, a Japanese bomb breached the *Princeton*'s flight deck, passed through the hangar deck, and blew up the bakery. Flames licked back upward to the hangar deck, engulfing six aircraft, fuel bunkers, and stacks of torpedoes. At 10:10 Captain William Buracker, who had been Halsey's *Enterprise* operations officer early in the war, ordered his 1,600 men to abandon the *Princeton*, keeping a small contingent of firefighters and antiaircraft gunners aboard. Hours later, a massive internal explosion blew away the carrier's stern, spewing enough shrapnel to kill 241 sailors on the nearby cruiser *Birmingham* and maim another 430 on both vessels. The light carrier had composed with the *Saratoga* the duo that had accomplished Sherman's daring raid on Rabaul in November 1942, but now Sherman directed that the *Princeton* be scuttled, just the third major American combatant loss since the *Chicago* at the tail end of the fight for Guadalcanal. Although the day's attacks had cost the Japanese as many as one hundred planes, many from Ozawa's already denuded flattops, the frantic activity had delayed Sherman's participation in Halsey's strike at Kurita's advancing column.[7]

In Davison's group to the south, pilots were also delayed but for different reasons. Through most of the morning, his fliers attacked Nishimura's ships in the Sulu Sea, drawn there not by any grand design but rather by the allure of such a juicy find. Led by a plucky band of *Enterprise* fliers, a series of attacks inflicted minor damage to a battleship and destroyer and uncoverd the one remaining Japanese surface force still unknown to the Americans: Shima's column of cruisers and destroyers steaming down the archipelago's interior seas for Surigao Strait. What they had not yet done, however, was aim toward Kurita's main force as Halsey had intended.

On the *New Jersey,* steaming with Bogan's center group of flattops, officers at first "had a devil of a time" deciphering the goings-on in the other carrier groups from fragmentary reports. Bogan had launched ninety planes toward Kurita shortly after Halsey ordered, but it was close to noon before Sherman and Davison could do the same, bringing the total of American attackers to 259 aircraft in four disparate waves, a far cry from the nearly 1,000 planes resident aboard Halsey's carriers when operating in unison at full strength. The first wave reached Kurita in the Sibuyan Sea at about 10:30 AM, damaging the *Yamato* with a bomb, the *Musashi* with a torpedo, and the cruiser *Myoko* with a few of each. Following attacks arrived near 1:00, 2:00, and 4:00 PM, denting the battleship *Nagato* and swarming to the monstrous bulk of the mighty *Musashi.* By late afternoon about nineteen torpedoes and seventeen bombs had found their mark on the great ship, rupturing power lines, riddling the hull, and leaving her ablaze. Throughout the day Kurita and Ugaki had pleaded with Fukudome to rush planes to their aid, but the land-based air commander had earlier elected to devote the bulk of his depleted strength to sinking the *Princeton,* leaving nothing left.[8]

Kurita, who within twenty-four hours had lost four cruisers, including his own flagship, been fished from oil-stained seas, and endured submarine and air attack, now watched the *Musashi* wallow from her sister *Yamato*'s bridge. He believed that to press ahead without air defenses "would merely make ourselves meat for the enemy." In late afternoon he retreated, leaving the *Musashi* behind and complaining to Toyoda in Tokyo of absent Japanese airplanes. Toyoda counter-marched the column, however, and Kurita turned back toward San Bernardino Strait as dusk approached. So it was that at about 7:00 PM Kurita's remaining able-bodied hulls steamed past the stricken *Musashi,* whose skipper had already ordered her battle ensign and national standard lowered and was then preparing to drown with his vessel. As Kurita passed and disappeared into the darkening eastern horizon, the *Musashi* rolled to port, stood on end, and plunged headlong into the ocean depths, killing 1,023 of her crew.

Kurita was now down one of the world's largest warships, but he still retained four powerful battlewagons, including the *Yamato,* eight cruisers, and ten destroyers. Aboard the *Yamato,* Ugaki believed the *Musashi* "had sacrificed herself" for the surviving column and re- solved to honor the bequest with a similar sacrifice on the morrow. Next to him stood Kurita, haggard and, with his temporary retreat aborted, some seven hours behind schedule for his rendezvous with the southern Japanese pincer early the next morning inside Leyte Gulf.[9]

On the *New Jersey* Halsey had eavesdropped on the attacks all day. He and his staff cheered as chatter of hit after hit crackled over the airwaves, and shouted in unison, "We've stopped them," at news of Kurita's initial retreat. At a cost of eighteen aircraft, American pi- lots reported and Halsey passed onto Nimitz news of a great victory: one super battleship afire and down at the bow, another battlewagon badly damaged, two more battleships hit, one cruiser sunk, three dam- aged, and, most importantly, Kurita's about-face. All this was not quite correct: only one ship beyond the *Musashi* suffered serious damage and by nightfall Kurita was headed toward San Bernardino Strait again. But for the time being, Halsey's report constituted ground truth, not only for him but for Nimitz in Hawaii and Kinkaid and MacArthur inside Leyte Gulf as well.[10]

As nightfall closed the first full day of the Battle of Leyte Gulf, only Ozawa's carriers, the sole Japanese force actually wishing to be spied, remained unseen and untouched. Halsey figured they were nearby; Nimitz had twice indicated their potential presence, Sherman had reported that some of the planes attacking the *Princeton* earlier that day had sported the telltale tail hook of carrier aircraft, and a series of incongruent contact reports in the afternoon seemed to suggest an enemy force lurking to the north. By his own admission, by that point in the war the enemy flattops had become an "obsession" to Halsey, the war having conditioned him and many others to view them as the central threat to American designs. As a result, he began to focus on the elusive carriers. In midafternoon, to both maintain a rearguard near Leyte and allow pursuit of the enemy flattops once found, Halsey issued a battle plan tagging four battleships, five cruisers, and nineteen destroyers under Lee as a provisional Task Force Thirty-Four to plug the San Bernardino narrows should Kurita reappear, and readied his carriers for a sprint north. Sending copies of this plan to Nimitz in Honolulu and King in Washington but not to Kinkaid in Leyte Gulf, who intercepted and read it nonetheless, most recipients understood Halsey's scheme as imperative and not conditional, and concluded Lee's powerful force had been left to cover San Bernardino Strait. Halsey corrected this confusion among his own ships at about 5:00 PM via short-range voice radio. "If," it clarified, "the enemy sorties" through San Bernardino Strait, "TF 34 will be formed when directed by me." As the sun dropped, then, Halsey's Third Fleet had a clear sense of the admiral's intentions. But no other Americans did, most believing Lee had trained his big guns at the exit of San Bernardino Strait.[11]

In early evening two search reports fixed at last Ozawa's force, identifying, alternatively, four carriers, two light cruisers, and five destroyers, or three carriers, four to six cruisers, and six destroyers, about 190 miles north of Sherman's flattops. It was too late to launch an air strike that day, so Halsey gathered his dirty tricksters at the long wardroom table and planned for the next morning. He knew through message traffic that Kinkaid would meet the southern pincer, then nearing Surigao Strait, with Oldendorf's battleships. He believed Kurita had retreated from his plunge toward San Bernardino Strait. And he now knew Ozawa's position, close enough to bypass the Third Fleet entirely in a nighttime dash to Leyte Gulf or, Halsey's worst nightmare, just far enough away to shuttle-bomb the American carriers with impunity early the next day, landing on Luzon airfields while Halsey's aircraft remained just out of range to strike back.[12]

He had three options. One, divide his fleet, leaving Task Force Thirty-Four to block San Bernardino Strait while his carriers sped north. Two, keep the entire force near the San Bernardino narrows. Three, strike Ozawa's flattops with all Third Fleet ships, leaving the strait unguarded. The first option was anathema to Halsey and nearly all Navy men. Since the days of Nelson, the highest admiral and lowest bluejacket alike worshipped at the altar of concentration; Spruance had not divided the fleet in the Marianas, and, despite his daring, Halsey's life in uniform had also left deep, traditional, and entirely conventional imprints. The second course, keeping the fleet tied to San Bernardino Strait, was contrary to Halsey's aggressive temperament, unnecessary if Kurita had indeed retreated, and at odds with prevailing sensibilities, not only on the *New Jersey* but also at Pearl Harbor and in Washington, to seek, in Nimitz's own orders to Halsey, the destruction of the enemy fleet if the opportunity arose—which for Halsey could only mean the enemy carriers.[13]

Halsey characterized deliberations on the *New Jersey* that night as penetrating and pervasive, telling King afterward, "It was a hard decision to make." Carney remembered a full exploration of options. "Every issue," Stassen proclaimed years later, "was thoroughly discussed." But Halsey's preference for a headlong thrust north with every available vessel was nearly preordained. It fit his character. It adhered to universal naval orthodoxy regarding concentration. And it matched Nimitz's own exhortations—orders, even. A silent witness to these deliberations, Solberg was nearer the truth than Stassen, Carney, or Halsey himself. "Probably," he wrote, "no argument could have held Halsey back." Near 8:00 PM, Halsey walked into the *New Jersey's* flag plot, pointed to Ozawa's reported position on a nautical chart, and said to Carney, "Here's where we're going, Mick. Start them north." Then he went to bed, exhausted, eager to catch a few hours' rest before the following morning's early attack.[14]

The decision left others unsettled. Halsey's plans officer, Riley, wondered, rather meekly, if Ozawa's force was a decoy to open up San Bernardino Strait for Kurita's force. Within an hour, search planes from the *Independence* reported that Kurita's force had indeed turned back toward San Bernardino Strait, leading to a "furious" argument between Cheek and Moulton. Kurita was "coming through" the narrows, Cheek exclaimed. "I know! I've played poker with them in Tokyo." But Moulton, the principal officer on duty in flag plot, rebuffed Cheek's exhortation. Orders to head north had already been issued, he intoned, and Halsey had retired to his cabin.[15]

Halsey *(left)* and Harold Stassen at sea, November 1944.
Courtesy of the U.S. National Archives.

Halsey *(left)* with Raymond Spruance at sea, May 1945.
Department of the Navy. Courtesy of the U.S. National Archives.

Halsey *(left)* with Marc Mitscher at sea, September 1944.
Courtesy of the U.S. National Archives.

Halsey *(right)* with John McCain Sr. at sea, December 1944.
Department of the Navy. Courtesy of the U.S. National Archives.
Photo 80-G-470859.

USS *St. Lo* shortly before sinking, Battle of Leyte Gulf, October 25, 1944.
Department of the Navy. Courtesy of the U.S. National Archives.
Photo 80-G-270511.

USS *Princeton* shortly before sinking, Battle of Leyte Gulf, October 25, 1944. Courtesy of the U.S. National Archives.

Japanese carrier *Zuiho* under attack by Third Fleet carrier planes,
Battle of Leyte Gulf, October 25, 1944.
Courtesy of the U.S. National Archives.

Halsey *(second from left)* playing deck tennis, USS *New Jersey,*
December 1944. Admiral Carney Collection. Courtesy of the
U.S. National Archives. Photo 80-G-470898.

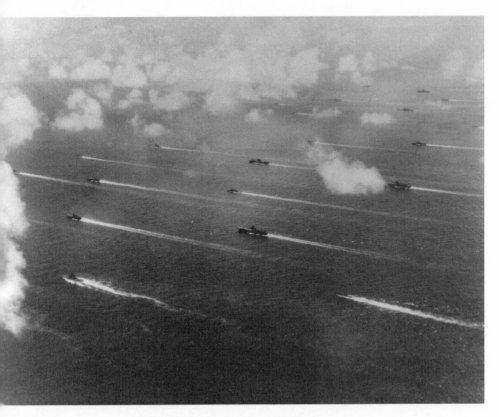

Third Fleet at sea, August 1945.
Department of the Navy. Courtesy of the
U.S. National Archives. Photo-80-G-427931.

Halsey and Fan Halsey with Franklin Roosevelt, March 1945.
Courtesy of the U.S. National Archives.

Halsey with Fan Halsey, hunting, Georgia, March 1945.
Courtesy of the U.S. National Archives.

Halsey at war's end, July 1945.
Courtesy of the U.S. National Archives.

Halsey *(middle)* with Robert Montgomery *(left)* and James Cagney *(right)*, on set of *The Gallant Hours*, May 1959. AP wirephoto.

Two hours later, Lieutenant Douglas Cox, a junior intelligence officer well outside Halsey's inner circle, marshaled the courage to challenge the decision again. Three weeks earlier, while at Ulithi, a captured Japanese document had reached the *New Jersey*. Titled "Z Operation Orders," it was, in Solberg's words, "the master matrix for Japanese defense plans," including the A-Plan employed in the Marianas and the Sho-Go plan now in effect in the Philippines. Each enemy scheme posited a major surface action to destroy not combatants but the soft auxiliaries of an amphibious fleet, a major departure from Mahanian decisive battle, and placed Japanese carriers beyond the range of enemy surface forces as a way to engage and distract mobile American forces supporting Allied landings. To Cox, the Z outline suggested that the Japanese were using Ozawa's flattops to lure Halsey from intercepting Kurita's forces, a notion that had also surfaced in various Seventh Fleet intelligence appreciations. He prevailed upon Cheek to bypass Moulton and raise concerns directly with Carney, whom he woke at about 10:00 PM. But Cheek had accumulated little of the personal capital necessary among his peers to effectuate a reversal, and in any event had failed to impress upon Carney or any other senior staffer the import of Cox's guess—after the war Carney, Moulton, Dow, Slonim, and Wilson all failed to recall having seen, heard, or talked of the elusive report. After listening, Carney declined to wake Halsey, declaring the admiral asleep and "not to be disturbed."[16]

Elsewhere in the Third Fleet at least three admirals were also flummoxed. Lee, aboard the *Washington*, had by early evening guessed that Ozawa's force was a snare with little offensive firepower and, after indications of Kurita's turnabout had reached him, sent two messages to the *New Jersey* conveying his views. He received a perfunctory "Roger" to the first and silence to the second. From the carrier *Intrepid*, Bogan raised the same point about Kurita. "Yes, yes, we have that information," Third Fleet staff officers replied, in a manner so brusque that Bogan resolved to say no more, though he believed Halsey was making "one hell of a mistake." A similar story prevailed on the *Lexington*, where Mitscher, bypassed as Halsey's carrier commander for days, had become little more than a passenger. When Third Fleet orders sending the entire fleet north reached the flattop about the same time as did reports of Kurita's resumed march toward San Bernardino Strait, Mitscher's chief of staff, Arleigh Burke, and his operations officer, James Flatley, woke the admiral and beseeched him to urge Halsey to form Lee's battle line. Mitscher, who had been at sea and at war for ten months, was by then "small," "frail," "extremely tired," and in no mood to try to muscle through Halsey's staff. If Halsey "wants my advice," he sulked before returning to bed, "he'll ask for it." So it was that aboard the *Independence* that the last of the night searchers returned at about midnight, certain their discovery of Kurita steaming through San Bernardino Strait had altered the tide of the emergent battle, and found to their astonishment the entire Third Fleet rushing north to confront Ozawa, leaving, as Morison put it, "nothing but empty air and ocean" between Kurita and the thin-skinned amphibians of MacArthur's invasion force.[17]

. . . .

To the south and inside Leyte Gulf, Kinkaid had spent October 24 laying plans to intercept the Japanese southern pincer then clearly steaming for Surigao Strait and meaning to force the narrows early the next day. Kinkaid bunched his amphibious ships behind a screen of destroyer escorts and sent Rear Admiral Jesse Oldendorf's battle line to the strait's upper narrows to plug its exit. For the task, Oldendorf had thirty-nine PT boats, twenty-eight destroyers, eight cruisers, and six battleships—five of them damaged or sunk and salvaged from the Pearl Harbor mud—a force far outpacing the combined strength of Nishimura's and Shima's columns, which together counted two battleships, four cruisers, and eight destroyers. "We were not at all concerned about the outcome of an encounter," Kinkaid's chief of staff remembered, and Oldendorf's only substantial worry was a shortage of ordnance: his vessels had shelled Japanese shore defenses since October 20, reducing some ships to 20 percent of their ammunition stores.[18]

Near 2:00 AM on October 25, Oldendorf thrust his destroyers along both edges of the Surigao channel just as Nishimura reached the most constricted portion of the strait, no wider than twelve miles. In near-perfect torpedo attacks followed by near-perfect battleship salvos, Oldendorf's combatants dominated one of the war's great surface clashes. By dawn's early light, five of Nishimura's seven ships were sunk, including both battlewagons, and the remaining two were seriously damaged, at a cost of damage to one American destroyer. This rout forced Shima, who had followed Nishimura's plunge through the strait, into hasty retreat, two of his three cruisers wounded, his four destroyers escaping unhurt. This Battle of Surigao Strait was as complete an American victory as any in the Pacific War. It was won by Oldendorf's canny disposition of his force, destroyer attacks of the kind Sims had championed, and an overwhelming American materiel advantage. According to Morison, the most intelligent Japanese act of the entire battle was Shima's retreat. For Kinkaid and Halsey, their loose and unspoken coordination had fared well. Halsey knew from the outset that Kinkaid's surface force under Oldendorf could intercept the southern pincer, and Kinkaid rose to the challenge.

Such happenstance would not again prevail in the broader Battle of Leyte Gulf. As Halsey had steamed north through the night to find Ozawa's carriers and as the Battle of Surigao Strait had commenced, Kurita's force passed one by one through San Bernardino Strait, every man on the eleven destroyers, eight cruisers, and four battleships dumbfounded to find the nighttime horizon free of American gun barrels. Turning south, they made their way toward Leyte. At about 5:30 AM Kurita learned of Nishimura's woes in Surigao Strait but pushed ahead, now more or less alone. An overcast dawn broke at 6:30, moments before lookouts found first the distinctive slim masts of American ships and then the boxy shapes of aircraft carriers. Thinking these were Halsey's fleet carriers, the chance to duel with proper warships and not weak transports heartened Kurita's martial spirit. At 6:44 he radioed Tokyo, "By heaven-sent opportunity, we are dashing to attack the enemy carriers."[19]

The vessels were actually a portion of Thomas Sprague's sixteen diminutive escort carriers and their modest destroyer screen, part of Kinkaid's cover force just outside the entrance to Leyte Gulf proper.

Sprague had divided his ships thrice, into Taffy 1, 2, and 3, and the northern group, Taffy 3, under the command of Rear Admiral Clifton Sprague (no relation), now sat in the crosshairs of the most powerful Japanese surface force to encounter American ships throughout the entire war. Escort carriers—dubbed baby flattops—had been slapped together atop merchant hulls and spit from American shipyards by the dozen; they possessed no armor, had a single five-inch gun, and, capable of a bare eighteen knots, lacked even the speed that is the last defense of the weak. Among old-time sailors, they were regarded "as interlopers— something like reservists, to be tolerated during the war but not taken too seriously," and at first blush seemed unable to offer any obstacle to Kurita. Compounding matters, Clifton Sprague's six escort carriers each carried a couple dozen aircraft prepared more for the support of troops ashore than for battle against the hardened steel of warships. Sprague and his officers had passed the early morning listening to Oldendorf wipe out Nishimura's ships, and as the distinctive pagoda shape of the Japanese warships came into view, some Americans believed them Nishimura's disheveled remnants.[20]

Just after 7:00 AM the first of Kurita's massive shells rained down. "That son-of-a-bitch Halsey," someone later remembered Sprague hissing, "has left us bare-assed." He ordered all ships to make smoke, his pilots to launch an all-out attack, his destroyers into the breach, and his carriers to hightail south and east toward Oldendorf's friendly if tired guns. He also begged immediately for help, in plain language and upon open radio channels, from any and all corners. He had no reasonable expectation beyond destruction and death for himself, but hoped for time enough for Oldendorf or Halsey to foul the Japanese plunge into Leyte Gulf.[21]

It was a weird battle without much precedent and plenty of fury. The only other time an aircraft carrier of any size had confronted surface guns occurred four years earlier, when two German battleships sank the British flattop *Glorious*. Kurita focused upon the flattops, unleashing his massive guns in a general as opposed to an ordered attack, contributing to an emerging melee. At 7:30 AM a squall line offered a crucial moment's respite to the Americans, allowing a small band of seven destroyers to close on the massive Japanese ships. In a two-hour free-for-all, the Japanese sank an escort carrier, two destroyers, and a destroyer escort, leaving many of the remaining hulls of Taffy 3 damaged but afloat. A kamikaze attack later doomed another escort carrier, but even with that kill the tally was less than Kurita had a right to expect given his overwhelming advantage. The Americans, on the other hand, had sent three Japanese cruisers to the sea floor and managed to damage another three and even land a punch on the mighty *Yamato*, a success far greater than Sprague could have reasonably presumed. Kurita's general attack had condemned the Japanese to a disorganized assault, and some of the war's most gallant American attacks helped account for this near miracle, including fearless destroyer attacks and aerial strikes with small cluster bombs, depth charges, flares, and, in two instances, a pilot's sidearm and a soda bottle.

Shortly after 9:00 AM Kurita, still convinced he was dueling with Halsey's fleet carriers, retreated to reform and, he insisted after the war, to plunge once again into the maelstrom. Then he hesitated. When an hour later a murky and erroneous contact report placed additional American carriers a mere sixty miles to his north, Kurita became wary of an enemy trap. His flagship *Yamato* was not seriously wounded, but his fleet, which had counted thirty-two powerful warships three days earlier, was now at half its strength, down a super battleship, eight cruisers, and seven destroyers. His remaining vessels had shrinking ammunition stores and dwindling fuel bunkers. He had slept little if at all for three days, and was in a state of near mental and physical shock. Right before noon he directed his fleet south again, but only for a moment. Shortly thereafter, Kurita turned away for good, making for San Bernardino Strait. The retreat shamed Ugaki, standing beside Kurita on *Yamato*'s bridge, stunned many other Imperial officers, and eventually cost Kurita his sea command—though the senior Japanese admiral may have simply shied from a headlong sacrifice of another 30,000 or so Japanese sailors to the Bushido code, however much damage he might have inflicted in the process.[22]

Throughout this Battle off Samar, as history has dubbed it, Sprague had beseeched Kinkaid and Halsey for help. Kinkaid had temporized.

He directed Oldendorf's combatants, their gun barrels still hot from the early morning's conquest in Surigao Strait, to form a line at the eastern entrance into Leyte Gulf, but he did not order them into the Philippine Sea until after Kurita broke off his attack, choosing instead to implore Halsey to race to Sprague's rescue, believing the Third Fleet commander had the greater obligation to do so, and in the process breaking MacArthur's prohibition of direct communications between the two naval fleets.

To the north on the *New Jersey*, Sprague's pleas and Kinkaid's exhortations led to crisis. Shortly before dawn Halsey had ordered all carriers to launch strikes toward Ozawa's carriers. Sensing a killing opportunity, he also formed Task Force Thirty-Four, with its six battlewagons, not to guard to the south but to lunge at Ozawa, sparking excitement on the *New Jersey* at the prospect of a fabled surface clash between capital ships with odds greatly favoring the Americans. At that moment, the first of many messages from Kinkaid arrived. Sent near 2:00 AM, it had become tangled in the massive communications network before finding Halsey ten minutes before 7:00. It outlined Oldendorf's looming action in Surigao Strait and queried whether Task Force Thirty-Four was guarding San Bernardino Strait. "Negative," replied Halsey. "Task Force 34 is with carrier group now engaging enemy carrier forces." At 8:22 a second message from Kinkaid, sent at 7:07, immediately after Kurita's ambush of Taffy 3, relayed Sprague's predicament. This information at first "surprised" but "did not greatly alarm" Halsey because Oldendorf's powerful guns hovered near Sprague. A third message arrived eight minutes later, pleading for Halsey's fast battleships "at once" in Leyte Gulf. A fourth missive reached Halsey at 9:00 AM, reporting Sprague's force in extremis, under direct attack by four battleships and eight cruisers, and urgently requesting Lee's battlewagons and a massive air strike from Halsey's fleet carriers. All told, Kinkaid shot Halsey nine urgent missives that morning, one note constituting nothing short of a shriek: "Where is Lee?" Kinkaid begged. "Send Lee."[23]

These dispatches annoyed Halsey. "It was not my job to protect the Seventh Fleet," he later explained. "My job was offensive, to strike with the Third Fleet, and we were even then rushing to intercept a force which gravely threatened not only Kinkaid and myself but the whole Pacific strategy." He sent word to McCain, then approaching the area, to make for Sprague's position at best speed, though a glance at charts showed that McCain's carriers could not reach Leyte until the following morning. Beyond that, Halsey insisted there "was nothing else I could do," given the distance between the Third Fleet's other carrier groups and Sprague's position, a fact he believed was surely known to Kinkaid even as the latter man repeated his appeals through the morning.[24]

Still, Halsey was in a bind. With Kinkaid's messages came confirmation that Kurita had indeed passed freely through the San Bernardino gauntlet the night before, a possibility Halsey had implicitly dismissed the previous evening. Now caught between responsibilities to MacArthur's landings, however distant he may have viewed them, and the chance of a lifetime to annihilate what he saw as the one remaining Japanese fleet between the American Navy and Tokyo Bay, his face became ashen. Settling upon the leather bench he often occupied in flag plot, Halsey muttered, to no one in particular, "When I get my teeth into something, I hate to let go." Then, Solberg recalled, Halsey "lapsed into silence, his jaw set like a bulldog's."[25]

News to the north acted as a temporary reprieve. At 8:00 AM Halsey's pilots found Ozawa's flattops, with a total of maybe two dozen operative planes among them, off northern Luzon's Cape Engaño, which in Spanish means, rather appropriately, "trick, deceit, or fraud." Led by McCampbell and another twenty-six aces, an incredible tally reflective of the rout the air war had become by late 1944, 130 American pilots dove toward the enemy ships, their excited voices filling the airwaves with reports of bombs hit, explosions heard, and Japanese ships burning and sinking. By 9:30 the hybrid carrier *Ise* and the fleet carrier *Zuikaku* sat aflame, the cruiser *Oyodo* was stricken, and the destroyer *Akizuki* lay on the ocean floor. A second American wave of thirty aircraft reached Ozawa fifteen minutes later, yielding hits on the cruiser *Tama* and the carrier *Chiyoda*. As the morning lengthened and Halsey's battlewagons edged ever nearer Ozawa's depleted scraps, officers on the *New Jersey* flag bridge all but stood on their toes and expected "Japanese masts to appear over the horizon any minute." By almost any measure, Halsey and his cohorts stood at the precipice of an epic naval victory, one for the ages, worthy of Drake or Nelson or Dewey.[26]

Almost. Others had spent the past twenty-four hours in silent observance, eavesdropping on what few dispatches among the Leyte Gulf forces they could pick up. In Washington, where it was evening, King's staff grew worried that Halsey had chased a feint, consistent with the captured Z documents that had so alarmed Cheek and Cox. At Pearl Harbor, where it was midafternoon, Nimitz knew Halsey had gone north, consistent with orders to seek maximum damage to Japanese forces, but the vagaries of radio reception kept him ignorant of the location of Task Force Thirty-Four. Over many months it had become Nimitz's habit to leave operational fighting to seagoing commanders, and he often pitched horseshoes to occupy himself as battle raged far over the horizon. But news reaching him that day had put him "on pins and needles" as Kinkaid's repeated pleas to Halsey reached Pearl Harbor radio receivers, prompting him at last to radio Halsey: "Where is Task Force 34? The World Wonders."[27]

Nimitz intended the precedent clause as a gentle nudge, and the antecedent, added by an indiscreet communications clerk as standard gibberish to foil enemy decryption efforts, should never had reached Halsey as part of a decoded dispatch. But it did. Exhausted and keyed to the sharp edge of anticipation, Halsey reacted badly when in the late morning aboard the *New Jersey* he read it. "I was stunned as if I had been struck in the face," he recalled after the war. "The paper rattled in my hands. I snatched off my cap, threw it on the deck and repeated something I am ashamed to remember." Solberg, standing nearby, was not. "What right does Chester have," he recorded Halsey saying, "to send me a God-damned message like that?" Halsey stormed about flag plot. Carney grabbed him. "Stop it," he ordered. "What the hell's the matter with you? Pull yourself together!"[28]

The dispatch and Halsey's reaction have produced a historical cottage industry of commentary, most of it negative toward the Third

Fleet commander, some of it telling of a sobbing Halsey or hinting that a round of drinking had impaired his capacities or claiming that his "psychosomatic skin rash" had interfered with decision making. There was, of course, nothing psychological about his skin maladies, and the charge of drunkenness, if true, condemned not only Halsey but also his entire staff, the *New Jersey* skipper, and the whole of naval culture from which they collectively sprang. This asks too much from the moment. Halsey's outburst had less dramatic roots; it was entirely consistent with a life lived on the outside, of a personality sensitive to external prompts, and of a sentimentality that placed emotion before reflection.[29]

Carney retreated with Halsey to the latter's sea cabin, where the two men huddled for the better part of half an hour. When they emerged, Halsey saw no choice but to countermarch his battle line. Although he was just forty-two miles from and within an hour of the first of Ozawa's cripples—and as much as a day from Sprague—he at last divided his force, taking himself with Task Force Thirty-Four and Bogan's carrier group to the south, leaving Mitscher, with Sherman and Davison's carriers, to tackle Ozawa's remaining vessels. Racing south at first thirty and then thirty-five knots, he received continuing dispatches from Kinkaid that oscillated between relief, fear, and relief again as Kurita retreated, returned, and finally retreated, reducing Halsey to hope that he might arrive in time to block the Japanese escape back through San Bernardino Strait. As Task Force Thirty-Four sped south through the early evening, *New Jersey* officers were crestfallen. One of them, contemplating what might have been to the north, lamented, "It could have been the greatest victory since Trafalgar," a sentiment roundly shared.[30]

Halsey's ships reached the San Bernardino narrows a bit after midnight, two hours after the first of Kurita's eighteen ships had stormed past at high speed, leaving three American warships the sad solace of a single trailing Japanese destroyer as war bounty. Aboard the *New Jersey* and the other majestic battlewagons, not one gun came alive. Halsey's rash decision to turn back late that morning, made in a pique of anger and disappointment, had condemned his big ships "to a kind of limbo," according to perhaps the best of the Leyte Gulf historians, "steaming on a tranquil sea" just beyond the edges of two great battles. Pug Henry, the fictionalized Mick Carney and the protagonist in Herman Wouk's *War and Remembrance,* voiced in literature what all in the *New Jersey*'s flag plot surely felt: "It was a bitter sight; bitter to be becalmed in this great Battle Line in the midst of vast engagements, yet not having fired a shot."[31]

. . . .

There were scant consolations. Mitscher's later attacks on Ozawa's fleet mortally wounded the carrier *Zuiho* and finished off the *Zuikaku,* the last of the flattops that had attacked Pearl Harbor to go to its grave, but they missed the hybrid flattops *Ise* and *Hyuga.* Later, the rump of Third Fleet surface forces remaining in the north sank the cruiser *Chiyoda* and the destroyer *Hatsuzuki,* meaning Ozawa had lost four carriers, a cruiser, and two destroyers, but that was a far cry from what Halsey's big ships could have accomplished had they also confronted Kurita. In the weeks to come, Halsey claimed that the decision to turn back in Sprague's defense was the worst decision of his wartime service, a judgment from which he never wavered and, as self-assessments go, fair enough.

Others found greater fault. There were mistakes aplenty: Kinkaid had assumed too much of Halsey's tactical dispositions and had kept Oldendorf's battlewagons from assisting Sprague's carriers; Nimitz's invitation to Halsey to seek the enemy fleet was a dangerous solicitation in the hands of an aggressive commander, a mistake even Nimitz's son, a submarine officer, recognized, telling his father afterward that the battle's snafu had been "your fault." But most observers focused on Halsey's blunder. Officers in Kinkaid's fleet decried Halsey's "free gift of passage" to the Japanese through San Bernardino Strait. Bogan believed if the Third Fleet had plugged the Bernardino channel, the result "would have been a slaughter. It could have meant the end of Japanese naval power right there. Completely." Most officers agreed. They believed Halsey had been fooled by the enemy, had impetuously chased Ozawa, and had imperiled the American landings at Leyte Gulf. To many observers, only Kurita's retreat and "the definite partiality of Almighty God," to use Sprague's phrase, had saved the day.[32]

Halsey sensed this criticism immediately. In a dispatch to Nimitz shortly after the battle, he explained he had "long ago adopted a policy of attacking first" and, in a choice of words revealing a defensive posture, wrote that it "seemed childish to me to guard statically San Bernardino Strait" once he knew of Ozawa's carriers. He also laid bare the myriad late, errant, and misidentified dispatches received during the battle, most stemming from a radio net unable in range or capacity to cope with massive message volume. He deprecated "the unsound employment of two separately commanded tactical fleets," found fault in the prohibition of direct communications between himself and Kinkaid, and explained that all this had required his staff to monitor twenty-eight separate radio circuits at all times, piecing together a portrait of the battle from disparate messages emanating from dissimilar sources and arriving on the *New Jersey* flag bridge at unrelated times.[33]

This was all correct, but truth is the product of more than mere accuracy. Halsey, who liked to say he believed in violating the rules and doing the unexpected, did neither at the Battle of Leyte Gulf. Although his massive fleet would have been sufficient both to cover San Bernardino Strait and to pursue Ozawa's fleet, he clung to the convention of concentration and hewed to the common sense—by that point in the war—of a carrier's supreme place among capital ships of consequence. His essential error at Leyte Gulf stemmed not from audacity but from orthodoxy.

A lifetime's worth of relaxed leadership also failed him. Halsey had for decades championed a liberal delegation to subordinate commanders, as long as—to recall William Sims's exhortations in the destroyer flotilla—each maintained fidelity to a common purpose. Such was not the case at Leyte Gulf, where Kinkaid and Halsey perceived different missions. Beyond that, what had worked well for Halsey in lower ranks and with less responsibility now undercut the candid expression and effective resolution of differing ideas. Halsey's brand of governance had always flirted with popularity and its close corollary, approval, a dalliance that had grown more dangerous with the trappings and deference of senior rank. Now, at the Battle of Leyte Gulf, those among his staff and within his fleet holding views contrary to prevailing opinion found little footing inside his inner circle. Cheek, Bogan, Sherman, Mitscher, and others regarded the fleet's headlong thrust north with deep reservation, especially after clear evidence arrived of Kurita's renewed march to San Bernardino Strait. Their voices received a perfunctory hearing within the *New Jersey*'s flag plot, and may not even have reached Halsey's ear, rendering them, in effect, mute, and Halsey deaf. Sims never envisioned leadership that way.

As it happened, Leyte Gulf was a crushing victory for the Americans. It comprised four smaller clashes, each a major engagement in its own right: the Battle of the Sibuyan Sea, the Battle of Surigao Strait, the Battle off Samar, and the Battle of Cape Engaño. Together these made for the supreme conflict of the naval war and among the greatest of all time. It spanned an area of 450,000 square miles, nearly the size of Western Europe. Rarely had a nation staked as much on a single engagement as the Japanese. The total number of ships engaged, 244, was but ten shy of that at the Battle of Jutland, though the Japanese losses at Leyte, twenty-nine combatants, were five times those of the Germans two decades earlier and more than the price Japan had paid across the multiyear South Pacific campaign. The battle reduced the Imperial Navy to nothing more than a coastal defense force, and it never again played an important surface role.[34]

Even had it been different, a Japanese victory at Leyte could not have altered the war in any profound sense. Very fine historians claimed that an Allied defeat would have equaled Athens's retreat at Syracuse in 413 B.C.E., one of the greatest military reversals of all time, or could have cost Roosevelt his reelection ten days later, or led to a negotiated peace, or reversed two centuries of growing American presence along the Pacific basin. This is hype. By October 1944, the basic outcome of the war was clear, made manifest by prior battles and ensured by the prowess of American industry: there were more American destroyers in the Battle of Leyte Gulf, 178, than Japanese carrier planes, 116, with more on the way; and the ships commissioned into the U.S. Navy from October 22 to 26 exceeded those American hulls lost during the same short period. In his concluding discussion of the clash, Morison dwelled at length on Halsey's mistakes as well as those of others, including Kinkaid, and then nevertheless declared, "The Battle of Leyte Gulf should be an imperishable part of our national heritage."[35]

Halsey's superiors recognized this nuance. MacArthur believed Halsey had erred, though he publicly proclaimed a "feeling of complete confidence and inspiration" in his old South Pacific partner and admonished his staff to "leave the Bull alone. He's still a fighting admiral in my book." Nimitz never formally chastised Halsey, but he told King he "regretted" the Third Fleet commander's dash north, adding, somewhat lamely, that it "never occurred" to him that Halsey would leave San Bernardino Strait unguarded. In Washington trying to decipher the battle, King was first as angry as he had been at any point in the war—quite an accomplishment—but then came to see many errors in the fight committed by Kinkaid and an array of commanders both near to and far from it. According to Halsey in an account never challenged by King, when the two first met again in February 1945, Halsey confessed to a "mistake in that battle." No, King replied, "you've got the green light in everything you did." With the principal commander at Leyte and his two naval superiors willing to let the matter rest, Halsey enjoyed a reasonably happy conclusion to the battle until he awakened antagonisms after the war and the whole affair became the shining light and largest kerfuffle in the retelling of the war's naval combat, or, as the eminent Civil War historian Douglas Southall Freeman phrased it, "the Navy's Gettysburg."[36]

Chapter Seventeen

An Old Man at Sea

THE WAR DID NOT WAIT on the controversies of the Battle of Leyte Gulf. While the Americans pushed inland on Leyte amid torrential November rainfall, the Japanese rushed reinforcements from Luzon and Formosa, making for a soggy Allied campaign to capture the middle Philippines. Delays in airfield construction undermined Kenney's air support to MacArthur's troops and, after most of the escort carriers retreated following their exhausting fight with Kurita, Halsey's fast carriers remained the major source of friendly aviation in the region. In the weeks to come the Third Fleet stayed nearby, though the close support mission was foreign to most naval aviators, Halsey's force was depleted, and he was tired. The commitment served as a foretaste of what was to come: as the war reached apogee, its ongoing operational demands taxed an increasingly weary Halsey, laying bare not only the boundaries of human endurance but also the limits of a lifetime spent adapting to the changing forms of naval warfare.

. . . .

Halsey waited mere hours after the Battle of Leyte Gulf to seek permission to withdraw for rest. "Seventeen days of battle," he radioed MacArthur on the evening of October 26, meant he could muster only two carrier groups for short periods as his pilots were "exhausted and the carriers are low in provisions, bombs, and torpedoes." But there was then only a single American field at Tacloban, with no immediate prospect of more amid the Philippine muck at the tail end of monsoon season, so Halsey continued air operations. On October 27 Sherman's group flew combat air patrol over Kinkaid's fleet and struck

Japanese airfields on nearby Cebu and southern Luzon, on October 28 fliers from Bogan's and Davison's groups did the same, and on October 29 Bogan's group hit airfields near Manila, claiming eighty-four planes shot down or destroyed on the ground at a cost of eleven aircraft and thirteen airmen. Although these missions provided needed succor to the Americans ashore, Halsey recognized the threat posed by his prolonged presence in the Philippine islands. Notwithstanding the success of his September and October air strikes, he believed his flattops could not bottle up enemy aviation indefinitely. The task, he told Nimitz, was "tough on our own flyers, there are a great many fields to cover, and the Empire can throw in a certain number of reinforcements." The longer his carriers milled off Philippine shores, the greater were the dangers of a counterstrike.[1]

On October 29 a Japanese flier eluded Bogan's combat patrol and crashed into the *Intrepid* as Halsey watched from the nearby *New Jersey*. The following day Imperial planes again broke through American fighter patrols. One grazed the *Enterprise;* another narrowly missed the *San Jacinto*. A third crashed upon the *Franklin's* flight deck, made a forty-foot hole, ruined a deck elevator, destroyed thirty-three planes, and killed fifty-six sailors. A fourth plane reached the *Belleau Wood,* punctured her flight deck, wrecked a dozen planes, and killed another ninety-two sailors. The attack forced both the *Franklin* and the *Belleau Wood* to Ulithi for extensive repairs, and heralded an astonishingly new, dangerous, and for a time extremely effective tactic by an increasingly desperate foe: the kamikaze attack.[2]

The Third Fleet's empty fuel bunkers and ammunition lockers forced a short retirement at month's end, no matter the state of the battle ashore. Once at Ulithi, Mitscher's exhaustion served as proxy for the entire force. Not a vigorous man, he now weighed barely one hundred pounds and appeared, as an observer once quipped, "not a day over eighty." On October 30 McCain replaced him as the carrier force commander, his own position as a group commander backfilled by Rear Admiral Alfred Montgomery. "There were few wiser or more competent officers in the Navy than 'Slew' McCain," wrote Nimitz's biographer, but a reputation for antics had sometimes hidden these talents: junior officers called him Popeye the Sailorman, and King believed McCain "was not very much in the way of brains, but he was a fighter." Others described him variously as "fearless, modest, extroverted, human," and "aggressive, profane, impulsive, volatile." Although he had written extensively for *Proceedings* before the war and fancied himself an author of short-form fiction, he was in other respects a near clone of Halsey, and in the months ahead he became, in Halsey's phrase, "not much more than my right arm."[3]

After nightfall on November 1 Japanese aircraft sank one of Kinkaid's destroyers and damaged five others inside Leyte Gulf, prompting MacArthur to request the Third Fleet's return to the area. Through most of November Halsey's weary fliers attacked enemy shipping, provided air defense for Kinkaid's surface combatants against kamikazes, and struck airfields on Cebu, Luzon, and Mindoro. On November 5 and 6 pilots claimed 439 enemy aircraft destroyed, most on the ground, and sank a cruiser. On November 11 they intercepted a convoy of four destroyers and half a dozen transports carrying 10,000 men bound for Leyte, sinking all ships and drowning most reinforcements at a cost of nine planes. On November 14 and 15 they sank a cruiser, four more destroyers, another seven transports, and wrecked eighty or so aircraft at a cost of twenty-five American planes. And on November 25 and 26 they sank two cruisers and two freighters. After the war, Japanese records proved insufficient to verify or challenge these high claims, but an exhaustive statistical analysis suggested that nearly 70 percent of them were correct, and in any event these November raids compelled the Japanese to abandon Manila as the port of entry for arriving ships. Earlier in the war, such a score across a single month would have elicited nothing less than euphoria among Americans, but in November 1944 it passed for par.[4]

These raids cost the Third Fleet. On the fifth, a kamikaze damaged the *Lexington*'s flight deck and superstructure, killing fifty men, and on November 26 a large suicide attack ruined the light carrier *Cabot*, crashed the *Essex*, and hit the *Intrepid*, killing 120. Since October 29, suicide planes had cost the Third Fleet 328 men, ninety planes, and the services of three carriers, a tally far greater than anything the Japanese had recently managed by other tactics. About one in four kami-kaze pilots had managed to find a target, and nearly one in thirty had managed to sink a ship, a worrisome rate. "The Japanese air command," Halsey reported, "has at last evolved a sound defensive plan against carrier attacks."[5]

This proved enough for him. By dispatch he irritably asked when Kenney's land-based aircraft would relieve his fliers from doing "the Army air forces' job." In letters to Nimitz, he added that numerous miscues coordinating the Third and Seventh Fleets' operations had created "day-to-day uncertainty and the continual need for counter-manding orders and changing plans," a condition sometimes "more wearing on the fleet than actual combat." Echoing his defense at Leyte Gulf, he believed that "two autonomous tactical fleet commands sup-porting the same operation" could not "be justified from a naval view-point." It invited "all the elements of confusion if not disaster" and was a "violation of every sound principle of command." And beyond all that, he stated that operations since early September—nearly three months—had proved "more strenuous and uninterrupted than any-thing the Fleet had heretofore experienced." Some of this was whining, but Halsey was also livid about criticism from Pearl Harbor over the absence of training exercises in the Third Fleet. In a curt note, he in-formed Nimitz that September had been "a busy month in enemy waters," and, since "departing Ulithi in early October we fueled in the wake of a typhoon, attacked Okinawa, Formosa, the Philippines, en-gaged the Nip Fleet, and went back to Luzon," concluding by saying that his force had had "lots of training—with the Nips furnishing the services."[6]

By the end of November, all of this made Halsey a beggar for re-spite. "Only strikes in great force for valuable stakes or at vital times," he pleaded, would continue to "justify exposure of the fast carriers to suicidal attacks." Following the kamikaze attack on November 26, Nimitz at last agreed, directing the Third Fleet to Ulithi to await refine-ment of better defensive tactics or another major assault of MacArthur's forces upon other Philippine islands, when the Pacific Fleet's flattops might mean the crucial difference. At Ulithi, on nothing more than a large sandbar, Kessing had established an advanced recreation center boasting a swimming beach, basketball courts, horseshoe pitches, baseball diamonds, and a football field. It was not Waikiki or even Nouméa, but to bluejackets long at sea it was welcome. Soft drinks were free; beer came from ships' welfare funds at a clip of two bottles per man per day, making teetotalers very popular as others vied for their coupons. Officers enjoyed a near-proper club, considering the distance to anything resembling civilization, and ordered up Scotch or bourbon for twenty cents a shot. Kessing may have had a mediocre prewar career, but he knew how to construct a way station in the middle of the Pacific Ocean in 1944.[7]

The brief holiday allowed bluejackets and officers alike to consider the two men who had led them across a year of sea combat, Halsey and Spruance, personal friends and professional associates of forty years' standing. Most would have agreed with Nimitz, who believed that "Halsey was a sailor's admiral and Spruance was an admiral's admiral." Rank and file thought Halsey was boisterous to the point of garrulous, Spruance reticent to the point of taciturn. Halsey was bold, Spruance cautious; Halsey instinctual and impetuous, Spruance intellectual and deliberate. Halsey's mantra of strategy, to arrive first with the most, contrasted with Spruance's view of war as "a game that requires cold and careful calculation. It might be a serious thing if we turned the wrong way, just once." When Spruance commanded the fleet, remembered one officer, "everybody knew what they were supposed to do and when they were supposed to do it." With Halsey, "it was a pretty razzle-dazzle affair."[8]

In outline these comparisons were fair enough. Differences between the two men long predated the war. Halsey loved the Naval Academy and Spruance hated his every moment as a midshipman. Whereas the *Lucky Bag* called Halsey an old salt with the head of Neptune, editors dubbed Spruance a "shy young thing with a rather sober, earnest face." More recently, wartime acclaim had made their differences virtual proxies for the major archetypes of military command, with Halsey as the heroic leader and Spruance as the military manager already seeping into popular commentary. In the decades since the war, distinctions between the two men became a basic staple of the Pacific War story: every extant description of Halsey hews to script, and differences between the two men constitute a subplot for Spruance's greatest biographer. Over time, their differences became a nearly necessary part of the backdrop to American operations in the Pacific War, simply a piece of the canvas upon which historians have applied their craft.[9]

Yet in detail these contrasts obscured truth. Halsey and Spruance's disparities sat in stark relief largely as a result of the proximity of their lives. Like Halsey, Spruance hailed from a New England family of "scholars, clergy, patriots, pioneers, and pilgrims." Like Halsey, he sought the Naval Academy for its promise of security and honor. And like Halsey, he eschewed religion. Their respective wives believed each was sensitive and high strung. They hated to write and make speeches. Halsey could be more tentative than legend has it, as he was at New Georgia, and Spruance more daring, as his carrier strikes in the Gilberts and Marshalls—well before the ascendancy of carriers against shore bases was clear—demonstrated. Halsey was a better thinker and Spruance more of a fighter than their respective reputations allowed. Both thrived in the Navy's closed fraternity. They shared a companionship unusual in the universe of Halsey's many acquaintances, and it asks too much of friendship to suppose their relationship across decades rested upon a foundation of contrasts. Once, in a quiet moment before the war, in the hours after dinner with their wives, Halsey asked Spruance, "If you did it all over, what would you be?" Spruance needed little time to reply: "A successful naval officer." Halsey nodded. "So would I."[10]

. . . .

Halsey and McCain used the time in Ulithi to prepare the Third Fleet to better fend off kamikaze strikes. They reorganized the fleet into three rather than four carrier groups, concentrating more carriers behind a heavier screen of escorts; they provided for a line of picket destroyers stationed sixty miles from the carriers and equipped with radar to provide advance warning of approaching enemy planes; and they increased the fighters and decreased the attack planes aboard the carriers to provide larger defensive patrols over the flattops, a solution

McCain acknowledged was a necessary compromise between the offensive and defensive requirements of the fleet. Together, these adjustments would mitigate but never eliminate the effectiveness of the suicide attacks.

On December 11 Halsey steered his force to sea again, where MacArthur, still short land-based air power, required Third Fleet planes for his next island hop to Mindoro, just south of Luzon and intended as a stepping stone toward Manila. Four days later and following suicide attacks on his ships, Kinkaid deposited some 10,000 Americans on the small island, where 1,200 defenders put up a brief, brisk defense before giving way to the onslaught. In support, Halsey's fast carriers struck airfields in southern Luzon on December 14, 15, and 16 before retiring to a point 500 miles east of Luzon to refuel on December 17. The Third Fleet commander intended an encore of these raids on December 19, 20, and 21, but a building typhoon belayed these plans and occupied Halsey for the better part of a week—and then dogged his reputation forever after.[11]

The first indications of foul weather arrived early on December 17. By noon thirty-knot gusts buffeted Third Fleet ships. Halsey, from the *New Jersey* flag bridge, could see a destroyer bobbing badly as it tried to fuel from the battleship's bunkers. After consulting his aerologist, Commander George Kosco, whom Halsey had known as a midshipman boxer in the late 1920s, Halsey canceled refueling operations and directed his fleet 200 miles to the northwest. Weather forecasts failed him, however, and he was now heading toward a powerful December typhoon. As the waves grew, he changed course again in midafternoon, to the southwest, a direction that merely established a course parallel to the storm track, ensuring indefinite hours of tough steaming by ships low on fuel and with little ballast.[12]

By 7:00 AM the next morning, with the weather no better anywhere near the fleet and in spots far worse, Halsey stubbornly resumed refueling to meet commitments to MacArthur's forces ashore. An hour later, amid forty-five-knot winds and visibility as little as 500 yards, he belayed the order amid what he called a "tropical disturbance." Turning south, Halsey was now matching wits with nature, and losing. Instead of heading northeast as Kosco had predicted, the storm dipped south and then headed westward, as if pursuing the Americans. At 9:00 the carrier *Independence* reported the first Third Fleet man overboard. Moments later, planes on the *Monterey* broke loose and caught fire. By 10:00 two additional men on the *Independence* had tumbled into the sea, two ships had lost steering, and another flattop had reported dangerous thirty-five-degree rolls. Halsey at last reported to MacArthur the postponement of the following day's strikes, and directed each Third Fleet ship to steer an independent course to better ride out the fury, a point of privilege granted at least half a day too late.[13]

By 1:00 PM Halsey had radioed Nimitz that the fleet was in extremis, with wind gusts approaching one hundred knots and seas seventy feet high. Sometime in midafternoon a mere twenty miles separated the center of the typhoon, now named Cobra, and the *New Jersey*. Aboard the big battlewagon, able to survive hits by sixteen-inch shells, Carney wondered if the mighty vessel would founder and he shuddered to think about conditions on smaller, lighter ships. Elsewhere, the *Hancock*'s flight deck, fifty feet above the waterline in calm seas, plunged below the surface wave after wave. Aboard the *Independence*, 1,000-pound bombs bounced around like empty beer kegs. Planes on the *San Jacinto* deck rolled into the sea.[14]

By 4:00 PM the worst was over. But Halsey's ships were scattered over 2,500 square miles of ocean, battered and beaten, not by any Japanese strike but by a sort of divine wind long a signal element of Imperial war mythology. The storm badly damaged seven ships and destroyed nearly 200 aircraft. The destroyers *Hull, Spence,* and *Monaghan* sank. Though Halsey searched for survivors until December 22, the maelstrom had taken all but 74 of their crew of more than 800 with them to the sea floor. Halsey had only rarely before incurred such loss at Japanese hands. "It was," he forthrightly acknowledged in his autobiography, "the Navy's greatest uncompensated loss since the Battle of Savo Island." Solberg probably spoke for most Third Fleet staffers, calling the brutal afternoon "an inglorious hour for our admiral."[15]

Halsey could do little but retreat to Ulithi to lick wounds and await the verdict of a three-man court of inquiry into the fiasco. The court convened on December 26. It was chaired by Vice Admiral John Hoover, once Halsey's chief of staff and briefly his deputy commander in the South Pacific, and included Vice Admiral George Murray, Halsey's *Enterprise* skipper early in the war. Although it found Halsey largely responsible for the debacle, the court offered a safe harbor, assigning a measure of blame to forecasting deficiencies aboard the *New Jersey* and inexperience among the destroyer skippers. It concluded that the Third Fleet commander had displayed no negligence and had acted instead out of an honorable commitment to stay near Luzon to aid MacArthur's Mindoro assault. Nimitz and King mostly agreed, and softened the court's verdict still further in their endorsements, Nimitz particularly mindful that Halsey had in the war's first months come "to my support and offered to lead the attack" in carrier raids when others had shied from the challenge, once even declaring, "I'll not be party to any enterprise that can hurt the reputation of a man like that." Morison added an early postwar defense of Halsey, writing, "One cannot quarrel with an officer who makes a mistake because of his single-minded devotion to his mission." But historical judgment demands adjudication of such squabbles, and the passage of seventy-five years makes manifest a conclusion not far from that of Third Fleet officers and men at the time: Bogan, Halsey's deputy at Pensacola a decade earlier, believed Halsey's mistakes constituted "just plain, goddam stubbornness and stupidity," and throughout the force, rumblings of a bumbling admiral wafted from bluejacket corridors where before mostly admiration had reigned.[16]

. . . .

By early January the fleet was back at sea, first to support MacArthur's invasion of Luzon at Lingayen Gulf and his march toward Manila, and then to push into the South China Sea to strike Japanese shipping along the Indochina coast, long a cherished Halsey ambition. His carrier aircraft—now nicknamed the Big Blue Blanket in light of their task to suppress kamikaze attacks—struck Formosa and Luzon airfields on January 3, 4, 6, 7, and 9, the last of these the day of Mac-

Arthur's landings at Lingayen. That night Halsey slid his flattops through the Luzon Strait and into the South China Sea, where heretofore only American submarines had trodden. On January 12 nearly 1,500 sorties aimed at merchant vessels at and near Cam Ranh Bay and, against losses of just twenty-three aircraft and a handful of pilots, the Third Fleet claimed forty-one enemy ships of 127,000 tons, a tally not far from the actual count of forty-four ships of 133,000 tons. Subsequent raids at Hong Kong and Hainan added incrementally to this score before Nimitz directed Halsey to retire back through the Luzon Strait on January 20, fearful of the risks inherent in an extended stay in the tight confines between the Philippines and Indochina and needing the Pacific Fleet for pending operations at Iwo Jima. The Third Fleet then capped the month with a series of raids along the Formosan coastline, incurring a large suicide attack on January 21 and bringing its total of enemy destruction for January to over 300,000 tons of shipping, including two cruisers and four destroyers, and about 600 enemy aircraft against American losses of 201 planes, 167 fliers, and 205 sailors killed in the kamikaze attack, prompting Nimitz to call Halsey's January forays "well-conceived and brilliantly executed."[17]

Halsey's blunder at Leyte Gulf has obscured the rest of his inaugural cruise as a fleet commander. But from October 30 to the end of January, Halsey's carriers flew more than 13,000 sorties over enemy targets and another 8,000 defending against kamikaze attacks, sinking 150 vessels of all types and damaging another 240. From the end of the Battle of Leyte Gulf, Halsey's fliers claimed nearly 1,200 Japanese planes destroyed while losing about 400 aircraft and 300 aircrew and suffering damage to nine vessels, most of them carriers wounded by kamikazes. The cruise had stripped away yet another layer of Japan's defensive perimeter and had rendered Indochina and the resource-rich Dutch East Indies isolated and useless empire outposts. Great as that triumph was, however, among Third Fleet officers then and historians since, most minds lingered over the disappointment of Leyte Gulf and the horror of the December typhoon. As January drew to a close, the Third Fleet staff looked toward rest and January 27, when Halsey and company turned over the Pacific Fleet to Spruance and the Fifth Fleet staff in a long-planned handoff. Then, as Spruance prepared for the assaults at Iwo Jima and Okinawa, Halsey and his cohort steamed for Hawaii.[18]

. . . .

At Pearl Harbor they spent a couple of weeks completing reports on their recent cruise. Most Third Fleet staff officers then dispersed for leave. Halsey went to Margaret's home in Delaware. His fame preceded him. Newspaper reporters regularly beseeched the admiral for a comment or quick picture. He usually obliged. At one point he crowed of someday riding Hirohito's ceremonial white horse amid Tokyo rubble, a boast that produced a slew of saddles, bridles, lariats, and spurs from an adoring public until, he lamented, he had become connected to the emperor's horse "as if I were a centaur." Fan was usually calm and collected amid the hullabaloo that followed Halsey wherever he went, but concern for her mental state kept her from attending a parade in Halsey's home town of Elizabeth. In late February, Carney arranged a hunting expedition for himself and Halsey and their wives at a large Georgia estate owned by John Hay Whitney, grandson of the great secretary of state John Hay and descendant of both the Pilgrim William Bradford and the Puritan John Whitney. Halsey was not nearly the hunter Carney was, but he enjoyed trading stories of common ancestry with Whitney, who retained far stronger ties to his New England bloodline than had the admiral.[19]

Across the first weeks in March, Halsey was in Washington making Navy Department rounds. On March 3 he went to the White House to receive from Roosevelt a decoration for recent Philippine operations and then chatted privately with the president for about an hour. It was the last time the two old acquaintances met, as Roosevelt died within six weeks. At the president's request, Halsey sent Stassen to San Francisco, where for six weeks the former Minnesota governor joined five other Americans and an international array of diplomats drafting the United Nations Charter. The august gathering stirred fanciful public concern of a Japanese raid aimed at the Golden Gate, and the Navy Department appointed Halsey the commander of a provisional

Mid-Pacific Striking Force, composed nominally of two fleet carriers and every surface ship then in West Coast ports, but made up mostly of Halsey's renown, as a counterweight to civic fears.

. . . .

Halsey reconvened his staff at Pearl Harbor on April 7 to plan further Third Fleet operations after they relieved Spruance's crew sometime toward the end of May. The Joint Chiefs had by then settled upon a two-pronged approach to Japan following MacArthur's return to the Philippines: an exterior line up through Iwo Jima to aid the Air Forces' massive B-29 bombers in their onslaught from Marianas airfields, and an interior line through Okinawa, necessary for yet more airfields as well as ground and sea staging areas for the invasion of Japan proper. To support these operations, Spruance's Fifth Fleet had launched a series of diversionary raids on Tokyo in mid-February, the first naval air strikes there since the Doolittle Raid, and then had pounded Iwo Jima defenses for three days prior to delivering Marines to its forlorn shore on February 19. Scheduled to take five days, the conquest of Iwo took nearly a month of vicious fighting and mutual slaughter of the kind seen at Tarawa and Peleliu. Nearly 7,000 Americans were killed and 19,000 wounded, and of Japan's garrison of 21,000 all but 216 chose death instead of surrender.

It was worse on Okinawa. Spruance's fast carriers and Army Air Forces had passed the last weeks of March softening targets and suppressing enemy air power in the area. On April Fools' Day, 1,418 ships of nearly fifty types helped push ashore the bow wave of over 180,000 troops, a ship tally and troop number second only to the Normandy invasion the previous June. Fighting ashore was brutal, and in the littorals it was ruthless. The Japanese unleashed the greatest sustained suicide attacks of the war. Using refined tactics, they launched seven massive kamikaze air waves comprising 1,260 aircraft during the first six weeks of the campaign, all aimed at Spruance's covering and supporting forces. One attack damaged the *Indianapolis*, Spruance's flagship, sending her to dry dock and the admiral to the *New Mexico*. There were American successes—on April 7 Spruance's fliers sank five warships, including the super dreadnought

Yamato—but mostly the campaign devolved into a depressing slug-fest. Through the end of May, Americans ashore had incurred the vast majority of the 7,500 deaths and 32,000 wounded that the campaign would ultimately extract, and at sea the Fifth Fleet had suffered most of the 10,000 casualties, thirty-two ships sunk, and 763 aircraft lost that the assault would require, making it the most costly naval campaign of the war by far and one seldom matched in naval history. Watching from afar, Halsey concluded that "once again the fleet was being held in static defense instead of being sent to hit the enemy where it would hurt."[20]

On May 27 Halsey, now aboard the *New Jersey*'s sister, *Missouri*, relieved Spruance off the coast of Okinawa. The Third Fleet then contained three carrier groups under Vice Admiral McCain: one still led by Sherman, another by the veteran carrier commander Jocko Clark, and a third by Arthur Radford, a strong-willed and aggressive rear admiral who later served as chairman of the Joint Chiefs of Staff. Halsey sent Sherman's group to Leyte for rest, and on June 2 and 3 commenced the first of many summertime raids with his remaining two groups, both supporting ground operations on Okinawa and hitting faraway airfields on Kyushu, the southernmost of the four major Japanese home islands.

The following day the first indication that a storm might again jeopardize Third Fleet vessels reached Halsey's flag plot. Through most of June 4 Halsey maneuvered his ships near the foul weather in an attempt to maintain station off Okinawa. At 1:30 AM on June 5, and perhaps recalling the faulty forecasts of the previous December, he dismissed weather reports as "not credible" and changed course from 110 degrees, heading generally east, to 300 degrees, generally west, in a bid to scoot across and in front of the storm track to the northwest and reach the typhoon's safer quadrant. This was a dangerous gambit, one that placed most of Clark's carrier group in jeopardy if it did not work but kept the Third Fleet near Okinawa if it did. Close to 3:00 Clark told McCain, his direct superior, that the new course was running his ships smack into the storm, and at 4:20 he requested permission to steer to 120 degrees, close to the fleet's original track and a course consistent with weather reporting to avoid the storm.²¹

Although Halsey told McCain to direct Clark to hold course, twenty minutes later McCain allowed Clark to maneuver independently. As with the December storm, this license was granted too late. By then Clark's ships were battling seventy-foot swells and wind gusts up to 127 knots. Nearly all his thirty-three vessels suffered damage, though none was sunk. Most battered was the cruiser *Pittsburgh,* which had a one-hundred-foot bow section sheared away. None of Clark's four flattops escaped unscathed. The forward flight decks of the *Hornet* and the *Bennington* collapsed. The *San Jacinto*'s hull buckled. The *Belleau Wood*'s forward catwalk washed to sea. Throughout the fleet, seventy-six planes were lost or destroyed, another sixteen were severely damaged, and six men were killed. On June 6, Halsey resumed air support for the troops ashore at Okinawa, but aboard every ship of the Third Fleet officers and bluejackets alike wondered how a second typhoon could have snookered Halsey. Clark was especially incensed: when in the storm's aftermath Carney inexplicably teased him about getting caught in the gale, Clark exploded: "Now Mick, you know who the typhoon king is!"²²

Weakening suicide attacks off Okinawa and mounting Army Air Forces strikes at Kyushu permitted Halsey to retire on June 10. On June 13 most of the Third Fleet arrived in Leyte Gulf, its seas now a placid forward anchorage. For eight days commencing on June 15, Halsey, McCain, Clark, and others were on Guam for an inquest into the typhoon damage, the court once again headed by Hoover and with Murray as a member. This time they brokered no apology for Halsey, whose defense rested, as it did in December, on deficiencies in meteorological reporting and pressing commitments to American troops ashore. Halsey's testimony was combative, contradictory, and evasive. Although he proclaimed "no wish to avoid my proper responsibility" in the affair, he plainly did. The court had none of it, concluding that Halsey's abrupt about-face early on June 5, from a course nearly due east to one west-northwest, was the primary cause of the debacle, and that McCain's twenty-minute hesitation before granting

Clark permission to change course was a secondary factor. The "remarkable similarity between the situations, actions, and results" of the December and June typhoons deeply troubled court members, and Halsey's decisions in this latest encounter had been "extremely ill-advised." In its report to higher authorities, the court suggested relieving both Halsey and McCain of their commands.[23]

Secretary of the Navy Forrestal agreed. King believed Halsey and McCain had blundered, but thought Forrestal too harsh. He agreed to consider another assignment for McCain, eventually sending him to duty at the Veterans Administration as punishment for his part in the fiasco. Halsey, however, was a national hero. In July, before the June typhoon had been widely reported and the court inquiry had submitted its report, Halsey made his second appearance on *Time*'s cover as a veritable bulldog, glaring at an ancient Japanese emperor with the caption "Kill Japs, Kill Japs, and then Kill More Japs." This adulation provided Halsey a protective cloak. His removal from command, King argued, would rejuvenate enemy morale and harm the Navy's shine as it approached its greatest hour. After Forrestal deferred to King's judgment, Halsey stayed at sea in command of the Third Fleet.[24]

As King protected Halsey's job, however, another verdict came from below, among those Halsey deigned to lead. The admiral's mistakes prompted open, widespread and previously rare snickers among bluejackets. A *Yorktown* variety skit portrayed Halsey as a publicity hound, raring to "rub out these yeller-bellied little monkey-men bastards," and a ditty disparaging him made the Third Fleet rounds:

> Bull is his name and bull his nature
> Bull his talk will always be
> But for me and many like me
> He's a perfect SOB
>
> Typhoons never worry the guy
> Though they come from north or south
> Typhoons, blah, he has one every
> Time he opens his month[25]

Halsey's second "inglorious hour" marred a needed rest in the Philippines for the Third Fleet. On June 21 Okinawa was declared secured and on July 1 the Third Fleet steamed from Leyte Gulf and turned north to attack Japanese naval and air forces, shipping, shipyards, and coastal objectives. Halsey's fleet consisted of a powerful battleship, cruiser, and destroyer screen to protect McCain's three American carrier task forces, each of which counted three fleet and two light carriers. Nearing Japan, they fueled on July 8 and commenced operation two days later over Tokyo, fulfilling Halsey's enduring aspiration to strike the city. Third Fleet fliers destroyed over one hundred aircraft on the ground, met no aerial opposition, and encountered only light antiaircraft fire.[26]

The fleet then pushed farther north, toward Honshu's upper reaches and Hokkaido, the most northern of the four main Japanese islands, which until then had been beyond the range of American air power. On July 14, from a point just eighty miles from shore, nearly 1,400 sorties aimed at airfields and shipyards, confronting virtually no aerial opposition. In the harbors of Muroran and Hakodate— crucial links between Honshu and Hokkaido—American pilots sank three destroyers, eight naval auxiliaries, thirteen freighters, and seven ferries. That same day, a surface force of four battlewagons, two cruisers, and nine destroyers under the command of John Shafroth approached sight of land and for two hours blasted the ironworks at Kamaishi, one of seven large Japan Iron Company plants, again without rousing a response from the enemy.[27]

The following day it was more of the same. American fliers focused on ferries, freighters, and colliers. They sank twelve of the first, ten of the second, and some seventy of the third. Another surface force of three battleships, two cruisers, and eight destroyers under the command of Rear Admiral Oscar Badger and including Halsey and the *Missouri* sailed boldly into the narrow waters between Honshu and Hokkaido and shelled Nihon Steel Company and the Wanishi Ironworks, the second largest producer of coke and pig iron in Japan. Halsey described the approach, bombardment, and retreat as the longest seven hours of his life, spent entirely within easy reach of land-based Japanese aircraft. These mid-July strikes astride Honshu and Hokkaido severed ferry traffic, reduced the delivery of coal from the northern island to the rest of Japan by 80 percent, and cost Japan a month's supply of pig iron and over two months' of coke production. The action was, according to one careful assessment, "the most devastating single strategic-bombing success of all the [naval] campaigns against Japan."[28]

Halsey refueled his ships on July 16 and added a British carrier group to his punching power. The Royal Navy had left the Pacific in early 1942, pulled from the region by pressing commitments elsewhere and pushed by the shocking loss of two capital vessels in the war's first week. As Allied fortunes improved in Europe, however, Winston Churchill wanted British hulls back in the Pacific, a move that American admirals feared would tax sea logistics and complicate well-developed tactical routines. Nonetheless, a fleet of four carriers carrying over 200 planes, two battleships, five cruisers, fifteen destroyers, and a fleet train arrived in time for the Okinawa campaign, where it registered valuable service as a flying buffer between the American invasion and Japanese aircraft on Sakishima Gunto, a bypassed enemy stronghold. The British ships had then retired to Sydney for upkeep and now joined Halsey, adding 26 men-of-war to the Third Fleet's 105, swelling further the most powerful maritime striking force in history.

Heading back to the Tokyo plain, an American contingent of five battleships with cruisers and destroyers raked six major copper, steel, and ammunition plants after darkness on July 17. The following day carrier planes struck the Yokosuka shipyard near Tokyo, where the principal target was the battleship *Nagato*, hiding from the Allies in a camouflaged mooring. That vessel survived, but a destroyer, two small escort vessels, and a patrol boat were sunk, at that point in the war a modest score for the fourteen planes and eighteen lives the Americans paid for the strike. From July 21 to 23 Service Squadron Six provided 6,369 tons of ammunition, 379,157 barrels of fuel, 1,635 tons of general provisions, ninety-nine replacement aircraft, and 412 replacement personnel to hungry Third Fleet ships. This was history's largest replenishment at sea—though not the war's most complex: those occurred in the war's first months, when the transfer of a few tons of fuel and food bedeviled the Navy as it struggled at the front end of a learning curve that now, after four hard years, had reached its apex.[29]

Its appetite satiated, Halsey's fleet continued its rampage. On July 24 perhaps the heaviest single carrier strike of the war flung almost 1,800 sorties toward Kobe, where most of Japan's heavy warships still afloat lurked, hidden in coves, like wounded but powerful animals at hunt's end. On July 28 pilots repeated these raids. The tandem strikes ruined the battleships *Haruna, Ise,* and *Hyuga,* along with five cruisers and five destroyers, whose hulls filled with water and whose forms settled in the shallow muck, half-sunk, their smoldering silhouettes reminiscent of American battlewagons at Pearl Harbor in December 1941.[30]

. . . .

A gathering typhoon on July 31 accomplished what feeble Japanese opposition could not, forcing Halsey's retreat to open sea to avoid another calamitous encounter with foul weather. In retrospect, the Third Fleet's July raids looked to some like mere thrashing in a war long since won but not yet over. Morison, for example, could do no better than aggregate them under late-war "miscellaneous operations." But this view is more apparent than real, distorted by a hindsight endowed with knowledge of all that would happen in August but that no one in July could know. The Japanese were surely defeated before they surrendered, though they had not yet raised the white flag, and modest indications that they would do so were eclipsed by massive evidence that they would fight to the bitter end, from the slugfest of Guadalcanal to the killing fields of Tarawa, Palau, Saipan, and Okinawa—where combatant fatality rates approached 100 percent and mass civilian suicides had been increasingly common. If the Third Fleet's July rampage along the Japanese coast resembled a series of drive-by shootings, it was also a part of a larger American strategy to impel a still-recalcitrant foe to unconditional surrender—as was the Army Air Force's revolutionary fire bombing that had by mid-June destroyed nearly three-quarters of Kawasaki; about half each of Tokyo, Yokohama, and Kobe; a third of Nagoya; and a fourth of Osaka, leaving millions homeless, 127,000 dead, and another 180,000 wounded, and rocking, in the words of a Japanese official, "the nation to its very foundations." But still the Japanese soldiered on, even adopting Ketsu-Go, a policy committing the nation to a fight to the finish and, in the judgment of the preeminent historian of the war's last days, "to choose extinction before surrender."[31]

As Halsey's fleet waited for the weather to clear, an admixture of factors at last catalyzed an incipient peace movement in Japan. In mid-July Halsey had been told to keep Hiroshima, Nagasaki, and three other cities off his target list, and on July 22 he had been informed of the Manhattan Project and the existence of atomic bombs, something Roosevelt had hinted at during their last meeting in March. Two bombs then obliterated Hiroshima and Nagasaki on August 6 and 9, respectively, killing as many as 120,000 Japanese instantly and many more eventually. Perhaps as important, on August 8 the Soviet Union entered the war with a general assault on Japanese positions in Manchuria—long of signal import to Imperial war aims—and within twenty-four hours had achieved a general dominance along a wide front. Together, these calamities loosened the intransigent elements pushing for prolonged war in Tokyo, though it would take days of high drama, personal intrigue, and close order negotiation among Japanese leaders before any substantial suggestion and confirmed intention of peace reached Allied ears.

. . . .

So on the same day that Nagasaki was bombed and amid excited rumors of peace, war, peace, and war again, Halsey, having replenished his fuel and supplies, resumed his carrier raids. In waters off northern Honshu, his fleet launched a large strike at airfields where some 200 Japanese kamikazes had assembled, foiling enemy plans to strike B-29 bases in the Marianas. On August 10 raids struck two previously unknown fields on Honshu where additional enemy warbirds had assembled as prospective kamikazes. The next day Halsey canceled operations to avoid a storm, but on August 13 Third Fleet fliers unleashed another large raid against airfields near Tokyo, claiming over 400 planes destroyed or damaged, a score at least a third too high but nonetheless part of the unremitting pressure upon Japan. Halsey refueled his ships on August 14 and the following morning launched two dawn strikes toward the Tokyo plain. Two hours later, word reached the Third Fleet to suspend all operations because the emperor had promised to surrender. Most American planes then jettisoned ordnance into the sea, but some had already begun attacking Tokoro-zawa airfield, where an encounter with as many as twenty Japanese planes netted nine enemy aircraft and cost four Hellcats in the final dogfight of the war.[32]

Near midday Nimitz ordered Halsey's fleet to "cease all offensive operations against Japan," a dispatch in postscript as momentous as the directive to commence unrestricted warfare against the Empire of Japan had been in prologue on December 7, 1941. Halsey's first thought was "Victory!" His second was "God be thanked, I'll never have to order another man out to die." His third was "I am grateful for the honor of being in command of the Third Fleet on this day." Then "plain joy took over. I yelled Yippee and pounded the shoulders of everybody within reach." Upon further reflection, he hoped history would remember "that when hostilities ended, the capital of the Japanese Empire had just been bombed, strafed, and rocketed by planes of the Third Fleet, and was about to be bombed, strafed, and rocketed again"—and that seven American pilots from that last war mission never returned. He broke out his four-star admiral's flag and celebrated with a full one-minute whistle and siren from the *Missouri* at 11:00, a point of privilege subordinate commanders exercised in turn for the better part of an hour. In the flag mess that night, Tulao conjured a feast worthy of Thanksgiving and Christmas put together, and throughout the fleet the outlines of hundreds of vessels met the darkening horizon with crews knowing that tomorrow meant peace. A sporadic and confused couple of days followed while higher authorities confirmed the surrender, during which time Halsey ordered combat air patrols to shoot down any approaching Japanese planes "in a friendly" fashion in case they menaced the Third Fleet. None did.[33]

Contingency plans for surrender had been in high gear for weeks. Nimitz had in late July designated the Third Fleet and about 10,000 embarked Marines and bluejackets as the leading edge of an American occupation force pending arrival of Army units under MacArthur's control. In early August the Joint Chiefs had designated MacArthur as supreme commander for the Allied powers, finally unifying command in the Pacific region when it largely no longer mattered. When reconnaissance teams discovered "indescribable hell holes of filth, disease, and death" at prisoner-of-war camps in the Tokyo area, Halsey rushed a small team to liberate as many captives as possible, freeing nearly 20,000 men within two weeks. They also seized the thoroughly wrecked Yokosuka naval base and began makeshift American operations from it.[34]

On August 27, Halsey brought the *Missouri* and other elements of the Third Fleet into Sagami Wan, the outer anchorage to Tokyo Bay, leaving the carriers at sea where they could conduct defensive patrols. In an ode to his home state, President Truman requested that the *Missouri* host the formal surrender ceremonies, slated for August 30 but postponed by yet another typhoon until September 2. As Halsey brought the mighty ship and a small escort into Tokyo Bay, Bill Kitchell worked, Halsey recalled, "like a Hong Kong coolie to organize the ceremony." The appointed day broke with scattered clouds, which soon gave way to glorious sunshine. American and Allied dignitaries began arriving shortly after dawn, the Soviet contingent looking, Halsey later recalled, like "gangsters." Nimitz came aboard at 8:05 AM, MacArthur at 8:43, and the Japanese delegation at 8:56. The atmosphere was frigid. Press reports had Halsey muttering a desire to kick each "Jap delegate in the face," something he steadfastly denied— though he had earlier refused the emperor's representatives the customary privilege of coffee and cigarettes. The affair was brief, officially over at 9:04 when the Japanese signed the instrument of surrender. MacArthur, Nimitz, and a few ranking military men retired to Halsey's flag quarters and enjoyed a few moments of subdued celebration. And then it was over.[35]

Eleven days later Halsey requested retirement from active duty. He had been headed to a twilight shore command in the months before Pearl Harbor, and although he was still a year away from mandatory retirement at sixty-four, he harbored no interest in delaying his return home. The war had taxed him as it had others; already John McCain was dead, passing away the week before as soon as he had arrived in San Diego, and many others of high rank and senior age would not long survive the fighting. Bureaucracy moved slowly, however, and for a time Halsey was "completely in a fog of bewilderment" regarding his request, spending the days overseeing occupation duties and posing for rather ridiculous pictures atop various white horses. His actions at Leyte Gulf and amid two typhoons had indicated his fatigue to nearly every disinterested observer, however, and Nimitz and King consented to Halsey's wishes by late September. "It will be difficult—if not impossible—to overestimate the value of Admiral Halsey's splendid service to our country" Nimitz opined, but all three men knew the time had come.[36]

On September 17 Spruance arrived in Tokyo Bay with the *New Jersey*. That evening the two old friends conferred aboard the *Mississippi*, Halsey's flagship after the *Missouri* had left for the West Coast. The next night the Fifth and Third Fleet commanders attended an inter-Allied party on board the *King George V*. "It was quite a celebration," Spruance reported to his wife, "and as Bill was having a thoroughly good time and feeling no pain whatever, it was 1:30 AM before we got back to our ships." On September 19 Halsey paid a final call on MacArthur. When they parted, the general opined, "When you leave the Pacific, Bill, it becomes just another damn ocean." That night the Third Fleet staff toasted Halsey in the ramshackle Yokosuka officer's club. At midnight, command of the massive American armada in the region passed to Spruance. Six hours later Halsey departed by air for Hawaii. On October 9 he boarded the *South Dakota* and assumed command of Task Force Thirty, composed of dozens of ships and thousands of servicemen returning to America. Halsey was more senior in age or rank than any other person in the task force. The war's last months had seen him struggle with the complexity of modern war, almost as if a lifetime of adjusting to new technologies had at last found its limits, and finally, at last, he was going home, whatever that meant.

Chapter Eighteen

At Home at Last

AS YOUTH FORESHADOWS what is to come, old age reflects what has been. Halsey returned home a famous hero, though in time the years stripped him of staff, pomp, and responsibility. As they did, essential traits reappeared, not seen clearly since before the war. The fabled Bull Halsey was real; he was flamboyant, charismatic, and forceful. A world war had midwifed that legend, however, and with the conflagration over, Bill Halsey emerged, somewhat unsteady after years at sea. On dry land, without war and, increasingly, the Navy as constant companions, Halsey was hesitant in his judgments and uncertain in his personal relationships. For him, the austerity of age revealed that his renowned confidence, boldness, and audacity were professional skills, not personal traits. This, of course, was a distinction he himself had helped obfuscate with his courtship of celebrity. But in the solitude of late life, Halsey came closer to the truth. "Only those people who don't know me," he once wrote a friend in those later years, "call me Bull."[1]

. . . .

Hubbub sustained the legend for a while. Stassen made elaborate arrangements for press coverage of the Third Fleet's homecoming voyage. Correspondents were assigned to ships with local significance to their respective newspapers and radio stations. Third Fleet public information officers prepared extensive publicity material on ships and crew members. Additional communications gear went into the *South Dakota* to transmit news copy. Photojournalists received liberal access to ship decks, bridges, and working spaces.[2]

In Honolulu, Colonel Julius Klein, formerly of the Hearst papers in Chicago and a onetime South Pacific staffer, scored Halsey's first formal sit-down press interview of the postwar era. The returning hero championed a strong postwar Navy, praised the joint team that had won the war, worried that atomic wizardry would lull Americans into a false sense of security, warned of the threat posed by international communism, and campaigned for universal military training, all soon staples of his speeches and interviews. Despite four stars and fame, Klein wrote, Halsey was "a regular guy" who wanted to "get reacquainted" with his family and then "look for a job." A mere six weeks of peace had peeled back the admiral's wartime patina, Klein wrote, and Halsey spoke in tones of "quiet intensity," "sensitivity," and "empathy," all in a manner "far removed from the loud, salty-tongued seadog written up through the war years. But I, who have known him on and off for 15 years, know this as the real Halsey," much more than the "half a man" portrayed by a wartime press.[3]

The *South Dakota* and Task Force Thirty reached America in mid-October. Various elements made for East Coast harbors via the Panama Canal, other units to West Coast ports from Seattle to San Diego. The *South Dakota,* with thirteen ships, went to San Francisco. On a gray October 15 morning, California governor Earl Warren, San Francisco mayor Roger Lapham, entertainer Bob Hope, and fifty more reporters and photographers came aboard. At noon the column passed under the Golden Gate Bridge, its twin towers ensconced in fog. Inside the bay, Halsey's flagship took station as the other vessels passed in review. The *South Dakota* band played "There'll Be a Hot Time in the Old Town Tonight," ship whistles and sirens blew, planes whizzed overhead, and thousands of spectators lined the bridge and shore, fewer than had crowded the nearby hills to see the Great White Fleet in 1909, but Halsey had been an anonymous ensign then, not the main attraction. "This is what we have dreamed of, hoped for, fought for, and prayed for," Halsey told the assembled crew and guests gathered on the main deck, "to return home again, knowing that our enemies have been vanquished, that now at last we are at peace." After the battleship moored to a pier along the city's embarcadero, Hope aired his radio show, which had the largest audience in America, from the *South Dakota,* with Halsey as his special guest. Halsey loved it all. "Oh he ate it up," recalled Carney. "He ate it up."[4]

Homecoming festivities occupied Halsey most of the fall of 1945, just as they did for a handful of other senior officers. Halsey headlined parades in San Francisco, Los Angeles, Houston, Saint Louis, India-napolis, Minneapolis, and Boston. People lined ten deep to get a glimpse of the admiral. There were national radio broadcasts and speeches. There was yet another Halsey Day in Elizabeth, where Fan joined him with the governor and the entire New Jersey congressional delegation. Afterward, he went to Wilmington to drop Fan back with Margaret and to visit his eighty-seven-year-old mother and his younger sister, Deborah, both of whom had taken up Delaware resi-dence during the war. He finished his homecoming circuit in Philadel-phia with yet another parade and ceremony. "I'm barnstorming in the interest of the children and grandchildren of all of us," he told news reporters at nearly every stop. "I am too damned old to fight another war, and I don't want them to have to fight one."[5]

There was one last orgy of fan mail and sentimentality. A shipmate from the *Don Juan de Austria* "rejoiced that your wonderful mother has lived to see your glory" and was certain "the soul of your father also must somehow, somewhere, know of it too." Another messmate proclaimed, "Long after you and I are gone, and our children and our children's children are no more, the generations yet unborn will re-member your valorous deeds and bless your name." A young woman wrote with "tears of joy" and exulted, "There is a God in Heaven, and next to that God in my admiration is you." In the months ahead, a survey of American college students identified Halsey as America's fa-vorite admiral. *Time* magazine declared that Halsey had been "a kind of seagoing General George Patton," the armored commander famous for his aggressive tank operations in Europe. Walter Winchell linked Halsey to John Paul Jones and George Dewey as the nation's preemi-nent naval heroes. Columbia, Lehigh, Washington, and American Universities all awarded Halsey honorary doctorate degrees. Juan

Trippe, the legendary chairman of Pan American Airways, offered Halsey a company vice presidency, and Charles Edison, the inventor's son and governor of New Jersey, twice implored Halsey to run as his replacement in Trenton.[6]

On November 20 Halsey was back in San Francisco and aboard the *South Dakota* to relinquish command of the Third Fleet and retire from a seagoing career of slightly over forty-five years. To a reporter, he remarked that leaving the Navy was like cutting off his right arm. It proved a long good-bye. The next month the Navy promoted him to its one remaining fleet admiral billet. Back in December 1944, Congress had authorized a quartet of five-star slots for each service. In the Army, George Marshall, Douglas MacArthur, Dwight Eisenhower, and Hap Arnold were logical choices. The Navy had three easy selections: William Leahy, Ernest King, and Chester Nimitz. Halsey's blunder at Leyte Gulf was then just six weeks old, however, and King was reluctant to promote Halsey while Spruance occupied the same echelon in the Pacific command hierarchy. So for the last Navy five-star slot, King endorsed to Forrestal every eligible officer: Halsey, Spruance, and four other admirals. The secretary was equally flummoxed, leaving the appointment unfilled for months before passing the buck to Truman. The president choose Halsey in recognition of his carrier raids early in the war and his contributions in the South Pacific, accomplishments Spruance could not match as Halsey's cruiser commander and Nimitz's chief of staff across the same months. Sentiment lingers still, however, that Truman bestowed the fifth star upon the wrong admiral, although Spruance maintained always and sincerely that the honorific was rightfully Halsey's before it was his.

In April 1946 Congress made the rank permanent, granting indefinite active-duty status to the eight men and providing a small office, modest administrative support, and pay and allowances of $15,750 a year in exchange for occasional obligations, usually of a ceremonial nature but sometimes in important capacities. Through 1947, these commitments propelled Halsey from coast to coast, usually about once a month, and upon a seven-nation South American goodwill tour. He served on numerous administrative, promotion, and retirement boards, and, for a while, engaged in nearly full-time speech making, where he dutifully "made a monkey out of myself for the benefit of the Navy." So ubiquitous were requests for his attendance in the years immediately following the war that three future presidents sought his presence, John Kennedy for the inaugural reunion of motor torpedo boat veterans in Boston, Lyndon Johnson to appear before a group of Texas businessmen, and Gerald Ford to headline a Michigan Navy Day parade, and so busy was the admiral that he turned them all down.[7]

This flurry of activity eventually faded. Testimony before Congress in 1947 on legislation to unify the War and Navy Departments and grant the Army Air Forces organizational autonomy constituted his last significant role as an officer. During the war and from his perch as the South Pacific commander, Halsey had forcefully supported defense unification, telling a high-powered committee investigating the matter that military leaders "ought to be made to do it" by congressional fiat after the war and, barring that, "have it beaten into their heads." Now that the fighting had stopped, however, he struggled to align his views with the Navy's official resistance to the initiative, first supporting a single department with the proviso that "the Commander of the Armed Forces be a naval officer," a preposterous requirement, before he abandoned altogether his support for defense unification, telling others that he had during the war conflated unification in Washington with unity of command in the field, an error it is hard to believe an experienced admiral could commit. His flip-flop invited press censure and, all in all, it was not a strong finish to a distinguished career.[8]

....

In the spring of 1946 Halsey undertook his memoir project. Literary agents, writers, and publishers had approached him on the subject since at least early 1944, including Robert McCormick of the *Chicago Tribune*. For a ghostwriter he chose Joseph Bryan, the son of a University of Virginia fraternity brother whose wartime *Saturday Evening Post* profile of the admiral had won wide acclaim. The *Post* paid $60,000 for the magazine rights and McGraw-Hill chipped in a

$20,000 advance for the book, from which Halsey's take was 60 percent, $48,000, or about $620,000 in 2015 dollars. For two weeks in February and another in March, Bryan and Halsey met in the Florida coastal home of Gene Tunney, the former heavyweight boxing champion whom Halsey knew through their mutual association with Spike Webb, the incomparable Academy boxing coach. There Halsey—with his wife, two Navy yeomen, an aide, and his daughter in tow—dictated recollections of his life. Bryan then composed a draft, passing it to Halsey and half a dozen wartime aides for review and comment, a cumbersome process guaranteed to invite untold third-party participation. Bryan soon complained that he had been unable "to salvage one single sentence" from Halsey's dictation and grew impatient when the first of numerous biographies, Ralph Jordan's *Born to Fight: The Life of Admiral Halsey,* beat him to press. Although Jordan's portrait was, in Halsey's view, "a combination of inaccuracies and gross exaggerations," Bryan fretted that he would never "get the whole bloody thing done," and, when he did finish, worried that his book was "about as timely as a report on Floyd Collins," whose dramatic death inside Mammoth Cave had captivated the nation in 1925.[9]

The *Post* installments began in June of 1947. Not long after the final segment appeared in late summer, McGraw-Hill published the autobiography under the title *Admiral Halsey's Story.* The magazine excerpts increased both subscription and newsstand sales for the *Post,* doing, the editor reported, "as well as the most exciting war stuff that we ran." The book underperformed, like most postwar memoirs of senior officers. Despite pleas from his literary agent, Halsey refused publicity tours for the book, eschewed bookstore signings, and declined to join a speaker's bureau at $500 to $750 per appearance, decisions that at the time and in the main were in accord with the dignity of his stature. *Admiral Halsey's Story* sold about 22,000 copies, never repaid its advance, and passed from print in 1951.[10]

By then the book had become an albatross to Halsey's legacy. There were passages warmly received then and worthy of admiration now, among them Halsey's robust defense of Admiral Husband

Kimmel, who had been dumped as the Pacific Fleet commander following the disaster at Pearl Harbor. But Halsey (or Bryan) could not quit wartime habits of embellishment. His bravado about drinking brought derision from prohibitionists, still a potent force in American society, and his account of wartime action tended toward the dramatic and the daring, obscuring the more studied aspects of his service.[11]

Most importantly, he courted argument with an ill-considered defense of his actions at Leyte Gulf. During the war and immediately after, naval officers had been content to bask in the battle's great success and keep its controversies in the shadows. Not Halsey. For public consumption he now described Kinkaid's mission as "defensive" and to "protect" MacArthur's forces; his own as "offensive" and to prowl "the ocean, striking at will." He "wondered how Kinkaid had let" Sprague's escort carriers "get caught" by Kurita's task force, and he had been "surprised" by Kinkaid's repeated pleas for help. He blasted the "inability" of George Kenney's land-based air forces "to give Leyte effective air support," thereby forcing the Third Fleet to attend to the Army's "knitting" in Philippine waters. He blamed divided command for an array of sins during the fight, which was true enough but had the effect of pointing fingers at his wartime superiors. His only mistake, he wrote, was the Third Fleet's fruitless return south to aid Sprague just as Halsey was closing on Ozawa's carriers, a blunder even then he attributed to Nimitz's corrupted message, "Where is Task Force 34? The World Wonders." It had always been Halsey's habit to praise liberally and censure carefully, but *Admiral Halsey's Story,* with its self-serving and churlish criticism of other commanders, opened wartime wounds that most of Halsey's naval associates would have preferred as healing scabs, taken to their graves.[12]

His version of events coincided with the first postwar assessments of the battle. In late 1946 the U.S. Strategic Bombing Survey published *Interrogations of Japanese Officials.* In early 1947 two books, James Field's *The Japanese at Leyte Gulf* and C. Vann Woodward's *The Battle for Leyte Gulf,* arrived. As Halsey's *Post* articles appeared, the *Virginia Quarterly Review* published an appraisal of the battle by Bernard Brodie, quickly becoming one of the nation's most prominent defense intellectuals. Finally, Kinkaid, who had earlier declined to compose his version of the battle, now helped Gilbert Cant pen, for *Life* magazine, "Bull's Run: Was Halsey Right at Leyte Gulf?" with the provocative subtitle, "Did a Japanese Blunder Save an American Army from a Halsey Mistake?" These accounts were variously sympathetic or hostile toward Halsey, but all focused on his decision to pursue the enemy carriers and none left any doubt that the Japanese had intended Ozawa's force as bait to lure him north, away from Leyte, a conclusion Halsey could never accept.[13]

To other officers, the budding literature had the whiff of a nasty family feud at a time when the Navy ought to have glowed in the aftermath of victory. Halsey's onetime mentor Bill Leahy thought Halsey's book uncharitable. "Personally," King wrote Halsey within a week of the *Post* edition covering Leyte Gulf, "I must say I did not like the tenor of the installment, neither as to Kinkaid" nor "as to the command set-up," suggesting that Halsey "review—and rewrite—the matter." Nimitz remained quiet, but Halsey knew his wartime boss took a dim view of the rush of postwar memoirs then flooding the market, and guessed correctly that Nimitz "did not care" for his contribution to the genre. As for the official Navy, Halsey heard "not a word," he told Bryan, "which is probably ominous. I imagine no one wants to get mixed up in a possible controversy." All this meant, he surmised, that "the fat is in the fire," adding, defiantly, "So what?"[14]

Disapproval did bite, however, especially when it came from senior members of the naval fraternity. Within weeks of his memoirs' publication, Halsey offered to step aside as honorary vice president of the Naval Historical Foundation, then headed by King. Within months, he told friends he had "no direct connection" with *Admiral Halsey's Story* "beyond hoping to collect a few shekels." Within three years, he wondered if its publication had rendered him "persona non-grata" in official circles. By 1951, he retained not a single copy, having to purchase one in preparation for a talk to the Air War College. In 1953 he concluded that it was a "mistake to write it," and two years after that he could not remember why he had been "foolish enough" to pen his memoirs.[15]

Once opened, however, the lesion of Leyte Gulf festered, flaring across the last decade of his life. From cocktail party comments, dinner speeches, school curricula, articles, and books, the controversy lived. On only a single occasion did Halsey as much as suggest culpability for his mistake in the battle, telling a historian writing a biography of Marc Mitscher in 1953 that he wished Spruance would have been at Leyte, where caution was demanded, and he in the Marianas, where boldness was needed. And on only a single occasion did he adopt a philosophical outlook toward the fight, telling a young girl who had solicited his help for a school paper in 1956 the "battle is very controversial and always will be."[16]

Throughout the 1950s Halsey engaged in a running battle with Samuel Eliot Morison, the dean of World War II naval historians then writing his seminal fifteen-volume history. The two had been friendly while Morison was with South Pacific forces in 1943 collecting information, and Halsey could find no fault with the scholar's volume on Guadalcanal, which feted the admiral. But in a 1951 lecture Morison opined that Halsey had blundered at Leyte, which convinced the aging admiral that Morison harbored a "personal animosity" toward him. The two commenced a dueling correspondence, occasionally directly and often by proxy, while Morison wrote his volume on Leyte. Published in 1958, *Leyte* dinged Halsey and his staff for sloppiness and poor judgment, infuriating the admiral. "Ham Dow came in to see me," Halsey reported to Carney shortly after its publication, "and we discussed a son-of-a-bitch named Morison." The book, Halsey declared, needed to be discredited "or I and my staff are going down in history as dubs." To Carney, Rollo Wilson, and any number of former staffers, he outlined a scheme to discredit Morison and, as he phrased it, "get the son-of-a-bitch's cajones in a vise." Halsey's former aides realized the battle had been a resounding American victory, and believed Morison's critique was rather akin to claiming that "a successful grand slam was played incorrectly." But they also saw no profit in a nasty paperclip war. "My Dear Admiral Bill," Carney wrote, Morison was a "widely acclaimed" writer and any attempt to hit back would likely "boomerang," further harming Halsey's standing.[17]

At any point before his autobiography appeared, a gracious mea culpa from Halsey would have secured the forgiveness that most of his contemporaries were willing to grant. But his contrived defense helped ensure a brouhaha that continued. The day Halsey died, Kinkaid wrote a Naval Academy professor that Halsey's lack of fealty to his mission was the "key to what happened at Leyte," and nothing else. When he learned of Halsey's death, he added a postscript: "The radio has just announced that Halsey died this morning at Fishers Island. All these comments were written before this announcement. I have not time to change them, nor do I desire to do so." The clash of memories and reputations extended well beyond the life span of any participant, and a bibliography prepared for the battle's fiftieth anniversary in 1994 listed 107 books devoted all or in part to the epic contest.[18]

. . . .

As he refought the Battle of Leyte Gulf, Halsey drifted from the Navy that had been his touchstone since birth. Nearly as soon as his return from the war he had fumbled for normalcy. There were mundane and necessary tasks. He filed his wartime tax returns. In 1946 he sold the Alexandria home for a $5,000 down payment and a $12,000 owner-financed note that later defaulted, forcing Halsey to sell it again in 1949, the place having done nothing but cost him money over the years. He worked to reestablish relations with Fan. Her mentality had brightened for a moment in the months following the war, but in May 1946 she was again hospitalized, this time at the Westbrook Sanatorium in Richmond, prompting Halsey to seek a regular routine, convinced that Fan would be "all but completely cured" if he could find some permanent and relaxed environment.[19]

In February 1947 he agreed to serve as the chairman of a University of Virginia capital fund drive to raise $18,000,000. His sentiment toward the university and the chance for Fan to live near family roots fueled enthusiasm for the task. He chaired meetings, traveled extensively, and made public appearances and speeches—forty-one in twelve different states from coast to coast in the second half of 1947 alone. He assimilated into the university, and commiserated with its president, Colgate Darden, when a federal appellate court compelled racial integration.[20]

He and Fan first rented a cottage at Farmington Country Club and then leased a comfortable residence with its own name, Four Acres, and a view of the Blue Ridge Mountains. "We're moved in," Halsey wrote a friend shortly thereafter, adding that they were "keeping house and thoroughly enjoying" a home of their own, the first in nearly fifteen years. Margaret's four children, aged four to sixteen, and young Bill's three-year-old delighted their grandparents with occasional visits, requiring babysitters for evenings out. "Ain't that something at our age?" Halsey squealed with delight to a friend. Halsey's mother died in 1948, but he renewed a kinship with his sister Deborah, whom he "loved being with." He even accepted with good grace a few outside speaking engagements: "Damn you!" he goaded Kitchell, then a promising executive with the Chemical Bank and Trust Company in New York, who had arranged an invitation to address a Maine bankers association. "To my dismay Fan said that it will be a fine trip, so I presume I am hooked, have swallowed the bait, and am sinking."[21]

Bliss did not last. Despite Halsey's hail-fellow gifts, the capital drive fell far short of the goal. A year after starting, pledges remained under $1,000,000 and expenses constituted a whopping 39 percent of promised donations. The university adjusted its target to $6,500,000, still a figure never met, and Halsey confronted a rare sense of professional failure. At home, Fan fell apart, again. Plagued by ill health, she established few close friends despite her family's two centuries in the region, and with Halsey often gone on business she was lonely, a typical trigger in past relapses. In November 1949, less than two years after moving to Charlottesville, she was back in arts and crafts class at Westbrook Sanatorium. To this development Halsey at first maintained a stiff upper lip, telling associates that Fan "was getting along very well, but it is going to be a long, up-hill fight." By early 1950 this optimism was gone. "I am sorry to tell you," he reported to Charlie Belknap, "that Fan is not a bit well. It is the same old trouble."[22]

Thus began Fan's final slide into a cerebral abyss and the end of Halsey's experiment with the ordinary. His fundraising efforts had offered introductions to scores of prominent men, them wishing to associate with a war hero, him interested in the gateway to another life that they could provide. One, a wealthy cotton merchant from Charlotte named Benjamin Gossett, became his initial conduit. The businessman provided $5,000 for a bust of Halsey later given to the Naval Academy, and through him Halsey became a member of a few small-time business boards, including that of the Pharis Tire and Rubber Company, and invested in numerous projects, among them the Liberia Company, a venture established by former secretary of state Edward Stettinius to capitalize on American trade with African nations. Halsey struck gold with none of these undertakings, most of which soon faded after Stettinius died in 1949 and Gossett passed away in 1951.[23]

But they gave the admiral a start in an upper-crust commercial world. Trips to New York offered admission to elite circles with the likes of Lowell Thomas, Babe Ruth, Jack Dempsey, Irving Berlin, Winthrop Rockefeller, and Eddie Rickenbacker. Coincident with Fan's return to the Westbrook Sanatorium in late 1949, one, Sosthenes Behn, the cofounder and chairman of the International Telephone and Telegraph Corporation, offered Halsey the board chairmanship of a subsidiary, the All-American Cable and Radio Corporation. Within a year Halsey was also a board member of ITT itself, and by early 1952 he had added to his portfolio the presidency of the International Tele-communications Laboratories and the chairmanship of the MacKay Radio and Telegraph Company, also ITT affiliates. Together with his military pay, investments, and other board memberships, Halsey earned about $40,000 per annum through most of the 1950s, or nearly $400,000 in 2015 dollars. Halsey's business interests sparked quiet heckles in naval circles as he technically remained on active duty and no other five-star officer had pursued commercial activity to the same extent. But his income allowed him to take first an apartment at 530 Park Avenue, where Bill Kitchell lived, and then a larger abode on the Upper East Side, on Eighty-Second Street, a move to accommodate the 1951 arrival of a frequent social companion, Barbara Cheney Watkins.[24]

Fan's decades-long struggle with mental illness and his own desire for something different had at last severed Halsey's marriage in all but legal name. Fan left Westbrook in the spring of 1950 and moved to Southern California, where young Bill, living in La Jolla, could act as family sentry. Halsey provided her with financial support and met expenses exceeding $15,000 for extended commitments at the Las Encinas Sanatorium in Pasadena in 1953 and 1955, a sum that reduced Halsey to inquire about two-dollar charges on hospital bills. But his distance sparked derision among Fan's extended family, including her cousin Armistead Dobie, a federal judge on the Fourth Circuit Court of Appeals, and for a time it strained relations with his son. By early 1953 Halsey reported that he had not seen or spoken to his wife for over two years, and communications with his son had become distant and clipped.[25]

When Fan's psychiatrist at Las Encinas suggested permanent institutional care in 1955, Halsey immediately concurred. "I am very much of the opinion that she will never be well," he told Dr. C. W. Thompson. Twenty years of struggle had confirmed a diagnosis of dementia praecox with homicidal tendencies, a disorder marked by cognitive disintegration known earlier as precocious madness and later recognized as a type of schizophrenia with violent tendencies. "I have not seen Mrs. Halsey for three and a half years," he told Thompson, admitting, "It was perfectly impossible for me to live in that atmosphere ever again. I know it is a very sad case but one with which I am completely unable to cope." He established a trust for his wife, who soon retired to a nursing home, and young Bill assumed legal guardianship. About the same time, Halsey agreed to become the chairman of the National Health Fund, a fundraising umbrella for state mental health commissions embarking upon a $5,000,000 appeal. "If I could save just one person from the hell I have gone through," he told Harold Stassen, "it would more than compensate me for my trouble." From that point forward, Halsey and Fan entered each other's distant orbits only when matters relating to trusts, wills, and estates required.[26]

. . . .

With his separation from Fan and his move to New York City, Halsey returned to the environs of his birth and took up a house far from where he had been. He enjoyed New York's stimulations while his health held. He maintained two offices, one at 67 Broad Street, ITT headquarters, and the other a few blocks away at 90 Church Street, the Navy building—both within a stone's throw of his grandfather James Drew Brewster's offices in the prior century. Duties with ITT were not strenuous; the nameplate on his office door carried the prior incumbent's name for months after his arrival, and he never learned much of ITT's business except, he told an acquaintance, that "it consists of a lot of wires, cables, and wireless." The Navy demanded less as well. Both, however, had the virtue of occasional travel: for seven weeks in the summer of 1951 he undertook a grand European tour to glad-hand for ITT, in 1952 he accompanied Behn to Buenos Aires, and in 1954 he made the long trek to Australia and New Zealand as a guest of the Canberra and Wellington governments, to commemorate Coral Sea Week with the former and his time as South Pacific commander with the latter.[27]

The Navy sent a physician with Halsey on that last trip, for by then he was in clear decline. As early as 1947 doctors had enjoined him from night driving, and in 1949 he had cataract surgery. Two years later he developed hypertension. By 1952, as he turned seventy, he wore hearing aids and gave up driving altogether. In 1956 he underwent an extensive operation to reconstruct part of a decaying jawbone, and his life had become, it seemed to him, merely one of "dodging in and out of hospitals." A moderate stroke in 1957 forced his retirement from ITT and its affiliated concerns, marked a general withdrawal from public life in all matters save a precious few, and triggered the addition of a Navy medical corpsman to Halsey's small staff of a naval aide and yeoman.[28]

As he aged, his interactions became uneven. He remained sentimental, always. He helped a slew of people soliciting his aid in this or that project. He jotted effusive notes to old shipmates predating World War II, and sometimes even to their widows. He tried to hire Benedicto

411

Tulao as a manservant when Tulao retired from the Navy. He toiled unsuccessfully for two years to get Hugh Barr Miller, who as a young lieutenant had survived a month on an enemy-held island in the South Pacific, the Medal of Honor. He battled a bout of flu to go to Sioux Falls to commemorate Joe Foss Airfield, named for a renowned Marine pilot in the South Pacific who was then governor of South Dakota. He chaired a losing bid to save his "sweetheart from World War II," the mighty *Enterprise,* from the scrap heap. And, to the end, he remained close to a small handful of former aides, among them Herb Carroll, who acted as informal liaison to the Navy Department; Harold Stassen, whom he had supported in a run for president in 1948 and who now served in Eisenhower's cabinet; Bill Kitchell, who became nothing short of Halsey's personal secretary and de facto guardian; and Mick Carney, who rose to the chief of naval operations in the mid-1950s but never escaped his role as Halsey's chief of staff. In the last years of his life, Halsey described Kitchell as "the best friend I have," and once closed a letter to Carney with "much love."[29]

Beyond these, however, Halsey's connections to the Navy atrophied and his relationships soured. He maintained social attachments to the Queenstown Destroyer Association, but kept up with almost no Navy peers from World War II. His attendance at a New York dinner honoring Chester Nimitz in 1954 was marked by its exception to Halsey's routine, and by the mid-1950s he "hated like hell" all "these Hip, Hip, Hooray shindigs" which required "hip hooray clothes." He grew tired of "autograph seekers" and the constant pressure "of a lot of damn bums on the telephone" seeking his time. In the few ceremonial gatherings he did attend, he took to feeling that "the Navy should change their plans to suit my liking." In 1957 a local chapter of the Navy League complained of hotel expenses associated with a Halsey dinner talk, including $168 for food and drink, $30 for long-distance calls, and $33 for flowers. Shortly after Miles Browning died in the mid-1950s, Halsey declined to assist his widow in substantiating Browning's illness in the spring of 1943, hidden as it was from the official record by the manner in which Halsey had sent him home at midwar, resulting in a reduction in Browning's death benefit. His friendship with Carnes Weeks, his Third Fleet physician, fractured with Weeks's unrelenting requests for favors, a long-unpaid $500 debt to Halsey, and a misunderstanding over the cost of a $10 lapel pin. "From the time you left my staff till the present," Halsey wrote Weeks in 1958, "you have appeared to me almost totally unreliable and untrustworthy." That may well have been, but Halsey's outburst sat at odds with a lifetime of tolerance for human foibles.[30]

Halsey's efforts to weasel out of obligations to Joe Bryan bordered on shameful. Bryan and his literary agent had for years worked to make a movie from *Admiral Halsey's Story,* but the admiral insisted that not a hint of his personal life or Fan's illness could appear in the script, frustrating potential producers eager to find some personal dramatic angle for a film. In 1958, Robert Montgomery, a onetime Halsey staffer in the South Pacific, and James Cagney teamed up to produce a Halsey movie that would shield the admiral's private life. Without including Bryan, Halsey sold Montgomery "the world-wide dramatic rights to my life story" for a $2,000 advance and 10 percent of net profits, afterward asking Bryan to waive his clear legal interest in any such project. Bryan declined to press the matter with the "old boy," as he took to calling the admiral, but he told his agent, "I'll never mention Halsey again."[31]

Like so much of Halsey's persona, the movie's façade proved a poor match with its subject. *The Gallant Hours* was filmed in 1959. It starred Cagney, whom Halsey's son thought a dead ringer for the wartime admiral, and premiered in 1960. The film's marketing promised much. "They called him the Bull of the Pacific," blurbed one typical ad, a fighting admiral whose order of the day was "to find the enemy and attack, repeat, attack." Navy bands played at larger theaters, Navy recruiters linked their efforts to the film's appearance, and its trailer suggested something of a Hollywood action blockbuster.[32]

The film was nothing of the sort. It was essentially a character study covering the five weeks in October and November 1942, when Halsey first commanded the South Pacific and the fate of Guadalcanal hung in the balance. Its cinematography rarely left the small, dark confines of Halsey's flag quarters on the *Argonne,* and then mostly to depict the analogous shipboard headquarters of Yamamoto, who was portrayed in an unusually evenhanded manner for the time. The movie's narrow focus was largely the result of Halsey's insistence that no personal matters pervade the film, and the *New York Times* movie critic Bosley Crowther wrote that the film could have easily masqueraded "as a stand out documentary." Despite good reviews, it fared poorly at the box office and today serves mostly as an artifact revealing Halsey's Janus face. Cagney, who interviewed Halsey twice and prepared diligently for the role, found his subject "far and away the most difficult" he had tried to capture on film. The actor got the admiral right, though. In his review, Crowther praised Cagney's performance, noting, "There is no braggadocio in it, no straining for bold or sharp effects." Instead, Cagney's Halsey "was one of the quietest, most reflective" characters the actor had portrayed across a long and distinguished career.[33]

. . . .

In the end Halsey retreated to an interior life. He saw his daughter Margaret regularly and young Bill periodically, their relationship having improved when Halsey resumed occasional visits to Fan after she entered a nursing home. Since the early 1950s Halsey had spent August at Fishers Island Country Club, known for its comfortable grace and seaside location just off the Connecticut coast near Mystic. He usually took a single room, most often on the second floor facing the ocean, at a rate of about $20 per day, although in 1957 he paid the princely sum of $1,000 for a two-week cottage rental to allow Margaret, now divorced, and her children to join him. In April 1959 he traveled with a Navy doctor, aide, and steward to Phoenix, as a guest at Kitchell's Arizona ranch, and La Jolla, to stay at Bill's California home, where he struck a young granddaughter as quiet and shy. A virus in June sent him into the hospital briefly and required the assignment of an additional medical corpsman to Halsey's staff. He returned to La Jolla in July, again with a doctor, aide, and steward, staying most of the month, visiting Fan on two occasions. He arrived at Fishers Island via Navy helicopter on August 1, 1959, for an intended stay through Labor Day, and checked into room forty-two. A little over two weeks later, at 11:10 AM on August 16, he was dead in his bed of a heart attack. Despite a life that ranged the globe, he died within a hundred miles of his birthplace, and, in sharp contrast to the large stage from which his renown sprang, he died alone.[34]

Halsey's last years traced an arc from the glory and fame known to a few to the solitude of death experienced by the many. A naval life had made his sea legs sturdy, but as he came ashore after World War II his equilibrium wavered. His ham-handed expression of his opinions on defense unification reminded careful observers that his career had been nearly devoid of staff or policy experience. His full-throated defense of Third Fleet action at Leyte Gulf was unwise, a folly he took to the grave. His pursuit of worldly success compared poorly to a lifetime of service, and sat at odds with the approach of every other five-star officer. He had never enjoyed a rich home life, and after the war he struggled toward companionship with his wife, a process made difficult by Fan's mental torments until at last he surrendered. Old age often strips acumen and even sanity. But well before infirmity, enough of Halsey's judgments were imperfect and enough of his personal relationships tentative to reveal something other than a man of supreme confidence, of calibrated boldness, and of constructive audacity.

As his funeral loomed, memory of him could at last begin.

Conclusion

A Naval Legacy

HALSEY'S FUNERAL BEFITTED a fleet admiral. A Navy plane carried his body to Washington on August 19. His remains lay in state at the National Cathedral until noon the following day. A military procession with caisson, Marine band, dozens of dignitaries, and honor troops from every branch of service accompanied him to Arlington National Cemetery. Chester Nimitz led honorary pallbearers to a hillside grave, near Halsey's father and close to a bevy of Navy heroes. A twenty-one-gun salute and military aircraft overhead pierced the still, humid air of late summer. Fan attended, and although there was much "apprehension as to how she would handle the situation," she played "the great lady" and would join her husband on the hill when her time came. A throng of press recorded the entire farewell, from the moment Halsey's body reached Anacostia Naval Air Station until they lowered the old man into the ground.[1]

From the periphery, persons great and ordinary commented. President Eisenhower mourned a "trusted friend" and joined with "countless other Americans who remember with gratitude and affection his inspiring leadership." Henry Cabot Lodge lamented the passing of an "unusually warm and magnetic man." The prime minster of New Zealand recalled Halsey's first visit to Wellington in early 1943, where Halsey "seemed an elemental force, like ocean weather." Those who knew Halsey best merely sighed, sad. "Our beloved Admiral Bill has passed from the scene," Carney wrote Halsey's son, "but he leaves one of the finest legacies ever bequeathed to our Service and our Country by a naval leader." He was "completely honest," endowed with "moral courage," and "unfailingly loyal," traits that created "greater affection and loyalty than I have ever seen rendered to any other military leader." Eisenhower proclaimed that Halsey's "name will be honored always by the country he loved and served so well," and Jerry Bogan, who had first served as Halsey's deputy at Pensacola and was with him at Leyte Gulf, declared that Halsey would "never be forgotten."[2]

How he would be remembered was history's province. To the Navy he remains a beloved figure best embraced from afar. His mistakes at Leyte Gulf and in two typhoons persist as great mars, and his impassioned wartime language grew crude as the years became decades. For its beau ideal of a fighter, the Navy adopted Marc Mitscher and commissioned an inspirational biography of that great carrier commander for its midshipmen. For World War II leaders, the Navy hews closer to Nimitz, whose talents as the Pacific Fleet commander remain indisputable, and Ray Spruance, who emerged after the war as a nearly "mystical figure in the hierarchy of the naval heroes." Nimitz's name adorns the Naval Academy library and an entire class of supercarriers, a ship type upon which he never served, and Spruance lends his name to a main academic building at the Naval War College and to a prominent postwar class of destroyers. In turn, Halsey got two small warships and an Annapolis gym named after him.[3]

For most, Halsey remains either a stereotype or an enigma. Soon after the war, the finest historian ever to write on Leyte Gulf devoted his penultimate paragraph to Halsey, comparing him to Hotspur, the outsized, impetuous counterweight to Shakespeare's philosophical and contemplative Hamlet. Seven decades later, a superb historian assessing wartime admirals could do no better than slice Halsey into two men—rather as an illusionist would—grading Halsey's contributions before 1944 as outstanding and his performance thereafter as poor, an analysis perfectly consistent with a public portrait of Halsey as legendary.[4]

But Halsey was human. He passed most of his days in obscure naval service. He inhabited the sea, sometimes to the detriment of life's other dimensions. He excelled in direct military leadership, especially within the intimacy of ship life and in combat, and often struggled to establish the same rich interactions when not on the quarterdeck.

Though war itself is worthy of no praise, it was for his career a happy accident that the First and Second World Wars bracketed his time in uniform—the first confirming Rear Admiral William Sims's gamble on Halsey following Halsey's mental collapse, and the second offering a stage upon which Halsey's particular traits could flourish, at least in the beginning. After the attack on Pearl Harbor, Halsey was for a time the nation's most successful sea commander, his carrier raids marked as much by the care of his training as by the pluck of his temperament. In the South Pacific he alone among senior officers established close working relations with both Douglas MacArthur and Chester Nimitz, making effective a raft of cockeyed compromises in strategy and command across the middle of the war. In Nouméa, he adapted better than nearly any peer to the unanticipated challenges of combined and joint operations, to the point that he later attributed Allied victory in the Pacific to, in order of importance, submarines, radar, airplanes, and bulldozers. Big warships did not make the list.[5]

At sea again with the Third Fleet, Halsey's grasp of change across a career of vast transitions weakened. He had displayed great mental agility through most of his career: He began his time in uniform as industrialization propelled the nation and her Navy toward new horizons, he later eschewed traditional tours on battleships for service aboard innovative destroyers, and he went boldly into aviation at an age few others did. By 1944, however, the war had become too large, too modern, and too bureaucratized for his deeply etched patterns of thought and habits of command, learned three decades earlier as part of Sims's small destroyer flotilla. At Leyte Gulf and in two typhoons, Halsey's ability to conform to an ever-changing world culminated, and the massive size and sprawling complexity of the Pacific Fleet proved better suited to Spruance's managerial approach than to Halsey's command instincts. His father had failed to keep apace of change at the front end of industrial-age war, and now Halsey faltered as the era reached an apogee with the atomic blasts over Hiroshima and Nagasaki. Halsey rode the riptide of twentieth-century progress better than many and longer than most, but at last he fell, his capacity to adapt exhausted.

It requires no magician's trick to understand this. From start to finish I have tried to impart humanity to Halsey, a task both central and elusive for biography, once the veneer of celebrity encrusted Halsey's outside and obscured everything within. But humanity is all that has ever been needed to grasp the complexities of his life and wartime service: the daring raids, the great victories, the giant personality, the inexplicable mistakes, and the grand blunders. Humanity encompasses this and more, and if Halsey's complexities were greater in their consequence than those of most people, they were not larger in their nature. Halsey was all that history accords: big, bold, and daring. In three dimensions, however, he was also a little bit more, and a little bit less, than the silhouette of his outsized legend.

NOTES

INTRODUCTION

1. All newspaper obituaries in Papers of William F. Halsey, box 48, Library of Congress.
2. E. B. Potter, ed., *Sea Power* (New York: Bramhall, 1960), 660, 700; Russell Weigley, *The American Way of War* (Bloomington: Indiana University Press, 1977), 300; Kenneth Hagan, *This People's Navy: The Making of American Sea Power* (New York: Free Press, 1991), 316; John Costello, *The Pacific War, 1941–1945* (New York: Quill, 1981), 275, 354; Bob Drury and Tom Clavin, *Halsey's Typhoon* (New York: Atlantic Monthly Press, 2007); Max Hastings, *Retribution* (New York: Knopf, 2008); Evan Thomas, *Sea of Thunder* (New York: Simon and Schuster, 2006); Clark Reynolds, *The Fast Carriers* (Annapolis: Naval Institute, 1968), xix, 163.
3. Ralph Jordan, *Born to Fight* (Philadelphia: David McKay, 1946); Chandler Whipple, *William F. Halsey: Fighting Admiral* (New York: Putnam, 1968), front plate, 218; Benis Frank, *Halsey* (New York: Ballantine, 1974), 9, 159; James Merrill, *A Sailor's Admiral: A Biography of William F. Halsey* (New York: Thomas Y. Crowell, 1976), 70; E. B. Potter, *Bull Halsey* (Annapolis: Naval Institute, 1985), xi; John Wukovits, *Admiral "Bull" Halsey* (New York: Palgrave, 2010), 1.
4. James Michener, *Tales of the South Pacific* (New York: Pocket Books, 1958); James Jones, *The Thin Red Line* (New York: Delta Books, 1998); Tom Clancy, *The Hunt for Red October* (Annapolis: Naval Institute, 1984).
5. William Halsey with Joseph Bryan, *Admiral Halsey's Story* (New York: McGraw-Hill, 1947), 81.
6. John Miller, *Cartwheel: The Reduction of Rabaul* (Washington, DC: U.S. Government Printing Office, 1959); Samuel Eliot Morison, *Breaking the Bismarcks Barrier* (Boston: Little, Brown, 1950).
7. Halsey and Bryan, *Admiral Halsey's Story*, 1.

1. AN AMERICAN ARISTOCRACY

1. William Halsey with Joseph Bryan, *Admiral Halsey's Story* (New York: McGraw-Hill, 1947), 2.
2. Unless otherwise noted, Halsey genealogy derived from Jacob Halsey, *Thomas Halsey of Hertfordshire, England, and South Hampton, Long*

Island, 1591–1679, with His American Ancestors to the Eighth and Ninth Generations (Morristown, NJ: Jerseyman Office, 1895).

3. John Adams, *New Jersey Journal,* November 18, 1788.

4. Clarence S. Brigham, *History and Bibliography of American Newspapers, 1690–1820* (New York: American Antiquarian Society, 1947), 510; Adams to Halsey, letter to the editor, *Newark Gazette,* November 4, 1800.

5. Robert Ernst, *Rufus King: American Federalist* (Chapel Hill: University of North Carolina Press, 1968), 410.

6. Edwin Burrows and Mike Wallace, *Gotham: A History of New York City to 1898* (Oxford: Oxford Paperbacks, 2000), 597; Brigham, *History and Bibliography of American Newspapers,* 607; *Dictionary of American Biography* (New York: Charles Scribner's Sons, 1936), 383. Halsey's published works were *A Memoir of the Construction of the Croton Aqueduct* (1843) and *Abridged Tactics for the School of the Soldier and of the Company* (1826).

7. *New York Herald,* May 3, 1855, 7.

8. William Bradford, *Of Plymouth Plantation, 1620–1647* (New York: McGraw-Hill, 1981), 324–328; Thomas Hutchinson cited in Emma Brewster Jones, *The Brewster Genealogy, 1566–1907* (Whitefish, MT: Kessinger Publishing, 2010), 212. Unless otherwise noted, Brewster genealogy derived from Jones.

9. 1850 Census, Philadelphia County, North Pennsylvania, 901.

10. Halsey to Walter Bateman, February 16, 1954, Halsey to Mrs. Roy N. Halsey, March 25, 1954, Halsey to Shelby Cullom Davis, June 2, 1952, and Halsey to Robert W. Spake, October 8, 1956, Papers of William F. Halsey, box 12, Library of Congress.

11. William F. Halsey Memoir, 11, in Joseph Bryan III Papers, Virginia Historical Society.

2. THE ADMIRAL'S CAPTAIN

1. Ric Burns and James Sanders, *New York: An Illustrated History* (New York: Knopf, 2003), 94; Edwin Burrows and Mike Wallace, *Gotham: A History of New York City to 1898* (Oxford: Oxford Paperbacks, 2000), 889–895.

2. Nathaniel Philbrick, *Sea of Glory* (New York: Penguin Books, 2004), 4.

3. William F. Halsey Memoir, 11, in Joseph Bryan III Papers, Virginia Historical Society (hereafter Halsey Memoir).

4. U.S. Naval Academy, *Annual Register of the United States Naval Academy, 1870* (Washington, DC: U.S. Government Printing Office, 1970), 16; Peter Karsten, *The Naval Aristocracy: The Golden Age of Annapolis and the*

Emergence of Modern American Navalism (New York: Free Press, 1972), 4; Robeson to Candidates, in U.S. Naval Academy, *Annual Register, 1870*, 27–28.

5. U.S. Naval Academy, Conduct Books, 1869–1870, 1870–1871, 1871–1872, and 1872–1873, U.S. Naval Academy Special Collections.

6. Charles Paullin, *Paullin's History of Naval Administration, 1775–1911* (Annapolis: Naval Institute, 2012), 313, 318, 341; Albert Barker, *Everyday Life in the Navy* (Philadelphia: Gorham Press, 1928), 98; *Alert* ship log, June 1876, Record Group 24, National Archives; Robley Evans, *A Sailor's Log: Recollections of Forty Years of Naval Life* (Annapolis: Naval Institute, 1994), 137; Kemp Tolley, *Yangtze Patrol: The U.S. Navy in China* (Annapolis: Naval Institute, 2012), 26.

7. *Alert* ship log, entries of September 30, 1876; December 31, 1876; March 31, 1877; and June 30, 1877.

8. Barker, *Everyday Life in the Navy*, 17, 100–111; *Alert* ship log, August 1896; Reynolds to Halsey, August 12, 1877, and secretary of the Navy to Halsey, September 8, 1877, both in Halsey Service Jacket, Record Group 24, National Archives.

9. *Iroquois* and *Ranger* ship logs, 1881–1884 and 1887–1890, respectively, Record Group 24, National Archives; secretary of the Navy to James Sands, April 11, 1884, Yates Stirling to secretary of the Navy, May 11, 1885, Robert Boyd to secretary of the Navy, April 18, 1878, and James Sands to secretary of the Navy, May 28, 1884, all in Halsey Service Jacket.

10. Halsey Memoir, 9.

11. *New York* ship log, 1896–1897, Record Group 24, National Archives; Officer Efficiency Report, July 1, 1896, Halsey Service Jacket; Winfield Scott Schley, *Forty-Five Years under the Flag* (New York: D. Appleton, 1904), 246.

12. Theodore Roosevelt, *The Works of Theodore Roosevelt, National Edition*, vol. 13 (New York: P. F. Collier, 1904), 184–186.

13. Edmund Morris, *The Rise of Theodore Roosevelt* (New York: Random House, 2001), 593, 596.

14. *Adams* ship log, April 1900, Record Group 24, National Archives; Medical Ticket, March 20, 1899, Halsey Service Jacket.

15. Bradley Fiske, *From Midshipman to Admiral* (New York: T. Werner Laurie, 1919), 348.

16. *General Alvara* ship log, August 1900, Record Group 24, National Archives.

17. G. Chase, W. Sexton, and E. Kalbfus to William Halsey, July 22, 1901, in *General Alvara* ship log.

18. Fiske, *From Midshipman to Admiral*, 317, 320; Yates Stirling, *Sea Duty: The Memoirs of a Fighting Admiral* (New York: Random House, 1939),

61; William F. Halsey Jr. to W. M. Callaghan, February 23, 1956, Papers of William F. Halsey, box 11, Library of Congress.

19. Report of Captain's Mast, November 7, 1900, December 7, 1900, January 19, 1901, May 6, 1901, and March 29, 1902, *General Alvara* ship log.

20. Paullin, *Paullin's History of Naval Administration,* 457; Stirling, *Sea Duty,* 271; Officer Efficiency Reports, December 31, 1901, and April 1, 1902, Halsey Service Jacket.

21. *Manila* ship log, April 1902, Record Group 24, National Archives.

22. William Halsey, "Some Experiences On Board the USS Manila," *Proceedings,* Fall 1902, 565–571.

23. Ibid., 567.

24. *Manila* ship log, June 1902.

25. Halsey, "Some Experiences On Board," 569.

26. *Manila* ship log, June 1902.

27. *Des Moines* ship log, September 1905, Record Group 24, National Archives.

28. *Des Moines* ship log, August 1906.

29. Medical Ticket, September 3, 1906, Halsey Service Jacket.

30. Ibid.

31. Ibid.

32. Fiske, *From Midshipman to Admiral,* 71, 163.

33. Karsten, *Naval Aristocracy,* 271; Paullin, *Paullin's History of Naval Administration,* 464–465, 473.

34. Karsten, *Naval Aristocracy,* 36, 50, 58, 86; Medical Ticket, September 3, 1906, Halsey Service Jacket.

35. Fiske, *From Midshipman to Admiral,* 379.

36. William Halsey, "Our National Flag: A Short History of Its Development; Its Lack of Uniformity in Government Displays; and Sentiment or Sentimentality in Its Use," *Proceedings,* Fall 1912, 879–884; William Halsey, "The Flag of the Chesapeake: A Plea for the Banner with Fifteen Stripes," *Proceedings,* Spring 1913, 790–792.

37. Questionnaire, 1912, Halsey Service Jacket.

3. A CAREFREE AND CAREFUL BOY

1. New York City Directories, 1865, 1870, 1880, New York Public Library.

2. William F. Halsey Memoir, 2, Joseph Bryan III Papers, Virginia Historical Society (hereafter Halsey Memoir).

3. Halsey Memoir, 3; John Lloyd to Halsey, October 3, 1944, Papers of William F. Halsey, box 3, Library of Congress (hereafter Halsey Papers).

4. Halsey Memoir, 5–6.
5. Ibid., 4; Halsey to William Brewster, February 2, 1955, Halsey Papers, box 11.
6. Halsey Memoir, 11; Halsey to Ronald Macdonald, January 7, 1947, Halsey Papers, box 6; Halsey to chief of police, San Diego, January 14, 1941, Halsey to J. A. Furer, December 14, 1942, Halsey Papers, box 2.
7. Halsey Memoir, 7.
8. Ibid.
9. Ibid.
10. William Halsey with Joseph Bryan, *Admiral Halsey's Story* (New York: McGraw-Hill, 1947), 3–4.
11. Chandler Whipple, *William F. Halsey: Fighting Admiral* (New York: Putnam, 1968), 22.
12. Halsey and Bryan, *Admiral Halsey's Story,* 5.
13. E. B. Potter, *Bull Halsey* (Annapolis: Naval Institute, 1985), 27.
14. William F. Halsey, Record of Naval Cadet, U.S. Naval Academy Special Collections.
15. Peter Karsten, *The Naval Aristocracy: The Golden Age of Annapolis and the Emergence of Modern American Navalism* (New York: Free Press, 1972), 10; Kenneth Hagan, *This People's Navy: The Making of American Sea Power* (New York: Free Press, 1991), 28.
16. Jack Sweetman, *United States Naval Academy: An Illustrated History* (Annapolis: Naval Institute, 1979), 149.
17. U.S. Naval Academy, *Annual Register of the United States Naval Academy, 1901* (Washington, DC: U.S. Government Printing Office, 1970).
18. William F. Halsey, Record of Naval Cadet, U.S. Naval Academy Special Collections.
19. Ibid.
20. Halsey Memoirs, 17; Halsey to William Dolan, February 26, 1957, Halsey Papers, box 12; Halsey and Bryan, *Admiral Halsey's Story,* 8.
21. Halsey and Bryan, *Admiral's Halsey's Story,* 6–7; Halsey to Edwin Johnson, April 8, 1957, Halsey Papers, box 12.
22. William F. Halsey, Record of Naval Cadet, U.S. Naval Academy Special Collections; Halsey Memoir, 29.
23. Halsey and Bryan, *Admiral Halsey's Story,* 7.
24. *Lucky Bag* (yearbook), 1904, 110.
25. Halsey and Bryan, *Admiral Halsey's Story,* 7; Halsey Memoir, 27–28; *Chesapeake* ship log, July 1903, Record Group 24, National Archives.
26. *Chesapeake* ship log, June 6, 1903.
27. *Lucky Bag,* 1904, 41.
28. *Lucky Bag,* 1904, 25.

29. *Lucky Bag,* 1904, 176.
30. Halsey and Bryan, *Admiral Halsey's Story,* 7.

4. NEW OFFICER, NEW NAVY, NEW CENTURY

1. William F. Halsey Memoir, 38, Joseph Bryan III Papers, Virginia Historical Society (hereafter Halsey Memoir).
2. Halsey Memoir, 43; Halsey to Don McLellan, May 11, 1938, Papers of William F. Halsey, box 2, Library of Congress (hereafter Halsey Papers); William F. Halsey with Joseph Bryan, *Admiral Halsey's Story* (New York: McGraw-Hill, 1947), 9.
3. Elting Morison, *Admiral Sims and the Modern American Navy* (Boston: Houghton Mifflin, 1942), 138–141; Yates Stirling, *Sea Duty: The Memoirs of a Fighting Admiral* (New York: Random House, 1939), 108.
4. Halsey and Bryan, *Admiral Halsey's Story,* 10; Frank Adams to Halsey, November 30, 1942, Halsey Papers, box 3; Halsey Memoir, 55.
5. Halsey Memoir, 55–56.
6. Edmund Morris, *Theodore Rex* (New York: Random House, 2001), 494; Samuel Carter, *The Incredible Great White Fleet* (New York: Crowell-Collier, 1971), 1.
7. *Harper's Weekly,* January 4, 1908, 10.
8. James Reckner, *Teddy Roosevelt's Great White Fleet* (Annapolis: Naval Institute, 2001), 23.
9. Ibid., 48; Halsey and Bryan, *Admiral Halsey's Story,* 12.
10. Reckner, *Teddy Roosevelt's Great White Fleet,* 27.
11. Halsey Memoir, 69–70.
12. Morris, *Theodore Rex,* 509; Reckner, *Teddy Roosevelt's Great White Fleet,* 59, 103.
13. Robert Hart, *The Great White Fleet: Its Voyage around the World, 1907–1909* (New York: Little, Brown, 1965), 193, 109; Reckner, *Teddy Roosevelt's Great White Fleet,* 101, 139.
14. Hart, *Great White Fleet,* 80–81.
15. Ibid., 99–101; Carter, *Incredible Great White Fleet,* 44; Henry Wiley, *An Admiral from Texas* (New York: Doubleday, Doran, 1934), 139; Halsey Memoir, 67.
16. Halsey Memoir, 72, 79, 69.
17. Philip Andrews, "With the Fleet," *Harper's Weekly,* March 21, 1908, 21; Reckner, *Teddy Roosevelt's Great White Fleet,* 88; Halsey Memoir, 69.
18. Robert Dunn, "The Work and Play of the Fleet," *Harper's Weekly,* January 25, 1908, 10–12; Henry Davis, "Leaves from the Log," *Harper's Weekly,* February 29, 1908, 16–17.

19. Officer Efficiency Reports, various dates, Halsey Service Jacket, National Personnel Records Center, St. Louis; Halsey Memoir, 84.
20. Morris, *Theodore Rex,* 549.
21. Ibid., 548–549; Halsey and Bryan, *Admiral Halsey's Story,* 14.
22. Reckner, *Teddy Roosevelt's Great White Fleet,* 82.
23. Francis Medhurst, "A Ballad of the Fleet," *Harper's Weekly,* March 20, 1909, 13.

5. A NAVAL BAND OF BROTHERS

1. William F. Halsey Memoir, 94, Joseph Bryan III Papers, Virginia Historical Society (hereafter Halsey Memoir).
2. Officer Efficiency Reports, William Halsey, various dates, 1909, Halsey Service Jacket, National Personnel Records Center, St. Louis (hereafter Halsey Service Jacket).
3. Halsey to R. B. Strassburger, March 12, 1910, Strassburger to Halsey, March 16, 1910, Papers of William F. Halsey, box 2, Library of Congress (hereafter Halsey Papers); William F. Halsey with Joseph Bryan, *Admiral Halsey's Story* (New York: McGraw-Hill, 1947), 17.
4. Jack Quimby and Alfred Reynold, Officer Efficiency Reports, various dates, 1911–1912, Halsey Service Jacket.
5. Halsey Memoir, 98.
6. Addie Bagley Daniels to Halsey, September 3, 1943, Halsey Papers, box 3.
7. Halsey and Bryan, *Admiral Halsey's Story,* 18.
8. Halsey Memoir, 130.
9. Sims to T. Knox, March 12, 1920, Papers of William Sims, box 69, Library of Congress (hereafter Sims Papers).
10. William Sims, "Naval War College Principles and Methods Applied Afloat," *Proceedings,* March–April 1915, 386, 385; Sims to wife, March 25, 1914, Sims Papers, box 7; Elting Morison, *Admiral Sims and the Modern American Navy* (Boston: Houghton Mifflin, 1942), 302.
11. Morison, *Admiral Sims and the Modern American Navy,* 295; Halsey to Charlie Belknap, August 13, 1943, Halsey Papers, box 3.
12. Dudley Knox, "The Great Lesson from Nelson for Today," *Proceedings,* March–April 1914, 308.
13. William Sims, "Notes on the Tactical Signals Book," Sims Papers, box 58.
14. Dudley Knox, "The Role of Doctrine in Naval Warfare," *Proceedings,* March–April 1915, 318; "Flotilla Tentative Doctrine," March 3, 1914, Sims Papers, box 58.
15. Sims to wife, February 10, 1914, and March 8, 1914, Sims Papers, box 7.

16. Sims to wife, February 23, 1914, Sims Papers, box 7; William Sims, "Memo to Commanding Officers, Torpedo Flotilla: Fleet Tactical Problem No. 37," Sims Papers, box 58.

17. Gerald Wheeler, *Admiral William Veazie Pratt, US Navy: A Sailor's Life* (Washington, DC: U.S. Government Printing Office, 1974), 75; Knox, "The Role of Doctrine in Naval Warfare," 314.

18. Sims to A. L. Bristol, July 11, 1916, Sims Papers, box 57; Halsey Thesis, Naval War College, 1933, Halsey Papers, box 45; Sims to William Barnes, June 3, 1915, Sims Papers, box 57.

19. Morison, *Admiral Sims and the Modern American Navy*, 302.

20. Sims Papers, box 57.

21. Halsey and Bryan, *Admiral Halsey's Story*, 47; William Sims, "General Comment on the Inspection of the Flotilla," November 14, 1913, Navy file 27364-131, Record Group 80, National Archives; Officer Efficiency Report, William Halsey, November 17, 1913, Halsey Service Jacket; Sims to J. J. Knapp, May 24, 1914, Sims Papers, box 21; Sims to Dudley Knox, October 26, 1914, Sims Papers, box 69; Sims, "Naval War College Principles," 396–397.

22. William Halsey Medical File, Halsey Service Jacket.

23. Ibid.

24. Officer Efficiency Reports, September 30, 1915, and January 4, 1916, Halsey Service Jacket.

25. Halsey Medical File, Halsey Service Jacket.

26. Victor Blue to Halsey, July 3, 1915, Halsey Papers, box 1; Yates Stirling, *Sea Duty: The Memoirs of a Fighting Admiral* (New York: Random House, 1939), 111.

27. Chandler Whipple, *William F. Halsey: Fighting Admiral* (New York: Putnam, 1968), 55–56.

28. Halsey and Bryan, *Admiral Halsey's Story*, 26.

29. Ibid., 26.

30. Sims to Navy Department, May 16, 1917, Sims Papers, box 95; Sims to secretary of Navy, May 30, 1917, Sims Papers, box 95; Sims to Navy Department, August 1, 1917, Halsey Service Jacket.

31. E. Keble Chatterton, *Danger Zone: The Story of the Queenstown Command* (Whitefish, MT: Kessinger, 2010), 138.

32. Lewis Bayly, *Pull Together: The Memoirs of Admiral Sir Lewis Bayly* (London: G. G. Harrap, 1939), 126; Morison, *Admiral Sims and the Modern American Navy*, 383.

33. Halsey and Bryan, *Admiral Halsey's Story*, 28; Joseph Taussig, "Destroyer Experiences during the Great War," *Proceedings*, January 1923, 47; Lewis

Bayly, "Sailing Orders," December 31, 1917, ADM 137 / 1528, National Archives, United Kingdom.

34. Halsey and Bryan, *Admiral Halsey's Story,* 31; Whipple, *William F. Halsey,* 61.

35. Halsey and Bryan, *Admiral Halsey's Story,* 35.

36. Halsey Memoir, 163.

37. Peter Macfarlane, "The Greatest Game," *Saturday Evening Post,* July 27, 1918, 26; Halsey and Bryan, *Admiral Halsey's Story,* 35.

38. Pringle to Sims, May 21, 1918, Sims Papers, box 54; chief of staff, destroyer flotilla, to Sims, "Historical Sketch of Activities during the War," March 12, 1919, Sims Papers, box 94; Bayly, *Pull Together,* 233; Halsey and Bryan, *Admiral Halsey's Story,* 27.

39. William N. Still, *Queenstown Patrol, 1917: The Diary of Joseph Knefler Taussig* (Darby, PA: Diane Publishing, 1996), 111; Halsey and Bryan, *Admiral Halsey's Story,* 36; Sims to Pringle, May 16, 1918, Sims Papers, box 79.

40. Macfarlane, "The Greatest Game," 13; Lewis Bayly, "Situation in Ireland," April 28, 1918, ADM 137 / 1512, 241, National Archives, United Kingdom; Sims to Bayly, June 8, 1918, Sims Papers, Bayly Special Correspondence, box 47; Bayly to Admiralty, "Protection of Naval Establishment in Ireland," April 16, 1918, ADM 137 / 1512, 199–204, National Archives, United Kingdom; Halsey Memoir, 165.

41. Joseph Taussig, "Destroyer Experiences during the Great War," *Proceedings,* February 1923, 234.

42. Halsey and Bryan, *Admiral Halsey's Story,* 39; Halsey to Sims, July 6, 1918, Halsey Papers, box 2; "Historical Summary of Destroyer Base 6," table 1, 4, Sims Papers, box 94.

43. Charles Wheeler Oral History, 250–252, U.S. Naval Institute.

44. Macfarlane, "The Greatest Game," 27; Peter Macfarlane, "Heroes All," *Saturday Evening Post,* April 19, 1919, 33; Pringle to Sims, May 12, 1918, Sims Papers, box 79; Fred Macfarlane to Halsey, June 8, 1941, and Halsey to MacFarlane, June 27, 1941, Halsey Papers, box 2.

45. Halsey diary, cited in Halsey Memoir, 167; Halsey Memoir, 166; Halsey and Bryan, *Admiral Halsey's Story,* 36; Halsey Memoir, 166–167; Halsey and Bryan, *Admiral Halsey's Story,* 36; Walter Delany, *Bayly's Navy* (Washington, DC: Naval Historical Foundation, 1980), 35; William Halsey, Book Reviews, *Proceedings,* September 1939, 1335.

46. Halsey Memoir, 185–201.

47. Henry Wiley, *An Admiral from Texas* (New York: Doubleday, Doran, 1934), 239; Wheeler, *Admiral William Veazie Pratt,* 156–160; E. P. Forrestel,

Admiral Raymond A. Spruance, USN: A Study in Command (Washington, DC: U.S. Government Printing Office, 1966), 9; Thomas Buell, *The Quiet Warrior: A Biography of Admiral Raymond A. Spruance* (Annapolis: Naval Institute, 1988), 46–47.

48. Halsey and Bryan, *Admiral Halsey's Story*, 42.
49. Ibid., 46.
50. Officer Efficiency Reports, William Halsey, July 24, 1920, March 31, 1921, November 14, 1919, January 13, 1920, October 30, 1920, and June 21, 1921, Halsey Service Jacket; commander, Destroyer Squadron Eleven, to commander, Destroyer Squadron Five, "Destroyer Division 2: Excellent Performance of, during Fleet Maneuvers, 29 September–2 October 1920," October 18, 1920, Halsey Service Jacket.
51. Robert Carney Oral History, 342, Columbia University Oral History Collection, Columbia University Special Collections; Halsey Memoir, 224; secretary of Navy to William Halsey, August 29, 1921, and Warren Harding to William Halsey, August 30, 1921, Halsey Service Jacket.
52. *Du Pont* ship log, May 29, 1909, and November 7, 1909, Record Group 24, National Archives; *Flusser* ship log, October 1913, and *Dale* ship log, July 1, 1924, September 26, 1924, and September 30, 1924, Record Group 24, National Archives; *Wickes* ship log, March 30, March 31, April 18, and May 3, 1921, Record Group 24, National Archives.
53. Whipple, *William F. Halsey*, 29.
54. Officer Efficiency Report, William Halsey, August 20, 1918, Halsey Service Jacket.
55. Halsey to Wiley, November 4, 1942, Halsey Papers, box 2.

6. BECOMING BILL HALSEY

1. William Halsey with Joseph Bryan, *Admiral Halsey's Story* (New York: McGraw-Hill, 1947), x–xv, 17; Charles Wheeler Oral History, 252, U.S. Naval Institute.
2. Halsey and Bryan, *Admiral Halsey's Story*, xii.
3. Halsey to J. B. Rutter, August 21, 1935, Papers of William F. Halsey, box 2, Library of Congress (hereafter Halsey Papers); Halsey to officer in charge, July 15, 1935, Halsey Papers, box 2; "Itemized Invoice," December 3, 1938, Halsey Papers, box 2; Halsey to Naval Mutual Aid Association, November 3, 7, 18, and 21, 1938, Halsey Papers, box 2; IRS to Halsey, September 29, 1941, and Halsey to IRS, November 7, 1941, and February 13 and March 23, 1942, Halsey Papers, box 2.
4. Halsey and Bryan, *Admiral Halsey's Story*, 44.
5. Halsey to L. W. Tostevin, August 8, 1939, Halsey Papers, box 2.

6. Halsey to Colgate Darden, May 23, 1952, Halsey Papers, box 9; Halsey to Roy Stratton, June 25, 1954, Halsey Papers, box 10; Thomas Moorer Oral History, U.S. Naval Institute, 76.
7. Rees Gillespie to Halsey, October 17, 1939, Halsey to Gillespie, November 25, 1939, Halsey Papers, box 2.
8. Wyman Packard, *A Century of U.S. Naval Intelligence* (Washington, DC: Naval Historical Center, 1996); Halsey and Bryan, *Admiral Halsey's Story,* 47.
9. Halsey and Bryan, *Admiral Halsey's Story,* 48; Packard, *A Century of U.S. Naval Intelligence,* 66.
10. Robert Murphy, *Diplomat among Warriors* (Garden City, NY: Doubleday, 1964), 13.
11. Packard, *A Century of U.S. Naval Intelligence,* 42.
12. Halsey to Office of Naval Intelligence, January 27, 1923, March 19, 1923, July 24, 1923, November 5, 1923, December 19, 1923, January 30, 1924, and March 12, 1924, in Register of Letters Received from Naval Attachés, 1901–1929, vol. 15, Record Group 38, National Archives (hereafter Register of Letters); Halsey and Bryan, *Admiral Halsey's Story,* 48.
13. Halsey to Office of Naval Intelligence, June 13, 1923, in Register of Letters.
14. Halsey to Gideon Timberlake, January 7, 1942, Halsey Papers, box 2.
15. Halsey and Bryan, *Admiral Halsey's Story,* 50–52.
16. Halsey to director of Naval Intelligence, March 19, 1923, entry 78, box 73, case 21060-191, Record Group 38, National Archives; secretary of state to secretary of the Navy, January 3, 1923, box 144, file 4790-168, Record Group 80, National Archives.
17. Halsey to director of Naval Intelligence, February 10, 1923, entry 78, box 2, Record Group 38, National Archives; Zachary Lansdowne to director of Naval Intelligence, July 3, 1923, entry 78, box 74, case 210-60-256, Record Group 38, National Archives; Halsey, "German Air Routes and Commercial Aviation, 1889–1939," entry 98, box 367, Record Group 38, National Archives; Halsey to Office of Naval Intelligence, June 10, 1923, box 367, Record Group 38, National Archives; Halsey to Office of Naval Intelligence, December 20, 1923, Register of Letters; Halsey to Office of Naval Intelligence, January 29, 1923, March 13, 1923, and March 26, 1923, Register of Letters; Halsey to Office of Naval Intelligence, November 29, 1922, and January 20, 1923, Register of Letters.
18. Clark Reynolds, *Admiral John H. Towers: The Struggle for Naval Air Supremacy* (Annapolis: Naval Institute, 1991), 181; William Trimble, *Jerome C. Hunsaker and the Rise of American Aeronautics* (Washington, DC: Smithsonian Institution Press, 2002), 182–194.

19. Halsey to Office of Naval Intelligence, May 28, 1923, September 4, 1923, September 5, 1923, January 23, 1923, July 3, 1923, July 11, 1923, and September 28, 1924, Register of Letters; Murphy, *Diplomat among Warriors,* 23.

20. Officer Efficiency Reports, William F. Halsey, October 13, 1922, March 12, 1924, and August 16, 1924, Halsey Service Jacket, National Personnel Records Center, St. Louis (hereafter Halsey Service Jacket).

21. Halsey Memoir, 185–187; Murphy, *Diplomat among Warriors,* 25.

22. Halsey to secretary of the Navy via director of Naval Intelligence, March 27, 1924, Andrews to Halsey, May 26, 1924, Bureau of Navigation to Andrews, June 3, 1924, Halsey Medical File, Halsey Service Jacket; Thomas Buell, *The Quiet Warrior: A Biography of Admiral Raymond A. Spruance* (Annapolis: Naval Institute, 1988), 51.

23. Halsey and Bryan, *Admiral Halsey's Story,* 49; Officer Efficiency Report, William Halsey, May 25, 1925, Halsey Service Jacket; Charles Minor to Department of Navy, August 5, 1926, Halsey Medical File, Halsey Service Jacket.

24. Officer Efficiency Report, William Halsey, July 16, 1926, Halsey Service Jacket.

25. Paul Ringer to Navy Department, August 7, 1926, Halsey Medical File, Halsey Service Jacket.

26. Medical Tickets, various dates, 1925–1926, Halsey Medical File, Halsey Service Jacket.

27. Secretary of Navy Curtis Wilbur to Halsey, July 21, 1928, Halsey Service Jacket.

28. Medical Tickets, various dates, 1925–1926, Halsey Medical File, Halsey Service Jacket; Halsey Memoir, 243.

29. U.S. Naval Academy, *Annual Register of the United States Naval Academy,* 1926, 1927, 1928, 1929, 1930 (Washington, DC: U.S. Government Printing Office); Halsey and Bryan, *Admiral Halsey's Story,* 52.

30. Rear Admiral Robinson to John Cremen, January 5, 1931, Records of Superintendent, Summer Education and Training, box 23, U.S. Naval Academy Special Collections; October 4, 1927, November 5, 1929, Halsey Medical File, Halsey Service Jacket.

31. Officer Efficiency Reports, William Halsey, March 30, 1932, and June 15, 1932, Halsey Service Jacket.

32. Harris Laning, "Opening Address to Class of 1933," Record Group 16, Naval War College Archives; John Hattendorf, B. Mitchell Simpson, and John R. Wadleigh, *Sailors and Scholars: The Centennial History of the U.S. Naval War College* (Newport, RI: Naval War College, 1984), 160, 73.

33. Hattendorf et al., *Sailors and Scholars,* 144–145.

34. William Halsey, Naval War College Thesis, "The Relationship in War of Naval Strategy, Tactics, and Command," 10–11, Halsey Papers, box 45.

35. E. B. Potter, *Nimitz* (Annapolis: Naval Institute, 1976), 136.

36. Halsey and Bryan, *Admiral Halsey's Story,* 54; Reading List for 1933, Record Group 4, Naval War College Archives; Halsey, "The Relationship in War," 1–11.

37. Orders, various dates, 1934, Halsey Service Jacket; Hattendorf et al., *Sailors and Scholars,* 148.

38. Harry Ball, *Of Responsible Command: A History of the U.S. Army War College* (Carlisle, PA: Alumni Association of the Army War College, 1994), 218; Halsey and Bryan, *Admiral Halsey's Story,* 54.

39. Harriet Holther to Halsey, July 27, 1938, Edward Van Devanter to Frances Halsey, August 20, 1935, Halsey to William Geary, May 20, 1940, Halsey to Captain Knight, January 19, 1935, Halsey to William Geary, May 20, 1940, and Halsey to Harriet Holther, September 18, 1939, Halsey Papers, boxes 2, 3, 5, and 6.

40. *Register of the Commissioned and Warrant Officers of the Navy of the United States and of the Marine Corps,* 1904, 1910, 1917, 1921, 1926, 1927, 1934 (Washington, DC: U.S. Government Printing Office).

41. Halsey, "The Relationship in War," 1–11.

7. THE OLDEST AVIATOR

1. William Halsey with Joseph Bryan, *Admiral Halsey's Story* (New York: McGraw-Hill, 1947), 55.

2. *Insurance Field,* October 14, 1932, 5, 17, in Statistical Addendum, Papers of William F. Halsey, box 19, Library of Congress (hereafter Halsey Papers); Halsey and Bryan, *Admiral Halsey's Story,* 55.

3. Halsey and Bryan, *Admiral Halsey's Story,* 56; Halsey Flight Training Records, Pensacola Naval Aviation Museum Special Collections (hereafter Halsey Flight Records); Leahy to Zogbaum, August 18, 1934, Halsey Flight Records; Zogbaum to Halsey, August 20, 1934, Leahy to Halsey, August 21, 1934, Leahy to Halsey, November 27, 1934, and Zogbaum to Halsey, December 4, 1934, Halsey Papers, box 2.

4. Memorandum for Commander Pownall from Commander J. C. Adams, Medical Corps, March 3, 1938, Halsey to Charles Pownall, February 10, 1938, Pownall to Halsey, March 3, 1938, Halsey Papers, box 2; chief of the Bureau of Medicine to chief of the Bureau of Navigation, January 15, 1937, chief of the Bureau of Aeronautics to chief of the Bureau of Navigation, February 4, 1937, Leahy to Halsey, February 6, 1937, chief of the Bureau of Medicine to chief of the Bureau of Navigation, December 20,

1937, and chief of the Bureau of Medicine to chief of the Bureau of Navigation, November 15, 1940, Halsey Papers, box 2.

5. "Students of Naval Aviation Class of 34-3," Records of the Bureau of Aeronautics, General Correspondence, NC 49, box 3985, Record Group 72, National Archives (hereafter Bureau of Aeronautics Correspondence); L. N. Medaris, November 5, 1934, Halsey Flight Records; G. A. Dussault, February 5, 1935, Halsey Flight Records; Fitzhugh Lee Oral History, 17, U.S. Naval Institute; Halsey and Bryan, *Admiral Halsey's Story*, 58–59.

6. "Commander Squadron VN5D8 to Halsey re: The Flying Jackass Trophy," April 1, 1935, Halsey Papers, box 2.

7. Halsey and Bryan, *Admiral Halsey's Story*, 60; Halsey to William Halsey III, March 17, 1934, Halsey Papers, box 2; Joseph Clark Oral History, 166, Columbia University Oral History Collection, Columbia University Special Collections.

8. Halsey Flight Records; Francis Foley Oral History, 163, U.S. Naval Institute.

9. Halsey Flight Certificates and Schedules, Halsey Flight Records.

10. *Saratoga* ship log, August 16, 1935, October 4, 5, 10, 16, 1935, and May 12, 1937, Record Group 24, National Archives; Donald Duncan Oral History, 252, Columbia University Oral History Collection, Columbia University Special Collections; Clark Reynolds, *Admiral John H. Towers: The Struggle for Naval Air Supremacy* (Annapolis: Naval Institute, 1991), 273, 275, 280; Officer Efficiency Reports, William Halsey, September 30, 1935, March 31, 1936, and June 9, 1936, Halsey Service Jacket, National Personnel Records Center, St. Louis (hereafter Halsey Service Jacket); Halsey and Bryan, *Admiral Halsey's Story*, 62; Halsey to Zogbaum, August 3, 1935, Halsey Papers, box 2.

11. Felix Stump to Halsey, July 11, 1935, Halsey to Stump, July 15, 1935, Halsey Papers, box 2; officer descriptions from Clark Reynolds, *The Fast Carriers* (Annapolis: Naval Institute, 1968), xix–xxi.

12. Halsey and Bryan, *Admiral Halsey's Story*, 62; Halsey to Frederick Horne, July 23, 1936, and August 14, 1936, Halsey Papers, box 2; Halsey to Cook, January 9, 1936, Sherman to Halsey, August 6, 1936, Duncan to Halsey, August 10, 1936, Halsey Papers, box 2; Gardner to Halsey, August 13, 1936, Halsey Papers, box 14.

13. Records Relating to U.S. Navy Fleet Problems I to XXII, 1923–1941, roll 21, frames 643–644, roll 22, frames 350–643, roll 23, frames 581–665, National Archives (hereafter Fleet Problems).

14. Hepburn, "Comments and Recommendations of Fleet Problem XVIII," June 13, 1937, roll 23, frames 598–599; Horne, "Comments and Recom-

mendations of Fleet Problem XVIII," June 13, 1937, Fleet Problems, roll 23, frame 610.

15. Officer Efficiency Reports, William Halsey, September 30, 1935, March 31, 1936, and June 9, 1936, Halsey Service Jacket.

16. U.S. Navy Department, *Register of the Commissioned and Warrant Officers of the Navy of the United States and of the Marine Corps, 1935, 1936* (Washington, DC: U.S. Government Printing Office); Thomas Buell, *Master of Sea Power: A Biography of Fleet Admiral Ernest J. King* (Boston: Little, Brown, 1980), 90.

17. "History of Naval Air Station Pensacola" and "Memo, Inspection of Naval Air Station, Pensacola," January 11, 1938, Bureau of Aeronautics Correspondence, box 3866; Halsey to American Surety Company of New York, November 24, 1939, Halsey Papers, box 2.

18. Commandant, Pensacola Naval Air Station, to chief, Bureau of Aeronautics, December 17, 1937, and January 21, 1938, Halsey Papers, box 1; William Ashford Oral History, 27, Papers of William Ashford, East Carolina University Special Collections (hereafter Ashford Oral History); commandant, Pensacola Naval Air Station, to judge advocate general of the Navy, December 31, 1931, Bureau of Aeronautics Correspondence, box 3866; chief of the Bureau of Aeronautics to commandant, Pensacola Naval Air Station, August 23, 1937, commandant, Pensacola Naval Air Station, to chief, Bureau of Aeronautics, September 13, 1937, Halsey Papers, box 1; W. D. Sample, "Inspection of Naval Air Station, Pensacola," January 11, 1938, Bureau of Aeronautics Correspondence, box 3866; Halsey to Park Trammell, March 19, 1936, Halsey Papers, box 2.

19. Ashford Oral History, 28.

20. Clark Reynolds, *Admiral John H. Towers: The Struggle for Naval Air Supremacy* (Annapolis: Naval Institute Press, 1991), xxi; Halsey to chief, Bureau of Navigation, January 12, 1938, Bureau of Aeronautics Correspondence, NC 49, box 3998; Gerald Bogan Oral History, 63, U.S. Naval Institute.

21. Halsey to Aubrey Fitch, March 14, 1938, Halsey Papers, box 2.

22. Halsey to Richard Foster, October 21, 1937, Halsey Papers, box 2; Halsey to Aubrey Fitch, May 6, 1938, Halsey Papers, box 2; "Claim for Travel of Dependent," Halsey to chief of the Bureau of Supplies and Accounts, October 13, 1938, Halsey Service Jacket; Halsey to Charles Pannill, October 13, 1938, Halsey Papers, box 1.

23. Halsey to King, May 16, 1938, Halsey Papers, box 13.

24. Thomas Moorer Oral History, 76, U.S. Naval Institute; Halsey to King, November 15, 1938, Halsey Papers, box 13.

25. Halsey to Cook, January 21, 1939, Halsey Papers, box 13.

26. Fleet Problem XX, Aircraft Battle Force, roll 29, frames 235–264, Fleet Problems; commander, Aircraft Battle Force, "Comments and Recommendations on Fleet Problem XX," roll 26, frame 149, Fleet Problems.

27. Narrative, Fleet Problem XX, Aircraft Battle Force, roll 29, frames 263–264; commander, Aircraft Battle Force, "Comments and Recommendations on Fleet Problem XX," roll 26, frame 150, Fleet Problems.

28. Carrier Division Two, General Comments on Fleet Problem XX, roll 29, frames 417–418; commander, Aircraft Battle Force, "Comments and Recommendations on Fleet Problem XX," roll 26, frame 151; Narratives of Fleet Problem XX, Aircraft Battle Force, and commander, Carrier Division Two, roll 29, frames 235–264 and 294–307, Fleet Problems; Buell, *Master of Sea Power,* 104–105.

29. Buell, *Master of Sea Power,* 76, 103; Ashford Oral History, 29; Halsey to King, June 22, 1939, Ernest King Papers, box 7, Library of Congress.

30. Halsey and Bryan, *Admiral Halsey's Story,* 66; Bogan Oral History, 66–67; George Anderson Oral History, 54–56, U.S. Naval Institute; John Hoover Oral History, 256, Columbia University Oral History Collection, Columbia University Special Collections.

31. William F. Halsey Memoir, 277, Joseph Bryan III Papers, Virginia Historical Society.

32. Saratoga Narrative, Fleet Problem XXI, roll 35, frames 163–170, Fleet Problems.

33. Narrative of Events, Commander Carrier Division One, Fleet Problem XXI, roll 33, frame 6; Narrative, Commander Carrier Division One, Fleet Problem XXI, roll 35, frames 132–140; Narrative, Task Force Nine, Fleet Problem XXI, roll 32, frames 327–329, Fleet Problems; Halsey and Bryan, *Admiral Halsey's Story,* 67–68; Admiral Halsey, Critique of Fleet Problem XXI, roll 36, frame 300, Fleet Problems.

34. Summary of Comments and Recommendations, Fleet Problem XXI, Commander Carrier Division One, roll 35, frame 101, Fleet Problems.

35. George Baer, *One Hundred Years of Sea Power: The U.S. Navy, 1890–1990* (Palo Alto, CA: Stanford University Press, 1994), 182–183.

36. Halsey and Bryan, *Admiral Halsey's Story,* 68; Halsey to Bristol, July 4, 1940, Halsey Papers, box 13; Halsey to Fitch, April 26, 1941, Halsey Papers, box 13.

37. John Lundstrom, *Black Shoe Carrier Admiral: Frank Jack Fletcher at Coral Sea, Midway, and Guadalcanal* (Annapolis: Naval Institute, 2006), 28.

38. Nimitz to Kimmel, February 28, 1941, Nimitz Papers, Naval Historical Center; John Hoover Oral History, 259–260.

39. Samuel Eliot Morison, *The Two Ocean War: A Short History of the United States Navy in the Second World War* (Boston: Little, Brown, 1963), 154;

Thomas H. Buell, *The Quiet Warrior: A Biography of Admiral Raymond A. Spruance* (Annapolis: Naval Institute, 1988), 140.

40. Halsey to Arthur Bristol, July 4, 1940, Halsey to Towers, July 11, 1940, Towers to Halsey, July 25, 1940, Halsey Papers, box 16; Thomas Moorer Oral History, 75; George Anderson Oral History, 54; Slade Cutter Oral History, 313, U.S. Naval Institute.

41. Thomas Wildenberg, *Destined for Glory: Dive Bombing, Midway, and the Evolution of Carrier Air Power* (Annapolis: Naval Institute, 2012); Craig C. Felker, *Testing American Sea Power: U.S. Navy Strategic Exercises, 1923–1940* (College Station: Texas A&M University Press, 2013), 58–59, 155; John Lundstrom, *The First Team: Pacific Naval Air Combat from Pearl Harbor to Midway* (Annapolis: Naval Institute, 2005), 16, 10–11.

42. Staff editorial, "The Case for the Naval Aviator," *Popular Aviation*, September 1939, 14; Halsey to Richardson, August 24, 1939, Halsey Papers, box 2; Halsey to Towers, December 13, 1940, Halsey Papers, box 13; Wildenberg, *Destined for Glory*, 166–170.

43. William Halsey, "Airpower and the US Navy," Halsey Papers, box 45, emphasis in original.

44. Microfilm collection, "Aviation in Fleet Exercises, 1911–1939," Rear Admiral W. F. Halsey, Fleet Problem XXI, Critique of Fleet Problem XXI, roll 36, frame 291; Prepared Remarks, Halsey Speech, 1941, Halsey Papers, box 45.

8. THE FIRST FIGHTER

1. Halsey to Charles Pannill, October 13, 1938, Papers of William F. Halsey, box 2, Library of Congress (hereafter Halsey Papers); Halsey to Purnall Galleries, November 27, 1940, Halsey to Buffum's, January 2, 1941, Halsey to W. Gearing, March 18, 1940, and March 30, 1940, Halsey to Wiley Grandy, October 19, 1940, Halsey to J. R. Hornberger, October 19, 1940, and Halsey to J. J. Gaffney, Halsey Papers, box 2; William Ashford Oral History, 39, Papers of William Ashford, East Carolina State University Special Collections; Halsey to *Honolulu Advertiser*, February 12, 1942, Halsey Papers, box 2.

2. Edwin Layton, *"And I Was There": Pearl Harbor and Midway—Breaking the Secrets* (Old Saybrook, CT: Konecky and Konecky, 1985), 215; William Halsey with Joseph Bryan, *Admiral Halsey's Story* (New York: McGraw-Hill, 1947), 73–74.

3. Richard Connolly Oral History, 94, Columbia University Oral History Collection, Columbia University Special Collections; commander, Task Force Eight, Action Report of December 7, 1941, box 85, Record Group

38, National Archives; Halsey Testimony, Hart Inquiry, 329, Halsey Papers, box 35.

4. Halsey and Bryan, *Admiral Halsey's Story,* 77; William F. Halsey Memoir, 313, Joseph Bryan III Papers, Virginia Historical Society (hereafter Halsey Memoir); Ashford Oral History, 47.

5. Halsey and Bryan, *Admiral Halsey's Story,* 77; Samuel Eliot Morison, *The Rising Sun in the Pacific* (Boston: Little, Brown, 1948), 212–215.

6. John Lundstrom, *The First Team: Pacific Naval Air Combat from Pearl Harbor to Midway* (Annapolis: Naval Institute, 2005), 16; Morison, *The Rising Sun in the Pacific,* 211–212.

7. Morison, *The Rising Sun in the Pacific,* 215; Ashford Oral History, 44; Lundstrom, *The First Team,* 18.

8. Lundstrom, *The First Team,* 21–22.

9. Halsey and Bryan, *Admiral Halsey's Story,* 80.

10. Ian Toll, *Pacific Crucible: War in the Pacific Islands, 1941–1942* (New York: Norton, 2012), 40; Halsey and Bryan, *Admiral Halsey's Story,* 81.

11. Halsey Testimony, Commission to Investigate the Japanese Attack of December 7, 1941, on Hawaii, Proceedings of the Roberts Commission, January 2, 1942, 605–632, and Halsey Testimony, Proceedings of the Hart Inquiry, April 12, 1944, 293–332, Halsey Papers, box 35; Halsey and Bryan, *Admiral Halsey's Story,* 82.

12. Paul Dull, *A Battle History of the Imperial Japanese Navy* (Annapolis: Naval Institute, 1978), 13; John Prados, *Combined Fleet Decoded: The Secret History of American Intelligence and the Japanese Navy in World War II* (Annapolis: Naval Institute, 1995), 195; Morison, *The Rising Sun in the Pacific,* 217.

13. Halsey to *Honolulu Advertiser,* February 12, 1942, and Halsey to William Calhoun, January 10, 1942, Halsey Papers, box 13.

14. Maurice Matloff and Edwin Snell, *Strategic Planning for Coalition Warfare, 1941–1942* (Washington, DC: U.S. Government Printing Office, 1953), 147; Ronald H. Spector, *Eagle against the Sun: The American War with Japan* (New York: Random House, 1985), 100.

15. Thomas B. Buell, *Master of Sea Power: A Biography of Fleet Admiral Ernest J. King* (Boston: Little, Brown, 1980), 150; Halsey Memoir, 325; Halsey and Bryan, *Admiral Halsey's Story,* 85.

16. Layton, *"And I Was There,"* 353; Toll, *Pacific Crucible,* 155; Thomas Wildenberg, *All the Factors of Victory: Admiral Joseph Mason Reeves and the Origins of Carrier Airpower* (Herndon, VA: Potomac Books, 2003), 239, 264; Richard Frank, "Picking Winners," *Naval History,* June 2011, 25; Buell, *Master of Sea Power,* 169.

17. Morison, *The Rising Sun in the Pacific,* 256–257.

18. Lundstrom, *The First Team*, 36; E. B. Potter, *Nimitz* (Annapolis: Naval Institute, 1976), 41; Buell, *Master of Sea Power*, 177; Layton, *"And I Was There,"* 391.

19. Halsey and Bryan, *Admiral Halsey's Story*, 85.

20. Ashford Oral History, 51; Lundstrom, *The First Team*, 62

21. Lundstrom, *The First Team*, 59–62; Morison, *The Rising Sun in the Pacific*, 262; Halsey and Bryan, *Admiral Halsey's Story*, 89.

22. Prados, *Combined Fleet Decoded*, 95–96; Lundstrom, *The First Team*, 61; Halsey Memoir, 333.

23. Halsey and Bryan, *Admiral Halsey's Story*, 90; Lundstrom, *The First Team*, 63.

24. Lundstrom, *The First Team*, 63.

25. Potter, *Nimitz*, 47; commander, Task Force Eight, "After Action Report," March 12, 1942, box 85, Record Group 38, National Archives; Halsey and Bryan, *Admiral Halsey's Story*, 93.

26. Halsey and Bryan, *Admiral Halsey's Story*, 93; Morison, *The Rising Sun in the Pacific*, 263.

27. Monohan to Halsey, August 6, 1947, and Halsey to Monohan, August 14, 1947, Halsey Papers, box 6; Prados, *Combined Fleet Decoded*, 238.

28. Commander, Task Force Eight, "After Action Report," March 12, 1942, box 85, Record Group 38, National Archives.

29. Ibid.; Morison, *The Rising Sun in the Pacific*, 263; John Lundstrom, *Black Shoe Carrier Admiral: Frank Jack Fletcher at Coral Sea, Midway, and Guadalcanal* (Annapolis: Naval Institute, 2006), 70; Halsey to Andrews, February 7, 1942, Halsey Papers, box 2.

30. Layton, *"And I Was There,"* 363; Matome Ugaki, *Fading Victory: The Diary of Admiral Matome Ugaki, 1941–1945* (Pittsburgh: University of Pittsburgh Press, 1991), 81–84, 104.

31. Lundstrom, *Black Shoe*, 65–67; Potter, *Nimitz*, 39; Halsey and Bryan, *Admiral Halsey's Story*, 96; "The War Summarized," *New York Times*, February 14, 1942, 1; "Tokyo Losses Heavy," *New York Times*, February 13, 1942, 1; "Pearl Harbor Well Repaid by Navy," *New York Times*, February 14, 1942, 5; Halsey and Bryan, *Admiral Halsey's Story*, 97.

32. Commander, Task Force Sixteen, "After Action Report," March 28, 1942, box 91, Record Group 38, National Archives.

33. Clarence Earle Dickinson, *The Flying Guns: Cockpit Record of a Naval Pilot from Pearl Harbor through Midway* (New York: Zenger Publications, 1980), 122.

34. Halsey Memoir, 348; Prange, *Fading Victory*, 94, 101; "Japanese Pounded," *New York Times*, March 26, 1942, 1.

35. Halsey and Bryan, *Admiral Halsey's Story*, 101.

36. Jimmy Doolittle, *I Could Never Be So Lucky Again* (New York: Bantam Books, 1991), 237.
37. Craig Nelson, *The First Heroes: The Extraordinary Story of the Doolittle Raid* (New York: Penguin Books, 2003), 61.
38. Edwin Layton Papers, Collection 69, box 34, Naval War College Archives (hereafter Layton Papers); Doolittle, *I Could Never Be So Lucky Again*, 61.
39. Toll, *Pacific Crucible*, 286; Doolittle, *I Could Never Be So Lucky Again*, 251.
40. Halsey and Bryan, *Admiral Halsey's Story*, 102.
41. Ibid., 103; Nelson, *The First Heroes*, 158; Halsey to Doolittle, April 24, 1942, Ernest J. King Papers, box 2, Operational Archives, Navy Yard, Washington, DC.
42. Commander, Task Force Sixteen, "War Diary," April 1942, box 61, Record Group 38, National Archives; "After Action Report, Doolittle Raid," box 10, Record Group 18, National Archives.
43. Layton, *"And I Was There,"* 387; Spruance Reminiscences, Collection 37, box 7, Naval War College Archives.
44. Prados, *Combined Fleet Decoded*, 288; Layton, *"And I Was There,"* 387; Layton Papers, Collection 39, box 34.
45. Halsey and Bryan, *Admiral Halsey's Story*, 97; Buell, *The Quiet Warrior*, 128.
46. Lundstrom, *Black Shoe*, 91; Buell, *The Quiet Warrior*, 158.
47. Clay Blair, *Silent Victory: The U.S. Submarine War against Japan* (Annapolis: Naval Institute, 2001), 114, 214; Frank, "Picking Winners," 25; Dickinson, *The Flying Guns*, 113; Gordon Prange, *At Dawn We Slept* (New York: Penguin, 1982), 118.
48. "Halsey of Naval Family," *New York Times*, February 13, 1942, 8; "Japanese Pounded," *New York Times*, March 26, 1942; "Seaman at Work," *Time*, April 6, 1942; Buell, *The Quiet Warrior*, 129.
49. Dickinson, *The Flying Guns*, 123, 113.
50. Halsey to W. H. Martin, February 12, 1942, Halsey Papers, box 2; Halsey to Benjamin Gossett, December 21, 1950, Halsey Papers, box 14; Layton, *"And I Was There,"* 364.

9. THE RIGHT MAN

1. *Enterprise* ship log, May 1942, Record Group 24, National Archives.
2. William Halsey with Joseph Bryan, *Admiral Halsey's Story* (New York: McGraw-Hill, 1947), 107.
3. Thomas H. Buell, *The Quiet Warrior: A Biography of Admiral Raymond A. Spruance* (Annapolis: Naval Institute, 1988), 135.

4. Nimitz to King, Message 280339, May 28, 1942, CinCPac Secret and Confidential Message File, reel 13, Record Group 38, National Archives; Nimitz to King, May 28, 1942, Chester Nimitz Papers, Operational Archives, Navy Yard, Washington, DC (hereafter Nimitz Papers).

5. William Ashford Oral History, 62–66, Papers of William Ashford, East Carolina University Special Collections; "Record of Study of Vice Admiral William F. Halsey, Jr, June 14–August 28, 1942, Warren T. Vaughan," Halsey Medical File, Halsey Service Jacket, National Personnel Records Center, St. Louis; Halsey to Vaughan, February 11, 1943, Papers of William F. Halsey, box 3, Library of Congress (hereafter Halsey Papers).

6. Bureau of Personnel to Nimitz, July 22, 1942, and Nimitz to Bureau of Personnel, July 26, 1942, CinCPac Secret and Confidential Message File, reel 19, Record Group 38, National Archives; "Souvenir of Hickory Hill," July 29, 1942, Halsey Papers, box 2; Halsey and Bryan, *Admiral Halsey's Story,* 108.

7. Ernest King, "Notes to Cominch-CinCPac conferences," Ernest King Papers, Library of Congress, box 4.

8. CinCPac to ComSoPac, October 17, 1942, Message 170249, SOPAC Incoming Messages, Top Secret Blue, Record Group 18, National Archives; Ashford Oral History, 72.

9. Maurice Matloff and Edwin Snell, *Strategic Planning for Coalition Warfare, 1941–1942* (Washington, DC: U.S. Government Printing Office, 1953), 162–164.

10. Louis Morton, *The War in the Pacific: The Fall of the Philippines* (Washington, DC: U.S. Government Printing Office, 1962), 144.

11. Ronald H. Spector, *Eagle against the Sun: The American War with Japan* (New York: Random House, 1985), 191; Richard Frank, *Guadalcanal* (New York: Random House, 1990), 57.

12. Frank, *Guadalcanal,* 366–367; Samuel Eliot Morison, *The Struggle for Guadalcanal* (Boston: Little, Brown, 1948), x.

13. Frank, *Guadalcanal,* 330, 317.

14. Morison, *The Struggle for Guadalcanal,* 178; Frank, *Guadalcanal,* 332–333.

15. Ghormley to Nimitz, September 7, 1942, Robert Ghormley Papers, East Carolina University Manuscript Collections; Frank, *Guadalcanal,* 227.

16. Command Diary, South Pacific War Diary, October 2, 1942, box 49, Record Group 38, National Archives; E. B. Potter, *Nimitz* (Annapolis: Naval Institute, 1976), 192–193; Frank, *Guadalcanal,* 333.

17. Hanson Baldwin Oral History, 349, U.S. Naval Institute; Henry Arnold, *Global Mission* (New York: Harper and Row, 1949), 240–342; Spector, *Eagle against the Sun,* 207; Nimitz to King, October 8, 1942, with

transcripts of the September 28 and October 2 *Argonne* conferences, Nimitz Papers; King to Nimitz, October 16, 1942, *Admiral Nimitz Command Summary, 1941–1945* (Graybook), microfilm frame 895.

18. William F. Halsey Memoir, 368, Joseph Bryan III Papers, Virginia Historical Society; Halsey and Bryan, *Admiral Halsey's Story*, 111; Potter, *Nimitz*, 197; James Hornfischer, *Neptune's Inferno: The U.S. Navy at Guadalcanal* (New York: Bantam Books, 2011), 424.

19. George Dyer, *The Amphibians Came to Conquer: The Story of Admiral Richmond Kelly Turner*, vol. 1 (Washington, DC: Department of the Navy, 1991), xix.

20. Millard Harmon, "Harmon Report," 705.04A, Historical Research Agency, Maxwell Air Force Base; Eric Bergerud, *Fire in the Sky: The Air War in the South Pacific* (Boulder, CO: Westview Press, 2000), 128.

21. Halsey and Bryan, *Admiral Halsey's Story*, 117; Archer Vandegrift, *Once a Marine: The Memoirs of General A. A. Vandegrift* (New York: Norton, 1964), 184; Halsey and Bryan, *Admiral Halsey's Story*, 17.

22. Frank, *Guadalcanal*, 355.

23. Morison, *The Struggle for Guadalcanal*, 199; Halsey and Bryan, *Admiral Halsey's Story*, 120.

24. John Lundstrom, *The First Team: Pacific Naval Air Combat from Pearl Harbor to Midway* (Annapolis: Naval Institute, 2005), 355; Halsey and Bryan, *Admiral Halsey's Story*, 121.

25. Vandegrift, *Once a Marine*, 190; Hornfischer, *Neptune's Inferno*, 222.

26. Halsey to Nimitz, October 31, 1942, Halsey Papers, box 15.

27. Frank, *Guadalcanal*, 397; Command Diary, South Pacific War Diary, October 26, 1942.

28. Halsey to E. S. Reynolds, August 14, 1947, Halsey Papers, box 6; "Secret Information Bulletin 3: Battle Experience, Solomon Islands, October 1942, 21–3," Operational Archives, Navy Yard, Washington, DC; Halsey to Nimitz, November 17, 1942, Nimitz Papers.

29. Vincent P. O'Hara, *The U.S. Navy against the Axis: Surface Combat, 1941–1945* (Annapolis: Naval Institute, 2007); Tameichi Hara with Fred Saito and Roger Pineau, *Japanese Destroyer Captain* (Annapolis: Naval Institute Press, 2011), 135.

30. Halsey to Nimitz, October 31, 1942, Halsey Papers, box 15.

31. Ibid.

32. Ibid.

33. Halsey to Nimitz, November 5, 1942, Halsey Papers, box 15.

34. Halsey to Nimitz, November 6, 1942, Halsey Papers, box 15.

35. Nimitz to King, November 14, 1942, King Papers, box 3.

10. THE THIN RED LINE

1. Command Diary, South Pacific War Diary, October 15, 1942, and October 17, 1942, box 49, Record Group 38, National Archives; Roosevelt to Joint Chiefs of Staff, October 24, 1942, Charles Cooke Papers, Hoover Institute, Stanford University (hereafter Cooke Papers); South Pacific War Diary, October 21, 1942; King to Roosevelt, October 26, 1942, Cooke Papers; Marshall to Roosevelt, October 26, 1942, Cooke Papers; Nimitz to Halsey, November 8, 1942, Halsey to Melvin Mass, December 15, 1942, Halsey to Nimitz, December 6, 1942, Papers of William F. Halsey, box 15, Library of Congress (hereafter Halsey Papers).

2. Halsey to secretary of the Navy, September 17, 1953, Halsey Papers, box 10; Halsey to Nimitz, October 31 and December 20, 1942, and January 1, 1943, Halsey Papers, box 15; South Pacific War Diary, November 30, 1942; Richard Leighton and Robert Coakley, *Global Logistics and Strategy, 1940–1943* (Washington, DC: U.S. Government Printing Office, 1955), 388–404.

3. Admiral Nimitz Command Summary, September 11, 1943 (Gray Book), Operational Archives, Navy Yard, Washington, DC (hereafter Nimitz Command Summary).

4. Clay Blair, *Silent Victory: The U.S. Submarine War against Japan* (Annapolis: Naval Institute Press, 2001), 203, 340; Charles Lockwood to Ralph Christie, June 23, 1943, and August 31, 1943, Charles Lockwood Papers, box 13, Library of Congress.

5. Louis Morton, *Strategy and Command: The First Two Years* (Washington, DC: U.S. Government Printing Office, 1962), 213; Wesley Craven and James Cate, *The Army Air Forces in World War II*, vol. 4 (London: Cambridge University Press, 1950), 16.

6. Craven and Cate, *The Army Air Forces*, 34; Henry Arnold, *Global Mission* (New York: Harper and Row, 1949), 337, 343.

7. Halsey to MacArthur, October 27, 1942, October 28, 1942, October 30, 1942, November 13, 1942, and November 14, 1942, MacArthur Memorial Archives and Library, Norfolk (hereafter MacArthur Archives); George Kenney, *General Kenney Reports: A Personal History of the Pacific War* (New York: Duell, Sloan, and Pearce, 1949), 44, 126–127, 176; Felix Johnson Oral History with D. Clayton James, MacArthur Archives, 41.

8. MacArthur to Halsey, November 23, 1942, November 28, 1942, and November 29, 1942, Nimitz Command Summary; Halsey to MacArthur, November 28, 1942, MacArthur Archives.

9. MacArthur to Marshall, November 26, 1942, and MacArthur to Halsey, November 28, 1942, MacArthur Archives; Ronald H. Spector, *Eagle against the Sun: The American War with Japan* (New York: Random House, 1985), 217; Samuel Eliot Morison, *Breaking the Bismarcks Barrier* (Boston: Little, Brown, 1950), 49–50.

10. David Evans, ed., *The Japanese Navy in World War II: In the Words of Former Japanese Naval Officers* (Annapolis: Naval Institute, 1986), 209.

11. Merrill B. Twining, *No Bended Knee: The Memoirs of Gen. Merrill B. Twining, USMC* (Novato, CA: Presidio Press, 1997), 126, 166; Archer Vandegrift, *Once a Marine: The Memoirs of General A. A. Vandegrift* (New York: Norton, 1964), 196; William F. Halsey Memoir, 384, Joseph Bryan III Papers, Virginia Historical Society (hereafter Halsey Memoir).

12. Richard Frank, *Guadalcanal* (New York: Random House, 1990), 425–426.

13. Secret Information Bulletin 4, "Battle Experience, Solomon Islands, November 1942," 17–27, Operational Archives, Navy Yard, Washington, DC; Frank, *Guadalcanal*, 431.

14. James Hornfischer, *Neptune's Inferno: The U.S. Navy at Guadalcanal* (New York: Bantam Books, 2011), 136, 144, 254.

15. Frank, *Guadalcanal*, 441.

16. William Halsey with Joseph Bryan, *Admiral Halsey's Story* (New York: McGraw-Hill, 1947), 126–127; Halsey to Nimitz, November 17, 1942, Halsey Papers, box 15.

17. Halsey to Charles Belknap, May 15, 1943, Halsey Papers, box 3; Action Report, "Circumstances of Loss of Juneau," November 22, 1942, box 71, Record Group 38, National Archives; Halsey and Bryan, *Admiral Halsey's Story*, 133–134.

18. Samuel Eliot Morison, *The Struggle for Guadalcanal* (Boston: Little, Brown, 1948), 258; Frank, *Guadalcanal*, 461.

19. Halsey and Bryan, *Admiral Halsey's Story*, 128.

20. Halsey to Nimitz, November 17, 1942, Halsey Papers, box 15.

21. Ibid.

22. Halsey Memoir, 388–389.

23. Ibid., 389.

24. H. P. Willmott, *The Last Century of Sea Power*, vol. 2 (Bloomington: Indiana University Press, 2010), 459.

25. Morison, *The Struggle for Guadalcanal*, 287; Hornfischer, *Neptune's Inferno*, 375.

26. Vandegrift, *Once a Marine*, 169; Halsey to Nimitz, November 17, 1942, Halsey Papers, box 15; Nimitz Command Summary, November 13, 1942, emphasis in original; Morison, *The Struggle for Guadalcanal*, 263; Hornfischer, *Neptune's Inferno*, 377.

27. E. B. Potter, *Nimitz* (Annapolis: Naval Institute, 1976), 208; Halsey and Bryan, *Admiral Halsey's Story*, 132.
28. Morison, *The Struggle for Guadalcanal*, 314; Halsey to Nimitz, January 1, 1943, and January 11, 1943, Halsey Papers, box 15; Morison, *The Struggle for Guadalcanal*, 314.
29. Twining, *No Bended Knee*, 156–157.
30. Frank, *Guadalcanal*, 527.
31. John Miller, *Guadalcanal: The First Offensive* (Washington, DC: U.S. Government Printing Office, 1978), 246.
32. Halsey to Nimitz, December 20, 1942, and January 11, 1943, Halsey Papers, box 15.
33. Potter, *Nimitz*, 216–217.
34. Nimitz Command Summary, January 23, 1943.
35. Morison, *The Struggle for Guadalcanal*, 317.
36. Frank, *Guadalcanal*, 542, 544; King to MacArthur, Nimitz, and Halsey, February 1, 1943, Halsey to Nimitz et al., February 1, 1943, Halsey to MacArthur, February 2, 1943, MacArthur to Halsey, February 3, 1943, and MacArthur to Marshall, February 3, 1943, box 16, Record Group 16, MacArthur Archives.
37. After Action Report, "Loss of *Chicago*," March 10, 1943, box 71, Record Group 38, National Archives.
38. Paul Dull, *A Battle History of the Imperial Japanese Navy* (Annapolis: Naval Institute, 1978), 268.
39. Halsey and Bryan, *Admiral Halsey's Story*, 148; South Pacific Operation Plan 4-43, January 27, 1943, box 90, Record Group 38, National Archives; Nimitz Command Summary, February 2–6, 1943; Frank, *Guadalcanal*, 597.
40. Twining, *No Bended Knee*, 166; Nimitz Command Summary, February 2, 1943; Frank, *Guadalcanal*, 597; John Prados, *Combined Fleet Decoded: The Secret History of American Intelligence and the Japanese Navy in World War II* (Annapolis: Naval Institute, 1995), 395.
41. Twining, *No Bended Knee*, ix; Morison, *The Struggle for Guadalcanal*, 373; James Michener, *Tales of the South Pacific* (New York: Pocket Books, 1958), 12.
42. Halsey and Bryan, *Admiral Halsey's Story*, 148.
43. H. K. Pickett to Halsey, November 18, 1942, Halsey Papers, box 2; *Time*, January 4, 1943, 21–22.

11. REAL TALES OF THE SOUTH PACIFIC

1. *New York Times*, October 25, 1942, 3; *Los Angeles Times*, October 26, 1942, 2; *Washington Post*, November 1, 1942, 5; *Detroit Free Press*,

November 18, 1942, 12; *Time,* November 20, 1942, 28–31. Halsey appeared on *Time*'s cover again on July 23, 1945. Only Douglas MacArthur (four times), Dwight Eisenhower (four times), and George Patton (three times) appeared more often.

2. *Roanoke Times,* November 19, 1942, 2; *New Zealand Herald,* January 7, 1943, 1; William Halsey and Joseph Bryan, *Admiral Halsey's Story* (New York: McGraw-Hill, 1947), 142–143; Houghton McBain, president, Marshall Field and Company, to Halsey, December 9, 1948, Papers of William F. Halsey, box 7, Library of Congress (hereafter Halsey Papers).

3. Elias Bernstein to Halsey, July 10, 1943, Halsey Papers, box 3.

4. Helen Zewaisis to Halsey, December 5, 1945, Halsey Papers, box 4.

5. Nolan Yates to Halsey, September 16, 1945, Halsey Papers, box 4; McCoy Taylor to Halsey, October 5, 1950, Halsey Papers, box 8; Walter Thomas to Halsey, August 27, 1945, Halsey Papers, box 4; Pat Sheedy to Halsey, September 21, 1945, Halsey Papers, box 4; Eleanor Herrmann to Halsey, May 18, 1945, Halsey Papers, box 4; Mabel Hudson, July 24, no year, Halsey Papers, box 4.

6. Daniel Boorstin, *The Image: A Guide to Pseudo-events in America* (New York: Harper and Row, 1961), 60–61; Richard Schickel, *Intimate Strangers: The Culture of Celebrity* (Garden City, NY: Doubleday, 1985), 55; *Time,* November 20, 1942, 28–31.

7. *Greensboro Record,* North Carolina, November 18, 1942, 1; E. B. Potter, *Nimitz* (Annapolis: Naval Institute, 1976), 40; *Baltimore Sun,* February 20, 1945, 4.

8. Kendal Wilkinson to Harry Truman, June 22, 1945, Halsey Papers, box 4.

9. Arthur King to author, July 7, 1998, Harold Stassen to author, June 2, 1998, in author's possession.

10. Mrs. Arthur Turner to Halsey, October 3, 1947, and Halsey to Turner, October 17, 1947, Halsey Papers, box 6; Halsey to Grace Gates, October 21, 1947, Halsey Papers, box 6; J. D. Custer to Harold Stassen, December 11, 1943, Harold Stassen Papers, Minnesota Historical Society; Thomas Buell, *The Quiet Warrior: A Biography of Admiral Raymond A. Spruance* (Annapolis: Naval Institute, 1988), 48–50; Halsey to all ships and stations, June 26, 1943, Halsey Papers, box 35; Shafroth to commanding officer, *Denver,* December 11, 1943, Halsey Papers, box 35; Shafroth to Randall Jacobs, January 24, 1944, Halsey Papers, box 35; John P. McLaughlin, Virginia Alcohol Control Board, to Halsey, December 23, 1947, Halsey Papers, box 6.

11. Halsey to South Pacific Force, November 24, 1942, Halsey to South Pacific Force, February 7, 1943, and Halsey to all naval establishments, South Pacific Force, November 21, 1942, Halsey Papers, box 35.

12. Halsey to R. S. Holmes, December 28, 1937, Halsey Papers, box 2; Halsey to J. W. Sands, August 27, 1949, Halsey Papers, box 7; Halsey to Right Reverend Maurice Sheehy, October 28, 1949, Halsey Papers, box 7; Halsey to Allen Geliman, September 24, 1952, Halsey Papers, box 9; Halsey to Maxwell Cohen, November 15, 1946, Halsey Papers, box 5; Halsey to Julius Klein, July 28, 1948, Halsey Papers, box 7.

13. John Dower, *War without Mercy: Race and Power in the Pacific War* (New York: Pantheon, 1987), 85; Halsey to Rufus Zogbaum, December 14, 1942, Halsey Papers, box 2.

14. Dower, *War without Mercy*, 13, 37, 91, 65; Fred Hardin to Halsey, February 28, 1945, Coy Taylor to Halsey, October 5, 1950, and Walter Thomas to Halsey, August 27, 1945, Halsey Papers, box 4.

15. Dower, *War without Mercy*, 54, 79.

16. Ibid., 113.

17. Halsey remarks aboard USS *Boise*, October 24, 1942, box 6597, Record Group 313, National Archives; Halsey to Melvin Mass, January 17, 1943, and Halsey to Nimitz, February 13, 1943, Halsey Papers, box 15; James Michener, *Tales of the South Pacific* (New York: Pocket Books, 1958), 2.

18. Halsey to Walter Woodfill, July 1, 1947, and Halsey to Paul Mueller, July 1, 1947, Halsey Papers, box 6; Halsey to Takashi Ihara, December 27, 1950, Halsey Papers, box 8; memorandum, C. R. Richardson to Halsey et al., September 11, 1953, Halsey Papers, box 10; Halsey to George Grant, March 23, 1955, Halsey Papers, box 11.

19. Halsey and Bryan, *Admiral Halsey's Story*, xv; Ernest King's Notes, no date, 1945, King Papers, box 4, Navy Yard; DeWitt Peck Oral History, Columbia University Oral History Collection, Columbia University Special Collections, 121.

20. Halsey and Bryan, *Admiral Halsey's Story*, 12, 13, 23, 27, 130, 138, 172.

21. Halsey to Markey, January 24, 1945, Halsey Papers, box 4; Halsey to Ken Jones, February 18, 1952, Halsey Papers, box 9.

22. Halsey remarks aboard USS *Boise*, October 24, 1942, box 6597, Record Group 313, National Archives.

23. "Health and Sanitation Report," American Consulate, Nouméa, December 9, 1943, box 5, Record Group 18, National Archives; "Report of Post War Usage of New Caledonia," House Naval Affairs Subcommittee, box 6303, Record Group 313, National Archives.

24. A. Bayardelle, "Report on the Events Which Preceded the Adhesion of New Caledonia to the Free French," 3, 72, box 6783, Record Group 313, National Archives; "Exchange Difficulty in Trade with New Caledonia," American Vice Consulate, Nouméa, October 23, 1941, Post Files, New Caledonia, box 1, Record Group 84, National Archives; "Decree 523

Concerning Customs Control," Post Files, New Caledonia, box 6, Record Group 84, National Archives; "Conditions in Noumea," November 8, 1940, unknown Australian merchant, box 5208, Record Group 59, National Archives; "Political Situation in New Caledonia," September 19, 1941, Post Files, New Caledonia, box 1, Record Group 84, National Archives.

25. Louis Morton, *Strategy and Command: The First Two Years* (Washington, DC: U.S. Government Printing Office, 1962), 209–210; Patch to Marshall, May 3, 1942, May 7, 1942, and Marshall to Roosevelt, May 8, 1942, Secretary File, box 83, Roosevelt Secretary Files, George Marshall, Franklin Roosevelt Library, Hyde Park, New York; Kim Munholland, *Rock of Contention: Free French and Americans at War in New Caledonia, 1940–1945* (New York: Berghahn Books, 2007), 42–44, 105–106.

26. Nimitz Command Summary, October 21, 1942, Chester Nimitz Papers, Operational Archives, Navy Yard, Washington, DC (hereafter Nimitz Papers); Halsey to M. Montchamp, October 26, 1942, October 29, 1942, November 16, 1942, December 8, 1942, and December 20, 1942, box 6748, Record Group 313, National Archives; Montchamp to Halsey, October 27, 1942, and December 22, 1942, Halsey Papers, box 2; Munholland, *Rock of Contention,* 120–121; Halsey to Nimitz, December 20, 1942, and Frank Knox to Halsey, February 17, 1943, Halsey Papers, box 14; Halsey to Knox, February 17, 1943, Halsey Papers, box 14.

27. Halsey and Bryan, *Admiral Halsey's Story,* 138.

28. "Base Data, Noumea," Halsey Papers, box 35; Henry Day to secretary of State, July 20, 1943, Halsey Papers, box 3; Munholland, *Rock of Contention,* 128.

29. US Navy liaison officer, Noumea, to director of Naval Intelligence, December 26, 1942, Halsey Papers, box 35.

30. "Investigation of Luitpold Blembell," November 26, 1942, and "Index of Suspicious Persons," October 21, 1942, both in box 6511, Record Group 313, National Archives; Counter Intelligence Unit, "Gentil, Rene," box 6511, Record Group 313, National Archives; Counter Intelligence Unit, "Sakanori, Arline," February 15, 1944, "Emile Solier," May 27, 1945, and confidential memorandum, "Milo Solier," January 29, 1944, all in box 6511, Record Group 313, National Archives.

31. "Index of Suspicious Persons," October 21, 1942, box 6511, Record Group 313, National Archives; Gene Markey to Julian Brown, January 26, 1943, Halsey Papers, box 3; Halsey to Walter Hertz, November 3, 1947, Halsey Papers, box 6; William Montgomery McGovern to Halsey, August 4, 1943, box 6399, Record Group 313, National Archives; William Don-

ovan to Halsey, April 26, 1943, Halsey Papers, box 13; Halsey to Nimitz, May 26, 1943, Halsey Papers, box 15.

32. Weekly reports, U.S. Treasury Checks and U.S. Currency Sold for Official Purposes, American Consulate, New Caledonia, Post Files, Nouméa, box 3, Record Group 84, National Archives; Munholland, *Rock of Contention,* 154; commanding general, First Marine Amphibious Corps, to commanding general, South Pacific Service Command, "Organized Pilferage," February 18, 1943, box 5612, Record Group 313, National Archives; "Report on Disturbances among Indentured Laborers in New Caledonia to the Secretary of State," n.d., and "Reform of the Indentured Labor System of Javanese and Indo-Chinese," March 25, 1944, both in box 5612, Record Group 313, National Archives; Munholland, *Rock of Contention,* 130.

33. "Schmidt, Gaetan, of Point Na (Shangri-La), Complaint of—Molestation of Sheep by Naval Personnel," March 1, 1944, box 6511, Record Group 313, National Archives; *Time,* January 3, 1944, 28; *Newsweek,* January 3, 1944, 22–23; "Rape Cases Involving Military Personnel," January 8, 1944, box 6511, Record Group 313, National Archives; Office of the Provost Marshal, I Island Command, "Assault Cases since February 1, 1943," January 8, 1944, box 6638, Record Group 313, National Archives.

34. William Ashford Oral History, 82, Papers of William Ashford, East Carolina University Special Collections; Halsey to Mark Clark, January 13, 1956, Halsey Papers, box 11; U.S. Department of Public Health for Nouméa, "Contagious and Infectious Disease Weekly Reports," various dates, 1943, box 9, Record Group 84, National Archives; Arthur King, *Vignettes of the South Pacific: The Lighter Side of World War II* (Cincinnati: privately published by the author, 1991), 57–59; Mason, *Destroyer,* 118–124.

35. Edward Niemeier, judge advocate, South Pacific Force, to Halsey, September 16, 1943, box 6607, Record Group 313, National Archives; John Shafroth to judge advocate general, South Pacific Force, November 15, 1943, box 6401, Record Group 313, National Archives; "List of Possible Homosexuals in the US Army, Compiled from Statements Taken from Naval Personnel," September 23, 1943, box 6511, Record Group 313, National Archives; statement, Charles Myron Clegg to E. M. Krieger, September 26, 1943, box 5611, Record Group 313, National Archives; "Report of Investigation of Homosexual Activity," Office of Naval Intelligence, South Pacific Command, box 5353, Record Group 313, National Archives; quote from Michener, *Tales of the South Pacific,* 177; Allan Bérubé, *Coming Out Under Fire: The History of Gay Men and Women in World War Two* (New York: Free Press, 1990), 215–227.

36. Shafroth to Randall Jacobs, October 18, 1943, Halsey Papers, box 3; commandant of the Marine Corps to commander, South Pacific, November 13, 1943, box 6611, Record Group 313, National Archives; John Shafroth to judge advocate general, South Pacific Force, November 15, 1943, box 6401, Record Group 313, National Archives; "List of Possible Homosexuals in the US Army, Compiled from Statements Taken from Naval Personnel," September 23, 1943, box 6511, Record Group 313, National Archives; E. M. Krieger to intelligence officer, Comsopac, n.d., box 6511, Record Group 313, National Archives.

37. "Roster," South Pacific Force Staff, October 1, 1943, box 6441, Record Group 313, National Archives; Edwin Layton, *"And I Was There": Pearl Harbor and Midway—Breaking the Secrets* (Old Saybrook, CT: Konecky and Konecky, 1985), 320.

38. Carney to Halsey, October 8, 1947, Halsey Papers, box 13; Officer Efficiency Reports, SOPAC, box 6591, Record Group 313, National Archives; Ashford Oral History, 32; Carney to Halsey, December 23, 1947, Halsey Papers, box 13.

39. Halsey to B. W. Fink, March 27, 1947, Halsey Papers, box 6; Ernest King to Halsey, August 3, 1943, Nimitz Papers; Halsey to Nimitz, December 20, 1942, Halsey Papers, box 15; Halsey and Bryan, *Admiral Halsey's Story*, 146.

40. Potter, *Nimitz*, 218, Ronald H. Spector, *Eagle against the Sun: The American War with Japan* (New York: Random House, 1985), 169; Nimitz to Halsey, December 18, 1942, Nimitz Papers.

41. Buell, *The Quiet Warrior*, 126; Halsey to Nimitz, January 1, 1943, Nimitz Papers.

42. Kitchell to Allen and Stark, Ltd, November 18, 1944, Halsey Papers, box 4.

43. Halsey to Barney Leonard, January 8, 1943, Halsey Papers, box 3; Calhoun to Halsey, June 18, 1943, Halsey Papers, box 13; C. W. Crosse to Halsey, May 29, 1943, and Halsey to T. W. Balfe, June 10, 1943, Halsey Papers, box 35.

44. Arthur Ageton, *The Jungle Seas* (New York: Signet Reprints, 1955), 13, 29; Halsey to Arthur Ageton, December 10, 1953, Halsey Papers, box 10; Calhoun to Halsey, December 11, 1945, March 31, 1948, Halsey Papers, box 13; Halsey to Mrs. Elsene Griggs, November 15, 1944, Halsey Papers, box 4.

45. Calhoun to Halsey, June 18, 1943, Halsey Papers, box 13; Kitchell to Herbert Fleishhacker, April 13, 1945, and April 30, 1945, Kitchell to Calhoun, May 16, 1945, Halsey Papers, box 13; King, *Vignettes*, 116; Theodore Mason, *Rendezvous with Destiny* (Annapolis: Naval Institute, 1997), 183–185; Kay Warford to Halsey, July 1, 1944, Halsey Papers, box 3.

46. "Itemized Schedule of Travel and Other Expenses," Halsey Service Jacket, National Personnel Records Center, St. Louis; Halsey to Marc Mitscher, November 18, 1943, Halsey Papers, box 15; Halsey to secretary of the Navy, April 3, 1946, Halsey Papers, box 5.
47. John Hoover Oral History, 330, Columbia University Oral History Collection, Columbia University Special Collections; Nimitz to Halsey, January 5, 1944, Halsey Papers, box 15.
48. Eleanor Roosevelt, *This I Remember* (New York: Harper and Row, 1949), 295; Joseph Lash, *Eleanor and Franklin* (New York: Norton, 1971), 688–690; Halsey and Bryan, *Admiral Halsey's Story*, 167; Stassen, interview with author, July 14, 1998.
49. Henry Day to secretary of state, August 8, 1943, box 6538, Record Group 313, National Archives; H. E. L. Priday, *Cannibal Island: The Turbulent Story of New Caledonia's Cannibal Coasts* (Wellington: A. W. Reed, 1944), 9; *National Geographic*, June 1942, 691–722; Arthur King, interview with author, December 7, 1999; Shafroth to secretary of the Navy, October 21, 1943, Halsey Papers, box 35; Halsey to secretary of the Navy, May 31, 1944, box 6781, Record Group 313, National Archives.

12. THE CROSSROADS OF COMMAND

1. Commander, Amphibious Force, South Pacific Force, "Report of Occupation of the Russell Islands, February 12 to April 17, 1943," box 72, Record Group 38, National Archives.
2. Ernest King to Nimitz, March 1, 1943, Nimitz Command Summary, Chester Nimitz Papers, Operational Archives, Navy Yard, Washington, DC (hereafter Nimitz Papers); Samuel Eliot Morison, *Breaking the Bismarcks Barrier* (Boston: Little, Brown, 1950), 98.
3. Marshall to King, December 21, 1942, Charles Cooke Papers, Hoover Institute, Stanford University (hereafter Cooke Papers); C. M. Cooke and A. C. Wedemeyer to King and Marshall, "Report by the Joint U.S. Staff Planners," no date but probably December 22, 1942, Cooke Papers; King to Marshall, December 30, 1942, and January 6, 1943, Cooke Papers.
4. Peck to Halsey, November 25, 1942, Papers of William F. Halsey, box 2, Library of Congress (hereafter Halsey Papers).
5. MacArthur to Nimitz and Halsey, January 13, 1943, South Pacific Files, MacArthur Memorial Archives and Library, Norfolk (hereafter MacArthur Archives); King to Nimitz and Halsey, January 31, 1943, Nimitz Command Summary.
6. March 4, 1943, Nimitz Command Summary.

7. D. Clayton James, *The Years of MacArthur, 1941–1945* (Boston: Houghton Mifflin, 1975), 310–311; Louis Morton, *Strategy and Command: The First Two Years* (Washington, DC: U.S. Government Printing Office, 1962), 300–399.

8. Morton, *Strategy and Command,* 250; Thomas Buell, *Master of Sea Power: A Biography of Fleet Admiral Ernest J. King* (Boston: Little, Brown, 1980), 147.

9. Geoffrey Perret, *Old Soldiers Never Die: The Life of Douglas MacArthur* (Holbrook, MA: Adams Media, 1996), 320–321; Carl Solberg, *Decision and Dissent: With Halsey at Leyte Gulf* (Annapolis: Naval Institute, 1995), 4.

10. Nimitz to Carpender, May 18, 1943, Nimitz Papers; MacArthur to Marshall, February 2, 1943, box 16, Record Group 4, MacArthur Archives, Norfolk; Russell Berkey Oral History with D. Clayton James, box 1, MacArthur Archives; Solberg, *Decision and Dissent,* 7.

11. Halsey to Nimitz, February 13, 1943, Halsey Papers, box 15.

12. MacArthur *Time* covers: March 25, 1935, December 29, 1941, and March 30, 1942.

13. William Manchester, *American Caesar: Douglas MacArthur, 1880–1964* (New York: Dell, 1978), 18.

14. Theodore Wilkinson Diary, April 9, 1943, Theodore Wilkinson Papers, Library of Congress; Felix Johnson Oral History, 158, U.S. Naval Institute; J. B. Colwell Oral History, 64, U.S. Naval Institute.

15. George Kenney, *General Kenney Reports: A Personal History of the Pacific War* (New York: Duell, Sloan, and Pearce, 1949), 205; Perret, *Old Soldiers Never Die,* 349; Manchester, *American Caesar,* 380.

16. MacArthur to Marshall, March 25, 1943, box 16, Record Group 4, MacArthur Archives.

17. Douglas MacArthur, *Reminiscences* (New York: McGraw-Hill, 1964), 173–174; Perret, *Old Soldiers Never Die,* 349; William Halsey with Joseph Bryan, *Admiral Halsey's Story* (New York: McGraw-Hill, 1947), 154–155; Carpender to Nimitz, May 18, 1943, and Nimitz to Halsey, May 14, 1943, Halsey Papers, box 15.

18. Halsey and Bryan, *Admiral Halsey's Story,* 157; Command Diary, South Pacific War Diary, March 15, 1943, box 50, Record Group 38, National Archives; "Troop Strength, South Pacific Bases," box 6781, Record Group 313, National Archives; "Supply of Food to South Pacific Area," September 5, 1944, Halsey Papers, box 35; Nimitz to King, June 22, 1943, Nimitz Papers; April 1, 1943, Nimitz Command Summary; South Pacific War Diary, April 3, 1943, box 50, Record Group 38, National Archives.

NOTES TO PAGES 265–273

19. Bruce Gamble, *Fortress Rabaul: The Battle for the Southwest Pacific, January 1942–April 1943* (Minneapolis: Zenith Press, 2010), 246, 295–298; James, *The Years of MacArthur,* 310–312.

20. Gamble, *Fortress Rabaul,* 316–327; John Prados, *Combined Fleet Decoded: The Secret History of American Intelligence and the Japanese Navy in World War II* (Annapolis: Naval Institute, 1995), 455–457; E. B. Potter, *Nimitz* (Annapolis: Naval Institute, 1976), 233; Halsey and Bryan, *Admiral Halsey's Story,* 155.

21. Mitscher to Halsey, "Investigation Concerning Leakages of Information Concerning the Fighter Sweep of the Kihili Area on April 18, 1943," May 30, 1943, Marc Mitscher Papers, box 2, Library of Congress.

22. Headquarters, Thirteenth Air Force, "Investigation, Specific Information Desired Concerning," June 7, 1943, Nathan Twining Papers, Library of Congress; Morison, *Breaking the Bismarcks Barrier,* 120.

23. "Air Combat Action Report," South Pacific, April 26, 1943, box 72, Record Group 38, National Archives; Marshall to King, July 28, 1943, and King to Marshall, August 31, 1943, Ernest King Papers, box 4, Naval Historical Center; Matome Ugaki, *Fading Victory: The Diary of Admiral Matome Ugaki, 1941–1945* (Pittsburgh: University of Pittsburgh Press, 1991), 360.

24. Halsey to Nimitz, December 8, 1942, Halsey Papers, box 15.

25. George Dyer, *The Amphibians Came to Conquer: The Story of Admiral Richmond Kelly Turner* (Washington, DC: Department of the Navy, 1991), 471, 474–478.

26. Millard Harmon, "Organization of Army Air Corps in SOPAC," 1–2, n.d., 705.040, Historical Research Agency, Maxwell Air Force Base; J. M. S. Ross, *Royal New Zealand Air Force* (Wellington: Department of Internal Affairs, 1955), 39, 108, 262; Air 118 / 81g, "RNZAF Historical Section Narrative of Operations," New Zealand National Archives, Wellington.

27. "Designation of Airfields and Sea Plane Bases," October 26, 1943, John Shafroth Papers, box 7, Library of Congress.

28. James Winnefeld and Dana Johnson, *Joint Air Operations: Pursuit of Unity of Command and Control, 1942–1991* (Annapolis: Naval Institute, 1991), 33–34.

29. Halsey and Bryan, *Admiral Halsey's Story,* 139, 186; Halsey to John McCain, December 11, 1943, Halsey Papers, box 15; Wesley Craven and James Cate, *The Army Air Forces in World War II,* vol. 4 (London: Cambridge University Press, 1950), 89, 204.

30. Nimitz to King, June 22, 1943, Nimitz Papers.

31. Halsey to Nimitz, May 14, 1943, and Halsey to Calhoun, June 29, 1943, Halsey Papers, box 13.

13. LOW TIDE

1. Command Diary, South Pacific War Diary, December 11, 1942, and March 4, 1943, box 49, Record Group 38, National Archives.

2. John Miller, *Cartwheel: The Reduction of Rabaul* (Washington, DC: U.S. Government Printing Office, 1959), 47; Eric Bergerud, *Fire in the Sky: The Air War in the South Pacific* (Boulder, CO: Westview Press, 2000), 227.

3. George Dyer, *The Amphibians Came to Conquer: The Story of Admiral Richmond Kelly Turner* (Washington, DC: Department of the Navy, 1991), 502–508; Miller, *Cartwheel,* 67–80; Samuel Eliot Morison, *Breaking the Bismarcks Barrier* (Boston: Little, Brown, 1950), 138–146.

4. Dyer, *The Amphibians Came to Conquer,* 533; Merrill B. Twining, *No Bended Knee: The Memoirs of Gen. Merrill B. Twining, USMC* (Novato, CA: Presidio Press, 1997), 182.

5. Nimitz to Holcomb, June 29, 1943, Chester Nimitz Papers, Operational Archives, Navy Yard, Washington, DC (hereafter Nimitz Papers); Twining, *No Bended Knee,* 181.

6. Holcomb to Nimitz, June 4, 1943, and Nimitz to Holcomb, June 29, 1943, Nimitz Papers.

7. Twining, *No Bended Knee,* 181; Alan Rems, "Halsey Knows the Straight Story," *Naval History,* August 2008; Holcomb to Nimitz, June 4, 1943, and Nimitz to King, June 22, 1943, Nimitz Papers; William Halsey with Joseph Bryan, *Admiral Halsey's Story* (New York: McGraw-Hill, 1947), 161.

8. Dyer, *The Amphibians Came to Conquer,* 511.

9. Ibid., 516–517; Miller, *Cartwheel,* 76; Halsey to Nimitz, "Action Occupation of Rendova Island, Solomon Islands, June 30 1943," 1, August 31, 1943, South Pacific Action Report, box 71, Record Group 38, National Archives.

10. Harmon to Halsey, July 11, 1943, box 6399, Record Group 313, National Archives; Miller, *Cartwheel,* 87–92.

11. Halsey to MacArthur and Nimitz, July 6, 1943, and July 7, 1943, Nimitz Command Summary, Nimitz Papers.

12. Vincent P. O'Hara, *The U.S. Navy against the Axis: Surface Combat 1941–1945* (Annapolis: Naval Institute, 2007), 180.

13. William F. Halsey Memoir, 421, Joseph Bryan III Papers, Virginia Historical Society (hereafter Halsey Memoir); Nimitz to Halsey, July 13, 1943, Papers of William F. Halsey, box 15, Library of Congress (hereafter Halsey Papers); Morison, *Breaking the Bismarcks Barrier,* 191.

14. Dyer, *The Amphibians Came to Conquer,* 577; Shafroth to R. S. Edwards, January 11, 1944, box 6441, Record Group 313, National Archives.

15. Miller, *Cartwheel,* 113; Bergerud, *Fire in the Sky,* 71.
16. Miller, *Cartwheel,* 121–122.
17. Turner to Raymond Spruance, November 30, 1943, Raymond Spruance Papers, box 1, Naval War College Archives, Newport; Bergerud, *Fire in the Sky,* 205–211.
18. Halsey to Nimitz, July 16, 1943, Halsey Papers, box 15; Nimitz Command Summary, July 7–July 22, 1942.
19. King to Halsey, August 3, 1943, Ernest King Papers, box 4, Naval Historical Center; Nimitz to Halsey, August 5, 1943, and King to Nimitz et al., August 6, 1943, Nimitz Command Summary; Wilkinson to Charles McMorris, September 25, 1943, Theodore Wilkinson Papers, box 1, Library of Congress (hereafter Wilkinson Papers); Theodore Wilkinson Diary, June 13, 1943, Wilkinson Papers.
20. Nimitz to Halsey, July 18, 1943, box 6399, Record Group 313, National Archives; Nimitz to Halsey, July 28, 1943, Halsey Papers, box 15.
21. Halsey and Bryan, *Admiral Halsey's Story,* 161; Millard Harmon, "The Army in the South Pacific," 8, Millard Harmon Papers, Historical Research Agency, Maxwell Air Force Base; Halsey, "Narrative Account of the South Pacific Campaign," 7, Halsey Papers, box 37; Third Fleet War Diary, July 6–15, 1943, box 49, Record Group 38, National Archives; Dyer, *The Amphibians Came to Conquer,* 584–587; Miller, *Cartwheel,* 126.
22. Robert Sherrod, *History of Marine Corps Aviation in World War II* (Novato, CA: Presidio Press, 1980), 180–181.
23. Miller, *Cartwheel,* 156–158; Nimitz to Halsey, August 8, 1943, and Halsey to Nimitz, August 19, 1943, Halsey Papers, box 15.
24. Miller, *Cartwheel,* 168–169.
25. Bergerud, *Fire in the Sky,* 375–376; Miller, *Cartwheel,* 165.
26. Halsey Memoir, 422–424; Rems, "Halsey Knows the Straight Story," 49; Miller, *Cartwheel,* 184; Morison, *Breaking the Bismarcks Barrier,* 223.
27. Halsey Memoir, 423.
28. Louis Morton, *Strategy and Command: The First Two Years* (Washington, DC: U.S. Government Printing Office, 1962), 512; Twining, *No Bended Knee,* 185; Rems, "Halsey Knows the Straight Story," 55; Halsey and Bryan, *Admiral Halsey's Story,* 161.
29. Carney to Halsey, June 10, 1952, Halsey Papers, box 13; Thurber Officer Efficiency Report, March 31, 1943, Halsey Papers, box 37.
30. Nimitz to Halsey, May 20, 1943, Halsey Papers, box 15; Nimitz to King, June 22, 1943, Nimitz Papers.
31. Robert Carney, "Staff Organization Afloat," *Proceedings,* December 1930, 1113–1125; Robert Carney, "Material Administration Aboard Ship," *Proceedings,* July 1938, 963–968; Betty Taussig, *A Warrior for Freedom*

(Manhattan, KS: Sunflower University Press, 1995), 67–68; Carney to William Ball, February 10, 1964, Nimitz Papers.

32. Robert Carney Oral History, 122, 123, 126, Columbia University Oral History Collection, Columbia University Special Collections; Taussig, *A Warrior for Freedom,* 80.

33. Taussig, *A Warrior for Freedom,* 97; James Merrill, *A Sailor's Admiral: A Biography of William F. Halsey* (New York: Thomas Y. Crowell, 1976), 129; William Halsey III, foreword to Taussig, *A Warrior for Freedom.*

34. Knox to Stassen, March 4, 1942, and March 28, 1942, Harold Stassen Papers, Minnesota Historical Society (hereafter Stassen Papers); Knox to Stassen, April 16, 1943, Stassen Papers; Stassen Officer Efficiency Report, March 31, 1944, May 24, 1944, and February 28, 1945, Stassen Papers.

35. Halsey to Belknap, November 15, 1944, Halsey Papers, box 4.

36. Carney Oral History, 293.

37. William Halsey, "Responsibilities of a Theater Commander, Armed Forces Staff College, April 7, 1947," William Riley Papers, box 2, Library of Congress.

38. Theodore Wilkinson, "Amphibious Operations in the South Pacific, Army and Navy Staff College, May 8, 1944," box 185, Record Group 334, National Archives; William Halsey, "Responsibilities of a Theater Commander, Armed Forces Staff College, April 7, 1947," William Riley Papers, box 2, Library of Congress.

39. O'Hara, *The U.S. Navy against the Axis,* 187–192; Morison, *Breaking the Bismarcks Barrier,* 212–222.

40. Calhoun to Halsey, August 20, 1943, Halsey Papers, box 36; War Diary, Scouting Squadron 58, August 1943, box 6671, Record Group 313, National Archives; Halsey and Bryan, *Admiral Halsey's Story,* 165–166.

41. Halsey and Bryan, *Admiral Halsey's Story,* 170.

42. Thurber to Halsey, June 21, 1952, Halsey Papers, box 16; Halsey to Turner, et al., July 11, 1943, Nimitz Command Summary; Third Fleet War Diary, July 11, 1943, box 49, Record Group 38, National Archives; Riley to Halsey, August 13, 1952, Halsey Papers, box 15.

43. Halsey to Nimitz, August 25, 1943, box 6400, Record Group 313, National Archives; Halsey to Prime Minister Peter Fraser, August 21, 1943, Halsey Papers, box 13; J. M. S. Ross, *Royal New Zealand Air Force* (Wellington: Department of Internal Affairs, 1955), 39, 108.

44. Commander, Acorn Flight Eight, "Resume of Developments of Munda Field," March 4, 1944, box 2729, Record Group 313, National Archives; Miller, *Cartwheel,* 183–184.

45. Miller, *Cartwheel,* 172; Halsey to Orlando Ward, August 27, 1952, Halsey Papers, box 16.

46. Morison, *Breaking the Bismarcks Barrier,* 226.

47. Halsey and Bryan, *Admiral Halsey's Story,* 172; O'Hara, *The U.S. Navy against the Axis,* 201–205; Miller, *Cartwheel,* 184–186; Morison, *Breaking the Bismarcks Barrier,* 239–242.

48. Bergerud, *Fire in the Sky,* 329–330.

49. John Toland, *The Rising Sun* (New York: Random House, 1970), 447; Morison, *Breaking the Bismarcks Barrier,* 252; Miller, *Cartwheel,* 186–187.

14. HIGH TIDE

1. King to Marshall, February 7, 1943, Charles Cooke Papers, Hoover Institute, Stanford University; King to Nimitz and Halsey, February 13, 1943, Nimitz Command Summary, Chester Nimitz Papers, Operational Archives, Navy Yard, Washington, DC (hereafter Nimitz Papers).

2. William Halsey, "Responsibilities of a Theater Commander, Armed Forces Staff College, April 7, 1947," William Riley Papers, box 2, Library of Congress (hereafter Riley Papers); Frederick Munson Oral History with D. Clayton James, 20, MacArthur Memorial Archives and Library, Norfolk (hereafter MacArthur Archives).

3. Robert Carney Staff Memorandum, "Pacific Ocean Areas Conference," October 7, 1943, Harold Stassen Papers, Minnesota Historical Society; September 1, 1943, Nimitz Command Summary.

4. MacArthur to Halsey, August 23, 1943, Papers of William F. Halsey, box 15, Library of Congress (hereafter Halsey Papers); Fitch, Harmon, Wilkinson, and Barrett to Halsey, September 7, 1943, box 6399, Record Group 313, National Archives.

5. Halsey to MacArthur, August 25, 1943, Halsey Papers, box 15; Nimitz to Halsey, September 6, 1943, Halsey Papers, box 15.

6. Halsey to King, August 21, 1943, Military Post Files, Roosevelt Library, Hyde Park; Halsey to MacArthur, September 15, 1943, and Halsey to Nimitz, September 15, 1943, box 167, Record Group 38, National Archives.

7. D. Clayton James, *The Years of MacArthur, 1941–1945* (Boston: Houghton Mifflin, 1942), 339.

8. William Halsey, "Items in Connection with Visit to CinCPac, September 17, 1943," Riley Papers, box 1; Halsey, Discussion Period Following "Responsibility of a Theater Commander, Armed Forces Staff College, April 7, 1943," Riley Papers, box 2.

9. Carney to John Heffernan, March 1, 1951, Halsey Papers, box 14; John Towers Diary, September 29, 1943, and September 30, 1943, John Towers Papers, Library of Congress; Nimitz to Halsey, September 16, 1943, Halsey Papers, box 15.

10. Henry Shaw and Douglas Kane, *Isolation of Rabaul* (Washington, DC: Headquarters, U.S. Marine Corps, 1963), 170–173.

11. Ibid., 170; Merrill B. Twining, *No Bended Knee: The Memoirs of Gen. Merrill B. Twining, USMC* (Novato, CA: Presidio Press, 1997), 182–186.

12. William Halsey with Joseph Bryan, *Admiral Halsey's Story* (New York: McGraw-Hill, 1947), 174; William Halsey, "Responsibility of a Theater Commander, Armed Forces Staff College, April 7, 1947," 13, William Riley Papers, box 2.

13. Twining, *No Bended Knee*, 189; Alan Rems, "Halsey Knows the Straight Story," *Naval History*, August 2008.

14. Record of Proceedings, "Court of Inquiry into the Circumstances Attending the Death of Charles Barrett, Late Major General, US Marine Corps, 8 October 1943," box 6607, Record Group 313, National Archives; Rems, "Halsey Knows the Straight Story," 90–93.

15. Rems, "Halsey Knows the Straight Story," 93; Halsey and Bryan, *Admiral Halsey's Story*, 174; Archer Vandegrift, *Once a Marine: The Memoirs of General A. A. Vandegrift* (New York: Norton, 1964), 227.

16. Rems, "Halsey Knows the Straight Story," 93.

17. Shaw and Kane, *Isolation of Rabaul*, 177, Vandegrift, *Once a Marine*, 227; Wilkinson to Halsey, October 14, 1943, Theodore Wilkinson Papers, box 1, Library of Congress (hereafter Wilkinson Papers); commander, South Pacific Force, "Operations Plans 16–43," box 91, Record Group 38, National Archives; George Kenney, *General Kenney Reports: A Personal History of the Pacific War* (New York: Duell, Sloan, and Pearce, 1949), 316–317; Robert Sherrod, *History of Marine Corps Aviation in World War II* (Novato, CA: Presidio Press, 1980), 180.

18. Sherrod, *History of Marine Corps Aviation*, 180–181; Robert Carney Oral History, 354, Columbia University Oral History Collection, Columbia University Special Collections; Halsey and Bryan, *Admiral Halsey's Story*, 176; William F. Halsey Memoir, 436, Joseph Bryan III Papers, Virginia Historical Society (hereafter Halsey Papers).

19. Sherrod, *History of Marine Corps Aviation*, 175–179; Samuel Eliot Morison, *Breaking the Bismarcks Barrier* (Boston: Little, Brown, 1950), 286.

20. Halsey and Bryan, *Admiral Halsey's Story*, 175.

21. Robert Sherrod, *History of Marine Corps Aviation in World War II* (Baltimore, MD: Nautical & Aviation Pub. Co. of America, 1987), 180–183; Shaw and Kane, *Isolation of Rabaul*, 207–218.

22. Vincent P. O'Hara, *The U.S. Navy against the Axis: Surface Combat, 1941–1945* (Annapolis: Naval Institute, 2007), 207–217.

23. Halsey and Bryan, *Admiral Halsey's Story*, 181; Betty Taussig, *A Warrior for Freedom* (Manhattan, KS: Sunflower University Press, 1995), 85.

24. Bruce Gamble, *Target Rabaul: The Allied Siege of Japan's Most Infamous Stronghold, March 1943–August 1945* (Minneapolis: Zenith Press, 2014), 213.
25. Halsey to Nimitz, November 18, 1943, Halsey Papers, box 15.
26. Morison, *Breaking the Bismarcks Barrier,* 353.
27. Ibid., 358.
28. John Miller, *Cartwheel: The Reduction of Rabaul* (Washington, DC: U.S. Government Printing Office, 1959), 255. Frederick Sherman, *Combat Command* (New York: Dutton, 1950), 206; Morison, *Breaking the Bismarcks Barrier,* 329–330.
29. Halsey and Bryan, *Admiral Halsey's Story,* 191–192; Shaw and Kane, *Isolation of Rabaul,* 207–293; Miller, *Cartwheel,* 352–377.
30. Halsey to South Pacific Force and Area, December 22, 1943, Halsey Papers, box 35; "Draft Remarks for Red Cross Magazine GISMO," Halsey Papers, box 3; Vandegrift, *Once a Marine,* 230.
31. Morison, *Breaking the Bismarcks Barrier,* 282; James Wellons, "General Roy S. Geiger, USMC, Marine Aviator, Joint Force Commander," MA thesis, School of Advanced Air and Space Studies, Maxwell Air Force Base, 2007.
32. Halsey to Norfolk Chamber of Commerce, December 4, 1945, Halsey Papers, box 18.
33. Carney to MacArthur, June 10, 1944, Richard Sutherland Correspondence, MacArthur Archives; Carney to E. M. Eller, May 3, 1956, Nimitz Papers.
34. "The Reduction of Rabaul, New Britain, 19 February to 15 May, 1944," box 91, Record Group 38, National Archives; "United States Pacific Fleet Aircraft, South Pacific Force," box 2720, Record Group 313, National Archives; Wesley Craven and James Cate, *The Army Air Forces in World War II,* vol. 4 (London: Cambridge University Press, 1950), 353–355; John Miller, "MacArthur and the Admiralties," in *Command Decisions,* ed. Kent Roberts Greenfield (Washington, DC: U.S. Government Printing Office, 1959), 295; Sherrod, *History of Marine Corps Aviation,* 211–213.
35. King to Nimitz, December 15, 1943, Ernest J. King Papers, box 4, Library of Congress.
36. Arthur Walsh to Halsey, January 11, 1944, Miles Trammell to Halsey, February 4, 1944, Halsey to Naval Uniform Service, February 5, 1944, and Halsey to Amon Carter, February 5, 1944, Halsey Papers, box 3; "T Buchanan Blakiston Radio Broadcast," January 7, 1944, Halsey Papers, box 3; "Pacific Lessons, SOPAC History Files," box 6787, Record Group 38, National Archives.
37. MacArthur to Marshall, January 19, 1944, box 16, Record Group 4, MacArthur Archives; Nimitz to Halsey, January 14, 1944, Halsey Papers,

box 15; Marshall to MacArthur, April 6, 1944, box 4, Record Group 4, MacArthur Archives; Joint Chiefs to MacArthur, and Joint Chiefs to Nimitz, January 23, 1944, box 16, Record Group 4, MacArthur Archives; Miller, *Cartwheel*, 306–309; Miller, "MacArthur and the Admiralties," 289–295.

38. Halsey to Wilkinson, December 22, 1943, Wilkinson Papers, box 1.
39. Wilkinson Diary, February 12, 1944, Wilkinson Papers; COMSOPAC Operation Plan 5-44, January 24, 1944, box 91, Record Group 38, National Archives; Wilkinson, "Amphibious Operations in the South Pacific, Army and Navy Staff College, May 8, 1944," box 185, Record Group 334, National Archives.
40. Miller, "MacArthur and the Admiralties," 295–300; MacArthur to Marshall, February 26, 1944, and February 27, 1944, MacArthur Archives.
41. Halsey and Bryan, *Admiral Halsey's Story,* 188–190.
42. Marshall to MacArthur, March 9, 1944, box 4, Record Group 4, MacArthur Archives.
43. COMSOPAC Operation Order 7-44, March 18, 1944, box 91, Record Group 38, National Archives; Wilkinson, "Amphibious Operations in the South Pacific, Army and Navy Staff College," May 8, 1944, box 185, Record Group 334, National Archives.
44. H. P. Willmott, *The Last Century of Sea Power,* vol. 2 (Bloomington: Indiana University Press, 2010), 371; Eric Bergerud, *Fire in Sky: The Air War in the South Pacific* (Boulder, CO: Westview Press, 2000), 441, 663.
45. Willmott, *The Last Century of Sea Power,* 456.
46. Wilkinson Diary, March 16, 1944, Wilkinson Papers.
47. "Base Facilities Report, South Pacific Area, January 1945," COMAIRSOPAC, box 2719, Record Group 313, National Archives; John Newton to King, "Naval Air Bases in the POA, October 19, 1945," box 255, Command File, World War II, Naval Historical Center; Halsey to MacArthur, June 10, 1944, MacArthur Correspondence, MacArthur Archives; MacArthur to Halsey, June 10, 1944, Halsey Papers, box 15; Nimitz to King et al., February 11, 1943, Flag Files, MacArthur Archives.
48. William Bernrieder to Halsey, June 2, 1955, Halsey Papers, box 11; Halsey to Nimitz, September 3, 1943, and Nimitz to King, September 15, 1943, Halsey Papers, box 15.
49. Halsey to David Wright, October 1, 1956, Halsey Papers, box 12; Bergerud, *Fire in Sky,* 635; Halsey and Bryan, *Admiral Halsey's Story,* 193.

15. AT SEA AT LAST

1. Robert Smith, *The Approach to the Philippines* (Washington, DC: U.S. Government Printing Office, 1953), 11.

2. Arleigh Burke Oral History, 327–328, U.S. Naval Institute; Clark Reynolds, *The Fast Carriers* (Annapolis: Naval Institute Press, 1992), 205; Spruance to Nimitz, July 4, 1944, Raymond Spruance Papers, box 1, Naval War College Archives, Newport; Samuel Eliot Morison, *New Guinea and the Marianas* (Boston: Little, Brown, 1953), 255

3. U.S. Fleet, "Statistical Analysis, Naval Intelligence, July 24, 1944, Table X," box 6640, Record Group 313, National Archives; Halsey to Frederick Sherman, March 11, 1944, and March 16, 1944, William F. Halsey Papers, box 15, Library of Congress (hereafter Halsey Papers).

4. Stassen to Carney, June 22, 1944, Stassen to Carney, May 14, 1944, Stassen to Carney, June 26, 1944, Harold Stassen Papers, Minnesota Historical Society (hereafter Stassen Papers); July 16, 1944, Third Fleet War Diary, Halsey Papers, box 37; Stassen to Carney, July 8, 1944, Stassen Papers; Staff Roster, Third Fleet, July 5, 1944, box 6799, Record Group 313, National Archives; June 28, 1944, Third Fleet War Diary, Halsey Papers, box 37.

5. Wilkinson to Halsey, May 4, 1944, Theodore Wilkinson Papers, box 1, Library of Congress; John Porter to Halsey, July 18, 1944, Halsey Papers, box 3; Halsey to Wilkinson, May 26, 1944, box 6711, Record Group 313, National Archives; June 18, 1944, Third Fleet War Diary, Halsey Papers, box 37.

6. Smith, *The Approach to the Philippines*, 67.

7. William Halsey Memoir, 470, Joseph Bryan III Papers, Virginia Historical Society (hereafter Halsey Memoir); Mitscher to Halsey, August 30, 1944, Halsey Papers, box 15.

8. Michael Bak Oral History, 186, U.S. Naval Institute; Carl Solberg, *Decision and Dissent: With Halsey at Leyte Gulf* (Annapolis: Naval Institute, 1995), 39; Halsey to Nimitz, September 9, 1944, Halsey Papers, box 15.

9. Theodore Taylor to Halsey, April 13, 1953, Halsey Papers, box 10.

10. William Halsey with Joseph Bryan, *Admiral Halsey's Story* (New York: McGraw-Hill, 1947), 198; Halsey to Nimitz, "Fleet Logistics," December 27, 1944, box 6771, Record Group 313, National Archives; Samuel Eliot Morison, *Leyte* (Boston: Little, Brown, 1958), 74–77, 415–432.

11. Thomas Cutler, *The Battle of Leyte Gulf* (New York: HarperCollins, 1994), 42; Halsey to Nimitz, September 15, 1944, Halsey Papers, box 15.

12. Halsey and Bryan, *Admiral Halsey's Story*, 200–201; Morison, *Leyte*, 13.

13. Frank Hough, *The Assault on Peleliu* (Nashville: Battery Press, 1990), 83.

14. Halsey and Bryan, *Admiral Halsey's Story*, 201.

15. Cutler, *The Battle of Leyte Gulf*, 69; H. P. Willmott, *The Battle of Leyte Gulf: The Last Fleet Action* (Bloomington: Indiana University Press, 2005), 43.

16. Nimitz to flag officers of the Pacific Ocean Areas, August 16, 1944, box 2715, Record Group 313, National Archives.

17. C. Vann Woodward, *The Battle for Leyte Gulf* (New York: Skyhorse Publishing, 2007), 27.
18. Cutler, *The Battle of Leyte Gulf,* 55; D. Clayton James, *The Years of MacArthur, 1941–1945* (Boston: Houghton Mifflin, 1975), 545, 548; Gerald Wheeler, *Kinkaid of the Seventh Fleet* (Washington, DC: Naval Historical Center, 1995), 381.
19. Morison, *Leyte,* 57; Cutler, *The Battle of Leyte Gulf,* 60.
20. Third Fleet Operation Plan 1-44, September 9, 1944, box 57, Record Group 38, National Archives; Halsey to Nimitz, September 28, 1944, Halsey Papers, box 15; Carney, Memorandum of Record, October 2, 1944, William Riley Papers, box 1, Library of Congress; Nimitz to Halsey, October 8, 1944, Halsey Papers, box 15.
21. Halsey to Nimitz, September 9, 1943, and October 6, 1944, Nimitz to Halsey, October 22, 1944, Halsey to Nimitz, October 22, 1944, and September 28, 1944, Mitscher to Halsey, August 30, 1944, Halsey Papers, box 15.
22. Morison, *Leyte,* 68–69; Nimitz to Halsey, October 8, 1944, Halsey Papers, box 15; Reynolds, *The Fast Carriers,* 286; Halsey to Nimitz, October 3, 1944, Halsey Papers, box 15.
23. Operation Order 21-44, Third Fleet, October 4, 1944, box 57, Record Group 38, National Archives; October 23, 1944, Third Fleet War Diary, Halsey Papers, box 37.
24. Betty Taussig, *A Warrior for Freedom* (Manhattan, KS: Sunflower University Press, 1995), 85; Carney to Mark Hersey, July 18, 1957, Robert Carney Papers, Naval Historical Center.
25. Solberg, *Decision and Dissent,* 125.
26. Taussig, *A Warrior for Freedom,* 106; Morison, *Leyte,* 91; Willmott, *The Battle of Leyte Gulf,* 64.
27. Willmott, *The Battle of Leyte Gulf,* 66.
28. Ibid., 64; Halsey and Bryan, *Admiral Halsey's Story,* 206; Halsey to Nimitz, "Report of Operations Preliminary to and in Support of the Leyte-Samar Operations, October, 1944," November 28, 1944, Halsey Papers, box 37.
29. Halsey and Bryan, *Admiral Halsey's Story,* 205–208.
30. Ibid., 209.
31. Willmott, *The Battle of Leyte Gulf,* 56, 61, 73; Morison, *Leyte,* 108; Halsey to Nimitz, "Report of Operations Preliminary to and in Support of the Leyte-Samar Operations, October, 1944," November 28, 1944, Halsey Papers, box 37.
32. Solberg, *Decision and Dissent,* 66; Woodward, *The Battle for Leyte Gulf,* 41.
33. Solberg, *Decision and Dissent,* 66; Halsey and Bryan, *Admiral Halsey's Story,* 209.

16. BULL'S RUN

1. D. Clayton James, *The Years of MacArthur, 1941–1945* (Boston: Houghton Mifflin, 1975), 557.
2. Halsey to Nimitz, October 22, 1944, Papers of William F. Halsey, box 15, Library of Congress (hereafter Halsey Papers); H. P. Willmott, *The Battle of Leyte Gulf: The Last Fleet Action* (Bloomington: Indiana University Press, 2005), 50.
3. Thomas Cutler, *The Battle of Leyte Gulf* (New York: HarperCollins, 1994), 93.
4. Carl Solberg, *Decision and Dissent: With Halsey at Leyte Gulf* (Annapolis: Naval Institute, 1995), 70.
5. Cutler, *The Battle of Leyte Gulf*, 115, 119; Solberg, *Decision and Dissent*, 80–84.
6. Halsey to King, "Action Report, Period 23–26 October 1944," November 13, 1944, Halsey Papers, box 35.
7. Cutler, *The Battle of Leyte Gulf*, 121–124, 131–133; Samuel Eliot Morison, *Leyte* (Boston: Little, Brown, 1958), 180–182.
8. Solberg, *Decision and Dissent*, 104; Morison, *Leyte*, 184; Cutler, *The Battle of Leyte Gulf*, 144–146.
9. Cutler, *The Battle of Leyte Gulf*, 150; Matome Ugaki, *Fading Victory: The Diary of Admiral Matome Ugaki, 1941–1945* (Pittsburgh: University of Pittsburgh Press, 1991), 491–492.
10. Solberg, *Decision and Dissent*, 108–109.
11. Ibid., 112; C. Vann Woodward, *The Battle for Leyte Gulf* (New York: Skyhorse Publishing, 2007), 68; Cutler, *The Battle of Leyte Gulf*, 161–164.
12. Halsey to King, "Action Report, Period 23–26 October 1944," November 13, 1944, Halsey Papers, box 35.
13. Solberg, *Decision and Dissent*, 117.
14. Halsey to King, "Action Report, Period 23–26 October 1944," November 13, 1944, Halsey Papers, box 35; Harold Stassen interview with author, July 17, 1996; Solberg, *Decision and Dissent*, 118; Cutler, *The Battle of Leyte Gulf*, 165.
15. Solberg, *Decision and Dissent*, 125.
16. Ibid., 122–124; Carney to Halsey, November 14, 1958, Wilson to Halsey, January 30, 1959, Moulton to Halsey, December 3, 1958, and Cheek to Halsey November 3, 1958, Halsey Papers, box 35; Solberg, *Decision and Dissent*, 125.
17. Clark Reynolds, *The Fast Carriers* (Annapolis: Naval Institute Press, 1992), 195–196; Evan Thomas, *Sea of Thunder* (New York: Simon and

Schuster, 2006), 233; Arleigh Burke Oral History, 398–399, U.S. Naval Institute; Morison, *Leyte,* 196.

18. Vincent P. O'Hara, *The U.S. Navy against the Axis: Surface Combat, 1941–1945* (Annapolis: Naval Institute, 2007), 244–259.

19. Ibid., 260.

20. Morison, *Leyte,* 242.

21. James Hornfischer, *The Last Stand of the Tin Can Sailors* (New York: Bantam Books, 2004), 136.

22. Willmott, *The Battle of Leyte Gulf,* 186; Cutler, *The Battle of Leyte Gulf,* 264; Thomas, *Sea of Thunder,* 173; Woodward, *The Battle for Leyte Gulf,* 186.

23. Solberg, *Decision and Dissent,* 150–151; O'Hara, *The U.S. Navy against the Axis,* 274; Cutler, *The Battle of Leyte Gulf,* 237–238.

24. Halsey quoted in Cutler, *The Battle of Leyte Gulf,* 237–238.

25. Solberg, *Decision and Dissent,* 153.

26. Woodward, *The Battle for Leyte Gulf,* 138.

27. Cutler, *The Battle of Leyte Gulf,* 249.

28. William Halsey with Joseph Bryan, *Admiral Halsey's Story* (New York: McGraw-Hill, 1947), 220; Solberg, *Decision and Dissent,* 154; Cutler, *The Battle of Leyte Gulf,* 251.

29. E. B. Potter, *Nimitz* (Annapolis: Naval Institute, 1975), 340–341; Thomas, *Sea of Thunder,* 227.

30. Halsey to King, "Action Report, Period 23–26 October 1944," November 13, 1944, Halsey Papers, box 35; Solberg, *Decision and Dissent,* 156.

31. Cutler, *The Battle of Leyte Gulf,* 252.

32. Potter, *Nimitz,* 343; Ralph Ofstie, "Special Report, Action of Samar Island, 25 October 1944," William Riley Papers, box 1, Library of Congress; Gerald Bogan Oral History, 111–113, U.S. Naval Institute.

33. Halsey to King, "Action Report, Period 23–26 October 1944," November 13, 1944, Halsey Papers, box 35; Halsey to Nimitz, "Report on Communications during Third Fleet Operations, September 1944–January 1945," January 26, 1945, Halsey Papers, box 37.

34. Woodward, *The Battle for Leyte Gulf,* 217.

35. Willmott, *The Battle of Leyte Gulf,* 242; Cutler, *The Battle of Leyte Gulf,* 284; Morison, *Leyte,* 338.

36. MacArthur to Halsey, October 29, 1944, Halsey Papers, box 15; James, *The Years of MacArthur,* 564–565; Cutler, *The Battle of Leyte Gulf,* 288; Joseph Clark Oral History, 488–501, U.S. Naval Institute; Halsey and Bryan, *Admiral Halsey's Story,* 226; Frank Britton Oral History, D. Clayton James Papers, box 1, Record Group 49, MacArthur Memorial Archives and Library.

17. AN OLD MAN AT SEA

1. Halsey to MacArthur, October 26, 1944, Papers of William F. Halsey, box 49, Library of Congress (hereafter Halsey Papers); E. B. Potter, *Bull Halsey* (Annapolis: Naval Institute, 1985), 309; Samuel Eliot Morison, *Leyte* (Boston: Little, Brown, 1958), 343; Halsey to Nimitz, October 22, 1944, Halsey Papers, box 15.

2. Morison, *Leyte*, 342.

3. Thomas Buell, *Master of Sea Power: A Biography of Fleet Admiral Ernest J. King* (Boston: Little, Brown, 1980), 348; Alton Gilbert, *A Leader Born: The Life of Admiral John Sidney McCain, Pacific Carrier Commander* (Philadelphia: Casement Publishing, 2006), 1–3.

4. Potter, *Bull Halsey*, 310–314; Samuel Eliot Morison, *The Liberation of the Philippines, Luzon, Mindanao, and the Visayas, 1944–1945* (Boston: Little, Brown, 1959), 13, 57.

5. "Third Fleet After Action Report, 27 October to 20 November," December 9, 1944, Halsey Papers, box 13.

6. Halsey to Nimitz, November 4, 1944, Halsey to Nimitz, November 8, 1944, Memorandum, Halsey to Nimitz, November 8, 1944, Halsey Papers, box 15.

7. William Halsey with Joseph Bryan, *Admiral Halsey's Story* (New York: McGraw-Hill, 1947), 231–232.

8. Ronald Spector, *Eagle against the Sun: The American War with Japan* (New York; Random House, 1985), 423; Buell, *Master of Sea Power*, 291; Andrew Jackson Oral History, 123, U.S. Naval Institute.

9. Thomas Buell, *The Quiet Warrior: A Biography of Admiral Raymond A. Spruance* (Annapolis: Naval Institute, 1987), 17.

10. Thomas Buell, *The Quiet Warrior: A Biography of Admiral Raymond A. Spruance* (Annapolis: Naval Institute Press, 1987), 3, 8, 35, 41.

11. Morison, *Liberation*, 52–59.

12. Ibid., 59–65.

13. Bob Drury and Tom Clavin, *Halsey's Typhoon* (New York: Atlantic Monthly Press, 2007), 152.

14. Morison, *Liberation*, 65–71.

15. Halsey and Bryan, *Admiral Halsey's Story*, 236; Carl Solberg, *Decision and Dissent: With Halsey at Leyte Gulf* (Annapolis: Naval Institute, 1995), 25.

16. Potter, *Bull Halsey*, 35; Morison, *Liberation*, 63; Gerald Bogan Oral History, 125–126, U.S. Naval Institute; Drury and Clavin, *Halsey's Typhoon*, 270–271.

17. Morison, *Liberation*, 177–183.

18. "Action Report, Commander Task Force Thirty-Eight, 30 October 1944–26 January 1945," John McCain Papers, box 1, Hoover Institute, Stanford University; War Diary, Third Fleet, January 1945, box 30, Record Group 38, National Archives.

19. Potter, *Bull Halsey*, 329.

20. Samuel Eliot Morison, *Victory in the Pacific, 1945* (Boston: Little, Brown, 1960), 108–109, 233, 272, 282; Halsey and Bryan, *Admiral Halsey's Story*, 251.

21. Morison, *Victory*, 298–309.

22. Potter, *Bull Halsey*, 337–339; Clark Reynolds, *On the Warpath in the Pacific* (Annapolis: Naval Institute, 2005), 425.

23. Morison, *Victory*, 308.

24. *Time* cover, July 23, 1945; Potter, *Bull Halsey*, 340.

25. Clark Reynolds, *The Fighting Lady: The New Yorktown in the Pacific War* (Missoula: Pictorial Histories Publishing, 1986), 300, 302.

26. Morison, *Victory*, 310.

27. Potter, *Bull Halsey*, 342; Morison, *Victory*, 312.

28. Morison, *Victory*, 311–313; Potter, *Bull Halsey*, 343; Richard Frank, *Downfall: The End of the Imperial Japanese Empire* (New York: Random House, 1999), 157–160.

29. Morison, *Victory*, 330–331.

30. Ibid., 331.

31. Ibid., 283; Frank, *Downfall*, 77; Morison, *Victory*, 93; Frank, *Downfall*, 95, 99, 230.

32. Morison, *Victory*, 331–333.

33. Morison, *Victory*, 334; Halsey and Bryan, *Admiral Halsey's Story*, 270–271.

34. Towers to Nimitz, "Report of Surrender and Occupation of Japan," February 11, 1946, Halsey Papers, box 23; Stassen to Joseph Bryan, no date, Harold Stassen Papers, Minnesota Historical Society.

35. John Hughes to Leo Gallagher, December 6, 1945, Halsey Papers, box 5; Halsey and Bryan, *Admiral Halsey's Story*, 281.

36. Halsey to secretary of Navy, "Request for Retirement," September 13, 1945, Halsey Papers, box 13; Halsey to Belknap, October 1, 1945, Halsey Papers, box 4; Nimitz to King, September 18, 1945, Halsey Papers, box 15.

18. AT HOME AT LAST

1. William Halsey with Joseph Bryan, *Admiral Halsey's Story* (New York: McGraw-Hill, 1947), 1; Halsey to Charlie Belknap, March 24, 1949, Pa-

pers of William F. Halsey, box 7, Library of Congress (hereafter Halsey Papers).

2. Harold Stassen, "Public Information Plan for Return of Third Fleet to Pearl Harbor and the United States," October 13, 1945, and Harold Stassen, "Public Relations on Mainland Trip," September 25, 1945, Papers of Harold Stassen, Minnesota Historical Society.

3. Julius Klein, "Notes of Interview with Halsey," Julius Klein Papers, MacArthur Memorial Archives and Library, Norfolk.

4. Talbert Johnson, "The Ships Come Home," Halsey Papers, box 38; Robert Carney Oral History, 478, Columbia University Oral History Collection, Columbia University Special Collections.

5. E. B. Potter, *Bull Halsey* (Annapolis: Naval Institute, 1985), 365.

6. Fritz Sandoz to Halsey, December 19, 1945, Francis Lucille to Halsey, September 18, 1945, Henry Steeger to Halsey, January 29, 1946, Halsey Papers, box 5; *Time*, November 10, 1947, 1; Walter Winchell transcript, radio commentary, June 13, 1948, Halsey Papers, box 7; Charles Edison to Halsey, May 31, 1945, and July 9, 1945, Halsey to Edison, June 24, 1945, and November 26, 1945, and Halsey to Air Marshal Len Isitt, September 25, 1946, Halsey Papers, box 5; Halsey to Doug Moulton, April 1, 1946, Halsey Papers, box 5.

7. Halsey to E. C. Ewen, September 27, 1948, Halsey Papers, box 7; Kennedy to Halsey, October 9, 1946, and J. W. Sands to Kennedy, November 4, 1946, Halsey Papers, box 5; Johnson to Halsey, April 1, 1948, and Halsey to Johnson, April 8, 1948, Halsey Papers, box 6; Ford to Tom Hamilton, July 14, 1948, and Halsey to Hamilton, July 21, 1948, Halsey Papers, box 7.

8. William Halsey, Testimony before the Richardson Committee, December 5, 1944, Halsey Papers, box 35; Halsey to Paul Hammond, February 24, 1954, Halsey Papers, box 10; William Huie, *The Case against the Admirals: Why We Must Have a Unified Command* (New York: Dutton, 1946), 208–210.

9. J. Loy Maloney to Halsey, November 12, 1945, Halsey Papers, box 5; Bryan to Carl Brandt, June 26, 1946, Joseph Bryan III Papers, Virginia Historical Society (hereafter Bryan Papers); Halsey to Bryan, September 11, 1946, and Halsey to Kenneth Crouch, October 21, 1946, Halsey Papers, box 5; Joseph Bryan to Carl Brandt, October 14, 1946, Bryan to Brandt, June 26, 1946, and Bryan to Brandt, December 1947 (1946?), Bryan Papers.

10. Ben Hibbs to Bryan, July 15, 1947, Halsey Papers, box 13; Carl Brandt to Halsey, various dates, 1947–1951, Halsey Papers, box 18.

11. Kimmel to Halsey, July 8, 1947, Halsey Papers, box 14.

12. William F. Halsey with Joseph Bryan, III, "Admiral Halsey Tells His Story," *Saturday Evening Post,* July 26, 1947, 64–71; Halsey and Bryan, *Admiral Halsey's Story,* 210, 219, 227; Potter, *Bull Halsey,* 371.

13. Thomas Cutler, *The Battle of Leyte Gulf* (New York: HarperCollins, 1994), 290; Potter, *Bull Halsey,* 377; Bernard Brodie, *Virginia Quarterly Review,* Summer 1947; Gilbert Cant, "Bull's Run: Was Halsey Right at Leyte Gulf?" *Life,* November 24, 1947, 73–90.

14. King to Halsey, July 30, 1947, Halsey Papers, box 14; Halsey to Bryan, November 17, 1947, Halsey Papers, box 13.

15. Halsey to Dudley Knox, November 17, 1947, Halsey Papers, box 21; Halsey to Margaret Zogbaum, November 5, 1947, Halsey Papers, box 6; Halsey to Scrappy Kessing, July 5, 1950, Halsey Papers, box 14; Halsey to Melvin Maas, March 6, 1953, Halsey Papers, box 9; Halsey to John Heffernan, April 18, 1955, Halsey Papers, box 14.

16. Halsey to Theodore Taylor, March 17, 1953, Halsey Papers, box 9; Halsey to Susan Brown, May 31, 1956, Halsey Papers, box 11.

17. Halsey to Carney, many dates, 1955–1959, Halsey Papers, box 13; Halsey to Wilson, many dates, 1958–1959, Halsey Papers, box 35; Carney to Halsey, November 14, 1958, with enclosure, Halsey Papers, box 35.

18. Gerald Wheeler, *Kinkaid of the Seventh Fleet* (Washington, DC: Naval Historical Center, 1995), 485; The Battle of Leyte Gulf, World War II Commemorative Bibliography, November 1995, Naval Department Library.

19. Halsey to Helen Marshall, July 2, 1946, Halsey Papers, box 5; Arlington County Deed Book, volumes 113, 241, 291, 565, 571, 573; Halsey to Deborah Wilson, July 1, 1946, Halsey Papers, box 5.

20. Memo, "The University of Virginia Development Fund, Immediate and Long Term Needs," August 8, 1947, Halsey Papers, box 23; Halsey to Colgate Darden, September 6, 1950, Halsey Papers, box 28.

21. Halsey to Gossett, January 19, 1948, Halsey Papers, box 13; Halsey to Betty and Hitch Saunders, April 16, 1948, Halsey Papers, box 23; Halsey to Gossett, April 16, 1948, Halsey Papers, box 13; Halsey to Deborah Halsey, December 28, 1953, Halsey Papers, box 10; Halsey to Kitchell, December 5, 1948, Halsey Papers, box 7.

22. Billing Statements, Westbrook Sanatorium, November 1949 to March 1950, Halsey Papers, boxes 7, 8; Halsey to Belknap, June 9, 1949, Halsey Papers, box 7; Halsey to Belknap, March 6, 1950, Halsey Papers, box 8.

23. Stettinius and Gossett and Halsey, many dates, 1948–1951, Halsey Papers, boxes 14, 15.

24. Halsey to Wheeler Sammons, April 11, 1952, Halsey Papers, box 23; Potter, *Bull Halsey,* 373; Gossett to Halsey, April 28, 1951, Halsey Papers,

box 14; Last Will and Testament of William F. Halsey Jr., New York City Surrogate Court, Liber Book 2267, 89.

25. Halsey to Halsey III, November 23, 1955, and Halsey to C. W. Thompson, January 19, 1955, Halsey Papers, box 11; Halsey to Beanie Grandy, February 18, 1953, Halsey Papers, box 9.

26. Halsey to C. W. Thompson, January 24, 1955, Halsey Papers, box 11; Halsey to Stassen, March 17, 1954, Halsey Papers, box 15.

27. Halsey to Edmund Fitzgerald, June 14, 1950, Halsey Papers, box 8.

28. Halsey to Edmund Fitzgerald, October 19, 1956, Halsey Papers, box 12; William Neville to Admiral Miles, September 2, 1957, Halsey Papers, box 12.

29. Halsey to Mrs. Alexander Peters, June 14, 1951, Halsey Papers, box 8; Potter, *Bull Halsey*, 376; Halsey to William Edgar, June 30, 1955, Halsey Papers, box 11; Carney to Halsey, July 2, 1951, and Halsey to Carney, December 29, 1954, Halsey Papers, box 13.

30. Halsey to William Smith, May 1955, Halsey Papers, box 11; Halsey to Gossett, September 10, 1947, Halsey Papers, box 13; Halsey to Lester McDowell, February 4, 1957, and George Gilman to George Beck, April 12, 1957, Halsey Papers, box 12; Halsey to Jane Browning, Halsey Papers, box 11; Weeks to Halsey, July 24, 1959, Halsey Papers, box 12.

31. Bryan to Frank McCarthy, May 16, 1956, Carl Brandt to Halsey, June 1, 1956, Carol Brandt to Halsey, May 22, 1957, Halsey to Brandt, May 20, 1957, Brandt to Frank McCarthy, May 24, 1957, and Bryan to Carl Brandt, April 18, 1958, Bryan Papers; Carol Brandt to Kitchell, May 7, 1957, Halsey Papers, box 18.

32. *The Gallant Hours* advertisement, Halsey Papers, box 40.

33. *New York Times,* June 23, 1960, F19; Cagney cited in trade newspaper account, n.d., Halsey Papers, box 40; *New York Times,* June 23, 1960, A24.

34. William Neville to Halsey III, June 11, 1959, Halsey Papers, box 12; Halsey to Fishers Island Country Club, many dates, 1955–1959, Halsey Papers, box 19.

CONCLUSION

1. Carney to Carroll, September 3, 1959, Chester Nimitz Papers, Naval Historical Center.

2. Eisenhower to Frances Halsey, August 18, 1959, Lodge to Margaret Halsey, statement by prime minister, September 2, 1959, Carney to Halsey III, August 19, 1959, and Bogan to Bill Halsey, August 23, 1959, Papers of William F. Halsey, box 48, Library of Congress.

3. Theodore Taylor, *The Magnificent Mitscher* (New York: Norton, 1954), xi; Thomas Buell, *The Quiet Warrior: A Biography of Admiral Raymond A. Spruance* (Annapolis: Naval Institute, 1988), xxx.
4. C. Vann Woodward, *The Battle for Leyte Gulf* (New York: Skyhorse Publishing, 2007), 221.
5. William Halsey with Joseph Bryan, *Admiral Halsey's Story* (New York: McGraw-Hill, 1947), 69.

ACKNOWLEDGMENTS

It took a long time to write *Admiral Bill Halsey: A Naval Life*. Along the way, I incurred debts I cannot possibly repay but wish to acknowledge. From the beginning, teachers gave me a love of ideas and the past, starting with my parents, Kevin and Joanne. Then there were the Mike Mullins and Fred Rupps and Bob Karns whom I recall even now as those who put me on my path. College professors Annette Atkins, David Bennett, Norm Ford, Joe Friedrich, and Ken Jones showed me I could buy groceries while doing what I love, and graduate mentors Joe Glatthaar and James Kirby Martin taught me how to do it. I hope I learned enough then to please them now.

A large number of people made this book feasible. Harold Stassen, my grandfather's friend, suggested the project before his death in 2001, indicating the book's long gestation. A summer research stipend from the Office of Naval History jump-started the venture, and Bill Trimble and Dom Pisano made possible a year as the Ramsey Fellow at the Smithsonian Institution's Air and Space Museum. Deans and department chairs at The Air University and the School of Advanced Air and Space Studies gave me time, among them John Albert, Sandy Cochran, Scott Gorman, Tom Griffith, Tom McCarthy, Tim Schultz, and Jeff Smith; and peers there offered encouragement when I felt like quitting, including Bill Allison, Steve Chiabotti, Everett Dolman, Jim Forsyth, James Kiras, Jim Tucci, Ed Westermann, Hal Winton, and especially Rich Muller, who carefully read the entire manuscript. Beyond that circle, John Lundstrom offered early guidance and Richard Frank read a final draft, saving me from many errors of fact. At the National Archives, Tim Nenninger and Barry Zerby saved me from many blind alleys, and Joe Caver at the Air Force Historical Research Agency did the same. My editor at Harvard University Press, Joyce Seltzer, and her right hand, Brian Distelberg, were models of patience as deadline after deadline slipped, and Joyce's incredible eye is present on every page. Most of Chapter 5 was originally published in a slightly different form as "Learning to Fight: Bill Halsey and the Early American Destroyer Force," in *Journal of Military History* 77 (January 2013): 71–90, and is reprinted here by permission. Philip Schwartzberg at Meridian Mapping did the excellent maps.

From start to finish I benefited from the best set of teachers, colleagues, and editors. Though they have helped immensely, the work is my own. What is good herein is a group effort, and what is bad is mine alone. I offer it to my wife, Alicia, and my daughters, Elizabeth and Katherine—the three people, I realize more and more as the days go by, for whom I live my life.

INDEX

INDEX

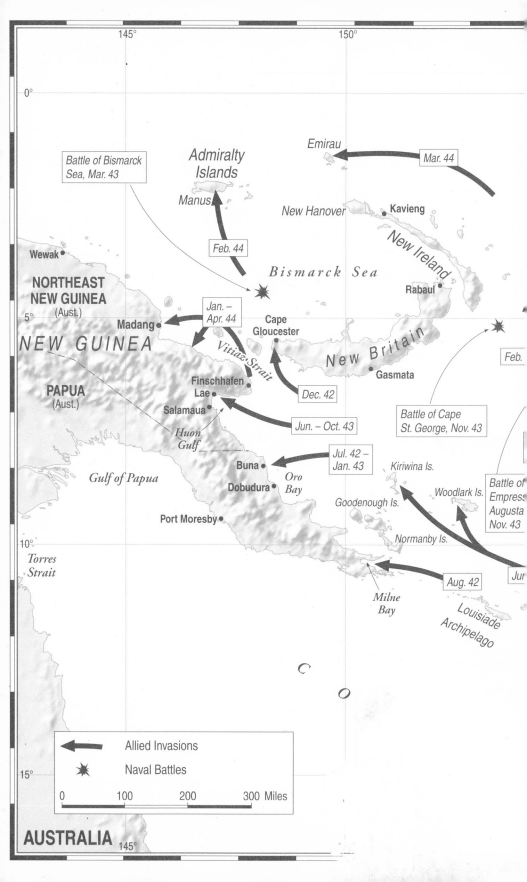

Battle of Bismarck
Sea, Mar. 43

Admiralty
Islands

Emirau

Mar. 44

Manus

New Hanover

Kavieng

New Ireland

Feb. 44

Bismarck Sea

Rabaul

Wewak

NORTHEAST
NEW GUINEA
(Aust.)

Madang

Jan. –
Apr. 44

Cape
Gloucester

New Britain

NEW GUINEA

Vitiaz Strait

PAPUA
(Aust.)

Finschhafen
Lae

Salamaua

Dec. 42

Gasmata

Feb.

Huon
Gulf

Jun. – Oct. 43

Battle of Cape
St. George, Nov. 43

Buna

Jul. 42 –
Jan. 43

Kiriwina Is.

Gulf of Papua

Dobudura

Oro
Bay

Woodlark Is.

Battle of
Empress
Augusta
Nov. 43

Goodenough Is.

Port Moresby

Normanby Is.

10°

Torres
Strait

Milne
Bay

Aug. 42

Jur

Louisiade
Archipelago

Allied Invasions

Naval Battles

0   100   200   300   Miles

15°

AUSTRALIA

145°